INDEX FOR FINDING CHAR

	SECTION[2]	GROUP AND PAGE N	
I →	1. 一	1	1一兰坦鱼 5卫上应 8俭 9工经 14士土在 20至王 26金生垂 30里
		2	32止业互五 36丑立豆 39且 40直盖监孟 43益血
		3	44继亡区 47世疟归彗当 50维届画凶齿 54山击摇 55出甘臼
	2. 口	4	58口石 64言合晤 69培占 72古告唐 75名 76召 77谷各 80沿台 81营官
		5	82日普 83借 89者 90白百 91目 95自临 97田由 101曲国 106面西
II ↓	3. 丨	6	107引个下 111斤昨卸节 116部十千 121干平 124午辛奉举 126半牛车
		7	129羊舞丰拜 131律革单 132中甲申斗纠耳
	4. 丿丨	8	137介侨齐非 138开并异升 142井川州肃
	5. ㇕	9	144今片
	6. 亅	10	144到剂 146刑 150丁街 153可予 155了子 158寸 165才于呼牙 167手争事
	7. ㇆	11	169门习司羽 173月丽角 180用辅而编 183高 184同摘周 186商南
		12	187纲网向 188巾布市雨 191内两离册 193再身
III ↙	8. 丿	13	194步少形 197厂广严产 199戶声伊岁多
	9. ㇇	14	200梦乡
	10. ㇆	15	200幻刀分万方 204约竭匈陶 205句物 207易场书巧号 208污考与
		16	209马乌鸟岛仍 210粥弯弱弟佛力 214办 215为母

1. The beginning page number for the subsequent characters/graphemes is shown in boldface type in each instance.
2. i.e. basic graphic element.

INDEX FOR FINDING CHARACTERS IN THE DICTIONARY[1]

	SECTION[2]	GROUP AND PAGE NUMBER	
IV ↘	11. ㇏	17	216人欠尺 219久爪长 221 大 223太头状 226夭天 227关矢夫 229夹块夷
		18	230木某 235术乐东 东 236本米未末朱 237来果策 238束乘兼
		19	238火 240水录膝 243求隶聚承蒙象畏 245丧派 衣表 247农跟走是 254定
	12. 㐅	20	255驳义文 256父交又服 260反发缓假搜 265度侵受
		21	266敲支皮 268没毁 270变攻致 277处及
	13. ㇏	22	278八入丈史 279更之 280逞 289挺
	14. ㇏	23	289纸民 290代战截 292咸线 294洩
	15. ㇗	24	295乱比犯 300纪已巷 302巴七托 304毛 303纯也 306电
	16. 儿	25	307儿元 309绕光先兄 310竟 312见鬼 314允 跳抛 315尤龙
		26	316无既耽 317免疏流
	17. ⺄	27	319讯气风飞
	18. ㇈	28	320几抗沉 322凡九瓦
	19. 乙	29	323亿
V ↘	20. 丶	30	324不以咳 326六兴兵共 328其具典只 329贝质负锁 333页黄 336小示京原
		31	340你素 341余赤恭 342心 348必黑私 352云去公 356 虫令专
	21. 丶	32	360女 361要安 362委
	22. ㇀	33	363尽 364冬

1. The beginning page number for the subsequent characters/graphemes is shown in boldface type in each instance.
2. i.e. basic graphic element.

A POCKET

CHINESE-RUSSIAN-ENGLISH DICTIONARY

A POCKET CHINESE-RUSSIAN-ENGLISH DICTIONARY

Arranged by the Rosenberg Graphical System

(Araushkin and Nadtochenko's Pocket Chinese-Russian Dictionary with an English Text)

JOHN S. BARLOW

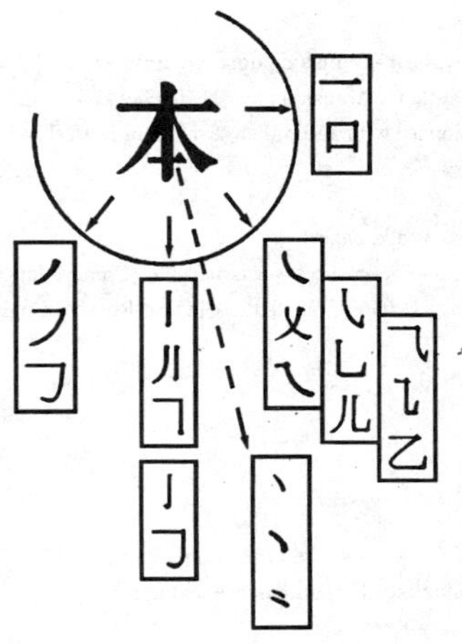

一 口 丨 刂 ㇕ 亅 ㇆ ノ フ ㇆ ㇏ 乂 ㇏ ㇃ ㇄ 儿 ㇅ ㇈ 乙 丶 ㇔ ⺀
1 2 3 4 5 6 7 8 9 10 11 12 13 14 15 16 17 18 19 20 21 22

University of Hawai'i Press • Honolulu

Printed in the United States of America

Chinese-Russian Text from: *Карманный Китайско-Русский Словарь,* Н. С. Араушкин и Б. Я. Надточенко, „Русский Язик", Москва, 1975, 208 стр. [*Karmannyi Kitaisko-Russkii Slovar',* N. S. Araushkin u B. Ya. Nadtochenko "Russkii Iazik," Moskva, 1975, 208p.]

05 04 03 02 01 00 5 4 3 2 1

Library of Congress Cataloging-in-Publication Data

Barlow, John S., 1925–

A pocket Chinese-Russian-English dictionary : arranged by the Rosenberg graphical system : Araushkin and Nadtochenko's pocket Chinese-Russian dictionary with an English text / John S. Barlow.

p. cm.

Includes index.

ISBN 0–8248–2294–3 (alk. paper)

1. Chinese language—Dictionaries—Russian. 2. Chinese language—Dictionaries—English. I. Title. II. Title: Chinese-Russian-English dictionary.

PL1459.R8B35 2000

413'.951—dc21 99–44237

CIP

University of Hawai'i Press books are printed on acid-free paper and meet the guidelines for permanence and durability of the Council on Library Resources.

Camera-ready copy prepared by John S. Barlow.

Printed by Edward Brothers Incorporated

CONTENTS

Preface

Most currently available Chinese-English dictionaries, including small or pocket ones, are alphabetically arranged according to pronunciation (e.g., pinyin), but if the pronunciation of the character is not known, an appended radical/stroke index must usually be consulted first. This can be a tedious and time-consuming process, and can discourage the use of dictionaries, especially by those at an early stage of study of the Chinese written language. By the same token, there is a dearth of small (pocket-book) dictionaries suitable for non-Chinese individuals. These difficulties arise because Chinese characters are not alphabetically based.

An alternative method of locating a character in a dictionary, long standard in Russia but little known elsewhere, is one in which the location is determined directly from inspection of the makeup of the character itself, without the necessity of first consulting a radical/stroke index. The system, which can be termed the Rosenberg Graphical System (after the Russian who perfected it in 1916), is founded on some 22 basic graphical elements (in contrast to 189, or 214, etc., radicals in the various radical systems). The system entails a systematic visual analysis of an unknown character into components of these basic graphic elements according to a simple set of rules, beginning at the right lower corner of the character. The approach can be considered somewhat analogous to that of finding a word in an alphabetically-based (e.g., English) dictionary.

For the present volume, which is arranged on the graphical system, a parallel English text has been added to the 2,273-character, 8,500-word *Pocket Chinese-Russian Dictionary* of Araushkin and Nadtochenko ("Russian Language," Moscow, 1975). That dictionary included the *List of the Most Frequently Used Characters*, published by the Ministry of Education of the People's Republic of China in 1952, and the *List of 3,000 Most Frequently Used Words of Putonghua,* published in 1959 by the Committee on Reform of the Chinese Written Language. Although the number of lead-entry characters is limited, the format of parallel equal-width columns of Chinese-Russian and of English has permitted an increased number of English renditions for each original Chinese entry. (The Russian text has not been altered.) The size of the word list approximates the 6,000 entries in *The Pocket English-Chinese (Pinyin) Dictio-*

nary (Wang Liangbi, Zhu Yuan, and Ren Yongchang, The Commercial Press, Beijing/Hong Kong, 1983).

In the preparation of the present volume, some corrections and updating have been made in the original Chinese text, e.g., replacement of a few unsimplified characters by their simplified forms (so that essentially all characters would appear in their simplified form), and inclusion of a number of characters that had been omitted from the alphabetical (pinyin) index. Page references have been added to the latter, facilitating its use as an alternative mode of entry to the body of the dictionary. A guide to the use of the graphical system has also been added. Some minor regrouping of the graphemes in the Grapheme Index (of which a running version is now included) and of the characters in the body of the dictionary has been carried out so as to be in agreement with the more recently published *Great Chinese-Russian Dictionary* (Oshanin, I.M. ed., Moscow, Nauka, 1983-84, 4 vols.), and the *Chinese-Russian Dictionary* (B.G. Mudrov, ed., Moscow, "Russian Language," 1980).

The English text was derived from the original Chinese text (quite independently of the Russian text), primarily with the aid of the recently published *ABC Chinese-English Dictionary* (John DeFrancis, ed., University of Hawai'i Press, 1996), and also *A Chinese English Dictionary, Revised Edition* (Wei Dongya, ed., Foreign Language Teaching and Research Press, Beijing, 1995). The relatively few phrases and idiomatic expressions of the original text have not been rendered into English. (In the author's opinion, phrases are best given triply: characters, pinyin, and English, as in Chinese-English phrase books usually; this would not have been feasible in the present undertaking.)

The present pocket dictionary can be considered as an introduction to the Rosenberg Graphical System, and as a smaller companion volume to my *A Chinese-Russian-English Dictionary Arranged by the Rosenberg Graphical System (Mudrov's Chinese-Russian Dictionary with an English Text and Appendices)* (University of Hawai'i Press, 1995), a medium-size dictionary of 5,700 characters and 60,000 words). The latter volume contains a more extensive guide to the use of the Graphical System as well as several appendices, including a history of the Graphical System, which dates from 1856.

Acknowledgments

It has been a pleasure to work with William Hamilton, Paul Herr, Cynthia Lowe, and Ann Ludeman of the University of Hawai'i Press, on the production of this book. As was the case with the previously mentioned large Chinese-Russian-English Dictionary, I am very grateful to Sibylle J. Barlow, my wife, for proofing the English text as well as the Chinese character lists.

GUIDE TO THE USE OF THE ROSENBERG GRAPHICAL SYSTEM

(Modified, after Grigor'ev[1] and Barlow[2])

The characters in the dictionary are ordered on the Rosenberg Graphical System, which is based on the following principles:

The 22 Basic Graphical Elements and Their 5 Principal Stroke Directions

Each (printed) Chinese character is imagined to be a square, and the graphical element (stroke) occupying the right lower corner of the square is taken as a basis for classification of the character as belonging to one of 22 basic graphical elements. If there is no stroke in the right lower corner, then the lowest distinguishable stroke that descends either vertically downwards or obliquely to the left is taken for classification. In the characters shown below, the basic graphical element is filled in:

上 下 片 門 多 勿 木 兆 飛 更

The 22 basic graphical elements, which correspond to the 22 sections of the dictionary (as well as to the 22 sections of the Grapheme Index appearing on the front and back inside covers—as described below), are as follows:

一	口	丨	川	乛	亅	コ	ノ	フ	㇆	㇏	乂	㇂	㇃	乚	儿	㇅	㇄	乙	丶	丶	㇀
1	2	3	4	5	6	7	8	9	10	11	12	13	14	15	16	17	18	19	20	21	22

These 22 basic graphical elements fall into 5 major categories of stroke-direction: I, horizontal; II, vertical; III, sloping downward to the left; IV, sloping downward to the right; and V, reverse curve downward (see also the left side of the facing pages of the inside covers):

Division	I	II	III	IV	V
Stroke-direction	→	↓	↙	↘	↘

A synthesis of the principal stroke directions, and a corresponding grouping of the 22 basic graphical elements can be found in the character, 本, if its lower horizontal stroke is taken to symbolize the fifth principal stroke direction; i.e., 一, 丨, ㇏, ノ, 丶. In turn, the 22 basic graphical elements can be grouped around this character, as follows:

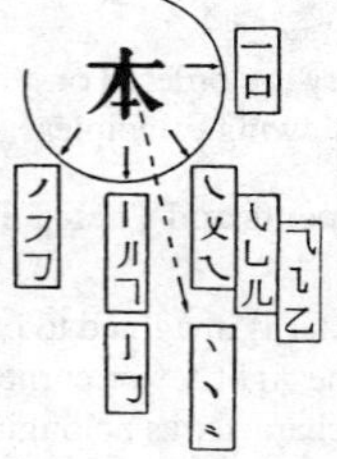

The Grapheme Index

These 22 basic graphical elements, taken individually and combined systematically, form the 407 graphemes of the Grapheme Index (inside covers of the book), which are in turn systematically combined with one or more of the 22 basic graphical elements and with one another to form the 2,273 characters in the dictionary. (There are thus an average of 5 characters to each grapheme.)

Location of a given character in the dictionary is thus accomplished by first establishing its basic graphic element, then its corresponding grapheme, and finally the character itself, as follows:

The graphemes within a section in the Grapheme Index are ordered as follows:
a) the simplest graphemes (which may be the same as the basic graphical element itself for that section) appear at the beginning;
b) then follow successively the graphemes formed by addition of other basic graphical elements (taking into account their own order) to a given basic graphical element in the following general sequence: on its left, on its upper left, on top of it, joining (touching) it, intersecting (crossing) it, and finally, inside it (i.e., enclosed by it). Some illustrative examples of these principles follow.

In Section 1, Group 1 (inside front/back covers, left side), the first grapheme, 一, is itself a basic graphical element. It is followed by the graphemes, 兰, 坦, and 鱼, which have additions on top of it (there are no additions at its left or its upper left). Then follow several graphemes, beginning with 卫 and 上,

that are formed by first touching it and then by intersecting it, in an orderly sequence. In Group 2 in the Grapheme Index, the graphemes are formed by two junctions with the first basic graphical element, —; some of the graphemes form enclosures.

In Section 6, the Basic Graphical Element for which is 丨, the first grapheme, 引, is formed by an addition to the left of the latter, the second, 个, by an addition on top of it, the third, 下, by two additions that touch it, the ninth, 十, by one that intersects it, and so on.

For convenience (described further below), the graphemes within each of the 22 sections (corresponding to the 22 basic graphical elements) are arbitrarily divided into 1 to 3 groups, for a total of 33 groups. For example, in Section 1 there are 3 groups, in Section 2 there are 2 groups, and so on.

The approximate position of the character within a section is established by determining the grapheme in the Grapheme Index that corresponds to that of the character being sought. Then, from the pagination (boldface numbers) given in the Grapheme Index, the character itself is located in the body of the dictionary from among those characters comprised of this particular grapheme, according to the sequence of combinations described above. (The inclusion of the pagination numbers results in further subdivision of the graphemes into arbitrary subgroups.)

The Arrangement of Characters Formed from Combinations of Graphemes

The sequence in the body of the dictionary of characters formed from two or more graphemes is as follows: first, those graphical complexes which are formed by addition of a grapheme on the left side of the original one, then those formed by addition of a grapheme at the upper left, and finally, by addition of a grapheme on top of the original one.

For example, compound forms of the character, 目, are arranged in the following sequence: 相, 眉, 冒, and compound forms of the character, 相, would be ordered as follows: 湘, 厢, 霜.

Such compound characters are arranged in order of the sequence of the basic graphical elements of the respective individual graphemes that are added to the base grapheme. For example, compound characters based on the grapheme,

登, would be arranged in the following sequence: 證, 橙, 燈, 澄, i.e., in the same sequence that these graphic elements appear alone.

It should be pointed out that the procedures outlined above serve more as guidelines than as a complete set of rules, which would be cumbersome in any case, and to which some exceptions would almost inevitably occur. (Note, for example, in the Grapheme Index, that some of the graphemes in Group 18 on p. 235 could alternatively have been included under Group 31 on p. 341. Typography can thus on occasion be a factor in the graphical classification of characters.) In any case, difficulties in using the graphical system can be expected to diminish with experience gained in using it.

The Running Grapheme Index

A running version of the Grapheme Index (including the Group numbers) is included at the top of each pair of facing pages. The basic graphical element appears at the top outer corners (in a square), and, in the top middle, a horizontal string of prior and subsequent graphemes is displayed, centered at the grapheme corresponding to the centerfold of the pair of pages, for a total of 30–40 graphemes. (The last grapheme of the string on a left-hand page is that for the last character on that page; the first grapheme of the string on a right-hand page is that for the first character on that page, or for the continuation of the character from the bottom of the paired left page.)

Summary of Steps in Finding a Character in the Dictionary

1. Determine the basic graphical element (1 of 22) from the lower right corner of the desired character. Locate the corresponding Section from among the 22 Sections in the Grapheme Index (inside front/back covers).

2. Determine from the Grapheme Index the corresponding grapheme (one of about 400) for the character in question, keeping in mind that other graphical elements are combined with a given one according to the following sequence: on the latter's left, on its upper left, on top, joining it, intersecting it, enclosed by it. (*It is very advisable to memorize this sequence, along with the 22 basic graphical elements themselves and their sequence.*) The approximate location of the corresponding grapheme is indicated by the pagination (boldface type), its exact location can be established from the Running Grapheme Index (top of each pair of pages). (The group numbers that are included in the Grapheme

Index and in the Running Grapheme Index indicate arbitrary subdivisions of graphemes, for convenience. The subgroupings of graphemes that result from insertion of page numbers in the Grapheme Index are likewise arbitrary.)

3. With the aid of the vertical lead-entry list of characters at the upper outer margin of each page, locate the desired character itself, keeping in mind that the order in the dictionary of compound characters that are made up of a combination of other graphemes with a given one is as follows: graphemes added to its left, then those added on its upper left, and finally, those added on top of it.

4. As a more expeditious alternative to Step 2, the basic graphical elements and the Running Grapheme Index (35–40 graphemes from the total of some 400, with their group numbers), which are displayed at the top of each pair of facing pages, can be used directly, without reference to the Grapheme Index (inside covers). The graphemes on the left page precede, those on the right page follow, the centerfold of a pair of pages. (The grapheme group numbers provide a means of coordination with the grapheme group numbers in the Grapheme Index (inside covers), if desired, the numbers being the same.)

With very few exceptions, only the simplified form of characters used in printed publications in the People's Republic of China are given in the dictionary.

Pinyin (Alphabetical) Index

A pinyin (phonetic, or alphabetical) index is included as Appendix B, thus providing a second mode of entry to the body of the dictionary in those instances in which the pronunciation is already known.

---

1. Grigor'ev, G.M. [*Short Chinese-Russian Dictionary*], State Publishing House for National Dictionaries, Moscow, 1962, 631 p.
2. Barlow, J.S. *A Chinese-Russian-English Dictionary,* University of Hawai'i Press, 1995, 830 p.

List of Abbreviations, Terms, and Symbols

abbr.—abbreviation
addr.—form of address
adj.—adjective
adv.—adverb
archi.—architecture
agri.—agriculture
anat.—anatomy
astron.—astronomy
attr.—attributive
aux.—auxiliary
av. —aviation
bot.—botany
Budd.—Buddhist
(C)CP—(Chinese) Communist Party
Ch. med.—Chinese medicine
chem.—chemistry
coll.—colloquial
comp.—computer/computing
conj.—conjunction
const.—construction(s)
court.—courteous/polite
ct. w.—counting word
derog.—derogatory
dial.—dialectical (non-Mandarin)
dipl.—diplomacy
econ.—economics
electr.—electrical
fig.—figuratively
finan.—financial
gov't.—government
gram.—grammatical
hon.—honorific
humb.—humbly
imper.—imperative
interj.—interjection
interr.—interrogatory
Jap.—Japanese
ling.—linguistics
lit.—literally
liter.—literature
loan w.—loan word
m.—meter
M.—measure (counting) word
mach.—machinery
med.—medicine
meteor.—meteorology
mil.—military
min.—mining
mus.—music
n. suf.—noun suffix
naut.—nautical
neg.—negation
no.—number
obj.—object
onom.—onomatopoeia
part.—particle
passive v.—passive voice
philos.—philosophy
phonet.—phonetic
photo.—photography
phys.—physics
physiol.—physiology
pl.—plural
pol.—politics
postp.—postposition
PRC—People's Republic of China
pref.—prefix
prep.—preposition
print.—printing

reflex.—reflexive
rr.—railroad
sb.—somebody
sing.—singular
sth.—something
suf.—suffix
surg.—surgical
theatr.—theater
topol.— topology
trad.—traditional
wr.—writing.

/—indicates alternative word(s)
//—continued on line above
\\—continued on line below

A POCKET

CHINESE-RUSSIAN-ENGLISH DICTIONARY

一

一 yī 1. оди́н; едини́ца; пе́рвый **2.** весь, цели́ко́м **3.** как то́лько	1. one; first 2. all, whole 3. as soon as
～些 yīxiē не́сколько, немно́го; не́которые	a number of, certain, some, a few/little
～直 yīzhí пря́мо, напрями́к	1. straight 2. continuously, always, all// //along
～倍 yībèi вдво́е	twice, double
～路平安 yīlù píng'ān счастли́вого пути́!	bon voyage!
～百 yībǎi сто	one hundred
～面 yīmiàn одна́ сторона́; ～面…, ～面… с одно́й стороны́…, с друго́й стороны́…; и…, и…	1. one side/aspect 2. simultaneously, both...and... ; on the one hand...on the other hand...
～下子 yīxiàz сра́зу, одни́м ма́хом	at one stroke, immediately, one fell swoop
～半 yībàn полови́на	one half; in part
～辈子 yībèiz вся жизнь; в тече́ние всей жи́зни	all one's life, a lifetime
～样 yīyàng подо́бный, одина́ковый	the same, equally, alike, as
～律 yīlǜ все как оди́н; все сра́зу	equally, without exception
～齐 yīqí вме́сте; одновре́ме́нно	simultaneously, in unison, together
～等 yīděng пе́рвого со́рта (кла́сса)	first-class/rate
～月 yīyuè янва́рь	January
～同 yītóng вме́сте, совме́стно; заодно́	together
～向 yīxiàng пре́жде; до сих по́р; всегда́	consistently, all along, up to now
～带 yīdài райо́н	district, region

一

一切 **yīqiè** все; всё	all, every, everything
～方面 **yīfāngmiàn** с одно́й стороны́	1. on one side 2. on the one hand...on the other hand..., for one thing...for \\
～天 **yī tiān** 1. одна́жды 2. весь день	1. one day, once 2. all day \\another -
～块儿 **yīkuàir** вме́сте	1. at the same place 2. together
～体化 **yītǐhuà** интегра́ция	to unify
～来 **yīlái** во-пе́рвых	since //all, altogether
～起 **yīqǐ** вме́сте, совме́стно	1. in the same place 2. together 3. in//
～定 **yīdìng** обяза́тельно, непреме́нно; наверняка́	1. fixed, definite; regular 2. certainly, surely, necessarily 3. given 4. proper
～般 **yībān** 1. обы́чный 2. в о́бщем, вообще́	general, ordinary, common -
～致 **yīzhì** 1. единогла́сно 2. еди́нство	1. identical 2. unanimous -
～边 **yībiān** одна́ сторона́; ～边..., ～边... с одно́й стороны́..., с друго́й стороны́...; и..., и...	1. one side 2. on the one hand...on the other hand... - -
～共 **yīgòng** итого́, всего́	all together, in all, all told
～小撮 **yī xiǎocuō** группиро́вка, го́рстка	a handful -
～系列 **yīxìliè** [це́лый] ряд	(whole) series
～点 **yīdiǎn** немно́го, чуть-чу́ть	1. point 2. an hour 3. a little, a bit -
～会儿 **yīhuìr** одна́ мину́та; мгнове́ние; то́тчас	a little while; one moment... the next... -
二 **èr** два; о́ба; второ́й	one or two, just a few/little
～十 **èrshí** два́дцать	twenty
～等 **èrděng** второ́го со́рта (кла́сса)	second class, second rate -
～月 **èryuè** февра́ль	February
～来 **èrlái** во-вторы́х	in the second place, secondly

仁 **rén** гума́нность; гума́нный	1. benevolence 2. humane, compassionate; esteemed 3. kernel
些 **xiē** не́которое коли́чество, не́сколько	a small quantity, a few, some
三 **sān** три; тре́тий	three; third
～月 **sānyuè** март	March
～角形 **sānjiǎoxíng** треуго́льник	triangle
～板 **sānbǎn** сампа́н	sampan
～轮车 **sānlúnchē** велори́кша	pedicab
兰 **lán** орхиде́я	1. orchid 2. fragrance 3. moral excellence
拦 **lán** прегражда́ть; препя́тствовать	to bar, block, hold back
～阻 **lánzǔ** заде́рживать; прегражда́ть	to obstruct, impede
～挡 **lándǎng** остана́вливать; меша́ть продвиже́нию	to block, obstruct, hinder
栏 **lán** **1.** пери́ла; по́ручни **2.** и́згородь **3.** коло́нка; столбе́ц	1. fence, railing, hurdle 2. pen, shed 3. column
～杆 **lángān** **1.** пери́ла; по́ручни **2.** барье́р; и́згородь	1. railing, banister, balustrade
烂 **làn** гнить, разлага́ться	1. to rot, fester; rotten, decayed 2. //mushy, sodden 3. dissolute
～纸 **lànzhǐ** макулату́ра	wastepaper
丝 **sī** **1.** шёлковая нить, шёлк **2.** про́волока; струна́ **3.** ничто́жное коли́чество	1. silk 2. threadlike thing 3. tiny bit/trace
～毫 **sīháo** чуть-чу́ть; *перед отриц.* ниско́лько не	in the slightest amount/degree
坦 **tǎn** **1.** и́скренний **2.** споко́йный	1. smooth, level 2. calm, composed 3. open, candid
～白 **tǎnbái** открове́нный, чистосерде́чный	1. honest, frank, candid 2. to confess
～克 **tǎnkè** танк; та́нковый	tank
～克手 **tǎnkèshǒu** танки́ст	tankman
但 **dàn** но, одна́ко; то́лько	1. but, yet, still, nevertheless 2. only, merely
～是 **dànshì** но, одна́ко	
担 **dān** **1.** нести́ *(на плечах)* **2.** брать на себя́ (нести́) отве́тственность	1. to carry on a shoulder pole 2. to take on, undertake
～ **dàn** **1.** коромы́сло **2.** *перен.* но́ша, бре́мя	1. (measure of wgt. = 50 # or 22.7 Kg) 2. load, burden; carrying pole

担任 **dānrèn** исполня́ть обя́занности	to assume the office of, take charge of
～当 **dāndāng** брать на себя́ отве́тственность	to take on, undertake, assume
～子 **dànz** *см.* 担 2	carrying pole plus load
～待 **dāndài** *см.* ～当	1. to show leniency 2. to look after
～保 **dānbǎo** руча́ться; гаранти́ровать	to guarantee
～架 **dānjià** носи́лки	stretcher, litter
～负 **dānfù 1.** нести́ *(на себе)* **2.** брать на себя́ (нести́) отве́тственность	to bear, shoulder, take on, be charged with
～心 **dānxīn** волнова́ться, беспоко́иться	to worry, feel anxious
胆 **dǎn 1.** жёлчь; жёлчный пузы́рь **2.** сме́лость, хра́брость	1. gallbladder 2. courage, bravery, audacity 3. internal parts
～量 **dǎnliàng** *см.* 胆 2	courage, guts
～子大 **dǎnz dà** сме́лый, хра́брый	bold, daring, audacious, brave
～子小 **dǎnz xiǎo** ро́бкий; трусли́вый	timid, shy; cowardly
～怯 **dǎnqiè** тру́сить; трусли́вый	timid; cowardly
宣 **xuān** объявля́ть; де́лать заявле́ние	1. to declare, proclaim, announce 2. to drain off (liquids)
～言 **xuānyán** манифе́ст; деклара́ция	declaration, manifesto
～誓 **xuānshì** дава́ть кля́тву; присяга́ть; кля́тва; прися́га	to take/swear an oath; vow
～告(布) **xuāngào(bù)** объявля́ть, провозглаша́ть; обнаро́довать	to declare, proclaim
～战 **xuānzhàn 1.** объявля́ть войну́; объявле́ние войны́ **2.** броса́ть вы́зов	to declare war
～传 **xuānchuán** агита́ция; пропага́нда	to propagate, disseminate, give publicity to
喧 **xuān** шуме́ть, галде́ть	noisy
～哗 **xuānhuá** сканда́лить; шум, галдёж	hubbub, uproar
～闹 **xuānnào** сканда́лить; сканда́л	to make a noise/racket
擅 **shàn 1.** захва́тывать, ов-	1. to arrogate to oneself, do on one's

ладева́ть **2.** де́йствовать самово́льно	own authority 2. to be good/expert at/in
擅自 **shànzì** самово́льно; **са**мово́льный	to do sth. without authorization
昼 **zhòu** дневно́е вре́мя, день; днём	daytime, daylight, day
～夜 **zhòu-yè** су́тки, день и ночь	day and night, around the clock
查 **chá** проверя́ть; выясня́ть	1. to check, investigate 2. to look up
～验 **cháyàn** освиде́тельствовать, осмотре́ть	to examine and approve
～看 **chákàn** осма́тривать; осмо́тр	to check up, go over, ferret out
～字典 **chá zìdiǎn** иска́ть иеро́глифы в словаре́	to look up a character in a dictionary
～对 **cháduì** сверя́ть; сопоставля́ть	to verify the amount/numbers
～问 **cháwèn** спра́шивать, справля́ться о	to interrogate
～明 **chámíng** выясня́ть	to ascertain
～考 **chákǎo** проверя́ть, обсле́довать	to ascertain
疆 **jiāng** грани́ца	boundary, border
～土 **jiāngtǔ** террито́рия *(страны́)*	territory
～界(域) **jiāngjiè(yù)** грани́цы; преде́лы *(страны́)*	territory; domain
鱼 **yú** ры́ба; ры́бный	1. fish 2. surname
～丝 **yúsī** ле́ска	fishing line
～盆 **yúpén** аква́риум	aquarium
～雷 **yúléi** торпе́да	torpedo
～肝油 **yúgānyóu** ры́бий жир	cod liver oil
～竿 **yúgān** у́дочка	fishing rod
～子 **yúzǐ** икра́	fish roe
～钩 **yúgōu** [рыболо́вный] крючо́к	fishhook
渔 **yú** лови́ть ры́бу; рыболо́вство; рыболо́вный	1. to catch fish 2. to usurp, gain by ruse
～业 **yúyè** рыболо́вство	fishery
～人 **yúrén** рыба́к, рыболо́в	fisherman
～民 **yúmín** рыбаки́	fisherfolk
卫 **wèi** охраня́ть, защища́ть; охра́на, карау́л	1. to guard, defend 2. guard
～生 **wèishēng** гигие́на; са-	hygiene, health; sanatarium; hygienic

卫上

нитари́я; здравоохране́ние; санита́рный	-
卫星 **wèixīng** *астр.* спу́тник; 人造卫星 искусственный спу́тник	satellite; artificial satellite
~国 **wèiguó** защища́ть ро́дину	to defend one's country
~国战争 **wèiguó zhànzhēng** оте́чественная война́	patriotic war
~兵 **wèibīng** охра́нник, карау́льный	guard, bodyguard
上 **shàng** **1.** верх; ве́рхний; све́рху **2.** вышеука́занный, предыду́щий **3.** вы́сшего со́рта, превосхо́дный **4.** поднима́ться, восходи́ть; направля́ться **5.** закрыва́ть, запира́ть **6.** *послелог обстоятельства места:* 海上 на мо́ре; 在桌子上 на столе́ **7.** *суф. наречий, указывающих на сферу деятельности:* 政治上 в полити́ческом отноше́нии, полити́чески	1. upper; upwards 2. higher, superior, better 3. first (part); preceding, previous 4. emperor 5. to mount, go up, board, get on 6. to go to, leave for 7. to present, submit 8. to go/forge ahead 9. to enter, appear on stage 10. to place/set/fix/apply 11. to be put on record, be carried in a publication 12. to wind/screw/tighten 13. (in questions) able/unable 14. third tone in Mandarin 15. (neutral tone) (after nouns) on; (after verbs) up
~班 **shàngbān** идти́ (выходи́ть) на рабо́ту [в свою́ сме́ну]	to go/start to work, be at work/on duty
~当 **shàngdàng** быть обма́нутым; попа́сть в глу́пое положе́ние	to be taken in, be fooled
~船 **shàngchuán** сади́ться на парохо́д (в ло́дку)	to board a boat/ship
~台 **shàngtái** *прям., перен.* появи́ться на сце́не; прийти́ к вла́сти	to mount a platform, appear on stage
~油 **shàngyóu** **1.** сма́зывать ма́слом **2.** накла́дывать мазь	1. to grease/oil 2. to cover with grease/oil
~面 **shàngmian** **1.** верх; наверху́ **2.** вы́ше, ра́ньше	1. above, on the surface/top of 2. higher authority 3. aspect, regard, respect
~下 **shàng-xià** **1.** верх и низ **2.** о́коло, приблизи́тельно	1. above and below, high and low 2. superior and inferior 3. more or less
~部 **shàngbù** **1.** ве́рхняя	1. upper part 2. first volume (of 2)

часть **2.** пе́рвая часть	-
(напр. произведения)	-
上午 **shàngwǔ** до полу́дня,	last year
в пе́рвой полови́не дня	-
~车 **shàngchē** сади́ться *(на*	to get into (a car/train/etc.)
поезд, в автобус и т. п.)	-
~升 **shàngshēng** повыша́ть	to rise
(-ся), поднима́ть(ся)	-
~街 **shàngjiē** выходи́ть на	1. to go into the street 2. to go shopping
у́лицу	-
~学 **shàngxué** посеща́ть	to attend school, be at school
шко́лу, учи́ться	-
~等 **shàngděng** вы́сший	first class, superior
сорт; первокла́ссный	-
~潮 **shàngcháo** прили́в	1. to go to court 2. to hold court
~马 **shàngmǎ 1.** сесть на	1. to mount a horse 2. to start a pro-
коня́; по ко́ням! **2.** взя́ть-	ject
ся за рабо́ту	-
~次 **shàngcì** в про́шлый раз	last time, previous occasion
~课 **shàngkè** идти́ на заня́-	1. to attend class, go to class 2. to give
тия (в шко́лу)	a lesson/lecture
~衣 **shàngyī** ве́рхняя оде́ж-	upper outer garment, jacket
да	-
~议院 **shàngyìyuàn** ве́рх-	upper house, senate
няя пала́та парла́мента;	-
сена́т	-
~级 **shàngjí** вышестоя́щая	higher level/authority
инста́нция; руково́дство	-
~层 **shàngcéng 1.** ве́рхний	upper strata/level
слой **2.** верхи́ *(общества)*	-
~层建筑 **shàngcéng jiànzhù**	superstructure
филос. надстро́йка	-
让 **ràng** уступа́ть; позво-	1. to yield 2. to allow 3. to induce sb. to
ля́ть; усту́пка; пусть	do sth. 4. to transfer possession of\\
~价 **ràngjià** уступи́ть, про-	to agree to reduce \\(signifies passive)
да́ть деше́вле	the price asked
~步 **ràngbù** *см.* 让	1. to yield, compromise 2. to step aside
应 **yīng 1.** сле́дует, ну́жно	1. should, ought to 2. to promise/
2. соглаша́ться	agree (to) 3. to answer, respond
~ **yìng 1.** отклика́ться, от-	1. to answer/reply/respond 2. to cor-
веча́ть **2.** соотве́тствовать	respond/conform to
~验 **yìngyàn** сбыва́ться;	to come true
подтвержда́ться	-
~当 **yīngdāng** *см.* 应 1	should, ought to

应付 **yìngfù** принимáть отвéтные мéры; реагúровать	1. to deal/cope with, handle 2. to do sth. perfunctorily 3. to make do
～得 **yìngdé** заслýженный; по заслýгам	to be (well) deserved, be due
～有 **yīngyǒu** необходúмый, надлежáщий	ought to have
～用 **yīngyòng** имéющий практúческое применéние; гóдный к употреблéнию, к испóльзованию	to apply, use
～邀 **yìngyāo** принимáть приглашéние; по приглашéнию	to receive an invitation
～战 **yìngzhàn** 1. принимáть вы́зов 2. вступáть в бой	1. to meet an enemy attack 2. to accept a challenge
～该 **yīnggāi** *см.* 应 1	should, ought to, must
俭 **jiǎn** эконóмить; эконóмный, бережлúвый	1. frugal, economical 2. meager 3. poor harvest
～省 **jiǎnshěng** эконóмить; эконóмия; эконóмный	frugal, thrifty
～朴 **jiǎnpǔ** 1. простóй, скрóмный 2. бережлúвый	economical, thrifty and simple
险 **xiǎn** 1. опáсность; опáсный 2. ýзкий, тéсный	1. vicious, venomous, malicious, dangerous 2. danger 3. nearly, narrowly
～要 **xiǎnyào** 1. вáжный стратегúческий пункт 2. жúзненно вáжный óрган	strategically located and difficult to access
脸 **liǎn** лицó; óблик	1. face, countenance 2. front
～盆 **liǎnpén** таз для умывáния	washbasin, washbowl
～面(子) **liǎnmiàn(z)** лицó; выражéние лицá	1. face 2. self-respect 3. sb.'s feelings
验 **yàn** 1. проверя́ть; осмáтривать 2. экзáмен 3. óпыт, эксперимéнт	1. to examine, check, test 2. to prove effective
～血 **yànxuè** анáлиз крóви	to do a blood test
～看 **yànkàn** осмáтривать; обслéдовать	1. to examine, inspect 2. to check closely
～收 **yànshōu** принимáть *(напр. строительный объект)*	to check on delivery
检 **jiǎn** проверя́ть, контролúровать; инспектúровать	1. to check, inspect, examine 2. to restrain 3. book label 4. form, pattern
～查(验) **jiǎnchá(yàn)** *см.* 检	1. to check, examine; examination

检讨 **jiǎntǎo** кри́тика; крити́ческий обзо́р	1. to discuss thoroughly 2. to self-criticize; self-criticism
～阅 **jiǎnyuè** 1. смотре́ть, наблюда́ть 2. принима́ть пара́д; пара́д	to review (troops, etc.); military review
～察 **jiǎnchá** рассле́довать; проверя́ть	to prosecute
～点 **jiǎndiǎn** проверя́ть по спи́ску	1. to examine/check carefully 2. to be cautious (in speech, deed)
签 **qiān** 1. подпи́сывать; по́дпись 2. накле́йка, этике́тка	1. to sign, autograph 2. bookmark 3. bamboo slips (for drawing lots, divination) 4. toothpick, pointed stick
～名 **qiānmíng** подпи́сываться, ста́вить по́дпись	to sign one's name, autograph
～订 **qiāndìng** подписа́ть, заключи́ть *(договор)*	to conclude and sign (a treaty, contract, etc.)
～收 **qiānshōu** распи́сываться в получе́нии	to sign after receiving sth. //to be versed in, good at
工 **gōng** рабо́та; ремесло́	1. work, productive labor 2. industry//
～程 **gōngchéng** 1. инжене́рные рабо́ты 2. сооруже́ние	engineering project
～程师 **gōngchéngshī** инжене́р	engineer
～业 **gōngyè** промы́шленность; промы́шленный, индустриа́льный	industry
～业品 **gōngyèpǐn** промы́шленные изде́лия	industrial products, manufactured goods
～业化 **gōngyèhuà** индустриализа́ция	industrialization
～作 **gōngzuò** рабо́тать; рабо́та	work, job
～作组 **gōngzuòzǔ** звено́ *(в с.-х. бригаде)*	work team/group
～间操 **gōngjiāncāo** произво́дственная гимна́стика	exercise during work-break
～商 **gōngshāng** промы́шленники и торго́вцы; торго́во-промы́шленный	industry and commerce
～商界 **gōngshāngjiè** торго́во-промы́шленные (делово́ые) круги́	industrial and commercial circles
～厂 **gōngchǎng** заво́д; фа́брика	factory, mill, plant, works

工场 **gōngchǎng** мастерска́я; фа́брика	workshop, atelier
～人 **gōngrén** рабо́чий	worker
～夫 **gōngfu** свобо́дное вре́мя, досу́г	1. time 2. workmanship; skill, art 3. work, labor, effort
～贼 **gōngzéi** штрейкбре́хер	scab, blackleg, strikebreaker
～钱 **gōngqián** зарпла́та	1. service charge 2. (coll.) wages, pay
～地 **gòngdì** стро́йка	building/construction site
～艺 **gōngyì** 1. ремесло́; ре́месленный 2. техноло́гия; технологи́ческий	technology, craft
～具 **gōngjù** ору́дие произво́дства; инструме́нт	tool, implement, instrument
～资 **gōngzī** за́работная пла́та	wages, pay
～会 **gōnghuì** профсою́з	trade/labor union
～龄 **gōnglíng** произво́дственный стаж	seniority, length of service
红 **hóng** 1. кра́сный, а́лый 2. счастли́вый, благоприя́тный 3. при́быль, дохо́д	1. red 2. revolutionary, communist 3. popular, in vogue 4. women's 5. bonus, dividend
～卫兵 **hóngwèibīng** хунвэйби́н(ы)	Red Guards
～宝石 **hóngbǎoshí** руби́н	ruby
～十字会 **hóngshízìhuì** О́бщество Кра́сного Креста́	Red Cross
～军 **hóngjūn** *ист.* Кра́сная А́рмия	1. Red Army 2. Red Army personnel
～茶 **hóngchá** ба́йховый чай	black tea
～色 **hóngsè** кра́сный цвет	1. red color 2. revolutionary
～旗 **hóngqí** кра́сное зна́мя	red flag
～枣 **hóngzǎo** жужу́б	date (fruit)
虹 **hóng** 1. ра́дуга 2. а́рка 3. дугообра́зный	rainbow
江 **jiāng** [больша́я] река́	1. river 2. Yangtze
～山 **jiāngshān** ре́ки и го́ры; страна́	1. rivers and mountains, land, landscape 2. country, state, power //country
～湖 **jiānghú** ре́ки и озёра	1. rivers and lakes 2. all corners of the//
差 **chā** ра́зница, разли́чие	difference
～ **chà** 1. про́мах; оши́бка 2. не соотве́тствовать; различа́ться	1. inferior, poor 2. to differ (by), be short, lack, be missing 3.wrong(ly)
～ **chāi** посыла́ть, командирова́ть; де́ло, поруче́ние	to send, dispatch

差距(错) **chājù(cuò)** упуще́ние; про́мах	spatial difference
～异 **chāyì** разли́чный, неодина́ковый	difference, divergence, discrepancy, diversity
～别 **chābié** различа́ть; ра́зница, разли́чие	difference
～得多(远) **chàde duō (yuǎn)** **1.** си́льно отлича́ться; о́чень больша́я ра́зница **2.** намно́го ху́же	to differ strongly/greatly; very large difference
～遣 **chāiqiǎn** посыла́ть, командирова́ть	to send, dispatch
～不离 **chàbùlí** **1.** почти́ **2.** ничего́, сойдёт!	almost, about; not bad
～不多 **chàbùduō** почти́; едва́ не	almost, about; good enough
磋 **cuō** полирова́ть; шлифова́ть	to grind, file, buff, polish
～商 **cuōshāng** согласо́вывать; догова́риваться	to consult, exchange views
左 **zuǒ** **1.** ле́вый **2.** непра́вильный, оши́бочный	1. left side 2. east 3. the Left
～证 **zuǒzhèng** доказа́тельство, ули́ка	to testify, give evidence
～右 **zuǒ-yòu** ле́вый и пра́вый	left and right
zuǒyòu приблизи́тельно, приме́рно	1. (suf.) about, around, nearly 2. to master, control, influence
～派 **zuǒpài** *полит.* ле́вые	1. the Left, the Left Wing 2. Leftist
～边 **zuǒbiān** ле́вая сторона́; вле́во; сле́ва	left side
～倾 **zuǒqīng** ле́вый укло́н; лева́цкий	left-leaning; progressive, inclined towards the revolution
揑 **niē** выду́мывать, измышля́ть; фабрикова́ть	1. to hold between the fingers, pinch 2. to knead, mold 3. to fabricate, trump up
～报 **niēbào** ло́жное сообще́ние; дезинформа́ция	false statement, disinformation
～造 **niēzào** фабрикова́ть; фальсифици́ровать; фальсифика́ция	to concoct, trump up
经 **jīng** **1.** проходи́ть *(через, мимо)* **2.** управля́ть, руководи́ть **3.** эксплуати́ровать *(предприятие)* **4.** *геогр.*	1. to pass through, undergo, stand, bear, endure 2. to manage, deal/engage in 3. longitude 4. scripture, canon, classics 5. constant, regular 6. menses

经 径 轻

меридиа́н; долгота́ **5.** в хо́де *чего;* по́сле	-
经验 **jīngyàn** о́пыт; о́пытный	to experience, go through; experience
～住 **jīngzhu** вы́держать, вы́стоять	to bear, endure, stand, sustain
～理 **jīnglǐ** **1.** управля́ть; управле́ние **2.** дире́ктор; управля́ющий	1. to manage, handle; manager, director
～营 **jīngyíng** *см.* 经 2, 3	to manage, run, engage in
～管 **jīngguǎn** управля́ть, име́ть в ве́дении; хозя́йствовать	to be in charge of
～济 **jīngjì** **1.** эконо́мика, хозя́йство; экономи́ческий, хозя́йственный **2.** эконо́мный, экономи́чный	1. economy 2. financial condition; income 3. economical, thrifty 4. of economic value
～济互助委员会 **jīngjì hùzhù wěiyuánhuì** Сове́т Экономи́ческой Взаимопо́мощи, СЭВ	Council of Mutual Economic Assistance (COMECON)
～手 **jīngshǒu** **1.** принима́ть ли́чное уча́стие **2.** посре́дник	to handle, deal with
～常 **jīngcháng** постоя́нный, обы́чный; всегда́, постоя́нно	1. day-to-day, everyday, daily 2. frequently, constantly, regularly, often
～历 **jīnglì** **1.** пережи́ть, испыта́ть **2.** про́шлое	to experience, go through, undergo; experience
～度 **jīngdù** *геогр.* долгота́	longitude
～受 **jīngshòu** терпе́ть, переноси́ть *(напр. страдания)*	to undergo, experience, withstand, stand
～过 **jīngguò** **1.** проходи́ть *(через, мимо)* **2.** пройти́ че́рез, испыта́ть **3.** по́сле того́, как **4.** ход собы́тий	1. to undergo, pass, go through 2. process, course 3. after, through, as a result of
～线 **jīngxiàn** *геогр.* меридиа́н	(geogr.) meridian
～费 **jīngfèi** расхо́ды, изде́ржки, затра́ты	funds, outlay, expenses
径 **jìng** **1.** тропи́нка, доро́жка **2.** диа́метр	1. path, track 2. diameter 3. directly, straight
～赛 **jìngsài** кросс; го́нки	(sports) track
轻 **qīng** **1.** лёгкий *(по весу)*; легко́ **2.** молодо́й **3.** легко-	1. light 2. agile 3. easy, simple 4. rash, reckless 5. unimportant 6. frivolous

мы́сленный **4.** презира́ть, пренебрега́ть; недооце́нивать	-
轻工业 **qīng gōngyè** лёгкая промы́шленность	light industry
～轻地 **qīngqīngde** слегка́, тихо́нько	lightly, gently
～信 **qīngxìn** дове́рчивый, легкове́рный	to be credulous/gullible
～年 **qīngnián** молодёжь; ю́ноша, молодо́й челове́к; ю́ность	youth, young people
～易 **qīngyì 1.** лёгкий; легко́ **2.** легкомы́сленно	lightly, rashly
～快 **qīngkuài** бы́стрый, прово́рный	brisk, lively, agile
～便 **qīngbiàn** лёгкий; удо́бный; портати́вный	light, portable, handy
～视 **qīngshì** презира́ть, пренебрега́ть; игнори́ровать	to despise, slight
～松 **qīngsōng** лёгкий, приво́льный	to relax, lighten up; light, relaxed
空 **kōng 1.** опусте́ть; пусто́й **2.** напра́сно, зря **3.** не́бо; возду́шный	1. to empty, exhaust; empty, hollow, void 2. vain and useless; unreal, impractical 3. high and vast 4. sky, space
～ **kòng 1.** свобо́дное вре́мя **2.** ме́сто, простра́нство **3.** вака́нсия	1. leisure, free/spare time 2. chance 3. room, space 4. spacious 5. wanting, blank
～虚 **kōngxū** пусто́й, поро́жний	hollow, void, devoid of meaning
～话 **kōnghuà** *см.* ～谈	empty/idle talk
～白 **kōngbái** про́пуск, пробе́л; незапо́лненный	blank space
～白点 **kōngbáidiǎn** про́пуск, пробе́л	blank, blank spot
～军 **kōngjūn** вое́нно-возду́шные си́лы, ВВС	air force
～降兵 **kōngjiàngbīng** возду́шный деса́нт; возду́шно-деса́нтные войска́	airborne force, paratroopers
～中 **kōngzhōng** в во́здухе; возду́шный; авиа-	open air/sky; aerial, overhead
～前 **kōngqián** неви́данный, небыва́лый	unprecedented

空间 **kōngjiān** простра́нство, промежу́ток	open air/sky/space
～谈 **kōngtán** пустозво́нство, болтовня́	prattle
～袭 **kōngxí** возду́шное нападе́ние, налёт	air raid
～运 **kōngyùn** возду́шные перево́зки	air transport
～战 **kōngzhàn** возду́шный бой	air battle
～气 **kōngqì** во́здух; атмосфе́ра	air; atmosphere
～想 **kōngxiǎng** фанта́зия, пусты́е мечты́	fantasy, daydream
控 **kòng 1.** подава́ть апелля́цию, апелли́ровать **2.** управля́ть; контроли́ровать	1. to accuse, charge 2. to control, dominate 3. to pour out, turn a vessel upside down
～告 **kònggào** обвиня́ть; обвине́ние	to charge, accuse
～诉 **kòngsù** подава́ть жа́лобу в суд	to accuse, denounce
～制 **kòngzhì** контроли́ровать; контро́льный	to control, dominate, command
腔 **qiāng 1.** *анат.* по́лость **2.** моти́в, мело́дия	1. (anat.) cavity 2. tune; accent; speech 3. (ct. w. for livestock)
～调 **qiāngdiào 1.** моти́в; а́рия **2.** интона́ция, акце́нт	1. tune 2. accent
诬 **wū** клевета́ть; ложь, клевета́	to accuse falsely
～告 **wūgào** оклевета́ть	to frame, falsely accuse
～蔑 **wūmiè** очерни́ть, опоро́чить	1. to slander, smear 2. to defile, tarnish
士 **shì 1.** учёный **2.** де́ятель **3.** солда́т	1. scholar; intelligentsia 2. person 3. soldier 4. specialist
～气 **shìqì** боево́й дух, мора́льное состоя́ние войск	morale
～兵 **shìbīng** солда́т, рядово́й; *сокр.* сержа́нты и солда́ты	rank-and-file soldiers
壮 **zhuàng 1.** си́льный, кре́пкий, здоро́вый **2.** взро́слый	1. strong, robust, sturdy 2. in the prime of life 3. magnificent 4. to improve
～年 **zhuàngnián** зре́лый во́зраст	prime of life
～丽 **zhuànglì** великоле́пный	majestic, magnificent

壮大 **zhuàngdà** **1.** кре́пкий, здоро́вый, си́льный **2.** грандио́зный	to grow in strength, expand
～气 **zhuàngqì** хра́брость; му́жество	(coll.) to urge on
土 **tǔ** **1.** земля́, по́чва, грунт **2.** грязь; пыль **3.** террито́рия **4.** ме́стный	1. soil, earth, clay 2. land 3. local, native, indigenous 4. crude, uncouth 5. opium
～豆 **tǔdòu** карто́фель	potato
～话 **tǔhuà** ме́стный го́вор, диале́кт	local/colloquial expressions/dialect
～产 **tǔchǎn** ме́стное произво́дство; ме́стная проду́кция	local product
～壤 **tǔrǎng** *см.* 土 1	soil
～堤 **tǔdī** на́сыпь; да́мба	embankment, dike
～地 **tǔdì** земля́; земе́льный, агра́рный	1. land, soil 2. territory
～地改革 **tǔdì gǎigé** агра́рная рефо́рма	agrarian reform
～货 **tǔhuò** това́р ме́стного произво́дства	local/native product
吐 **tǔ** **1.** плева́ть **2.** выба́лтывать	1. to expectorate, spit 2. to speak out, tell, utter
～ **tù** тошни́ть; рвать	to let/blurt out, blab
～露 **tǔlù** вы́болтать, проговори́ться	to reveal, tell
～痰 **tǔtán** ха́ркать; плева́ть	to spit, expectorate
社 **shè** **1.** о́бщество, объедине́ние **2.** комму́на; кооперати́в **3.** реда́кция; аге́нтство **4.** социа́льный, обще́ственный	1. organized body, agency, society; club 2. people's commune 3. (sacrifices to) god of the land
～评 **shèpíng** передова́я статья́; обзо́р	editorial
～论 **shèlùn** передова́я (редакцио́нная) статья́	editorial
～员 **shèyuán** **1.** член кооперати́ва (комму́ны) **2.** сотру́дник реда́кции	commune member
～会 **shèhuì** о́бщество; обще́ственный, социа́льный	society
～会主义 **shèhuìzhǔyì** социали́зм; социалисти́ческий	socialism; socialist

牡 **mǔ** саме́ц *(животного)*	male (of some birds and animals)
肚 **dù** живо́т; брю́хо	belly, abdomen, stomach
～ **dǔ** желу́док	tripe
杜 **dù** затыка́ть; зава́ливать;	to stop, prevent; to shut out
загора́живать	-
～塞 **dùsè** прегражда́ть; за-	to stop, block up
ва́ливать	-
～绝 **dùjué** пресе́чь; ликви-	to stop, put an end to
ди́ровать; прерва́ть *(отно-*	-
шения)	- //canteen
灶 **zào** оча́г; плита́	1. kitchen stove 2. kitchen; mess, //
庄 **zhuāng** 1. населённый	1. village, hamlet 2. manor 3. place of
пункт; дере́вня 2. серьёз-	business 4. banker (in gambling game)
ный	5. serious, grave
～重 **zhuāngzhòng** серьёз-	serious, grave, solemn
ный, ва́жный	-
～严 **zhuāngyán** ва́жный,	solemn, dignified, stately
торже́ственный; стро́гий	-
～户 **zhuānghù** крестья́н-	peasant household
ское хозя́йство, двор	-
～稼 **zhuāngjia** посе́вы; хле-	crops
ба́	-
脏 **zāng** па́чкать, загряз-	dirty, filthy
ня́ть; гря́зный	-
～ **zàng** вну́тренности, вну́т-	viscera, internal organs
ренние о́рганы	-
桩 **zhuāng** столб; сва́я	1. stake, pile 2. M. for items/matters
粧 **zhuāng** 1. наряжа́ться	1. to apply makeup; makeup 2. woman's
2. притворя́ться 3. украше́-	personal adornments 3. trousseau,
ния; косме́тика	dowry
赃 **zāng** по́дкуп; взя́тка;	1. booty, spoils 2. bribe
награ́бленное	-
～物 **zāngwù** награ́бленное;	1. booty, spoils 2. bribe
добы́тое нече́стным путём	-
～款 **zāngkuǎn** взя́тка	illicit money
在 **zài** 1. быть, находи́ться	1. to be, exist, live 2. (to be) at/in/on
2. быть в живы́х, жить	3.(indicates action in progress); while
3. состоя́ть, заключа́ться в	<while he was writing>
4. *перед гл. указывает на*	-
длительный характер дей-	-
ствия или состояние: 他	-
在写字 он пи́шет	-
～座 **zàizuò** прису́тствовать;	to be present
заседа́ть	-

在世 **zàishì** быть в живы́х, жить	to be living
~于(乎) **zàiyú(hu)** состоя́ть, заключа́ться в	1. to lie in, rest with 2. to be determined by, depend on
~内 **zàinèi** **1.** находи́ться внутри́ **2.** в том числе́, включа́я и	to be included; including
~场 **zàichǎng** прису́тствовать; принима́ть уча́стие	to be on the scene/spot, be present
~职 **zàizhí** находи́ться на слу́жбе (при исполне́нии служе́бных обя́занностей)	to be on the job
~心(意) **zàixīn(yì)** по́мнить, держа́ть в мы́слях	to feel concerned, mind, be attentive
鞋 **xié** о́бувь; ту́фли; боти́нки	shoes
~匠 **xiéjiàng** сапо́жник	shoemaker, cobbler
~油 **xiéyóu** крем для о́буви; гутали́н	shoe polish
挂 **guà** **1.** ве́шать; висе́ть **2.** регистри́ровать, запи́сывать	1. to hand, put up/aside, ring up 2. to hitch 3. to register, check in 4. to worry 5. (M. for sth. stringshaped)
~帅 **guàshuài** идти́ впереди́, вести́ за собо́й	to assume command/leadership (of a large army); to dominate
~彩 **guàcǎi** **1.** разукра́шивать **2.** получи́ть ране́ние	1. to decorate for festive occasions 2. to be wounded in action
~钩 **guàgōu** **1.** взять на букси́р **2.** установи́ть связь, войти́ в конта́кт	1. to couple (railway cars) 2. to articulate 3. to link up with, establish contact with 4. hook; coupling links
~号 **guàhào** регистри́ровать; нумерова́ть	1. to register 2. to send by registered mail
桂 **guì** кори́чное де́рево	1. cassia bark tree 2. laurel, bay tree 3.// //short name for Guangxi Auton. Region
娃 **wá** **1.** ребёнок **2.** ку́кла; игру́шка	1. baby; child 2. newborn animal
~娃 **wáwa** *см.* 娃	1. baby; child 2. doll
洼 **wā** впа́дина; овра́г	low-lying, hollow; low-lying area, de-// //pression
~地 **wādì** низи́на; впа́дина	depression, low-lying land
崖 **yá** обры́в	precipice, cliff
堂 **táng** **1.** зал; храм **2.** вели́чественный, торже́ственный **3.** родня́; двою́родный	1. hall 2. main room of a building/house
~屋 **tángwū** приёмная; зал	1. central room (in a trad. house) 2. // //main hall
~兄弟 **tángxiōngdì** двою́родные бра́тья	male cousins on paternal side

膛 **táng** **1.** грудна́я (брюшна́я) по́лость **2.** по́лое простра́нство	1. thorax, chest 2. inside cavity, chamber
堑 **qiàn** оборони́тельный ров; я́ма; кюве́т	moat, defensive ditch; chasm
～壕 **qiànháo** транше́я	trench, entrenchment
壁 **bì** стена́	1. wall 2. cliff 3. rampart, breastwork
型 **xíng** **1.** лите́йная фо́рма **2.** моде́ль, образе́ц; тип	1. mold 2. model, type, pattern
～式 **xíngshì** фо́рма; тип; образе́ц	form, type, pattern
塑 **sù** лепи́ть, ва́ять	model, mold
～料 **sùliào** пластма́сса, пла́стик	plastics
堕 **duò** **1.** па́дать **2.** приходи́ть в упа́док	to fall, sink
～落 **duòluò** опуска́ться *(мора́льно)*; приходи́ть в упа́док	to degenerate, sink low
～胎 **duòtāi** де́лать або́рт; або́рт	to have an (induced) abortion; induced abortion
基 **jī** осно́ва, фунда́мент, ба́за; основно́й	base, foundation
～金 **jījīn** фонд *(дене́жный)*	fund, endowment
～础 **jīchǔ** осно́ва, основа́ние, фунда́мент, ба́зис	base, foundation; basic, fundamental
～本 **jīběn** основно́й, капита́льный	basic, fundamental, elementary, essential, main; in the main, on the whole
～地 **jīdì** ба́за, опо́рный пункт	base
～层 **jīcéng** первичный, низово́й	grass-roots unit; primary level
塞 **sāi** затыка́ть; зава́ливать; прегражда́ть	to fill, stuff in; stopper, cork
～ **sài** кре́пость, форт	place of strategic importance
～ **sè** заткну́ть; заку́порить	to stop up, cork up
墓 **mù** моги́ла	grave, tomb, mausoleum
～地 **mùdì** кла́дбище	burial ground, cemetery
堡 **bǎo** **1.** кре́пость, форт **2.** глинобитное строе́ние	fort, fortress
～垒 **bǎolěi** **1.** кре́пость, форт **2.** ла́герь, оплот	fort, fortress
垦 **kěn** распа́хивать *(цели́ну)*; целина́	to cultivate, reclaim (wasteland)

垦地(荒) **kěndì(huāng)** под-	to cultivate land
нимáть целинý	-
圣 **shèng** **1.** святóй; свящéн-	1. sage, saint 2. emperor 3. genius 4.
ный **2.** совершéнный	sacred, holy 5. imperial 6. eminent
怪 **guài** **1.** удивúтельный,	1. surprising, strange; to find sth.
стрáнный; чýдо **2.** удив-	strange 2. to blame 3. quite, very 4.
ля́ться **3.** выговáривать,	monster, evil spirit
упрекáть	-
～话 **guàihuà** абсýрд	1. cynical remark 2. complaint
～物 **guàiwù** привидéние,	1. monster, freak 2. eccentric fellow
прúзрак; чудóвище	-
～不得 **guàibùdé** неудиви́-	1. no wonder, so that's why 2. not to
тельно, что	blame
坚 **jiān** **1.** крепúть, укреп-	1. hard, solid, strong, firm; firmly,
ля́ть; прóчный, твёрдый,	resolutely 2. stronghold, fortification
крéпкий **2.** решúтельный,	-
настóйчивый	-
～苦 **jiānkǔ** трýдный; на-	adamant
пряжённый	-
～固 **jiāngù** прóчный, крéп-	firm, solid, sturdy
кий	-
～持 **jiānchí** **1.** крéпко дер-	1. to persist in 2. to inisist on
жáться **2.** настáивать на,	-
отстáивать; твёрдо при-	-
дéрживаться	-
～守 **jiānshǒu** прóчно удéр-	to stick to, hold fast to
живать *(позиции)*	-
～实 **jiānshí** прóчный, твёр-	1. solid, substantial 2. robust
дый, надёжный	-
～决 **jiānjué** решúтельный	firm, determined; firmly, resolutely
～定 **jiāndìng** твёрдый, не-	firm, staunch, steadfast; to strength-
поколебúмый	en
～硬 **jiānyìng** *см.* 坚 2	hard, solid
～忍 **jiānrěn** вынóсливый,	steadfast and persevering
терпелúвый	-
～强 **jiānqiáng** укрепля́ть;	strong, firm, staunch; to strengthen
сúльный; мóщный; крéп-	-
кий	-
垄 **lǒng** **1.** бороздá **2.** холм;	1. ridge in a field 2. raised path be-
нáсыпь	tween fields
～断 **lǒngduàn** монопóлия;	to monopolize
монополизúровать; моно-	-
пóльный	- //2. to advance money 3. cushion
垫 **diàn** **1.** подпóрка **2.** под-	1. to put sth. under sth. else; to fill up//

сти́лка; сиде́нье **3.** ода́л-	-
живать; аванси́ровать	-
尘 **chén** пыль	1. dust, dirt 2. this world
～土(埃) **chéntǔ(āi)** пыль	dust
墨 **mò** **1.** тушь; черни́ла	1. ink, ink cake 2. handwriting 3. black;
2. тёмный; чёрный **3.** а́лч-	pitch-dark 4. corrupt, venal
ный	-
～守成规 **mòshǒu chéngguī**	to stick to conventions
цепля́ться за ста́рое; при-	-
де́рживаться консервати́в-	-
ных взгля́дов	- //learning
～水 **mòshuǐ** тушь; черни́ла	1. prepared Chinese ink 2. ink 3. book//
垒 **lěi** кре́пость, форт; укреп-	1. to build by piling up 2. rampart 3.
лённый пункт	baseball base
至 **zhì** **1.** доходи́ть, дости-	1. to, until, till 2. extreme(ly), most 3. to
га́ть **2.** в вы́сшей сте́пени,	arrive, reach
весьма́ **3.** что каса́ется	-
～今 **zhìjīn** до сего́дняшне-	until now, up to now; still, for the pre-
го дня, до сих по́р	sent
～于 **zhìyú** что каса́ется	as for/to; (go) so far as to
～少 **zhìshǎo** са́мое ма́лое,	at (the) least
минима́льно, ми́нимум	-
～多 **zhìduō** са́мое бо́льшее,	at (the) most
максима́льно, ма́ксимум	-
侄 **zhí** племя́нник	brother's son, nephew
～女 **zhínǚ** племя́нница	woman weaver
屋 **wū** ко́мната; дом; жильё;	1. house 2. room
помеще́ние	-
～顶 **wūdǐng** кры́ша	roof, housetop
握 **wò** **1.** держа́ть, сжима́ть	to hold, grasp
(в руке) **2.** при́го́ршня	-
～手 **wòshǒu** пожа́ть ру́ку;	to shake/clasp hands
рукопожа́тие	-
～拳 **wòquán** сжима́ть кула-	to make/clench fist
ки́	-
室 **shì** помеще́ние; ко́мната;	1. room 2. house 3. work unit 4. wife
кабине́т	-
坐 **zuò** **1.** сесть; сиде́ть	1. to sit (down) 2. to travel by (plane,
2. е́хать на (в)	etc.) 3. to sink 4. recoil 5. to be pun-\\
～位 **zuòwèi** ме́сто; сиде́нье	place, seat \\ished 6. seat 7. because
～落 **zuòluò** местоположе́ние	to be situated/located
～下 **zuòxia** сесть; сади́тесь!	to sit down
～视 **zuòshì** быть сторо́нним	to sit by and watch
наблюда́телем	-

挫 **cuò 1.** неуда́ча **2.** уни́зить; сломи́ть	1. to defeat, frustrate 2. to subdue, deflate
～折 **cuòzhé** неуда́ча	setback, reverse
座 **zuò 1.** сиде́нье; ме́сто **2.** трон **3.** *сч. сл. для гор и фундаментальных сооружений*	1. seat, place 2. stand, pedestal, base 3. constellation 4. fare 5. (restaurant) customer 6. (M. for mountains, bridges, etc.)
～谈会 **zuòtánhuì** собесе́дование; пресс-конфере́нция; семина́р	forum, symposium - -
压 **yā 1.** дави́ть; прессова́ть **2.** угнета́ть; гнёт	1. to press, push/hold down 2. to control; to quell 3. to pigeonhole, shelve\\
～倒 **yādǎo** превосходи́ть; довле́ть	to overwhelm, overpower \\4. pressure -
～倒多数 **yādǎo duōshù** подавля́ющее большинство́	overwhelming majority -
～制 **yāzhì** подавля́ть; притесня́ть; подверга́ть репре́ссиям	1. to suppress, stifle, inhibit 2. (mach.) press -
～力 **yālì** давле́ние; нажи́м	pressure
～伏(服) **yāfú(fú)** подчиня́ть; принужда́ть си́лой	to force/compel sb. to submit -
～迫 **yāpò** угнета́ть; гнёт; и́го	1. to oppress, repress 2. to constrict -
～死(坏) **yāsǐ(huài)** раздави́ть, задави́ть	to crush, overwhelm, run over -
任 **rèn 1.** ве́рить; полага́ться на **2.** назнача́ть *(на должность)* **3.** слу́жба; до́лжность **4.** попусти́тельствовать; допуска́ть **5.** любо́й, вся́кий	1. to serve in a position 2. to appoint to a position 3. to allow 4. official post 5. no matter (what/how) - - -
～命 **rènmìng** *см.* 任 2	human life
～何 **rènhé** любо́й, вся́кий	any, whatever
～务 **rènwù** зада́ча, зада́ние	assignment, job
～职 **rènzhí** *см.* 任 2	to hold a position
呈 **chéng** рапортова́ть; ра́порт, донесе́ние	1. to assume (a form/color/etc.) 2. to submit, present 3. petition, memorial
～报 **chéngbào** докла́дывать; предста́вить докла́д (ра́порт)	to submit a report - -
程 **chéng 1.** путь, маршру́т **2.** пра́вило; образе́ц **3.** проце́сс; после́довательность	1. rule, regulation 2. order, procedure 3. journey 4. distance -

程望王旺狂班

程序 **chéngxù** поря́док; програ́мма; процеду́ра	1. order, procedure, course, sequence 2. program
～序化 **chéngxùhuà** программи́рование	programming
～度 **chéngdù** сте́пень, у́ровень	level, degree, extent
望 **wàng 1.** смотре́ть вдаль **2.** наде́яться; ожида́ть	1. to observe 2. to visit 3. to hope, expect 4. to approach 5. reputation
～远镜 **wàngyuǎnjìng** бино́кль	telescope
～见 **wàngjiàn** посети́ть, нанести́ визи́т	1. to see 2. to meet/see one another
王 **wáng** коро́ль; прави́тель; князь	1. king, sovereign, prince 2. grand, great, honorable
旺 **wàng 1.** све́тлый; блестя́щий **2.** расцве́т, процвета́ние	prosperous, flourishing, vigorous
～盛 **wàngshèng** процвета́ть; процвета́ние	vigorous, exuberant
狂 **kuáng 1.** беси́ться; бе́шенство **2.** сумасбро́дный; распу́щенный	1. mad, crazy 2. violent, wild, unrestrained 3. arrogant, overbearing 4. mania, insanity
～言 **kuángyán** враньё; пустозво́нство	1. ravings 2. bragging
～喜 **kuángxǐ** ликова́ние, восто́рг	wild with joy
～人 **kuángrén** манья́к	1. madman, maniac 2. (derog.) unbalanced/conceited person
～犬病 **kuángquǎnbìng** *мед.* бе́шенство	(med.) rabies
～风 **kuángfēng** урага́н; бу́ря	gale-force wind
～热 **kuángrè** ажиота́ж; аза́рт	fanatical, feverish
班 **bān 1.** расставля́ть; располага́ть **2.** гру́ппа; *воен.* отделе́ние **3.** сме́на; о́чередь; дежу́рство	spot, speck, stripe; spotted, striped
～次 **bāncì 1.** о́чередь; в поря́дке о́череди **2.** рейс	1. order of school classes/grades 2. number of runs/flights
～长 **bānzhǎng** бригади́р *(на произво́дстве);* ста́роста *(гру́ппы);* команди́р *(отделе́ния)*	1. class monitor 2. squad leader 3. (work) team leader
～机 **bānjī** ре́йсовый самолёт	1. airliner 2. regular air service; scheduled flight

枉 **wǎng 1.** искажáть; искажённый **2.** зря, напрáсно	1. to distort, pervert 2. to wrong 3. to deign 4. crooked, bent 5. vainly
~然 **wǎngrán** *см.* 枉 2	futile, purposeless
~法 **wǎngfǎ** нарушáть закóн; незакóнный	to pervert the law -//4. scheduled, regular 5. (M. for crowds,etc.)
斑 **bān** пёстрый; пятни́стый	1. class, team 2. shift, duty 3. squad//
~点 **bāndiǎn** пятнó; пя́тна	spot, stain, speckle
汪 **wāng** поливáть; увлажня́ть	1. to collect, accumulate (of liquid) 2. to soak 3. puddle, pool
~洋 **wāngyáng** неогля́дный, необозри́мый	vast, boundless (of water) -
皇 **huáng** имперáтор; царь	1. emperor, sovereign 2. imperial, royal
~宫 **huánggōng** имперáторский дворéц	(imperial) palace -
~帝 **huángdì** имперáтор; богдыхáн	emperor -
惶 **huáng** смятéние; страх; пáника	1. afraid, fearful 2. anxious, uneasy 3. hurried, flurried
~恐 **huángkǒng** испугáться; страх; пáника	terrified -
煌 **huáng** сверкáть; сия́ющий; свéтлый	bright, brilliant -
全 **quán** весь, цéлый; целикóм; совершéнно	to make perfect/complete; keep intact; complete(ly), whole(ly)
~盘 **quánpán** весь, целикóм, пóлностью	total, overall, comprehensive, complete -
~国 **quánguó** вся странá; общегосудáрственный	the whole country/nation; nationwide; national
~面 **quánmiàn** всесторóнний; всеóбщий	comprehensive, overall, all-round, all-out
~部 **quánbù** весь, целикóм, всецéло	whole, complete, total, all -
~局 **quánjú** óбщая обстанóвка (ситуáция)	overall situation -
~集 **quánjí** пóлное собрáние сочинéний	complete/collected works -
~体 **quántǐ** все; всеóбщий; пленáрный	whole body, plenary assembly; all, unanimously
~球战略 **quánqiú zhànlüè** глобáльная стратéгия	global strategy -
~权 **quánquán** полномóчия; полномóчный	full/plenary powers -
~民 **quánmín** весь нарóд; всенарóдный	whole/entire people, all the people -

全景电影 **quánjǐng diànyǐng** кинопанора́ма	panoramic movie -
玉 **yù** **1.** я́шма; нефри́т **2.** прекра́сный; благоро́дный	1. jade 2. fair, beautiful (of women) 3. (polite) your -
～米 **yùmǐ** кукуру́за	maize, (Indian) corn
宝 **bǎo** сокро́вище; драгоце́нный, дорого́й	treasure; precious, treasured -
～座 **bǎozuò** трон	throne
～石 **bǎoshí** драгоце́нный ка́мень	gem, precious stone -
～库 **bǎokù** сокро́вищница	treasure-house, treasury
～藏 **bǎozàng** бога́тства недр	precious (mineral) deposits
～贝 **bǎobèi** сокро́вище; драгоце́нность	1. treasured object 2. darling 3. cowry 4. good-for-nothing 5. to treasure
～贵 **bǎoguì** це́нный, дорого́й	to value; valuable, precious
主 **zhǔ** **1.** хозя́ин; нача́льник; заве́дующий; управля́ющий **2.** гла́вный; ва́жный **3.** приде́рживаться; стоя́ть за	1. master 2. owner 3. host 4. to direct, manage 5. main, principal 6. to indicate 7. to advocate 8. opinion, view 9. god 10. ancestral tablet 11. person/party concerned
～任 **zhǔrèn** *см.* 主 1	director, head, chair
～语 **zhǔyǔ** *грам.* подлежа́щее	(gram.) subject -
～管 **zhǔguǎn** ве́дать; заве́довать; компете́нтный	to be responsible for, be in charge of; person in charge of
～旨 **zhǔzhǐ** гла́вная устано́вка; основна́я иде́я	purport, substance, gist -
～子 **zhǔz** джентльме́н	master, boss
～持 **zhǔchí** возглавля́ть; заве́довать; управля́ть	1. to take charge/care of, manage, direct 2. to uphold, stand for
～编 **zhǔbiān** гла́вный реда́ктор	editor-in-chief, chief editor/compiler; to edit, supervise publication
～席 **zhǔxí** председа́тельствовать; председа́тель, председа́тельствующий	1. chair (of a meeting) 2. chair/president (of organization/state) -
～席团 **zhǔxítuán** прези́диум	presidium
～力 **zhǔlì** гла́вная (основна́я) си́ла	(mil.) main force -
～动 **zhǔdòng** инициати́ва; веду́щий; де́йствующий	initiative; on one's own initiative; (mach.) driving
～办 **zhǔbàn** возглавля́ть, руководи́ть	to direct, sponsor, host -
～人 **zhǔrén** хозя́ин; шеф	1. master 2. host 3. owner

主张 **zhǔzhāng** то́чка зре́ния; приде́рживаться *(како́го-л. взгля́да)*; стоя́ть за	to advocate, stand for, maintain, hold; view, position, stand, proposition
~义 **zhǔyì** 1. основно́й при́нцип; уче́ние 2. *суф. сущ.* =изм; =ство	doctrine, -ism
~权 **zhǔquán** суверените́т; сувере́нные права́	sovereign rights; sovereignty
~观 **zhǔguān** субъекти́вный	subjectivity; subjective
~观主义 **zhǔguānzhǔyì** субъективи́зм	subjectivism
~要 **zhǔyào** са́мый ва́жный, гла́вный; госпо́дствующий	main, chief, principal, major
住 **zhù** 1. остана́вливаться; жить, прожива́ть 2. прекраща́ться	1. to live, reside, stay 2. to stop, cease 3. (suf.) tightly, firmly
~址 **zhùzhǐ** а́дрес	address
~戶 **zhùhù** жиле́ц, кварти-ра́нт	household; resident
~房 **zhùfáng** прожива́ть; квартирова́ть	household, lodging
~家 **zhùjiā** жить до́ма	to reside; residence
~宅 **zhùzhái** жили́ще; кварти́ра	residence, dwelling
往 **wǎng** 1. идти́, отправля́ться, направля́ться 2. про́шлый; пре́жде	1. to go toward 2. past, previous
~往 **wǎngwǎng** ча́сто; постоя́нно	often, frequently
~后 **wǎnghòu** наза́д	henceforth, from now on, later, in the future
~后退 **wǎnghòu tuì** отходи́ть (отступа́ть) наза́д	to retreat, step back, recede
~日 **wǎngrì** пре́жде, в пре́жние времена́	(in) former days
~年 **wǎngnián** в про́шлом	(in) former years
~前 **wǎngqián** вперёд	ahead
~前走 **wǎngqián zǒu** идти́ вперёд	to go ahead
~来 **wǎnglái** 1. уходи́ть и приходи́ть; туда́ и обра́тно 2. теку́щий *(о счёте)* 3. отноше́ния, свя́зи	1. to come and go 2. contact, intercourse
~复 **wǎngfù** туда́ и обра́тно	back and forth

往返(还) **wǎng-fǎn(huán)** туда́ и обра́тно; уходи́ть и возвраща́ться	to go and return; there and back
驻 **zhù 1.** пребыва́ть, находи́ться *(временно)*; дислоци́роваться; быть расквартиро́ванным **2.** быть аккредито́ванным	1. to halt, stay 2. to be stationed at
～华 **zhùhuá** аккредито́ванные (находя́щиеся) в Кита́е	to be accredited to (stationed in) China
～军 **zhùjūn** расквартиро́ванные войска́; гарнизо́н	billeted troops; garrison
～守 **zhùshǒu** обороня́ть; уде́рживать	to garrison, defend
～防 **zhùfáng** быть расквартиро́ванным	to be on garrison duty, garrison
～扎(屯) **zhùzhá(tún)** расквартиро́вывать войска́	to be stationed, quartered
柱 **zhù 1.** коло́нна; столб; подпо́рка **2.** подде́рживать, служи́ть подпо́ркой	post, upright, pillar, column
～石 **zhùshí 1.** коло́нна; столб **2.** осно́ва, костя́к	pillar, mainstay
注 **zhù 1.** обраща́ть *(внимание)* **2.** разъясня́ть, комменти́ровать **3.** де́лать заме́тки; запи́сывать **4.** влива́ть(ся); впада́ть *(о реке)*	1. to pour 2. to annotate 3. to concentrate 4. to record, register 5. stakes (in gambling) 6. notes, annotation 7. (M. for business deals)
～重 **zhùzhòng** обраща́ть серьёзное внима́ние	to lay stress on, pay attention to
～射 **zhùshè** впры́скивать; инъе́кция	to inject
～明 **zhùmíng** разъясня́ть, поясня́ть	to indicate/note clearly
～定 **zhùdìng** предопределя́ть	to be doomed/destined
～记 **zhùjì** де́лать заме́тки; запи́сывать	to note, make notes, write down
～视 **zhùshì** следи́ть, наблюда́ть	to watch attentively, gaze at
～意 **zhùyì** обраща́ть внима́ние; внима́ние	to pay attention to, take note of
金 **jīn 1.** мета́лл; зо́лото;	1. metals 2. gold; golden 3. money 4. // //precious 5. durable 6. Jin (dynasty)

де́ньги **2.** золоти́стый;	-
жёлтый	-
金星 **jīnxīng 1.** золота́я звез-	(astron.) Venus
да́ **2.** *астр.* Вене́ра	-
～刚石 **jīngāngshí** алма́з;	diamond
бриллиа́нт	-
～子 **jīnz** зо́лото	gold
～属 **jīnshǔ** мета́ллы; ме-	metals (in general)
талли́ческий	-
～矿 **jīnkuàng** золоты́е при́-	gold mine
иски	-
～融 **jīnróng** де́нежное обра-	finance, banking
ще́ние; фина́нсы	-
鉴 **jiàn 1.** рассма́тривать;	1. to reflect, mirror 2. inspect, examine
определя́ть **2.** предостере-	3. warning, object lesson 4. (polite)
га́ть	to peruse (a letter)
～于 **jiànyú** принима́я во	in view of, seeing that
внима́ние, что...	-
～定 **jiàndìng** характеризо-	to appraise, identify, authenticate; ap-
ва́ть; определя́ть; харак-	praisal
тери́стика; аттеста́ция	-
～戒 **jiànjiè** предостереже́-	warning, object lesson
ние	-
生 **shēng 1.** роди́ть(ся);	1. to give birth to, bear 2. to grow 3.
рожда́ть(ся) **2.** жить, су-	to get, have, cause to happen 4. to
ществова́ть **3.** производи́ть	make (a fire) 5. to exist, live; living, a-
4. появля́ться, возника́ть	live; existence, life 6. unripe, green,
5. необрабо́танный; сыро́й	raw, uncooked 7. unfamiliar, strange
6. нео́пытный	8. stiff, mechanical 9. very keenly \\
～理 **shēnglǐ** физиологи́че-	physiology \\10. pupil, student,scholar
ские проце́ссы; физиоло-	-
ги́ческий	-
～理学 **shēnglǐxué** физиоло́-	physiology
гия	-
～殖 **shēngzhí** размножа́ть-	(biol.) to reproduce
ся; размноже́ние	-
～活 **shēnghuó** жизнь	1. life; existence 2. livelihood, profes-\\
～日 **shēngrì** день рожде́ния	birthday \\sion 3. to live
～命 **shēngmìng** жизнь; судь-	life
ба́	-
～存 **shēngcún** жить, суще-	to subsist, exist, live
ствова́ть; существова́ние	-
～字 **shēngzì** незнако́мый ие-	unfamiliar/new word
ро́глиф	-

生育 **shēngyù** рожда́ть; рожда́емость	to give birth to, bear
～病 **shēngbìng** заболе́ть	to fall ill
～产 **shēngchǎn** **1.** роди́ть **2.** производи́ть; произво́дство; произво́дственный	1. to produce, manufacture 2. to give birth to a child
～物学 **shēngwùxué** биоло́гия	biology
～力 **shēnglì** жи́зненные си́лы	fresh (of reinforcements)
～动 **shēngdòng** живо́й; жи́зненный	lively, vivid
～长 **shēngzhǎng** расти́; вы́расти	to grow, develop
～水 **shēngshui** сыра́я вода́	unboiled water
～效 **shēngxiào** вступа́ть в си́лу	to go into effect, become effective
～气 **shēngqì** **1.** серди́ться **2.** [жи́зненная] эне́ргия; живо́й	1. information 2. physical/spiritual relations/affinity
～货 **shēnghuò** сырьё; полуфабрика́т	semifinished product
～意 **shēngyì** сде́лка	business, trade
性 **xìng** **1.** сво́йство; хара́ктер **2.** *биол.* пол; полово́й	1. nature, character, disposition; property, quality 2. sex, gender 3. (suf.)\\ \\ -ty, -ness
～格 **xìnggé** ка́чества челове́ка; темпера́мент	nature, temperament
～质 **xìngzhì** сво́йство; хара́ктер	quality, nature, character
牲 **shēng** живо́тное; скот	1. domestic animal 2. animal sacrifice
～畜 **shēngchù** скот	livestock, domestic animal
胜 **shèng** **1.** брать верх, побежда́ть **2.** превосходи́ть **3.** прекра́сный **4.** спосо́бный	1. to win victory, succeed, surpass, excel 2. victory 3. scenic view 4. triumphant, superb, distinctive
～任 **shèngrèn** справля́ться **с** обя́занностями	to be competent/qualified
～利 **shènglì** побе́да	to win victory/success; victory
～过 **shèngguo** превосходи́ть *в чём*	to excel, surpass
～负 **shèng-fù** исхо́д борьбы́; оконча́тельный результа́т	victory and/or defeat; success and/or failure
姓 **xìng** носи́ть фами́лию; фами́лия	surname, family/clan name

姓名 **xìngmíng** фами́лия и и́мя	full name
星 **xīng** небе́сное те́ло; звезда́	1. star; heavenly body 2. particle, bit 3. weight marks on steel yard
～期 **xīngqī** неде́ля	1. week 2. Sunday
～期一(二,三,四,五,六,日) **xīngqīyī (èr, sān, sì, wǔ, liù, rì)** понеде́льник (вто́рник, среда́, четве́рг, пя́тница, суббо́та, воскресе́нье)	Monday (Tuesday, Wednesday, Thursday, Friday, Saturday, Sunday)
～火 **xīnghuǒ** и́скра; бы́стрый, стреми́тельный	1. spark 2. shooting star, meteor
～际 **xīngjì** межпланéтное простра́нство	interplanetary, interstellar
醒 **xǐng** пробужда́ться, просыпа́ться	1. to come to, sober up 2. to wake up, be awake 3. to be clear in mind\\
～悟 **xǐngwù** 1. очну́ться, прийти́ в себя́ 2. поня́ть, осозна́ть	to come to realize, \\4. to be striking wake up to reality
腥 **xīng** за́тхлый; ду́рно па́хнущий	raw meat/fish; fishy smell
～臭 **xīngchòu** воню́чий	stench
～味儿 **xīngwèir** дурно́й за́пах	interest, tastes
隆 **lóng** 1. ще́дрый; оби́льный; процвета́ющий 2. возвыша́ться; высо́кий	1. prosperous, brisk, booming 2. lofty, eminent, glorious 3. abundant, ample 4. generous and kind 5. rumbling
～重 **lóngzhòng** вели́чественный; торже́ственный	grand, solemn, ceremonious
～起 **lóngqǐ** поднима́ться, вздыма́ться	to swell, bulge
垂 **chuí** висе́ть; све́шиваться; вертика́льный	1. to hang down, let fall 2. to hand down 3. to approach 4. to condescend
～直 **chuízhí** вертика́льный, отве́сный	perpendicular, vertical
～危 **chuíwēi** смерте́льно опа́сный	to be critically ill
睡 **shuì** спать; сон	to sleep
～着 **shuìzháo** засну́ть; во сне́	to fall asleep
～觉 **shuìjiào** спать	to go to bed, to sleep
锤 **chuí** мо́лот	1. hammer 2. mace 3. weight 4. to shape
～炼 **chuíliàn** кова́ть	to hammer into shape, forge; polish
谨 **jǐn** 1. осторо́жный, осмот-	1. careful, cautious, circumspect 2. so-

姓星醒腥隆垂睡锤谨

谨里埋理

ри́тельный, внима́тельный	lemnly, sincerely
2. почти́тельный	-
谨严 **jinyán** 1. осторо́жно	precise, cogent
2. стро́го	-
～慎 **jinshèn** внима́тельно;	cautious, circumspect
осторо́жно	-
里 **lǐ** 1. ли *(мера длины, рав-*	1. lining, inside 2. neighborhood 3.
ная 0,5 км) 2. подкла́дка	hometown, native place 4. Ch. mile: =
3. *послелог* внутри́, в; 皮	1/2 km, 1/3 mile 5. internal, interior,
包里 в портфе́ле 4. *суф.*	inside 6. suf. for place
наречий места и времени:	-
那里 там; 夜里 но́чью	-
～程 **lǐchéng** расстоя́ние	1. mileage 2. course (of development)
～程碑 **lǐchéngbēi** верстово́й	milestone
столб; ве́ха	-
～面 **lǐmian** внутри́, в	inside, interior
～子 **lǐz** подкла́дка	lining
～头(边) **lǐtóu(biān)** внут-	inside, interior
ри́, в	-
埋 **mái** зары́ть в зе́млю, за-	to bury
копа́ть; похорони́ть	-
～葬 **máizàng** хорони́ть	to bury
～头 **máitóu** уйти́ с голово́й	to immerse oneself up to one's ears in
(в какое-л. занятие)	-
～伏 **máifu** устро́ить заса́ду;	to hide, lie low; to ambush
заса́да	-
理 **lǐ** 1. при́нцип; зако́н; те-	1. texture/grain 2. reason, logic, truth
о́рия 2. моти́в, до́вод	3. natural science 4. law, principle,
3. приводи́ть в поря́док	theory 5. to manage, run 6. to put in
4. управля́ть, вести́ дела́	order, tidy up 7. to take notice, ac-
5. рациона́льный, разу́м-	knowledge 8. to administer, govern,
ный	operate
～性 **lǐxìng** рассу́док; ра́зум,	reason
интелле́кт	-
～智 **lǐzhì** ра́зум, интелле́кт	reason, intellect
～由 **lǐyóu** причи́на; аргу-	reason, grounds, argument
ме́нт	-
～解 **lǐjiě** поня́ть, разобра́ть-	to understand, comprehend
ся	-
～事 **lǐshì** управля́ть дела́ми	council member; director
～事会 **lǐshìhuì** правле́ние;	council; board of directors
сове́т	-
～发 **lǐfà** стри́чься; де́лать	haircut, hairdressing
причёску	-

理发馆 lǐfàguǎn парикма́херская	barbershop; hairdresser
～论 lǐlùn тео́рия; уче́ние	theory
～论家 lǐlùnjiā теоре́тик	theoretician, theorist
～想 lǐxiǎng 1. идеа́л 2. гипо́теза, предположе́ние	ideal, ideal (attr.)
～会 lǐhuì поня́ть, разобра́ться	1. to understand, comprehend 2. to take notice of, pay attention to
哩 lǐ ми́ля *(английская, равная 1,609 км)*	statute/British mile (=1.6 km)
缠 chán обма́тывать; перевя́зывать	1. to wind, twine 2. to tangle, tie up 3. to pester
量 liáng ме́рить, измеря́ть; взве́шивать	to measure
～ liàng 1. ме́ра; вес; объём; разме́р 2. коли́чество	1. capacity 2. quantity, amount, volume 3. to estimate, measure
～具 liángjù измери́тельные прибо́ры	measuring tool
童 tóng ребёнок; подро́сток; ю́ный	boy servant
～工 tónggōng 1. де́тский труд 2. рабо́чий-подро́сток	1. child laborer 2. child labor
～话 tónghuà де́тские расска́зы; ска́зки	children's stories, fairy tales
～年 tóngnián де́тские го́ды; о́трочество	childhood
撞 zhuàng 1. ударя́ть, бить; стуча́ть 2. толкну́ть; столкну́ться	1. to run into, strike, collide 2. to meet by chance 3. to rush, dash 4. to dupe
～倒 zhuàngdǎo опроки́нуть, переверну́ть	1. to overturn, overthrow, overrun 2. to turn over
～骗 zhuàngpiàn обману́ть	to swindle
重 zhòng 1. тя́жесть; вес; тяжёлый 2. придава́ть значе́ние; цени́ть 3. ва́жный	1. weight 2. heavy, weighty, important 3. serious, solemn 4. to lay stress on, attach importance to
～ chóng повторя́ть; сно́ва, опя́ть, вновь	to repeat, duplicate; again, once more; (suf.) -fold; (M. for layers)
～工业 zhòng gōngyè тяжёлая промы́шленность	heavy industry
～量 zhòngliàng вес	weight
～新 chóngxīn сно́ва, вновь; возобнови́ть; пере=; воз=	again, anew, afresh
～力 zhònglì тя́жесть; *физ.* си́ла тя́жести	gravity, gravitational force

重懂止址耻扯企正

重大 **zhòngdà** значи́тельный, ва́жный	great, weighty, significant, major, important
～复 **chóngfù** повторя́ть; дубли́ровать	to repeat, duplicate; repetition
～视 **zhòngshì** придава́ть серьёзное значе́ние; цени́ть	to attach importance to, take sth. seriously, value
～心 **zhòngxīn** центр тя́жести	1. (phys.) center of gravity 2. heart, core, focus
～点 **zhòngdiǎn** ва́жный уча́сток; *перен.* центр тя́жести; суть, су́щность	focal point, stress, emphasis
～要 **zhòngyào** ва́жный, значи́тельный	important, significant, major
懂 **dǒng** поня́ть, уясни́ть	to understand, know
止 **zhǐ 1.** остана́вливать(ся); прекраща́ть(ся) **2.** включи́тельно **3.** то́лько	1. to stop, halt, arrive at 2. to suppress, prohibit 3. to stay; to detain 4. only, merely 5. demeanor, bearing
～痛 **zhǐtòng** успоко́ить боль; болеутоля́ющий	to relieve/stop pain
～步 **zhǐbù** останови́ться	to halt, stop, go no farther
～渴 **zhǐkě** утоли́ть жа́жду	to quench thirst
～境 **zhǐjìng** преде́л, коне́ц	end, limit
址 **zhǐ** местоположе́ние; а́дрес	location, site
耻 **chǐ** позо́р; униже́ние; стыд	shame, disgrace, humiliation
～辱 **chǐrǔ** *см.* 耻	shame, disgrace, humiliation
扯 **chě 1.** тащи́ть, тяну́ть **2.** рвать *(бумагу)* **3.** пустосло́вить	1. to pull, tear 2. to buy (cloth) 3. chat, gossip
～谎 **chěhuǎng** лгать, врать	to tell a lie
企 **qǐ** предпринима́ть; пыта́ться; попы́тка	1. to stand on tiptoe 2. to expect sth. anxiously, look forward to
～望 **qǐwàng** наде́яться; жела́ть	to hope, look forward to; hope
～业 **qǐyè** предприя́тие	enterprise, business
～图 **qǐtú** наме́рение; за́мысел; попы́тка	to attempt, scheme
正 **zhèng 1.** исправля́ть; упоря́дочивать **2.** пра́вильный, то́чный **3.** и́стинный, настоя́щий **4.** справедли́вый **5.** как ра́з; то́чно	1. straight, upright 2. central 3. exact, due 4. obverse, rector, right 5. pure, unmixed (of flavors/etc.) 6. correct, orthodox 7. main 8. positive 9. honest 10. to rectify 11. precisely, punctually

正在 **zhèngzài** как ра́з в; в проце́ссе	to be in the process/course of
～理 **zhènglǐ** основны́е при́нципы	correct principle/reason/argument/procedure
～当 **zhèngdàng** норма́льный, пра́вильный	proper, legitimate
～面 **zhèngmiàn** лицева́я сторона́; фаса́д; анфа́с	1. obverse/right side 2. front, facade 3. positive 4. directly, openly
～午 **zhèngwǔ** по́лдень	high noon
～门 **zhèngmén** гла́вный вход	main entrance
～确 **zhèngquè** то́чный, достове́рный	correct, right, proper
～常 **zhèngcháng** обы́чный, норма́льный	normal, regular
～常化 **zhèngchánghuà** нормализа́ция	normalization
～方 **zhèngfāng** квадра́т; квадра́тный	square
～大 **zhèngdà** справедли́вый; че́стный	upright, honest
～派 **zhèngpài** че́стный, поря́дочный	upright, honest, decent
～是 **zhèngshì** как ра́з, и́менно	to be exactly/precisely
～义 **zhèngyì** справедли́вость; справедли́вый	justice
～式 **zhèngshì** официа́льный	formal (of actions/speeches/etc.)
～规 **zhèngguī** норма́льный; регуля́рный	regular, standard
～负 **zhèng-fù** плюс и ми́нус	1. plus-minus 2. positive and negative
征 **zhēng 1.** покоря́ть; усмиря́ть **2.** собира́ть *(налоги)* **3.** призыва́ть *(в армию);* вербова́ть **4.** похо́д	1. to go on a journey 2. to start a campaign 3. to levy taxes/etc. 4. to take, seize, demand 5. evidence, proof, sign
～集 **zhēngjí** призыва́ть *(в армию);* вербова́ть; призы́в	1. to collect 2. to draft, call up, recruit
～服 **zhēngfú** завоёвывать; покоря́ть	to conquer, subjugate
～税 **zhēngshuì** взима́ть нало́ги	to levy/collect taxes
～兵 **zhēngbīng** призыва́ть *(в армию);* вербова́ть солда́т	to draft, call up
证 **zhèng 1.** доказа́тельство,	1. to prove, testify, demonstrate; evi-

свидéтельство, подтверждéние **2.** удостоверéние, докумéнт	dence, proof, testimony 2. certificate, card, credentials
证据 **zhèngjù** доказáтельство, свидéтельство; ули́ка	evidence, testimony, proof
～明 **zhèngmíng** докáзывать; свидéтельствовать, удостоверя́ть	1. to prove, testify, bear out 2. certificate, identification, testimonial, proof
～明书 **zhèngmíngshū** удостоверéние, свидéтельство	certificate, testimonial
～实 **zhèngshí** докáзывать, подтверждáть	to confirm, verify
～见 **zhèngjiàn** свидéтельствовать, удостоверя́ть	1. evidence 2. eyewitness, witness
整 **zhěng** **1.** устрáивать; приводи́ть в поря́док, упоря́дочивать **2.** весь, цéлый	1. entire, whole, full 2. neat, tidy 3. to arrange, put in order, consolidate 4. to repair, mend
～理 **zhěnglǐ** *см.* 整 1	to put in order, arrange
～日 **zhěngrì** весь день	the whole day, all day
～备 **zhěngbèi** комплектовáть	to reorganize and outfit (troops)
～年 **zhěngnián** весь (кру́глый) год	all/whole year
～编 **zhěngbiān** реорганизóвывать; реорганизáция	to reorganize (troops)
～体 **zhěngtǐ** еди́ное цéлое; моноли́т	whole, entirely
～体化 **zhěngtǐhuà** консоли́дáция	consolidation
～风 **zhěngfēng** упоря́дочивать стиль рабóты	(politics) to rectify incorrect work styles
～顿 **zhěngdùn** приводи́ть в поря́док; налáживать	to rectify, reorganize
歪 **wāi** искажáть; кривóй; неправильный	1. askew, crooked, inclined 2. devious, underhand(ed)
～曲 **wāiqū** искажáть, извращáть	to distort, misrepresent, twist
～风 **wāifēng** порóчный стиль *(в работе)*	unhealthy trend (in work)
虚 **xū** **1.** пустотá; пустóй **2.** лóжный **3.** дря́хлый	1. empty 2. diffident, timid 3. false 4. modest 5. weak 6. void 7. theory 8. in vain
～构 **xūgòu** вы́думка; фи́кция	to fabricate, make up
～弱 **xūruò** слáбый, хи́лый	in poor health, weak, debilitated

虚伪 **xūwěi** ло́жный; фальши́вый	sham, false, hypocritical
～报 **xūbào** ло́жное сообще́ние; дезинформа́ция	to make a false report
～假 **xūjiǎ** фальши́вый; ло́жный	false, sham
～线 **xūxiàn** пункти́р	line of dots/dashes
业 **yè** 1. ремесло́; заня́тие; профе́ссия 2. иму́щество, со́бственность	1. line of business, trade 2. occupation, profession, job 3. school studies 4. enterprise 5. property 6. to engage in 7.\\ \\already
～务 **yèwù** де́ятельность, заня́тие; слу́жба	professional work, business
～余 **yèyú** свобо́дное от рабо́ты вре́мя; люби́тельский; самоде́ятельный	1. spare time, after-hours 2. amateur
～余学校 **yèyú xuéxiào** ве́черняя шко́ла	part-time school
亚 **yà** 1. второ́й; второсте́пе́нный; сле́дующий за 2. *сокр.* Азия	1. inferior 2. second 3. (abbr.) Asia
哑 **yǎ** немо́й	1. mute, dumb 2. hoarse, husky
～吧 **yǎba** немо́й	dumb person, mute
显 **xiǎn** 1. я́сный, отчётливый 2. вы́явить, обнару́жить, прояви́ть	1. to appear, be obvious 2. to demonstrate, show, display 3. illustrious and powerful
～露 **xiǎnlù** вы́явиться, обнару́житься	to become visible, appear
～著 **xiǎnzhù** я́вный, я́сный	notable, marked, striking, outstanding
～明 **xiǎnmíng** я́сно вы́раженный, заме́тный	1. bright (of color) 2. distinct, distinctive
～微镜 **xiǎnwēijìng** микроско́п	microscope
～示 **xiǎnshì** я́сно показа́ть; прояви́ть	to show, display, demonstrate, manifest
～然 **xiǎnrán** очеви́дно; коне́чно, разуме́ется	obviously, evidently, clearly
湿 **shī** отсыре́ть; промо́кнуть; вла́жный; сыро́й	wet, damp, humid
～度 **shīdù** вла́жность	humidity
碰 **pèng** 1. натолкну́ться; уда́риться 2. встре́титься, столкну́ться	1. to touch, knock against 2. to meet, encounter, run into 3. to take one's chances, explore
～钉子 **pèngdīngz** встре́тить затрудне́ние (отка́з)	to meet with rebuff

碰头 **pèngtóu** встре́титься, столкну́ться	1. to see each other 2. to meet and discuss, put heads together
～见 **pèngjiàn** уви́деться, встре́титься *(случайно)*	to meet unexpectedly, run into -
～杯 **pèngbēi** чо́кнуться	to clink glasses
壶 **hú** ча́йник; фля́га	1. kettle, pot 2. bottle, flask
互 **hù** взаи́мный, обою́дный; вме́сте, сообща́	mutual, each other -
～相 **hùxiāng** взаи́мно; взаи́мный	mutually, each other -
～助 **hùzhù** взаимопо́мощь	to help each other
～助组 **hùzhùzǔ** брига́да взаимопо́мощи	mutual aid group/team -
～不侵犯 **hùbùqīnfàn** взаи́мное ненападе́ние	nonagression treaty/pact -
五 **wǔ** пять; пя́тый	five
～一节 **wǔ-yījié** пра́здник 1 Ма́я	May Day (1 May) - //iron, tin) 2. metals 3. hardware
～金 **wǔjīn** мета́ллы	1. the 5 metals (gold, silver, copper,//
～官 **wǔguān** о́рганы чувств	the 5 sense organs (eyes, ears, lips,\\
～月 **wǔyuè** май	May \\nose, tongue)
～角宫 **wǔjiǎogōng** Пентаго́н	the Pentagon -
～彩 **wǔcǎi** цветно́й, разноцве́тный	1. the 5 colors (blue, yellow, red, white, black) 2. multicolored
伍 **wǔ** отря́д; шере́нга; строй; ряды́	1. five (on checks/etc.) 2. associates; ranks; (5-man) squad
丑 **chǒu** 1. осрами́ться; позо́р 2. ни́зкий, по́длый 3. уро́дство	1. ugly, unsightly 2. shameful, scandalous, disgraceful 3. clown role 4. 2nd of the 12 Earthly Branches
～剧 **chǒujù** фарс	farce
～事 **chǒushì** сканда́л; позо́рное де́ло	scandal -
～化 **chǒuhuà** опоро́чить, очерни́ть	to defame, make ugly -
～恶 **chǒu'è** отврати́тельный; непригля́дный	repulsive, hideous -
纽 **niǔ** завя́зывать; застёгивать; у́зел	1. handle, knob 2. button 3. pivot, key position 4. bond, tie
～扣 **niǔkòu** застёжка; пу́говица	button -
扭 **niǔ** крути́ть; закру́чивать	1. to twist, wrench 2. to sway 3. to seize
～转 **niǔzhuǎn** крути́ть(ся); повора́чивать(ся)	1. to turn around/back, reverse 2. to remedy (a situation)

钮 **niǔ** пу́говица; пе́тля; застёжка	button
羞 **xiū** 1. стесня́ться, робе́ть, стыди́ться 2. позо́рить; позо́р	1. to shame 2. bashful, shy 3. shameful, disgraceful 4. ashamed, embarrassed 5. to embarrass (sb.)
～耻 **xiūchǐ** стыди́ться, стесня́ться	(sense of) shame
～辱 **xiūrǔ** позо́рить; оскорбля́ть; позо́р	to humiliate, put sb. to shame
立 **lì** 1. стоя́ть; сто́я 2. устана́вливать; создава́ть, учрежда́ть 3. неме́дленно, то́тчас	1. to stand 2. to erect, set up 3. to exist, live 4. upright, erect, vertical 5. immediate, instantaneous
～正 **lìzhèng** стоя́ть навы́тяжку; сми́рно!	to stand at attention; (mil.) attention!
～国 **lìguó** основа́ть госуда́рство	to found a state
～脚点 **lìjiǎodiǎn** то́чка опо́ры	1. foothold, footing 2. standpoint, stand
～即 **lìjí** неме́дленно, то́тчас	immediately, at once, promptly
～刻 **lìkè** сра́зу же, неме́дленно	immediately, at once
～方 **lìfāng** куб; куби́ческий	1. cube 2. cubic meter
～场 **lìchǎng** платфо́рма *(полити́ческая)*, подхо́д, пози́ция	position, stand(point)
～功 **lìgōng** отличи́ться; соверши́ть по́двиг	to render meritorious service
～体 **lìtǐ** стереоскопи́ческий, объёмный	1. a solid (body) 2. three-dimensional, stereoscopic
～定 **lìdìng** 1. установи́ть(-ся); утверди́ть(ся) 2. стой!	halt; halt!
～志 **lìzhì** реши́ть(ся); отва́житься	to resolve, be determined
～法 **lìfǎ** устана́вливать зако́ны; законода́тельный	legislation
垃:～圾 **lājī** му́сор, отбро́сы	refuse, garbage
位 **wèi** 1. помести́ть, устро́ить 2. ме́сто; пост 3. трон 4. лицо́, персо́на 5. *сч. сл. для людей*	1. place, location 2. status, position
～置 **wèizhì** 1. местоположе́-	seat, place, position; to post/place (sb.)

拉 啦 粒 竖 豆 短 痘 登

ние, расположе́ние **2.** ме́сто; пост	-
拉 **lā 1.** тяну́ть, тащи́ть **2.** тяну́ть за собо́й, увлека́ть	1. to pull, draw, drag 2. to haul 3. to move (troops) 4. to drag out 5. to help 6. to implicate 7. to win over
～开 **lākai 1.** раздви́нуть(ся) **2.** оттащи́ть	1. to pull open 2. to draw back 3. to space out
～丁 **lādīng** латы́нь; лати́нский	Latin
啦 **la** *эмфатическая частица (в конце предложений)*	(particle at end of sentence indicating excitement/doubt)
粒 **lì** зёрнышко, крупи́нка	1. grain, granule, pellet 2. (M. for sth.// //grain-like)
竖 **shù** водружа́ть; ста́вить пря́мо; прямо́й; отве́сный	to set upright, erect, stand ; vertical, upright
豆 **dòu** бобы́; горо́х; фасо́ль, со́я; бобо́вый	legumes, beans, peas, pulses
～油 **dòuyóu** бобо́вое ма́сло	soybean oil
～腐 **dòufu** со́евый тво́ро́г; бобо́вый сыр	beancurd, tofu
短 **duǎn 1.** коро́ткий **2.** не хвата́ть, недостава́ть **3.** недоста́ток, поро́к	1. short, brief 2. to lack, owe 3. weak point
～评 **duǎnpíng** заме́тка; о́черк	short commentary, brief comment
～裤 **duǎnkù** тру́сики; шо́рты	shorts
～期 **duǎnqī** краткосро́чный	short time
～篇小说 **duǎnpiān xiǎoshuō** расска́з	short story
～波 **duǎnbō** коротково́лновый	short wave
～处 **duǎnchù** недоста́ток; отрица́тельные сто́роны	shortcoming
痘 **dòu** о́спа	1. smallpox 2. smallpox pustule
登 **dēng 1.** подниматься наве́рх, восходи́ть **2.** регистри́ровать **3.** опублико́вывать	1. to ascend, climb, mount 2. to publish, record 3. harvest 4. pedal 5. to step on
～陆 **dēnglù** выса́живаться *(на берег)*; деса́нт	to land, disembark
～场 **dēngchǎng 1.** подня́ться на сце́ну **2.** появи́ться на полити́ческой аре́не **3.** поступи́ть на ры́нок	1. to be taken to the threshing ground 2. to come on stage

登报 **dēngbào** опубликова́ть в пре́ссе	1. to publish in a newspaper 2. to make an announcement in the newspaper
~载 **dēngzǎi** напеча́тать, помести́ть *(в прессе)*	to publish (in a periodical)
~记 **dēngjì** записа́ть; зарегистри́ровать	to register, check in
瞪 **dèng** при́стально смотре́ть, уста́виться	to stare at, open (one's eyes) wide, glare at
~眼 **dèngyǎn** пя́лить глаза́, уста́виться	1. to stare 2. to stare down, glower
橙 **chéng** апельси́н	orange (color)
澄 **chéng** све́тлый; прозра́чный, чи́стый	clear, transparent
~ **dèng** фильтрова́ть; отста́ивать *(жидкость)*	to settle (of liquids)
~清 **dèngqīng** очища́ть *(напр. воду)*	to settle, become clear (of liquids)
且 **qiě** **1.** ещё, всё ещё **2.** и́ли же, ли́бо **3.** *союз, связывающий сказ.:* 且...且...и..,и..	1. moreover, still, further 2. while, as; both...and...
组 **zǔ** **1.** организо́вывать, образо́вывать, создава́ть **2.** гру́ппа; звено́; брига́да	section, group
~合 **zǔhé** **1.** объединя́ть, организо́вывать **2.** арте́ль; това́рищество	1. to make up, compose 2. to unite, form a partnership 3. company, corporation, union
~成 **zǔchéng** составля́ть; формирова́ть	to form, make up (into), compose
~成部分 **zǔchéng bùfen** составна́я часть, компоне́нт	component part
~织 **zǔzhī** организова́ть; организа́ция	1. to organize, form; organization 2. tissue, nerve 3. to weave
~织性 **zǔzhīxìng** организо́ванность	orderliness, (good) organization, self-discipline
祖 **zǔ** пре́док; родонача́льник	1. progenitor 2. grandfather
~国 **zǔguó** ро́дина, оте́чество	1. homeland, native land 2. China (used only by Chinese)
~母 **zǔmǔ** ба́бушка	(paternal) grandmother
~父 **zǔfù** де́душка	(paternal) grandfather
~先(宗) **zǔxiān(zōng)** пре́дки	ancestors, forebears
阻 **zǔ** заде́рживать; меша́ть; прегра́да, препя́тствие	to prevent, obstruct, stop, detain, proscribe

阻拦(挡) **zǔlán(dǎng)** преграждáть; мешáть	to stop, obstruct
～止 **zǔzhǐ** остановúть, прекратúть	to prevent, stop, prohibit
～难 **zǔnàn** затруднéния	to obstruct, impede
～碍 **zǔ'ài** препя́тствовать, мешáть; преграда	to hinder, block, impede, bar; obstruction, obstacle, hindrance
～力 **zǔlì** сúла сопротивлéния	obstruction, resistance
～挠 **zǔnáo** задéрживать; противодéйствовать; помéхи, препóны	to obstruct, thwart, prevent
粗 **cū** **1.** грýбый, необрабóтанный **2.** небрéжный; черновóй **3.** невéжественный	1. wide (in diameter), thick 2. coarse, crude, rough 3. gruff, husky 4. careless, negligent 5. rude 6. roughly
～略 **cūlüè** приблизúтельный; черновóй	rough, sketchy
～笨 **cūbèn** неуклю́жий, неповорóтливый	clumsy, unwieldy
～米 **cūmǐ** чумúза	unpolished rice
～暴 **cūbào** жестóкий; грýбый	rude, rough, crude
～心 **cūxīn** небрéжный, халáтный	careless, thoughtless
租 **zū** нанимáть, арендовáть; сдавáть в арéнду; рéнта; арéндная плáта	1. to rent, lease 2. to tax
～金 **zūjīn** арéндная плáта	rent, rental
～借 **zūjiè** арендовáть; сдавáть в арéнду	to rent, hire, lease
～钱 **zūqian** *см.* ～金	(coll.) rent, rental
姐 **jiě** стáршая сестрá	1. (elder) sister 2. young woman
～姐 **jiějiě** *см.* 姐	elder sister
～妹 **jiěmèi** сёстры	1. sisters 2. brothers and sisters, siblings
宜 **yí** **1.** соответствующий, подходя́щий **2.** нýжно, слéдует	1. right, suitable 2. a matter
直 **zhí** **1.** выпрямля́ть; прямóй **2.** чéстный; справедлúвый **3.** напрямúк **4.** тóлько, всегó лишь	1. straight 2. vertical 3. just, righteous, honest 4. frank, forthright 5. stiff, numb 6. to straighten 7. directly, straight, continuously, simply, just
～径 **zhíjìng** диáметр	diameter
～译 **zhíyì** дослóвный перевóд	to translate literally

直升机 **zhíshēngjī** вертолёт	helicopter, chopper
~到 **zhídào** вплоть до	1. until 2. up to
~属 **zhíshǔ** непосре́дственное подчине́ние	to be directly subordinate to
~爽 **zhíshuang** открове́нный	candid, forthright
~觉 **zhíjué** интуи́ция	1. conscious 2. perception
~接 **zhíjiē** прямо́й, непосре́дственный	direct, intermediate
值 **zhí** **1.** сто́ить; цена́; сто́имость **2.** дежу́рить; дежу́рство	1. to be worth 2. to happen 3. to be on duty, take one's turn at sth. 4. value, price
~班 **zhíbān** дежу́рить; стоя́ть на ва́хте	to be on duty
~日 **zhírì** дежу́рить; дежу́рный; ва́хта	to be on duty for the day
~得 **zhídé** сто́ить, заслу́живать	to merit, deserve, be worth; merit
殖 **zhí** **1.** дава́ть пото́мство, размножа́ться **2.** колонизи́ровать, заселя́ть	to breed, multiply
~民主义 **zhímínzhǔyì** колониали́зм	colonialism
~民地 **zhímíndì** коло́ния	colony
植 **zhí** выра́щивать; сажа́ть	1. to plant, grow 2. to set up, establish
~物 **zhíwù** расти́тельность, расте́ния	plant; flora
~物学 **zhíwùxué** бота́ника	botany
置 **zhì** **1.** положи́ть; поста́вить **2.** монти́ровать; устана́вливать **3.** осно́вывать, учрежда́ть **4.** покупа́ть, закупа́ть	1. to place, put 2. to set up, install 3. to buy
~备 **zhìbèi** загото́вить впрок	to purchase (equipment/etc.)
盖 **gài** **1.** кры́шка; накрыва́ть *(крышкой)* **2.** стро́ить *(дом);* крыть *(крышу)* 3. прикла́дывать *(печать)*	1. to cover, seal, affix seal 2. to surpass, top, prevail over 3. to build, construct 4. about, around
~章 **gàizhāng** поста́вить печа́ть	to stamp, affix seal
~子(儿) **gàizi(r)** кры́шка	1. lid, cover, cap, top 2. shell (of //tortoise/etc.)
盒 **hé** коро́бка; шкату́лка	box, case
温 **wēn** **1.** тёплый; теплота́ **2.** греть, согрева́ть, нагрева́ть **3.** ла́сковый; до́брый	1. warm, mild (of temperament) 2. to warm up 3. to review

直值殖植置盖盒温

温盐监蓝篮孟猛盟

温室 **wēnshì** оранжерéя, теплúца	hothouse, greenhouse
~带 **wēndài** умéренный пóяс	temperate zone
~泉 **wēnquán** горя́чий истóчник	hot spring
~暖 **wēnnuǎn** теплó; тёплый	warm
~度 **wēndù** температýра	temperature
~度计 **wēndùjì** термóметр	thermograph
盐 **yán** соль; солёный	salt
~田 **yántián** соляны́е поля́ (разрабóтки)	saltfield, salina
~场 **yánchǎng** соляны́е прóмыслы	saltworks, saltern
监 **jiān** **1.** надзирáть, наблюдáть, контролúровать **2.** сажáть в тюрьмý; тюрьмá	1. prison, jail 2. inspector, supervisor 3. to supervise, watch, inspect //supervisor
~督 **jiāndū** *см.* 监 **1**	to supervise, superintend, control;//
~制 **jiānzhì** систéма контрóля *(на производстве)*	to supervise the manufacture of
~狱 **jiānyù** тюрьмá	prison, jail
~犯 **jiānfàn** заключённый, арестáнт	prison convict
~视 **jiānshì** наблюдáть, смотрéть за	to keep a watch on, keep a lookout over
~察 **jiānchá** контролúровать; инспектúровать	to supervise, control
蓝 **lán** сúний	1. blue 2. indigo plant
篮 **lán** корзúна	1. basket 2. basketball goal/basket
~球 **lánqiú** баскетбóл	basketball
孟 **mèng** **1.** стáрший, пéрвый *(о братьях, сёстрах)* **2.** грýбый, неотёсанный	1. the first month of a season 2. eldest brothers
猛 **měng** **1.** жестóкий, свирéпый **2.** отвáжный, хрáбрый **3.** внезáпно	1. fierce, valiant 2. fearsome, severe 3. suddenly, abruptly
~兽 **měngshòu** хúщный зверь, хúщник	beast of prey
~烈 **měngliè** я́ростный; ожесточённый	fierce, vigorous
~然 **měngrán** внезáпно, неожúданно	suddenly, abruptly
盟 **méng** сою́з; блок; лúга	1. alliance, pact 2. (mongol) league
~国 **méngguó** странá-сою́зник	allied country, ally

盟约 **méngyuē** до́говор о сою́зе	oath/treaty of alliance
～员 **méngyuán** член сою́за (бло́ка)	league/bloc member
盘 **pán** **1.** таре́лка; блю́до **2.** скла́дывать; свёртывать **3.** враща́ться **4.** спира́ль	1. tray, plate, dish 2. current price 3. game, set 4. to coil, wind, twist 5. to build (stove, etc.) 6. to examine, check
～查 **pánchá** рассле́довать; рассма́тривать; осма́тривать	to interrogate and examine
～据 **pánjù** захвати́ть; укрепи́ться; обоснова́ться	to occupy forcibly/illegally; to be entrenched
～算 **pánsuan** высчи́тывать, вычисля́ть	to calculate, figure, plan
～剝 **pánbō** обира́ть; вымога́ть	to practice usury
～子 **pánz** таре́лка; блю́до	tray, plate, dish
～问 **pánwèn** допра́шивать; допро́с	to cross-examine, interrogate
～儿 **pánr** *см.* ～子	tray, plate, dish
盆 **pén** таз	basin, tub, pot
～堂 **péntáng** ба́ня	bathtub cubicle
盈 **yíng** **1.** превыша́ть **2.** изли́шек; при́быль	1. to be full of, be filled with 2. to have a surplus of
～利 **yínglì** при́быль	to make a profit/gain; profit, gain
～余 **yíngyú** изли́шек	surplus; profit
盗 **dào** гра́бить; граби́тель; банди́т	to steal, rob, misappropriate
～窃 **dàoqiè** гра́бить; расхища́ть	to steal
～取 **dàoqǔ** огра́бить, отня́ть си́лой; грабёж	to steal, take unlawfully
益 **yì** **1.** по́льза, вы́года; поле́зный **2.** увели́чивать	benefit, good, advantage
～处 **yìchù** по́льза, вы́года; преиму́щество	benefit, profit, good
隘 **ài** **1.** уще́лье; у́зкий прохо́д **2.** у́зкий; стеснённый	1. narrow 2. a narrow pass
～口 **àikǒu** *см.* 隘 1	(mountain) pass
～路 **àilù** дефиле́; у́зкая го́рная доро́га	narrow passage, defile
盛 **shèng** процвета́ть; цвету́щий; оби́льный; великоле́пный	1. prosperous 2. vigorous, energetic 3. magnificent, grand 4. abundant, plentiful 5. popular 6. greatly, deeply

盛 **chéng** наполня́ть; вмеща́ть	1. to fill, ladle 2. to hold, contain
~名 **shèngmíng** широ́кая изве́стность; сла́ва	great reputation
~行 **shèngxíng** име́ть широ́кое распростране́ние; широко́ распространённый	to be current, be in vogue
~大 **shèngdà** грандио́зный, вели́чественный	grand, magnificent
~况 **shèngkuàng** расцве́т; процвета́ние	grand occasion, spectacular event
~典 **shèngdiǎn** торжество́, торже́ственная церемо́ния	grand ceremony
~宴 **shèngyàn** пы́шный приём (банке́т)	grand banquet, sumptuous dinner
血 **xuè 1.** кровь; крова́вый **2.** кро́вное родство́; кро́вный	1. blood 2. related by blood
~压 **xuèyā** кровяно́е давле́ние	blood pressure
~管 **xuèguǎn** кровено́сные сосу́ды	blood vessel
~案 **xuè'àn** уби́йство	murder case
~脉 **xuèmài 1.** пульс; кровено́сные сосу́ды **2.** родосло́вная	1. blood vessels 2. blood relationship
~战 **xuèzhàn** кровопроли́тные бои́	bloody/sanguinary battle
恤 **xù 1.** жале́ть; соболе́зновать, сочу́вствовать **2.** помога́ть, ока́зывать по́мощь (подде́ржку)	1. to pity, sympathize 2. to give relief, compensate
~金 **xùjīn** пе́нсия	pension; relief payment
继 **jì 1.** продолжа́ть(ся); сле́довать за; вслед за **2.** быть прее́мником, продолжа́ть *(чьё-л. дело)*	1. to continue, succeed, follow 2. then, afterwards 3. step- (e.g., step-father)
~任 **jìrèn** быть прее́мником *(по должности)*	to succeed sb. in a post
~母 **jìmǔ** ма́чеха	stepmother
~续 **jìxù** продолжа́ть; продолже́ние	to continue, go on
~承 **jìchéng** *см.* 继 1	to inherit, carry on
~承者 **jìchéngzhe** насле́д-	heir, successor, continuer

ник; преéмник, продолжá-	-
тель	-
～父 **jìfù** óтчим	stepfather
亡 **wáng** **1.** гúбнуть; уми-	1. to flee 2. to lose 3. to die 4. to des-
рáть; гúбель **2.** бежáть;	troy 5. deceased
бéгство	-
～命 **wángmìng** бежáть *(под*	1. to flee, seek refuge, go into exile
чужим именем); эмигрú-	2. to be desperate
ровать	-
忙 **máng** **1.** торопúться, спе-	1. to hurry, hasten, make haste 2. busy,
шúть **2.** быть зáнятым	fully occupied
～碌 **mánglù** быть óчень зá-	to be busy, bustle about
нятым	-
～乱 **mángluàn** суетúться;	slapdash
хлопотáть	-
茫 **máng** **1.** ширóкий; без-	1. boundless and indistinct 2. ignorant,
брéжный **2.** неясный, непо-	in the dark
нятный	-
～然 **mángrán** неясно, непо-	ignorant, in the dark
нятно	- //sharp point
芒 **máng** **1.** остриё **2.** ость	1. beard/awn of wheat 2. spike,//
～鞋 **mángxié** солóменные	straw sandals
сандáлии	-
匹 **pǐ** **1.** пáра; четá **2.** штýка	1. to match 2. companion, mate 3. pair
(ткани) **3.** *сч. сл. для ло-*	4. female and male 5. equal 6. lone 7.
шадей	common 8. (M. for horses, mules, etc.)
甚 **shèn** óчень, чересчýр	1. very, extremely 2. more than 3. what
～至 **shènzhì** дáже; вплоть	even (to the point of), so much so that
до	-
汇 **huì** **1.** переводúть дéньги	1. to converge; to gather together 2.
(по почте); перевóд *(де-*	to remit 3. collection, assemblage,
нежный) **2.** сливáться *(о*	things collected
реках) **3.** собирáть(ся)	-
～合 **huìhé** сливáться *(о ре-*	to join, meet, converge, assemble; con-
ках)	fluence, fusion
～款 **huìkuǎn** переводúть	to remit money; remittance
дéньги *(по почте);* пере-	-
вóд *(денежный)*	-
～报 **huìbào** свóдка	to report, give an account of
框 **kuàng** рáма; опрáва	frame, case
匠 **jiàng** мáстер; ремéслен-	(suf.) craftsman, artisan
ник; *суф. специальностей*	-
～人 **jiàngrén** ремéсленник	artisan, craftsman //candy, etc
匣 **xiá** шкатýлка; ящичек	1. small box/case; casket 2. (M. for//

匪 **fěi** **1.** банди́ты; разбо́йни-	1. bandit, brigand, robber 2. not
ки; бродя́ги **2.** непутёвый,	-
дурно́й	-
～帮 **fěibāng** ша́йка, ба́нда	bandit gang
～徒 **fěitú** *см.* 匪 1	gangster, bandit
医 **yī** медици́на; врач	1. physician, doctor 2. medicine 3.\\
～生 **yīshēng** врач, до́ктор	physician, doctor \\to treat, cure
～治(疗) **yīzhì(liǎo)** лечи́ть;	to cure, treat, heal
лече́ние	-
～学 **yīxué** медици́на	medical science, medicine
～师 **yīshī** *см.* ～生	physician
～药 **yīyào** лека́рство	medicine (for treatment)
～院 **yīyuàn** больни́ца; го́с-	hospital
питаль	-
区 **qū** **1.** райо́н; о́круг	1. region, area 2. district 3. cottage 4.
2. классифици́ровать, рас-	to discriminate, classify, subdivide 5.
пределя́ть по гру́ппам	unimportant, little
～别 **qūbié** различа́ть; ра́з-	to distinguish, differentiate; distinc-
ница, отли́чие	tion, difference
～划 **qūhuà** разби́ть на уча́-	to divide into districts
стки, разграни́чить	-
～分 **qūfēn** различа́ть; раз-	to differentiate, set apart
грани́чивать	-
～域 **qūyù** райо́н; о́круг; уча́-	region, zone, district
сток	-
呕 **ōu, ǒu** рво́та; рвать	to vomit
～吐 **ǒutù** тошни́ть; рвать	to vomit
抠 **kōu** ковыря́ть; скобли́ть	1. to dig/carve out 2. to delve into\\
～伤 **kōushāng** расковыря́ть	to pick/scratch open \\3. stingy
躯 **qū** те́ло; ко́рпус, ту́лови-	the (human) body/torso/trunk
ще	-
～干 **qūgàn** те́ло; торс	trunk, torso
～体 **qūtǐ** те́ло; ко́рпус *(напр.*	body, carcass
корабля)	-
驱 **qū** **1.** гнать, погоня́ть **2.**	1. to drive (horse/car/etc.) 2. to ex-
изгоня́ть, прогоня́ть **3.** то-	pel 3. to simulate
ропи́ться	-
～使(遣) **qūshǐ(qiǎn)** ко-	to prompt, urge, spur on
мандирова́ть, посыла́ть	-
～逐 **qūzhú** пресле́довать;	to expel, get rid of
изгоня́ть	-
～除 **qūchú** изгоня́ть, выго-	to drive out, eliminate
ня́ть	-
枢 **shū** **1.** ось; сте́ржень	pivot, hub, center

2. ко́рень, осно́ва **3.** основно́й, кардина́льный; фундамента́льный	-
枢纽 **shūniǔ** ось; сте́ржень	pivot, center
～纽部 **shūniǔbù** узлово́й пункт, у́зел	junction, central point
巨 **jù** огро́мный, колосса́льный	huge, gigantic
～型 **jùxíng** гига́нтский; гига́нт	gigantic (in size)
～人 **jùrén** гига́нт, велика́н	giant, colossus (person)
～大 **jùdà** *см.* 巨	huge, gigantic
距 **jù** отстоя́ть; расстоя́ние; отдалённый от	1. to be apart/away from 2. to oppose 3. distance 4. huge 5. spur
～离 **jùlí** расстоя́ние, диста́нция	to be apart/away from; distance
拒 **jù 1.** отража́ть *(нападе́ние);* противостоя́ть **2.** уклоня́ться; отка́зываться	1. to relinquish, abandon 2. to contribute, subscribe 3. tax
～绝 **jùjué** отказа́ться, отве́ргнуть	to refuse, reject, decline
矩 **jǔ 1.** уго́льник **2.** пра́вило, но́рма	1. carpenter's square, square 2. rules, regulations
～形 **jǔxíng** прямоуго́льник	rectangle
柜 **guì 1.** шкаф; сейф **2.** прила́вок	cupboard, cabinet
臣 **chén** чино́вник, сано́вник; мини́стр	1. subject 2. (humble) I
世 **shì 1.** мир; мирово́й **2.** эпо́ха; век **3.** поколе́ние **4.** совреме́нный	1. generation 2. life, lifetime 3. age, epoch 4. world
～界 **shìjiè** мир; мирово́й	world
～界观 **shìjièguān** мировоззре́ние	world view
～代 **shìdài 1.** эпо́ха **2.** поколе́ние	1. generation 2. epoch, period 3. from generation to generation
～纪 **shìjì** столе́тие, век	century
泄 **xiè 1.** протека́ть; проса́чиваться **2.** разглаша́ть	1. to let out, discharge, release 2. to leak (e.g., news) 3. to give vent to
～露(漏) **xièlù(lòu)** разгласи́ть, вы́дать *(тайну)*	to leak, divulge
～气(愤) **xièqì(fèn)** изли́ть гнев; сорва́ть зло	1. to lose heart 2. disappointing, frustrating
疟 **nüè** малярия́	malaria

疟疾 **nüèji** маляри́я	malaria, ague
～蚊 **nüèwén** маляри́йный кома́р	malarial mosquito
虐 **nüè** истяза́ть; жесто́кий, бесчелове́чный	cruel, tyrannical
～待 **nüèdài** жесто́ко обраща́ться; истяза́ть, му́чить	to maltreat, tyrannize, abuse
～政 **nüèzhèng** тирани́я; деспоти́зм	tyrannical government, tyranny
归 **guī** **1.** возвраща́ться **2.** принадлежа́ть; перейти́ к **3.** зако́нчиться	1. to go back to, return 2. to return sth. to 3. to come together 4. to put in sb.'s charge 5. to belong 6. despite
～宿 **guīsù** обобща́ть, резюми́ровать; заключе́ние	(a) home to return to
～罪 **guīzuì** обвиня́ть	to put blame on, impute to
～并 **guībìng** слива́ться; воссоединя́ться	1. to incorporate/merge into 2. to add up
～根 **guīgēn** в конце́ концо́в, в ито́ге	in the end, after all, as a result
～还 **guīhuán** верну́ть(ся), возврати́ть(ся)	to return, revert
～总 **guīzǒng** в ито́ге	to put together, sum up
扫 **sǎo** мести́, подмета́ть; вымета́ть	1. to sweep 2. to sweep away, eliminate 3. to glance at 4. to paint (eyebrows)
～ **sào** ве́ник; метла́	broom
～盲 **sǎománg** ликвиди́ровать негра́мотность	to eliminate illiteracy
～射 **sǎoshè** обстре́ливать	to strafe
～清 **sǎoqīng** вы́мести; очи́стить; изба́виться	to clear away
～帚 **sàozhou** ве́ник; метла́	broom
～荡 **sǎodàng** смести́ [с лица́ земли́], уничто́жить	to mop up, destroy
～地 **sǎodì** подмета́ть пол	1. to sweep; make a clean sweep 2. to// //reach a nadir (of repute)
～除 **sǎochú** **1.** вы́мести **2.** ликвиди́ровать	to clear away, wipe out; clean up
妇 **fù** жена́; же́нщина; сноха́	1. woman 2. married woman 3. wife
～科 **fùkē** гинеколо́гия	(department of) gynecology
～女 **fùnü** же́нщины; же́нский	women
彗 **huì** **1.** метла́; ве́ник **2.** коме́та	1. broom 2. comet
～星 **huìxīng** коме́та	comet
雪 **xuě** **1.** снег **2.** оправда́ть	1. snow 2. to avenge; wipe out (a hu-// //miliation)

雪耻 **xuěchǐ** смыть позо́р	to avenge an insult/humiliation
～白 **xuěbái** белосне́жный	snow-white; snowy white
～板 **xuěbǎn** лы́жи	skis
当 **dāng 1.** быть; явля́ться; станови́ться **2.** выполня́ть обя́занности **3.** сле́дует, до́лжно **4.** соотве́тствовать **5.** коне́чно, безусло́вно **6.** *предлог* в; на	1. to undertake, accept 2. to be equal 3. to be in sb.'s presence 4. to be just as 5. should
～日 **dāngrì** в те дни; в тот же день	the same day, that very day
～面 **dāngmiàn** в прису́тствии; на глаза́х у	face-to-face, in one's presence
～年 **dāngnián** в те го́ды; в том году́	1. that year, those years 2. bygone years 3. prime of life
～中 **dāngzhōng** среди́; посреди́, в середи́не	1. in the middle/center 2. among
～前 **dāngqián** предстоя́щий; ближа́йший; очередно́й, сле́дующий	1. before/facing one 2. the present, here and now
～时 **dāngshí** в то вре́мя, тогда́	1. at that time, then 2. right away, immediately
～局 **dāngjú** вла́сти; администра́ция	(appropriate/concerned) authorities
～场 **dāngchǎng** здесь же, на ме́сте	on the spot, then and there
～权 **dāngquán** стоя́ть у вла́сти	to hold power
～做 **dāngzuò 1.** служи́ть, рабо́тать в ка́честве *кого* **2.** счита́ть, полага́ть	to consider/treat as
～兵 **dāngbīng** служи́ть в а́рмии; быть солда́том	to serve in the army
～心 **dāngxīn** остерега́ться, бере́чься	to be careful, take care, look out
～然 **dāngrán** коне́чно, разуме́ется, очеви́дно	1. as it should be, only natural 2. without doubt, certainly, of course
挡 **dǎng** заслоня́ть(ся), загора́живать(ся)	1. to ward off, block 2. to get in the way of 3. screen, blind, fender 4. gear
～住 **dǎngzhù** прегражда́ть путь	to block, impede, hinder, obstruct
档:～案 **dàng'àn** архи́в, архи́вное де́ло	file, record, dossier, archives
维 **wéi 1.** свя́зывать; соеди-	1. to join, connect 2. to maintain, save//from damage 3. thinking 4. net

维 堆 唯 雅 推

ня́ть **2.** оберега́ть; **сохра-**	-
ня́ть	-
维生素 **wéishēngsù** витами́ны	vitamin
～持 **wéichí** подде́рживать	to keep, preserve
～护 **wéihù 1.** оберега́ть; за-	to safeguard, defend, uphold
щища́ть **2.** уха́живать *(за*	-
животными); обслу́живать	-
(технику)	-
堆 **duī 1.** ку́ча **2.** на́сыпь	to pile/heap up; pile, heap
3. нагроможда́ть, нава́ли-	-
вать	-
～积 **duījī** свали́ть в ку́чу,	1. to heap/pile up 2. (geogr.) accumu-
нагромозди́ть	lation
唯 **wéi 1.** лишь, то́лько; но	only, alone
2. алло́!	-
～一 **wéiyī** еди́нственный	only, sole
～物 **wéiwù** материалисти́че-	materialistic
ский	-
～物主义 **wéiwùzhǔyì** мате-	materialism
риали́зм	-
～心 **wéixīn** идеалисти́че-	idealistic
ский	-
～心主义 **wéixīnzhǔyì** идеа-	idealism
ли́зм	-
雅 **yǎ 1.** пра́вильный, класси́-	1. refined, elegant 2. (polite) your 3.
ческий **2.** изя́щный, изы́с-	acquaintance, friendship 4. very 5. us-
канный	ually, often
～观 **yǎguān** привлека́тель-	refined, tasteful
ный; элега́нтный	-
推 **tuī 1.** толка́ть **2.** выдви-	1. to push 2. to cut (with clippers),
га́ть *(кандидатуру)* **3.** от-	pare 3. to infer, deduce, investigate
клоня́ть; отка́зываться **4.**	4. to decline, refuse, reject 5. to
иссле́довать; дои́скивать-	delay, postpone, put off
ся **5.** стричь маши́нкой *(во-*	-
лосы)	-
～土机 **tuītǔjī** бульдо́зер	bulldozer
～算 **tuīsuàn** вычисля́ть, рас-	to calculate, reckon
счи́тывать	-
～子 **tuīz** маши́нка для	hair clippers; clippers
стри́жки воло́с	-
～翻 **tuīfān 1.** све́ргнуть **2.**	1. to overturn, topple 2. to repudiate,
oпроки́нуть, переверну́ть	reverse
～销 **tuīxiāo** сбыва́ть, реали-	to promote the sale of, peddle
зова́ть; сбыт	-

推广 **tuīguǎng** распространя́ть(ся); внедря́ть	to popularize, spread, extend
～动 **tuīdòng 1.** привести́ в движе́ние **2.** стимули́ровать	to push forward, promote
～迟 **tuīchí** заде́рживать, затя́гивать	to postpone, defer
～论 **tuīlùn** де́лать вы́вод (заключе́ние)	to infer; inference, deduction, corollary
～想 **tuīxiǎng** предполага́ть	to imagine, guess, reckon
雕 **diāo** выреза́ть; гравирова́ть; вая́ть	to carve, engrave
～塑 **diāosù** скульпту́ра	sculpture
～刻 **diāokè** гравирова́ть; гравю́ра; резьба́	to carve, engrave
帷 **wéi** заслоня́ть; по́лог; што́ра	bed-curtain
～幕 **wéimù** занаве́ска; по́лог	heavy curtain
难 **nán** затрудне́ние; тру́дный, тяжёлый	1. difficult, hard, troublesome 2. unpleasant 3. to make difficulties
～ **nàn** бе́дствие	1. calamity, adversity 2. to blame
～看 **nánkàn** непригля́дный, непривлека́тельный	1. ugly, unsightful 2. shameful, embarrassing
～听 **nántīng** неприя́тный для слу́ха	1. unpleasant to hear 2. offensive, coarse 3. scandalous
～关 **nánguān** тру́дный моме́нт	difficulty, crisis
～友 **nànyǒu** това́рищ по несча́стью	fellow sufferer
～受 **nánshòu 1.** труднопереноси́мый **2.** тяжело́, тоскли́во	to feel unwell/unhappy/pained
～道 **nándào** неуже́ли?, ра́зве?	really? do you really mean to say that? (questioning particle)
～过 **nánguò** тяжело́ *(на сердце);* си́льно пережива́ть	1. to have a hard time 2. to feel sorry/sad/bad
～民 **nànmín** бе́женцы	refugee
～免 **nánmiǎn** неизбе́жно; неизбе́жный	hard to avoid
～吃 **nánchī** невку́сный; несъедо́бный	unpalatable
摊 **tān 1.** разверну́ть; рас-	1. to spread out, unfold 2. to contri-

滩雄准谁锥雇催摧罐灌

кры́ть 2. разложи́ть 3. распредели́ть	bute, take share in 3. to befall 4. vendor's stall/stand 5. (M. for liquids)
滩 **tān** мель, о́тмель	1. beach sands 2. shoal
雄 **xióng 1.** си́льный **2.** хра́брый, отва́жный; геро́йский 3. саме́ц	1. powerful/influential person/state/etc. 2. male 3. grand, imposing 4. powerful, mighty
～壮 **xióngzhuàng 1.** си́льный, могу́чий **2.** му́жественный, хра́брый	magnificent, majestic
～厚 **xiónghòu** си́льный, мо́щный	rich, solid, abundant
准 **zhǔn 1.** разреша́ть, позволя́ть **2.** утвержда́ть **3.** в соотве́тствии, согла́сно **4.** образе́ц; пра́вило **5.** то́чный, пра́вильный	1. to allow, grant, permit 2. standard, norm, criterion 3. accurate, exact 4. definitely, certainly 5. in accordance with 6. quasi-, para-
～备 **zhǔnbèi** гото́вить(ся); подгото́вка; гото́вность	1. to prepare, get ready 2. to intend, plan
～许 **zhǔnxǔ** *см.* 准 1	to permit, allow
～则 **zhǔnzé** но́рма	norm, standard, criterion
～时 **zhǔnshí** своевре́менно, во́время	punctually
～确 **zhǔnquè** то́чный, пра́вильный; ме́ткий	accurate, exact, precise
谁 **shuí 1.** кто?; чей?; кого́? **2.** тот; кто́-либо; вся́кий **3.** *с отриц.* никто́; ниче́й	1. (interrog.) who 2. someone, anyone
锥 **zhuī** ши́ло	1. awl 2. (math) cone 3. to bore/drill\\ \\with an awl
雇 **gù** нанима́ть; наёмный	to hire, employ
～佣 **gùyōng** нанима́ть *(на работу)*	to hire, employ
～农 **gùnóng** батра́к	hired farmhand
催 **cuī** торопи́ть, подгоня́ть	1. to urge, hurry 2. to hasten, expedite
～促 **cuīcù** спосо́бствовать	to urge, hasten, press
摧 **cuī** разруша́ть; лома́ть; уничтожа́ть	to break, destroy
～毁 **cuīhuǐ** *см.* 摧	to destroy, smash, wreck
～残 **cuīcán** разгроми́ть; разру́шить	to wreck, destroy, devastate
罐 **guàn** кувши́н; кру́жка; ба́нка	1. vessel, container 2. jug, jar
～头 **guàntóu** консе́рвы	1. tin can 2. canned goods
灌 **guàn 1.** полива́ть; ороша́ть **2.** набива́ть; впихи-	1. to irrigate; to fill, pour 2. to photograph 3. to offer libation

вать **3.** наливáть; заполнять водóй	-
灌木 **guànmù** кустáрник	bush, shrub
~溉 **guàngài** орошáть; орошéние, ирригáция	to irrigate
耀 **yào** сверкáть, блестéть; сиять	1. to shine, illuminate, dazzle 2. to boast of, laud 3. honor, credit
霍 **huò** мгновéнно; внезáпно, вдруг	suddenly, quickly
~乱 **huòluàn** холéра	1. cholera 2. (Ch. med.) acute gastroenteritis
雀 **qiǎo** птичка; воробéй	sparrow
届 **jiè 1.** назнáченный срок; наступáть *(о сроке)* **2.** созы́в; сéссия	1. year (of graduation) 2. session (of conference/meeting) 3. to fall due
画 **huà 1.** рисýнок; картина; иллюстрированный **2.** рисовáть; чертить; чертá, штрих	1. to draw, paint 2. to mark, draw a line/sign 3. to decorate with painting/pictures 4. plan 5. stroke in a Ch. character
~图 **huàtú** чертить; рисовáть	1. to draw designs/maps/etc. 2. picture
~片 **huàpiān** открытка *(художественная)*	1. picture postcard 2. miniature reproduction of a painting
~象 **huàxiàng** портрéт	to draw a portrait; portrait, portrayal
~报 **huàbào** иллюстрированный журнáл	illustrated magazine/newspaper; pictorial
~儿 **huàr** картинка; рисýнок	picture, painting
函 **hán 1.** деловóе письмó **2.** футляр; конвéрт	1. case, big envelope; letter 2. casket
~授[学习] **hánshòu [xuéxí]** заóчное обучéние	to teach by correspondence; correspondence course
凶 **xiōng 1.** злой; жестóкий, свирéпый **2.** опáсный	1. inauspicious, ominous 2. fiendish, murderous 3. terrible 4. violence, murder
~手 **xiōngshǒu** убийца, злодéй	murderer, assassin
~暴 **xiōngbào** жестóкий	fierce and brutal
~恶 **xiōng'è** злой; отвратительный; преступный	ferocious, fiendish
齿 **chǐ 1.** зýбы **2.** зубцы́; зубчáтый **3.** вóзраст	1. tooth 2. sth. tooth-like 3. age
恼 **nǎo** сердиться; негодовáть; гнев; досáда	1. to exasperate, anger; angered, irritated 2. unhappy, worried 3. irritating
~火 **nǎohuǒ** гнев; злость	(coll.) to burn with anger
~恨 **nǎohèn** ненавидеть	to resent, hate

恼怒 **nǎonù** гне́ваться; зли́ться; гнев	to be angry/indignant/furious
脑 **nǎo** головно́й мозг	brain
～子 **nǎoz** головно́й мозг	1. brain 2. brains, mind, head
～力 **nǎolì** интелле́кт, у́мственные спосо́бности	brains, mental capability
～筋 **nǎojīn** мозг; ум	brains, mind, head
～袋 **nǎodài** голова́	head
山 **shān** гора́; холм; го́рный	hill, mountain
～口 **shānkǒu** го́рный прохо́д	mountain pass
～谷 **shāngū** го́рное уще́лье	mountain valley
～羊 **shānyáng** [го́рный] козёл	(mountain) goat
～峰 **shānfēng** го́рная верши́на, пик	mountain peak
～洞 **shāndòng** пеще́ра	cave, cavern
～坡 **shānpō** склон горы́; отко́с	hillside, mountain slope
～地 **shāndì** го́рная (холми́стая) ме́стность	1. mountainous/hilly country 2. hillside field
～岭 **shānlǐng** го́рный хребе́т	mountain ridge
仙 **xiān** 1. отше́льник; свято́й 2. ге́ний	celestial being, immortal
岳 **yuè** 1. го́рная верши́на, пик 2. роди́тели жены́	1. mountain peak 2. wife's parents
～母 **yuèmǔ** тёща	wife's mother, mother-in-law
～父 **yuèfù** тесть	wife's father, father-in-law
岔 **chà** разветвле́ние доро́г, разви́лка	to branch; branch
～路(道) **chàlù(dào)** разви́лка доро́г; перекрёсток	branch road
密 **mì** 1. та́йный, секре́тный 2. бли́зкий, инти́мный 3. густо́й, пло́тный 4. шифр; код	1. dense, thick 2. intimate, close 3. fine, meticulous 4. secret 5. density
～语 **mìyǔ** код	1. ciphered/code words 2. to talk//secretly
～切 **mìqiè** те́сный, бли́зкий	close, intimate; carefully, intently, closely
～约 **mìyuē** та́йный до́гово́р	secret agreement/treaty
～码 **mìmǎ** шифр	cipher/secret code
～集 **mìjí** 1. спла́чиваться 2. масси́рованный *(удар, огонь)*	concentrated, crowded together

密谋 **mìmóu** та́йные за́мыслы	to conspire, plot, scheme
~友 **mìyǒu** бли́зкий друг	close/bosom friend
~度 **mìdù** пло́тность	density, thickness
~电 **mìdiàn** шифро́ванная телегра́мма	1. cipher telegram 2. to telegraph sb. secretly
击 **jī 1.** уда́рить; атакова́ть; уда́р; ата́ка **2.** стуча́ть	1. to strike, hit, beat, knock 2. to attack, assault 3. to bump into
~落 **jīluò** сбить *(самолёт)*	to shoot down (a plane)
~中 **jīzhòng** попа́сть *(в цель)*	to hit the point/target
~伤 **jīshāng** подби́ть *(танк, самолёт)*	to damage/wound
~败 **jībài** разгроми́ть	to defeat
~退 **jītuì** отби́ть *(атаку)*; отбро́сить *(врага)*	to beat back, repel
陆 **lù** су́ша; контине́нт; сухопу́тный	land
~上 **lùshàng** на су́ше; назе́мный	on land; ground (attr.), surface (attr.)
~军 **lùjūn** сухопу́тные войска́	ground/land force/army
~地 **lùdì** су́ша; контине́нт; сухопу́тный	dry land
摇 **yáo 1.** кача́ть(ся); трясти́(сь) **2.** маха́ть	1. to shake, wave 2. to row, scull 3. to agitate
~篮 **yáolán** колыбе́ль	cradle
~手 **yáoshǒu** маха́ть руко́й; отма́хиваться	to wave the hand horizontally to show disapproval
~动 **yáodòng** *прям., перен.* колеба́ться; кача́ться	to wave, sway, rock
~头 **yáotóu** покача́ть голово́й	to shake one's head
谣 **yáo 1.** клевета́; сплéтни **2.** наро́дные пе́сни	1. ballad, rhyme, folk song 2. rumor
~言 **yáoyán** *см.* 谣 1	rumors
~传 **yáochuán** ло́жные слу́хи; ложь	rumor
窑 **yáo 1.** печь; гонча́рня **2.** у́гольная ша́хта **3.** пеще́ра	1. kiln 2. (coal) pit 3. cave dwelling
~洞 **yáodòng** пеще́ра	cave dwelling
出 **chū 1.** выходи́ть; вы́ход **2.** удаля́ться; покида́ть	1. to go/come out, exit 2. to exceed, go beyond 3. to issue, put out, post 4. to

出

3. производи́ть *(потомство);* рожда́ть 4. выпуска́ть; издава́ть 5. вывози́ть; э́кспорт 6. происходи́ть, случа́ться 7. выделя́ться; выходи́ть за преде́лы	produce, turn out 5. to arise, happen 6. to put forth, vent 7. to rise well (in cooking) 8. to pay out, expend - - - -
出差 **chūchāi** уезжа́ть в командиро́вку; командиро́вка	to be away on official business or on a business trip -
~租 **chūzū** сдава́ть в аре́нду	to hire, rent out //driving a vehicle
~租车 **chūzūchē** такси́	1. to dispatch a vehicle 2. to be out//
~口 **chūkǒu** 1. вы́ход; вы́езд 2. вы́воз, э́кспорт	1. to speak, utter 2. to export 3. exit -
~品 **chūpǐn** проду́кция; изде́лия	to produce, manufacture, make; product
~名 **chūmíng** изве́стный, просла́вленный	1. famous, well-known 2. to become famous/well-known 3. to lend one's name
~路 **chūlù** вы́ход *(из положения)*	1. way out, outlet 2. employment opportunities
~国 **chūguó** вы́ехать *(за границу)*	to go abroad (from one's own country) -
~汗 **chūhàn** поте́ть	to perspire
~事 **chūshì** случи́лось происше́ствие	to deal with affairs/matters -
~门 **chūmén** вы́йти из до́ма; уе́хать	to be away from home, go on a journey, go out
~席 **chūxí** прису́тствовать *(на собрании)*	to attend, be present -
~身 **chūshēn** происхожде́ние; происходи́ть из	1. class origin, family background 2. one's previous experience/occupation
~产 **chūchǎn** выпуска́ть, производи́ть; вы́работка	to produce, manufacture; product -
~卖 **chūmai** 1. пуска́ть в прода́жу 2. предава́ть	1. to sell, offer for sale 2. to sell out, betray
~来 **chūlai** выходи́ть *(сюда)*	to come out, emerge; out (toward one) -
~版 **chūbǎn** издава́ть; изда́ние	to come off the press, publish, come out
~版社 **chūbǎnshè** изда́тельство	publisher, press -
~发 **chūfā** отпра́виться, вы́ступить *(в поход)*	1. to set out, start off 2. to start/proceed from
~入 **chūrù** 1. вход и вы́ход 2. ра́зница	1. to come in and go out 2. discrepancy, divergence

出色 **chūsè** выделя́ться; заме́тный, незауря́дный	outstanding, remarkable, splendid
～现 **chūxiàn** появля́ться; появле́ние	to appear, arise, emerge
～兵 **chūbīng** дви́нуть войска́	to dispatch troops
～其不意 **chūqíbùyì** неожи́данно	to take sb. by surprise
～去 **chūqù** выходи́ть *(отсю́да)*	to go/get out, exit
础 **chǔ** осно́ва, фунда́мент, ба́зис	plinth, stone base of a column
拙 **zhuō** тупо́й, неспосо́бный	foolish, stupid, silly, inane; meaningless
～劣 **zhuōliè** *см.* 拙	ignorant, dull, clumsy, inferior
屈 **qū 1.** сгиба́ть(ся); криво́й, изо́гнутый **2.** подчиня́ться **3.** несправедли́вость	1. to bend 2. to suffer wrong 3. crooked 4. wrong, incorrect 5. injustice, wrong
～辱 **qūrǔ** быть опозо́ренным; позо́р	to be humiliated/insulted; humiliation, disgrace //crossed
～膝 **qūxī** проси́ть поща́ды	1. to kneel, genuflect 2. to sit with knees//
～服 **qūfú** подчини́ть(ся); покори́ть(ся)	to surrender, yield
倔 **juè** упо́рный; упря́мый	gruff, surly
掘 **jué** копа́ть, рыть	to dig
～土机 **juétǔjī** экскава́тор	excavator, power shovel
窟 **kū** я́ма; пеще́ра; отве́рстие	hole, cave, den
甘 **gān 1.** вку́сный; сла́дкий **2.** охо́тно, с удово́льствием	1. sweet, pleasant, satisfactory 2. willing, of one's own accord 3. Gansu
～居 **gānjū** мири́ться, дово́льствоваться	to accept (a low position) willingly
～薯 **gānshǔ** бата́т, сла́дкий карто́фель	sweet potato
～心 **gānxīn** *см.* 甘 2	1. to be willing 2. to be reconciled/re-\\
～蔗 **gānzhè** са́харный тростни́к	sugar cane \\signed to
甜 **tián** сла́дкий; вку́сный	1. sweet 2. agreeable
～瓜 **tiánguā** ды́ня	muskmelon
酣 **hān 1.** попо́йка **2.** вдо́воль, до́сыта	rapturously; to one's heart's content
钳 **qián 1.** сжима́ть; зажима́ть **2.** выдёргивать *(гвозди)* **3.** щипцы́; клёщи́; тиски́	1. pincers, pliers, clamps, forceps 2. to pinch, clamp 3. to restrain, gag

钳工 **qiángōng** слéсарь	1. benchwork 2. fitter
~制 **qiánzhì** скóвывать	to clamp down on, suppress
臼 **jiù** стýпка	1. mortar 2. joint (of bones)
陷 **xiàn** **1.** упáсть **2.** попáсть в неприя́тное положéние **3.** оккупи́ровать **4.** ловýшка, западня́	1. to get stuck/bogged down 2. to become sunken/caved in 3. to frame/trump up 4. to be captured, fall 5. pitfall, trap 6. defect, deficiency
~害 **xiànhài** **1.** приноси́ть вред; губи́ть **2.** изменя́ть, предавáть	to frame, trump up charges against
~落 **xiànluò** провали́ться; упáсть	1. to subside, sink/cave in 2. to fall into enemy hands (of territory)
~阱 **xiànjing** попáсть в ловýшку; западня́	pitfall, pit, trap
焰 **yàn** плáмя; огóнь	flame, blaze
蹈 **dǎo** **1.** топтáть; попирáть, нарушáть **2.** слéдовать, подражáть	1. to tread, stamp the feet 2. to skip, trip 3. to follow
稻 **dào** рис *(на корню)*	paddy, rice
~田 **dàotián** ри́совое пóле	paddy field, rice farm
~草 **dàocǎo** ри́совая солóма	rice straw
~米 **dàomǐ** рис *(очищенный)*	rice paddy
滔 **tāo** **1.** выходи́ть из берегóв, разливáться **2.** бýрный, бурля́щий	to inundate, flood
插 **chā** **1.** встáвить; водрузи́ть **2.** сажáть *(рассаду)* **3.** вти́скиваться **4.** вклáдыш; вставка	to insert, interpose
~画 **chāhuà** иллюстрáция	(inserted) illustration (in book)
~言(话) **chāyán(huà)** вмéшиваться в разговóр; перебивáть; рéплика	to interpose a remark; a remark interposed; digression, episode
~嘴 **chāzuǐ** вмéшиваться в разговóр; перебивáть	to interrupt, break in

口

口 **kǒu** **1.** рот; пасть **2.** вход; вы́ход **3.** дырá; отвéрстие **4.** гóрлышко *(сосуда)* **5.** порт; гáвань **6.** ýстно; **ýстный** **7.** **глотóк; затя́ж-**	1. mouth 2. opening, entrance 3. hole, cut 4. knife edge 5. Great Wall gateway 6. (M. for mouthfuls/people/wells, etc.)

ка **8.** *сч. сл. а) для людей (едоков); б) для предметов с крышкой или отверстием, лезвий и ножей*	-
口红 **kǒuhóng** губна́я пома́да	lipstick
～径 **kǒujìng** кали́бр *(орудия)*; диа́метр *(отверстия)*	1. bore, caliber 2. requirements, specifications, line of action
～腔 **kǒuqiāng** по́лость рта, рот	oral cavity
～音 **kǒuyīn** произноше́ние; вы́говор	1. voice 2. local/regional accent
～罩 **kǒuzhào** повя́зка на рот; респира́тор	antiseptic mask
～琴 **kǒuqín** губна́я гармо́ника	harmonica
～子 **kǒuz 1.** дыра́; отве́рстие **2.** рты, едоки́ **3.** у́стье	opening, cut, tear
～号 **kǒuhào** ло́зунг, призы́в	slogan, watchword
～头 **kǒutóu** у́стно; у́стный	1. oral, in words 2. flavor (of fruit, etc.)
～味 **kǒuwèi** вкус	1. a person's taste 2. taste of food
～袋 **kǒudài** карма́н; мешо́к	pocket
～是心非 **kǒushì-xīnfēi** лицеме́рие, двули́чие	hypocritical
～述 **kǒushù** *см.* ～头	to recount orally
～吃 **kǒuchī** заика́ться	stuttering, stammering
～令 **kǒulìng 1.** кома́нда **2.** паро́ль	1. (oral) command 2. password, watchword, countersign
器 **qì 1.** прибо́р; аппара́т; инструме́нт **2.** посу́да **3.** о́рганы *(животных, растений)*	1. talent, aptitude 2. (suf. for utensil, ware, instrument, (body) organ)
～官 **qìguān** *см.* 器 3	organ, apparatus
～具 **qìjù 1.** прибо́ры, аппарату́ра; инструме́нты **2.** посу́да; у́тварь	utensil, implement, appliance
品 **pǐn 1.** предме́т, вещь, изде́лие **2.** класс; чин; разря́д **3.** сво́йство, ка́чество **4.** оце́нивать	1. article, product, goods 2. grade, class, rank, rate 3. character, quality 4. to taste, sample, judge 5. to blow (an instrument) 6. light/pale (color)
～格 **pǐngé** хара́ктер *(человека)*; досто́инства; ка́чества	1. one's character and morals 2. style and quality (of literary/artistic works)
～目 **pǐnmù** номенклату́ра	list of articles

品评 **pǐnpíng** оце́нивать; классифици́ровать	to judge, comment on
～种 **pǐnzhǒng** ассортиме́нт	1. breed 2. variety, assortment
～类 **pǐnlèi** сорт; разнови́дность	category, class
～质 **pǐnzhì** сво́йства, ка́чества; хара́ктер	character, quality
扣 **kòu 1.** закрыва́ть; застёгивать; застёжка **2.** удéрживать, вычита́ть **3.** ски́дка **4.** пу́говица **5.** задéрживать	1. to button/buckle/tie up 2. to detain, arrest 3. to deduct, discount; discount 4. knot, button, buckle 5. (M. for bundles/bunches/etc.) 6. to cover with a concave object
～上 **kòushàng** застегну́ть	to fasten, button up
～留 **kòuliú** арестова́ть, задержа́ть	to detain, arrest
～押 **kòuyā** наложи́ть аре́ст *(на имущество)*	to detain, hold in custody
～除 **kòuchú** удержа́ть, вы́честь; вы́чет	to deduct
加 **jiā 1.** увели́чивать; умножа́ть; прибавля́ть; плюс **2.** присоединя́ться	1. to increase, augment 2. to put in, add, append 3. to confer
～上 **jiāshàng 1.** приба́вить, доба́вить **2.** плюс ко всему́, к тому́ же	to add to
～工 **jiāgōng** обраба́тывать; отдéлывать	1. to process 2. machining, working
～倍 **jiābèi 1.** удва́ивать; вдво́е **2.** увели́чивать в нéсколько раз	to double, redouble
～油 **jiāyóu** заправля́ть *(машину)*	1. to oil, lubricate 2. to refuel 3. to make an extra effort
～剧 **jiājù** обостря́ться *(об обстановке)*	to aggravate, intensify
～多 **jiāduō** увели́чивать(ся)	to add more
～快 **jiākuài** ускоря́ть, убыстря́ть	to speed up, accelerate
～入 **jiārù** вступа́ть, присоединя́ться	1. to add, mix, put in 2. to join, accede
～速 **jiāsù** ускоря́ть, форси́ровать	to accelerate, quicken, expedite
～以 **jiāyǐ 1.** приба́вить; плюс к э́тому **2.** подвéргнуть *(напр. критике)*	1. (before polysyllabic verbs or verbal nouns) to handle, treat 2. in addition, moreover

加紧 **jiājin** обостря́ть(ся), уси́ливать(ся)	to speed up, intensify
~强 **jiāqiáng** уси́ливать, укрепля́ть	to strengthen, augment, reinforce
咖: ~啡 **kāfēi** ко́фе	coffee
~啡馆 **kāfēiguǎn** кафе́	café
嘉 **jiā** прекра́сный, превосхо́дный; досто́йный	1. good, fine 2. to praise, commend
~奖 **jiājiǎng** награ́да	to commend, cite
~礼 **jiālǐ** сва́дебный обря́д	wedding ceremony
茄 **qié** баклажа́н	eggplant
知 **zhī** знать; познава́ть; понима́ть; ра́зум; зна́ния	1. to know, realize, sense 2. to inform, notify 3. to administer 4. to be expert in
~名 **zhīmíng** широкоизве́стный	noted, famous
~道 **zhīdào** знать, быть в ку́рсе	to know, realize, be aware of
~觉 **zhījué** созна́ние; ощуще́ние, восприя́тие	1. consciousness 2. perception
~识 **zhīshí** зна́ния, эруди́ция	knowledge
~识分子 **zhīshi fēnz** интеллиге́нция	1. educated person (high school or college equivalent) 2. intelligentsia
~心 **zhīxīn** задуше́вный	intimate, close; understanding
~照 **zhīzhào** уве́домить, извести́ть	to inform, notify, tell
痴 **chī** глу́пый; идио́т	1. silly, idiotic 2. crazy about 3. insane
和 **hé 1.** мир, согла́сие; ми́рный **2.** мя́гкий; тёплый; смягча́ть **3.** *союз или предлог* и; с; 我和他 я и он, мы с ним	1. gentle, mild, moderate 2. harmonious 3. (together) with 4. sum 5. peace 6. (sports) tie, draw
~ **huó** меси́ть; заме́шивать	to mix (with water, etc.), knead
~睦 **hémù** дру́жно, в согла́сии	harmony, amity
~平 **hépíng 1.** мир; ми́рный **2.** доброду́шный	1. peace 2. mild
~平主义 **hépíngzhǔyì** пацифи́зм	pacificism
~好 **héhǎo** помири́ться; дру́жный; ми́рный	1. to become reconciled 2. friendly
~尙 **héshang** будди́йский мона́х	Buddhist monk
~约 **héyuē** ми́рный до́говор	peace treaty

和如钮石岩碧磨

和缓 **héhuǎn** смягча́ть(ся); уме́ренный	1. to ease up, relax 2. gentle, mild
～气 **héqì** **1.** ми́рная атмосфе́ра; согла́сие **2.** сми́рный, кро́ткий	kind, polite, amiable
如 **rú** **1.** походи́ть; подо́бно; вро́де; как **2.** наприме́р **3.** е́сли; е́сли бы **4.** согла́сно, по	1. to be like 2. to measure up to 3. to go to 4. according to, in accordance with 5. such as, as if, like, for example 6. if, supposing
～上 **rúshàng** вышеизло́женный	as above
～下 **rúxià** нижесле́дующий	as follows
～今 **rújīn** тепе́рь, ны́не	nowadays
～何 **rúhé** как?; како́й?	how, how about it
～果 **rúguǒ** е́сли, в слу́чае	if
～此 **rúcǐ** так; тако́в; таки́м о́бразом	thus, like this, such
～意 **rúyì** быть дово́льным; с удово́льствием	1. as one wishes 2. ornamental scepter
钮 **kòu** застёгивать; пу́говица	to fasten, button; button
～子 **kòuz** пу́говица; застёжка	1. knot, button 2. bottle neck 3. story break to create suspense
石 **shí** ка́мень; минера́л; ка́менный	1. stone, rock 2. stone inscription
～ **dàn** дань (*мера объёма, равная 100 л*)	(M. for grain, = 1 hectoliter)
～器 **shíqì** изде́лия из ка́мня	1. stone implement/artifact 2. stone//vessel, stoneware
～榴 **shíliú** *бот.* грана́т	pomegranate
～油 **shíyóu** нефть; нефтяно́й	petroleum, oil
～头 **shítóu** ка́мень; ка́менный	stone, rock
～灰 **shíhuī** и́звесть; изве́стковый	lime
～炭 **shítàn** ка́менный у́голь	coal
岩 **yán** скала́, утёс; обры́в	1. rock 2. cliff, crag
～石 **yánshí** го́рные поро́ды	rock
碧 **bì** **1.** нефри́т; я́шма **2.** лазо́ревый	bluish/emerald green; blue; jasper, green jade
～玉 **bìyù** я́шма	jasper, emerald
磨 **mó** тере́ть, растира́ть; полирова́ть; точи́ть	1. to rub, grind, polish 2. to wear down/out 3. to trouble, pester
～ **mò** **1.** точи́льный ка́мень;	1. to grind, mill; millstone, mill 2. to

жёрнов 2. молóть, перемáлывать	turn around/about
磨盘 **mòpán** мéльничный жёрнов	lower/nether millstone; mill, millstones
~房 **mòfáng** мéльница	mill
~床 **móchuáng** точи́льный станóк	grinding machine
~练 **móliàn** тренировáться, упражня́ться; усéрдно рабóтать над	to temper/steel oneself
右 **yòu** прáвый; напрáво	1. right side; the right 2. the Right //3. west 4. conservative
~派 **yòupài** *полит.* прáвые	the right; rightist
~边 **yòubiān** прáвая сторонá; спрáва	the right-hand side, the right
若 **ruò** 1. éсли 2. как бýдто; подóбно	1. if, as if 2. like, similar 3. to seem, appear to; seemingly
~干 **ruògān** нéкоторое числó, нéсколько	1. a certain number/amount 2. how many?
~非 **ruòfēi** éсли бы не	if not for
~是 **ruòshì** éсли; éсли бы	if, supposing
诺 **nuò** 1. обещáть 2. утверди́тельный отвéт; хорошó; да	promise
~言 **nuòyán** обещáние; соглáсие	promise, consent
君 **jūn** 1. князь; госудáрь, прави́тель 2. Вы; господи́н	1. monarch, sovereign, supreme ruler 2. gentleman, sir
~主 **jūnzhǔ** монáрх; корóль; госудáрь	monarch, sovereign
~子 **jūnz** благорóдный человéк; джентльмéн	1. man of noble character, gentleman 2. sovereign
裙 **qún** юбка; перéдник	skirt, apron, petticoat
后 **hòu** 1. императóр; императри́ца 2. зáдний; сзáди, позади́, за 3. пóсле тогó, как; пóсле 4. послéдующий; грядýщий; чéрез	1. rear, back, behind 2. offspring, descendant 3. (coll.) day after tomorrow 4. empress, queen 5. afterwards, later
~卫 **hòuwèi** арьергáрд	1. rear guard 2. (sports) fullback; guard
~备 **hòubèi** резéрв, запáс; запаснóй, резéрвный	reserve
~备队 **hòubèiduì** резéрвы, резéрвные чáсти	(mil.) reserve
~面 **hòumiàn** зáдняя сторонá; позади́, сзáди, за	1. at the back of, in the rear, behind 2. later

后启言信

后辈 **hòubèi** послéдователи; бýдущее поколéние	1. younger generation 2. posterity -
~年 **hòunián** чéрез два гóда	year after next
~方 **hòufāng** тыл; тыловóй	rear
~悔 **hòuhuǐ** раскáиваться, сожалéть	to regret, repent -
~人 **hòurén** наслéдники; потóмки	1. later generations 2. posterity, descendants 3. to lag behind others
~头 **hòutou** 1. позади́ 2. потóм, затéм; в бýдущем	1. rear, behind 2. in the future -
~天 **hòutiān** послезáвтра, чéрез день	1. day after tomorrow 2. postnatal; acquired
~来 **hòulái** затéм, потóм; впослéдствии	1. afterwards, later 2. latecomers -
~果 **hòuguǒ** послéдствия; конéчный результáт	consequences, aftermath -
~边 **hòubiān** *см.* ~面	rear, back, behind
~代 **hòudài** послéдующие эпóхи (поколéния)	1. later periods/ages 2. later generations, descendants, posterity, progeny
启 **qǐ** 1. открывáть, раскрывáть 2. начинáть 3. объявля́ть	1. to open (up) 2. to enlighten, expound 3. note 4. to open (a letter/etc.) -
~事 **qǐshì** объявлéние; объявля́ть	notice, announcement -
~发 **qǐfā** разъясня́ть, спосóбствовать понимáнию	to enlighten, stimulate; enlightenment, inspiration
言 **yán** 1. словá, речь; язы́к 2. говори́ть	1. speech, word, talk 2. character 3. to say, talk, speak
~语 **yányǔ** язы́к; речь	1. to speak, talk 2. to answer
~行 **yánxíng** словá и делá	words and deeds
~词 **yáncí** словá; выражéния	words, expressions -
~谈 **yántán** бесéдовать; бесéда	content/manner of speech -
~论 **yánlùn** выскáзывания	open discussion, speech
信 **xìn** 1. вéрить, доверя́ть; вéра 2. письмó; извéстие 3. сигнáл, знак	1. confidence, trust, faith 2. sign, evidence 3. letter, mail 4. message, word, information 5. to believe 6. true 7.\\
~任 **xìnrèn** доверя́ть; довéрие	to trust, have confidence in \\random -
~箱 **xìnxiāng** почтóвый я́щик	1. mailbox, letter box 2. post-office box -
~仰 **xìnyǎng** вéра; убеждéния; идеáлы	to believe -

信件 **xìnjiàn** корреспонде́нция; пи́сьма	letter; mail
～封 **xìnfēng** конве́рт *(почто́вый)*	envelope
～用 **xìnyòng** креди́т; креди́тный	trustworthiness, credit
～号 **xìnhào** сигна́л	signal
～义 **xìnyì** договорённость	(good) faith
～教 **xìnjiào** ве́ровать; вероиспове́дание	to profess a religion
～托 **xìntuō** доверя́ть; поруча́ть	to trust, entrust
～心 **xìnxīn** уве́ренность, ве́ра	confidence, faith
～念 **xìnniàn** убежде́ния; ве́ра; кре́до	faith, belief, conviction
誓 **shì** кля́сться; присяга́ть; кля́тва; прися́га	to vow, pledge, swear; oath, pledge, vow
～言(词) **shìyán(cí)** кля́тва; прися́га	oath, pledge
譬 **pì** сра́внивать; приме́р; наприме́р	example, analogy
～如 **pìrú** наприме́р	for example, such as
誊 **téng** перепи́сывать; копи́ровать	to transcribe, copy out
～写 **téngxiě** переписа́ть; снять ко́пию	to transcribe, copy out
警 **jǐng** **1.** предупрежда́ть, предостерега́ть **2.** трево́га **3.** охраня́ть, оберега́ть **4.** поли́ция	1. to warn 2. to guard against 3. alarm 4. police 5. alert, vigilant
～卫 **jǐngwèi** **1.** охра́на **2.** гва́рдия; гварде́йский	1. (security) guard 2. to guard against
～告 **jǐnggào** предупрежда́ть, предостерега́ть; предупрежде́ние	to warn, caution, admonish; (disciplinary) warning
～备 **jǐngbèi** **1.** быть насторо́же **2.** гарнизо́нная слу́жба	guard, garrison
～备军 **jǐngbèijūn** охра́нные войска́; гарнизо́н	guard troops, garrison
～惕 **jǐngtì** бди́тельный; насторожи́ться	to be on guard against
～惕性 **jǐngtìxìng** бди́тельность	vigilance

警报 **jǐngbào** трево́га *(напр. боевая)*	alarm, warning, alert
～戒 **jǐngjiè** предосторо́жность	1. to warn, admonish 2. to guard against, keep close watch on
～察 **jǐngchá** поли́ция; мили́ция	police, policeman
誉 **yù** прославля́ть, восхваля́ть; изве́стность, сла́ва	reputation, fame; to praise, eulogize
～望 **yùwàng** изве́стность, сла́ва	fame, reputation
兽 **shòu** живо́тное; зверь; звери́ный	beast, animal
～医 **shòuyī** ветерина́р	veterinarian, vet
合 **hé** 1. соединя́ть(ся); смыка́ть(ся) 2. объединя́ть(-ся); коопери́ровать(ся) 3. соотве́тствовать, совпада́ть	1. to close, shut 2. to pool/join/combine (efforts/etc.) 3. to be equal to, amount to 4. to be fitting 5. whole, together, jointly 6. (astron.) conjunction
～金 **héjīn** сплав мета́ллов	alloy
～理 **hélǐ** целесообра́зный, рациона́льный	rational, reasonable, equitable
～理化 **hélǐhuà** рационализа́ция	to rationalize
～格 **hégé** отвеча́ть тре́бованиям; быть го́дным; удовлетвори́тельный	to qualify, reach a standard, pass
～营 **héyíng** совме́стное управле́ние	jointly owned/operated
～唱 **héchàng** петь хо́ром; хорово́е пе́ние	to sing in a chorus; chorus
～唱队 **héchàngduì** хор	chorus, choral group
～作 **hézuò** сотру́дничать; сотру́дничество; коопера́ция	to cooperate, collaborate, work together
～作社 **hézuòshè** кооперати́в; коопера́ция	co-op, cooperative
～并 **hébìng** соединя́ть, присоединя́ть; анне́ксия	to merge, amalgamate
～同 **hétóng** 1. до́гово́р, контра́кт 2. взаимоде́йствовать	contract, agreement
～适 **héshì** подходя́щий; целесообра́зный; в са́мый раз	suitable, appropriate, becoming, right
～成 **héchéng** 1. комбини́ро-	1. (chem.) to compose, compound 2. to//synthesize

ванный; составнóй **2.** сúнтез; синтетúческий	-
合法 **héfǎ** закóнный, легáльный	lawful, legitimate, rightful
给 **gěi 1.** давáть, предоставля́ть **2.** *перед косвенным доп. обозначает адресата:* 给我拿来 принесú мне **3.** *употр. вм.* 被 *в пассивной конструкции:* 他的话给父亲打断了 егó речь былá прéрвана отцóм	1. to give (to) 2. for, to 3. (in passive constructions) by
～ **jǐ** давáть, снабжáть; снабжéние	1. to supply, provide 2. ample, well provided for
～养 **jǐ(gěi)yǎng** содержáние; снабжéние, довóльствие	provisions, victuals
～予(与) **gěi yǔ(yǔ)** давáть, предоставля́ть; окáзывать *(помощь)*	to give to
～以 **gěiyi 1.** давáть, предоставля́ть **2.** наносúть *(удар)*	to give, grant
哈 **hā** хохотáть; ха-хá!	1. to exhale, sip 2. stoop 3. aha!
～哈 **hāhā** ха-хá!	ha-ha!
～哈大笑 **hāhā dàxiào** расхохотáться; хóхот	to roar with laughter
恰 **qià 1.** как рáз; кстáти, вóвремя; к счáстью **2.** чуть-чýть, сáмая мáлость	appropriately, properly, just, exactly
～当 **qiàdāng** соответствующий, надлежáщий	appropriate, proper, suitable, fitting
～恰 **qiàqià** *см.* 恰 1	1. coincidentally 2. exactly, just right
～恰相反 **qiàqià xiāngfǎn** как рáз наоборóт	precisely the opposite
～好 **qiàhǎo** к счáстью; кстáти	1. by luck/coincidence 2. exactly, just right
～巧 **qiàqiǎo** *см.* 恰 1	by chance, fortunately
拾 **shí 1.** подбирáть, поднимáть **2.** собирáть, убирáть *(урожай)* **3.** убирáть(ся), наводúть поря́док	1. to pick up, collect 2. ten (on checks/etc.)
塔 **tǎ** бáшня; пáгода	1. pagoda 2. stupa 3. tower
～斯社 **tǎsishè** ТАСС (Те-	TASS (former Soviet News Agency)

леграфное агентство Советского Союза)	-
搭 **dā** 1. сбить, сколоти́ть 2. присоедини́ться, соста́вить компа́нию 3. погрузи́ться, сесть на	1. to put up, construct 2. to hang over 3. to join together 4. to travel by or take (a conveyance) 5. to lift together 6. to add (money/etc.)
～乘 **dāchéng** е́хать на *чём*	to travel (by conveyance)
～救 **dājiù** вы́ручить, оказа́ть по́мощь	to rescue, go to the rescue of
～载 **dāzài** 1. перевози́ть пасса́жиров 2. грузи́ть(ся) *(на суда)*	to carry (passengers)
答 **dá** 1. отвеча́ть; отве́т 2. отозва́ться, откли́кнуться	1. to answer, reply 2. to return (a call/etc.), reciprocate
～应 **dáyìng** 1. обеща́ть; соглаша́ться 2. отвеча́ть, отзыва́ться	1. to answer, reply 2. to agree to, promise
～复 **dáfù** отвеча́ть; отве́т	answer, reply
吉 **jí** сча́стье; счастли́вый, ра́достный	1. lucky, auspicious, propitious 2. Jilin (prov.)
～它 **jítā** гита́ра	guitar
结 **jié** 1. свя́зывать; завя́зывать *(узел)* 2. нала́живать *(отношения)*; заключа́ть *(договор)* 3. результа́т, ито́г, вы́вод	1. to tie, knot, knit, weave; knot 2. to congeal, form, forge, cement 3. to settle, conclude 4. written guarantee 5. affidavit 6. (electr.) junction 7. (physiol.) node
～ **jiē** про́чный, кре́пкий	to bear (fruit), form (seed)
～盟 **jiéméng** заключа́ть сою́з	to form an alliance, ally, align
～合 **jiéhé** свя́зывать(ся); соединя́ть(ся); сочета́ние	1. to combine, unite, integrate, link 2. to be joined in wedlock
～婚 **jiéhūn** вступа́ть в брак, жени́ться, выходи́ть за́муж; брак	to marry, get married; marriage, wedding
～局 **jiéjú** результа́т; фина́л	final result, outcome, ending
～构 **jiégòu** структу́ра, строе́ние; констру́кция; устро́йство	1. structure, composition, construction 2. (geol.) structure
～实 **jiēshí** кре́пкий, про́чный	1. to bear fruit 2. strong, solid, durable
～果 **jiéguǒ** результа́т, ито́г; в результа́те	result, outcome, consequence
～束 **jiéshù** 1. зако́нчить(ся);	to end, conclude, close

коне́ц, фина́л **2.** заключа́ть,	-
резюми́ровать	-
结冰 **jiébīng** обледене́ть; за-мёрзнуть	to freeze, ice up/over
~论 **jiélùn** вы́вод, заключе́ние	conclusion; verdict
洁 **jié** **1.** чи́стить; чи́стый **2.** улучша́ть, соверше́нствовать	to clean
善 **shàn** **1.** де́лать добро́; до́брый **2.** уме́ть, быть иску́сным в	1. good; charitable, kind, friendly; kindness, good deed 2. familiar 3. to do sth. well, make perfect 4. to be apt/prone to\\
~于 **shànyú** быть иску́сным в	to be good at, be adept in \\5. properly
~良 **shànliáng** до́брый	good and kind, decent
~意 **shànyì** доброжела́тельный	goodwill
晤 **wù** встре́титься, уви́деться	to meet face to face
悟 **wù** **1.** прийти́ в созна́ние **2.** заста́вить поня́ть; просвети́ть	to realize, awaken (to)
语 **yǔ** **1.** язы́к; слова́ **2.** разгова́ривать, говори́ть	1. language, tongue, words; to speak, say 2. saying, proverb 3. means of \\
~汇 **yǔhuì** слова́рный соста́в, ле́ксика	vocabulary \\communication
~言 **yǔyán** язы́к; речь	language
~音 **yǔyīn** произноше́ние	1. speech sounds 2. pronunciation
~词 **yǔcí** сло́во; выраже́ние	words and phrases
~句 **yǔjù** предложе́ние, фра́за	sentence
~文 **yǔwén** язы́к *(устный и письменный)*	1. (spoken and written) language 2. language and literature
~法 **yǔfǎ** грамма́тика	grammar; syntax
培 **péi** **1.** оку́чивать **2.** воспи́тывать; выра́щивать	1. to bank up with earth 2. to foster, train, educate
~植 **péizhì** **1.** выра́щивать, культиви́ровать **2.** внедря́ть	to cultivate, foster, train
~养(育) **péiyǎng(yǔ)** воспи́тывать, выра́щивать	1. to foster, train, develop 2. (biol.) culture
倍 **bèi** удва́ивать; вдво́е; двойно́й; 一倍 вдво́е; 两倍 втро́е	1. times, -fold 2. twice as much

倍陪赔喜嘻售占站

倍数 **bèishù** крáтное числó	(math) multiple //compensate
陪 **péi** сопровождáть	1. to accompany 2. to assist 3. to//
～伴(同) **péibàn(tóng)** быть вмéсте; составля́ть компáнию	to accompany, keep sb. company
赔 **péi 1.** возмещáть, компенси́ровать **2.** нести́ убы́тки **3.** признавáть винý, извиня́ться	1. to compensate, pay for 2. to stand a loss
～罪 **péizuì** признавáть винý	to apologize
～偿 **péicháng** компенси́ровать, возмещáть; компенсáция	to compensate, pay for
喜 **xǐ 1.** счáстье; рáдость; счастли́вый; рáдостный **2.** люби́ть; нрáвиться	1. to be fond of, be keen on; happy, delighted, pleased 2. to be happy/elated
～剧 **xǐjù** комéдия	comedy
～事 **xǐshì** прáздникство; свáдьба; рáдостное собы́тие	happy event, joyous occasion
～欢 **xǐhuān** нрáвиться; люби́ть	1. to like, love, be fond of 2. to be happy/elated
嘻 **xī** хихи́кать; хи-хи́!	1. Alas!, My! 2. he! he!; giggle
～笑 **xīxiào** смея́ться; хихи́кать	to be laughing and playing //cepted
售 **shòu** продавáть; продáжа	1. to sell 2. to get (a plan/etc.) ac-//
～货员 **shòuhuòyuán** продавéц	shop assistant, clerk
～票处 **shòupiàochǔ** билéтная кáсса	ticket office
～票员 **shòupiàoyuán** касси́р *(билетный)*	ticket seller
占 **zhàn 1.** захвáтывать, занимáть, оккупи́ровать **2.** составля́ть *(часть)*	1. to occupy, take 2. to constitute, make up; to account for
～据 **zhànjù** *см.* 占 1	to occupy, hold
～有 **zhànyǒu** присвáивать, захвáтывать	1. to own, have 2. to occupy, hold
～领 **zhànlǐng** *см.* 占 1	to occupy, hold
站 **zhàn 1.** встать; стоя́ть **2.** останови́ться; остано́вка; стáнция; вокзáл	1. to (take a) stand 2. to stop, halt 3. station, stop
～主 **zhànzhǔ** останови́ться; стой!	1. to stop, halt 2. to hold one's ground 3. to hold water, be tenable

站岗 **zhàngǎng** стоя́ть на посту́	to stand sentry
~队 **zhànduì** постро́иться ряда́ми	to line up, fall in
~长 **zhànzhǎng** нача́льник ста́нции	station/center/etc. head
~起来 **zhànqilai** подня́ться; встать!	to rise, get up; get up!
帖 **tiē** пригласи́тельный биле́т	1. note, card 2. invitation 3. (M. for doses)
黏 **nián** **1.** вя́зкий; ли́пкий **2.** скле́иваться; слипа́ться; прикле́ивать	1. sticky, glutinous 2. to adhere, stick
~土 **niántǔ** гли́на	clay
~膜 **niánmò** сли́зистая оболо́чка	mucous membrane, mucosa
贴 **tiē** **1.** прикле́ивать; закле́ивать **2.** стипе́ндия; посо́бие	1. to paste, glue, stick to 2. to subsidize; subsidies, allowance 3. to sentence to death
~补 **tiēbǔ** ока́зывать по́мощь *(материальную)*; субсиди́ровать	to subsidize, help financially
沾 **zhān** **1.** промо́кнуть **2.** косну́ться, затро́нуть **3.** переня́ть; зарази́ться	1. to moisten, soak 2. to be stained with 3. to profit from 4. to touch
~染 **zhānrǎn** **1.** окра́ситься **2.** зарази́ться; зараже́ние	to be infected by
钻 **zuàn** **1.** сверло́; бура́в **2.** алма́з *(для резки стекла)*	1. to drill, auger 2. diamond, watch, jewel 3. to bore, drill, get/dig into
~ **zuān** **1.** проткну́ть **2.** дои́скиваться, дока́пываться	to drill, bore, get/dig into
店 **diàn** **1.** магази́н; ла́вка **2.** гости́ница; харче́вня	1. shop, store 2. inn
~铺 **diànpù** магази́н; ла́вка	store, shop
惦 **diàn** по́мнить; забо́титься, беспоко́иться	to remember with concern, be concerned about, keep thinking about
~念 **diànniàn** скуча́ть; беспоко́иться о	to keep thinking about, be anxious about
掂 **diān** взве́шивать, прики́дывать	to weigh in the hand
哲 **zhé** **1.** проница́тельный; му́дрый **2.** филосо́фия	1. wise, sagacious 2. wise man, sage
~学 **zhéxué** филосо́фия	philosophy
~学家 **zhéxuéjiā** фило́соф	philosopher

站帖黏贴沾钻店惦掂哲

古估枯姑居据锯

古 **gǔ** дре́вний, стари́нный;	1. ancient, age-old 2. not following cur-
дре́вность	rent customs/practice
～物 **gǔwù** предме́ты стари-	ancient objects, antiquities
ны́	-
～物学 **gǔwùxué** археоло́гия	archeology
～迹 **gǔjì** истори́ческие па́-	historic site
мятники; достопримеча́-	-
тельности	-
～代 **gǔdài** дре́вность; дре́в-	antiquity
ний; анти́чный	-
估 **gū** вычисля́ть; измеря́ть	to estimate, appraise
～计 **gūjì** **1.** оце́нивать; оце́н-	to estimate, appraise, reckon
ка **2.** учи́тывать, брать на	-
учёт	-
枯 **kū** **1.** вя́нуть; со́хнуть	1. withered (of plants/etc.) 2. dried
2. худо́й, то́щий	(of wells/etc.) 3. dull 4. emaciated
姑 **gū** **1.** свекро́вь; тётка; зо-	1. father's sister 2. husband's sister
ло́вка **2.** де́вушка	3. husband's mother 4. nun 5. tempo-\\
～母 **gūmǔ** тётка	father's married sister \\rary
～娘 **gūniáng** де́вушка; не-	1. girl 2. (coll.) daughter
заму́жняя же́нщина	-
～息 **gūxī** **1.** балова́ть *(де-*	to appease, indulge, tolerate
тей) **2.** попусти́тельство-	-
вать; либера́льничать	-
居 **jū** жить, прожива́ть; ме-	1. to reside, live 2. to occupy 3. to as-
стожи́тельство	sert, claim 4. to store up 5. residence
～住 **jūzhù** жить, прожива́ть	to live, reside
～留 **jūliú** пребыва́ть, нахо-	to reside
ди́ться	-
～民 **jūmín** жи́тели, населе́-	resident, inhabitant
ние	-
～然 **jūrán** **1.** по́просту **2.** не-	1. unexpectedly, to one's surprise 2.
ожи́данно	going so far as to
据 **jù** **1.** осно́вываться на;	1. according to, on the grounds of 2. to
су́дя по **2.** ба́за, опо́рный	occupy, seize 3. to rely/depend on 4.
пункт **3.** свиде́тельство,	evidence, proof, certificate
доказа́тельство, аргуме́нт	-
～闻 **jùwén** по слу́хам	by ear
～说 **jùshuō** как говоря́т; пе-	it is said that
редаю́т, что	-
～点 **jùdiǎn** опо́рный пункт;	fortified point, stronghold
ключева́я пози́ция	-
锯 **jù** пили́ть; пила́; зубча́-	saw; to saw
тый	-

锯木厂 **jùmùchǎng** лесопи́льный заво́д	sawmill, lumber mill -
苦 **kǔ 1.** го́рький; тяжёлый, тру́дный **2.** страда́ния, муче́ния **3.** упо́рно; изо все́х сил	1. hardship, suffering, pain 2. to cause sb. suffering 3. to suffer from, be troubled by 4. painstakingly 5. excessive 6. bitter
～工 **kǔgōng 1.** тяжёлый труд **2.** чернорабо́чий	hard manual work -
～难 **kǔnàn** бе́дствия; страда́ния	suffering, misery, distress -
～刑 **kǔxíng** пы́тка	torture
～力 **kǔlì** ку́ли, чернорабо́чий	1. laborer, coolie 2. strenuous effort, hard work
～头 **kǔtóu** страда́ния, муче́ния	1. suffering 2. bitter taste -
～战 **kǔzhàn** упо́рные бой	to struggle hard; hard struggle
～心 **kǔxīn** стара́ние, усе́рдие	trouble taken, pains
舌：～头 **shétóu** *анат.* язы́к	1. (anat.) tongue 2. ability to talk
括 **kuò** включа́ть, охва́тывать	1. to draw together, contract 2. to include -
～号 **kuòhào** ско́бки	brackets; parentheses; braces
活 **huó 1.** жить; живо́й; жизнь **2.** де́йствовать; де́ятельный **3.** рабо́та, заня́тие; 一学活用 изуча́ть и применя́ть на пра́ктике	1. to live 2. to save (sb.'s life) 3. alive, live, living 4. moving 5. vivid, lively 6. exactly; simply 7. work 8. product 9. livelihood -
～动 **huódòng 1.** де́йствовать; де́ятельность **2.** дви́гаться; подви́жный	1. to move about, exercise 2. activity, maneuver 3. behavior 4. unsteady 5. movable, mobile 6. to use influence
～跃 **huóyuè** оживля́ться; оживлённый; оживле́ние	to enliven, animate, invigorate; brisk, active, dynamic
～泼 **huópō** бо́дрый, энерги́чный, живо́й	lively , vivacious, vivid -
话 **huà 1.** слова́; речь, язы́к **2.** разгово́р, бесе́да	1. speech, talk, conversation, words, sayings, story 2. language 3. to talk
～剧 **huàjù** спекта́кль, пье́са	modern drama, stage play
舍 **shè** жили́ще; общежи́тие; гости́ница	1. room, dorm 2. school building 3. pen/ shed for animals 4. (M. distance, =30 li)
～ **shě** отка́зываться; броса́ть	1. to give up, abandon 2. to give alms -
～弃 **shěqì** бро́сить, оста́вить	to give up, abandon
～身 **shěshēn** поже́ртвовать собо́й	to give/sacrifice one's life -

舍不得 **shěbude** не в си́лах отказа́ться	1. to loathe to part with 2. to begrudge doing sth.
告 **gào 1.** объявля́ть; докла́дывать; сказа́ть *кому* **2.** обвиня́ть; жа́ловаться **3.** обраща́ться с про́сьбой, проси́ть	1. to tell, inform, explain 2. to accuse, go to law against 3. to ask for, request 4. to make known, state clearly, announce
~知 **gàozhi** оповести́ть, уве́домить	to inform, notify
~诉 **gàosù 1.** сказа́ть, сообщи́ть **2.** пожа́ловаться *(в суд)*	to tell, let know, inform
~别 **gàobié** проща́ться; проща́ние, расстава́ние	1. to leave, part from 2. to bid farewell to //important
~成 **gàochéng** заверши́ться	to announce completion of sth. //
酷 **kù** му́чить; жесто́кий	1. oppressive 2. very 3. (slang) cool
浩 **hào** безбре́жный, необъя́тный	1. great, vast, grand 2. many, much
~大 **hàodà** огро́мный; вели́кий	huge, vast
~繁 **hàofán** оби́льный; многочи́сленный	vast and numerous
害 **hài 1.** губи́ть; по́ртить; вреди́ть; уще́рб; бе́дствие **2.** страда́ть *чем*	1. to harm, injure 2. to kill 3. to contract an illness 4. to feel 5. disaster, harm, evil; harmful
~羞 **hàixiū** стесня́ться, смуща́ться	to be bashful/shy
~怕 **hàipà** боя́ться, тру́сить	to be afraid/scared
~臊 **hàisào** стыди́ться, стесня́ться	to feel ashamed, be bashful
~处 **hàichù** вред, уще́рб	harm
~虫 **hàichóng** насеко́мые-вреди́тели	destructive insect, pest
瞎 **xiā 1.** осле́пнуть; слепо́й **2.** наугáд, как попа́ло	1. to become blind; blind 2. groundlessly, to no end 3. to become tangled
~话 **xiāhuà** чепуха́, вздор	lie, untruth
~子 **xiāz** слепо́й	blind person
~眼 **xiāyǎn** осле́пнуть; слепо́й	to be blind //govern
辖 **xiá** управля́ть, ве́дать	to have jurisdiction over, administer,//
唐 **táng 1.** хвастовство́ **2.** дина́стия Тан	1. exaggerative, boastful 2. in vain, for nothing 3. Tang dynasty (618—907)
塘 **táng 1.** земляна́я плоти́на **2.** водоём	1. embankment 2. pool, pond

糖 **táng** сáхар; слáдости; конфéты; сáхарный	1. sugar 2. sweets, candy 3. carbohydrates
～果 **tángguǒ** слáсти; конфéты	sweets, candy
～尿病 **tángniàobìng** сáхарный диабéт	diabetes
含 **hán** **1.** содержáть в себé; вмещáть **2.** сдéрживать (-ся)	1. to keep in the mouth 2. to contain 3. to nurse, cherish, harbor
～泪 **hánlèi** глотáть слёзы	to have tears in one's eyes
～有 **hányǒu** содержáть в себé; обладáть *(каким-л. свойством)*	to contain, have
～怒 **hánnù** гнéвно, с негодовáнием	to be angry/resentful
名 **míng** **1.** именовáть, называ́ть; и́мя **2.** слáва, извéстность; репутáция **3.** *сч. сл. для людей*	1. name 2. fame, reputation 3. number, order of selection 4. famous 5. to name, describe 6. (M. for persons)
～望 **míngwàng** извéстность, слáва	fame, renown
～胜 **míngshèng** достопримечáтельности	place famous for its scenery or historical relics; scenic spot
～誉 **míngyù** *см.* ～望	fame, reputation
～单 **míngdān** спи́сок *(поимённый)*	name list
～片 **míngpiàn** визи́тная кáрточка	visiting/calling card, name-card
～利主义 **mínglìzhǔyì** карьери́зм	careerism
～子(字) **míngz(zì)** наименовáние, назвáние; и́мя	name
～词 **míngcí** **1.** [и́мя] существи́тельное **2.** тéрмин	1. noun, substantive 2. term; phrase 3. name
～声 **míngshēng** репутáция	reputation, repute, renown
～义 **míngyì** и́мя; звáние; номинáльный; 代表…名义 от и́мени	name; nominal, titular, in name
～额 **míng'é** штат; штáтное расписáние	quota of people
～称 **míngchēng** назвáние, наименовáние	name
召 **zhào** звать, созывáть, приглашáть	1. to call, convene, summon 2. to solicit, recruit

召回 **zhàohuí** отзывáть	to recall (e.g., a diplomat)
～开 **zhāokāi** открывáть	to convene, convoke
(съезд)	-
～唤 **zhàohuàn** вызывáть,	to call, summon
звать	-
～集 **zhàojí** собирáть, созы-	to call together, convene
вáть; сбор	-
招 **zhāo 1.** звать, подзывáть	1. to beckon 2. to enlist, recruit 3. to
2. приглашáть; принимáть	attract, incur 4. to provoke 5. to
3. признавáть *(вину)*	confess 6. to infect 7. trick, device
～生 **zhāoshēng** набирáть	to recruit students
(принимáть) учáщихся	-
～牌 **zhāopai** вы́веска	shop sign, signboard
～待 **zhāodài** принимáть, об-	to receive (guests); to serve (custo-
слýживать *(гостей)*	mers)
～呼 **zhāohū 1.** звать; манúть	1. to call 2. to greet 3. to notify, tell 4.
2. забóтиться; присмáтри-	to take care of 5. to take care lest 6.
вать	to work hard 7. to get into a fight
～致 **zhāozhì** привестú к,	1. to seek, recruit (followers/etc.) 2. to
навлéчь	incur, lead to
～兵 **zhāobīng** вербовáть сол-	to recruit soldiers
дáт	-
沼 **zhǎo** болóто	natural pond
～地 **zhǎodì** болóтистая мéст-	swampy/marshy area
ность	-
谷 **gǔ 1.** ущéлье; оврáг	1. valley, gorge 2. cereal, grain; millet
2. хлебá; злáки	3. unhusked rice
～物 **gǔwù** зерновы́е; злáки	cereal, grain
俗 **sú 1.** нрáвы, обы́чаи **2.**	1. vulgar 2. popular, common, current
обы́чный, простóй **3.** вуль-	3. secular 4. custom, convention
гáрный; банáльный	-
～话 **súhuà 1.** пословица; по-	(coll.) common saying, proverb
говóрка **2.** просторéчие	-
～气 **súqì** обывáтельщина	vulgar, in poor taste
裕 **yù** обúльный, богáтый	abundant, plentiful
容 **róng 1.** вмещáть; содер-	1. to contain 2. to allow, tolerate 3.
жать в себé; ёмкость; объ-	looks, appearance
ём **2.** позволя́ть, допус-	-
кáть **3.** нарýжность, óблик	-
4. свобóдно, легкó	-
～让 **róngràng** уступáть, по-	to make a concession, yield, give in
зволя́ть; терпúмость	-
～量 **róngliàng** объём; ём-	capacity (of a container)
кость	-

容许 **róngxǔ** допускáть, позволя́ть	to permit, tolerate
～纳 **róngnà** вмещáть	to have a capacity for, accommodate
～易 **róngyì** лёгкий; легкó	easy
～貌 **róngmào** óблик, внéшний вид	facial features, looks
～忍 **róngrěn** терпéть; терпели́вый	to tolerate, condone
熔 **róng** плáвить *(металл)*; расплáвленный	to melt, smelt, fuse
～铸 **róngzhù** отливáть; плáвить	founding, casting
～铁炉 **róngtiělú** дóменная печь	blast furnace
溶 **róng** растворя́ть(ся); раствóр	to dissolve
咨 **zī** **1.** отношéние, официáльная бумáга **2.** обсуждáть, совещáться	to consult, take counsel
～文 **zīwén** официáльное письмó, послáние	official report/message (by head of state/etc.)
吞 **tūn** **1.** проглоти́ть **2.** присвóить; поглоти́ть; аннекси́ровать	1. to swallow, gulp down 2. to annex, absorb
～并 **tūnbìng** аннекси́ровать; аннéксия	to gobble, swallow up; to annex (territory)
～服 **tūnfú** покори́ть, подчини́ть	to take (medicine)
～没 **tūnmò** поглоти́ть; завладéть	1. to embezzle 2. to engulf
杏 **xìng** абрикóс; абрикóсовый	apricot
唇 **chún** губá; гýбы	lip
各 **gè** кáждый, вся́кий; различный; все	each, every, different; separately, differently
～位 **gèwèi** **1.** вы; ваш **2.** господá!; товáрищи!	1. you-all 2. everybody
～个 **gègè** кáждый в отдéльности; отдéльный	each, every, various; one by one, separately
～种各样 **gèzhǒnggèyàng** разнообрáзный, всевозмóжный	all sorts/varieties
～界 **gèjiè** все слои́ (круги́) óбщества	all walks of life

各别 **gèbié** отде́льный; инди-	1. out of the ordinary, peculiar 2. odd,
видуа́льный	eccentric 3. distinct, different
～方面 **gèfāngmiàn** во всех	from all sides/points of view
отноше́ниях; всесторо́нний	-
～人 **gèrén** ка́ждый [челове́к];	each one, everyone
вся́кий	-
～尽所能，按需分配 **gèjin suǒ-**	from each according to his ability, to
néng, ànxū fēnpèi от ка́ж-	each according to his need
дого — по спосо́бностям,	-
ка́ждому — по потре́бно-	-
стям	-
～尽所能，按劳分配 **gèjin suǒ-**	from each according to his ability, to
néng, ànláo fēnpèi от ка́ж-	each according to his labor/work done
дого — по спосо́бности,	-
ка́ждому — по труду́	-
络 **luò 1.** свя́зывать; обвя́зы-	1. to enmesh 2. to wind, twine 3. net
вать; сеть **2.** связь, кон-	4. vein 5. threads of thought
та́кт	-
路 **lù 1.** доро́га, путь; у́лица;	1. road, path, way 2. journey; distance
доро́жный **2.** карье́ра; жи́з-	3. means, way 4. sequence, logic, line
ненный путь	5. region, district 6. route 7. sort, grade
～程 **lùchéng** маршру́т; рейс	distance traveled; journey
(маши́ны)	-
～线 **lùxiàn 1.** путь, марш-	1. route, itinerary 2. line
ру́т **2.** *полит.* ли́ния, курс	-
～费 **lùfèi** путевы́е расхо́ды;	traveling expenses
подъёмные [де́ньги]	-
露 **lù 1.** обнару́жить(ся), по-	1. dew 2. syrup 3. to show, reveal, be-
каза́ть(ся) **2.** откры́тый,	tray
обнажённый **3.** роса́	-
～天 **lùtiān** под откры́тым	in the open air, outdoors
не́бом; откры́тый	-
～水 **lùshui** роса́	(coll.) dew
略 **lüè 1.** немно́жко, чуть-	1. to omit, delete, leave out 2. to cap-
-чу́ть **2.** кра́ткий, сокращён-	ture, seize 3. to invade 4. to super-
ный **3.** план; за́мысел;	vise 5. summary, outline 6. strategy,
страте́гия **4.** отнима́ть, гра́-	plan, scheme 7. brief, sketchy; cur-
бить	sorily, somewhat, slightly
～微 **lüèwēi** немно́жко, чуть-	to do sth., briefly/roughly
-чу́ть	-
胳：～臂 **gēbei** рука́ *(до ки-*	arm
сти)	-
骆：～驼 **luòtuó** верблю́д	camel
格 **gé 1.** графа́; кле́тка	1. lattice, grid, squares 2. case

2. станда́рт, но́рма 3. *грам.* паде́ж 4. дра́ться врукопа́шную	3. standard, pattern, style 4. to resist, obstruct
格外 **géwài** исключи́тельно, осо́бенно	especially, all the more
～斗 **gédòu** рукопа́шная схва́тка	to grapple, wrestle, fistfight
～子 **géz 1.** [бума́га] в клётку 2. моде́ль; шабло́н	check, pattern in squares
～式 **géshì** фо́рма; образе́ц, моде́ль	form, pattern
落 **luò 1.** спуска́ться; па́дать; опада́ть **2.** ги́бнуть; приходи́ть в упа́док **3.** попа́сть, перейти́ *(в руки)*	1. to fall, drop; go down, set; lower; decline, come down; sink 2. to fall/leave/stay behind 3. to get, receive, have 4. to fall into, rest with 5. settlements \\
～空 **luòkōng** ру́хнуть; оста́ться ни с чем	to come to nothing, fail \\6. whereabouts
～后 **luòhòu** отстава́ть; отста́лый	1. to fall/lay behind 2. backward
～下 **luòxià** спуска́ться; па́дать; опада́ть	to fall down, descend, drop
～脚儿 **luòjiǎor** зацепи́ться за	to stop over, put up
～网 **luòwǎng** попа́сться в се́ти	to be captured (of a criminal)
～实 **luòshí** осуществи́ть; поста́вить на про́чную осно́ву; закрепи́ть	1. to fix, decide in advance, ascertain 2. to fulfill, implement 3. practicable, workable 4. to feel at ease
～成 **luòchéng** зако́нчить(ся) *(о стройке)*	to be completed (of a building/etc.)
客 **kè 1.** гость; посети́тель 2. путеше́ственник; пассажи́р **3.** гости́ть; остана́вливаться	1. visitor, guest 2. traveler, passenger 3. traveling merchant 4. customer 5. objective 6. to settle/live in a strange place, be a stranger
～堂 **kètáng** приёмная; гости́ная	living/reception room
～车 **kèchē** пассажи́рский по́езд (ваго́н)	1. passenger train 2. bus
～厅 **kètīng** гости́ная	drawing/living room, parlor
～人 **kèrén 1.** гость; посети́тель **2.** пассажи́р	1. visitor, guest 2. guest (at a hotel, etc.), traveler
～观 **kèguān** объекти́вный	objectivity; objective
～气 **kèqi** церемо́ниться; учти́вость; ве́жливый	to be polite, stand on ceremony; polite, courteous; modest

船沿铅否台抬胎始

船 **chuán** су́дно, кора́бль; ло́дка	boat, ship
～舶 **chuánbó** суда́, корабли́	shipping; boats and ships
～厂 **chuánchǎng** судове́рфь	shipyard
～仓 **chuáncāng** каю́та; трюм	1. ship's hold 2. cabin
沿 **yán** 1. вдоль; по кра́ю 2. край	1. to follow (a pattern/etc.) 2. to trim (border/etc.); edge, border 3. along
～岸 **yán'àn** вдоль бе́рега; прибре́жный	to skirt a bank/coast; littoral, riparian
～用 **yányòng** продолжа́ть по́льзоваться; продолжа́ть тради́цию	to continue to use (old methods, etc.)
～海 **yánhǎi** вдоль морско́го побере́жья; примо́рский	along the coast; coast; coastal, littoral
铅 **qiān** свине́ц; свинцо́вый	lead
～笔 **qiānbi** каранда́ш	pencil
否 **fǒu** нет; и́ли нет?; не так ли?	to negate, deny; nay, no
～则 **fǒuzé** е́сли не так, то; в проти́вном слу́чае	otherwise, if not, or else
～认 **fǒurèn** отрица́ть, не признава́ть	to deny, repudiate
～决 **fǒujué** отклоня́ть; голосова́ть про́тив	to vote down, veto, overrule
～决权 **fǒujuéquán** пра́во ве́то	veto (power)
～定 **fǒudìng** отрица́ть; отрица́тельный	to negate, deny; negation
台 **tái** 1. ба́шня; платфо́рма; сце́на; аре́на; трибу́на 2. *сч. сл. для машин, спектаклей*	1. platform, stage, terrace; stand, support 2. table, desk 3. station 4. Taiwan 5. (in letters) you 6. (M. for performances/engines/etc.)
～灯 **táidēng** насто́льная ла́мпа	desk/table/reading lamp
～布 **táibù** ска́терть	tablecloth
抬 **tái** 1. подня́ть; нести́ 2. повы́сить *(напр. цену)*	1. to lift, raise 2. to carry (together) 3. (slang) to betray 4. to argue
～头 **táitóu** подня́ть го́лову	1. to raise one's head 2. to gain, go up
胎 **tāi** 1. заро́дыш; плод 2. ка́мера; покры́шка	1. fetus, embryo 2. padding, stuffing 3. roughcast 4. (loan w.) tire
始 **shǐ** 1. начина́ть; нача́ло 2. лишь тогда́	1. to begin, start 2. not...until, only then
～终 **shǐzhōng** от нача́ла до конца́; всегда́	from beginning to end

冶 **yě** пла́вить; распла́вить	to smelt
~金 **yějīn** пла́вить мета́лл; металлурги́ческий	metallurgy
~金工业 **yějīn gōngyè** металлу́ргия	metallurgical industry
~铸 **yězhù** лить, отлива́ть; литьё	to smelt metals and cast utensils
~炼 **yěliàn** пла́вить	to smelt
治 **zhì** 1. управля́ть; ве́дать 2. лечи́ть	1. to rule, administer 2. to treat, cure 3. to control 4. to eliminate 5. to study
~理 **zhìlǐ** 1. управля́ть 2. приводи́ть в поря́док	1. to administer, govern 2. put in order, bring under control
~疗 **zhìliáo** лечи́ть	to treat, cure; treatment, cure
~病 **zhìbìng** лечи́ть; лече́бный; целе́бный	to treat illness
~安 **zhì'ān** установи́ть обще́ственный поря́док	public order/security
营 **yíng** 1. вое́нный ла́герь 2. батальо́н; дивизио́н 3. предпринима́ть; промышля́ть; стро́ить	1. to seek/strive for 2. to operate, run, manage 3. to nourish 4. camp, barracks 5. battalion
~业 **yíngyè** 1. предприя́тие; про́мысел 2. торго́вля	to do business; business
~养 **yíngyǎng** пита́ться; пита́ние; пита́тельный	nutrition, nourishment
~房 **yíngfáng** каза́рма	barracks
宫 **gōng** 1. дворе́ц; за́мок 2. храм; монасты́рь	1. palace 2. place for cultural activities and recreation 3. womb, uterus
~殿 **gōngdiàn** дворе́ц	palace
官 **guān** 1. чино́вник; чин 2. прави́тельственный; госуда́рственный 3. о́рганы чувств	1. government official, office holder 2. organ 3. government-owned, official 4. public
~话 **guānhuà** 1. официа́льный язы́к 2. гуаньхуа́ *(диалект кит. языка)*	1. Chinese common language 2. Mandarin
~方 **guānfāng** официа́льные круги́; официа́льный	government; official
~本 **guānběn** официа́льное изда́ние	1. government share 2. official publication
~报 **guānbào** 1. официа́льное сообще́ние 2. прави́тельственная газе́та; официо́з	official journal

官馆管日

官运 **guānyùn** 1. продвижéние по слýжбе, карьéра 2. служéбные перевóзки	official career, fortunes of officialdom - -
~气 **guānqì** канцеля́рщина	bureaucratic airs
~员 **guānyuán** официáльное лицó; должностны́е ли́ца	official (person) -
~僚 **guānliáo** бюрокрáт	bureaucrat; bureaucracy
~僚主义 **guānliáozhǔyì** бюрократи́зм	bureaucratism -
馆 **guǎn** 1. гости́ница; ресторáн 2. учреждéние, канцеля́рия	1. accommodation for guests 2. embassy, legation, consulate 3. shop 4. place for cultural activities
管 **guǎn** 1. трубá; трýбы 2. управля́ть, вéдать 3. имéть отношéние к	1. to run, manage, administer 2. to discipline 3. to provide 4. tube, pipe; wind musical instrument 5. to guarantee
~理 **guǎnlǐ** управля́ть, завéдовать, руководи́ть	to manage, supervise, take care of -
~理局 **guǎnlǐjú** управлéние *(учреждение)*	management office/bureau, administration
~理处 **guǎnlǐchù** контóра; управлéние	administrative/management office -
~辖 **guǎnxiá** управля́ть, вéдать; имéть в подчинéнии	to have jurisdiction over -
~制 **guǎnzhì** контроли́ровать; контрóль	1. to control 2. to put under surveillance
~子 **guǎnz** трубá; трýбка	tube, pipe
~事 **guǎnshì** управля́ть делáми; рабóтать *(в учреждении)*	to run things, be in charge; manager, steward; efficacious, useful -
日 **rì** 1. сóлнце 2. день 3. числó; дáта; срок	1. sun 2. day 3. daytime 4. daily -
~程 **rìchéng** повéстка (поря́док) дня	schedule, itinerary -
~落 **rìluò** захóд сóлнца, закáт	sunset -
~子 **rìz** дни; дáта; 过日子 жить	1. day, days 2. life, livelihood -
~期 **rìqī** срок; дáта	date
~用 **rìyòng** повседнéвный, обихóдный	for daily use; daily expenses -
~用品 **rìyòngpǐn** предмéты ширóкого потреблéния	articles for daily use -
~常 **rìcháng** обы́чный, заурядный	day-to-day, everyday -

日历 **rìlì** календа́рь; дневни́к	calendar
～报 **rìbào** ежедне́вная газе́та	daily newspaper
～记 **rìjì** дневни́к; журна́л; заме́тки	diary, journal
～光 **rìguāng** со́лнечный (дневно́й) свет	sunlight
晶 **jīng 1.** криста́лл **2.** прозра́чный; блестя́щий	1. crystal 2. clear, brilliant, radiant
旧 **jiù 1.** ста́рый, пре́жний, давни́шний 2. ве́тхий; поно́шенный	1. past, bygone, old 2. used, worn, old 3. former, one-time 4. old friendship/ friend
～历 **jiùlì** ста́рый стиль [календаря́]; лу́нный календа́рь	lunar calendar
阳 **yáng 1.** со́лнце; свет; со́лнечный 2. мужско́й; положи́тельный; плюс	1. (Ch. philos.) positive/active/male principle in nature 2. sun 3. open 4. male genitals 5. of this world
～性 **yángxìng 1.** мужско́й пол **2.** *грам.* мужско́й род	1. (med.) positive 2. (gram.) masculine gender
～历 **yánglì** со́лнечный календа́рь	solar calendar
鲁 **lǔ** тупо́й, глу́пый	1. stupid, dull 2. vulgar 3. rash, im-\\ \\ petuous, blunt
普 **pǔ** популя́рный; распространённый; всео́бщий; повсеме́стный	generous, universal
～及 **pǔjí** популяризи́ровать; распространя́ть(ся); всео́бщий	to popularize, disseminate, spread; universal, popular
～通 **pǔtōng 1.** обы́чный **2.** популя́рный; о́бщий	ordinary, common, average
～通话 **pǔtōnghuà** путунхуа́	Mandarin Chinese, standard language
～遍 **pǔbiàn** всео́бщий; распространённый	universal, general, widespread
～选 **pǔxuǎn** *сокр.* всео́бщие вы́боры	general election
醋 **cù 1.** у́ксус; ки́слый **2.** ревнова́ть; ре́вность	1. vinegar 2. jealousy
惜 **xī 1.** жале́ть; жа́лость **2.** дорожи́ть, бере́чь	1. to cherish, care for tenderly 2. to grudge 3. to feel sorry for sb.
～别 **xībié** сожале́ть о расстава́нии	to be reluctant to part, hate to see sb. go
借 **jiè 1.** одолжи́ть; взять взаймы́; дать в долг	1. to borrow 2. to lend 3. to make use of, take advantage of (opportunity,

借措腊猎籍蜡错音暗

2. полагáться, опирáться 3. под предлóгом	etc.) 4. to use as a pretext 5. if, supposing
借口 **jièkǒu** предлóг, пóвод; под предлóгом	to use as a pretext/excuse; excuse, pretext
～钱 **jièqián** занимáть (брать) дéньги	to borrow money
措 **cuò** 1. размещáть, располагáть 2. распоряжáться, принимáть мéры	1. to arrange, handle, manage 2. to make plans
～施 **cuòshī** мéры; мероприя́тия	measure, step
腊 **là** солúть; солёное мя́со; солёная ры́ба	1. 12th lunar month 2. 12th month 3. cured fish/meat/etc.
猎 **liè** охóтиться	hunt, chase
～狗 **liègǒu** охóтничья собáка	hunting dog, hound
～人 **lièrén** охóтник	hunter
籍 **jí** 1. литератýра; кнúги 2. записáть; внестú в спúсок; спúски населéния; пéрепись	1. books, works 2. native place, birthplace 3. membership
蜡 **là** 1. воск; восковóй; вощёный 2. свечá	1. candle 2. polish 3. yellowish, sallow
错 **cuò** 1. ошибáться; ошúбка; ошúбочный 2. пýтать; смéшивать	1. to be interlocked 2. to rub 3. to let slip; to evade 4. to alternate, stagger 5. wrong, mistaken 6. bad
～字 **cuòzì** ошúбка; непрáвильно напúсанный иерóглиф	1. incorrectly written characters 2. misprint
～误 **cuòwù** ошúбка; оплóшность	wrong, mistaken; error, blunder
音 **yīn** звук; тон; произношéние; чтéние *(иероглифа)*	1. sound 2. tone 3. news, tidings
～调 **yīndiào** 1. тон; интонáция 2. мелóдия; нóта	tone, tonality
～响 **yīnxiǎng** звук; звучáние; акустúческий	1. sound, acoustics 2. stereo, hi-fi 3. music center
～乐 **yīnyuè** мýзыка	music
～乐队 **yīnyuèduì** оркéстр	orchestra
～乐家 **yīnyuèjiā** музыкáнт	musician
～乐会 **yīnyuèhuì** концéрт	concert
暗 **àn** 1. темнéть; тёмный, мрáчный; темнотá 2. тáйный, скры́тый, секрéтный	1. dark, dim, dull 2. hidden, secret; secretly 3. unclear

暗害 **ànhài** вред; вреди́тельство	1. to plot murder 2. to stab in the back
～中 **ànzhōng** 1. в темноте́ 2. вта́йне	1. in the dark 2. in secret, surreptitiously
～号 **ànhào** паро́ль; усло́вный знак	secret signal/sign; countersign; cipher
～杀 **ànshā** террористи́ческий акт; уби́йство из-за угла́	to assassinate
～示 **ànshì** намекну́ть; намёк	to (drop a) hint, suggest; hint, suggestion
智 **zhì** ум, ра́зум; му́дрость	wisdom, resourcefulness, wit
～力(能) **zhìlì(néng)** у́мственные спосо́бности, ум	intelligence, intellect
～慧 **zhìhuì** му́дрость; ра́зум	wisdom, intelligence
昌 **chāng** 1. процвета́ть; процвета́ние 2. блестя́щий, великоле́пный	prosperous, flourishing
～盛 **chāngshèng** процвета́ть; процвета́ющий	prosperous
唱 **chàng** петь; пе́ние	to sing
～片 **chàngpiàn** 1. грампласти́нка 2. музыка́льный фильм	disc, record (phonograph)
～歌 **chànggē** петь пе́сни; пе́ние	to sing a song
倡 **chàng** 1. восхваля́ть; рекламировать 2. класть нача́ло	to initiate, advocate
～导 **chàngdǎo** вести́ за собо́й; затева́ть; класть нача́ло	to initiate, propose
～议 **chàngyì** проявля́ть инициати́ву; инициати́ва	to propose
～议者 **chàngyìzhě** инициа́тор	initiator
猖:～狂 **chāngkuáng** неистовствовать; безу́мный	savage, furious
曾 **céng** когда́-то, в про́шлом	once, ever, before
～ **zēng** *в терминах родства*	relationship between great-grand-\\children & gr.-gr. parents
～经 **céngjīng** пре́жде, когда́-то	once, ever
～祖母 **zēngzǔmǔ** праба́бушка	great-grandmother (of same surname)
～祖父 **zēngzǔfù** праде́душка	great-grandfather (of same surname)
增 **zēng** увели́чивать(ся);	to increase, gain, add

增 贈 糟 暂 暮 替 潜

возрастáть; прибавля́ть (-ся); уси́ливать(ся)	-
增加 **zēngjiā** *см.* 增	to increase, raise, add
~产 **zēngchǎn** увели́чивать вы́пуск (произвóдство)	to increase production
~多 **zēngduō** увеличéние *(напр. продукции)*	to increase (in number/quantity)
~长 **zēngzhǎng** увели́чивать (-ся); возрастáть; рост	to increase, grow
~进 **zēngjìn 1.** продвигáться; продвижéние **2.** уси́ливать, укрепля́ть	to enhance, promote, further
~强 **zēngqiáng** уси́ливать, укрепля́ть	to strengthen, enhance
贈 **zèng** дари́ть, преподноси́ть	to give as a present
~品 **zèngpǐn** подáрок, сувени́р; дáрственный экземпля́р	gift, giveaway
~给 **zènggei** *см.* ~送	to give, make a present of, present
~送 **zèngsòng** дари́ть, преподноси́ть	to present as a gift
糟 **zāo 1.** гнить, пóртиться **2.** плóхо дéло	1. rotten, spoiled (lit./fig.) 2. infirm 3. dregs 4. pickle
~糕 **zāogāo** не повезлó; всё пошлó прáхом	(coll.) What a mess!; Too bad!
暂 **zàn** врéменно, покá; врéменный	temporary; temporarily
~时 **zànshí** *см.* 暂	temporarily
暮 **mù 1.** вéчер, закáт **2.** конéц *(сезона)*	1. dusk, evening, sunset 2. towards the end
~年 **mùnián** глубóкая стáрость	declining years, old age
替 **tì 1.** заменя́ть; вмéсто; за **2.** для	1. to take the place of, replace, substitute 2. decline 3. for, on behalf of
~罪羊 **tìzuìyáng** козёл отпущéния	scapegoat
~换(代) **tìhuan(dài)** сменя́ть; подменя́ть	to replace, displace
潜 **qián 1.** скрывáться, пря́таться **2.** погружáться в вóду; ныря́ть **3.** скры́тый, потенциáльный **4.** подвóдный	1. to dive, hide 2. to submerge 3. to ford a stream 4. latent, hidden, secret 5. stealthily 6. weir, barrage

潜在 **qiánzài** скры́тый, потенциа́льный	latent, potential
～力 **qiánlì** скры́тые (потенциа́льные) возмо́жности	latent capacity, potential(ity)
～水 **qiánshuǐ** 1. находи́ться под водо́й 2. ныря́ть	to dive, go under water
～水艇 **qiánshuǐtǐng** подво́дная ло́дка	submarine
～水员 **qiánshuǐyuán** водола́з	diver, frogman
春 **chūn** весна́; весе́нний	1. spring (season) 2. love, lust 3. life,//vitality
～节 **chūnjié** пра́здник весны́; нового́дний пра́здник *(в Китае по лунному календарю)*	Spring Festival (Lunar New Year)
～天 **chūntiān** весна́; весе́нний	spring(time)
香 **xiāng** арома́т; души́стый, арома́тный	1. fragrant, scented 2. savory 3. popular, welcome 4. with relish 5. perfume
～品 **xiāngpǐn** парфюме́рные това́ры	perfumery, perfume shop
～烟 **xiāngyān** папиро́сы; сигаре́ты; таба́к	1. cigarette 2. incense smoke 3. posterity
～粉 **xiāngfěn** пу́дра	face powder
～水 **xiāngshuǐ** духи́; одеколо́н	perfume, scent
～皂 **xiāngzào** туале́тное мы́ло	perfumed/scented soap
～气 **xiāngqì** арома́т	fragrance, aroma
～槟酒 **xiāngbīnjiǔ** шампа́нское	champagne
～蕉 **xiāngjiāo** бана́н	banana
踏 **tà** ступа́ть; наступа́ть; топта́ть	to step on, tread, stamp
～步 **tàbù** то́пать нога́ми	(mil.) to mark time
昏 **hūn** 1. су́мрак; темнота́ 2. глу́пый, тупо́й 3. теря́ть созна́ние	1. to faint, swoon 2. dark, dim 3. confused, muddled 4. dusk
～脑 **hūnnǎo** тупо́й; неве́жда	stupid, dull; ignoramus
～暗 **hūn'àn** темнота́, мрак	dim, dusky
～倒 **hūndǎo** упа́сть в о́бморок	to faint
～迷 **hūnmí** быть ослеплённым; заблужда́ться	stupor, coma

潜春香踏昏

昏婚旨指脂

昏乱 **hūnluàn** смяте́ние; па́ника; неразбери́ха	decrepit and muddle-headed
婚 **hūn** жени́ться; брак; жени́тьба	to wed, marry; marriage, wedding
～礼 **hūnlǐ** сва́дьба, церемо́ния бракосочета́ния	wedding ceremony
旨 **zhǐ 1.** значе́ние, смысл **2.** наме́рение, цель	1. meaning, intention, aim 2. decree, edict
～意 **zhǐyì** устремле́ния	decree, order
指 **zhǐ 1.** па́лец **2.** ука́зывать, пока́зывать	1. finger 2. fingerbreadth 3. to point at/to/out 4. to refer to 5. to rely on
～望 **zhǐwàng** рассчи́тывать, наде́яться; наде́жды	1. to look to, count on 2. prospect, hope
～出 **zhǐchū** ука́зывать, отмеча́ть	to point out (that)
～挥 **zhǐhuī** кома́ндовать; управля́ть; руководи́ть	to command, direct, conduct; commander, director, conductor
～挥部 **zhǐhuībù** штаб; кома́ндование	command post, headquarters
～挥员 **zhǐhuīyuán** команди́р	commander
～甲 **zhǐjiǎ** но́готь	fingernail
～导 **zhǐdǎo** направля́ть; вести́; руководи́ть; инструкти́ровать	to guide, direct
～导员 **zhǐdǎoyuán 1.** руководи́тель; инстру́ктор **2.** гид, проводни́к	(mil.) PLA political instructor
～明 **zhǐmíng** ука́зывать; определя́ть; подчёркивать	to demonstrate, point out
～南针 **zhǐnánzhēn** ко́мпас	compass
～头 **zhǐtou** па́лец	finger; toe
～定 **zhǐdìng** намеча́ть; назнача́ть; ука́зывать	to appoint, assign
～战员 **zhǐzhànyuán** бойцы́ и команди́ры	PLA officers and men
～责 **zhǐzé** осужда́ть, порица́ть; обвиня́ть	to censure, criticize
～示 **zhǐshì** ука́зывать; ука́зание	1. to indicate, point out 2. to instruct 3. directions, instructions
～标 **zhǐbiāo** указа́тель; и́ндекс	target, quota, norm, index
～令 **zhǐlìng** директи́ва	to order, direct; order, instructions
脂 **zhī 1.** жир, са́ло; жи́рный **2.** крем; пома́да	1. fat, grease, tallow 2. rouge

脂肪 **zhīfáng** жир, са́ло	fat
者 **zhě 1.** тот, кото́рый; то,	(nominal suf.) one who
что **2.** *суф. сущ., обозна-*	-
чающих лиц различных	-
профессий, а также деяте-	-
лей: 参加者 уча́стник	-
绪 **xù 1.** нача́ло, исто́ки **2.** пе-	1. the beginning of a matter 2. thread
режи́ток	ends, remnants 3. task, undertaking
堵 **dǔ 1.** загора́живать; за-	1. to stop up; stifled 2. wall
ва́ливать; заку́поривать **2.**	-
стена́	-
～塞 **dǔsè** загора́живать; за-	to block up
ва́ливать; блоки́ровать	-
猪 **zhū** свинья́	pig, hog, swine
赌 **dǔ** аза́ртная игра́; риско-	to gamble, bet
ва́ть	-
～注 **dǔzhù** де́лать ста́вку	stake (in gambling/venture)
(напр. в игре)	-
～博 **dǔbó** аза́ртная игра́	to gamble
诸 **zhū** все; ка́ждый	all; various
～位 **zhūwèi** господа́!; гра́ж-	Ladies and Gentlemen!; Sirs!; Everyone!
дане!	-
储 **chǔ** нака́пливать; запа-	to store up
са́ть	-
～备 **chǔbèi** запаса́ть; запа́с	1. to lay in, stock up 2. to reserve
～备品 **chǔbèipǐn** запа́сы; на-	supplies, reserves; accumulation
копле́ния	-
～蓄银行 **chǔxù yínháng** сбе-	savings bank
рега́тельная ка́сса	-
～存 **chǔcún** сберега́ть; хра-	to lay in/up, store, stockpile
ни́ть	-
屠 **tú** убива́ть	to slaughter
～杀 **túshā 1.** осуществля́ть	to massacre, butcher; massacre,
ма́ссовые уби́йства; ис-	butchery
требля́ть; распра́ва; резня́	-
2. забива́ть *(скот)*	-
暑 **shǔ** жара́; сезо́н жары́	heat, hot weather
～假 **shǔjià** ле́тние кани́кулы	summer vacation
署 **shǔ 1.** учрежде́ние; ве́дом-	1. to arrange (for) 2. to deputize 3. to
ство; управле́ние **2.** подпи́-	sign one's name 4. government office
сывать **3.** вре́менно испол-	-
ня́ть обя́занности	-
～名 **shǔmíng** подпи́сывать	to sign one's name
(-ся), ста́вить по́дпись	-

著 **zhù 1.** я́сный, очеви́дный **2.** изве́стный, знамени́тый **3.** сочиня́ть; сочине́ние, труд	1. to show, manifest, prove 2. to write (a book/etc.); book; work 3. outstanding, notable
～名 **zhùmíng** *см.* 著 2	famous, celebrated
～作 **zhùzuò** произведе́ние, творе́ние; труды́	to write; book; writings; work
白 **bái 1.** бе́лый; чи́стый; све́тлый **2.** я́сный, поня́тный **3.** по́пусту, напра́сно	1. white 2. clear 3. pure, plain 4. free 5. wrongly written/pronounced 6. in vain 7. colloquial 8. to turn white
～话 **báihuà** байхуа́	1. vernacular 2. empty talk
～糖 **báitáng** са́хар; рафина́д	(refined) white sugar
～宫 **báigōng** Бе́лый дом	White House
～白的 **báibáid 1.** зря, понапра́сну **2.** да́ром, беспла́тно	in vain, for nothing, to no purpose
～酒 **báijiǔ** во́дка	spirits distilled from sorghum
～干儿 **báigānr** гаоля́новая во́дка	spirits distilled from sorghum
～种人 **báizhǒngrén** челове́к бе́лой ра́сы	white person, Caucasian
～天 **báitiān** днём, в дневно́е вре́мя	daytime, day
～菜 **báicài** капу́ста	Chinese cabbage
～米 **báimǐ** [очи́щенный] рис	(polished) rice
～费 **báifèi** напра́сно, зря	waste
怕 **pà 1.** боя́ться, опаса́ться **2.** бою́сь, что; пожа́луй	1. to fear, dread 2. perhaps, I'm afraid
～事 **pàshì** ро́бкий, нереши́тельный	to fear getting into trouble
伯 **bó** дя́дя	1. father's elder brother, uncle 2. eldest brother
～伯 **bóbo** дя́дя	father's eldest brother, uncle
～母 **bómǔ** тётка	wife of father's eldest brother, aunt
～父 **bófù** *см.* ～伯	father's older brother, uncle
拍 **pāi 1.** ударя́ть, хло́пать **2.** снима́ть, фотографи́ровать	1. to clap, pat 2. to take a picture, shoot a movie 3. to send a telegram 4. racket; bat 5. (mus.) beat, time
～打 **pāidǎ** стуча́ть, хло́пать	to pat, slap
～子 **pāiz 1.** *муз.* ритм, такт **2.** раке́тка *(теннисная)*	1. bat; racket 2. (mus.) beat, time
～手 **pāishǒu** аплоди́ровать	to applaud, clap one's hands
～卖 **pāimài** аукцио́н	to auction, sell at reduced price; auction
～摄(照) **pāishè(zhào)** *см.* 拍 2	to take a picture, shoot a film
柏 **bǎi, bó** кипари́с	cypress

泊 **bó 1.** причáлить; пришвартовáться; стать на я́корь **2.** óзеро	to be at anchor, moor
皆 **jiē** все; всё	all, everyone
百 **bǎi 1.** сто; сóтня **2.** мнóгие; многочи́сленный	1. hundred 2. numerous; all kinds of
~姓 **bǎixìng** простóй нарóд; нарóд	(the) common people
~科全书 **bǎikē-quánshū** энциклопéдия	encyclopedia
~闻不如一见 **bǎi wén bùrú yī jiàn** лу́чше оди́н раз уви́деть, чем сто раз услы́шать	one seeing is better than a hundred hearings (one picture is worth a thousand words)
~万 **bǎiwàn** миллиóн	million
~战百胜 **bǎizhàn - bǎishèng** непобеди́мый	(to) be ever victorious; invincible
~货商店 **bǎihuòshāngdiàn** универсáльный магази́н	small department store
宿 **sù 1.** останови́ться; переночевáть **2.** стáрый, дáвний	1. to stay overnight 2. long-standing, old; veteran
~舍 **sùshè** общежи́тие	dormitory
~愿 **sùyuàn** завéтное желáние	long-cherished wish
缩 **suō 1.** отступáть **2.** сокращáть(ся), уменьшáть (-ся)	1. to contract, shrink 2. to withdraw, recoil
~短 **suōduǎn** укорáчивать (-ся); сокращáть(ся); корóткий *(о сроке)*	to shorten, curtail, cut down
~写 **suōxiě** стенографи́ровать	to abridge; abbreviation
~尺 **suōchǐ** масштáб	reduced scale
~减 **suōjiǎn** сокращáть, уменьшáть; уменьшéние	to reduce, cut; subtractive
~小 **suōxiǎo 1.** умéньшиться **2.** преуменьшáть, занижáть	to reduce, narrow, shrink
目 **mù 1.** глаз; взгляд; зрéние **2.** подзаголóвок; оглавлéние; указáтель; и́ндекс	1. eye 2. item, section 3. list, catalogue
~击 **mùjī 1.** ви́деть сóбствен-	to see with one's own eyes

目 相

ными глазáми **2.** бросáться в глазá	-
目前 **mùqián** в настоя́щее врéмя, тепéрь, сейчáс; тепéрешний, текýщий	at present, at the moment
～的 **mùdì** цель; глáвная идéя	purpose, aim, goal, objective, end
～的地 **mùdìdì** мéсто назначéния	destination
～力 **mùlì** зрéние	eyesight, vision
～次(录) **mùcì (lù)** оглавлéние; указáтель; и́ндекс; спи́сок; каталóг	table of contents
～光 **mùguāng** взгляд, взор	1. sight, vision, view 2. gaze, look
～标 **mùbiāo** мишéнь, цель; объéкт	objective, target, goal
相 **xiāng** взаи́мный, обою́дный	1. each other, mutually 2. to size up by appearance
～ **xiàng** фóрма; внéшний вид	1. looks, appearance 2. bearing, posture 3. to look at and appraise
～应 **xiāngyìng** **1.** соответствовать **2.** откликáться; поддéрживать	1. to act in response to 2. relevant, corresponding
～互 **xiānghù** взаи́мно, обою́дно; взаи́мный	mutually, reciprocally
～当 **xiāngdāng** соотвéтствующий, надлежáщий	1. to match, balance, correspond to, be equal to 2. suitable, fit 3. fairly, quite
～信 **xiāngxìn** вéрить, доверя́ть	to believe in, be convinced of
～合 **xiānghé** совпадáть; соотвéтствовать	to conform, coincide
～片 **xiāngpiàn** фотосни́мок	photograph, photo
～对 **xiāngduì** **1.** относи́тельный **2.** противостоя́ть	1. to be opposite, be face to face 2. relative(ly)
～同 **xiāngtóng** одинáковый, тождéственный	to be identical/alike
～反 **xiāngfǎn** противополóжный; наоборóт	opposite, contrary, reverse
～貌 **xiàngmào** внéшний вид, óблик	looks, appearance
～似 **xiāngsì** похóжий, подóбный	to resemble, be similar/alike; alike, similar
～称 **xiāngchèng** соотвéтствовать, подходи́ть	to address each other (as)

霜 **shuāng** и́ней	1. frost 2. frost-like 3. white, hoary\\
箱 **xiāng** чемода́н; я́щик; коро́бка	chest, box, case, trunk \\4. rigorous
泪 **lèi** слёзы	tear, teardrop
着 **zhuó** **1.** надева́ть, носи́ть *(одежду)* **2.** приступа́ть к	1. to put on (clothes) 2. to touch 3. to apply 4. to send
~ **zháo** **1.** подверга́ться, испы́тывать **2.** приём, спо́соб **3.** *суф. результативных гл., напр.:* 买着 купи́ть	1. to touch, come into contact with 2. to feel, be affected by (cold/etc.) 3. to catch fire 4. (suf. for accomplishment/hitting the mark)
~ **zhe** *гл. суф., указывающий на продолженный характер действия или состояние, напр.:* 他坐着看书 он си́дя чита́ет кни́гу	(suf. indicating continuing progress/state or for emphasis)
~重 **zhuózhòng** придава́ть значе́ние, подчёркивать	to stress, emphasize
~陆 **zhuólù** приземля́ться; поса́дка *(самолёта)*	to land, touch down
~手 **zhuóshǒu** приступа́ть *(к делу),* начина́ть	to put a hand to, set about
~火 **zháohuǒ** загоре́ться, вспы́хнуть	to catch fire, be on fire
~凉 **zháoliáng** простуди́ться	to catch cold/chill
~急 **zháojí** **1.** волнова́ться, беспоко́иться **2.** спеши́ть, торопи́ться	to worry, be anxious; worried, anxious
眉:~毛 **méimao** бро́ви	eyebrow, brow
看 **kàn** **1.** смотре́ть; чита́ть **2.** осма́тривать *(о враче)* **3.** навеща́ть **4.** рассма́тривать; счита́ть; принима́ть за **5.** в зави́симости от	1. to see, look at, watch 2. to read 3. to think, consider 4. to regard, look upon 5. to treat 6. to look after 7. to call on, visit 8. to depend on 9. to watch out, mind 10. to present (tea/wine)
~ **kān** присма́тривать, уха́живать	1. to look after, tend 2. to keep under surveillance
~轻 **kànqing** недооце́нивать, пренебрега́ть	to underestimate, look down on
~重 **kànzhòng** цени́ть, придава́ть значе́ние	to value, set store by
~齐 **kànqí** равня́ться; 向...看齐 равня́ться на (по)	1. to arrange in a line, dress 2. to emulate, keep up with
~得起 **kàndeqǐ** относи́ться с уваже́нием; придава́ть значе́ние	to think highly of

霜箱泪着眉看

看待 **kàndài** обраща́ться, обходи́ться; принима́ть за	to look upon, regard, treat
~守 **kānshǒu** охраня́ть, карау́лить	to watch, guard
~穿 **kànchuān** распознава́ть; разга́дывать	to see through
~门的 **kānménd** швейца́р	door/gate keeper, watchman
~病 **kànbìng** осма́тривать больно́го; лечи́ть	1. to see a patient 2. to see a doctor
~护 **kānhù** оберега́ть, забо́титься	to nurse; hospital nurse
~书 **kàn shū** чита́ть *(про себя)*	to read a book
~来 **kànlai** как ви́дно; похо́же, что	it seems, it looks as if
~戏 **kànxì** смотре́ть спекта́кль; ходи́ть в теа́тр	to watch/look at a performance/spectacle
~成 **kànchéng** счита́ть, рассма́тривать как	to take for/as
~见 **kànjian** ви́деть; увиде́ть	to catch sight of, see
~不起 **kànbuqi** презира́ть; ни во что́ не ста́вить	to scorn, despise
~法 **kànfa** то́чка зре́ния, взгляд; подхо́д	view, way of looking at sth.
盲 **máng** 1. слепо́й; ослепля́ть 2. неве́жественный, тёмный	blind
~目 **mángmù** 1. слепо́й; слепота́ 2. сле́по, безрассу́дно	blind
~动主义 **mángdòngzhǔyì** авантюри́зм	putschism
~人 **mángrén** слепо́й; слепе́ц	blind person
~从 **mángcóng** сле́по сле́довать (подчиня́ться)	to follow blindly
盾 **dùn** щит	shield
循 **xún** 1. сле́довать *чему,* приде́рживаться *чего;* согла́сно 2. враща́ться, верте́ться	to follow, abide by
~序 **xúnxù** после́довательно, по поря́дку	in proper order/sequence
~环 **xúnhuán** обраща́ться,	to circulate, cycle

циркули́ровать; цикл; цир-	-
куля́ция	-
冒 **mào 1.** вырыва́ться нару́-	1. to emit 2. to risk, brave 3. to claim
жу **2.** не обраща́ть внима́-	falsely 4. careless, rash
ния, пренебрега́ть	-
～险 **màoxiǎn** рискова́ть;	to take risks/chances
риск; авантю́ра	-
～险主义 **màoxiǎnzhǔyì** аван-	adventurism
тюри́зм	-
～名 **màomíng** выдава́ть се-	to assume another's name
бя́ за *кого-л.*	-
帽 **mào 1.** головно́й убо́р;	1. headgear, hat, cap 2. cap-like cover
шля́па; ша́пка **2.** колпа́к;	-
наконе́чник	-
～子 **màoz 1.** *см.* 帽 1 **2.** кли́ч-	1. headgear, hat, cap 2. label, tag
ка; ярлы́к	-
省 **shěng 1.** прови́нция; про-	1. to save, economize 2. to omit, leave
винциа́льный **2.** эконо́мить,	3. province 4. provincial capital
бере́чь	-
～城 **shěngchéng** гла́вный го́-	provincial capital
род прови́нции	-
～钱 **shěngqián** эконо́мить	to save money, be economical
де́ньги	-
督 **dū 1.** контроли́ровать, ин-	to superintend and direct
спекти́ровать **2.** руково-	-
ди́ть, управля́ть	-
～促 **dūcù** 1. контроли́ровать	to supervise and urge
2. подта́лкивать, подгоня́ть	-
自 **zì 1.** сам, ли́чно; свой	1. self, oneself, one's own; personally
2. из; от; с тех по́р как	2. certainly, of course 3. from, since
3. коне́чно, разуме́ется	-
～卫 **zìwèi** самозащи́та, са-	to defend oneself
мооборо́на	-
～在 **zìzài** быть дово́льным	free, unrestrained
～立 **zìlì** самостоя́тельный,	to stand on one's own feet
незави́симый	-
～治 **zìzhì** автоно́мия, само-	autonomy, self-government
управле́ние	-
～由 **zìyóu** свобо́да, во́ля;	freedom, liberty; free, unrestrained
свобо́дный; либера́льный	-
～由主义 **zìyóuzhǔyì** либера-	liberalism
ли́зм	-
～新 **zìxīn** обновля́ться; об-	to make a fresh start
новле́ние	-

自 咱

自制 **zìzhì** сдéрживаться; самообладáние	1. to make by oneself 2. self-control, self restraint
～行 **zìxíng** самохóдный	1. by oneself 2. of oneself, voluntarily 3. to move by oneself
～行车 **zìxíngchē** велосипéд; самокáт	bicycle, bike
～满自足 **zìmǎn-zìzú** самодовóльство; самодовóльный	self-satisfied
～力更生 **zìlì gēngshēng** опирáться на сóбственные сúлы	to regenerate/reconstruct through one's own efforts 2. self-reliance
～动 **zìdòng** 1. автоматúческий 2. добровóльно, по сóбственной инициатúве	1. voluntarily, of one's own accord 2. automatic
～动化 **zìdònghuà** автоматизáция	automation
～从 **zìcóng** с тех пóр как, начинáя с	since
～大 **zìdà** кичúться; занóсчивость, чвáнство	self-important, arrogant
～决 **zìjué** самоопределéние	self-determination
～决权 **zìjuéquán** прáво на самоопределéние	right to self-determination
～杀 **zìshā** покóнчить с собóй; самоубúйство	to commit suicide
～来 **zìlái** автоматúческий	originally, from the beginning, in the first place
～来水 **zìláishuǐ** водопровóд	running/tap water
～发 **zìfā** 1. автоматúческий 2. стихúйный	to be spontaneous
～我 **zìwǒ** сам себя́; само=	1. self, oneself 2. ego
～我检讨(批评) **zìwǒjiǎntǎo(pīpíng)** самокрúтика	self-criticism
～己 **zìji** сам; сóбственный, свой	1. oneself 2. closely related, own
～觉 **zìjué** самосознáние; сознáтельный	to be conscious/aware (of)
～愿 **zìyuàn** добровóльный	to act voluntarily; voluntary act
～然 **zìrán** прирóда; естéственный; натурáльный	1. the natural world 2. naturally, of course, in the usual course of events
～～ **zìran** конéчно, разумéется	(coll.) natural, free from affectation
～传 **zìzhuàn** автобиогрáфия	autobiography
咱 **zán** я; мы с вáми	1. we, you and I 2. I
～们 **zánmen** мы; мы с вáми	1. we, you and I 2. I 3. you

首 **shǒu** **1.** головá **2.** главá, ли́дер **3.** пéрвый; глáвный **4.** сначáла, прéжде всегó	1. head 2. leader, chief 3. first 4. to bring charge against sb. 5. to confess - -
～脑 **shǒunǎo** главá, ли́дер	head
～相 **shǒuxiàng** премьéр-ми́нистр	prime minister -
～都 **shǒudū** столи́ца	capital (of a country)
～次 **shǒucì** пéрвый раз, впервы́е	first (time) -
～长 **shǒuzhǎng** начáльник; руководи́тель, главá; командйр	senior officer - -
～先 **shǒuxiān** сначáла, прéжде всегó	first; in the first place, first of all -
～领 **shǒulǐng** вождь, ли́дер, главá	chieftain, leader -
临 **lín** **1.** подходи́ть, приближáться к **2.** наступáть *(о моменте);* пéред	1. to face, overlook 2. to arrive, be present 3. to copy 4. on the point of, just before, be about to 5. facing
～时 **línshí** **1.** врéменный **2.** э́кстренный; чрезвычáйный	1. at the time when sth. happens 2. temporary, provisional -
～近 **línjìn** **1.** прибли́зиться **2.** близлежáщий, бли́зкий	close -
田 **tián** пóле; обрабóтанная земля́	field, farmland -
～径 **tiánjìng** лёгкая атлéтика	(sports) track and field -
～径赛 **tiánjìngsài** соревновáния (состязáния) по лёгкой атлéтике	(sports) track and field meet - -
～野 **tiányě** поля́; полевóй	field, open country
～产 **tiánchǎn** земéльная сóбственность	real estate -
～地 **tiándì** поля́, пáшни; полевóй	1. farmland, cropland 2. plight -
细 **xì** **1.** тóнкий; мéлкий; изя́щный **2.** подрóбный, детáльный; тщáтельно, подрóбно	1. thin, slender 2. fine, in small particles 3. thin and soft 4. exquisite, delicate 5. careful, meticulous, detailed 6. minute, trifling
～工 **xìgōng** тóнкая рабóта	fine workmanship
～菌 **xìjūn** бактéрии, микрóбы; бактериологи́ческий	germ, bacterium -

细佃亩奋福辐幅富

细菌战 **xìjūnzhàn** бактериологи́ческая война́	bacteriological/germ warfare
~致 **xìzhì** то́нкий, ажу́рный	careful, meticulous, painstaking
~微 **xìwēi** незначи́тельный, ме́лкий; кро́шечный	slight, fine, subtle
佃 **diàn** арендова́ть зе́млю	to rent land (from landlord)
~租 **diànzū** аре́ндная пла́та за зе́млю	land rent
~户(农) **diànhù (nóng)** аренда́тор *(земли́)*	tenant (farmer)
亩 **mǔ** му *(ме́ра пло́щади, ра́вная 0,06 га)*	(measure of area = 0.06 hectare or 1/6 acre)
奋 **fèn** 1. воодушевля́ться; пы́лкий 2. на́тиск; эне́ргия	1. to exert oneself, act vigorously 2. to raise, lift
~斗 **fèndòu** герои́ческая борьба́	to struggle, fight, strive
~勇 **fènyǒng** му́жественный, бесстра́шный; сме́лость, отва́га	1. to summon up all one's courage and energy
福 **fú** сча́стье, уда́ча; счастли́вый	good fortune, blessing, happiness
~利 **fúlì** благосостоя́ние	material benefits, well-being, welfare
~气 **fúqi** уда́ча, сча́стье, везе́ние	happy lot, good fortune
辐 **fú** 1. спи́ца *(колеса́)* 2. собира́ть(ся), концентри́ровать(ся)	spoke
~射 **fúshè** излуча́ть; излуче́ние, радиа́ция	(phys.) radiation; to radiate
~辏(凑) **fúcòu** собира́ть(ся), концентри́ровать(ся)	to converge
幅 **fú** 1. поло́тнище, полоса́ мате́рии 2. *сч. сл. для карти́н, плака́тов, карт*	1. width of cloth 2. size 3. (M. for cloth/paintings/etc.)
~员 **fúyuán** пове́рхность, пло́щадь; протяже́ние	extent of a country
富 **fù** бога́тство; бога́тый, зажи́точный	wealthy, abundant
~裕 **fùyù** зажи́точный, состоя́тельный	well-to-do, well-off
~利 **fùlì** благосостоя́ние	welfare, well-being
~有 **fùyǒu** быть бога́тым; име́ть в изоби́лии	1. to be rich/wealthy 2. to be rich in; be full of

富农 **fùnóng** зажи́точный крестья́нин; кула́к	rich peasant
～余 **fùyu** 1. изли́шки 2. бога́тый, оби́льный	to have more than needed; surplus
苗 **miáo** ростки́, всхо́ды	young plant, seedling
瞄 **miáo** прице́ливаться, наводи́ть на цель	to concentrate, gaze on
～准 **miáozhǔn** це́литься, наводи́ть ору́дие; прице́льный	to take aim at
描 **miáo** опи́сывать, изобража́ть	1. to trace, copy 2. to touch up, retouch
～写(述) **miáoxiě(shù)** опи́сывать, изобража́ть	to describe, depict, portray
猫 **māo** ко́шка; кот	cat
雷 **léi** 1. гром; греме́ть 2. ми́на; фуга́с	1. thunder 2. mine
～雨 **léiyǔ** гроза́	thunderstorm
～达 **léidá** радиолока́тор, рада́р	(loan w.) radar
留 **liú** 1. остава́ться; остана́вливаться 2. оставля́ть; заде́рживать	1. to remain, stay 2. to ask sb. to stay 3. to reserve, keep, save 4. to (let) grow 5. to accept 6. to leave (sth.)
～下 **liúxià** оста́вить; оста́ться	to stay behind, remain
～学 **liúxué** обуча́ться за грани́цей	to study abroad
～声机 **liúshēngjī** патефо́н	phonograph, gramophone
榴 **liú** 1. грана́товое де́рево 2. грана́та	pomegranate
～弹 **liúdàn** грана́та	high-explosive shell
溜 **liū** 1. скользи́ть 2. ускольза́ть, убега́ть 3. броди́ть, гуля́ть	1. to slide, glide 2. to sneak off, slip away 3. smooth
～达 **liūda** гуля́ть, прогу́ливаться	1. (coll.) to stroll, saunter, take a walk 2. to leave, be on one's way
番 **fān** о́чередь; раз	1. kind 2. turn, time 3. foreign countries
播 **bō** 1. се́ять 2. разбра́сывать; распространя́ть	1. to sow, seed 2. to broadcast
～音 **bōyīn** радиовеща́ние	to transmit, broadcast
～种 **bōzhǒng** се́ять	to sow (seeds)
～送 **bōsòng** передава́ть по ра́дио, трансли́ровать	to broadcast, beam
备 **bèi** 1. подготовля́ть, при-	1. to be equipped with, have 2. to prepare

富苗瞄描猫雷留榴溜番播备

готовля́ть; запаса́ть **2.** по́лностью, всё	get ready 3. to provide against 4. fully
备有 **bèiyǒu** пригото́вить, име́ть нагото́ве	to stock, carry
～用 **bèiyòng** загото́вить, име́ть в запа́се	to keep in reserve; spare, backup, standby
～而不用 **bèi ér bùyòng** име́ть на вся́кий слу́чай; про запа́с	to have sth. ready just in case
～战 **bèizhàn** гото́виться к войне́	to prepare for war
～忘录 **bèiwànglù** па́мятная запи́ска; мемора́ндум	memorandum
畜 **chù** скот	domestic animal, livestock
～ **xù** занима́ться животново́дством	to raise domestic animals
～牧 **xùmù** скотово́дство; занима́ться скотово́дством	to raise/rear livestock/poultry
蓄 **xù 1.** нака́пливать, собира́ть; накопле́ние **2.** вмеща́ть; вмести́мость	1. to store/save up 2. to grow 3. to entertain (an idea), harbor
～水池 **xùshuǐchí** водохрани́лище	cistern, reservoir
～电池 **xùdiànchí** аккумуля́тор	storage battery, accumulator
～积 **xùjī** нака́пливать, собира́ть	to store, save up
～意 **xùyì** у́мысел; умы́шленный	deliberately, premeditatively
由 **yóu 1.** из; от; че́рез, посре́дством **2.** причи́на **3.** *см.* 被	1. to let (sb. do sth.) 2. reason, cause 3. owing/due to 4. by, through
～于 **yóuyú** благодаря́, вследствие, по причи́не	owing/due/thanks to
～此可见 **yóu cǐ kě jiàn** из э́того сле́дует; отсю́да ви́дно, что	thus it can be seen (that)
袖 **xiù** рука́в; пря́тать в рука́в	to tuck inside a sleeve; sleeve
轴 **zhóu** ось; сте́ржень	// (M. for thread/paintings/etc.) 1. axle, shaft 2. axis 3. spool, rod 4. //
抽 **chōu 1.** тяну́ть; вытаскивать **2.** взы́скивать, вычита́ть	1. to remove 2. to obtain by drawing/etc. 3. to shrink 4. to lash, whip 5. to put forth (of certain plants)

抽屉 **chōuti** выдвижно́й я́щик	(cabinet/desk) drawer
～烟 **chōuyān** кури́ть *(таба́к)*	to smoke (cigarette/pipe)
～水机 **chōushuǐjī** насо́с, по́мпа	water pump
～象 **chōuxiàng** отвлечённый, абстра́ктный	abstract
油 **yóu** 1. ма́сло; жир 2. кероси́н; нефть; бензи́н 3. сма́зывать ма́слом	1. oil, fat, grease; oily, greasy 2. glib, slick 3. to apply paint/oil/varnish 4. to be stained with oil/grease 5. spon-\\taneously 6. abundantly
～画 **yóuhuà** жи́вопись *(ма́сло)*	oil painting
～田 **yóutián** нефтепро́мыслы	oil field
～料 **yóuliào** нефтепроду́кты	oil-bearing crops
～井 **yóujǐng** нефтяна́я сква́жина	oil well
～灯 **yóudēng** кероси́новая ла́мпа	oil lamp
～布 **yóubù** клеёнка	oilcloth; tarpaulin
～纸 **yóuzhǐ** прома́сленная бума́га; перга́мент	oiled paper
庙 **miào** храм; монасты́рь	1. temple, shrine 2. temple fair
笛 **dí** ду́дка; свисто́к; сире́на	1. bamboo flute 2. whistle
曲 **qū** 1. изо́гнутый, криво́й 2. непра́вый, несправедли́вый	1. bent, crooked 2. false, wrong 3. unjust 4. evil, dishonest
～ **qǔ** мело́дия, моти́в; пе́сня	1. song 2. drama, opera
～折 **qūzhé** затрудне́ния, осложне́ния	1. tortuous, winding, complicated 2. complications of an event
～子 **qǔz** пе́сня; а́рия	tune, song, melody
国 **guó** 1. госуда́рство, страна́; госуда́рственный; национа́льный 2. ца́рство, кня́жество	1. country, state, nation 2. of the state, national 3. of our country, Chinese
～立 **guólì** госуда́рственный; национа́льный	state/nationally maintained/run
～语 **guóyǔ** гоюй	national language written and spoken
～营 **guóyíng** госуда́рственный	state-operated/run

国

国营农场 **guóyíngnóngchǎng** госхо́з; совхо́з	state farm
～籍 **guójí** гражда́нство; по́дданство	nationality
～外 **guówài** вне́шний, иностра́нный	overseas
～都 **guódū** столи́ца госуда́рства	national capital
～界 **guójiè** госуда́рственная грани́ца	national boundaries
～有化 **guóyǒuhuà** национализи́ровать; национализа́ция	nationalization
～内 **guónèi** вну́тренний; внутри́ страны́	interior (of a country), internal, domestic, home
～内战争 **guónèi zhànzhēng** гражда́нская война́	civil war
～防 **guófáng** оборо́на страны́	national defense
～书 **guóshū** вери́тельные гра́моты	1. credentials 2. documents exchanged between nations
～[务]卿 **guó[wù]qīng** госуда́рственный секрета́рь *(США)*	(U.S.) Secretary of State
～务院 **guówùyuàn** Госуда́рственный сове́т *(КНР)*; Госуда́рственный департа́мент *(США)*	1. State Council 2. U.S. State Department
～歌 **guógē** госуда́рственный гимн	national anthem
～庆节 **guóqìngjié** национа́льный пра́здник	National Day
～体 **guótǐ** госуда́рственное устро́йство	1. state system 2. national prestige
～家 **guójiā** госуда́рство, страна́; госуда́рственный	country, state, nation
～徽 **guóhuī** госуда́рственный герб	national emblem
～民 **guómín** наро́д; наро́дный; граждани́н	citizen; people, nationals
～民经济 **guómín jīngjì** наро́дное хозя́йство	national economy
～民党 **guómíndǎng** гоминьда́н	Kuomintang (KMG), Nationalist Party

国境 **guójìng** *см.* ～界	national territory
～旗 **guóqí** госуда́рственный флаг	national flag
～际 **guójì** междунаро́дный, интернациона́льный	international
～际主义 **guójìzhǔyì** интернационали́зм	internationalism
～际歌 **guójìgē** Интернациона́л *(гимн)*	The Internationale
～会 **guóhuì** парла́мент	parliament, congress
回 **huí** **1.** возвраща́ться, повора́чивать обра́тно **2.** отвеча́ть *(на вопрос, письмо)* **3.** мусульма́нин; дунга́нин **4.** раз; о́чередь	1. to circle, wind 2. to answer, reply 3. to refuse, decline 4. to return, go back 5. to turn around 6. chapter 7. times 8. Moslem 9. Hui ethnic minority
～任 **huírèn** верну́ться на пре́жнюю до́лжность	to return to an old post
～信 **huíxìn** отве́тное письмо́	1. to write in reply 2. to write back 3. letter in reply
～答 **huídá** отвеча́ть; отве́т	to answer, reply; answer, reply
～音 **huíyīn** о́тклик, о́тзвук, э́хо	1. echo 2. reply 3. (mus.) turn
～国 **huíguó** возвраща́ться на ро́дину	to return to one's country
～拜 **huíbài** нанести́ отве́тный визи́т	to pay a return visit
～声 **huíshēng** э́хо, о́тзвук	echo //to repent 3. later, by and by
～头 **huítóu** огляну́ться	1. to turn one's head, turn around 2. //
～族 **huízú** мусульма́не; дунга́не	Hui ethnic minority
～来 **huílai** возвраща́ться *(сюда)*; 拿…～回来 принести́ обра́тно *(сюда)*	to return, come/be back
～家 **huíjiā** возвраща́ться домо́й	to return home //ing sb.)
～避 **huíbì** уклоня́ться	1. to evade, dodge 2. to avoid (meet-//
～电 **huídiàn** телегра́фный отве́т	to wire back; reply (telegram)
～忆 **huíyì** вспомина́ть; воспомина́ние	to recollect, recall
～去 **huíqu** возврати́ться; уйти́ обра́тно; 拿…回去 отнести́ обра́тно *(туда)*	to return, go/be back
墙 **qiáng** стена́; огра́да	wall

墙报 **qiángbào** стенная газета	wall newspaper
固 **gù** **1.** прочный, твёрдый **2.** упрямый, упорный **3.** конечно, несомненно, безусловно	1. originally 2. as a matter of course 3. certainly 4. indeed 5. solid, secure, firm, steadfast 6. to consolidate, strengthen
～体 **gùtǐ** твёрдое тело; твёрдый	solid
～定 **gùdìng** **1.** прочно установить; устойчивый **2.** стационарный, постоянный	to fix, regularize
～然 **gùrán** конечно, несомненно, безусловно	1. no doubt 2. of course, admittedly
团 **tuán** **1.** организация; союз; группа; коллектив **2.** объединяться, сплачиваться **3.** полк	1. to roll sth. into a ball 2. to unite, assemble 3. group, society, organization 4. round, circular 5. regiment 6. Communist Youth League 7. roundish mass
～结 **tuánjié** сплачивать(ся), соединять(ся); сплочение	to unite, rally; union, rally
～长 **tuánzhǎng** **1.** командир полка **2.** глава делегации	1. regimental commander 2. head of delegation/troupe/etc.
～体 **tuántǐ** организация; коллектив	organization, group, team
～员 **tuányuán** член организации; *сокр.* комсомолец	member (of delegation/organization/ etc.)
围 **wéi** **1.** окружать, охватывать; окружение **2.** вокруг	1. to surround, enclose, corral 2. (all) around 3. curtain 4. (M. for measure of outstretched arms)
～裙 **wéiqún** фартук, передник	apron
～巾 **wéijīn** кашне, шарф	scarf, muffler
～攻 **wéigōng** осаждать; осада	to besiege, attack from all sides
～绕 **wéirǎo** **1.** окружать; вокруг **2.** обращаться вокруг	1. to move around 2. to center on, revolve around
因 **yīn** **1.** причина **2.** вследствие того, что; ввиду того, что	1. cause, reason; because, as, on account of, on the basis of 2. to carry on, continue
～而 **yīn'ér** поэтому, следовательно	consequently
～为 **yīnwei** **так как, ибо, потому что**	because of, for, on account of

因此 **yīncǐ** поэ́тому, ввиду́ э́того	therefore, consequently
～素 **yīnsù** фа́ктор	factor, element
咽 **yān** го́рло; гло́тка	pharynx
～ **yàn** глота́ть; проглоти́ть	to swallow
烟 **yān** 1. дым 2. таба́к 3. ко́поть	1. smoke 2. mist, vapor 3. tobacco, cigarette 4. opium 5. to be irritated by smoke
～叶 **yānyè** листово́й таба́к	tobacco leaf
～斗 **yāndǒu** тру́бка; чубу́к	tobacco/opium pipe
～筒 **yāntong** труба́ *(дымохо́д)*	chimney, funnel, stovepipe
～幕 **yānmù** дымова́я заве́са	smoke screen
～卷儿 **yānjuǎnr** сигаре́та; папиро́са	cigarette
困 **kùn** 1. испы́тывать тру́дности; тру́дное положе́ние 2. утоми́ться, уста́ть	1. to surround 2. stranded, hard-pressed 3. sleepy, tired 4. poor, hard up
～难 **kùnnan** тру́дности, затрудне́ния; тру́дно	1. difficulty 2. straitened circumstances, dire straits
～苦 **kùnkǔ** страда́ть; терпе́ть лише́ния	privation
～境 **kùnjìng** тяжёлое положе́ние; тупи́к	difficult position, predicament, straits
捆 **kǔn** обвя́зывать, свя́зывать; тюк, ки́па	to tie, truss, bundle; bundle
菌 **jūn** бакте́рии, микро́бы; пле́сень	fungus, bacterium
圈 **quān** круг, окру́жность; кольцо́; пе́тля	to circle, encircle; circle, ring, corral
四 **sì** четы́ре; четвёртый	four, 4
～面 **sìmiàn** все сто́роны; со всех сторо́н, круго́м	(on) four/all sides
～郊 **sìjiāo** окре́стности; при́город	suburbs, outskirts
～月 **sìyuè** апре́ль	1. April 2. fourth lunar month
～肢 **sìzhī** коне́чности	-
园 **yuán** парк; сад	1. garden 2. place for public recreation
圆 **yuán** 1. кру́глый; круг 2. по́лный; вполне́ 3. юа́нь; до́ллар	1. circle 2. round, circular, spherical 3. satisfactory; comprehensive 4. to justify, make plausible 5. Ch. monetary unit
～规 **yuánguī** ци́ркуль	(math.) compass
图 **tú** 1. ка́рта; план; чертёж; схе́ма 2. пыта́ться;	1. picture, drawing, chart, map 2. plan 3. intention 4. to plan, seek, pursue

图窗面西

замышля́ть; за́мысел; попы́тка	-
图画 **túhuà** карти́на; рису́нок	drawing, picture, painting
～章 **túzhāng** печа́ть, печа́тка *(личная)*	seal, stamp
～样 **túyàng** чертёж; эски́з; план	pattern, design, draft
～书馆 **túshūguǎn** библиоте́ка	library
～谋 **túmóu** замышля́ть; пла́ны, за́мыслы; за́говор	to plot, scheme, conspire; plot, scheme
～表 **túbiǎo** схе́ма; диагра́мма; гра́фик	-
窗 **chuāng** окно́; витри́на	window
～户 **chuānghu** окно́	window, casement
面 **miàn** **1.** лицева́я сторона́; лицо́ **2.** поверну́ться лицо́м к **3.** пове́рхность; сторона́ **4.** ли́чный; ли́чно **5.** мука́; те́сто; лапша́ **6.** *сч. сл. для флагов, зеркал*	1. face 2. surface, top 3. cover, outside 4. side, aspect 5. extent, range, scale, scope 6. (wheat) flour 7. powder 8. noodles 9. to face 10. superficial 11. soft and floury 12. entire area 13. (M. for mirrors/flags/etc.)
～目 **miànmù** лицо́, физионо́мия; о́блик	1. face, features, visage 2. appearance, aspect 3. self-respect, honor, face
～临 **miànlín** стоя́ть пе́ред; быть обращённым к	to be faced with, be up against
～前 **miànqián** **1.** пе́ред; пе́ред лицо́м **2.** впереди́; в ближа́йшее вре́мя	in the face of, in front of, before
～向 **miànxiàng** лицо́м к	face toward
～粉 **miànfěn** мука́	wheat flour
～条 **miàntiáo** лапша́; вермише́ль	noodles
～孔 **miànkǒng** *см.* ～目	face
～包 **miànbāo** хлеб; бу́лка	bread
～貌 **miànmào** нару́жность, вне́шность, о́блик; лицо́	1. face, features 2. appearance, look, aspect
～具 **miànjù** ма́ска	mask
～积 **miànji** пло́щадь; пове́рхность	surface area
西 **xī** за́пад; за́падный	(the) west; Occidental, Western
～红柿 **xīhóngshì** помидо́ры, тома́ты	tomato

西南 **xīnán** юго-за́пад	1. (the) southwest 2. Southwest China
～方 **xīfāng** за́пад; за́падный	1. the west 2. the West, the Occident
～瓜 **xīguā** арбу́з	watermelon
～服 **xīfú** костю́м европе́йского покро́я	Western-style clothes
～北 **xīběi** се́веро-за́пад	1. northwest 2. Northwest China
晒 **shài** **1.** загора́ть **2.** суши́ть на со́лнце	1. to shine on 2. to sun-dry, soak up the sun 3. (coll.) to cold-shoulder
～太阳 **shài tàiyáng** загора́ть на со́лнце	to sun-bathe
牺 **xī** **1.** же́ртвенное живо́тное **2.** же́ртвовать	sacrificial beast (of a uniform color)
～牲 **xīshēng** поже́ртвовать жи́знью; же́ртва	1. to sacrifice oneself, die a martyr's death 2. to do sth. at sb.'s expense
洒 **sǎ** разбры́згивать; опры́скивать; ороша́ть	1. to sprinkle, spray 2. to spill, shed
酒 **jiǔ** вино́; спиртны́е напи́тки	wine, liquor, spirits
～醉 **jiǔzuì** опьяне́ть; опьяне́ние	to become drunk
～精 **jiǔjīng** спирт	ethyl alcohol
～鬼 **jiǔguǐ** пья́ница, пропо́йца	drunkard, toper, alcoholic
～杯 **jiǔbēi** бока́л; рю́мка	wine cup/glass
～会 **jiǔhuì** банке́т	cocktail party
酱 **jiàng** со́евая па́ста	thick sauce; cooked/pickled in soy sauce
～油 **jiàngyóu** со́евый со́ус	soy sauce

丨

引 **yǐn** **1.** вести́ *(за собой)* **2.** вовлека́ть, втя́гивать **3.** вызыва́ть, возбужда́ть **4.** цити́ровать	1. to draw, pull, stretch 2. to lead, guide 3. to seduce 4. to quote, cite 5. introduction, preface 6. (M. of length, = 33.3 meters)
～言 **yǐnyán** введе́ние, предисло́вие	foreword, introduction
～到 **yǐndào** доводи́ть до; подводи́ть к	to lead to; to bring to
～导 **yǐndǎo** направля́ть, вести́ за собо́й	to guide, lead
～用 **yǐnyòng** приводи́ть *(цитату)*, ссыла́ться на	1. to quote, cite 2. to recommend, appoint
～起 **yǐnqǐ** вызыва́ть, возбужда́ть	to give rise to, lead to

引个卧仆补

引入 **yǐnrù** вводи́ть; вовлека́ть	to lead/draw into
～接 **yǐnjiē** встреча́ть, принима́ть *(гостей)*	to meet (with), receive, greet, welcome (guests/visitors)
个 **gè** **1.** шту́ка **2.** отде́льный, индивидуа́льный **3.** *универсальное сч. сл.*	(non-specific M. word)
～个 **gègè** ка́ждый *(в отдельности)*	each and every one, all
～别 **gèbié** отде́льный, индивидуа́льный	1. individual, specific 2. very few; exceptional
～子 **gèz** рост	height, stature, build
～人 **gèrén** отде́льный челове́к, индиви́дуум	individual (person); personal
～人迷信 **gèrén míxìn** культ ли́чности	personality cult
～体 **gètǐ** **1.** единоли́чный **2.** *биол.* индиви́д, о́собь	individual
卧 **wò** **1.** лежа́ть; ложи́ться **2.** спать; спа́льный	1. to lie down 2. to crouch, sit (of animals/birds) 3. to poach (eggs)
～室 **wòshì** спа́льня	bedroom
～车 **wòchē** спа́льный ваго́н	1. sleeping car/carriage 2. auto, car
～倒 **wòdǎo** упа́сть на́взничь; ложи́сь!	to fall prone
～铺 **wòpù** спа́льное купе́	sleeping berth, sleeper
～具 **wòjù** посте́льные принадле́жности	bedding (on a train/ship)
仆 **pú** слуга́, прислу́жник	servant
～从 **púcóng** **1.** прислу́живать **2.** сателли́т	footman, retainer
补 **bǔ** **1.** пополня́ть, дополня́ть; дополни́тельный **2.** чини́ть; што́пать **3.** возмеща́ть, компенси́ровать	1. to mend, patch 2. to fill, supply 3. to nourish 4. (wr.) to benefit 5. supplementary
～贴 **bǔtiē** субси́дия; дота́ция	to subsidize; subsidy
～习 **bǔxí** дополни́тельные заня́тия	to take lessons after schoolwork
～助 **bǔzhù** помога́ть; вспомога́тельный	1. to help financially, subsidize 2. subsidy, allowance
～助金 **bǔzhùjīn** субси́дия	grant-in-aid
～足(充) **bǔzú(chōng)** пополня́ть, дополня́ть; дополни́тельный	to bring up to full strength, make up a deficiency

扑 **pǔ 1.** уда́рить; прихло́пнуть **2.** заглуши́ть; погаси́ть *(пламя)*	1. to fling oneself at 2. to beat, pat, tap
~灭 **pūmiè** туши́ть, гаси́ть *(огонь)*	1. to stamp out, extinguish 2. to exterminate, wipe out
外 **wài 1.** вне́шний, нару́жный; вне, за **2.** кро́ме, исключа́я	1. outside 2. appearance 3. abroad 4. other 5. foreign, external 6. informal, unofficial 7. on mother's/dau./sis. side
~国 **wàiguó** иностра́нное госуда́рство; иностра́нный	foreign country
~国语(话) **wàiguóyǔ(huà)** иностра́нный язы́к	foreign language
~国人 **wàiguórén** иностра́нец	foreigner
~面 **wàimiàn** нару́жная сторона́; вне́шний; снару́жи	outside, exterior
~部 **wàibù** вне́шняя сторона́ (часть); вне́шний	outside, exterior, surface
~科 **wàikē** хирурги́я	surgical department
~行 **wàiháng** профа́н, неве́жда	1. layman, nonprofessional 2. sb. working outside his/her line
~号 **wàihào** про́звище, кли́чка	nickname
~人 **wàirén** чужо́й, посторо́нний челове́к	1. stranger, outsider 2. foreigner, alien 3. bystander
~长 **wàizhǎng** мини́стр иностра́нных дел	(abbr.) foreign minister, minister of foreign affairs
~头 **wàitou** снару́жи	outside, out
~衣 **wàiyī** ве́рхняя оде́жда	1. outer clothing/garment 2. appearance, semblance
~交 **wàijiāo** вне́шние сноше́ния; диплома́тия; дипломати́ческий	foreign affairs, diplomacy
~交部 **wàijiāobù** министе́рство иностра́нных дел	Foreign Ministry
~交家 **wàijiāojiā** диплома́т	diplomat
~援 **wàiyuán** иностра́нная по́мощь	foreign aid, outside help
~边 **wàibiān** снару́жи; вне	1. outside, exterior 2. place other than where one lives
~货 **wàihuò** и́мпортный това́р	foreign goods
朴 **pǔ** просто́й, бесхи́тростный	simple, plain

朴 讣 下

朴素 **púsù** простóй, скрóмный	simple, plain
讣 **fù** извещáть о смéрти	to announce sb.'s death; obituary
～告 **fùgào** трáурное объявлéние; некролóг	1. announcement of sb.'s death 2. obituary
下 **xià** **1.** низ; ни́жний; вниз; внизу́ **2.** нижеслéдующий **3.** ху́дший **4.** спускáть(ся) **5.** класть *(яйца)*; метáть *(икру)* **6.** раз; удáр	1. lower, inferior 2. next, latter, second 3. down, downward 4. below, under, underneath 5. to descend, go downwards, alight 6. to go into 7. to leave, exit 8. to issue 9. to take away
～工(班) **xiàgōng(bān)** уйти́ пóсле окончáния рабóты; закóнчить смéну	to leave work, come/go/knock off work
～雪 **xiàxuě** идёт снег; снегопáд	to snow
～台 **xiàtái** сойти́ со сцéны; лиши́ться влáсти	1. to step down from the stage/platform 2. to fall out of power
～面 **xiàmian** внизу́, под	1. lower level, subordinate 2. next
～午 **xiàwǔ** вторáя полови́на дня; пóсле полу́дня	afternoon
～半年 **xiàbànnián** вторóе полугóдие	second half of the year
～降 **xiàjiàng** **1.** снижáться, опускáться **2.** пáдать вниз	to descend, go/come down, drop, fall, decline
～车 **xiàchē** сойти́ с пóезда; вы́йти из вагóна	to get off/out of a vehicle
～列 **xiàliè** нижеслéдующий	listed below, following
～剩 **xiàshèng** остáток	(coll.) to be left (over)
～月 **xiàyuè** слéдующий мéсяц; в бу́дущем мéсяце	next month
～雨 **xiàyǔ** идёт дождь; дождь	to rain
～属 **xiàshǔ** подчинённый	(a) subordinate
～乡 **xiàxiāng** идти́ (направля́ться) в дерéвню	to go to the countryside
～场 **xiàchǎng** **1.** итóг, финáл **2.** сойти́ со сцéны	1. to go off stage, exit 2. (sports) to leave the playing field 3. next show
～次 **xiàcì** в слéдующий раз	next time
～来 **xiàlai** спускáться, сходи́ть *(сюда)*	1. to come down from a higher place 2. to go among the masses
～课 **xiàkè** кончáться *(об урóке)*	to finish/get out of class
～水 **xiàshuì** **1.** спусти́ть нá воду **2.** спусти́ть вóду	1. to enter the water, be launched 2. to take to evildoing 3. downriver/stream

下议院 **xiàyìyuàn** ни́жняя пала́та парла́мента	1. lower house/chamber 2. House of Commons
~放劳动 **xiàfàng láodòng** направля́ть на рабо́ту в	to be sent/directed to a lower (level of) work
низы́	-
~级 **xiàjí** нижестоя́щий,	1. lower level 2. (a) subordinate
подчинённый	-
~边 **xiàbiān** внизу́, сни́зу, под	1. lower level, subordinate; below, under, underneath 2. next, following
~达 **xiàdá** доводи́ть до све́-	to transmit to a lower level
дения *(нижестоящих)*; 下	-
达命令 отдава́ть прика́з	-
~流 **xiàliú 1.** ни́жнее тече́-	1. mean, low-down, obscene, dirty 2.
ние *(реки́)* **2.** низкопро́б-	lower reaches (of a river)
ный **3.** низы́, подо́нки *(об-*	-
щества)	-
~棋 **xiàqí** игра́ть в ша́хма-	to play chess
ты	-
~层 **xiàcéng** низы́ *(общест-*	lower level/strata
ва)	-
~去 **xiàqu** спусти́ться, сой- ти́ *(вниз)*	1. to go down, descend 2. to go on, continue
吓 **xià** пуга́ть, запу́гивать	to frighten, scare, intimidate
虾 **xiā** рак; креве́тка	shrimp //customs barrier, guardhouse
卡 **kǎ** *фон. знак*	1. to block, check 2. to strangle 3. //
~车 **kǎchē** грузови́к	truck, lorry
~片 **kǎpiàn** ка́рточка *(ви-*	card
зитная, библиотечная)	-
斤 **jīn** цзинь *(мера веса,*	(M. of weight, =1/2 kilogram)
равная 0,5 кг)	-
断 **duàn 1.** разруба́ть; отсе- ка́ть **2.** прекраща́ть, пре-	1. to break, cut off 2. to give up 3. to decide 4. absolutely, decidedly
рыва́ть **3.** реши́тельно,	-
определённо	-
~言 **duànyán** заявля́ть ка-	to affirm, assert categorically
тегори́чески, утвержда́ть;	-
утвержде́ние	-
~面 **duànmiàn** разре́з; по-	section
пере́чное сече́ние	-
~片 **duànpiàn** отры́вок,	part, fragment, extract
фрагме́нт	-
~绝 **duànjué** разорва́ть; пре-	to break off, sever
рва́ть	-
听 **tīng 1.** слу́шать, прислу́-	1. to listen, hear 2. to heed, obey 3. to

下吓虾卡斤断听

听 斩 渐 折 所

шиваться 2. слу́шаться, повинова́ться	allow, let 4. to administer 5. (M. for cans)
听话 **tīnghuà** слу́шаться; послу́шный	1. to await a reply 2. to heed advice 3. to obey; obedient
～讲 **tīngjiǎng** слу́шать (посеща́ть) ле́кции	to listen to a talk/lecture
～到 **tīngdào** услы́шать	to hear
～写 **tīngxiě** дикта́нт	dictation
～从 **tīngcóng** *см.* 听 2	to obey, heed, comply with
～众 **tīngzhòng** слу́шатели, аудито́рия	audience, listeners
～取 **tīngqǔ** заслу́шать, вы́слушать	to listen to
～说 **tīngshuō** говоря́т, что; по слу́хам	to hear/understand that; hearsay
～见 **tīngjiàn** услы́шать	to hear
斩 **zhǎn** отруби́ть; отре́зать	1. to chop, cut 2. to behead
渐 **jiàn** постепе́нно	gradually, by degrees
～渐 **jiànjiàn** постепе́нно, ма́ло-пома́лу	gradually, by degrees, little by little
折 **zhé** 1. перегиба́ть; сгиба́ть 2. криво́й, ло́маный 3. де́лать (производи́ть) перерасчёт	1. to break, snap 2. to lose 3. to turn back 4. to admire 5. to humiliate 6. to discount 7. to fold, bend 8. to die young 9. bent, twisted 10. discount\\ \\11. folder 12. act
～扣 **zhékòu** 1. удержа́ние 2. ски́дка	discount, rebate
～断 **zhéduàn** переломи́ть, слома́ть	to snap, break
所 **suǒ** 1. ме́сто, местонахожде́ние 2. учрежде́ние; конто́ра 3. *сч. сл. для домов, построек* 4. *префикс, при котором гл. получает значение объекта действия:* 所作 то, что де́лают; сде́ланное	1. (suf.) place; office, bureau, institute 2. that which 3. (M. for houses)
～在[地] **suǒzài[dì]** местонахожде́ние, местопребыва́ние	place, location
～有 **suǒyǒu** 1. всё, что име́ется; всё 2. иму́щество, со́бственность	to own, possess; all
～有制 **suǒyǒuzhì** систе́ма со́бственности	(system of) ownership

所谓 **suǒwèi** так называ́емый	so-called
～以 **suǒyǐ** поэ́тому; таки́м о́бразом	so, therefore, as a result
析 **xī** анализи́ровать	1. to divide, separate 2. to analyze, dissect, resolve
新 **xīn** но́вый; обновля́ть; за́ново	1. new, fresh, up-to-date 2. Xin dynasty (9–24 A.D.)
～殖民主义 **xīnzhímínzhǔyì** неоколониали́зм	neocolonialism
～华社 **xīnhuáshè** аге́нтство Синьхуа́	Xinhua (New China) News Agency
～鲜 **xīnxiān** но́вый, све́жий	1. fresh 2. new, novel, strange
～年 **xīnnián** но́вый год	New Year
～闻 **xīnwén** но́вости, изве́стия; хро́ника	news
～闻处 **xīnwénchù** пресс-це́нтр, пресс-бюро́	office of information, information service
～闻记者 **xīnwénjìzhě** корреспонде́нт; журнали́ст	reporter, journalist
～式 **xīnshì** но́вый, но́вого образца́	new-style
～兴国家 **xīnxīng guójiā** развива́ющиеся стра́ны	developing countries
～兵 **xīnbīng** новобра́нец	new recruit
薪 **xīn** 1. окла́д 2. дрова́; хво́рост	1. firewood, fuel 2. salary
～金(水) **xīnjīn(shuǐ)** зарпла́та	salary
斯 **sī** *фон. знак*	1. then, thus, therefore 2. this
撕 **sī** разорва́ть, уничто́жить	to tear, rip
～破(毁) **sīpò(huǐ)** порва́ть, разорва́ть	to tear, rip
斧 **fǔ** топо́р	axe, hatchet
～头 **fǔtóu** топо́р	axe, hatchet
拆 **chāi** 1. разбира́ть; демонти́ровать 2. лома́ть, разруша́ть	1. to tear open, take apart 2. to pull down, dismantle
～台 **chāitái** подрыва́ть; подрывно́й	to undercut (sb.)
～卸 **chāixiè** *см.* 拆 1	to dismantle, dismount
～开 **chāikāi** разобра́ть; разорва́ть; распако́вывать	to take apart, open, separate
诉 **sù** 1. жа́ловаться; обви-	1. to tell, relate, inform 2. to complain, accuse 3. to appeal/resort to

ня́ть; жа́лоба **2.** расска́зывать, сообща́ть	-
昨 **zuó** вчера́; вчера́шний	yesterday
~天 **zuótiān** *см.* 昨	yesterday
作 **zuò** **1.** де́лать; создава́ть, твори́ть **2.** быть, явля́ться; станови́ться	1. to make, produce, manufacture 2. to cook, prepare 3. to do, act, engage in 4. to be/become 5. to write, compose 6. to feign
~工 **zuògōng** рабо́тать, труди́ться	to work, toil, labor
~业 **zuòyè** рабо́та, заня́тие	1. school assignment 2. work, operation
~品 **zuòpǐn** произведе́ние *(искусства)*	works (of art/literature)
~客 **zuòkè** быть го́стем	to sojourn, live away from home
~者 **zuòzhě** а́втор	author, writer
~曲家 **zuòqǔjiā** компози́тор	composer
~事 **zuòshì** рабо́тать; служи́ть	1. to handle matters 2. to work, have a job
~用 **zuòyòng** роль, значе́ние; примене́ние	1. action, function, effect 2. intention, motive 3. to act on, affect
~物 **zuòwù** [сельскохозя́йственная] культу́ра	crop
~为 **zuòwéi** приня́ть за; в ка́честве	1. action, conduct, deed 2. to accomplish 3. to regard as, take for 4. as
~家 **zuòjiā** писа́тель	writer
~战 **zuòzhàn** вести́ войну́, воева́ть	to fight, do battle
~成 **zuòchéng** сде́лать, соверши́ть	to complete successfully
~风 **zuòfēng** стиль рабо́ты	style of work, way
~法 **zuòfǎ** стиль; спо́соб, ме́тод	way of doing/making sth.
炸 **zhà** взрыва́ть(ся)	1. to explode, burst 2. to blow up, bomb, blast 3. to flee in terror
~ **zhá** жа́рить	to deep-fry
~弹 **zhàdàn** бо́мба	bomb
~药 **zhàyào** взры́вчатое вещество́	explosive (charges), dynamite
~毁 **zhàhuǐ** взорва́ть; взрыв	to blow up, demolish
诈 **zhà** обма́нывать; моше́нничать; вымога́ть; шантажи́ровать	1. to cheat, swindle, dupe 2. to feign 3. to beguile, fish for information
窄 **zhǎi** у́зкий, те́сный	1. narrow 2. petty 3. hard up
榨 **zhà** выжима́ть *(напр. масло)*; пресс	to press, extract; extract; press
卸 **xiè** **1.** разгружа́ть, вы-	to unload, discharge, lay down, take sth. off

гружа́ть 2. слага́ть с себя́ *(обязанности)*	-
卸任 **xièrèn** *см.* ～责	to leave office
～下 **xièxià** разгружа́ть, выгружа́ть	1. to strip, disassemble 2. to unload
～责 **xièzé** снять с себя́ отве́тственность; сложи́ть полномо́чия	to shirk responsibility
御 **yù** противостоя́ть; обороня́ться	1. to drive (a carriage/etc.) 2. to resist, ward off 3. to control, manage
命 **mìng** 1. жизнь 2. судьба́ 3. прика́зывать; прика́з; ука́з 4. называ́ть, дава́ть и́мя (назва́ние)	1. life 2. lot, fate, destiny 3. order, instruction 4. to order, command 5. to assign (a title, etc.)
～名 **mìngmíng** дать назва́ние, назва́ть	1. to name (sb. sth.) 2. denomination
～中 **mìngzhòng** попа́сть *(в цель)*; попада́ние	to hit a target/mark
～脉 **mìngmài** арте́рия	lifeblood, lifeline
～运 **mìngyùn** судьба́, у́часть, до́ля	destiny, fate, lot
～令 **mìnglìng** *см.* 命 3	to order, command; order, command
印 **yìn** 1. печа́ть; клеймо́; о́ттиск 2. след 3. печа́тать; печа́тный	1. to print, engrave 2. seal, stamp, chop 3. mark, trace, print
～刷 **yìnshuā** печа́тать, издава́ть *(книги)*; печа́тный	to print; print
～刷品 **yìnshuāpǐn** печа́тные изда́ния	printed matter
～刷所 **yìnshuāsuǒ** типогра́фия	typography
～象 **yìnxiàng** впечатле́ние	impression
柳 **liǔ** и́ва	willow
～树 **liǔshù** и́ва	willow tree
却 **què** 1. отступа́ть(ся); отверга́ть, отка́зываться 2. всё же, тем не ме́нее	1. to step back, retreat 2. to repulse 3. to reject, refuse 4. but, yet 5. indeed 6. now 7. just 8. however, but
脚 **jiǎo** нога́; ступня́; подо́шва	1. foot 2. base 3. dregs, residue 4. leg
～踏车 **jiǎotàchē** велосипе́д; самока́т	bicycle
～印 **jiǎoyìn** след (отпеча́ток) ноги́; следы́	footprint, track
～步 **jiǎobù** шаг, по́ступь	step, pace

即 **jí** **1.** и́менно, а и́менно **2.** да́же; да́же е́сли **3.** сейча́с же, неме́дленно	1. to approach, reach, be near 2. to assume, undertake 3. to be, mean 4. at present, in the immediate future, then
～刻 **jíkè** неме́дленно, то́тчас	at once, immediately
～使 **jíshǐ** е́сли бы да́же, пусть да́же	even, even if/though
仰 **yǎng** **1.** смотре́ть вверх **2.** опира́ться, полага́ться	1. to face upward 2. to admire, respect 3. to rely/depend on
节 **jié** **1.** абза́ц; пара́граф; пункт **2.** сезо́н **3.** пра́здник **4.** эконо́мить	1. joint, node, knot 2. segment, part 3. festival 4. item 5. moral integrity 6. to economize, save, 7. to restrain
～俭 **jiéjiǎn** эконо́мный, бережли́вый	thrifty, frugal
～日 **jiérì** пра́здник	festival, holiday
～目 **jiémù** **1.** програ́мма **2.** разде́л; подзаголо́вок	program, item (on program), number
～省 **jiéshěng** эконо́мить, сокраща́ть расхо́ды	to economize, save, cut down; frugal
～约 **jiéyuē** эконо́мия; режи́м эконо́мии	1. to economize, save 2. to conclude a treaty/etc.
爷 **yé** **1.** оте́ц **2.** дед **3.** господи́н	1. grandfather 2. father 3. (polite) uncle 4. master
卵 **luǎn** *биол.* яйцо́	1. egg, ovum, spawn 2. fish roe
部 **bù** **1.** отде́л, разде́л, часть **2.** министе́рство	1. part, section 2. unit 3. headquarters, office, board, ministry 4. troops
～署 **bùshǔ** **1.** расположи́ть; расположе́ние; дислока́ция **2.** за́мыслы, пла́ны	to dispose, deploy
～门 **bùmén** о́трасль; отде́л	1. department, branch 2. classification
～属 **bùshǔ** подчинённый; подве́домственный	1. troops under one's command 2. subordinate 3. affiliated to a ministry
～分 **bùfen** часть, до́ля; части́чный	part, section
～队 **bùduì** войска́, а́рмия; войскова́я часть	1. army 2. troops
～长 **bùzhǎng** мини́стр	minister; head of a section
～长会议 **bùzhǎng huìyì** сове́т мини́стров	Council of Ministers
～族 **bùzú** пле́мя; наро́дность	tribe, clan
都 **dōu** *обобщающая частица* все; всё	1. all 2. even 3. already
～ **dū** столи́ца	capital; metropolis

邮 **yóu** по́чта; почто́вый	mail, post
~汇 **yóuhuì** почто́вый перево́д	to remit by post/mail
~[政]局 **yóu[zhèng]jú** почто́вое отделе́ние; почта́мт	post office
~票 **yóupiào** почто́вая ма́рка	postage stamp
鄙 **bǐ** **1.** по́длый, ни́зкий **2.** захолу́стье	1. low, mean, vulgar 2. (humb.) my 3. to despise, scorn 4. out-of-the-way place
~视 **bǐshì** презира́ть; презре́ние	to despise, disclaim
耶 **yē** *фон. знак*	abbr. for Jehovah, God
邪 **xié** **1.** ло́жный **2.** поро́чный **3.** вре́дный *(о климате)*	1. evil 2. heretical, irregular 3. (Ch. med.) unhealthy influences that cause disease
邦 **bāng** госуда́рство, страна́	nation, state, country
~交 **bāngjiāo** межгосуда́рственные отноше́ния	diplomatic relations
绑 **bǎng** **1.** привя́зывать, свя́зывать **2.** перевя́зывать **3.** похища́ть *(людей)*	1. to bind, tie 2. to bind sb.'s hands behind him, truss up
那 **nà** **1.** тот; то **2.** там **3.** так; тогда́, в тако́м слу́чае	1. that 2. then, in that case
~ **nǎ** **1.** како́й?, кото́рый? **2.** где?; куда́?	(interrog.) which, what, how
~一个 **nàyīgè, nèiyīgè** тот	that
nǎyīgè кото́рый?	(interrog.) which?
~里 **nàlǐ** там; туда́	that place, over there
nǎli **1.** где?; куда́? **2.** где уж там!	1. (interrog.) where 2. how could this be possible? 3. whenever, when
~样 **nàyàng** **1.** таки́м о́бразом, так **2.** тако́й	1. that kind of, like that 2. such, so, in that case
~边儿 **nàbiār** там; туда́	that side, there
nǎbiār где?; куда́?	which side?
~么 **nàme** таки́м о́бразом; сле́довательно	1. like that, in that way 2. then, in that case
哪 **nǎ** **1.** како́й?, кото́рый? **2.** где?; куда́?	(interrog.) which?, what?, how?
~怕 **nǎpà** несмотря́ на; хотя́ бы	even; even if/though; no matter how
挪 **nuó** передвига́ть(ся)	to move, shift

邮
鄙
耶
邪
邦
绑
那
哪
挪

挪动 **nuódòng** передви́нуть (-ся)	to move, shift
郑 **zhèng** ва́жный; торже́ственный	solemn, ceremonial, festive, gala; grand
掷 **zhì** броса́ть; мета́ть; толка́ть	to throw, cast, fling, hurl
郎 **láng** молодо́й мужчи́на; муж	(polite) young man
郊 **jiāo** при́город; предме́стье	1. suburbs, outskirts 2. sacrifices to heaven and earth
～区(外) **jiāoqū (wài)** при́городы, окре́стности	suburban districts, outskirts
邻 **lín** 1. сосе́д; сосе́дний 2. примыка́ть, грани́чить	1. neighbor 2. neighborhood, community 3. basic community unit 4. near, adjacent, neighboring
～居 **línjū** жить по сосе́дству; сосе́д	neighbor
～接 **línjiē** примыка́ть, прилега́ть	to border on, be next/contiguous to, adjoin
十 **shí** 1. де́сять; деся́тый 2. целико́м, по́лностью	ten, 10
～一月 **shíyīyuè** ноя́брь	1. November 2. eleventh lunar month
～二月 **shí'èryuè** дека́брь	1. December 2. twelfth lunar month
～月 **shíyuè** октя́брь	1. October 2. tenth lunar month
～月革命 **shíyuè gémìng** Октя́брьская револю́ция	(Russian) October Revolution (1917)
～分 **shífēn** 1. целико́м, по́лностью 2. о́чень, весьма́	very, fully, utterly, extremely
～万 **shí wàn** сто ты́сяч	one hundred thousand
～亿 **shíyì** миллиа́рд	one billion (U.S.)
叶 **yè** 1. лист; ли́стья 2. страни́ца	1. leaf, foliage 2. page, leaf 3. epoch
什 **shí** 1. де́сять, деся́ток 2. вся́кая вся́чина	1. (used in fractions or multiples) ten 2. assorted, varied, miscellaneous
～么 **shénme** 1. что?; како́й? 2. что́-либо; како́й-либо	what?
汁 **zhī** сок; жи́дкость	juice
计 **jì** 1. счита́ть, подсчи́тывать, вычисля́ть 2. план, за́мысел	1. to count, compute, calculate 2. to plot, plan 3. gauge, meter 4. idea
～算 **jìsuàn** рассчи́тывать, вычисля́ть; расчёт	to count, calculate, compute; consideration, planning
～算机 **jìsuànjī** вычисли́тельная маши́на; арифмо́метр	1. computer 2. calculating machine, calculator

计划 **jìhuà** плани́ровать; план; пла́новый	plan, project, program
针 **zhēn** **1.** игла́; була́вка **2.** стре́лка *(прибора)* **3.** коло́ть; уко́л	1. needle, pin 2. stitch 3. injection, shot 4. acupuncture
～对 **zhēnduì** направля́ть на	to be directed at/against, counter
～法 **zhēnfǎ** иглоука́лывание, акупункту́ра	needle technique (in acupuncture/knitting, etc.)
早 **zǎo** **1.** у́тро **2.** ра́но; ра́нний **3.** давно́	1. morning; Good morning! 2. early, long ago 3. in advance 4. premature(ly)
～上 **zǎoshàng** у́тром	1. morning 2. (suf.) earlier
～操 **zǎocāo** у́тренняя гимна́стика	morning (setting-up) exercises
～晨 **zǎochén** у́тро; у́тром	(early) morning
～饭 **zǎofàn** за́втрак	breakfast
～已 **zǎoyǐ** задо́лго; давно́ уж	long ago/since
～晚 **zǎowǎn** **1.** у́тро и ве́чер **2.** ра́но или по́здно	1. morning and evening 2. sooner or later
～安 **zǎo'ān** до́брое у́тро!	Good morning!
章 **zhāng** **1.** глава́; разде́л **2.** статья́; о́черк **3.** уста́в; пра́вила **4.** герб; о́рден; значо́к **5.** печа́ть	1. chapter; section 2. composition; structure 3. rules, regulations, constitution 4. seal, stamp 5. badge, medal, emblem 6. to make known
～程 **zhāngchéng** уста́в; положе́ние; регла́мент	rules, regulations, constitution
障 **zhàng** препя́тствовать; препя́тствие; прегра́да	to hinder, obstruct; obstacle, obstruction, barrier, impediment
～碍物 **zhàng'àiwù** препя́тствие, загражде́ние	obstacle, barrier
卓 **zhuó** приме́тный, выдаю́щийся	1. tall and erect 2. eminent, outstanding
～越 **zhuóyuè** превосхо́дный; выдаю́щийся	outstanding, brilliant
悼 **dào** печа́литься; скорбь; тра́ур	to mourn, lament
～念 **dàoniàn** чтить па́мять	to mourn, grieve
掉 **diào** **1.** урони́ть; упа́сть, свали́ться **2.** теря́ть **3.** *гл. суф., указывающий на завершение действия*	1. to drop, fall, come off 2. to lose, be missing 3. to fall behind 4. to change 5. to turn 6. (suf.) away/down/out/ etc.
～色 **diàosè** полиня́ть; вы́цвести	to lose color, fade
棹:～子 **zhuōz** стол	table, desk

罩 **zhào** **1.** чехóл; покрышка **2.** абажýр	1. to cover, shade; cover, hood 2. overalls 3. bamboo fish trap
草 **cǎo** **1.** травá; солóма; сéно **2.** черновóй; грýбый	1. grass, straw 2. female (of animals) 3. careless, hasty, rough 4. to draft;\\ \\draft
~鞋 **cǎoxié** солóменные сандáлии	straw sandals
~字 **cǎoz** скóропись	cursive characters
~稿 **cǎogǎo** рýкопись; черновúк	(rough) draft
~约 **cǎoyuē** проéкт договóра	draft treaty/protocol
~书 **cǎoshū** скóропись	cursive/running hand
~写 **cǎoxiě** писáть скóрописью; скóропись	cursive/running hand
~案 **cǎo'àn** проéкт, наброóсок	draft
~本 **cǎoběn** черновúк	herbaceous (plant)
~地(原) **cǎodì(yuán)** луг; степь	1. grassland, meadow 2. lawn
卑 **bēi** пóдлый, нúзкий	low, inferior; modest, humble
~劣 **bēiliè** мéрзкий; пóдлый, гнýсный	base, mean, despicable
牌 **pái** **1.** табличка; вывеска; таблó **2.** мáрка *(торговая)*; этикéтка **3.** кáрты *(игральные)*	1. plate, tablet 2. brand 3. cards, dominoes, etc.
脾 **pí** селезёнка	spleen
~性(气) **píxìng(qì)** харáктер, нрав; 发脾气 сердúться	1. complexion 2. (coll.) disposition, nature, temperament
碎 **suì** разбúть(ся), раздробúть(ся)	1. broken, fragmentary 2. garrulous, gabby 3. to break to pieces, smash
醉 **zuì** **1.** опьянéть; пьяный **2.** увлекáться; увлечéние	1. drunk, tipsy 2. addicted to 3. marinated in wine
~心 **zuìxīn** *см.* 醉 2	-
华 **huá** **1.** прекрáсный, великолéпный **2.** Китáй; китáйский	1. glory, splendor 2. essence 3. China 4. resplendent 5. gray (of hair) 6. (polite) you
~侨 **huáqiáo** китáйцы, проживáющие за границей	overseas Chinese
毕 **bì** **1.** закóнчить(ся); конéц **2.** всё, пóлностью	to finish, accomplish, conclude; fully, altogether
~业 **bìyè** окóнчить учéбное заведéние; выпускнóй	to graduate, finish school

毕业生 **bìyèshēng** выпускни́к учебного заведе́ния	graduate
～业证书 **bìyèzhèngshū** дипло́м; аттеста́т	diploma
～竟 **bìjìng** наконе́ц; всё-таки	after all, when all is said and done
率 **shuài** вести́ *(за собой)*, возглавля́ть	1. to lead, command 2. direct 3. cursory 4. handsome 5. generally, mostly
～ **lǜ** но́рма; тари́ф; коэффицие́нт	(suf.) rate, proportion, ratio
～領 **shuàilǐng** вести́ *(за собой)*, возглавля́ть; кома́ндовать	to lead, head, command
摔 **shuāi** па́дать; броса́ть; роня́ть	1. to fall, tumble 2. to move backward and forward, swing 3. to cast/throw\\
～倒 **shuāidǎo** опроки́нуть(-ся); упа́сть	1. to fall down 2. to fell an \\down/off opponent
伞 **sǎn** 1. зонт 2. парашю́т	umbrella
～兵 **sǎnbīng** 1. возд吗шно-деса́нтные войска́ 2. парашюти́ст	paratrooper; parachuter
千 **qiān** 1. ты́сяча 2. мно́жество 3. всеми сре́дствами	thousand
～方百计 **qiānfāng-bǎijì** во что́ бы то ни ста́ло	by hook or by crook
歼 **jiān** уничтожа́ть, истребля́ть	to annihilate, destroy
～击机 **jiānjījī** *ав.* истреби́тель	fighter plane
～灭 **jiānmiè** уничто́жить, истреби́ть	to annihilate, destroy
干 **gān** 1. каса́ться, име́ть отноше́ние 2. вме́шиваться; наруша́ть	to have to do with, be implicated in, involve
～ **gān** 1. вы́сушить; сухо́й 2. чи́стый; до́чиста	1. dry, hollow 2. free 3. in vain 4. helplessly 5. only, simply 6. shield
～ **gàn** 1. рабо́тать; де́лать 2. ствол 3. магистра́ль 4. *сокр.* ка́дры	1. to do, work 2. to hold the post of 3. to fight 4. trunk
～活 **gànhuó** рабо́тать	to work on a job
～部 **gànbù** 1. ка́дры, ка́дровые рабо́тники 2. кома́ндный соста́в	cadre

干肝杆奸汗岸旱捍悍焊

干草 **gāncǎo** сéно	hay
～掉 **gāndiào** распрáвиться;	(coll.) to kill, get rid of, liquidate
расправа	-
～淨 **gānjìng** 1. чúстый	1. clean, neat and tidy 2. complete,
2. дóчиста, целикóм	total
～事 **gànshì** вестú делá; ра-	to work, do things
бóтать	-
～涉 **gānshè** вмéшиваться;	to interfere, intervene, meddle;
интервéнция; вмешáтель-	(phys.) interference
ство	-
～劲 **gānjìn** энтузиáзм, энéр-	enthusiasm, drive, vigor
гия	-
～脆 **gāncuì** я́сно, недву-	clearcut, straightforward
смы́сленно	-
～扰 **gānrǎo** мешáть; нару-	to disturb, interfere; (electr.) inter-
шáть; помéхи	ference, jamming
～杯 **gānbēi** осушúть бо-	to drink a toast; Cheers, Bottoms up!
кáл; пей до дна!	-
～吗 **gànmá** зачéм?	1. what to do; what's up? 2. why on \\
肝 **gān** пéчень; печёнка	liver \\earth?, whatever for?
～脏 **gānzàng** пéчень	liver
杆 **gān** 1. жердь: столб	pole, staff
2. дрéвко	-
奸 **jiān** 1. ковáрный, веро-	1. evil, treacherous 2. (coll.) self-seek-
лóмный 2. распу́тный	ing and wily 3. traitor 4. illicit sexual
3. предáтель; предáтель-	relations, adultery
ский	-
～细 **jiānxì** шпиóн; агéнт	1. spy 2. intriguer
汗 **hàn** пот; испáрина	sweat, perspiration
岸 **àn** бéрег; побережье	bank, shore, coast
旱 **hàn** зáсуха; засу́шли-	1. dry spell, drought 2. dry land
вый	-
～灾 **hànzāi** зáсуха	drought
～地 **hàndì** 1. пусты́ня 2. не-	non-irrigated farmland, dry land
поливны́е зéмли	-
捍 **hàn** оборонять, защи-	to defend, guard
щáть	-
～卫 **hànwèi** защищáть, от-	to defend, guard, protect
стáивать	-
悍 **hàn** 1. смéлый, отвáж-	1. brave, bold 2. fierce, ferocious
ный 2. дéрзкий; нáглый	-
～然 **hànrán** нáгло	brazenly, flagrantly
焊 **hàn** паять; свáривать;	to weld, solder
свáрка	-

焊接 **hànjiē** сва́ривать; сва́рка; па́йка	welding, soldering
罕 **hǎn** ре́дкий, необы́чный	rarely, seldom
～见 **hǎnjiàn** неви́данный	rare, rarely seen
平 **píng** **1.** ро́вный, пло́ский; равни́на **2.** мир; ми́рный **3.** ра́вный; по́ровну **4.** обы́чный, зауря́дный	1. flat, level, even 2. ordinary, common, uniform 3. safe, peaceful, calm 4. fair, just 5. to level 6. to make peace 7. to weigh and pay 8. peace 9. Beiping
～坦 **píngtǎn** гла́дкий, ро́вный	level, even, smooth, flat (of land/etc.)
～面 **píngmiàn** пло́скость; пло́ский	plane
～行 **píngxíng** паралле́льный	1. equal rank, parallel 2. simultaneous
～衡 **pínghéng** уравнове́шивать; равнове́сие	to balance; equilibrium, balance
～时 **píngshí** **1.** ми́рное вре́мя **2.** повседне́вно, постоя́нно	1. in ordinary/normal times; ordinarily 2. in peacetime
～等 **píngděng** ра́венство, равнопра́вие	equal; equality
～静 **píngjìng** тишина́, споко́йствие; ти́хий	calm, quiet, tranquil
～常 **píngcháng** обы́чный; обы́чно	ordinary, common; generally, usually, ordinarily, as a rule
～方 **píngfāng** квадра́т; квадра́тный	square; square (of area, e.g., meters, etc.)
～均 **píngjūn** сре́дний; в сре́днем; по́ровну	average; equally
～权 **píngquán** равнопра́вие, ра́венство	equal rights
～反 **píngfǎn** реабилити́ровать	to redress (a mishandled case); to rehabilitate
～原 **píngyuán** равни́на	plain, flatlands
～安 **píng'ān** споко́йствие	1. safe and sound 2. quiet and stable
抨 **pēng** обвиня́ть; разоблача́ть	to impeach
～击 **pēngjī** осужда́ть, упрека́ть	to attack (in speech/writing), assail
秤 **chèng** взве́шивать; весы́; безме́н	balance, steelyard, scale
评 **píng** оце́нивать; критикова́ть; определя́ть	1. to comment, criticize, review 2. to judge, appraise
～价 **píngjià** оце́нивать; оце́нка	to appraise, evaluate

评判 **píngpàn** выносить приговóр	to judge, pass judgment on; judgment
～定 **píngdìng** постановить, определить	to pass judgment on, evaluate, assess
～比 **píngbǐ** оцéнивать; оцéнка	to compare and assess
～论 **pínglùn** обозрéние; рецéнзия; обсуждéние	to comment on, discuss; commentary, review, comment
～论员 **pínglùnyuán** обозревáтель	commentator
苹:～果 **píngguǒ** я́блоко	apple
～果树 **píngguǒshù** я́блоня	apple tree
午 **wǔ** пóлдень; врéмя от 11 до 13 часóв	noon, midday
～饭 **wǔfàn** обéд	midday meal, lunch
许 **xǔ** 1. разрешáть, позволя́ть, допускáть 2. вероя́тно; мóжет быть 3. óчень, весьмá	1. to praise 2. to promise 3. to allow, permit 4. to be bethrothed (to) 5. maybe, perhaps 6. somewhat 7. and more 8. place
～可 **xǔkě** разрешáть, позволя́ть; разрешéние	to permit, allow; permit
～多 **xǔduō** мнóго, мнóжество	many, much, a lot of
辛 **xīn** 1. гóрький; óстрый 2. гóрестный, скóрбный 3. трýдный, тяжёлый	1. bitter 2. hard-working
～苦 **xīnkǔ** 1. старáться изо всéх сил 2. мýчиться, страдáть	1. hard, laborious 2. to work hard 3. to endure hardship
辞 **cí** 1. словá; речь 2. откáзываться 3. подавáть в отстáвку	1. diction, phraseology 2. to take leave 3. to decline 4. to dismiss, discharge 5. to shrink from, shirk
～别 **cíbié** прощáться	to bid farewell
～典 **cídiǎn** словáрь	dictionary
～职 **cízhí** увóлиться с рабóты; уйти́ в отстáвку	to resign
辨 **biàn** различáть; определя́ть	to differentiate, discriminate, distinguish
～别 **biànbié** различáть, распознавáть	to discriminate, differentiate
辩 **biàn** спóрить; спор; ди́спут	to argue, dispute, debate
～证 **biànzhèng** диалекти́ческий	to discriminate and verify; dialectical

辩证法 biànzhèngfǎ диалéктика	dialectics
～解 biànjiě защищáть, оправдывать	to provide an explanation, try to defend oneself; plea
～护 biànhù защищáть(ся), опрáвдывать(ся)	1. to speak in defense of 2. to plead, defend
～护士 biànhùshì апологéт; защи́тник	apologist
～论 biànlùn спóрить; спóры; дебáты	to argue, debate
～论会 biànlùnhuì ди́спут	debate
辜 gū провини́ться; винá	guilt; crime
～负 gūfù обманýть ожидáния; подвести́	to let down, fail to live up to, disappoint
幸 xìng счáстье, удáча	1. luck 2. to come, arrive (of an emperor)
～福 xìngfú счáстье; счастли́вый	happiness; happy
～得 xìngdé к счáстью	1. fortunately 2. to obtain by chance
～运 xìngyùn счастли́вая судьбá; удáча	very fortunate
奉 fèng 1. получáть, принимáть *(от высшего по положению)* 2. подноси́ть; прислýживать	1. to give, present 2. to receive 3. to esteem, revere, respect 4. to believe in 5. to wait upon, attend to 6. (polite) to have the honor to
～命(令) fèngmìng(lìng) получи́ть прикáз; по прикáзу	to receive orders, act under orders
捧 pěng подноси́ть	1. to hold /carry sth. level in both hands 2. to boost, boast, flatter
棒 bàng пáлка; дуби́нка	1. stick, club 2. good, fine, strong
择 zé выбирáть, отбирáть	1. to select, choose 2. to differentiate
释 shì 1. объяснять, разъяснять 2. освобождáть	1. to explain, elucidate 2. to let go, be relieved of 3. to clear up 4. to release
～放 shìfàng отпускáть, давáть свобóду	to release, set free
泽 zé 1. óзеро 2. глáдкий; блестя́щий	1. pool, pond 2. luster
译 yì переводи́ть; расшифрóвывать	to translate, interpret
举 jǔ 1. нести́; поднимáть 2. выдвигáть; избирáть 3. дéйствие, акт 4. весь, целикóм	1. to lift, raise, hold up 2. to act, move 3. to start 4. to nominate, choose 5. to cite 6. to praise 7. to propose 8. to give birth to 9. act, deed 10. whole, all
～例子 jǔ lìz приводи́ть примéр	to give an example

辩辜幸奉捧棒择释泽译举

举半绊伴拌胖牛件牵

举行 **jǔxíng** осуществля́ть, проводи́ть	to hold (a meeting/etc.)
～手 **jǔshǒu** поднима́ть ру́ку; ру́ки вверх!	to raise one's hand(s)
～办 **jǔbàn** устра́ивать; организо́вывать	to conduct, hold, run
半 **bàn** полови́на; полу-	1. half, semi- 2. very little, the least bit\\
～径 **bànjìng** ра́диус	radius \\3. partly, about half
～殖民地 **bànzhímíndì** полуколо́ния	semi-colony
～年 **bànnián** полго́да; полугодово́й	half a year
～制品 **bànzhìpǐn** полуфабрика́т	semi-manufactured goods
～导体 **bàndǎotǐ** полупроводни́к; транзи́стор	semiconductor
～岛 **bàndǎo** полуо́стров	peninsula
～天 **bàntiān** 1. полдня́ 2. до́лго	1. half a day 2. a long time, quite a while
～球 **bànqiú** полуша́рие	hemisphere //half a night
～夜 **bànyè** по́лночь	1. midnight, middle of the night 2.//
绊 **bàn** 1. пу́ты; арка́н 2. свя́зывать 3. спотыка́ться	1. to stumble 2. to trip 3. to entangle 4. impediment, obstruction
～倒 **bàndǎo** упа́сть, свали́ться	to trip over, trip, stumble
伴 **bàn** партнёр, компаньо́н; спу́тник	to accompany; companion, partner
～奏 **bànzòu** аккомпани́ровать	to accompany (with musical instruments)
拌 **bàn** сме́шивать, разме́шивать	to mix
胖 **pàng** жи́рный, то́лстый	fat, stout, plump
牛 **niú** коро́ва; бык; вол	1. ox, cattle 2. arrogant
～肉 **niúròu** говя́дина	beef
～马 **niú-mǎ** рабо́чий скот	1. oxen and horses 2. beasts of burden
～奶 **niúnǎi** молоко́	cow's milk
件 **jiàn** 1. вещь, предме́т; шту́ка 2. *сч. сл. для одежды, документов*	1. correspondence, paper, document 2. (M. for articles/items/etc.)
牵 **qiān** 1. тяну́ть 2. уде́рживать; ско́вывать	1. to lead along (by holding hand/halter/etc.); to pull 2. to involve, implicate
～引 **qiānyǐn** тяну́ть; вовлека́ть, втя́гивать	to tow, draw, haul

牵引车 **qiānyǐnchē** тяга́ч	tractor, tractor truck
～制 **qiānzhì** свя́зывать, ограни́чивать, ско́вывать	to pin down, contain, curb
～涉 **qiānshè** косну́ться, затро́нуть	to involve, drag in
牢 **láo** **1.** кре́пкий, про́чный **2.** тюрьма́	1. pen, fold 2. sacrifice 3. prison, jail 4. firm
～固 **láogù** *см.* 牢 1	firm, secure
～狱 **láoyù** тюрьма́	prison, jail
～不可破 **láo bùkě pò** про́чный, неруши́мый	unbreakable, indestructible
犁 **lí** **1.** плуг **2.** паха́ть	to plow; plow
解 **jiě** **1.** рассека́ть; разделя́ть **2.** освобожда́ть **3.** ликвиди́ровать **4.** разъясня́ть, растолко́вывать	1. to separate, divide, cut apart 2. to untie, undo 3. to dispel, dismiss 4. to explain 5. to understand 6. to relieve oneself 7. to take off 8. to discharge\\
～雇 **jiěgù** увольня́ть, лока́ут	to discharge, dismiss \\9. ideas, views
～答 **jiědá** отвеча́ть на вопро́сы	to answer, explain; answer, explanation
～释 **jiěshì** разъясня́ть, объясня́ть	to expound, interpret, analyze; analysis
～开 **jiěkai** отвя́зывать, развя́зывать	to untie, undo
～剖 **jiěpōu** вскрыва́ть, анатоми́ровать	to dissect
～决 **jiějué** реша́ть, разреша́ть *(вопрос)*	1. to solve, resolve, settle 2. to dispose of, finish off
～散 **jiěsàn** распуска́ть; расформиро́вывать; разгоня́ть; разойди́сь!	1. to dismiss 2. to dissolve, disband
～放 **jiěfàng** освобожда́ть; освобожде́ние; освободи́тельный	to liberate, emancipate; liberation
～除 **jiěchú** **1.** ликвиди́ровать; искореня́ть **2.** лиша́ть *чего* **3.** отка́зываться от	1. to remove, relieve, get rid of 2. to fire (sb.)
懈 **xiè** лени́ться; лени́вый	slack, lax, inattentive
车 **chē** **1.** теле́га, пово́зка; автомаши́на; ваго́н **2.** стано́к	1. vehicle 2. wheeled machine/instrument 3. to lathe, turn 4. to lift water with a water-wheel
～站 **chēzhàn** ста́нция; вокза́л; остано́вка; стоя́нка	station

车阵库裤军

车箱 **chēxiāng** вагóн	railway car/carriage
～间 **chējiān** цех; цеховóй	(work)shop
～辆 **chēliàng** вагóны; повóзки; автомоби́ли	vehicle, car
～头 **chētóu** паровóз	1. front of a vehicle 2. engine (of a train), locomotive
～床 **chēchuáng** станóк	lathe
阵 **zhèn** 1. ряды́; строй; пози́ция 2. *сч. сл. для явлений природы, действий*	1. battle array 2. a period of time 3. to battle, fight 4. (M. for passing phase, spell)
～亡 **zhènwáng** поги́бнуть в бою́	to die in action
～营 **zhènyíng** лáгерь	interest group; clique
～地 **zhèndì** пози́ция; позициóнный	battlefield
库 **kù** кладовáя; склад; храни́лище	1. warehouse, storehouse 2. treasury
裤 **kù** брю́ки; штаны́	trousers, pants
军 **jūn** áрмия, войскá	armed forces, army, troops
～区 **jūnqū** воéнный óкруг	military region
～官 **jūnguān** офицéр	officer
～备 **jūnbèi** воéнная подготóвка; вооружéние	armament, arms
～备竞赛 **jūnbèi jìngsài** гóнка вооружéний	arms race
～国主义 **jūnguózhǔyì** милитари́зм; милитаристи́ческий	militarism
～训 **jūnxùn** боевáя подготóвка, воéнное обучéние	military training
～衔 **jūnxián** вóинское звáние	military rank
～事 **jūnshì** воéнное дéло; воéнный	military affairs
～事犯 **jūnshìfàn** воéнный престýпник	war criminal
～阀 **jūnfá** милитари́сты; воéнщина	warlord
～用 **jūnyòng** воéнный; для воéнных целéй	for military use, military
～人 **jūnrén** военнослýжащий	soldier, serviceman, armyman
～队 **jūnduì** войскá, áрмия	armed forces, army, troops
～服 **jūnfú** воéнная фóрма	military uniform
～役 **jūnyì** воéнная слýжба	military service

军舰 **jūnjiàn** воéнный корáбль	warship, naval vessel
挥 **huī** **1.** руководи́ть, управля́ть **2.** махáть, размáхивать **3.** разбрáсывать	1. to brandish 2. wipe off/away 3. to command (an army) 4. to scatter, disperse 5. to squander (money/etc.)
浑 **hún** **1.** мýтный **2.** хаоти́ческий, сумбýрный **3.** целикóм, пóлностью	1. muddy, turbid 2. stupid 3. unsophisticated 4. entire, all over
晕 **yūn** **1.** теря́ть сознáние **2.** крýжится головá; укáчивает	to faint; dizzy
～船 **yūnchuán** морскáя болéзнь	to become seasick
辈 **bèi** **1.** поколéние **2.** век, жизнь	1. lifetime, generation 2. people of a certain kind
羊 **yáng** барáн; козёл	sheep
～肉 **yángròu** барáнина	mutton
鲜 **xiān** свéжий; нóвый	1. fresh, new 2. bright-colored 3. tasty 4. delicacy 5. seafood
～明 **xiānmíng** я́сный, отчётливый	1. bright (of color) 2. distinct, distinctive
～花 **xiānhuā** свéжие (живы́е) цветы́	fresh flower
群 **qún** **1.** мáсса, толпá **2.** стáдо; стáя	1. group, crowd 2. (M. for group/swarm/flock/etc.)
～岛 **qúndǎo** архипелáг	archipelago
～众 **qúnzhòng** [нарóдные] мáссы; мáссовый	the masses/people
祥 **xiáng** добрó; счáстье; дóбрый	auspicious, propitious, lucky
样 **yàng** **1.** образéц; фасóн; модéль **2.** вид; спóсоб; стиль	1. appearance, shape, form 2. sample, model, pattern 3. (M. for kind/type/class)
～品 **yàngpǐn** образцы́ товáров	sample (product), specimen
～子 **yàngz** **1.** вид; óбраз **2.** образéц	1. appearance, shape 2. manner, air 3. sample, model, pattern 4. tendency
～式 **yàngshì** фасóн; модéль	pattern, type, style, form
洋 **yáng** **1.** океáн **2.** замóрский, инострáнный **3.** совремéнный	1. ocean 2. silver coin 3. vast 4. foreign 5. modern
～车 **yángchē** ри́кша	rickshaw
～铁 **yángtiě** жесть; жестянóй	1. tin-plate 2. galvanized iron

洋火 **yánghuǒ** спи́чки	matches
详 **xiáng** растолко́вывать; подро́бный, дета́льный	1. detailed, minute; detail 2. clear 3. to explain in detail
～细 **xiángxì** подро́бный, дета́льный	detailed, minute
～明 **xiángmíng** вы́яснить; я́сный, подро́бный	full and clear
舞 **wǔ** 1. танцева́ть, пляса́ть; та́нец 2. игра́ть, забавля́ться 3. злоупотребля́ть	1. to dance; dance 2. to flourish, brandish
～蹈 **wǔdǎo** та́нец, пля́ска	dance
～台 **wǔtái** сце́на; аре́на	stage, arena
～剧 **wǔjù** бале́т	dance drama, ballet
～会 **wǔhuì** танцева́льный ве́чер, бал	dance (party), ball
瞬 **shùn** миг, мгнове́ние	wink, twinkling (of an eye)
降 **jiàng** спуска́ть(ся), снижа́ть(ся); па́дать	to fall, drop, lower
～ **xiáng** сдава́ться, капитули́ровать	1. to surrender, capitulate 2. to subdue, tame
～落 **jiàngluò** спуска́ться; приземля́ться	1. to descend, land 2. to drop (in water level/etc.)
～落伞 **jiàngluòsǎn** парашю́т	parachute
～服 **xiángfú** сда́ться, покори́ться	to yield, surrender
～低 **jiàngdī** снижа́ть(ся); сниже́ние	to reduce, cut down, drop, lower
年 **nián** 1. год 2. во́зраст 3. эпо́ха, пери́од	1. year 2. age 3. New Year 4. period in one's life 5. a period in history 6. harvest
～轻(青) **niánqīng(qīng)** молодо́й	young
～初 **niánchū** нача́ло го́да; в нача́ле го́да	beginning of a/the year
～级 **niánjí** курс; класс	grade, year (in school/etc.)
～底 **niándǐ** коне́ц го́да	end of a/the year
～代 **niándài** поколе́ние; эпо́ха, пери́од	1. age, years, time 2. decade
～龄 **niánlíng** во́зраст	age
～终 **niánzhōng** коне́ц го́да	year-end
丰 **fēng** 1. бога́тый, оби́льный 2. пы́шный, густо́й	1. abundant, plentiful 2. great
～富 **fēngfù** изоби́лие; бога́тый	1. to enrich 2. rich, abundant, plentiful

丰满 **fēngmǎn** оби́льный; по́лный	1. plentiful 2. well-developed, full-grown 3. shapely, well-padded
～收 **fēngshōu** бога́тый урожа́й	bumper harvest
～收年 **fēnghōunián** урожа́йный год	bumper-harvest year
峰 **fēng** го́рная верши́на, пик	peak, summit, hump
～岭 **fēnglǐng** го́рный хребе́т	mountain ridge/range
蜂 **fēng** пчела́; оса́	1. wasp 2. bee
～密 **fēngmì** мёд	honey
锋 **fēng** 1. остриё *(копья)*; о́стрый 2. аванга́рд; аванга́рдный	1. sharp point/cutting edge (of a knife/sword/etc.) 2. vanguard 3. (meteor.) front
拜 **bài** 1. кла́няться; покло́н 2. наноси́ть визи́т	1. to do obeisance, salute 2. to make a courtesy call
～年 **bàinián** поздравля́ть с Но́вым го́дом	to pay a New Year's call, wish sb. Happy New Year
～访 **bàifǎng** нанести́ визи́т, посети́ть	to pay a visit, call on
律 **lǜ** пра́вило; зако́н	law, rule, regulation, statute
～师 **lǜshī** адвока́т; юри́ст	lawyer, attorney
肆 **sì** своево́льничать; распу́щенный	1. four (on checks/etc.) 2. wantonly 3. shop, store
～意 **sìyì** самово́льно, произво́льно	wantonly, recklessly
津 **jīn** 1. брод, перепра́ва 2. посо́бие *(денежное)*	1. ferry crossing, ford 2. saliva 3. sweat 4. moist, damp 5. Tianjin
～贴 **jīntiē** стипе́ндия; посо́бие	to subsidize; subsidy, allowance
革 **gé** 1. устраня́ть; смеща́ть 2. реорганизо́вывать, преобразо́вывать, реформи́ровать	1. to dismiss, expel 2. leather, hide
～新 **géxīn** обновля́ть; обновле́ние	to innovate; innovation
～新家 **géxīnjiā** нова́тор	innovator
～命 **gémìng** револю́ция; революцио́нный	revolt, revolution; to revolt
～命家 **gémìngjiā** революционе́р	revolutionary, revolutionist
单 **dān** 1. просто́й, элемента́рный 2. оди́н; едини́ч-	1. single, sole 2. odd (numbered) 3. weak 4. singly, alone

单 弹 輝 中

ный **3.** нечётный **4.** спи́сок; счёт	-
单位 **dānwèi** едини́ца *(измерения; организационная)*	unit (in measurement or organization)
～干戶 **dāngànhù** единоли́чник	peasant family farming on its own
～子 **dānz** спи́сок, пе́речень	1. list, bill, form 2. bedsheet
～纯 **dānchún** чи́стый, без при́меси; просто́й	1. simple, pure, plain, artless 2. alone
～独 **dāndú** отде́льный; самостоя́тельный; оди́н	alone, solely, singly, individually, on one's own
弹 **dàn** снаря́д; пу́ля; патро́н; грана́та	1. pellet, ball 2. bullet 3. bomb
～ **tán 1.** эласти́чный, упру́гий **2.** игра́ть *(на муз. инструменте)*	1. to catapult, shoot 2. to flick, flip, fluff 3. to pluck/play 4. to accuse, impeach 5. (suf.) done for, tired
～片 **dànpiàn** оско́лки *(снаряда, бомбы)*	shell fragment, shrapnel
～药 **dànyào** боеприпа́сы	ammunition
～药库 **dànyàokù** склад боеприпа́сов	ammunition depot
～丸 **dànwán** пу́ля	1. pellet, shot 2. tiny (area)
～簧 **tánhuáng** пружи́на	(mach.) spring
輝 **huī 1.** блесте́ть; блеск **2.** сла́ва	1. brightness, splendor 2. to shine
～煌 **huīhuáng** блестя́щий, великоле́пный	brilliant, glorious
中 **zhōng 1.** центр, середи́на; сре́дний **2.** внутри́; среди́ **3.** Кита́й; кита́йский	1. center, middle, interior 2. China 3. mid 4. medium, intermediate 5. mean 6. all right, OK
～ **zhòng 1.** попа́сть в цель **2.** подве́ргнуться *чему*	1. to hit (a target), attain 2. be hit by 3. to pass an exam 4. (suf.) accurately
～立 **zhōnglì** нейтралите́т	neutrality
～医 **zhōngyī** кита́йская медици́на	1. traditional Chinese medicine 2. doctor of traditional Chinese medicine
～断 **zhōngduàn** прерыва́ть	to suspend, break off
～部 **zhōngbù** центра́льная (сре́дняя) часть	1. central section 2. middle
～学 **zhōngxué** сре́дняя шко́ла	1. middle school 2. traditional Chinese learning
～等 **zhōngděng** сре́дний; сре́днего ка́чества	1. medium, middling 2. secondary
～间 **zhōngjiān** промежу́ток; ме́жду; среди́	center, middle

中毒 **zhōngdú** отрави́ться	to be poisoned
~央 **zhōngyāng** центр; центра́льный; *сокр.* ЦК (Центра́льный Комите́т)	1. center, middle 2. central authorities (of state/party/etc.)
~农 **zhōngnóng** середня́к	middle peasant
~文 **zhōngwén** кита́йский язы́к; кита́йская пи́сьменность	Chinese written language
~途 **zhōngtú** в пути́, на полдоро́ге	halfway, midway
~共 **zhōnggòng** *сокр.* КПК (Коммунисти́ческая па́ртия Кита́я)	Chinese Communist Party
~心 **zhōngxīn** центр; центра́льный, основно́й	center, heart, hub
肿 **zhǒng** опуха́ть; о́пухоль; отёк	to swell; swelling; swollen
种 **zhǒng 1.** се́мя; семена́ **2.** поро́да; сорт; ра́са; разнови́дность	1. species 2. race 3. seed, strain, breed 4. guts, grit 5. (M. for kind/sort/type)
~ **zhòng 1.** се́ять; сажа́ть 2. обраба́тывать зе́млю 3. де́лать приви́вку	to plant, cultivate, sow
~植 **zhòngzhí** се́ять; сажа́ть	to plant, grow
~田 **zhòngtián** обраба́тывать зе́млю	to till land, farm
~子 **zhǒngz** семена́	seed
~类 **zhǒnglèi** вид; род	kind, type, variety
~族 **zhǒngzú** ра́са; ра́совый	race, ethnic group
~族主义 **zhǒngzúzhǔyì** раси́зм	1. racism 2. ethnocentrism
~地 **zhòngdì** *см.* ~田	to till/cultivate land
冲 **chōng 1.** размыва́ть; смыва́ть **2.** уда́рить; атакова́ть	1. to rinse, flush 2. to charge, rush, dash 3. to clash, collide 4. to develop (film) 5. thoroughfare
~击 **chōngjī** атакова́ть; ата́ка	1. to lash, pound 2. to charge, assault
~锋 **chōngfēng** атакова́ть, штурмова́ть; ата́ка	to charge, assault
~锋枪 **chōngfēngqiāng** *воен.* автома́т	submachine/tommy gun; assault rifle
~突 **chōngtū** столкну́ться; столкнове́ние, конфли́кт	conflict, clash

冲淡 **chōngdàn** разбавля́ть, разжижа́ть	1. to dilute 2. to water/play down, weaken
～洗 **chōngxǐ** промыва́ть; смыва́ть	1. to rinse, wash 2. to develop (film) -
钟 **zhōng** **1.** часы́ *(настенные, настольные)* **2.** час *(единица времени)* **3.** ко́локол	1. bell 2. clock 3. time 4. handleless cup 5. to concentrate (affection/etc.) - -
～头 **zhōngtóu** час	hour
～表 **zhōngbiǎo** часы́ с бо́ем	timepiece -
串 **chuàn** нани́зывать; свя́зка, нить	1. to string together 2. to conspire, gang up 3. to get things mixed up
窜 **cuàn** убега́ть, ускольза́ть	1. to flee 2. to exile, expel 3. to alter
～逃 **cuàntào** скрыва́ться; бежа́ть	to flee in disorder, scurry off -
甲 **jiǎ** **1.** пе́рвый; гла́вный **2.** скорлупа́; па́нцирь; броня́ **3.** но́гти; ко́гти	1. indefinite person/thing 2. first 3. shell, carapace 4. nails 5. armor, crust 6. tithing 7. to excel
～板 **jiǎbǎn** па́луба	-
押 **yā** **1.** отдава́ть в зало́г **2.** заде́рживать; брать под стра́жу; конвои́ровать **3.** подпи́сывать	1. to mortgage, pawn, pledge 2. to detain 3. to escort 4. to shelve 5. to rhyme 6. signature, mark in lieu of signature
～送 **yāsòng** доста́вить под конво́ем	to send under escort -
申 **shēn** доноси́ть; подава́ть *(жалобу)*	to state, express, explain -
～斥 **shēnchì** осужда́ть, порица́ть	to reprimand -
～诉 **shēnsù** подава́ть жа́лобу; жа́лоба	to appeal, complain -
～辩 **shēnbiàn** опроверга́ть, оспа́ривать	to defend oneself, plead one's case -
～请 **shēnqǐng** хода́тайствовать; подава́ть заявле́ние	to apply for - -
～请书 **shēnqǐngshū** хода́тайство	application form -
伸 **shēn** **1.** протя́гивать **2.** выпрямля́ть, распрямля́ть, вытя́гивать	to stretch, extend - -
～开 **shēnkāi** раздви́нуть; растяну́ть	to stretch out (e.g., one's arms) -

伸手 **shēnshǒu** протяну́ть ру́ку	to stretch/hold out one's hand
～张 **shēnzhāng** распространя́ть(ся); расширя́ть(ся)	to uphold, promote
神 **shén** **1.** бог, божество́; дух **2.** таинственный, непостижи́мый **3.** эне́ргия, жи́зненная си́ла	1. god, deity, divinity 2. spirit, soul, mind 3. vitality, energy 4. supernatural, magical 5. smart, clever
～经 **shénjīng** не́рвы; не́рвный	nerve
～圣 **shénshèng** свято́й, свяще́нный	sacred, holy
～话 **shénhuà** леге́нда; миф; преда́ние	mythology, myth, fairy tale
～父 **shénfu** свяще́нник	(Catholic) father, priest
～气 **shénqì** жи́зненная си́ла, дух	1. expression, air, manner 2. spirited, vigorous 3. cocky, overweening 4. triumphant
～志 **shénzhì** рассу́док, ум, ра́зум	state of mind, consciousness
～秘 **shénmì** волшебство́; ми́стика; волше́бный	mysterious, mystical
审 **shěn** рассле́довать; допра́шивать	1. to examine, go over 2. to interrogate, try 3. to know 4. carefully 5. indeed
～查 **shěnchá** рассле́довать; проверя́ть; рассма́тривать	to examine, investigate
～判 **shěnpàn** суди́ть; суде́бный проце́сс, суд	to try a legal case; trial
～判厅 **shěnpàntīng** суд	court(room)
～判员 **shěnpànyuán** судья́	judge, judicial officer
～问(讯) **shěnwèn(xùn)** допра́шивать; допро́с	to interrogate, question
斗 **dòu** **1.** боро́ться; дра́ться **2.** соревнова́ться, состяза́ться	1. to fight 2. to vie 3. to denounce 4. to purge 5. to make animals fight (as a game) 6. to fit together, pool
～ **dǒu** **1.** до́у *(мера сыпучих тел, равная 10 л)* **2.** ковш, черпа́к	1. sth. shaped like a cup/dipper 2. whorl (of fingerprint) 3. Big Dipper 4. (M. for grain, = 1 decaliter)
～子 **dǒuz** воро́нка	1. coal scuttle 2. wooden container
～争 **dòuzhēng** боро́ться; борьба́	1. to fight 2. to accuse and denounce at a meeting 3. to strive/fight for
～篷 **dǒupeng** плащ; наки́дка	cape, cloak
～志 **dòuzhì** боево́й дух, боево́е настрое́ние	will to fight

斟 **zhēn** поду́мать, сообрази́ть	to pour (tea/wine)
抖 **dǒu** трясти́, встря́хивать	1. to tremble, shake, shiver 2. to rouse,//stir up
～动 **dǒudòng** встряхну́ть	to shake, tremble, vibrate
料 **liào** **1.** предполага́ть; рассчи́тывать **2.** материа́л; сырьё	1. to expect, anticipate; to infer, foresee; to consider, calculate 2. (raw) material; stuff, makings 3. grain, feed
～理 **liàoli** вести́ хозя́йство; приводи́ть в поря́док	1. to arrange, manage, attend to, take care of 2. Japanese cuisine
～子 **liàoz** материа́л; ткань	1. clothing material 2. woolen fabric
～想 **liàoxiǎng** предполага́ть, ду́мать	to expect, think, presume
科 **kē** **1.** учéбный предмéт, дисципли́на **2.** отделéние, отдéл	1. branch of study 2. administrative section 3. (animal) family 4. stage directions 5. rules, laws 6. to mete out
～目 **kēmù** **1.** учéбный предмéт, дисципли́на **2.** пункт *(программы)*	1. school subject/course 2. category of subjects 3. headings in an account book
～学 **kēxué** нау́ка; нау́чный	science, scientific knowledge; scientific,//rational
～学家 **kēxuéjiā** учёный	scientist
～长 **kēzhǎng** нача́льник отделéния	section chief
斜 **xié** наклóнный; косóй	oblique, inclined, tilted
～度 **xiédù** у́гол наклóна; уклóн	gradient
～坡 **xiépō** склон; спуск	slope
纠 **jiū** **1.** исправля́ть **2.** соединя́ть(ся) **3.** вовлека́ть	1. to correct, rectify 2. to entangle 3. to denounce 4. to reunite 5. to probe
～正 **jiūzhèng** исправля́ть, корректи́ровать	to correct, redress
～纷 **jiūfēn** раздóры; разноглáсия; конфли́кт	dispute, issue
～察 **jiūchá** расслéдовать; проверя́ть	1. to maintain order at a public gathering 2. picket
～察队 **jiūcháduì** пикéт; патру́ль	pickets
叫 **jiào** **1.** звать; называ́ть (-ся) **2.** велéть, заставля́ть 3. *употр. для выражения пассивной формы:* 叫敌人发现了 [был] обнару́жен врагóм	1. to cry, shout 2. to call, greet 3. to hire, order 4. to name, call 5. to cause 6. by (in passive constr.) 7. male (of animals)
～做 **jiàozuò** называ́ться, именова́ться	to be called, be known as

叫唤 **jiàohuan** звать, вызывать	to cry/call out
耳 **ěr** **1.** ýхо **2.** ушкó, рýчка	1. ear 2. (prefix) side, flanking
~聋 **ěrlóng** глухóй	3. to be deaf
缉 **jí** задéрживать; арестóвывать	to catch, seize, detain, delay
~捕 **qìbù** *см.* 缉	to seize, arrest
辑 **jī** собирáть, составля́ть	1. to compile, collect, edit 2. volume, part
耸 **sǒng** **1.** возвышáться; высóкий **2.** пугáться; боя́ться	1. to be towering/lofty 2. to arouse attention; to alarm/shock
聋 **lóng** глухотá; глухóй	deaf, hard-of-hearing

儿

介 **jiè** посрéдничать; рекомендовáть	1. to interpose, be situated between 2. to take seriously 3. upright 4. tiny\\
~居 **jièjū** находи́ться посреди́не	to be in the middle \\ 5. armor, shell
~绍 **jièshào** рекомендовáть; знакóмить, представля́ть	1. to introduce, present 2. to recommend, suggest 3. to brief, inform
价 **jià** стóимость; ценá	1. price 2. value
~值 **jiàzhí** цéнность; стóимость; ценá	value, worth
~格 **jiàgé** *эк.* ценá	price
~钱 **jiàqian** ценá	price
阶 **jiē** **1.** этáп; пери́од **2.** класс; стéпень **3.** ступéни *(лестницы)*	1. steps, stairs 2. rank
~段 **jiēduàn** этáп; ступéнь; отрéзок	1. stage, phase 2. (minimum) level
~级 **jiējí** **1.** класс *(общества)*; клáссовый **2.** ранг, звáние	social class
养 **yǎng** воспи́тывать; содержáть; корми́ть	1. to support 2. to raise, maintain 3. to give birth 4. to form 5. to rest
~活 **yǎnghuo** содержáть, корми́ть	1. to support, feed 2. to raise (animals) 3. to give birth to
~成 **yǎngchéng** воспитáть; вскорми́ть	to cultivate, raise
~老金 **yǎnglǎojīn** пéнсия по стáрости	old-age pension //group, division
界 **jiè** **1.** грани́ца, рубéж	1. boundary 2. scope, extent 3. circles,//

叫耳缉辑耸聋介价阶养界

2. преде́лы, ра́мки **3.** сре-	-
да́, круги́	-
界限 **jièxiàn** **1.** грани́ца	limits, bounds
2. преде́л, ра́мки	-
～线 **jièxiàn** демаркацио́н-	1. boundary/dividing line 2. limits,
ная ли́ния	bounds
侨 **qiáo** **1.** эмигра́нт **2.** жить	1. emigrant 2. to live abroad
на чужби́не	-
～民 **qiáomín** эмигра́нты	alien residents
～胞 **qiáobāo** соотéчествен-	overseas compatriots
ники, прожива́ющие за	-
грани́цей	-
轿 **jiào** носи́лки; паланки́н	sedan chair
骄 **jiāo** го́рдый; высокомéр-	1. proud, arrogant, conceited 2. un-
ный, зано́счивый	tamed 3. severe
～傲 **jiāo'ào** зазнава́ться;	to be proud, take pride in; pride; ar-
го́рдый; высокомéрный	rogant, conceited
桥 **qiáo** мост; насти́л	bridge
～梁 **qiáoliáng** мост	bridge (lit./fig.)
娇 **jiāo** краси́вый; милови́д-	1. tender, lovely, charming 2. fragile,
ный	frail, delicate 3. finicky 4. to pamper
齐 **qí** **1.** ро́вный **2.** вмéсте,	1. (to make) even/equal 2. together 3.
заодно́ **3.** целико́м, по́л-	(suf.) complete, prepared
ностью	-
挤 **jǐ** **1**. толка́ть(ся); тес-	1. to squeeze, press 2. to jostle, push
ни́ть(ся); да́вка; теснота́	against 3. to crowd, cram
2. отта́лкивать **3**. выжи-	-
ма́ть, выда́вливать	-
济 **jì** помога́ть, выруча́ть	1. to cross (a river) 2. to aid, relieve,
(материально)	help 3. to benefit, be of help
鼻 **bí** **1.** нос **2.** нача́ло; пéр-	nose
вый	-
～子 **bíz** нос	nose
非 **fēi** **1**. не явля́ется; не=,	1. not, no, non- 2. mistake, error, wrong
без= **2.** непра́вда **3**. отри-	3. evildoing 4. not to conform, to run
ца́ть, отверга́ть	counter to 5. to censure, blame
～常 **fēicháng** исключи́тель-	1. extraordinary, unusual, special 2.
ный, необыкновéнный;	very, extremely, highly
чрезвыча́йный	-
～法 **fēifǎ** незако́нный; не-	illegal, unlawful, illicit; illegally
лега́льный	-
排 **pái** **1.** ста́вить в ряд; ряд;	1. to arrange, put in order 2. to remove
ли́ния **2.** *воен.* взвод	with force, discharge 3. to push open
3. выта́лкивать	4. to rehearse 5. row, line 6. raft

排外 **páiwài** бойкоти́ровать иностра́нцев	anti-foreign, parochial
～斥 **páichì** отта́лкивать, отбра́сывать; отстраня́ть	to repel, exclude, eject
～挤 **páiji** **1.** оттесня́ть **2**. дискримина́ция	(pol.) to push aside, push/elbow out
～列 **páiliè** ста́вить в ряд	to arrange, put in order
～队 **páiduì** стро́иться; стро́ем	to stand in line
～水量 **páishuiliàng** водоизмеще́ние	1. displacement (of ships) 2. discharge capacity (of spillway/etc.)
～球 **páiqiú** волейбо́л	volleyball
～除 **páichú** вытесня́ть, устраня́ть; исключа́ть	to remove, eliminate
诽:～谤 **fĕibàng** клевета́ть; клевета́	to slander, libel
靠 **kào** **1.** опира́ться; примыка́ть к; о́коло **2.** в зави́симости от; исходя́ из	1. to lean against 2. to come up to, keep to, get near 3. to depend/rely on 4. near, by 5. make-believe armor
～岸 **kào'àn** прича́лить, приста́ть к бе́регу	to pull/draw into shore
～得住 **kàodezhù** надёжный	to be reliable
～近 **kàojìn** прибли́зиться; побли́зости, во́зле, о́коло	to be nearby, be close to
～拢 **kàolŏng** сближа́ться; пло́тный	1. to draw close, close up 2. to sit/stand closer 3. to shift allegiance
～不住 **kàobuzhù** ненадёжный	unreliable
罪 **zuì** преступле́ние; вина́	crime; guilt
～行 **zuìxíng** преступле́ние	criminal acts
～人 **zuìrén** престу́пник	offender, sinner
～状 **zuìzhuàng** обстоя́тельства преступле́ния	nature of offense
～犯 **zuìfàn** престу́пник; обвиня́емый	criminal, culprit
开 **kāi** **1.** открыва́ть **2.** начина́ть; осно́вывать, учрежда́ть **3.** исключа́ть **4**. выступа́ть, отправля́ться **5.** управля́ть; вести́ *(машину)* **6.** распуска́ться; расцвета́ть **7.** кипе́ть **8.** выпи́сывать *(документ, рецепт)*	1. to open; open 2. to open up, reclaim (land) 3. to open out 4. to come loose 5. to start, begin, operate 6. to drive 7. to turn on (a light) 8. to run (a business) 9. to hold (a meeting/etc.) 10. to eliminate 11. to divide into 12. to reveal 13. to boil

开

开 ⁼kai *гл. суф., указывающий на отделение, разделение:* 离开 уе́хать из, поки́нуть	(v. suf.) away, off, out
～工 **kāigōng** начина́ть рабо́ту; вступа́ть в строй *(о предприятии)*	to start up (construction, etc.)
～垦 **kāikěn** осва́ивать *(новые земли)*	to reclaim wasteland
～始 **kāishǐ** приступа́ть, начина́ть; нача́ло	to begin, start; beginning, initial stage
～辟 **kāipì** прокла́дывать *(путь)*; начина́ть *(дело)*	1. to open/set up, start 2. to build (a road)
～车 **kāichē 1.** отправля́ться *(о поезде, машине)* **2.** вести́ *(автомашину)*	1. to drive/start a car/train 2. to get a machine going
～门 **kāimén 1.** откры́ть дверь **2.** быть откры́тым *(напр. о магазине)*	to open a door (lit./fig.)
～端 **kāiduān** нача́ло, нача́льный эта́п	beginning, start
～幕 **kāimù 1.** подня́ть за́навес **2.** откры́ть, нача́ть *(собрание, спектакль)*	1. (theatr.) to raise the curtain 2. to open, inaugurate (a meeting, etc.)
～步走 **kāibùzǒu** зашага́ть; ша́гом марш!	(mil.) Forward, march!; Quick march!
～动 **kāidòng** ввести́ в де́йствие	1. to start, set in motion 2. to move, march
～火 **kāihuǒ** откры́ть ого́нь; нача́ть вое́нные де́йствия	to open fire
～展 **kāizhǎn** развива́ть(ся); развёртывать(ся); разви́тие	1. to develop, launch, unfold 2. open-minded, politically progressive
～饭 **kāifàn** накрыва́ть на стол	to serve (up) a meal
～支 **kāizhī** расхо́довать; расхо́ды, затра́ты	to pay (expenses/wages, etc.); expenses
～设 **kāishè** основа́ть, учреди́ть	to open (a shop/etc.); to offer (a course/etc.)
～放 **kāifàng 1.** откры́ть *(доступ)*; откры́тый **2.** распусти́ться *(о цветке)*	1. to come into bloom 2. to lift a ban/etc. 3. to open to traffic/the world 4. to be turned on, be in operation
～战 **kāizhàn** нача́ть войну́	to make war, to battle against
～化 **kāihuà** цивилиза́ция	to become civilized

开花 **kāihuā** расцвета́ть; распуска́ться	1. to blossom, bloom, flower 2. to feel elated 3. to break/split apart, explode
～枪 **kāiqiāng** стреля́ть, открыва́ть ого́нь	to fire (a gun), shoot
～除 **kāichú** исключи́ть; уво́лить	to expel, discharge
～会 **kāihuì** открыва́ть собра́ние; заседа́ть	to hold/attend a meeting
研 **yán** 1. иссле́довать, изуча́ть 2. тере́ть, растира́ть, натира́ть	1. to study 2. to grind
～究 **yánjiū** изуча́ть, иссле́довать	to study, research; study, research
～究生 **yánjiūshēng** аспира́нт	graduate student
～究所 **yánjiūsuǒ** нау́чно-иссле́довательский институ́т	research institute
并 **bìng** 1. соединя́ть; па́рный; паралле́льный 2. *перед отриц.* во́все не, совсе́м не	1. to combine, merge 2. equally, simultaneously 3. (intensifier before a negative) actually, truly 4. and
～立 **bìnglì** стоя́ть ря́дом	to coexist
～且 **bìngqiě** вме́сте с тем; а та́кже	and, besides, moreover
～行 **bìngxíng** идти́ бок о́ бок; паралле́льный	1. to run parallel 2. to implement together
～肩 **bìngjiān** плечо́м к плечу́	shoulder-to-shoulder
併 **bìng** соединя́ть; присоедини́ть(ся)	to join, unite, connect
～合 **bìnghé** *см.* 併	to join, unite, connect
拼 **pīn** 1. собира́ть; скола́чивать 2. сража́ться	1. to put/piece together 2. to risk one's life 3. to spell
～音 **pīnyīn** транскриби́ровать; транскри́пция; фонети́ческий	to spell, phoneticize; pinyin (official Chinese alphabetic system)
～命 **pīnmìng** 1. стара́ться изо всех сил 2. дра́ться на́смерть	1. to risk one's life 2. to make a death-defying effort
饼 **bǐng** лепёшка; блин; пече́нье	round flat cake, pancake, tortilla
～干 **bǐnggān** пече́нье	biscuit, cracker, cookie
弄 **nòng** 1. де́лать 2. игра́ть, забавля́ться 3. доводи́ть	1. to play with 2. to make, do, handle, engage in 3. to obtain 4. to play tricks

弄算弊葬异弃奔升井耕

до **4.** *образует гл. от основ*	-
прил.: ～清楚 вы́яснить,	-
внести́ я́сность	-
弄错 **nòngcuò** ошиба́ться	to make a mistake; to misunderstand
～权 **nòngquán** злоупотреб-ля́ть вла́стью	to abuse one's power
	-
～坏 **nònghuài** испо́ртить	to spoil, harm, cause damage/loss to
算 **suàn** **1.** счита́ть, вычис-ля́ть **2.** счита́ть, полага́ть; рассчи́тывать	1. to calculate, compute, figure; to in-clude, count 2. to plan 3. to suppose, think 4. to carry weight 5. let it pass
～计 **suànjì** **1.** вычисля́ть **2.** обду́мывать	1. to calculate 2. to consider, plan 3. to expect 4. scheme, plot
～了吧 **suànleba** дово́льно, хва́тит; пусть	1. settled, concluded (of a case) 2. That's enough!, Forget about it!
～清 **suànqīng** рассчита́ться	to settle accounts with, reckon with
～帐 **suànzhàng** **1.** подво-ди́ть ито́г; подсчи́тывать **2.** своди́ть счёты	1. to reckon accounts, ask for (make out) a bill 2. to get even with sb., set-tle old scores
～术 **suànshù** арифме́тика;	arithmetic
арифмети́ческий	- //vantage, harm
弊 **bì** зло; поро́к	1. fraud, abuse, malpractice 2. disad-//
葬 **zàng** хорони́ть; по́хоро-ны	1. to bury, inter 2. (coll.) offensive
	-
异 **yì** **1.** неодина́ковый; ино́й **2.** необы́чный; выдаю́щий-ся	1. different; strange, unusual; other, another 2. foreign (place) 3. disloyal 4. to separate 5. to feel surprised
～常 **yìcháng** необыкнове́н-ный	unusual(ly), extraordinary, abnormal
	-
弃 **qì** броса́ть; оставля́ть,	to discard, abandon
покида́ть; отка́зываться	- //flee 3. to approach
奔 **bēn** бежа́ть; торопи́ться	1. to head for 2. to hurry, rush, hasten,//
升 **shēng** поднима́ть(ся); возраста́ть, повыша́ться	1. to rise, ascend 2. to promote 3. liter 4. pint (dry measure)
～降机 **shēngjiàngjī** эскала́-тор; лифт	freight elevator
	-
～级 **shēngjí** **1.** продвига́ть-ся по слу́жбе; повыше́-ние **2.** эскала́ция	1. to go up (in grade/etc.) 2. to esca-late
	-
井 **jǐng** коло́дец; ша́хта	1. well 2. neat, orderly
耕 **gēng** обраба́тывать зе́м-лю; паха́ть	to plow, till
	-
～田 **gēngtián** обраба́тывать по́ле	to plow, till
	-
～畜 **gēngchù** рабо́чий скот	farm animal

耕种 **gēngzhǒng** *см.* 耕田	to till, cultivate
~地 **gēngdì** обрабáтывать зéмлю; пáхотная землá	to plow, till; cultivated land
讲 **jiǎng 1.** говорúть, разговáривать **2.** преподавáть; читáть *(лекцию)* **3.** объяснúть	1. to speak, say, tell 2. to explain, interpret 3. to discuss, negotiate 4. to stress, pay attention to 5. discourse, lecture 6. concerning, as for
~话 **jiǎnghuà** разговáривать, говорúть	1. to speak, talk, address; speech, talk 2. guide, introduction (in book titles)
~台 **jiǎngtái** трибýна	platform, dais, rostrum
~解 **jiǎngjiě** разъяснúть, толковáть; толковáние, пояснéние	to explain, narrate
~解员 **jiǎngjiěyuán** экскурсовóд	guide
~清 **jiǎngqīng** объяснúть, разъяснúть	to intercede, plead for sb.
~师 **jiǎngshī** лéктор	lecturer
~究 **jiǎngjiū** тщáтельно изучáть; быть знатокóм	1. to be particular about, pay attention to 2. to stress, strive for 3. to back-\\
~演 **jiǎngyǎn** лéкция; речь	lecture \\bite 4. exquisite, tasteful
~坛 **jiǎngtán** трибýна; кáфедра	1. platform, rostrum 2. forum
川 **chuān** рекá; течéние	1. river 2. plain
训 **xùn** учúть; тренировáть; инстрýкция; директúва, указáние	1. to lecture, teach, train; teachings, instruction 2. standard, model, example
~练 **xùnliàn** обучáть; тренировáть; подготóвка	to train, drill
~~班 **xùnliànbān** кýрсы	training class/course
~令 **xùnlìng** инстрýкция	instructions, order, directive
州 **zhōu** óкруг; штат; óбласть	1. administrative division 2. (autonomous) prefecture
酬 **chóu** вознаградúть; отблагодарúть	1. to propose a toast 2. to fulfill, realize 3. reward, payment 4. friendly \\
~报 **chóubào** отблагодарúть	reward, requite \\exchange
洲 **zhōu** континéнт, матерúк	1. continent 2. river islet, sand bar,\\
~际 **zhōujì** межконтиненттáльный	intercontinental \\shoal
肃 **sù 1.** велúчественный, торжéственный **2.** уничтóжить, искоренúть	1. respectful 2. solemn 3. to clean, mop up
~清 **sùjīng** очúстить, искоренúть; покóнчить с	solemnly silent

今琴片剑到倒

㇆

今 **jīn** сейча́с; сего́дня	today
~后 **jīnhòu** впредь, отны́не	henceforth, hereafter
~日 **jīnrì** сего́дня; сего́дняшний; совреме́нный	1. today 2. now, the present
~年 **jīnnián** ны́нешний год; в теку́щем году́	this year
~天 **jīntiān** сего́дня	1. today 2. the present, now
琴 **qín** лю́тня; стру́нный инструме́нт	1. stringed instrument 2. zither-like instrument
片 **piàn** **1.** поло́ска; стру́жка **2.** откры́тка; визи́тная ка́рточка **3.** лепесто́к	1. to slice; to pare; slice, flake 2. part 3. incomplete, partial 4. small, brief 5. (M. for tablets, stretches of land)
~ **piān** **1.** кинофи́льм **2.** грампласти́нка	1. (movie) film 2. phonograph record
~面 **piànmiàn** односторо́нний	1. unilateral 2. one-sided

亅

剑 **jiàn** меч	sword, saber
到 **dào** **1.** достига́ть; прибыва́ть **2.** *предлог* в; к; до; на **3.** *суф. результативности*	1. to arrive, reach 2. to go to 3. up to 4. thoughtful, considerate 5. (suf., indicating completion of verbal action)
~期 **dàoqī** пора́; в срок	1. to become due 2. to mature 3. to expire
~场 **dàochǎng** яви́ться; прису́тствовать	to be present, show/turn up
~来 **dàolái** наста́ть, наступи́ть	to arrive
~处 **dàochù** повсеме́стно	everywhere
~达 **dàodá** прибы́ть	to reach, arrive
~底 **dàodǐ** в конце́ концо́в; до конца́	1. to the end 2. at last 3. after all
倒 **dǎo** упа́сть; опроки́нуть (-ся)	1. to fall over, collapse 2. to exchange, move around, shift 3. to become hoarse
~ **dào** **1.** переверну́ть **2.** нали́ть; вы́лить **3.** одна́ко, тем не ме́нее; наоборо́т	1. to invert, move backwards, place upside down 2. to pour 3. in reverse order, back 4. actually 5. but, still, nevertheless
~闭 **dǎobì** закры́ться, обанкро́титься	to go bankrupt
~霉 **dǎoméi** не везёт	to be out of luck

倒茶 **dàochá**	налить чаю, подать чай	to pour tea
剖 **pōu**	вскрывать; рассекать	1. to cut/split open 2. to analyze, dissect
～面 **pōumiàn**	разрез; сечение	cross section, sectional view
創 **chuàng**	создавать, творить	to initiate (sth.)
～ **chuāng**	рана	to wound, injure, hurt; wound
～立 **chuànglì**	создавать; учреждать; становление	to found, originate
～始 **chuàngshi**	учреждать	to originate, initiate
～作 **chuàngzuò**	создавать, творить; творчество	to create, produce, write; creation, creative work
～举 **chuàngjǔ**	почин, начало	pioneering work/undertaking
～伤 **chuāngshāng**	рана; раны	wound, trauma
～造 **chuàngzào**	создавать, творить; творчество; творческий	to create, produce, bring about
剧 **jù**	1. резко, сильно 2. спектакль; пьеса	1. theatrical work, drama, play, opera 2. acute, severe, intense
～团 **jùtuán**	труппа	theatrical company; operatic troupe
～场 **jùchǎng**	театр; зрительный зал	theater
～烈 **jùliè**	острый; резкий	violent, fierce
刮 **guā**	1. скоблить 2. брить 3. дуть *(о ветре)*	1. to scrape, shave 2. to daub/smear (with paste/etc.) 3. to plunder, extort 4. to blow
～脸 **guāliǎn**	бриться	to shave (the face)
～脸刀 **guāliǎndāo**	бритва	razor
～风 **guāfēng**	дует ветер; ветрено	the wind is blowing
割 **gē**	1. отрезать 2. урезать; отторгать 3. жать; косить	to cut
～据 **gējù**	захватить; отторгнуть	to set up a separatist regime by force of arms
～断 **gēduàn**	отсечь; отрезать; ампутировать	to cut off, sever
～裂 **gēliè**	расколоть; разделить	to cut apart, separate
副 **fù**	1. помощник; заместитель; вице- 2. дубли-	1. deputy, assistant, vice- 2. auxiliary, subsidiary 3. to conform to, fit 4. (M.

ка́т; ко́пия; побо́чный	for sets of things, facial expressions)
3. *сч. сл. для комплектов,*	-
наборов	-
副业 **fùyè** подсо́бное хозя́й-	sideline, side occupation
ство	-
～官 **fùguān** адъюта́нт	adjutant, aide-de-camp
～本 **fùběn** дублика́т; ко́пия	duplicate, copy; transcript //dose
剂 **jì** до́за	1. medicinal/chemical preparation 2.//
刑 **xíng 1.** наказа́ние; казнь	1. punishment 2. torture, corporal pun-
2. уголо́вный	ishment
～罚 **xíngfá** наказа́ние *(за*	penalty, punishment
уголовное преступление)	-
～事 **xíngshì** уголо́вный	criminal, penal
愉:～快 **yúkuài** ра́доваться;	happy, cheerful
ра́достный	-
偷 **tōu 1.** ворова́ть **2.** испод-	1. to steal 2. secretly
тишка́, укра́дкой **3.** нера-	-
ди́вый; ко́е-ка́к	-
～空 **tōukòng** вы́брать вре́-	1. to snatch a moment (to do sth. else)
мя	2. to take time off (from work)
～看 **tōukàn** подгля́дывать	to steal a glance, peek (at)
～听 **tōutīng** подслу́шивать	to eavesdrop, bug
～窃 **tōuqiè** красть; кра́жа	to steal, pilfer
～懒 **tōulǎn** безде́льничать;	to idle, loaf, goldbrick
отлы́нивать	-
输 **shū 1.** перевози́ть **2.** про-	1. to transport, convey 2. to contri-
и́грывать	bute, donate 3. to lose, be defeated
～血 **shūxuè** перелива́ние	1. to transfuse blood 2. to give aid and
кро́ви	support
～出 **shūchū** вывози́ть, экс-	1. to export 2. (electr.) output
порти́ровать; э́кспорт	-
～入 **shūrù** ввози́ть, импор-	1. to import 2. (electr.) input
ти́ровать; и́мпорт	-
～送 **shūsòng** перевози́ть,	to carry, transport, convey
транспорти́ровать	-
前 **qián 1.** пе́ред; пере́дний;	1. front 2. forward, former, preced-
впереди́ **2.** проше́дший;	ing, first 3. formerly, ago, ahead, be-
бы́вший; пре́жде; до; до	fore
того́, как	- //guard 3. halfback
～卫 **qiánwèi** аванга́рд	1. avant-garde 2. advance guard, van-//
～任 **qiánrèn** бы́вший, пре́ж-	1. forefathers, predecessors 2. above-
ний	mentioned persons
～往 **qiánwǎng** направля́ть-	to go, leave for, proceed to
ся в	-

前后 **qiánhòu 1.** до и по́сле **2.** спе́реди и сза́ди	front and rear, around or about, altogether
～言 **qiányán** предисло́вие, введе́ние	1. earlier remarks 2. preface, foreword, introduction
～者 **qiánzhě** предше́ственник	the former
～面 **qiánmian** впереди́; пе́ред	in front, ahead, above, preceding
～辈 **qiánbèi** ста́ршее поколе́ние	senior (in age, experience/etc.), elder, older generation
～年 **qiánnián** позапро́шлый год	year before last
～锋 **qiánfēng** аванга́рд	1. vanguard, van 2. (sports) forward
～门 **qiánmén** гла́вные воро́та; гла́вный вход	front door/gate
～夕 **qiánxī** накану́не; кану́н	eve, the day before
～天 **qiántiān** позавчера́	the day before yesterday
～提 **qiántí** предпосы́лка	premise, presupposition, prerequisite
～进 **qiánjìn** продвига́ться; передово́й; вперёд!	to advance, go forward, proceed, progress
～途 **qiántú** перспекти́ва, бу́дущее	future career, prospects
～线 **qiánxiàn** фронт; передова́я ли́ния	front, frontline
～景 **qiánjǐng 1.** перспекти́ва **2.** пере́дний план	foreground, prospects, vista, perspectives
箭 **jiàn** стрела́	arrow //to cut, chop
削 **xiāo** обреза́ть; строга́ть	1. to pare/peal with a knife 2. (sport)//
刚 **gāng 1.** твёрдый, про́чный **2.** как ра́з; то́лько что	1. firm, strong, indomitable 2. just, exactly 3. barely, only just 4. only a short while ago
～刚 **gānggāng** *см.* 刚 2	1. just, only, exactly 2. a moment ago,\\
～才 **gāngcái** то́лько что; едва́	just now, a moment ago \\just now
刷 **shuā** чи́стить щёткой; щётка	1. to brush, scrub 2. to daub, paste up 3. to eliminate, remove 4. to fire
～白 **shuàbái** вы́чистить добела́; побели́ть	white, pale
～子 **shuāz** щётка	brush
～牙 **shuāyá** чи́стить зу́бы	to brush one's teeth
制 **zhì 1.** систе́ма; режи́м, строй **2.** подавля́ть; ограни́чивать **3.** вырабáты-	1. to make, manufacture, create 2. to work out, formulate, stipulate 3. to restrict, control, govern 4. system,

制删刊判列例

вать; изготовля́ть **4.** устана́вливать; создава́ть	institution 5. 3-yr. mourning period for parents
制止 **zhìzhi** останови́ть; пресе́чь	to curb, prevent, stop -
~订 **zhìdìng** вы́работать, установи́ть	to work/map out, formulate -
~定 **zhìdìng** утверди́ть; установи́ть	to formulate, draft -
~服 **zhìfú** фо́рменная оде́жда	uniform -
~度 **zhìdù** *см.* 制 **1**	system, institution
~造 **zhìzào** производи́ть, выра́батывать	1. to make, manufacture 2. to engineer, create, fabricate
删 **shān** сокраща́ть, уре́зывать	to delete, leave out -
刊 **kān 1.** печа́тать; изда́ние **2.** выреза́ть; гравирова́ть	1. to print, publish 2. to delete/correct 3. to inscribe on stone/wood 4.\\
~物 **kānwù** печа́тные изда́ния; печа́ть	publication, \\publication, periodical periodical
判 **pàn 1.** определя́ть, реша́ть **2.** разграни́чивать, различа́ть	1. to distinguish, discriminate 2. to decide, judge 3. to sentence, condemn 4. disparate, separate
~断 **pànduàn** определя́ть; оце́нивать; реша́ть; реше́ние	to judge, determine; judgment - -
~决 **pànjué** суди́ть; пригова́ривать; пригово́р	court decision, judgment -
列 **liè** ста́вить в ряд; шере́нга, ряд	1. to arrange, line up 2. to list 3. each and every, various 4. row, file, rank\\
~车 **lièchē** по́езд, соста́в	train \\5. kind, sort 6. (M. for rows,etc.)
~宁主义 **lièníngzhǔyì** ленини́зм	Leninism -
~入 **lièrù** вступа́ть в ряды́; зачисля́ть	to be listed/placed -
~强 **lièqiáng** вели́кие держа́вы	(the) great powers -
例 **lì** пра́вило; поря́док; приме́р	1. example, instance 2. precedent 3. instance, case 4. rule, regulation
~如 **lìrú** наприме́р	for instance/example, e.g., such as
~外 **lìwài** исключе́ние *(из правил)*	exception -
~子 **lìz** приме́р	example, case, instance
~会 **lìhuì** очередно́й пле́нум; очередна́я се́ссия	regular meeting -

别 **bié** **1.** различáть **2.** разлучáться **3.** инóй, другóй **4**. нельзя́, не нáдо	1. other, another 2. don't 3. to leave 4. to differentiate 5. to fasten 6. to stick in (one's belt/etc.)
～墅 **biéshù** дáча	villa //separate, detached
～的 **biéd** другóй, инóй	1. (an)other, different 2. independent,//
～动队 **biédòngduì** отря́д осóбого назначéния; диверсиóнный отря́д	special detachment, commando - -
～人 **biérén** другúе	others, other people, another person
剃 **tì** брить	to shave
刺 **cì** **1.** колóть; пронзáть; укóл **2.** колю́чка; шип	1. to stab, prick 2. to assassinate 3. to irritate, stimulate 4. to criticize 5. \\
～刀 **cìdāo** штык	dagger, bayonet \\thorn, splinter
～杀 **cìshā** заколóть, убúть	to stab to death; bayonet fighting
～激 **cìjī** **1.** возбуждáть; раздражáть **2.** стимулúровать; стúмул	1. to stimulate; stimulation 2. to upset, irritate, provoke -
喇 **lǎ** *фон. знак*	(phonetic sign/symbol)
～嘛 **lǎma** *будд.* лáма	lama //loudspeaker
～叭 **lǎba** трубá, горн	1. brass wind instrument, trumpet 2.//
利 **lì** **1.** пóльза, вы́года **2.** успéх, удáча **3.** прúбыль, дохóд; вы́годный, прúбыльный **4.** удóбный, благоприя́тный	1. profit, interest 2. advantage, benefit 3. to do good to, benefit 4. sharp 5. favorable - -
～益 **lìyì** интерéсы; пóльза; полéзный	interest, benefit, profit -
～害 **lì-hài** пóльза и вред	advantages and disadvantages
lìhai **1.** сúльный **2.** ужáсный	1. terrible, devastating 2. tough 3. sharp
～润 **lìrùn** прúбыль	profit
～用 **lìyòng** применя́ть, испóльзовать, пóльзоваться	1. to use, utilize 2. to take advantage of, exploit
～息 **lìxī** процéнты	interest
痢:～疾 **lìjī** дизентерúя	dysentery
剩 **shèng** оставáться в избы́тке; остáток; излúшек	to be left (over), remain -
～下 **shèngxia** оставáться; в остáтке	to be left (over), remain -
～余 **shèngyú** остáток; избы́ток	to be left over, remain; surplus, remainder
剝 **bō** отнимáть, лишáть	to peel, flay
～削 **bōxuē** эксплуатúровать; эксплуатáция	to exploit -

剥刈划刻则侧测厕罚丁打

剥夺 **bōduó** отобра́ть; экспроприи́ровать	to deprive, expropriate, strip (away/off) -
刈 **yì** жать; коси́ть	to mow, cut; to reap, crop
划 **huà 1.** плани́ровать; план **2.** начерти́ть **3.** разграни́чить	1. to delimit, differentiate 2. to transfer, assign 3. to plan 4. to draw, mark 5. stroke (of a Ch. character)
~ **huá** грести́	1. to paddle, row 2. to pay, be to one's\\profit
~船 **huáchuán** грести́; гре́бля	to paddle/row a boat -
~清 **huàqīng** чётко разграни́чить	to make clear a distinction -
~分 **huàfēn** разби́ть на; разграни́чить	to divide, differentiate -
刻 **kè 1.** гравирова́ть; выре́зывать **2.** че́тверть ча́са **3.** неме́дленно	1. to engrave, carve, cut, etch 2. cruel, savage, inhuman, callous 3. 1/4 hour 4. time, moment
~苦 **kèkǔ** насто́йчивый, упо́рный	1. assiduous, hard working, painstaking 2. simple and frugal
则 **zé 1.** зако́н; пра́вило; статья́; пара́граф **2.** то; в тако́м слу́чае	1. rule, regulation 2. standard, criterion 3. to imitate 4. to do, make 5. then, in that case 6. (M. for written items)
侧 **cè** фланг; сторона́; фланго́вый	to lean, incline; side -
~面 **cèmiàn** про́филь; бок; боково́й; сбо́ку	side, flank -
测 **cè 1.** ме́рить, измеря́ть **2.** вычисля́ть	1. to survey, fathom; measure 2. to conjecture, infer
~验 **cèyàn** проверя́ть; испы́тывать; обме́р и осмо́тр	to test, quiz; test, quiz - -
~量 **cèliáng** измеря́ть; производи́ть съёмку *(местности)*; съёмка	to survey, measure - -
~绘 **cèhuì** де́лать съёмку и составля́ть ка́рту *(местности)*	to survey and map - -
厕: ~所 **cèsuǒ** туале́т, убо́рная	toilet -
罚 **fá** нака́зывать; наказа́ние; штраф	to punish, penalize -
丁 **dīng** совершенноле́тний, взро́слый	1. man 2. population 3. cubes 4. 4th of the 10 Heavenly Stems
打 **dǎ 1.** бить, ударя́ть; разбива́ть **2.** сража́ться;	1. (generalized v. of doing) to strike, hit, fight; construct; forge; mix 2. from

дра́ться 3. *универсальный гл., широко сочетающийся с именами сущ.*	-
打 **dá** дю́жина	dozen
～量 **dǎliang** прики́нуть; дать оце́нку	1. to measure with the eye, estimate 2. to think
～扫 **dǎsǎo** подмести́, вы́мести	to sweep, clean
～击 **dǎjī** уда́рить, нанести́ уда́р; уда́р	to strike, hit, attack
～猎 **dǎliè** охо́титься	to hunt
～雷 **dǎléi** гром греми́т; гром	to thunder
～断 **dǎduàn** 1. переби́ть *(речь)* 2. переломи́ть	1. to break 2. to interrupt, cut short
～听 **dǎtīng** разузнава́ть; справля́ться о	to inquire, ask about
～针 **dǎzhēn** сде́лать уко́л	to give/have an injection
～开 **dǎkāi** откры́ть(ся), раскры́ть(ся), распахну́ть (-ся)	1. to open, unfold 2. to turn/switch on
～算 **dǎsuàn** рассчи́тывать; намерева́ться	to plan, intend, prepare
～倒 **dǎdǎo** све́ргнуть, опроки́нуть; доло́й!	to overthrow
～字 **dǎzì** печа́тать на маши́нке	1. to type(write) 2. to do typing work
～字机 **dǎzìjī** пи́шущая маши́нка	typewriter
～闪 **dǎshǎn** сверка́ть *(о молнии)*	to flash (of lightning)
～扮 **dǎbàn** наряжа́ться	1. to dress, make up, deck out 2. to//pose as
～架 **dǎjià** ссо́риться; дра́ться; дра́ка	to fight, scuffle, come to blows
～火机 **dǎhuǒjī** зажига́лка	lighter
～破 **dǎpò** разру́шить; слома́ть; ～破记录 поби́ть реко́рд	to break, smash
～败 **dǎbài** разгроми́ть, нанести́ пораже́ние	1. to defeat 2. to be defeated
～仗 **dǎzhàng** сража́ться, воева́ть	to wage war, fight a battle
～成 **dǎchéng** сколоти́ть, сплоти́ть	1. to gather, collect 2. to join, unite, assemble

打灯订钉厅亭停宁

打成一片 **dǎchéng yīpiàn** сплоти́ть(ся) воеди́но	to integrate
～死 **dǎsǐ** уби́ть	to kill, murder, slay, assassinate
～盹 **dǎdǔn** дрема́ть	to doze, take a nap
～电话 **dǎ diànhuà** звони́ть по телефо́ну	to make a telephone call
～电报 **dǎ diànbào** посыла́ть телегра́мму	to send a telegram
～扰 **dǎrǎo** беспоко́ить; меша́ть	to disturb, trouble
灯 **dēng** ла́мпа; фона́рь	1. lamp, lantern, light 2. (electr.) tube// //burner
～塔 **dēngtǎ** мая́к	lighthouse, beacon
～罩 **dēngzhào** абажу́р	lampshade, (oil) lamp chimney
～泡 **dēngpào** ла́мпочка	1. light bulb 2. (slang.) chaperone
～光 **dēngguāng** свет ла́мпы; освеще́ние	lamplight
～心 **dēngxīn** фити́ль	wick
订 **dìng 1.** заключа́ть *(догово́р)* **2.** подпи́сываться на; зака́зывать	1. to draw up, agree on 2. to subscribe to, book (seats) 3. to revise
～立 **dìnglì** заключа́ть *(до́говор, контракт)*	to conclude, reach (e.g., an agreement)
～购 **dìnggòu** зака́зывать; закупа́ть; контрактова́ть	1. to order goods 2. system of fixed quotas for purchasing
钉:～子 **dīngz** гвоздь; болт	1. nail 2. snag
～ **dìng** вбива́ть; прибива́ть	1. to nail 2. to sew on
厅 **tīng 1.** зал **2.** управле́ние; комиссариа́т	1. hall 2. office 3. provincial government department
亭 **tíng** павильо́н; кио́ск; бесе́дка	1. pavilion, kiosk 2. erect
停 **tíng** остана́вливать(ся), прекраща́ть(ся)	1. to stop, pause 2. to stop over 3. (coll.) part, portion
～工 **tínggōng** прекрати́ть рабо́ту	to stop work, shut down
～止 **tíngzhǐ** остнови́ть(ся), прекрати́ть(ся); прекраще́ние, остано́вка	to stop, suspend, call off
～泊 **tíngbó** прича́лить; стать на я́корь	anchor, berth
～留 **tíngliú** задержа́ться, оста́ться	to stay for a time
宁 **níng** ти́хий, споко́йный; споко́йствие	1. peaceful, tranquil 2. Ningxia 3. Nanjing
～ **nìng** лу́чше [уж]	1. rather, would rather 2. could there be

宁愿 **nìngyuàn** лу́чше уж; предпоче́сть	would rather, better
拧 **nǐng** крути́ть; завёртывать *(винт)*	1. to screw 2. to differ, disagree 3. wrong, mistaken
~ **níng** выжима́ть, отжима́ть	1. to twist, wring 2. to pinch, tweak
贮 **zhù** накопля́ть, собира́ть	to store, save, lay aside
街 **jiē** у́лица	1. street 2. county fair, market
行 **xíng 1.** ходи́ть, идти́ **2.** де́йствовать; посту́пок **3.** мо́жно; ла́дно	1. to go, travel 2. to be current, prevail, circulate 3. to do, perform, carry out, engage in 4. to be OK 5. behavior
~ **háng 1.** строй, ряд **2.** профе́ссия	1. row, business 2. seniority in family 3. shop, firm 4. line of business
~程 **xíngchéng** рейс, маршру́т	1. route/distance of travel, itinerary 2. (mach.) stroke, throw, travel
~业 **hángyè** профе́ссия, заня́тие	1. trade, profession 2. industry
~军 **xíngjūn** марш, похо́д	march
~列 **hángliè** ряды́; строй; шере́нга	ranks, procession
~李 **xíngli** бага́ж	luggage, baggage
~动 **xíngdòng** де́йствовать; де́йствие; поведе́ние	1. to act, take action; action, operation 2. to move, get about
~为 **xíngwéi** посту́пки, де́йствия; поведе́ние	action, behavior, conduct
~政 **xíngzhèng** администра́ция; администрати́вный; исполни́тельный	administration
~政权 **xíngzhèngquán** исполни́тельная власть	executive power, executive
衡 **héng** взве́шивать; уравнове́шивать	1. to weigh, measure, judge 2. weighing apparatus 3. graduated arm of a scale
衍 **yǎn 1.** ли́ться че́рез край **2.** обши́рный; оби́льный, изоби́льный	1. to spread out, develop 2. redundant, superfluous 3. low-lying flatland; marsh, swamp, bog
衔 **xián** ранг; зва́ние	1. to hold in the mouth 2. to harbor,\\
竹 **zhú** бамбу́к	bamboo \\ bear 3. rank, title
可 **kě 1.** мо́жно; возмо́жно **2.** подходя́щий, го́дный **3.** но, одна́ко; а	1. can, may; need to 2. to be worth/worthy 3. to approve 4. to fit, suit 5. to be estimated at 6. but, yet 7. but\\
~耻 **kěchǐ** позо́рный	shameful, disgraceful \\8. actually
~惜 **kěxī** жаль, к сожале́нию; досто́йный сожале́ния	unfortunately, it's a pity!

可怕 **kěpà** стра́шно; стра́ш-	fearful, terrible
ный	-
~靠 **kěkào** надёжный, вéр-	reliable, trustworthy
ный	-
~笑 **kěxiào** смешнóй	ridiculous, funny
~恨 **kěhèn** ненави́стный	hateful, detestable //3. is indeed
~是 **kěshì** но, однáко	1. but, yet, however 2. Is it that...? //
~爱 **kě'ài** ми́лый, слáвный	lovable, likeable, lovely
~能 **kěnéng** возмóжный;	possible, probable; probably, maybe;
возмóжно, мóжет быть	possibility
~能性 **kěnéngxìng** возмóж-	possibility
ность	- //not bad
~以 **kěyǐ** мóжно; мочь	1. can, may 2. passable, pretty good,//
~怜 **kělián** жáлкий	1. pitiable, poor 2. meager, wretched\\
何 **hé** как?; какóй?; где?; ку-	who?, what?, why?, how? \\3. to have\\
дá?; почемý?	- \\pity on
~处 **héchù** где?, в какóм	where?
мéсте?	-
~必 **hébì** зачéм?, к чемý?	why must...?; there is no need
荷 **hé** лóтос	lotus
阿 **ā** *фон. знак*	(prefix used familiarly before names)
啊 **ā** *межд. удивления, удов-*	(interj. indicating elation)
летворения	-
~ **a** *частица воскл., вопр.*	(part. used as phrase suf. in: 1. enum-
и побуд. предложений	eration 2. exclamation 3. impatience,\\
河 **hé** рекá	1. river 2. Yellow River \\confirmation)
~岸 **hé'àn** бéрег реки́	river bank
哥 **gē** стáрший брат	1. (elder) brother 2. brothers, boys
~哥 **gēge** *см.* 哥	elder brother
奇 **qí** изумля́ться, удивля́ть-	1. strange, queer, rare 2. extremely
ся; удиви́тельный, необык-	-
новéнный	-
~怪 **qíguài** удивля́ться; уди-	1. strange, odd, amazing 2. amazed
ви́тельный	-
~异 **qíyì** необы́чный, стрáн-	strange, queer, bizarre, odd
ный	-
~迹 **qíjì** чýдо	miracle, wonder, marvel
骑 **qí** éхать верхóм	to ride/sit astride; cavalry; cavalryman
~马 **qímǎ** éхать верхóм *(на*	to ride (horseback)
лошади)	-
~兵 **qíbīng** кавалéрия; ка-	cavalryman; cavalry
валери́ст	-
椅:~子 **yǐz** стул	chair
寄 **jì** **1.** посылáть; пересы-	1. to send, mail, post 2. to entrust, de-

ла́ть 2. поруча́ть, доверя́ть	posit, place 3. to lodge at 4. to depend on, attach oneself to 5. foster,\\ \\adopted
寄生虫 **jìshēngchóng** парази́т	parasite
～托 **jìtuō** 1. поруча́ть 2. полага́ться	1. to entrust to the care of 2. to place (hope/etc.) on
予 **yǔ** предоставля́ть, дава́ть; жа́ловать	to give
～以 **yǔyǐ** дава́ть, предоставля́ть	to give, grant
野 **yě** 1. ди́кий; ва́рварский 2. по́ле; пусты́рь; захолу́стье; за́городный; полево́й	1. wild, undomesticated; boorish, rude 2. open country 3. limits, bounds 4. people not in power 5. extremely
～兽 **yěshòu** зверь; хи́щник	wild animal
～营 **yěyíng** ла́герь	camp, bivouac
～外 **yěwài** за го́родом; в полевы́х усло́виях	open country, field
～战 **yězhàn** *воен.* полево́й	field operations, battle
～心 **yěxīn** а́лчность; кова́рные за́мыслы, а́лчные устремле́ния	wild ambition, careerism
～蛮 **yěmán** ва́рварство; ди́кий; ва́рварский, бесчелове́чный	1. uncivilized, savage 2. barbarous, cruel
舒 **shū** 1. расправля́ть; растя́гивать 2. споко́йный; медли́тельный 3. удо́бный	1. to open up, relax, unfold 2. to be relaxed/leisurely
～服 **shūfu** удо́бно; прия́тно; удо́бный, ую́тный; 不舒服 нездоро́виться	1. comfortable 2. well
序 **xù** 1. после́довательность, поря́док 2. предисло́вие	1. order, sequence 2. preface 3. village school 4. introductory, initial 5. to arrange in order
～列 **xùliè** строй; поря́док	1. alignment, array 2. order, sequence,\\ \\succession
矛 **máo** пи́ка; копьё	lance, pike, spear
～盾 **máodùn** противоре́чия	contradictory; contradiction
～头 **máotóu** остриё	spearhead
了 **liǎo** 1. зако́нчить 2. поня́ть, уясни́ть 3. *гл. суф. возможности или невозможности совершения действия*	1. to understand, know clearly 2. to end, finish, settle, dispose of 3. entirely 4. (suf. used with *de* and *bu* to indicate possibility)
～ **liào** обозрева́ть, наблюда́ть	to inspect, examine, look at closely

了 疗 子 仔 好 存 荐 游

了 **le** *гл. суф. завершённого вида*	1. (v. suf. indicating completed action) 2. (part. indicating new situation)
～望 **liàowàng** наблюда́ть, смотре́ть вдаль	to watch
～解 **liǎojiě** поня́ть, уясни́ть	1. to understand, comprehend 2. to find out, acquaint oneself with
～不得 **liǎobude** 1. пло́хо де́ло!, беда́! 2. невероя́тный, порази́тельный	1. terrific, extraordinary 2. terrible, awful
～不起 **liǎobuqǐ** изуми́тельный; невероя́тный	amazing, terrific, extraordinary
疗: ～养院 **liáoyǎngyuàn** санато́рий	sanatorium, convalescent hospital/home
子 **zǐ** 1. сын; де́ти 2. семена́; плод; я́йца *(насекомых)* 3. *суф. имён сущ.*	1. son, child, offspring 2. person 3. seed 4. egg 5. copper (coin) 6. young, tender, small 7. cartridge
～弹 **zǐdàn** патро́н; пу́ля	bullet, cartridge
仔: ～细 **zǐxì** тща́тельный; аккура́тный	1. to be careful, look out 2. careful, attentive 3. frugal, economical
好 **hǎo** 1. хоро́ший; хорошо́ 2. дру́жественный, ми́рный 3. удо́бный; удо́бно 4. весьма́; о́чень 5. *гл. суф. результата действия*	1. good 2. easy to 3. good to 4. quite, very 5. so as to, so that 6. may, can, should 7. (suf. indicating completion) 8. (prefix indicating disapproval)
～ **hào** люби́ть; увлека́ться	1. to like, be fond of 2. to be liable to
～看 **hǎokàn** краси́вый	1. good-looking, nice 2. interesting, delightful 3. honored
～听 **hǎotīng** благозву́чный	pleasant to hear
～久 **hǎojiǔ** давно́	for a long time
～象 **hǎoxiàng** как бу́дто; похо́же, что	to seem, be like
～处 **hǎochu** 1. досто́инство, преиму́щество 2. по́льза, вы́года	1. benefit, advantage, good 2. gain, profit
～战 **hàozhàn** вои́нственный	bellicose, warlike
～吃 **hǎochī** вку́сный	tasty, good to eat
～意 **hǎoyì** дру́жеские чу́вства; доброта́	good intentions, kindness
存 **cún** 1. существова́ть 2. храни́ть, сберега́ть	1. to exist, live 2. to store, keep 3. to collect, gather 4. to deposit 5. to leave with 6. to retain
～在 **cúnzài** существова́ть; существова́ние, бытие́	to exist, be
荐 **jiàn** рекомендова́ть, представля́ть	1. to recommend 2. grass, straw; straw mat
游 **yóu** 1. пла́вать 2. броди́ть, кочева́ть	1. to swim, float 2. to travel, rove 3. reaches of a river

游击队 **yóujīduì** партизáнский отря́д	guerrilla force
～击战 **yóujīzhàn** партизáнская войнá	guerrilla warfare
～行 **yóuxíng** демонстрáция; шéствие	to parade, march, demonstrate
～泳 **yóuyǒng** плáвать	to swim
～泳池 **yóuyǒngchí** плáвательный бассéйн	swimming pool
享 **xiǎng** пóльзоваться	to enjoy
～有 **xiǎngyǒu** обладáть, пóльзоваться	to enjoy (rights, etc.)
～用 **xiǎngyòng** пóльзоваться, имéть в распоряжéнии	to enjoy (use of)
～受 **xiǎngshòu** наслаждáться; пóльзоваться	to enjoy
厚 **hòu 1.** толщинá; тóлстый **2.** щéдрый, обúльный	1. thick 2. deep, profound 3. kind, magnanimous 4. large, generous 5. rich in\\
～度 **hòudù** толщинá	thickness \\flavor 6. to favor, stress
字 **zì** иерóглиф; бу́ква; слóво	1. character, script, writing 2. word 3. receipt, contract 4. courtesy name
～母 **zìmǔ** бу́квы; алфавúт	letter of an alphabet, letter
～典 **zìdiǎn** словáрь *(иероглифов)*	dictionary, thesaurus
脖: ～子 **bóz** шéя	neck
学 **xué 1.** учúться; учéние; нау́ка **2.** шкóла; учúлище; учéбное заведéние	1. to study, learn; learning, knowledge, subject of study, branch of learning 2. school, college 3. to imitate, mimic
～生 **xuésheng** студéнт; учáщийся, ученúк	1. student, pupil 2. disciple, follower
～位 **xuéwèi** учёная стéпень	academic degree, degree
～者 **xuézhě** учёный	scholar, learned person
～年 **xuénián** учéбный год	school/academic year
～制 **xuézhì** систéма обучéния (образовáния)	1. educational/school system 2. length of schooling //amples 2. to learn well
～好 **xuéhǎo** вы́учить(ся)	1. to learn from or emulate good ex-//
～问 **xuéwen** знáния, эрудúция	learning, scholarship, knowledge
～习 **xuéxí** учúться; учёба	to study, learn, emulate
～期 **xuéqī** учéбный семéстр	school term, semester
～徒 **xuétú 1.** ученúк, подмастéрье **2.** послéдователь	apprentice, trainee
～校 **xuéxiào** *см.* 学 2	school, educational institution

学院 **xuéyuàn** институ́т, акаде́мия	college, academy, institute
～说 **xuéshuō** уче́ние, тео́рия	theory, doctrine
～员 **xuéyuán** слу́шатель, курса́нт	1. member of an institution of learning 2. (court.) student
～会 **xuéhuì** 1. научи́ться, вы́учиться 2. нау́чное о́бщество	1. learned society, (scholarly) association 2. to learn, master
孕 **yùn** забере́менеть	to be pregnant; pregnancy
李 **lǐ** сли́ва	plum
季 **jì** сезо́н, вре́мя го́да; пери́од	1. season 2. yield in one season 3. 4th/ youngest (brother) 4. last month of\\
～节 **jìjié** вре́мя го́да, сезо́н; сезо́нный	season \\(a season)
～度 **jìdù** кварта́л *(четверть года)*; кварта́льный	quarter of a year //war; captive
俘 **fú** брать в плен; пле́нный	to capture, take prisoner; prisoner of//
～虏 **fúlǔ** пле́нный	to capture, take prisoner; captive,\\
～获 **fúhuò** захва́тывать в плен	to capture \\P.O.W.
浮 **fú** 1. пла́вать 2. легкомы́сленный, пусто́й	1. to float 2. to exceed, be superfluous 3. flighty, unstable 4. temporary 5.\\
～桥 **fúqiáo** понто́нный мост	pontoon \\hollow, inflated 6. excessive
～水 **fúshuǐ** пла́вать	to swim //decimeter)
寸 **cùn** цунь, вершо́к	1. very little/short 2. (Ch. inch, = 1/3//
封 **fēng** 1. запеча́тывать *(конверт)* 2. блоки́ровать 3. конве́рт	1. to seal 2. to bank (a fire) 3. to confer (a title/territory/etc.) upon 4. envelope 5. (M. for letters)
～面 **fēngmiàn** 1. обло́жка 2. лицева́я сторона́ конве́рта	1. title page of a threadbound book 2. front and back cover of a book 3. front cover
～闭 **fēngbì** опеча́тывать; запира́ть	1. to seal 2. to seal off, close
～建 **fēngjiàn** феода́льный	1. system of enforcement 2. feudalism,\\
～建主义 **fēngjiànzhǔyì** феодали́зм	feudalism \\feudal
～锁 **fēngsuǒ** блоки́ровать; блока́да	to blockade, block, seal off
厨 **chú** стря́пать; ку́хня	cabinet, closet
～师 **chúshī** шеф-по́вар; по́вар	cook, chef
～房 **chúfáng** ку́хня	kitchen
橱: ～窗 **chúchuāng** витри́на	show/display window; showcase
时 **shí** 1. вре́мя; срок; пери́-	1. time (when) 2. period, season 3. hour,

од; эпо́ха **2.** час **3.** посто-янно, всегда́ **4.** совреме́нный; мо́дный **5.** *конечное сл. грам. конструкции времени*	o'clock 4. opportunity, chance 5. current, present 6. now and then, occasionally, from time to time
时评 **shípíng** фельето́н; статья́ на зло́бу дня	news commentaries
~刻 **shíkè** моме́нт; вре́мя	time, hour, moment; constantly, always
~刻表 **shíkèbiǎo** расписа́ние	timetable, schedule
~事 **shíshì** теку́щие дела́ (собы́тия)	current event/affair
~间 **shíjiān** вре́мя; промежу́ток вре́мени	time, duration
~期 **shíqī** пери́од, срок	period (of time)
~常 **shícháng** ча́сто; постоя́нно	often, frequently
~局 **shíjú** совреме́нное положе́ние; теку́щий моме́нт	current political situation
~候 **shíhou** вре́мя	1. (duration of) time 2. moment, (a point in) time
~代 **shídài** эпо́ха; пери́од	1. times, age, era, epoch 2. period in one's life
~髦 **shímáo** мо́да; мо́дный	fashionable, in vogue
~机 **shíjī** моме́нт; слу́чай	opportunity, opportune moment
付 **fù 1.** вруча́ть **2.** доверя́ть, поруча́ть **3.** плати́ть	1. to hand/turn over to, commit to 2. to pay
~款 **fùkuǎn** плати́ть; платёж	to pay a sum of money
附 **fù 1.** прилага́ть; присоединя́ть; приложе́ние; дополни́тельный **2.** прилега́ть, примыка́ть	1. to add, attach, enclose 2. to get close to, be near 3. to agree to
~加 **fùjiā** добавля́ть, дополня́ть; дополни́тельный	to add, attach; additional, attached, appended
~件 **fùjiàn** приложе́ние	1. appendix, annex 2. enclosure 3. accessories, attachments
~庸 **fùyōng** прида́ток; васса́льный, подчинённый	1. dependency, vassal state 2. appendage
~属 **fùshǔ 1.** подчинённый, подопе́чный **2.** принадлежа́ть	subsidiary, auxiliary, attached, affiliated
~录 **fùlù** приложе́ние, дополне́ние	appendix
~近 **fùjìn** окре́стности; о́коло, вблизи́	nearby, neighboring; vicinity
府 **fǔ 1.** прису́тственное мес-	1. seat of government, government office 2. official residence/mansion

то; канцеля́рия **2.** рези-	-
де́нция	-
俯 **fǔ 1.** смотре́ть вниз	to bow (one's head)
2. пики́ровать	-
~首 **fǔshǒu** поко́рно; подо-	to bow one's head (in submission)
бостра́стно	-
符 **fú 1.** совпада́ть, сходи́ть-	1. to tally/accord with; tally 2. symbol
ся **2.** усло́вный знак; аму-	3. magic figures
ле́т	-
~合 **fúhé** совпада́ть; отве-	to accord/tally with, conform to; coin-
ча́ть, соотве́тствовать	cidence
~号 **fúhào** зна́ки препина́-	1. symbol, mark 2. insignia
ния	- //neath 2. to set off, contrast with
衬 **chèn** ни́жнее бельё	1. to line; lining; to place sth. under-//
~衫 **chènshān** соро́чка	shirt
耐 **nài** терпе́ть, переноси́ть;	1. to bear, endure 2. talent
упо́рный	-
~性 **nàixìng** терпе́ние	patience, endurance
~力 **nàili** выно́сливость	endurance, stamina
~劳 **nàiláo** уси́дчивый; при-	diligent, able to stand hard work
вы́чный к труду́	-
~火砖 **nàihuǒzhuān** огне-	firebrick
упо́рный кирпи́ч	-
~心 **nàixīn** выно́сливость,	patient; patience, endurance
терпе́ние	-
射 **shè 1.** стреля́ть **2.** впры́с-	1. to shoot, fire 2. to emit, discharge 3.
кивать **3.** излуча́ть	to allude to, insinuate
~击 **shèjī** стреля́ть, вести́	to shoot, fire; fire
ого́нь	-
谢 **xiè 1.** благодари́ть **2.** от-	1. to thank 2. to decline 3. to apologize
ка́зываться; отклоня́ть	4. to wither (of flowers/leaves/etc.)
~谢 **xièxie** благодарю́!, спа-	thank you
си́бо!	-
~意 **xièyì** благода́рность,	gratitude
призна́тельность	-
村 **cūn** дере́вня; село́, селе́-	village, hamlet; rustic; boorish
ние	-
~庄 **cūnzhuāng** *см.* 村	village, hamlet
~落 **cūnluò** посёлок; дере́в-	village, hamlet
ня	-
对 **duì 1.** противостоя́ть;	1. to answer, reply 2. to treat 3. to be
про́тив, напро́тив **2.** отно-	trained on 4. to suit, agree 5. to com-
си́ться к; по отноше́нию к	pare, check 6. to set, adjust 7. to mix,
3. ве́рно, пра́вильно **4.** со-	add 8. to divide into halves 9. mu-

поставля́ть, сверя́ть **5.** па́ра; па́рный **6.** *предлог направления действия:* 我对他说 я сказа́л ему́	tual 10. opposite 11. right, correct 12. by 13. (M. for pair/couple)
对立 **duìlì** противостоя́ть; противопоставля́ть; антагони́зм	to oppose, set sth. against, be antagonistic to; opposition, contrast
~准 **duìzhǔn** прице́ливаться	to aim at; alignment
~话 **duìhuà** диало́г	to (carry on) a dialogue; dialogue
~面 **duìmiàn** противополо́жная сторона́; напро́тив	1. (the) opposite 2. right in front 3. face-to-face
~外 **duìwài** вне́шний *(о политике, торговле)*	external, foreign, concerned with the outside world
~外政策 **duìwài zhèngcè** вне́шняя поли́тика	foreign policy/politics
~了 **duìle** ве́рно!, пра́вильно!	Right!, Correct!
~付 **duìfu** реаги́ровать; применя́ть ме́ры	1. to deal/cope with, counter, tackle 2. to make do
~待 **duìdài** относи́ться к; обраща́ться с	to treat, approach, handle
~等地 **duìděngdi** на парите́тных нача́лах	on a par (with), on an equal footing (with)
~于 **duìyú** по отноше́нию к; относи́тельно	(in regard) to, toward, at, for
~手 **duìshǒu** партнёр	1. opponent, adversary 2. match
~方 **duìfāng** **1.** противополо́жная сторона́ **2.** проти́вник	other side/party
~换 **duìhuàn** обменя́ться; обме́н	to exchange, convert
~象 **duìxiàng** **1.** объе́кт **2.** партнёр	1. target, object 2. boy/girl friend
~比 **duìbǐ** сопоставля́ть; соотноше́ние	1. to contrast 2. ratio, correlation
~抗 **duìkàng** **1.** сопротивля́ться **2.** антагони́зм	to resist, oppose; antagonism, confrontation
~不住(起) **duìbuzhù(qǐ)** извини́те!, винова́т!	1. to let sb. down, be unfair to 2. I'm sorry, excuse me
~称 **duìchèng** симметри́я; симметри́чный	symmetry, symmetrical
~照 **duìzhào** сопоставля́ть, сра́внивать; сравне́ние	to contrast, compare; contrast, comparison
树 **shù** **1.** де́рево **2.** сажа́ть,	1. tree 2. to plant, cultivate 3. to set// //up, establish, uphold

выра́щивать 3. воздвига́ть, ста́вить	-
树立 **shùlì** сооружа́ть; ста́вить	to set up, establish
～木 **shùmù** дере́вья; де́рево	to plant trees; trees
～林 **shùlín** лес	woods, grove
～根 **shùgēn** ко́рень де́рева	tree roots
讨 **tǎo** 1. нака́зывать; кара́ть 2. идти́ войно́й 3. допы́тываться 4. тре́бовать	1. in demand, dun 2. to discuss, study 3. to marry (a woman) 4. to incur 5. to denounce, condemn 6. to deal with\\ \\militarily
～价 **tǎojià** торгова́ться	to ask/name a price
～伐 **tǎofá** идти́ войно́й; кара́тельная экспеди́ция	to send a punitive expedition
～论 **tǎolùn** обсужда́ть; обсужде́ние	to discuss, talk over
寿 **shòu** долголе́тие; во́зраст	1. longevity 2. life, age 3. birthday 4. sth. used for burial
～命 **shòumìng** 1. долголе́тие; долгове́чность 2. судьба́	life
铸 **zhù** отлива́ть; литьё	to cast, found
筹 **chóu** рассчи́тывать, стро́ить пла́ны	1. to prepare, plan 2. chip, counter
～备 **chóubèi** подготовля́ть; подготови́тельный	to prepare, arrange, plan
碍 **ài** меша́ть, препя́тствовать; загора́живать	to hinder, obstruct, be in the way of
得 **dé** 1. приобрета́ть, получа́ть 2. зака́нчивать, заверша́ть 3. разреша́ется, мо́жно 4. хва́тит, ла́дно	1. to get 2. to result in 3. to be fit/proper 4. to be satisfied 5. to be finished
～ **de** 1. *показатель обстоятельства, следующего за сказ.:* 他跑得快 он бежи́т бы́стро 2. *гл. инфикс, выражающий возможность совершения действия:* 他买得起 он в состоя́нии купи́ть	(in v. constructions, indicates able to, possibility of, being in a condition to do sth.)
～ **děi** ну́жно, сле́дует	(coll.) 1. need 2. should be
～到 **dédào** получи́ть, приобрести́	to succeed in obtaining, gain, receive
～了 **déle** 1. доста́л, получи́л 2. дово́льно!, хва́тит!	Stop it!, Hold it!, Enough!

得逞 **déchěng** добиться успеха; удалось!	to prevail
寺 **sì** буддийский храм (монастырь)	temple
待 **dài** 1. ждать, ожидать 2. обходиться с; принимать *(гостей)*	1. to treat, entertain 2. to wait for 3. to need 4. pending
~ **dāi** задерживаться, находиться	(coll.) to stay
~遇 **dàiyù** 1. уход за; обхождение 2. условия (труда); обеспечение *(материальное)*	treatment (salary/etc.)
特 **tè** 1. специальный, особый 2. обособленный 3. нарочно, намеренно	1. special, particular, exceptional 2. spy, secret agent
~征 **tèzhēng** особенность, характерная черта	characteristic, feature, trait
~种 **tèzhǒng** особый, особого сорта	special type, particular kind
~命 **tèmìng** чрезвычайный *(о дип. представителях)*	special command
~命全权大使 **tèmìng quánquán dàshi** чрезвычайный и полномочный посол	ambassador extraordinary and plenipotentiary
~别 **tèbié** особый; чрезвычайный; в особенности	special, particular
~号 **tèhào** знак качества	extra-large size
~务 **tèwu** шпион; агент	special/secret agent, spy
~殊 **tèshū** особый, своеобразный	special, particular, peculiar
~权 **tèquán** привилегии	privilege, prerogative
~意 **tèyì** намеренно, специально	purposely, specially
~点 **tèdiǎn** особенность, своеобразие	characteristic, peculiarity, trait
持 **chí** 1. держать *(в руке)* 2. удержаться, устоять 3. поддерживать	1. to hold, grasp 2. to support, maintain 3. to manage, run 4. to oppose
~久 **chíjiǔ** длительный, затяжной; стойкий	lasting, protracted
诗 **shī** стихи; стихотворение; поэзия	poetry, verse, poem
~人 **shīrén** поэт	poet

等寻尊蹲守博搏

等 **děng 1.** сте́пень; класс; сорт **2.** ждать, ожида́ть **3.** ра́вный, одина́ковый **4.** та-ки́е как	1. class, grade 2. to be equal 3. to wait 4. and so on
～价 **děngjià** эквивале́нт; равноце́нный, равнозна́чный	equal (in) value
～待 **děngdài** ждать, ожида́ть	to wait for, await
～等 **děngděng** и так да́лее	and so on
～于 **děngyú** равня́ться *чему*; равно́	to be equivalent/tantamount to
～候 **děnghòu** ожида́ть	to wait, await, expect
～级 **děngjí** сте́пень; чин; ранг; ступе́нь	1. grade, rank 2. order and degree, social status
寻 **xún** иска́ть, разы́скивать; доискиваться	1. to search, seek 2. ordinary
～查 **xúnchá** изуча́ть, иска́ть	to make a tour of inspection, make one's rounds
～访 **xúnfǎng** навести́ть	to try to locate, inquire about
～求 **xúnqiú** иска́ть; добива́ться	to seek, explore
～找 **xúnzhǎo** иска́ть; по́иск	to seek, look for //your 3. senior
尊 **zūn** почита́ть; уважа́ть	1. to respect, venerate 2. (court.)//
～重 **zūnzhòng** чтить, уважа́ть	to respect, value, esteem
～敬(崇) **zūnjìng(chóng)** уважа́ть; уваже́ние	respect, honor, esteem
蹲 **dūn** сиде́ть на ко́рточках	1. to squat on the heels 2. to stay
守 **shǒu 1.** защища́ть; охраня́ть **2.** сохраня́ть; уде́рживать	1. to guard, defend 2. to keep watch 3. to observe, abide by 4. to be close to
～卫 **shǒuwèi** карау́лить, охраня́ть	to guard, defend
～住 **shǒuzhù** уде́рживать, защища́ть	to hold, retain; to defend, protect
博 **bó 1.** широ́кий, обши́рный **2.** учёность; зна́ющий	1. abundant, plentiful 2. to win, gain //or craft
～士 **bóshì** до́ктор нау́к	1. Ph.D. 2. (coll.) master of any trade//
～物馆 **bówùguǎn** музе́й	museum
～览会 **bólǎnhuì** вы́ставка	exhibition, trade fair
搏 **bó 1.** бить руко́й **2.** подра́ться	1. to wrestle, fight 2. to pounce on 3. to pulsate, beat

搏斗 **bódòu** схвáтка; стычка	to wrestle, fight
膊 **bó** плечó; рукá *(выше локтя)*	arm
薄 **báo** тóнкий; жи́дкий; слáбый	1. thin, flimsy 2. weak, light 3. lacking in warmth, cold 4. infertile
~ **bó** слáбый; жи́дкий	1. thin, flimsy 2. weak, light 3. lacking in warmth, cold, infertile
~弱 **bóruò** слáбый, нéмощный	frail, weak
簿 **bù** счётная книга; журнáл учёта; реéстр	book
将 **jiāng** 1. в бýдущем; *показатель буд. времени* 2. *показатель прямого доп., стоящего перед сказ.*	1. to take 2. to be about to 3. to handle 4. to checkmate 5. (prep., introducing object of main v.) 6. just, a short time ago 7. partly...partly...
~ **jiàng** генерáл; полковóдец	1. general 2. commander-in-chief 3. to command, lead 4. king (chess piece)
~官(军) **jiàngguān(jūn)** генерáлы	general-rank military officers
~来 **jiānglái** бýдущий; в бýдущем	(the) future; in the future
~要 **jiāngyào** в бýдущем; вот-вóт	going to, will, shall
夺 **duó** лиши́ть; отня́ть; захвати́ть; огрáбить	1. to take by force 2. to force one's way 3. to contend for 4. to deprive
~取 **duóqǔ** *см.* 夺	1. to capture, seize, wrest 2. to strive
~权 **duóquán** лиши́ть прав	to seize power
辱 **rǔ** позóрить; позóр; стыд	1. to insult; insult, disgrace 2. court. to be honored
褥 **rù** матрáц, тюфя́к	cotton-padded mattress
导 **dǎo** руководи́ть; вести́	1. to guide, lead, instruct 2. to transmit
~弹 **dǎodàn** управля́емая ракéта	1. guided missile 2. (slang) to cause trouble
~师 **dǎoshī** учи́тель, настáвник	1. tutor, teacher, supervisor 2. leader in a cause
~火线 **dǎohuǒxiàn** фити́ль	1. (blasting) fuse 2. direct cause
~演 **dǎoyǎn** режиссёр	to direct (a film/play/etc.); director
才 **cái** 1. спосóбности; даровáние, талáнт 2. тóлько что; тóлько тогдá	1. talent, ability 2. then and only then 3. just now 4. only (before a number)
~能 **cáinéng** спосóбность; талáнт	ability, talent
材 **cái** веществó; сырьё; материáл	1. timber 2. material 3. ability, talent 4. capable person
~料 **cáiliào** 1. материáл,	1. material 2. data 3. ingredients, stuff

搏膊薄簿将夺辱褥导才材

сырьё **2.** да́нные; исто́чники	-
财 **cái** 1. це́нности; сре́дства, фина́нсы **2.** со́бственность	wealth, riches
～产 **cáichǎn** со́бственность, иму́щество	property
～物 **cáiwù** иму́щество; со́бственность	property, belongings
～政 **cáizhèng** фина́нсы; фина́нсовый	finance
～源 **cáiyuán** ресу́рсы	financial resources, sources of revenue
于 **yú** *предлог лит. языка* к; от; в; из; с; для	1. in, at, to, from, out of, by 2. than
～是 **yúshì** таки́м о́бразом; в тако́м слу́чае	thereupon, hence, consequently, as a result
～此 **yúcì** здесь; в э́том	here, at this point, about this/it; in this
宇 **yú** вселе́нная; не́бо; мир; ко́смос; мирово́й; косми́ческий	1. eaves 2. house 3. space, universe, world
～宙 **yǔzhòu** *см.* 宇	universe, cosmos
～宙船 **yǔzhòuchuán** косми́ческий кора́бль	spaceship, spacecraft
芋 **yù** сла́дкий карто́фель, бата́т	1. taro 2. tuber crops
呼 **hū** 1. крича́ть, звать; обраща́ться **2.** дыша́ть; дыха́ние	1. to breathe out, exhale 2. to shout, cry out, call
～应 **hūyìng** отозва́ться, откли́кнуться	to echo; to work in concert with
～声 **hūshēng** во́зглас, восклица́ние	cry; voice
～号 **hūhào** позывно́й сигна́л; клич	1. to wail, cry out in distress 2. (radio) call sign
～唤 **hūhuàn** призыва́ть, звать; призы́в	1. to call, shout 2. to summon
～吸 **hūxī** дыша́ть; дыха́ние	to breathe, respire
牙 **yá** 1. зуб; клык; би́вень **2.** зубе́ц; зубча́тый	1. tooth 2. ivory 3. broker
～齿 **yáchi** зу́бы	tooth
～刷 **yáshuā** зубна́я щётка	toothbrush
～粉 **yáfěn** зубно́й порошо́к	tooth powder
呀 **yā** *коне́чная части́ца вопр. и воскл. предложе́ний*	1. (interj.) ah, oh 2. (onom.) creak

芽 **yá** побéги, росткú; пóчка	bud, sprout, shoot
穿 **chuān** 1. проникáть, проходúть насквóзь 2. нанúзывать 3. надевáть, носúть *(платье)*	1. to penetrate, pierce through 2. to pass through, cross 3. to wear, put on, be dressed in
~堂 **chuāntáng** проходнáя кóмната	hallway
~通 **chuāntōng** проникнуть, пройтú насквóзь	to penetrate, go through, pass through
手 **shǒu** 1. рукá 2. держáть в рукáх 3. мáстер, знатóк	1. hand 2. person skilled in sth. 3. to hold, have in the hand
~工业 **shǒugōngyè** кустáрная промы́шленность	handicraft industry, handicraft
~帕 **shǒupà** носовóй платóк	handkerchief
~榴弹 **shǒuliúdàn** ручнáя гранáта	hand grenade
~面 **shǒumiàn** на рукáх, в рукáх	the way a person handles his/her money
~下 **shǒuxià** под рукóй; подрýчный	1. leadership 2. one's present financial condition 3. at hand 4. at the hands of
~掌 **shǒuzhǎng** ладóнь	palm
~巾 **shǒujīn** полотéнце; носовóй платóк	towel
~册 **shǒucè** 1. блокнóт 2. спрáвочник	handbook, manual
~续 **shǒuxù** процедýра; формáльности	procedure
~条 **shǒutiáo** запúска	note, memo
~术 **shǒushù** [хирургúческая] оперáция; 动手术 дéлать оперáцию	surgery
~表 **shǒubiǎo** ручны́е часы́	wristwatch
~段 **shǒuduàn** срéдство, спóсоб, приём	1. means, method 2. trick, artifice
~纸 **shǒuzhǐ** туалéтная бумáга	(coll.) toilet paper
~枪 **shǒuqiāng** пистолéт, револьвéр	pistol
~套 **shǒutào** перчáтки; рукавúцы	gloves
~法 **shǒufǎ** приёмы; искýсство, мастерствó	1. skill, technique 2. trick, gimmick
拿 **ná** 1. взять, брать	1. to hold, take 2. to seize, capture 3.//(introduces instrument or target)

芽穿手拿

拿掌撑拳摩争

2. схватить, арестовать	-
3. *перед сказ.: а) вводит*	-
инструментальное доп. вм.	-
用; *б) вводит прямое доп.*	-
вм. 把	-
拿来 **nálái** принести	to bring, fetch
~起 **náqi** поднять	to raise, lift
~去 **náqù** унести, отнести	to take/carry away/off
掌 **zhǎng** 1. ладонь; лапа 2. управлять; держать в руках	1. palm (of hand) 2. feet, pad, sole 3. shoe sole/heel 4. horseshoe
~握 **zhǎngwò** 1. овладеть; освоить 2. взять; захватить	1. to grasp, master 2. to have in the hand; to control
~管 **zhǎngguǎn** управлять; заведовать	to be in charge of
~声 **zhǎngshēng** аплодисменты	clapping, applause
撑 **chēng** поддерживать; подпора	1. to prop up, brace 2. to move with a pole 3. to maintain 4. to open, unfurl
拳 **quán** кулак	1. fist 2. boxing, pugilism 3. punch
~斗(术) **quándòu(shù)** бокс	fisticuffs, Chinese boxing
摩 **mó** 1. тереть, растирать 2. гладить (ощупывать) рукой	1. to rub, scrape, touch 2. to mull over, study
~登 **módēng** модный; новый, современный	(loan w.) modern, fashionable
~托 **mótuō** мотор	(loan w.) motor
~托化 **mótuōhuà** механизация	motorized
~擦 **mócā** 1. тереть; трение 2. конфликты	1. to rub 2. friction
争 **zhēng** 1. бороться; соперничать, соревноваться; борьба 2. спорить	1. to contend, vie 2. to argue, disagree 3. to be short of, be wanting 4. straightforward
~辩 **zhēngbiàn** спорить, диспутировать; спор	to argue, contend
~得 **zhēngdé** завоевать *(победу)*	to win, gain, get
~夺 **zhēngduó** захватить, завладеть; отнять	to vie with sb. for sth.
~端 **zhēngduān** предмет спора	conflict, dispute, controversy

争取 zhēngqu завоёвывать; боро́ться за; добива́ться — to strive/fight for
～论 zhēnglùn спо́рить; спор — to dispute, controvert
挣:～扎 zhēngzha выбива́ться из сил; аго́ния — to struggle
静 jìng неподви́жный; споко́йный; поко́й, тишина́ — still, quiet, calm
净 jìng 1. прозра́чный; чи́стый 2. очища́ть(ся) 3. по́лностью, до́чиста — 1. clean 2. net (price/etc.) 3. completely 4. only, merely, nothing but 5. (opera) painted-face role
事 shì 1. де́ло; собы́тие; происше́ствие 2. заня́тие, рабо́та — 1. matter, affair, thing, event 2. trouble, accident 3. job, work 4. responsibility, involvement 5. to wait on, serve
～业 shìyè профе́ссия; де́ло, про́мысел — 1. cause, undertaking 2. enterprise; facilities
～件 shìjiàn собы́тие; инциде́нт, слу́чай — incident, event
～情 shìqíng де́ло, обстоя́тельство; факт — affair, matter, thing, business
～物 shìwù предме́т, вещь — thing, object
～务 shìwù дела́; слу́жба — 1. work, routine 2. general affairs
～实 shìshí действи́тельность, факт — fact
～变 shìbiàn собы́тие, инциде́нт — 1. incident 2. emergency, exigency
～故 shìgù 1. ава́рия 2. инциде́нт — accident, mishap
～先 shìxiān заблаговре́менно, зара́нее — in advance, beforehand
～项 shìxiàng пункт, вопро́с; де́ло — item, matter

门

门 mén 1. воро́та; дверь 2. специа́льность, о́трасль 3. *сч. сл. для артиллерийских орудий* — 1. opening, door, gate 2. valve, switch 3. knack, way to do sth. 4. family, house 5. sect, school 6. class, category; phylum 7. (M. for courses,\\ \\branches of sci.)
～口 ménkǒu вход; подъе́зд — entrance, doorway
～牌 ménpái но́мер до́ма — 1. (house) no. plate 2. house no.
～诊部 ménzhěnbù амбулато́рия — clinic, outpatient/ambulatory department
～户 ménhù 1. две́ри, вход 2. дом, семья́; двор — 1. door 2. strategic gateway 3. faction, sect 4. family status

们 **men** *суф. мн. ч. личных мест. и сущ., например:* 同志们 товáрищи; 他们 они	(suf. pluralizer after pronouns and nouns of persons)
闰: ～年 **rùnnián** високóсный год	leap (intercalary) year
～月 **rùnyuè** добáвочный мéсяц *(по лунному календарю)*	additional (intercalary) (13th) month (in the lunar calendar)
润 **rùn** смáчивать, увлажнять	1. moist 2. soft to the touch 3. to lubricate, moisten 4. to embellish
问 **wèn** спрáшивать	1. to ask; inquire after 2. to examine
～答 **wèndá** диалóг	to question; questions and answers
～好 **wènhǎo** здорóваться; передавáть привéт	to send one's regards to, say hello to
～事处 **wènshìchù** спрáвочное бюрó	information desk
～候 *см.* ～好	to send one's regards/respects to
～题 **wèntí** вопрóс, проблéма; 成问题 представлять собóй проблéму; сомнúтельный	1. question, problem, issue 2. trouble, mishap
阔 **kuò 1.** простóрный, ширóкий **2.** щéдрый; роскóшный	1. wide, broad, vast 2. wealthy, rich 3. separated, living apart
～大 **kuòdà** обшúрный, большóй, расшúренный	capacious, spacious, broad (space/viewpoint)
～气 **kuòqì** рóскошь	luxurious, extravagant, lavish
阁 **gé 1.** дворéц; палáты **2.** правúтельственный óрган; кабинéт минúстров	1. pavilion 2. woman's chamber 3. cabinet 4. rack, shelf
～下 **géxià** Вáше превосходúтельство; Вы	-
间 **jiān 1.** мéжду; промежýток **2.** помещéние **3.** *послелог* в течéние; мéжду; средú **4.** *сч. сл. для комнат*	1. room 2. locality 3. duration of time 4. (M. for rooms)
～ **jiàn 1.** разделять, разобщáть **2.** развéдывать, шпиóнить	1. to separate 2. to thin out (seedlings) 3. to sow discord 4. space between, opening 5. crevice 6. mixed
～断 **jiànduàn** прерывáть (-ся); оборвáть; оборвáться	to be disconnected/interrupted

间隔 **jiàngé** промежу́ток, интерва́л	interval, intermission; to be separated
～谍 **jiàndié** шпио́н; аге́нт; агенту́рный	spy
～隙 **jiànxì** промежу́ток, простра́нство	1. interval, gap, space 2. (mach.) clearance 3. animosity, discord
～接 **jiànjiē** ко́свенно; ко́свенный	indirect, secondhand
简 **jiǎn** 1. просто́й; кра́ткий, сокращённый 2. небре́жный, хала́тный	1. simple, simplified, brief 2. letter 3. bamboo slips 4. to select, choose
～短 **jiǎnduǎn** сокраща́ть; кра́ткий	brief
～直 **jiǎnzhí** пря́мо-таки; по́просту	1. simply, really 2. straightforward
～略 **jiǎnlüè** сокращённый; резюме́	simple, brief, sketchy
～单 **jiǎndān** просто́й; упрощённый; про́сто	1. simple, uncomplicated 2. (derog). commonplace, ordinary 3. casual, over-\\
～便(易) **jiǎnbiàn(yì)** упроща́ть; облегчённый	simple and convenient, handy \\simplified
～化 **jiǎnhuà** упроща́ть; упроще́ние	to simplify
～要 **jiǎnyào** сокращённый, сжа́тый; резюме́	concise and to the point
闸 **zhá** шлюз	1. sluice gate 2. (car) brake 3. switch
闻 **wén** 1. слы́шать 2. изве́стия; слу́хи 3. обоня́ть	1. to hear 2. to smell 3. news, story 4. repugnance 5. famous, well-known
～人 **wénrén** изве́стное лицо́	well-known figure, famous person
闭 **bì** 1. закрыва́ть, замыка́ть 2. прегражда́ть; блоки́ровать	1. to shut, close 2. to stop up 3. to obstruct
～幕 **bìmù** закры́ть(ся) *(о собрании, выставке)*	1. curtain falls 2. to close, conclude
～关 **bìguān** закры́ть, замкну́ть	closed off; closed-door (e.g., policy)
闹 **nào** 1. шуме́ть, сканда́лить; шу́мный, оживлённый 2. разрази́ться, разыгра́ться *(о событиях)*	1. to make a noise 2. to stir up trouble 3. to vent anger 4. to suffer from, be troubled by 5. to go in for, do, make 6. noisy
～钟 **nàozhōng** буди́льник	alarm clock
～乱 **nàoluàn** сканда́лить; создава́ть беспоря́дки	1. to cause trouble //flash 6. flash //a mishap 4. to leave behind 5. to//
闪 **shǎn** сверка́ть; мелька́ть	1. to dodge 2. to twist, sprain 3. to have//

闪电 **shǎndiàn** сверка́ть; мгнове́нный, молниено́сный	1. lightning; to flash lightning
闲 **xián** пра́здный; свобо́дный; беззабо́тный	1. not busy, unoccupied 2. not in use 3. idle 4. leisure, spare time
阅 **yuè 1**. чита́ть **2**. инспекти́ровать, осма́тривать; смотр	1. to read, go over 2. to review, inspect 3. to experience, go through
～兵 **yuèbīng** пара́д, смотр	to review troops //closed
闷 **mèn** скуча́ть, уныва́ть	1. bored, depressed 2. sealed, tightly//
～ **mēn** ду́шный; духота́	1. muffled 2. stuffy 3. to cover, seal
习 **xí 1**. упражня́ться, практикова́ться **2**. привы́чка, обы́чай	1. practice, exercise, review 2. to get accustomed to 3. habit, custom
～惯 **xíguàn** привы́чка, на́вык; привы́кнуть	habit, custom; to be accustomed/used to
司 **sī 1**. заве́довать, управля́ть **2**. управле́ние; ве́домство	1. to take charge of, attend to, manage 2. department (of a ministry)
～机 **sījī** шофёр; машинист	driver
～法 **sīfǎ** юсти́ция	administration of justice, judicature
～令 **sīlìng** кома́ндующий	commander, commanding officer
～令部 **sīlìngbù** штаб	headquarters, command
饲 **sì** корми́ть; выра́щивать, выка́рмливать	1. to raise, rear 2. forage, fodder, feed
～料 **sìliào** корм, фура́ж	forage, fodder, feed
词 **cí** сло́во; те́рмин	1. word, term 2. speech, statement
～汇 **cíhuì** ле́ксика, слова́рный соста́в	vocabulary, words and phrases
～典 **cídiǎn** слова́рь	dictionary
羽 **yǔ** пе́рья, опере́ние	1. feather, plume 2. wing
～毛球 **yǔmáoqiú** бадминто́н	1. badminton 2. shuttlecock
翻 **fān 1**. перевора́чивать (-ся); опроки́дывать(ся) **2**. переводи́ть; расшифро́вывать	1. to turn over (to) 2. to cross, get over 3. to rummage, search 4. to translate 5. to reverse 6. to multiply 7. to fall out, break up
～新 **fānxīn** обнови́ть(ся); обновле́ние	to renovate, recondition
～译 **fānyì** переводи́ть; перево́д; перево́дчик	to translate, interpret; translator, interpreter
～身 **fānshēn** освободи́ться; нача́ть но́вую жизнь	1. to turn over 2. to free oneself, stand up
～案 **fān'àn** реабилита́ция	to reverse a verdict

翔 **xiáng** пари́ть, кружи́ть	to circle in the air
扇 **shàn** ве́ер	1. fan 2. leaf 3. (M. for doors/etc.)
～ **shān** 1. обма́хиваться ве́ером 2. возбужда́ть, подстрека́ть	1. to fan 2. to incite, instigate, stir up
～动 **shāndòng** 1. подстрека́ть 2. демаго́гия	1. to fan, flap 2. to incite, instigate (a strike/etc.)
塌 **tā** ру́хнуть, обвали́ться	1. to collapse 2. to droop 3. to settle\\ \\down
月 **yuè** луна́, ме́сяц; ме́сячный	1. moon 2. month
～台 **yuètái** перро́н, железнодоро́жная платфо́рма	railway platform
～初 **yuèchū** в нача́ле ме́сяца	beginning of the month
～分 **yuèfèn** ме́сяц; ме́сячный	month
～底 **yuèdǐ** в конце́ ме́сяца	end of the month
～亮 **yuèliàng** луна́	1. moon 2. moonlight
胡 **hú** 1. глу́пый; безрассу́дный 2. усы́; борода́	1. mustache, beard, whiskers 2. dewlap 3. recklessly, wantonly 4. why?; when?; how?
～子 **húz** усы́; борода́	1. beard, mustache, whiskers 2. bandit
～闹 **húnào** сканда́лить, шуме́ть	to horse around
～同 **hútong** переу́лок	(loan w.) lane, alley
～说 **húshuō** говори́ть ерунду́, болта́ть	to talk nonsense/drivel; drivel
～涂 **hútu** бестолко́вый, глу́пый	1. muddle, confused, bewildered 2. stupid, foolish
糊 **hú** 1. кле́ить; клей; кле́йстер 2. глу́пый, бестолко́вый	1. to paste, plaster; paste, plaster 2. muddy, unclear 3.overcooked until mushy
蝴:～蝶 **húdié** ба́бочка; мотылёк	butterfly
湖 **hú** о́зеро	1. lake 2. Hunan/Hubei (prov.)
明 **míng** 1. све́тлый, я́сный 2. понима́ть; поня́тливый; поня́тный 3. за́втра	1. bright 2. clear, distinct 3. open, overt, obvious 4. sharp-eyed, clear-sighted 5. next (day/year) 6. to under-\\ \\stand 7. clearness
～显 **míngxiǎn** я́сный, очеви́дный	clear, obvious
～信片 **míngxìnpiàn** откры́тка	postcard
～白 **míngbai** понима́ть; поня́тный	1. to understand, realize, know 2. clear, obvious, plain 3. sensible, reasonable
～确 **míngquè** уточня́ть; оп-	clear-cut, explicit; to make clear

明萌阴朝嘲潮霸丽朋

ределя́ть; чёткий; досто-	-
ве́рный	-
明天 **míngtiān** за́втра; ～天	1. tomorrow 2. the near future
见 до за́втра!	-
～文 **míngwén** я́сно, чётко	precise/formal text
～亮 **míngliàng** све́тлый, я́р-	1. well-lit, bright 2. bright, shining
кий, я́сный	-
萌 **méng** зарожда́ться; пус-	1. to put out buds/sprouts/shoots 2.
ка́ть ростки́; по́чки *(рас-*	to become pregnant
тений)	-
～芽 **méngyá** зача́тки; пе́р-	to sprout; sprout (lit./fig.)
вые ростки́	-
阴 **yīn** **1.** тень; тенево́й	1. female/passive/negative principle
2. скрыва́ть; та́йный, сек-	in nature 2. the moon 3. shaded orien-
ре́тный **3.** тёмный, мра́ч-	tation 4. overcast 5. covert, concealed
ный **4.** отрица́тельный	hidden 6. sinister 7. female sex organs
～郁 **yīnyù** угрю́мый	gloomy, dismal
～历 **yīnlì** лу́нный кален-	lunar calendar
да́рь	-
～谋 **yīnmóu** та́йные за́мыс-	plot, scheme
лы; за́говор; интри́га	-
朝 **cháo** **1.** быть обращён-	1. court, government 2. dynasty 3. an
ным к; в; на **2.** дина́стия	emperor's reign 4. facing, towards
～ **zhāo** у́тро; день	1. early morning, morning 2. day
嘲 **cháo** **1.** шути́ть; насме-	to ridicule, deride
ха́ться **2.** щебета́ть, чири́-	-
кать	-
潮 **cháo** **1.** прили́в, прибо́й	1. tide 2. (social) upsurge, current 3.
2. мо́крый; вла́жный, сы-	damp, moist
ро́й	-
～湿 **cháoshī** **1.** сыро́й,	moist, damp
вла́жный **2.** промока́ть,	-
пропи́тываться	-
～气 **cháoqì** сы́рость; вла́ж-	humidity
ность	-
霸 **bà** узурпи́ровать, захва́-	1. hegemon, overlord 2. tyrant, bully 3.
тывать; де́спот, тира́н	hegemonic power 4. to dominate,\\
～占 **bàzhàn** узурпи́ровать;	to occupy forcibly, seize \\lord over
оккупи́ровать	-
～权 **bàquán** гегемо́ния; гос-	hegemony, supremacy
по́дство; тирани́я	-
丽 **lì** краси́вый, прекра́сный;	beautiful
изя́щный	-
朋 **péng** друг; прия́тель	friend

朋友 **péngyou** прия́тель; друг; друзья́	1. friend 2. boy/girl friend
绷 **bēng** бинтова́ть; бинт, повя́зка	1. to stretch tight 2. to spring, bounce
～带 **bēngdài** бинт, повя́зка; банда́ж	bandage
棚 **péng** шала́ш; наве́с; тент	1. canopy/awning of reed mats, etc. 2. shed, shack
崩 **bēng** обру́шиться; обва́л	1. to collapse 2. to burst 3. to execute//by shooting 4. to be hit
～溃 **bēngkuì** разва́л; крах, катастро́фа	to collapse, fall apart
朗 **lǎng** 1. я́сный, прозра́чный 2. отчётливый *(о звуке)*	1. light, bright 2. loud and clear
～读 **lǎngdú** чита́ть вслух; деклами́ровать	to read aloud; to read loudly and clearly
期 **qī** 1. срок; пери́од 2. ожида́ть 3. вы́пуск *(журнала)*	1. period of time, stage, phase 2. to hope, expect 3. issue (of a periodical), term
～待 **qīdài** ожида́ть	to look forward to
～间 **qījiān** срок; пери́од	time, period
～满 **qīmǎn** по истече́нии сро́ка	to expire, run out
～限 **qīxiàn** срок	time limit, deadline
钥 **yào** ключ	key
～匙 **yàoshi** ключ	key
肩 **jiān** плечо́	to shoulder; shoulder
～章 **jiānzhāng** пого́ны; эполе́ты	1. shoulder loop 2. epaulet
～负 **jiānfù** нести́ на плеча́х	to undertake, bear
有 **yǒu** 1. име́ть(ся); быть в нали́чии; есть 2. не́кий, не́кто; не́которые	1. to have, possess 2. to be, exist
～一天 **yǒu-yi-tiān** одна́жды	once, one day
～些 **yǒuxiē** не́которые	some; somewhat, rather
～理 **yǒulǐ** пра́вильный; обосно́ванный	1. reasonable, justified, in the right 2. (math.) rational
～益 **yǒuyì** поле́зный	profitable, beneficial, useful
～害 **yǒuhài** вре́дный	harmful, detrimental, pernicious
～名 **yǒumíng** знамени́тый, изве́стный	well-known, famous
～利 **yǒulì** вы́годный; дохо́дный	to be advantageous/beneficial

朋 绷 棚 崩 朗 期 钥 肩 有

有的 **yǒud** не́которые	some
~的是 **yǒudeshì** мно́го; поря́дочно	to have plenty of, there's no lack of
~力 **yǒulì** си́льный	strong, forceful, powerful
~关 **yǒuguān** име́ть отноше́ние к; заинтересо́ванный; соотве́тствующий	to have a bearing on, concern, be relevant
~限 **yǒuxiàn** ограни́ченный	limited, finite
~趣 **yǒuqù** интере́сный	interesting, fascinating, amusing
~效 **yǒuxiào** действи́тельный	efficacious, effective, valid
~机 **yǒujī** органи́ческий	organic
~意 **yǒuyì** умы́шленно, созна́тельно	1. to have a mind to 2. to be interested in 3. intentionally, deliberately
贿 **huì** взя́тка, по́дкуп	bribe
~赂 **huìlù** подкупа́ть; по́дкуп	to bribe; bribery
惰 **duò** лени́вый	lazy, indolent
~性 **duòxìng** лень, ине́ртность	inertia
肯 **kěn** хоте́ть; соглаша́ться, быть согла́сным	to be willing/ready to
~定 **kěndìng** определённый; положи́тельный *(ответ)*	to affirm, approve, regard as positive; positive, affirmative; definitely, surely
捐 **juān** 1. дава́ть де́ньги; же́ртвовать; поже́ртвование 2. взима́ть нало́ги 3. отверга́ть; отка́зываться от	1. to relinquish, abandon 2. to contribute, subscribe 3. tax
~款 **juānkuǎn** внести́ де́ньги; поже́ртвовать	to contribute money; contribution, donation, subscription
膏 **gāo** 1. мазь; па́ста 2. жир, са́ло; жи́рный, ту́чный	1. fat, grease, oil 2. paste, cream, ointment
胃 **wèi** желу́док	stomach
~口 **wèikǒu** аппети́т	1. appetite 2. liking
~病 **wèibìng** желу́дочное заболева́ние	stomach/gastric disease/distress
谓 **wèi** говори́ть; сказа́ть; называ́ть	1. to say 2. to call, name 3. meaning, sense
骨 **gǔ, gú** 1. кость; костяно́й 2. скеле́т; карка́с, о́стов	1. bone 2. skeleton, framework 3. character, spirit
~干 **gǔgàn** 1. скеле́т, о́ст-	backbone, mainstay

ов 2. костя́к, основны́е ка́дры	-
骨头 **gútou** кость	1. bone 2. strong character
～气 **gǔqì** твёрдость; твёрдый хара́ктер	moral integrity, backbone
滑 **huá** 1. скользи́ть; ско́льзкий, гла́дкий 2. хи́трый	1. slippery, smooth 2. cunning, crafty 3. to slip, slide
～雪 **huáxuě** ката́ться на лы́жах	to ski
～翔机 **huáxiángjī** планёр	glider, sailplane
～冰 **huábīng** ката́ться на конька́х	to skate
臂 **bèi** рука́ *(от плеча до кисти)*	upper arm
脊 **jǐ** позвоно́чник	1. spine, backbone 2. mountain ridge
～背 **jǐbèi** спина́	back (of a vertebrate)
背 **bèi** 1. спина́ 2. ты́льная (обра́тная) сторона́ 3. измени́ть; нару́шить 4. учи́ть наизу́сть	1. back of body/object 2. to turn one's back, turn away 3. to hide sth. from 3. to learn by heart, recite from memory 4. to faint 5. to die //to shoulder
～ **bēi** нести́ на спине́	1. to carry on the back 2. to bear, //
～信 **bèixìn** изме́на, вероло́мство	to break faith
～面 **bèimiàn** ты́льная (обра́тная) сторона́	back, reverse side
～弃 **bèiqì** 1. броса́ть, отбра́сывать 2. отходи́ть, отка́зываться 3. предава́ть, изменя́ть	to abandon, renounce
～影 **bèiyǐng** 1. фон 2. подоплёка	view of sb.'s back
～书 **bèishū** вы́учить наизу́сть	1. to recite from memory 2. endorsement (on a check)
～袋 **bēidài** *см.* 背包	knapsack, field pack, shoulder bag
～叛 **bèipàn** измени́ть; изме́на	1. to betray, rebel against 2. treason
～包 **bēibāo** ра́нец; рюкза́к; вещево́й мешо́к	1. knapsack, field pack, shoulder bag 2. blanket roll
～景 **bèijǐng** 1. за́дний план; фон 2. декора́ция 3. подоплёка	background, backdrop
～心 **bèixīn** жиле́т; ма́йка	sleeveless garment, vest
哨 **shào** 1. пост; дозо́р; карау́л 2. гудо́к, свисто́к	1. to warble, chirp, whistle; whistle 2. sentry, patrol 3. (coll.) to harangue

哨兵 **shàobīng** часовóй, караýльный	sentinel, sentry
稍 **shāo** немнóго, чуть-чýть, слегкá	slightly
～微 **shāowēi** слегкá; чуть-чýть	slightly, a bit
～息 **shāoxī** передохнýть; вóльно!	(mil.) At ease!
消 **xiāo** **1.** исчезáть; растворя́ться; рассéиваться **2.** потребля́ть, расхóдовать **3.** уничтожáть **4.** пасси́вный	1. to disappear, vanish 2. to eliminate, dispel, remove 3. to while away (time) 4. need, take
～防队 **xiāofángduì** пожáрная комáнда	fire brigade
～毒 **xiāodú** **1.** дезинфéкция **2.** дегазáция	to disinfect, sterilize
～灭 **xiāomiè** уничтожáть, ликвиди́ровать	1. to perish, die out, pass away 2. to eliminate, abolish, exterminate
～极 **xiāojí** **1.** отрицáтельный пóлюс **2.** пасси́вный **3.** отрицáтельный	1. negative 2. passive, inactive
～化 **xiāohuà** растворя́ть (-ся); перевáривать(ся), усвáивать(ся)	to digest; digest
～耗 **xiāohào** расхóдовать; истощáть, измáтывать	to consume, use up, deplete
～费 **xiāofèi** потребля́ть; потреблéние	to consume; consumption
～除 **xiāochú** устраня́ть; отменя́ть, упраздня́ть	to eliminate, dispel, remove, clear up
～息 **xiāoxī** нóвости, извéстия	news, information, tidings
销 **xiāo** **1.** отменя́ть; ликвиди́ровать **2.** продавáть, сбывáть	1. to melt (metal) 2. to cancel, annul 3. to sell, market 4. to pin, peg; pin, peg 5. to expend, spend
～售 **xiāoshòu** сбывáть, реализовáть; сбыт, реализáция	to sell, market
育 **yù** **1.** корми́ть; воспи́тывать; расти́ть **2.** роди́ть	1. to give birth to 2. to rear, raise 3. to educate
青 **qīng** **1.** си́ний; зелёный; тёмный; чёрный **2.** молодóй	1. nature's color, green, blue, greenish-black 2. not ripe 3. young (of people) 4. Qinghai (prov.) 5. Qingdao (city)

青春 **qīngchūn** **1.** веснá **2.** молоды́е гóды	one's youth; young adulthood
～年 **qīngnián** ю́ноша; мóлодость; молодёжь	youth, young people
～菜 **qīngcài** óвощи; зéлень	green vegetables, greens, Ch. cabbage
晴 **qíng** я́сный день; проя́сниться	fine, clear (of weather)
睛 **jīng** зрачóк; хрустáлик	eyeball
情 **qíng** **1.** чу́вства, эмóции **2.** любóвь; страсть **3.** симпáтии **4.** положéние, обстанóвка, ситуáция	1. sentiment, sensibility 2. inclination, interest, affection 3. love, passion 4. situation, circumstances, condition
～绪 **qíngxù** настроéние	emotions, feelings, mood
～形 **qíngxíng** обстоя́тельства; положéние дел; обстанóвка	circumstances, situation
～报 **qíngbào** информáция, свéдения	intelligence, information
～报局 **qíngbàojú** развéдывательное управлéние	intelligence agency
～况 **qíngkuàng** *см.* 情形	circumstances, situation
～感 **qínggǎn** чу́вства, эмóции	emotion, feeling, friendship
猜 **cāi** отгáдывать; догáдываться	1. to guess 2. to suspect
～测 **cāicè** предугáдывать; догáдка	to guess, surmise
精 **jīng** **1.** очищáть; отбóрный **2.** сéмя; спéрма **3.** энéргия; си́ла дýха	1. refined 2. perfect, excellent 3. meticulous, precise 4. sharp, clever 5. skilled, proficient 6. essence 7. spirit, energy 8. semen, seed 9. demon 10. very
～密 **jīngmì** тóнкий; тóчный; аккурáтный	precise, accurate
～粹 **jīngcuì** чи́стый; отбóрный	succinct, pithy, terse
～神 **jīngshén** дух; душá; морáльное состоя́ние; пси́хика	1. spirit, mind, consciousness 2. essence, gist
～简 **jīngjiǎn** упрощáть	to retrench, simplify, reduce
～确 **jīngquè** тóчный, мéткий	accurate, exact, precise
～力 **jīnglì** энéргия, си́ла	energy, vigor
清 **qīng** **1.** чи́стый; я́сный, свéтлый **2.** очи́стить **3.** сполнá; до концá	1. to clear up, settle 2. pure, clean 3. fresh, cool 4. lonely, poor 5. (suf.) fully, clearly 6. Qing (Manchu) dynasty

清算 **qīngsuàn** **1.** рассчи́тываться **2.** своди́ть счёты	1. to clear/square accounts 2. to expose and criticize 3. liquidation
～茶 **qīngchá** зелёный чай	1. green tea 2. tea without refreshments
～楚 **qīngchǔ** я́сный, отчётливый	1. clear, distinct, without ambiguity 2. to understand clearly
～洗 **qīngxǐ** чи́стить, вы́чистить; чи́стка	to rinse, wash, purge
～凉 **qīngliáng** прохла́дный	fresh and cool, refreshing
请 **qǐng** **1.** проси́ть; пожа́луйста! **2.** приглаша́ть, принима́ть *(гостей)*	1. to request, ask (a favor) 2. to engage, hire (a teacher, etc.) 3. please
～帖 **qǐngtiě** пригласи́тельный биле́т	written invitation
～客 **qǐngkè** приглаша́ть госте́й	1. to invite/entertain guests 2. to treat sb. (to a meal/show/etc.)
～问 **qǐngwèn** разреши́те спроси́ть	excuse me; may I ask...
～求 **qǐngqiú** проси́ть; про́сьба	to ask, request, entreat
～假 **qǐngjià** проси́ть о́тпуск	to ask for leave
～示 **qǐngshì** проси́ть указа́ний (инстру́кций)	to ask for instructions
角 **jiǎo** **1.** рог; рога́ **2.** у́гол **3.** грань	1. horn, bugle 2. corner 3. angle 4. cape, promontory 5. (M. for money)
～落 **jiǎoluò** у́гол, приста́нище	corner, nook
～度 **jiǎodù** **1.** у́гол [в гра́дусах] **2.** то́чка зре́ния, подхо́д	1. angle 2. perspective
～色 **jiǎosè** роль; де́йствующее лицо́	haughty look
确 **què** достове́рный, то́чный; надёжный	1. true, reliable, authentic 2. firmly, indeed, truly
～切 **quèqiè** определённый, то́чный	definite, exact, precise, accurate, clear and unambiguous
～实 **quèshí** по́длинный, достове́рный	definitely true/real/certain/reliable; really, certainly, truly, indeed
～定 **quèdìng** определи́ть; определённый	to define, fix, determine, settle, decide firmly; definitely
嘴 **zuǐ** рот; клюв	mouth, snout, bill
～巴 **zuǐbā** **1.** мо́рда **2.** щёки **3.** пощёчина	mouth, cheeks
用 **yòng** **1.** применя́ть; употребля́ть, испо́льзовать	1. to use, employ, apply 2. to eat, drink 3. to spend 4. expense 5. use, good

2. с по́мощью, посре́дством; 用笔写字 писа́ть ру́чкой	-
~品 yòngpǐn предме́ты потребле́ния	articles for use
~户 yònghù потреби́тель; абоне́нт	consumer, user
~处 yòngchu по́льза; примене́ние	use, practical application
~途 yòngtú [пред] назначе́ние, примене́ние, употребле́ние	to use
~具 yòngjù принадле́жности; предме́ты обихо́да	utensil, appliance
佣 yōng нанима́ть; наёмный	
拥 yōng 1. обнима́ть 2. подде́рживать	1. to embrace, hold 2. to gather around, surround 3. to swarm, throng 4. to support, uphold
~挤 yōngjǐ сти́снуть, сдави́ть; да́вка	crowded, pushed and squeezed together
~护 yōnghù подде́рживать; подде́ржка	consumer, user
~抱 yōngbào обнима́ть; объ́ятия	to embrace
踊 yǒng скака́ть, пры́гать	to leap/jump up
~跃 yǒngyuè с энтузиа́змом	1. to leap, jump 2. eagerly, enthusiastically
桶 tǒng бо́чка; ка́дка; ведро́	tub, pail, barrel
痛 tòng 1. боль; бо́льно 2. сожале́ть, скорбе́ть 3. весьма́, о́чень	1. to ache, pain; ache, pain 2. deeply, bitterly
~苦 tòngkǔ страда́ть, му́читься; му́ка	pain, suffering
~斥 tòngchì ре́зко осужда́ть; клейми́ть позо́ром	1. to attack bitterly 2. to recount with pain
~快 tòngkuai ра́достный, весёлый	1. joyful, delighted 2. to one's heart's content 3. forthright
~恨 tònghèn ненави́деть; не́нависть	to hate bitterly
辅 fǔ помога́ть, подде́рживать	1. to assist, complement, supplement 2. side-pole guards of cart wheels
~导 fǔdǎo направля́ть, руководи́ть; консульти́ровать	tutor, coach

辅捕铺庸而端喘需编

辅助 **fǔzhù** помогáть; вспомогáтельный	1. to assist 2. supplementary, auxiliary, subsidiary
捕 **bǔ** ловить; хватáть, арестóвывать	to catch, seize, arrest
～获(捉) **bǔhuò(zhuō)** схватить, арестовáть	to catch, capture, seize
铺 **pū** стелить, расстилáть; подстилка; постéль	1. to spread, extend, unfold 2. to pave, lay 3. thoroughly, throughout
～ **pù** магазин; лáвка	1. store, shop 2. bed 3. to spread 4. to set in order
～盖 **pūgài** постéльное бельё; постéль	bedding, bedclothes
～张 **pūzhāng** 1. развернýть, раскинуть 2. преувеличивать	extravagant, exaggerated
庸 **yōng** обычный; рядовóй, заурядный	1. commonplace, mediocre 2. inferior, second-rate 3. (no) need 4. how
～俗 **yōngsú** мещáнский, пóшлый, обывáтельский	vulgar, philistine
而 **ér** но; а; к томý же	and, and yet, right after
～且 **érqiě** к томý же, притóм	furthermore, and
端 **duān** 1. конéц; оконéчность 2. начáло	1. end, extremity 2. beginning 3. point 4. reason 5. to hold sth. level, carry
喘 **chuǎn** тяжелó дышáть; задыхáться	1. to gasp for breath, pant 2. asthma
需 **xū** нуждáться, трéбоваться; потрéбность, нуждá, необходимость	to need, want, require; need, want
～求 **xūqiú** спрос, потрéбность	requirement, demand
～要 **xūyào** нýжно, необходимо; нуждáться	to need, want, require, demand; need, demand, requirement
编 **biān** 1. плести, сплетáть 2. формировáть, комплектовáть, составлять	1. to weave, plait 2. to organize, group 3. to edit, compile 4. to write, compose 5. to fabricate 6. book, volume
～辑 **biānjí** редактировать; редáктор	to edit, compile; editor, compiler
～制 **biānzhì** комплектовáть; формировáть; организáция; штат	1. to weave, plait 2. to work out, organize 3. organized staff/force
～写 **biānxiě** написáть; состáвить; разрабóтать	1. to compile 2. to write, compose
～队 **biānduì** *воен.* формировáние; строй	1. to form columns 2. to make name assignments to a team/unit 3. formation

编入 **biānrù** вводи́ть *(в соста́в)*; зачисля́ть	1. to include (in a budget) 2. to enlist, recruit
～织 **biānzhī** ткать; плести́	to weave, knit, plait, braid
偏 **piān** **1.** отклоня́ться; отклоне́ние **2.** односторо́нний; пристра́стный	1. inclined, partial, prejudiced 2. side 3. special 4. to incline 5. to insist on 6. (polite) to have already eaten\\
～差 **piānchā** отклоне́ние; про́мах; переги́б	deviation, error \\7. stubbornly\\ - \\8. on the contrary
～偏 **piānpiān** **1.** как ра́з, кста́ти **2.** как назло́	1. just 2. but 3. only -
～向 **piānxiàng** укло́н; скло́нность	1. to be partial to 2. to load the dice 3. to tend to 4. erroneous tendency
～见 **piānjiàn** **1.** предубежде́ние, предвзя́тое мне́ние **2.** предрассу́дки	prejudice, bias - -
騙 **piàn** обма́нывать, моше́нничать	1. to deceive, fool, hoodwink 2. to leap on a horse
～局 **piànjú** обма́н, моше́нничество	fraud, hoax - //etc.) 3. (M. for chapters, etc.)
篇 **piān** статья́; глава́; часть	1. piece of writing 2. sheet (of paper,//
高 **gāo** **1**. высо́кий; высота́ **2.** гро́мкий; высо́кого то́на **3.** возвы́шенный; выдаю́щийся	1. tall, high 2. above average 3. loud - - -
～空 **gāokōng** больша́я высота́; высо́тный	high altitude, upper air -
～射炮 **gāoshèpào** зени́тное ору́дие	anti-aircraft gun/artillery -
～等 **gāoděng** вы́сший; вы́сшего со́рта	higher, advanced -
～潮 **gāocháo** прили́в, подъём	1. high tide/water 2. upsurge, climax -
～尚 **gāoshàng** возвы́шенный, благоро́дный	noble, lofty -
～炉 **gāolú** до́менная печь, до́мна	blast furnace -
～涨 **gāozhǎng** поднима́ться; подъём, рост	to rise, surge up, run high -
～梁 **gāoliáng** гаоля́н	Chinese sorghum
～度 **gāodù** высота́ *(при измерении)*	1. altitude, height 2. high degree -
～级 **gāojí** вы́сший у́ровень; вы́сший; вышестоя́щий	high in rank/grade/quality -
～[级]中[学] **gāo[jí] zhōng-**	senior middle school

[**xué**] сре́дняя шко́ла вто-	-
ро́й ступе́ни *(10—12 год*	-
обучения)	-
高[级]小[学] **gāo[jí] xiǎo-**	higher primary school
[**xué**] нача́льная шко́ла	-
второ́й ступе́ни *(5—6 год*	-
обучения)	-
~地 **gāodì** высота́, возвы́-	upland, elevation, height
шенность	-
~兴 **gāoxìng** ра́доваться	1. glad, happy 2. willing
~原 **gāoyuán** плоского́рье	plateau, tableland
搞 **gǎo 1.** занима́ться, де́-	1. to do, carry on, be engaged in 2. to
лать **2.** добива́ться, полу-	make, produce, work out 3. to set up,
ча́ть	start, organize 4. to get (hold of),\\
~臭 **gǎochòu** дискредити́ро-	to discredit, put to shame \\secure
вать	- //sketch 3. original manuscript
稿 **gǎo** ру́копись; чернови́к	1. stalk of cereal crops 2. draft,//
尚 **shàng 1.** почита́ть, ува-	1. to esteem, value 2. respectfully 3.
жа́ть **2.** [всё] ещё	still, yet 4. fairly, rather
~且 **shàngqiě** да к тому́	even, still, yet
же; пока́ что; да́же	-
倘 **tǎng** е́сли; допу́стим, что	if, supposing
躺 **tǎng** лечь; лежа́ть	-
同 **tóng 1**. совпада́ть; оди-	1. to be the same as; same, similar 2.
на́ковый, о́бщий **2.** сооб-	together, in common 3. harmony, con-
ща́, вме́сте; с	cord 4. with 5. for
~一 **tóngyī** оди́н и то́т же	same, identical
~性 **tóngxìng** одноро́дный	-
~温层 **tóngwēncéng** стра-	stratosphere
тосфе́ра	-
~盟 **tóngméng** сою́з, блок;	alliance, league
сою́зный	-
~盟国 **tóngméngguó** сою́з-	ally, allied nation
ное госуда́рство	-
~样 **tóngyàng** ра́вным о́б-	same, equal, similar
разом; тако́й же	-
~行 **tóngháng** колле́га; со-	person of same profession
служи́вец	- //dent, schoolmate
~学 **tóngxué** однока́шник	to be in the same school; fellow stu-//
~时 **tóngshí** в то́ же вре́мя,	(at) the same time, meanwhile
одновре́ме́нно	- //worker
~事 **tóngshì** *см.* 同行	to work together; colleague, fellow//
~情 **tóngqíng** сочу́вствие;	to sympathize with
солида́рность; симпа́тии	-

同步 **tóngbù** синхро́нный	synchronism
～乡 **tóngxiāng** земля́к	fellow villager/townsman
～谋 **tóngmóu** соуча́стие	to conspire; conspirator
～化 **tónghuà** ассимили́ровать; ассимиля́ция	to assimilate -
～胞 **tóngbāo** соотéчественники	1. offspring of same parents 2. compatriots
～心 **tóngxīn** единоду́шие; единоду́шно	1. concentric 2. to be of one heart; of one heart
～志 **tóngzhì** това́рищ, единомы́шленник	comrade -
～意 **tóngyì** соглаша́ться	to agree, consent, approve
桐 **tóng** ту́нговое дéрево	tung (oil) tree
～油 **tóngyóu** ту́нговое ма́сло	tung oil -
洞 **dòng** отвéрстие, дыра́; пещéра	1. hole, cavity 2. penetratingly, thoroughly
铜 **tóng** медь; бро́нза	copper
筒 **tǒng** труба́; цили́ндр	1. tube-shaped object 2. a section of thick bamboo
摘 **zhāi** 1. срыва́ть, собира́ть 2. отбира́ть; вы́держка из	1. to pick, pluck 2. to make extracts 3. to point out (mistakes) 4. to borrow money
～要 **zhāiyào** резюмé	to make a summary; summary, abstract
滴 **dī** ка́пля; ка́пать; стека́ть	to drip; (M. for drop)
周 **zhōu** 1. оборо́т, круг; цикл 2. вокру́г, круго́м, вездé 3. годовщи́на 4. недéля	1. to circle 2. to overturn 3. circumference, circle, ring, periphery 4. whole, entirety 5. week 6. (electr.) cycle 7. perfect, complete 8. Zhou dynasty
～密 **zhōumì** 1. густо́й, пло́тный 2. тща́тельный, дета́льный	careful, thorough - -
～知 **zhōuzhī** всем извéстно	everybody knows, widely known
～围 **zhōuwéi** окружа́ть; вокру́г; окружа́ющий	vicinity, surrounding, all around -
～年 **zhōunián** годовщи́на	anniversary
～刊 **zhōukān** еженедéльник	weekly (publication) -
绸 **chóu** шёлк; чесуча́	silk, silk fabric
稠 **chóu** густо́й, пло́тный	1. thick 2. dense
～密 **chóumì** *см.* 稠	dense
调 **tiáo** 1. согласо́вывать; регули́ровать 2. настра́ивать (*музыкальный инструмент*)	1. to regulate, adjust 2. to mediate 3. to tease - -

调商

调 diào 1. перемещáть, перебрáсывать 2. обслéдовать 3. интонáция; тон; мелóдия	1. to transfer 2. accent 3. tune, air 4. (ling.) tone 5. (mus.) key
～查 diàochá обслéдовать	to investigate, look into, survey
～整 tiáozhěng упорядóчивать, регулúровать	to adjust, readjust, regulate, restructure, balance
～和 tiáohé примирять; примирéние	1. to mediate, reconcile 2. to be in harmony 3. to mix, blend 4. to season
～解 tiáojiě посрéдничать; посрéдничество	to mediate, accommodate, make peace
～动 diàodòng перемещáть, перебрáсывать; перебрóска	1. to transfer 2. to move (troops), muster 3. to bring into play
～人 tiáorén посрéдник	mediator
～度 diàodù регулúровать, управлять	1. to dispatch (buses/etc.) 2. to manage 3. dispatcher
～皮 tiáopí озорнóй; упрямый	1. naughty, noisy and mischievous 2. tricky, artful
～配 diàopèi расстáвить; распределúть	to allocate, deploy
商 shāng 1. совещáться, обсуждáть 2. торговáть; торгóвля	1. to discuss, consult 2. trade, business 3. merchant, business person 3. quotient 4. Shang dynasty
～量 shāngliàng совéтоваться, совещáться, консультúроваться	to consult, talk over
～业 shāngyè торгóвля, коммéрция	commerce, trade, business
～品 shāngpǐn товáры	commodity, goods, merchandise
～店 shāngdiàn магазúн; лáвка	shop, store
～船 shāngchuán торгóвое сýдно	merchant ship
～界 shāngjiè торгóвые кругú	busines circles
～务 shāngwù торгóвля; торгóвый	business affairs
～谈 shāngtán вестú переговóры	to confer, discuss, negotiate
～定 shāngdìng услóвиться, договорúться	to settle through discussion
～议 shāngyì совещáться; вестú переговóры	to confer, discuss

隔 **gé** 1. быть отделённым; отделя́ться 2. отстоя́ть от	1. to separate, cut off, impede 2. at a distance from, after an interval of
南 **nán** юг; ю́жный	south
～部 **nánbù** ю́жная часть; юг	southern part, the south
～方 **nánfāng** юг; ю́жный	1. the south 2. the southern part of a//country
～瓜 **nánguā** ты́ква	pumpkin, cushaw
纲 **gāng** програ́мма; те́зисы	1. outline, program 2. key link, guiding//principle
～领 **gānglǐng** програ́мма	program, guiding principle
～要 **gāngyào** 1. основны́е положе́ния, те́зисы 2. о́черк, набро́сок	outline, compendium
钢 **gāng** 1. сталь; стально́й 2. твёрдый	steel
～琴 **gāngqín** роя́ль; пиани́но	piano
～骨水泥 **gānggú shuǐní** железобето́н	reinforced concrete
～铁 **gāngtiě** сталь; стально́й	iron and steel
～笔 **gāngbǐ** перо́; ру́чка	fountain pen
岗 **gǎng** 1. холм, со́пка; возвыше́ние 2. пост	1. hillock, mound 2. ridge, welt, wale 3. sentry post
～位 **gǎngwèi** пост *(карау́льный, служе́бный)*	post, station
网 **wǎng** сеть, се́тка	to net; net
～球 **wǎngqiú** те́ннис	1. tennis 2. tennis ball
向 **xiàng** 1. быть обращённым к; в направле́нии; к; на; у 2. направле́ние, курс	1. to face, turn towards 2. to side with, be partial to 3. direction 4. to, toward 5. always, all along
～日葵 **xiàngrìkuí** подсо́лнух	sunflower
～例 **xiànglì** прецеде́нт, слу́чай	custom
～导 **xiàngdǎo** экскурсово́д; гид	guide
～来 **xiànglái** и́здавна; всегда́; *с отриц.* никогда́	always, all along
响 **xiǎng** 1. звук; э́хо 2. звуча́ть; греме́ть; гро́мкий	1. to make a sound; sound, noise 2. loud, noisy
～应 **xiǎngyìng** отклика́ться, отзыва́ться; о́тклик; реа́кция	to respond, answer
～声 **xiǎngshēng** звук	sound, noise

晌 **shǎng** по́лдень	1. a short period of time 2. noon
巾 **jīn** плато́к; полоте́нце; ска́терть; головна́я повя́зка	cloth
帅 **shuài 1.** полково́дец; ма́ршал; генерали́ссимус **2.** вести́, предводи́тельствовать	1. to command (an army) 2. commander-in-chief 3. handsome, chic
布 **bù 1.** полотно́; холст **2.** расставля́ть, располага́ть **3.** публикова́ть	1. cloth 2. to declare 3. to spread, distribute
～置 **bùzhì** расположи́ть, расста́вить; *воен.* дислока́ция	1. to arrange, fix up 2. to assign
～匹 **bùpǐ** тка́ни	cloth; piece goods
～告 **bùgào** объявле́ние; обраще́ние	notice, bulletin
～雷 **bùléi** мини́ровать	to lay mines, mine
～景 **bùjǐng** фон; декора́ция	1. (art) composition 2. (drama) setting
～尔什维克 **bù'ěrshíwéikè** большевики́; большеви́стский	Bolshevik
怖 **bù** боя́ться; пуга́ть; терроризи́ровать	to fear, be afraid of
希 **xī 1.** ре́дкий; ре́дко **2.** наде́яться	1. to hope 2. rare, scarce, uncommon
～望 **xīwàng** наде́яться; наде́жда	to hope, wish; hope, wish
稀 **xī 1.** ре́дкий, непло́тный **2.** дико́винный	1. rare, scarce, uncommon 2. sparse, scattered 3. watery, thin
～有 **xīyǒu** ре́дкостный, ре́дкий	rare, unusual
饰 **shì** украша́ть; приукра́шивать; украше́ния; наря́д	1. to adorn, dress up; decoration, ornament 3. to play the role of
席 **xí 1.** цино́вка; подсти́лка **2.** ме́сто *(за столом)*	1. mat 2. seat, place 3. feast, banquet, dinner
～子 **xíz** цино́вка	(coll.) mat
～卷 **xíjuǎn** охва́тывать, вовлека́ть	1. to take away everything 2. to sweep across, engulf
吊 **diào 1.** висе́ть; подвесно́й **2.** поднима́ть	1. to hang 2. to lift up/let down 3. to mourn 4. to revoke, withdraw
常 **cháng 1.** ча́стый; постоя́нный; регуля́рно **2.** обы́чный, рядово́й	1. ordinary, common, normal 2. invariable, constant 3. often, usually, frequently

常驻代表 **chángzhù dàibiǎo** постоя́нный представи́тель	permanent representative
～备军 **chángbèijūn** регуля́рная а́рмия	standing army
～用 **chángyòng** употреби́тельный	to use often; in common use
～务委员会 **chángwù wěiyuánhuì** постоя́нный комите́т	standing committee
～规 **chángguī** обы́чный, норма́льный	convention, rule, common practice, routine
～识 **chángshí** а́збучные зна́ния, элемента́рное представле́ние	1. general knowledge 2. common sense
～会 **chánghuì** очередно́е собра́ние; се́ссия	regular meeting/session
棉 **mián** хло́пок; ва́та; ва́тный	cotton; cotton-padded
～布 **miánbù** хлопчатобума́жная ткань	cotton cloth
～衣 **miányī** **1.** оде́жда из хлопчатобума́жной тка́ни **2.** ва́тная оде́жда	cotton-padded clothes
～花 **miánhuā** хло́пок-сыре́ц; ва́та	cotton
锦 **jǐn** парча́; расши́тый	1. brocade 2. bright and beautiful
～标 **jǐnbiāo** приз; вы́мпел	prize, title
带 **dài** **1.** по́яс; реме́нь **2.** райо́н; зо́на **3.** име́ть (носи́ть) при себе́ **4.** вести́ за собо́й; вме́сте с	1. to take, bring, bear 2. to lead 3. to look after, raise 4. belt, band, girdle 5. tire 6. zone
～路 **dàilù** вести́, пока́зывать доро́гу	to show/lead the way
～子 **dàiz** по́яс; ле́нта	belt, girdle, band, tape
～头(领) **dàitóu(lǐng)** руководи́ть, вести́	to pioneer, initiate, be the first
滞 **zhì** заде́рживать; заде́ржка; засто́й	stagnant, sluggish
～销 **zhìxiāo** затова́ривание	to be unsalable/unmarketable
帝 **dì** **1.** императо́р; влады́ка **2.** божество́; бог	1. Supreme Being, God 2. emperor 3. imperialism 4. imperial
～王 **dìwáng** короли́, мона́рхи	emperor, monarch

帝国 **dìguó** монáрхия, импé-	empire
рия	-
～国主义 **dìguózhǔyì** импе-	imperialism
риали́зм; империалисти́че-	-
ский	-
缔 **dì** свя́зывать; тéсная	to form (a friendship), conclude (a
связь; у́зел	treaty)
～结 **dìjié** заключáть *(дого-*	to conclude, establish
вор)	-
～造 **dìzào** твори́ть, создa-	to found, create
вáть	-
蹄 **tí** копы́то	hoof
币 **bì** дéньги; валю́та	money, currency
～制 **bìzhì** валю́тная систé-	currency system
ма	-
帮 **bāng** 1. помогáть; по-	1. to help, assist 2. gang 3. side 4. up-
мóщник 2. грýппа; артéль	per (of shoe) 4. (M. for groups)
～忙 **bāngmáng** помогáть	to help, do the favor (of), give a hand
～凶 **bāngxiōng** посóбник,	accomplice, accessory to a crime
приспéшник	-
～手 **bāngshǒu** помóщник,	assistant, accomplice
подрýчный	-
～助 **bāngzhù** помогáть; пó-	to help, assist; help, assistance
мощь	-
幕 **mù** 1. зáнавес 2. экрáн	1. curtain, screen, tent 2. (M. for thea-
3. акт, дéйствие	trical acts)
～后 **mùhòu** за кули́сами;	behind the scenes, backstage
закули́сный	-
帘 **lián** зáнавеси; штóры;	1. flag as a shop sign 2. curtain
жалюзи́	-
师 **shī** 1. диви́зия; дивизиóн-	1. teacher, master 2. model, example 3.
ный 2. учи́тель, настáв-	person skilled in a certain profession
ник; мáстер	4. (army) division 5. troop, army 6.\\
～部 **shībù** штаб диви́зии	division headquarters \\to imitate
～长 **shīzhǎng** команди́р ди-	1. (court.) teacher 2. division com-
ви́зии	mander
～范 **shīfàn** 1. нормáльный;	1. pedagogical, teacher-training 2.
образцóвый 2. педагоги́-	normal school
ческий	-
～范大学 **shīfàn dàxué** педа-	teachers' training college
гоги́ческий институ́т	-
狮 **shī**: 狮子 **shīz** лев	lion
筛 **shāi** просéивать; решетó;	1. to sift, sieve; sifter 2. to heat up
си́то	wine 3. to pour wine

市 **shì** **1.** ры́нок, база́р **2.** го́род	1. market 2. city, municipality 3. to buy, sell, deal in
～郊 **shìjiāo** при́город; окре́стности го́рода	suburb, outskirts
～场 **shìchǎng** база́р, ры́нок	market, bazaar
～长 **shìzhǎng** мэр го́рода; председа́тель горсове́та	mayor
～集 **shìjí** я́рмарка, база́р	1. fair 2. small town
～政府 **shìzhèngfǔ** городска́я упра́ва; муниципалите́т	municipal administration (offices)
～民 **shìmín** городско́е населе́ние, горожа́не	townspeople
肺 **fèi** лёгкие	lungs
～脏 **fèizàng** лёгкие	lungs
～病 **fèibìng** лёгочное заболева́ние	pulmonary tuberculosis (TB)
～炎 **fèiyán** воспале́ние лёгких, пневмони́я	pneumonia
柿 **shì** хурма́	persimmon
雨 **yǔ** дождь	rain
～量 **yǔliàng** коли́чество оса́дков	rainfall
～衣 **yǔyī** плащ, дождеви́к	raincoat
漏 **lòu** **1.** протека́ть, проса́чиваться **2.** разглаша́ть **3.** де́лать про́пуск *(в те́ксте)*	1. to leak out 2. divulge, leak 3. to be missing, be left out 4. water clock; hourglass 5. depravity
～斗 **lòudǒu** воро́нка	funnel
～水 **lòushuǐ** пропуска́ть во́ду, дава́ть течь	to leak water
内 **nèi** **1.** внутри́; вну́тренний **2.** в; в тече́ние	1. inside 2. one's wife or her relatives
～容 **nèiróng** содержа́ние	content, substance
～部 **nèibù** вну́тренняя часть; внутри́	inside, interior; internal
～科 **nèikē** вну́тренние боле́зни; терапи́я	internal medicine (as a specialty)
～行 **nèiháng** знато́к	expert, adept
～阁 **nèigé** кабине́т мини́стров	(govt.) cabinet
～衣 **nèiyī** бельё	underwear
～政 **nèizhèng** вну́тренняя поли́тика	(govt.) domestic affairs

市 肺 柿 雨 漏 内

内纳肉腐柄病祸锅窝两俩满

内战 **nèizhàn** гражда́нская война́	civil war
～燃机 **nèiránji** дви́гатель вну́треннего сгора́ния	internal-combustion engine
纳 **nà** **1.** вноси́ть, плати́ть **2.** брать, принима́ть	1. to receive, admit 2. to accept 3. to enjoy 4. to pay, offer 5. to restrain
肉 **ròu** **1.** мя́со **2.** мя́коть *(фруктов)*	1. meat, flesh 2. (coll.) spongy (of fruit) 3. slow-moving
～饼 **ròubing** котле́ты	meat patty
～刑 **ròuxíng** теле́сные наказа́ния	corporal punishment
～眼 **ròuyǎn** невооружённым гла́зом	naked eye
腐 **fǔ** гнить, разлага́ться; гнило́й	1. rotten, putrid 2. stale 3. corroded 4. corrupt
～烂 **fǔlàn** *см.* 腐	1. decomposed, putrid 2. corrupt, rotten
～朽 **fǔxiǔ** разложи́вшийся, гнило́й	1. rotten, decayed 2. decadent, degenerate
～败 **fǔbài** загнива́ть, разлага́ться	1. rotten, putrid, decayed 2. corrupt
柄 **bìng** рукоя́тка; ру́чка	1. handle 2. stem 3. power, authority
病 **bìng** **1.** боле́ть; боле́знь **2.** недоста́ток; поро́к	1. disease 2. fault, defect 3. to fall sick/ill
～历 **bìnglì** исто́рия боле́зни	pathology
～人 **bìngrén** больно́й [челове́к]	patient
祸 **huò** несча́стье, бе́дствие	1. to ruin, bring disaster to 2. misfortune, disaster, calamity
锅 **guō** котёл; кастрю́ля	1. pot, wok, pan, boiler 2. (pipe) bowl
～炉 **guōlù** парово́й котёл	boiler
窝 **wō** **1.** гнездо́; ло́гово; прито́н **2.** дом, семья́ **3.** вы́водок	1. to harbor, shelter 2. to hold in, check 3. to bend, crease 4. nest 5. lair, den 6. hollow part of human body 7. place
两 **liǎng** **1.** два; па́ра **2.** лян *(мера веса, равная 50 г)*	1. two 2. both (sides), either (side) 3. a few, some 4. (M. for ounce, tael)
～口子 **liǎngkǒuz** супру́ги, муж и жена́	(coll.) husband and wife, couple
～脚规 **liǎngjiǎoguī** ци́ркуль	1. compasses 2. dividers
俩 **liǎ** два; о́ба	(coll.) 1. two 2. some, several
满 **mǎn** **1.** наполня́ть; по́лный; целико́м; весь **2.** истека́ть *(о сроке)* **3.** удовлетворя́ть; дово́льный **4.** маньчжу́р; маньчжу́рский	1. to fill 2. to reach a limit, expire, be over 3. complete, full 4. satisfied 5. conceited 6. entirely, wholly 7. Manchus

满堂红 **mǎntánghóng** по́лный успе́х	1. red decorations on auspicious occasions 2. successful 3. crepe myrtle
～足 **mǎnzú** удовлетворя́ть по́лностью	1. to be satisfied/content 2. to satisfy, meet
～意 **mǎnyì** быть дово́льным; дово́льный	satisfied, pleased
离 **lí** **1.** покида́ть, расстава́ться **2.** отстоя́ть от	1. to leave, part from, be away from 2. to separate 3. to defy, go against 4.\\
～婚 **líhūn** развести́сь; разво́д	divorce \\distant/apart from
～开 **líkāi** уезжа́ть из, покида́ть	to leave, depart/deviate from
～别 **líbié** расстава́ться	to take leave of
～间 **líjiàn** се́ять вражду́, разобща́ть	to sow discord, drive a wedge between
属 **shǔ** **1.** принадлежа́ть, относи́ться **2.** подчиня́ться; подчинённый	1. to be subordinate to 2. to belong to 3. category; genus 4. family member, dependent
～于 **shǔyú** *см.* 属 1	to belong to, be a part of
偶 **ǒu** **1.** ку́кла; и́дол **2.** па́ра; па́рный **3.** неожи́данно; случа́йно	1. image, idol 2. mate, spouse 3. even (number) 4. by chance 5. occasionally, casually 6. together
～然 **ǒurán** случа́йно, вдруг	1. fortuitous, chance; accidentally 2.\\
册 **cè** кни́жка; том; па́пка	1. volume, book 2. copy \\occasionally
栅 **zhà** забо́р; решётка; барье́р	railings, paling, bars
丹 **dān** **1.** ки́новарь; кра́сный **2.** пилю́ля	1. red 2. (Ch. med.) pellet, powder //and then, not before 3. to return
再 **zài** ещё, сно́ва, опя́ть	1. again, once more, further(more) 2.//
～三 **zàisān** неоднокра́тно	over and over again, repeatedly
～生产 **zàishēngchǎn** воспроизво́дство	reproduction
～来 **zàilái** **1.** приходи́те сно́ва! **2.** ещё раз!, бис!	once again, once more; Encore!
～说 **zàishuō** повтори́ть *(сказанное)*	furthermore, besides
～见(会) **zàijiàn(huì)** до свида́ния!	goodbye, see you again
身 **shēn** **1.** те́ло, ту́ловище **2.** ко́рпус; ствол **3.** ли́чно	1. body 2. life, incarnation 3. child in womb 4. in person 5. (M. for suits)
～上 **shēnshang** с собо́й, при себе́	1. on one's body 2. at/on hand
～分 **shēnfen** **1.** положе́ние *(социальное)* **2.** ли́чность	1. identity, status; capacity 2. dignity

身步涉少纱吵

身分证 **shēnfenzhèng** удостоверéние ли́чности	identity/identification card
～体 **shēnti** 1. тéло; телосложéние 2. здорóвье	1. body 2. health

ノ,㇆

步 **bù** 1. шагáть; слéдовать за; шаг 2. пехóта; пехóтный	1. step 2. condition, state 3. to tread 4. to pace off
～行 **bùxíng** [идти́] пешкóм	1. won't do/work 2. to be no good 3. not to be permitted
～骤 **bùzhòu** шаги́, мéры	
～兵 **bùbīng** пехóта; пехоти́нец	1. infantry; infantryman, foot soldier
涉 **shè** 1. касáться, имéть отношéние 2. переходи́ть вброд	1. to wade, ford 2. to go through, experience 3. to involve, implicate
～及 **shèjí** касáться, затрáгивать	to involve, touch upon
少 **shǎo** 1. малочи́сленный; мáло 2. недоставáть, не хватáть	1. few, little 2. less 3. to lack, be deficient 4. to lose, be missing 5. to stop, quit
～ **shào** молодóй	young
～年 **shàonián** подрóсток; молодóй человéк	1. early youth (10—16 years) 2. juvenile
～[年]先[锋]队 **shào[nián] xiān[fēng]duì** пионéрская организáция	Young Pioneers
～数 **shǎoshù** меньшинствó	1. a few, a small number 2. minority
～数民族 **shǎoshù mínzú** национáльные меньши́нства	1. ethnic minority 2. national minority, minority nationality
～见 **shǎojiàn** *вежл.* давнó не ви́делись!	1. to see seldomly 2. seldom seen, unique, rare
～不了 **shǎobuliǎo** быть необходи́мым	1. to be indispensable 2. to be unavoidable
～女 **shàonǚ** дéвочка	young girl
纱 **shā** тюль; газ	1. yarn 2. gauze
～布 **shābù** мáрля; бинт	gauze
吵 **chǎo** кричáть, шумéть	1. to make a noise 2. to quarrel, wrangle
～嘴 **chǎozuǐ** пререкáться, спóрить	to quarrel, bicker
～架 **chǎojià** скандáлить	to quarrel, have a row/spat

抄 **chāo** **1.** переписа́ть, снять ко́пию **2.** конфискова́ть	1. to copy, transcribe 2. to plagiarize 3. to search and confiscate 4. to go off with 5. to fold
~件(本) **chāojiàn(běn)** ко́пия	to copy, duplicate
~袭 **chāoxí** копи́ровать, подража́ть; плагиа́т	1. to plagiarize 2. to copy indiscriminately from others 3. to launch a surprise attack
秒 **miǎo** секу́нда	second (of time)
炒 **chǎo** жа́рить, поджа́ривать	to stir-fry, fry, sauté
妙 **miào** **1.** прекра́сный, очарова́тельный **2.** то́нкий, иску́сный	1. wonderful, excellent, fine 2. ingenious, clever, subtle 3. mystery, charm
沙 **shā** песо́к; песча́ный	1. sand 2. sth. granulated 3. hoarse, husky 4. gritty
~鱼 **shāyú** аку́ла	shark
~皇 **shāhuáng** царь; ца́рский	tsar, czar
~滩 **shātān** о́тмель	sandy beach
~糖 **shātáng** са́харный песо́к	granulated sugar
~场(漠) **shāchǎng(mò)** пусты́ня	battlefield
~文主义 **shāwénzhǔyì** шовини́зм	chauvinism
~发 **shāfā** дива́н, софа́	(loan w.) sofa
钞 **chāo** бума́жные де́ньги	1. bank note, paper money 2. collected writings
~票 **chāopiào** банкно́та; ассигна́ция	bank note, paper money, bill
膨 **péng** пу́хнуть, распуха́ть	to expand, inflate
~胀 **péngzhàng** **1.** распуха́ть **2.** расширя́ться, увели́чиваться	to expand, swell, inflate
衫 **shān** руба́шка; блу́зка	1. unlined upper garment 2. shirt
形 **xíng** вид; фо́рма	1. form, shape 2. body, entity 3. to look
~容 **xíngróng** **1.** изобража́ть, опи́сывать **2.** нару́жность, вне́шний вид	1. to describe 2. appearance, countenance
~势 **xíngshì** обстано́вка, ситуа́ция	1. terrain, topographical features 2. situation, circumstances
~状 **xíngzhuàng** вне́шний вид, фо́рма	form, appearance, shape
~象 **xíngxiàng** о́браз; изображе́ние	1. image, form, figure 2. (art) imagery
~式 **xíngshì** тип; вид; фо́рма	form, shape

抄秒炒妙沙钞膨衫形

形彩影谚珍诊谬参

形式主义 **xíngshìzhǔyì** формали́зм	formalism
~成 **xíngchéng** формирова́ться, скла́дываться	to form, take shape
~态 **xíngtài** **1.** фо́рма; вид **2.** положе́ние, состоя́ние	1. form, shape, pattern 2. morphology
彩 **cǎi** **1.** разноцве́тный, пёстрый **2.** приз; вы́игрыш	1. color 2. brilliance, splendor 3. prize 4. blood from wound 5. ornamented,\\
~色 **cǎisè** цветно́й; пёстрый	1. color 2. variegation \\colorful
~票 **cǎipiào** лотере́йный биле́т	lottery ticket
	//3. picture, photograph 4. movie
影 **yǐng** тень; отраже́ние	1. shadow, reflection, image 2. trace//
~片 **yǐngpiān** кинофи́льм	film, movie
谚 **yàn** посло́вица; погово́рка	proverb, saying, adage, saw
~语 **yànyǔ** *см.* 谚	proverb, saying, adage, saw
珍 **zhēn** жемчу́жина; драгоце́нность; сокро́вище	1. treasure 2. precious, valuable, rare 3. to value highly, treasure
~宝 **zhēnbǎo** сокро́вище	jewelry, treasure
~珠 **zhēnzhū** же́мчуг	pearl
诊 **zhěn** осма́тривать *(больного)*; ста́вить диа́гноз	to examine (a patient)
~断 **zhěnduàn** [ста́вить] диа́гноз	to diagnose
~疗所 **zhěnliáosuǒ** амбулато́рия	clinic, dispensary, ambulatory department
谬 **miù** **1.** оши́бка, заблужде́ние **2.** абсу́рд	wrong, false, erroneous, mistaken
~误 **miùwù** *см.* 谬 **1**	falsehood; error
~论 **miùlùn** абсу́рд; измышле́ние, вы́мысел	fallacy, absurd theory
参 **cān** **1.** уча́ствовать **2.** проверя́ть	1. to join, enter, take part in 2. to refer, consult 3. to call to pay one's \\
~ **shēn** **1.** женьше́нь **2.** трепа́нги	counselor, advisor \\respects to
~加 **cānjiā** уча́ствовать, принима́ть уча́стие; прису́тствовать	1. to join, attend, take part in 2. to give (advice/etc.)
~考 **cānkǎo** наводи́ть спра́вки	1. to consult, refer to 2. reference
~议院 **cānyìyuàn** ве́рхняя пала́та парла́мента	senate
~战 **cānzhàn** уча́ствовать в войне́, воева́ть	to enter or take part in war

参观 **cānguān** осма́тривать; посеща́ть, соверша́ть экску́рсию	to visit, tour
惨 **cǎn 1.** жесто́кий, бесчелове́чный **2.** печа́литься, скорбе́ть; траги́ческий	1. miserable, pitiful, tragic 2. cruel, savage 3. to a serious degree, disastrously
～酷 **cǎnkù** *см.* 惨 1	cruel, brutal, merciless
～败 **cànbài** жесто́кое пораже́ние	to be crushingly/disastrously defeated
修 **xiū 1.** приводи́ть в поря́док; исправля́ть, ремонти́ровать **2.** стро́ить, сооружа́ть	1. to embellish, decorate 2. to repair, mend, overhaul 3. to write, compile 4. to study, cultivate 5. to build, construct 6. to trim, prune
～理 **xiūlǐ** ремонти́ровать; ремо́нт	1. to repair, mend, fix 2. (slang) to punish
～正 **xiūzhèng** вноси́ть попра́вки	1. to revise, amend, correct 2. to mutilate, revise pervertedly
～正主义 **xiūzhèngzhǔyì** ревизиони́зм	revisionism
～盖(建) **xiūgài(jiàn)** стро́ить *(здание)*	to build, rebuild
厂 **chǎng** заво́д; фа́брика; мастерска́я	1. factory, mill, plant, works 2. yard, depot
～长 **chǎngzhǎng** дире́ктор заво́да (фа́брики)	factory director/manager
广 **guǎng** широ́кий, обши́рный	1. wide, vast 2. numerous 3. to expand, spread 4. Guangzhou/Guandong
～告 **guǎnggào** объявле́ние; рекла́ма	advertisement
～播 **guǎngbō** радиовеща́ние	to broadcast, air; broadcast
～播电台 **guǎngbō diàntái** широковеща́тельная радиоста́нция	broadcasting/radio station
～阔 **guǎngkuò** *см.* 广	vast, broad
～场 **guǎngchǎng** пло́щадь *(напр. городская)*	public square
～泛 **guǎngfàn** широ́кий; широко́	extensive, wide-ranging
矿 **kuàng 1.** минера́лы; ископа́емые **2.** рудни́к, при́иск; ша́хта	1. mineral deposit, ore 2. mine
～工 **kuànggōng** шахтёр	miner
～业 **kuàngyè** горнодобыва́ющая промы́шленность	mining industry

矿扩严产

矿山 **kuàngshān** рудни́к, при́иск	mine
～物 **kuàngwù** ископа́емые; минера́лы	mineral
～泉水 **kuàngquánshuǐ** минера́льная вода́	mineral water
～藏 **kuàngcàng** поле́зные ископа́емые	mineral resources
扩 **kuò** расширя́ть, увели́чивать	to expand, enlarge, extend
～音器 **kuòyīnqì** репроду́ктор	1. megaphone 2. audio amplifier
～张 **kuòzhāng** **1.** расширя́ть(ся) **2.** расшире́ние; экспа́нсия	1. to expand, enlarge, extend 2. to dilate; dilation //swell, dilate
～大 **kuòdà** расширя́ть	1. to enlarge, expand, extend 2. to//
严 **yán** **1.** пло́тный, густо́й **2.** стро́гий; непреклóнный, реши́тельный **3.** ва́жный, значи́тельный	1. tight, strict, rigorous 2. majestic, imposing 3. (trad.) father
～重 **yánzhòng** ва́жный, серьёзный	serious, grave, critical
～密 **yánmì** **1.** со́бранный, подтя́нутый **2.** стро́го секре́тный	tight, close
～格 **yángé** стро́гий; то́чный, чёткий	strict, rigorous
～肃 **yánsù** **1.** суро́вый; стро́гий **2.** торже́ственный	serious, solemn
产 **chǎn** **1.** роди́ть **2.** выра́щивать **3.** произво́дство **4.** иму́щество, со́бственность	1. to give birth to, be delivered of 2. to produce 3. product, produce 4. property, estate
～生 **chǎnshēng** **1.** рожда́ть(-ся) **2.** производи́ть	1. to produce, engender 2. to emerge, come into being
～量 **chǎnliàng** **1.** объём произво́дства **2.** производи́тельность	output, yield
～业 **chǎnyè** **1.** промы́шленность; о́трасль произво́дства **2.** иму́щество	1. estate, property 2. industry
～品 **chǎnpǐn** проду́кция, проду́кты произво́дства	product, produce
～科 **chǎnkē** акуше́рство	obstetrical department; obstetrics

戶 **hù** двор, хозя́йство; семья́	1. door 2. household, family (bank) account 3. person of a certain status
～口 **hùkǒu** 1. жильцы́ 2. пропи́ска	1. number of households and total population 2. registered permanent res-\\
护 **hù** защища́ть; охраня́ть; забо́титься	1. to protect, guard\\ \\idents \\2. to shield, cover, be partial to
～士 **hùshi** медици́нская сестра́	(hospital) nurse -
～送 **hùsòng** сопровожда́ть, эскорти́ровать	escort, convoy -
～照 **hùzhào** па́спорт *(заграничный)*	passport -
驴 **lǘ** осёл	donkey, ass
炉 **lú** печь; жаро́вня	1. stove, furnace 2. heat
声 **shēng** 1. го́лос; звук; тон 2. репута́ция, сла́ва	1. sound, voice 2. tone 3. reputation, fame, prestige 4. to make a sound\\
～名 **shēngmíng** репута́ция	reputation, fame \\5. to declare
～音 **shēngyīn** го́лос; звук	sound, voice
～讨 **shēngtǎo** разоблача́ть, облича́ть	to denounce, condemn -
～明 **shēngmíng** де́лать заявле́ние; заявле́ние	1. to state, announce, make clear; announcement, statement 2. Buddhist\\
～明书 **shēngmíngshū** заявле́ние	communiqué \\chanting -
～调 **shēngdiào** тон, интона́ция	tone, note -
～援 **shēngyuán** подде́рживать мора́льно	to give support to -
伊 **yī** *фон. знак*	he/she
～斯兰 **yīsīlán** исла́м	Islam
岁 **suì** во́зраст; год	1. year 2. year (of age) 3. year (for
～数 **suìshu** во́зраст	crops)
罗 **luó** сеть, силки́	1. to collect; to net birds 2. to display\\
～马字 **luómǎzì** лати́нский алфави́т	Roman/Latin alphabet \\3. to sift, sieve -
萝: 萝卜 **luóbo** ре́дька; ре́па	radish
多 **duō** 1. увели́чивать(ся); мно́го 2. свы́ше, бо́лее	1. many, much, more 2. excessive, too much 3. far more 4. how 5. (pref.)\\
～ **duó** как..!, до чего́ же..!	how! \\poly-, multi-
～咱 **duōzan** когда́?	what time? when?
～少 **duōshao** ско́лько?	how much/many?
～数 **duōshù** большинство́	majority
～么 **duōme** до како́й сте́пени; до чего́ же...!	how?, what? -

戶护驴炉声伊岁罗萝多

够 **gòu** достáточно, хватáет	1. to suffice 2. to reach, be up to
移 **yí 1.** перемещáть(ся); переселя́ть(ся) **2.** переменúть, изменúть	1. to move, remove, shift 2. to transform, change, alter
～植 **yízhí** пересáживать растéния	1. to transplant 2. (med.) to graft
～动 **yídòng** перемещáть(ся), передвигáть(ся)	to move, shift
～民 **yímín** переселéнцы; колонúсты	to emigrate; emigrant, immigrant
梦 **mèng** сон, сновидéние	to dream; dream
～见 **mèngjiàn** вúдеть во сне	to dream about sb./sth.
～想 **mèngxiǎng** мечтáть; мечты́, фантáзия	to dream of, hope vainly; fond dream
乡 **xiāng 1.** дерéвня, селó **2.** рóдина	1. country(side), village, rural area 2. native place, home village/town
～村 **xiāngcūn** дерéвня	village, countryside, rural area
～亲 **xiāngqīn** земля́к	1. fellow villager 2. villagers

刀

幻 **huàn** иллю́зия; фантáзия	1. unreal, imaginary 2. to change magically
～灯片 **huàndēngpiàn** диапозитúв	slide
～象 **huànxiàng** мирáж	mirage, phantom, phantasm
～想 **huànxiǎng** мечтáть; фантáзия; иллю́зия	to imagine, dream; illusion, fancy, fantasy
局 **jú 1.** управлéние; бюрó; контóра **2.** положéние, ситуáция **3.** лимитúровать, огранúчивать	1. bureau, office 2. situation, condition, state 3. pattern (of events) 4. moral character 5. tolerance 6. gathering 7. chessboard 8. to limit, confine 9. (M. for innings)
～面 **júmiàn** ситуáция, обстанóвка	aspect, phase, situation
～部 **júbù 1.** часть; отдéл **2.** частúчный, огранúченный	part
～势 **júshì** положéние, ситуáция	situation
～限 **júxiàn** огранúчивать (-ся); ограничéния	to limit, confine
刀 **dāo** нож; меч; брúтва	1. knife, sword, blade 2. knife-shaped

刀片 **dāopiàn** лéзвие *(для безопасной бритвы)*	1. razor blade 2. (tool) bit, blade
～把子(儿) **dāobǎz(r)** власть	1. knife handle 2. sword hilt 3. (mil.) power
初 **chū** **1.** начáло; пéрвый **2.** первобы́тный; рáнний	1. at the beginning of, in the early part of 2. (prefix) first
～期 **chūqī** начáльный периóд	initial stage, early days
～步 **chūbù** пéрвый шаг; первоначáльный	initial, preliminary, tentative
～级 **chūjí** начáльный, элементáрный; перви́чный	elementary, primary
～[级]中[学] **chū[jí] zhōng[xué]** срéдняя шкóла пéрвой ступéни *(7—9 год обучения)*	junior middle school
～[级]小[学] **chū[jí] xiǎo[xué]** начáльная шкóла пéрвой ступéни *(1—4 год обучения)*	primary school
切 **qiē** рéзать; колóть	1. to cut, slice 2. to rip off
～ **qiè** **1.** настоя́тельный, насýщный **2.** надлежáщий	1. to correspond to, be close to 2. to feel the pulse 3. absolutely, exactly 4. ardently
～断 **qiēduàn** отрезáть; перерезáть	to sever, amputate
～削 **qiēxiāo** рéзать; рéзание	(mach.) cutting, chipping
～忌 **qièjì** остерегáться; воздéрживаться от	to avoid by all means
沏 **qī** завáривать чай	to infuse (tea)
窃 **qiè** **1.** воровáть, красть **2.** укрáдкой, втихомóлку, тайкóм	1. to steal 2. secretly 3. (humble) I
～据 **qièjù** узурпи́ровать	to occupy (by rebels)
剪 **jiǎn** **1.** нóжницы; щипцы́ **2.** стричь, подстригáть; разрезáть; вырезáть; срезáть	1. to exterminate, wipe out 2. to cut, clip, trim 3. scissors, shears, clippers
寡 **guǎ** **1.** вдовá **2.** одинóкий	1. widowed 2. few, scant, 3. bland, tasteless
～妇 **guǎfu** вдовá	widow
～情 **guǎqíng** апáтия	unfeeling, cold-hearted
分 **fēn** **1.** дели́ть; распределя́ть **2.** различáть; разграни́чивать **3.** филиáл, отделéние **4.** деся́тая (сóтая) часть *чего*	1. to divide, separate 2. to distribute, allot 3. to distinguish, differentiate, discriminate 4. fraction 5. 1/10th 6. percent 7. (M. for length/area/, weight/money/time/etc.)
～ **fèn** часть; дóля	1. ingredient, component 2. one's duty, right

刀
初
切
沏
窃
剪
寡
分

分 纷 粉

分工 **fēngōng** разделéние трудá	to divide the work; division of labor
～红 **fēnhóng** распределя́ть при́быль	to share a bonus, draw extra dividends
～量 **fènliang** вес; мéра	weight
～外 **fènwài** осóбенно; чрезвычáйно	1. especially, particularly 2. beyond one's duty
～析 **fēnxı** анализи́ровать; анáлиз	to analyze
～辨 **fēnbiàn** разбирáться в, различáть	1. to distinguish, differentiate 2. to defend oneself (against a charge)
～开 **fēnkāi** дели́ть; раздéльно	1. to separate, part 2. separately
～别 **fēnbié** 1. рáзница 2. расставáться, разлучáться	1. to part, leave each other 2. to distinguish, differentiate 3. difference 4. separately, respectively
～子 **fēnzǐ** *физ.* молéкула	1. molecule 2. numerator
fènzǐ 1. составнáя часть, элемéнт 2. прослóйка; элемéнты	1. share for a joint undertaking (e.g., buying a gift) 2. gift of money
～清 **fēnqīng** разграни́чить, вы́делить	to distinguish, draw a clear distinction between
～布 **fēnbù** 1. располагáть; расставля́ть 2. распространя́ть	to be distributed (over an area), be scattered; distribution
～队 **fēnduì** *воен.* подразделéние	1. unit 2. gang 3. platoon
～类 **fēnlèi** классифици́ровать, систематизи́ровать	to classify, sort; classification division
～裂 **fēnliè** раскóл; распáд	to split, divide, break up; (biol.) fission,//
～歧 **fēnqí** разноглáсия	difference, divergence
～散 **fēnsàn** рассéивать; рассредотóчивать	to disperse, scatter, decentralize
～数 **fēnshù** 1. дробь 2. оцéнка	1. (math.) fraction 2. mark, grade
～配 **fēnpèi** распределя́ть	to distribute, allot, assign; distribution
～泌 **fēnmì** выделя́ть; *физиол.* секрéция	1. (biol.) to secrete; secretion 2. (geol.) material oozing from cracks in rocks
纷 **fēn** 1. мнóжество 2. беспоря́док, пу́таница	1. confused, tangled, disorderly 2. numerous, profuse, many and various
～乱 **fēnluàn** беспоря́док, хаóс	numerous and disorderly, helter-skelter
粉 **fěn** 1. порошóк, пу́дра; мукá 2. бели́ть	1. powder 2. noodles/vermicelli 3. whitewash 4. white 5. pink

粉碎 **fěnsuì 1.** разби́ть вдрéбезги **2.** разгроми́ть	1. to smash, shatter, crush 2. broken to pieces
~刷 **fěnshuā** бели́ть	1. to whitewash 2. to plaster
~条 **fěntiáo** прозра́чная вермишéль из горóховой муки́	noodles of bean or sweet potato starch -
~笔 **fěnbǐ** мел	chalk
券 **quàn 1.** билéт **2.** облига́ция	ticket, certificate -
万 **wàn 1.** дéсять ты́сяч **2.** мнóжество; всё	1. ten thousand 2. myriad, multitudinous 3. absolutely, extremely, by all means
~一 **wànyī** éсли вдруг	1. just in case, if by any chance 2. contin-\\
~岁 **wànsuì** да здра́вствует...!; ура́!	1. long life!\\ \\gency, eventuality 3. 1/10,000 \\2. Your/His Majesty
~能 **wànnéng 1.** всемогу́щий **2.** универса́льный	1. universal, all-purpose 2. all-powerful, omnipotent
厉 **lì** жестóкий; свирéпый; стрóгий	1. strict, rigorous 2. stern, severe -
~害 **lìhài 1.** опа́сный, врéдный **2.** óчень	1. terrible, devastating 2. tough 3. sharp
方 **fāng 1.** страна́ свéта; сторона́; направлéние **2.** квадра́т **3.** мéсто **4.** мéтод, спóсоб	1. direction 2. side, party 3. place, region 4. recipe, prescription 5. method, way 6. square 7. upright, honest 8. just, only just/then 9. (M. for sq./cu. m.)
~言 **fāngyán** диалéкт, нарéчие	dialect (non-Mandarin) -
~面 **fāngmiàn 1.** сторона́ **2.** аспéкт; óбласть	aspect, side, facet -
~针 **fāngzhēn** курс, ориента́ция	policy, guiding principle - //for mixing chemicals
~子 **fāngz** рецéпт	1. prescription 2. formula; directions//
~向 **fāngxiàng** направлéние, курс	direction, orientation -
~案 **fāng'àn** проéкт; план	scheme, plan, program
~便 **fāngbiàn** удóбный, комфорта́бельный	1. convenient 2. (coll.) to go to the lavatory 3. to have money to spare/lend
~式 **fāngshì 1.** тип; образéц; фóрма **2.** мéтод, спóсоб	way, fashion, pattern - -
~法 **fāngfǎ** мéтод, спóсоб	method, way, means
纺 **fǎng** прясть	1. to spin 2. thin silk cloth
~织业 **fǎngzhīyè** тексти́льная промы́шленность	textile industry -
仿 **fǎng 1.** похóже; подóбно	1. to imitate, copy 2. to resemble, be like

仿 防 妨 访 房 旁 磅 镑 约

2. подражáть, имитúровать	-
仿制 **fǎngzhì** имитáция, поддéлка	to copy, imitate
～佛 **fǎngfú** как бýдто, якобы	1. to seem; as if 2. to be more or less the same, be alike
防 **fáng** оборонять; защищáть	1. to guard/prepare against, prevent 2. to defend, guard 3. dike, embankment
～卫 **fángwèi** *см.* 防	to defend
～空 **fángkōng** противовоздýшная оборóна	air defense, antiaircraft
～治 **fángzhì** профилáктика и лечéние	prevention and cure; prophylaxis
～御 **fángyù** оборóна	defense
～毒 **fángdú** противохимúческая защúта	to defend against (poison) gas
妨 **fáng** препятствовать; вредúть	to hinder, impede, obstruct
～害 **fánghài** мешáть; вредúть	to impair, jeopardize, be harmful to
～碍 **fáng'ài** препятствовать	to hamper, impede, obstruct
访 **fǎng** 1. навещáть, посещáть; наносúть визúт 2. брать интервью	1. to visit, call on 2. to seek by inquiry/search, try to get
～问 **fǎngwèn** *см.* 访 1	to visit, call on, interview
房 **fáng** дом; кóмната	1. house 2. room 3. house-like structure
～间 **fángjiān** 1. кóмната; нóмер *(в гостинице)* 2. купé	room
旁 **páng** 1. обóчина 2. óколо, вóзле 3. посторóнний	1. side 2. other, else 3. lateral part of a Ch. character
～听 **pángtīng** быть наблюдáтелем	1. to be a visitor at a class meeting/etc. 2. to audit a class
～边 **pángbiān** в сторонé; óколо	side
磅 **bàng** 1. фунт 2. весы́; взвéшивать	1. (loan w.) pound 2. (print.) point, type 3. to weigh; scales
镑 **bàng** фунт стéрлингов	(loan w.) pound (currency)
约 **yuē** 1. услóвиться, договорúться; договóр 2. сдéрживать, ограничивать	1. to make an appointment 2. to ask, invite 3. to restrict, restrain 4. pact 5. about 6. brief 7. indistinct 8. frugal
～束 **yuēshù** свя́зывать; ограничивать	to control, restrain, bind; restraint

药 **yào 1.** лекáрство **2.** пóрох	1. medicine, drug, remedy 2. to poison 3. to cure 4. certain chemicals
～铺(房) **yàopù(fáng)** аптéка	herbal medicine shop
～丸 **yàowán** пилю́ли	pill
的 **de, d** *служ. сл., оформляющее определительные связи*	(syntactic w. and suffix forming a definition/attribute indicating possession, etc.)
～ **dí** и́стинный; тóчный	true, exact, accurate
～当 **dídāng** прáвильный; соотвéтствующий	accurate, proper
～确 **díquè** действи́тельный, пóдлинный; в сáмом дéле	certainly, sure
钓 **diào 1.** крючóк **2.** уди́ть ры́бу	to fish with hook and line, to angle
均 **jūn** рáвный, одинáковый	1. equal, even, uniform 2. without exception 3. potter's wheel
竭 **jié** истощи́ть, исчерпáть	1. to make the utmost effort 2. to exhaust, use up
～力 **jiélì** всячески	to do one's utmost
喝 **hē** пить	1. to drink 2. to shout (a command)
揭 **jiē** вскрывáть, разоблачáть; разгáдывать	1. to tear/take off 2. to uncover, lift (lid/etc.) 3. to expose 4. to proclaim
～露 **jiēlù** обличáть	1. to expose, unmask 2. to announce
～穿 **jiēchuān** разоблачáть	to expose, lay bare
渴 **kě 1.** испы́тывать жáжду **2.** надéяться	thirsty
匈 **xiōng** *фон. знак*	(archaic) breast
胸 **xiōng** грудь, груднáя клéтка	1. chest, bosom, thorax 2. mind, heart
～怀 **xiōnghuái** чу́вства	mind, heart
陶 **táo** керáмика; гончáрные издéлия	1. to make pottery; pottery, earthenware 2. to cultivate, educate, mold
～器 **táoqì** керами́ческие издéлия	pottery, earthenware
掏 **tāo 1.** выбирáть, отбирáть **2.** доставáть, вынимáть	1. to take out with the hand 2. to hollow/scoop out
淘 **táo 1.** промывáть; полоскáть **2.** шали́ть, баловáться	1. to rinse, wash clean 2. to clean out, dredge 3. to eliminate the inferior 4. to tax (one's energy) 5. naughty
～汰 **táotài** отбирáть; отбóр	1. to eliminate through selection or competition 2. to die out
～气 **táoqì** капри́зничать; баловáться	mischievous
句 **jù** предложéние, фрáза	1. sentence 2. (M. for poems/songs)
～号 **jùhào** тóчка	period, full stop

句 拘 狗 旬 询 葡 勾 构 购 沟 物

句法 **jùfǎ** си́нтаксис	syntax
拘 **jū** задержа́ть, схвати́ть, арестова́ть	1. to arrest, detain 2. to restrain, constrain 3. inflexible, restrained
～留 **jūliú** арестова́ть; интерни́ровать	to detain, intern
～禁 **jūjìn** взять под стра́жу	to take into custody
狗 **gǒu** соба́ка	1. dog 2. damned, cursed
～腿子 **gǒutuiz** посо́бник	(coll.) hired thug, henchman
旬 **xún** дека́да	1. period of 10 days 2. period of 10 yrs.
询 **xún** спра́шивать, выясня́ть; допра́шивать	to ask, inquire
葡 **pú** виногра́д	grape
～萄 **pútao** виногра́д	grape
～萄酒 **pútaojiǔ** виногра́дное вино́	grape wine
～萄干 **pútaogān** изю́м	raisin
勾 **gōu** 1. крюк 2. завле́чь, втяну́ть	1. to cancel, cross out 2. to delineate, portray 3. to induce, evoke, attract
～ **gòu** вступи́ть в за́говор	shady business
～当 **gòudang** махина́ции; проде́лки	shady deal/business
～结 **gòujié** войти́ в сго́вор	to collude/collaborate with
构 **gòu** стро́ить, сооружа́ть	1. to construct, compose 2. to fabricate\\ \\3. lit. composition
～筑 **gòuzhu** стро́ить; сооруже́ние	to construct, build
～想(思) **gòuxiǎng(sī)** за́мысел; воображе́ние	1. to visualize, conceptualize 2. proposition
购 **gòu** покупа́ть, закупа́ть	to buy
～买力 **gòumǎilì** покупа́тельная спосо́бность	purchasing power
沟 **gōu** ров; кана́ва	1. ditch, channel, trench 2. groove, rut,// //furrow 3. gully, ravine
物 **wù** 1. вещь, предме́т 2. *филос.* мате́рия; материа́льный	1. think, matter 2. the world vs. oneself
～理学 **wùlixué** фи́зика	physics
～价 **wùjià** це́ны	commodity prices
～质 **wùzhì** мате́рия, вещество́; материа́льный	matter, substance, material
～质条件 **wùzhì tiáojiàn** материа́льное положе́ние	material conditions
～质鼓励 **wùzhì gǔlì** материа́льное стимули́рование (поощре́ние)	material reward/incentive

物资 **wùzī** материа́льные ресу́рсы	materials, goods
易 **yì** **1.** лёгкий, удо́бный **2.** меня́ться, изменя́ться	1. easy 2. amiable, gentle 3. to change 4. to exchange
踢 **tī** бить ного́й, пина́ть	to kick
～球 **tīqiú** игра́ть в футбо́л	1. to kick a ball 2. to play soccer/football
锡 **xī** о́лово	tin
场 **chǎng** **1.** пло́щадь *(напр. городская)* **2.** ме́сто де́йствия **3.** сеа́нс; спекта́кль	1. gathering place 2. level open space, yard, stage 3. market, country fair 4. (M. for games/performances, etc.)
扬 **yáng** **1.** поднима́ть(ся) **2.** повыша́ть *(голос)*	1. to raise 2. to wave, flutter 3. to praise 4. to winnow 5. to make known
～言 **yángyán** угрожа́ть; угро́за	to broadcast threats
肠 **cháng** кишка́; кишки́	intestines
～子 **chángz** **1.** кишки́ **2.** колбаса́; соси́ски	intestines
汤 **tāng** **1.** кипято́к **2.** суп; бульо́н	1. hot/boiling water 2. hot springs 3. soup, broth
书 **shū** **1.** кни́га **2.** писа́ть; каллигра́фия **3.** письмо́; докуме́нт	1. book 2. letter 3. document 4. style of calligraphy, script 5. to write
～摊 **shūtān** кни́жный ларёк	bookstall, bookstand
～信 **shūxìn** корреспонде́нция, перепи́ска	letter, written message
～店 **shūdiàn** кни́жный магази́н	bookstore
～籍 **shūjí** кни́ги, литерату́ра	books, works, literature
～面 **shūmiàn** **1.** пи́сьменный **2.** обло́жка *(книги)*	written, in written form, in writing
～册 **shūcè** брошю́ра	booklet, pamphlet, brochure
～架 **shūjià** кни́жная по́лка; стелла́ж	bookshelf, bookcase
～桌 **shūzhuō** пи́сьменный стол	(writing) desk
～记 **shūji** секрета́рь *(парторганизации)*	1. secretary 2. clerk
～法 **shūfǎ** каллигра́фия; по́черк	calligraphy
巧 **qiǎo** **1.** ло́вкий, иску́сный **2.** кста́ти, как ра́з	1. clever, intelligent 2. skillful 3. deceiving 4. cute 5. fortuitous
～克力 **qiǎokèlì** шокола́д	(loan w.) chocolate
号 **hào** **1.** назва́ние; про́зви-	1. name 2. assumed name 3. firm, shop 4.

号亏污夸考烤与写

ще, кли́чка **2.** но́мер; число́	mark, signal 5. number in a series 6. size 7. date 8. order 9. to make a mark
号 **háo** звать, крича́ть	to howl (of humans/wind)
～召 **hàozhào** призыва́ть к	to call, appeal (for supporters)
～外 **hàowài** э́кстренный вы́пуск	newspaper extra
～叫 **háojiào** крик; плач	to howl, wail
～码 **hàomǎ** ци́фра; но́мер	(serial) number
亏 **kuī 1.** недоста́ча; уще́рб, убы́ток **2.** к сча́стью	1. to lose (money/etc.), have a deficit 2. to treat unfairly 3. fortunately
污 **wū 1.** па́чкать; гря́зный **2.** клевета́ть **3.** а́лчный	1. dirty, filthy, foul 2. corrupt 3. dirt, filth 4. to defile, smear
～辱 **wūrǔ** уни́зить; оскорби́ть; надруга́ться	1. to humiliate, insult; insult 2. to defile, sully
～蔑 **wūmiè** клевета́ть; облива́ть гря́зью	1. to slander, smear 2. to defile, tarnish
～点 **wūdiǎn** позо́р	stain, spot, blemish
夸 **kuā 1.** хва́стать(ся); преувели́чивать **2.** хвали́ть; похвала́	1. to exaggerate, overstate, boast 2. to praise 3. big 4. lavish
～张 **kuāzhāng** *см.* 夸 1	to exaggerate, overstate; hyperbole
～大 **kuādà** преувели́чивать	to exaggerate, magnify
～奖 **kuājiang** *см.* 夸 2	to praise, commend
考 **kǎo 1.** про́бовать, проверя́ть; иссле́довать **2.** экзаменова́ть	1. to give/take a test 2. to check, inspect 3. to study, investigate, verify
～验 **kǎoyàn** [жи́зненные] испыта́ния	to test; test, trial
～上 (中) **kǎoshàng(zhōng)** вы́держать экза́мен	to pass an entrance examination
～选 **kǎoxuǎn** ко́нкурсный экза́мен	to select by competition; competitive examination
～试 **kǎoshì** экзаменова́ться; экза́мен	to examine; examination, test
～虑 **kǎolǜ** проду́мать, взве́сить; уче́сть	to think over, consider
烤 **kǎo 1.** гре́ться у огня́ **2.** жа́рить *(на открытом огне)*	1. to bake, roast, toast 2. to warm (hands and feet) near a fire
与 **yǔ 1.** *союз* и; с; 和平与战争 война́ и мир; **2.** дава́ть, предоставля́ть	1. to give, offer 2. to commend, support, assist 3. to get along with 4. to; with 5. and, together with
写 **xiě** писа́ть; опи́сывать	1. to write, compose 2. to describe, de-\\\\pict 3.to paint,draw
～作 **xiězuò** занима́ться ли-	to write; writing

тературной деятельностью	-
	-
马 **mǎ** лóшадь, конь; кóнный	1. horse 2. horse chess piece
	-
～上 **mǎshàng** тóтчас, немéдленно	at once, right away
	-
～路 **mǎlù** мостовáя; дорóга; шоссé	road, street
	-
～列主义 **mǎlièzhǔyì** маркси́зм-ленини́зм	Marxism-Leninism
	-
～克斯主义 **mǎkèsīzhǔyì** маркси́зм	Marxism
	-
～马虎虎 **mǎmǎhūhū** кóе-кáк, небрéжно	1. careless, casual 2. fair, so-so
	-
～戏 **mǎxì** цирк	circus
～铃薯 **mǎlíngshǔ** картóфель	potato
码 **mǎ** **1.** ци́фра; нóмер **2.** шифр	1. (coll.) to pile up, stock 2. code (number) 3. (M. for clothes/happenings)
～头 **mǎtou** при́стань; причáл; нáбережная	1. wharf, dock, port city, commercial/ transportation center
妈 **mā**, 妈妈 **māma** мáма	(coll.) mama
骂 **mà** ругáть(ся)	1. to abuse, call names 2. to reprove
驾 **jià** управля́ть *(маши-ной)*	1. to harness 2. to draw (a cart, etc.) 3. to drive, pilot, sail 4. carriage, cart
～驶 **jiàshǐ** управля́ть, вести́; пилоти́ровать	to drive (a vehicle), pilot (a ship/plane)
	-
乌 **wū** **1.** вóрон **2.** чёрный	1. black, dark 2. crow
鸟 **niǎo** пти́ца	bird
鸽 **gē** гóлубь	duck
鸭 **yā** ýтка	crow
鸦 **yā** вóрон	(loan w.) opium
～片 **yāpiàn** óпиум	chicken
鸡 **jī** кýры	(loan w.) cocktail
～尾酒 **jīwěijiǔ** коктéйль	goose
鹅 **é** гусь	island, isle //3. to thresh, hull, unhusk
岛 **dǎo** óстров	1. to attack, harass 2. to beat, pound//
捣 **dǎo** нарушáть поря́док	to cause a disturbance, make trouble
～乱 **dǎoluàn** безобрáзничать, хулигáнить; стрóить	-
	-
кóзни	to play tricks, gossip and cause mischief, sow discord
～鬼 **dǎoguǐ** интриговáть; наговáривать	pigeon, dove
仍 **réng** по-прéжнему; как обы́чно	still, yet
	-

仍扔奶携秀绣诱锈粥弯湾弱弔弟梯第佛力

仍然 **réngrán** *см.* 仍	still, yet
扔 **rēng 1.** бросáть, метáть **2.** выбрáсывать	1. to throw, toss 2. to throw away
奶 **nǎi 1.** сосóк *(грудú)*; вы́мя **2.** молокó	1. breasts 2. milk 3. (coll.) to nurse, breast-feed
～油 **nǎiyóu** сли́вочное мáсло	cream
～类 **nǎilèi** молóчные продýкты	milk/dairy products
携 **xié 1.** вести́ зá руку **2.** имéть при себé, нести́	1. to carry, take along 2. to take/hold of sb. by the hand
～带 **xiédài** *см.* 携 2	to carry, take along
～带行李 **xiédài xíngli** ручнáя кладь	hand luggage/baggage
秀 **xiù** прелéстный, изя́щный	1. elegant, beautiful 2. excellent 3. to put forth flowers/ears (of grains)
绣 **xiù** вышивáть; вы́шивка	to embroider; embroidery
诱 **yòu** завлекáть, замáнивать; совращáть	1. to guide, lead, induce 2. to lure, seduce, entice
～惑 **yòuhuò** очарóвывать; обольщáть	to tempt, seduce, lure
锈 **xiù** ржáветь; ржáвчина	to rust; rust
粥 **zhōu** отвáр; жи́дкая кáша	gruel, porridge, congee
弯 **wān** кривóй, изóгнутый	1. to bend, flex 2. to draw (a bow) 3.// //bent, curved, crooked 4. curve
～曲 **wānqū** *см.* 弯	1. to distort 2.winding, crooked, curved
湾 **wān** зали́в, бýхта; порт	1. bend in a stream 2. gulf, bay
弱 **ruò 1.** слáбый; бесси́льный **2.** мéньше, мéнее	1. weak, feeble 2. inferior 3. young 4. a bit less than
～点 **ruòdiǎn** слáбое (уязви́мое) мéсто	weak point
弔 **diào 1.** соболéзнование; трáур **2.** висéть	1. to hang 2. to lift up or let down with rope 3. to mourn 4. to withdraw, revoke
弟 **dì** млáдший брат	1. younger brother 2. junior 3. I
～兄 **dìxiong** брáтья; брáтский	1. brother 2. soldiers
梯 **tī** лéстница; ступéни	1. ladder, steps, stairs 2. terraced
第 **dì** *префикс порядк. числ.*	1. (prefix) sequence, order 2. rank 3.\\ \\marker of nos.
佛 **fó** Бýдда; будди́зм; будди́йский	Buddha; Buddhism
力 **lì 1.** си́ла, мощь **2.** спосóбности, возмóжности	1. power, strength, ability; force 2. to make every effort 3. earnestly
～量 **lìliang** си́ла, мощь; си́лы	1. physical strength 2. power, force. 3. ability

力争 **lìzhēng** борóться за	1. to work hard for, do all one can
～求 **lìqiú** старáться, стремúться	to do one's best to, strive for
	-
～气 **lìqi** сúла; бóдрость	physical strength, effort
功 **gōng 1.** заслýга; пóдвиг **2.** дéло, занятие	1. meritorious service, exploit 2. achievement, result, effect 3. skill
～率 **gōnglǜ** *тех.* мóщность	(phys.) power
～劳 **gōngláo** трудовы́е заслýги (пóдвиги)	contribution, credit, merit
	-
～效 **gōngxiào 1.** успéхи **2.** эффéкт	efficacy, effect
	-
～绩 **gōngjì** заслýги; успéхи; успевáемость	contribution, merits and achievements
	-
劲 **jìn** сúльный; сúла; усúлия	(coll.) vigor, energy, strength, interest
	-
～儿 **jìr 1.** дух, сúла **2.** интерéс; смысл, суть	(coll.) vigor, energy, strength, interest
	-
勤 **qín 1.** прилежáние, усéрдие **2.** обслýживание	1. diligent, hardworking 2. solicitous 3. service, attendance
～俭 **qínjiǎn** трудолюбúвый и бережлúвый	hardworking and thrifty
	-
～劳 **qínláo** трудолюбúвый	industrious, hardworking
～务 **qínwù** слýжба	1. service 2. non-combatant service
助 **zhù** помогáть; пóмощь	to help, assist, aid
～手 **zhùshǒu** помóщник, ассистéнт	assistant, aid
	- //obtrusive veins 4. fiber
筋 **jīn** мы́шцы, мýскулы	1. muscle 2. (coll.) tendon, sinew 3.//
劝 **quàn** убеждáть, уговáривать	to exhort, urge, persuade
	-
～告 **quàngào** совéтовать; убеждáть	to advise, counsel, exhort
	-
勋 **xūn** заслýга; пóдвиг	merit, meritorious service achievement
～章 **xūnzhāng** óрден	medal, decoration //3. disaster
劫 **jié** грáбить; грабёж	1. to rob, plunder, raid 2. to coerce//
～夺 **jiéduó** грáбить; отнимáть	to seize by force, plunder
	-
动 **dòng 1.** двúгаться, передвигáться **2.** дéйствовать; дéйствие	1. to move 2. to act, get moving 3. to change 4. to use 5. to arouse
	-
～摇 **dòngyáo** качáться; колебáться	to shake, vascillate, waver
	-
～作 **dòngzuò** дéйствия, постýпки	to act, start moving; movement, motion, action //3. to strike, hit
～手 **dòngshǒu 1.** начинáть,	1. to start action 2. to touch, handle//

力功劲勤助筋劝勋劫动

приступа́ть **2.** дава́ть во́-лю рука́м	-
动身 **dòngshēn** отпра́виться в путь	to leave on a journey
～物 **dòngwù** живо́тные	animal
～人 **dòngrén** тро́гательный, волну́ющий	moving, touching, poignant
～机 **dòngjī** моти́в, побужде́ние	motive, intention
～员 **dòngyuán** мобилизова́ть	to mobilize, arouse
～态 **dòngtài** **1.** ситуа́ция; положе́ние **2.** о́браз де́йствий	1. trends, development 2. situation 3. dynamic state
幼 **yòu** младе́нец; младе́нческий; де́тство	1. young, under age 2. situation, the young
～稚 **yòuzhì** **1.** молодо́й; де́тский **2.** незре́лый, нео́пытный	1. young 2. childish, puerile, naive
～儿园 **yòu'éryuán** де́тский сад	kindergarten, nursery school, infant school
历 **lì** **1.** проходи́ть, минова́ть **2.** испы́тывать, пережива́ть **3.** календа́рь	1. experience 2. calendar 3. era, age 4. to calculate, count 5. to undergo, experience 6. last 7. through(out)
～书 **lìshū** календа́рь	almanac
～史 **lìshǐ** исто́рия; истори́ческий	history, past records
～代 **lìdài** на протяже́нии веко́в	successive/past dynasties
虏 **lǔ** брать в плен; пле́нный	to take prisoner; captive, prisoner-of-war
伤 **shāng** ра́нить; ра́на	1. to injure, wound; injury, wound, wounded 2. to fall ill from
～口 **shāngkǒu** ра́на; поре́з	wound, cut
～害 **shānghài** вред, уще́рб; зло	to injure, harm
～亡 **shāng-wáng** ра́неные и уби́тые	injuries and deaths, casualties
～疤 **shāngbā** шрам, рубе́ц	scar
～气 **shāngqì** упа́сть ду́хом	to feel frustrated, feel disheartened
～风 **shāngfēng** просту-жа́ться; просту́да	to catch cold; cold
～心 **shāngxīn** горева́ть; печа́льный	to be sad/grieved
另 **lìng** друго́й; специа́льный, осо́бый	1. other, another, separate, extra 2. in addition, besides 3. to separate, divide

另外 **lìngwài** другóй; крóме тогó	in addition, moreover, besides
拐 **guǎi** **1.** поворáчивать *(за угол)* **2.** хромáть; костыль	1. to turn, change direction 2. to limp 3. to swindle 4. to abduct 5. crutch, cane
～弯 **guǎiwān** **1.** повернýть зá угол **2.** увиливать, уклоня́ться, хитри́ть	1. to turn a corner, turn 2. to turn around, pursue a new course 3. at the corner
男 **nán** мужчи́на; муж; мужскóй	1. man, male 2. son, boy
劳 **láo** **1.** труди́ться; труд **2.** уставáть **3.** благодари́ть за труды́	1. to put sb. to the trouble of 2. to express one's appreciation 3. work 4. accomplishment 5. hard, wearisome
～驾 **láojià** извини́те за беспокóйство	Excuse me, May I trouble you (to)
～动 **láodòng** труди́ться; труд	(coll./court.) to bother/trouble (sb.)
捞 **lāo** **1.** вылáвливать *(из воды)* **2.** чéрпать *(воду)*	1. to dredge up, drag for 2. to get by improper means
勇 **yǒng** хрáбрость, герóйство, отвáга	1. brave, valiant, courageous 2. soldier, conscript
～敢 **yǒnggǎn** смéлый, хрáбрый	brave, courageous
～气 **yǒngqì** смéлость, мýжество	courage, nerve
劣 **liè** плохóй, дурнóй; ни́зкий	bad, inferior, of low quality
～绅 **lièshēn** деревéнские эксплуатáторы	evil gentry; intellectual bully
～势 **lièshì** неблагоприя́тная обстанóвка	inferior strength/position
募 **mù** вербовáть; призывáть *(в армию)*	to raise, collect, enlist, recruit
努 **nǔ** напрягáть си́лы; энерги́чно	1. to put forth strength 2. to pour 3. to injure oneself by over-exertion
～力 **nǔlì** прилагáть уси́лия; старáться; старáтельный	to make a great effort, try hard; great effort
务 **wù** **1.** дéло, заня́тие **2.** обя́занность; задáча	1. affair, business 2. to strive for/to 3. to devote oneself to 4. must, should
雾 **wù** тумáн, мгла	fog, mist //to exhaust 4. limit, end
穷 **qióng** бéдность, нищетá	1. poor, impoverished 2. exhausted 3.//
～苦 **qióngkǔ** бéдный, ни́щий	destitute; destitution
势 **shì** **1.** си́ла, влия́ние,	1. power, force, influence 2. appear-

另拐男劳捞勇劣募努务雾穷势

势办协胁苏

власть 2. усло́вия, обстоя́тельства	ance, configuration 3. situation, circumstance 4. sign, gesture 5. male\\
势力 shìli си́ла, мощь, могу́щество	force, power, influence \\genitals
～力范围 shìli fànwéi сфе́ра влия́ния	sphere of influence //up 3. to buy 4. to punish (by law)
办 bàn де́лать, выполня́ть	1. to do, handle, manage 2. to run, set//
～理 bànli вести́ дела́; де́йствовать; исполня́ть	to handle, conduct, transact
～法 bànfǎ 1. спо́соб, ме́тод 2. вы́ход *(из положения)*	way, means, measure
～公 bàngōng служи́ть; рабо́тать	1. to handle official business, work (usu. in an office)
～公室 bàngōngshì кабине́т; канцеля́рия	office
协 xié 1. сотру́дничать; сотру́дничество 2. согла́сие, гармо́ния	1. joint, common 2. to assist
～和 xiéhé *см.* 协 2	to meditate, harmonize
～作 xiézuò *см.* 协 1	cooperation, coordination
～同 xiétóng совме́стный; совме́стно	to work in coordination with, cooperate with
～调 xiétiáo 1. согласо́вывать 2. гармо́ния	to coordinate, harmonize, bring into line
～商 xiéshāng совеща́ться, консульти́роваться; консульта́ция	to consult, talk things over
～定 xiédìng соглаше́ние; конве́нция	agreement, accord, pact
～会 xiéhuì сою́з; о́бщество; ассоциа́ция	association, society
胁 xié 1. рёбра 2. угрожа́ть; угро́за	1. to force, coerce 2. upperside of human body
～从 xiécóng посо́бничество	to accompany by force
苏 sū *сокр.* 1. СССР (Сою́з Сове́тских Социалисти́ческих Респу́блик); сове́тский 2. *пров.* Цзянсу́	1. (abbr.) Suzhou 2. (abbr.) Jiangsu prov. 3. (abbr.) former U.S.S.R. (Soviet Union)
～维埃 sūwéiāi сове́т; Сове́ты; сове́тский	(loan w.) Soviet, soviet
～共 sūgòng КПСС (Коммунисти́ческая па́ртия Сове́тского Сою́за)	(abbr.) Communist Party of the Soviet Union (CPSU)

为 **wéi** **1.** де́лать; сде́лать **2.** быть, явля́ться	1. to do, accomplish 2. act/serve as 3. to be, become 4. to govern 5. by
～ **wèi** ра́ди, для; что́бы	1. to stand for, support 2. for, on account of, to, up to, till, until
～止 **wéizhǐ** по, включи́тельно по	-
～难 **wéinán** ста́вить в затрудни́тельное положе́ние	1. to create difficulties (for sb.) 2. to be in a quandary 3. embarrassed
～首 **wéishǒu** возглавля́ть	to head, be headed by
～什么 **wèishénme** почему́?	why?, why is it that?
伪 **wěi** **1.** подде́лывать; фальши́вый **2.** марионе́точный	1. false, fake 2. puppet
～军 **wěijūn** марионе́точная а́рмия	puppet army/soldier
～装 **wěizhuāng** притворя́ться; маскирова́ться	1. to pretend, feign 2. to disguise; disguise, mask 3. camouflage
～造 **wěizào** подде́лывать, фальсифици́ровать	to forge, counterfeit
母 **mǔ** **1.** мать **2.** са́мка	1. mother 2. female elders 3. nut 4. fe-//male 5. alphabet, sound element
～亲 **mǔqin** мать	mother
～校 **mǔxiào** родна́я шко́ла	one's old school, alma mater
每 **měi** **1.** ка́ждый, вся́кий **2.** ка́ждый раз	1. every, each 2. frequent, often
悔 **huì** раска́иваться, сожале́ть	to regret, repent
侮 **wǔ** обижа́ть, оскорбля́ть	to insult, bully
～辱 **wǔrǔ** оскорбля́ть, унижа́ть	to insult, humiliate
梅 **méi** **1.** сли́ва **2.** си́филис	plum
海 **hǎi** **1.** мо́ре; морско́й **2.** мно́жество, ма́сса	1. sea 2. big lake 3. a huge group of people/things 4. a great capacity
～难 **hǎinán** кораблекруше́ние	perils of the sea
～外 **hǎiwài** иностра́нный	overseas, abroad
～岸 **hǎi'àn** бе́рег мо́ря	seacoast, seashore
～军 **hǎijūn** вое́нно-морски́е си́лы	navy
～洋 **hǎiyáng** моря́ и океа́ны	seas and oceans; ocean
～带 **hǎidài** морска́я капу́ста	kelp
～参 **hǎishēn** трепа́нг	sea cucumber, sea slug
～湾 **hǎiwān** зали́в, бу́хта	bay, gulf
～关 **hǎiguān** тамо́жня	custom house, customs
～峡 **hǎixiá** проли́в	strait, channel

海味 **hǎiwèi** продýкты мóря	seafood
～拔 **hǎibá** высотá над ýровнем мóря	elevation, height above sea level
～运 **hǎiyùn** морскúе перевóзки	to transport by sea; sea transportation, ocean shipping
～滨 **hǎibīn** взмóрье	seashore, seaside
莓 **méi** землянúка; малúна	berry
霉 **méi** плéсень	mold, mildew
毒 **dú** 1. яд; ядовúтый 2. жестóкий, злóбный	1. poison, toxin 2. narcotics 3. to kill with poison 4. poisonous 5. malicious
～害 **dúhài** повредúть, погубúть; отравлéние	to poison (sb.'s mind)
～药 **dúyào** яд	poison, toxicant
～气 **dúqì** отравля́ющие веществá	poison(ous) gas

㇏

人 **rén** 1. человéк; человéческий 2. лúчность, осóба, персóна	person, people; human
～工 **réngōng** искýсственный	1. man-made 2. manual work; manpower
～口 **rénkǒu** 1. населéние 2. члéны семьú	population
～种 **rénzhǒng** рáса	race (of humans)
～行道 **rénxíngdào** тротуáр	sidewalk
～间 **rénjiān** 1. человéческий род 2. на лю́дях	the human world
～参 **rénshēn** женьшéнь	ginseng
～物 **rénwù** дéятель; лúчность; персонáж	1. character, personage 2. character in literature 3. figure painting
～类 **rénlèi** человéчество	human being/species
～家 **rénjiā** 1. лю́ди 2. чужúе, посторóнние	1. sb. else 2. I (used by women)
～象 **rénxiàng** портрéт	portrait, image
～造 **rénzào** искýсственный	synthetic, artificial
～道 **réndào** гумáнность; гумáнный	human sympathy; humane
～道主义 **réndàozhǔyì** гуманúзм	humanitarianism
～民 **rénmín** нарóд, населéние	the people

人员 **rényuán** персона́л; штат	1. personnel, staff
队 **duì** отря́д; кома́нда; брига́да; подразделе́ние	1. a row of people, line 2. team, group
~伍 **duìwǔ** отря́д; коло́нна	1. troops 2. ranks, contingent
从 **cóng 1.** сле́довать, сопровожда́ть **2.** посвяти́ть себя́ *чему* **3.** *предлог* из; от; с	1. to crowd together; crowd, collection 2. clump, thicket, grove
~前 **cóngqián** пре́жде, в про́шлом	before, formerly, in the past
~事 **cóngshì** занима́ться *чем;* посвяща́ть себя́ *чему*	1. to go in for, be engaged in 2. to deal with
~来 **cónglái** всегда́; *перед отриц.* никогда́ ещё	always, at all times, all along
纵 **zòng 1.** освобожда́ть, отпуска́ть **2.** вертика́льный; продо́льный	1. to release, set free 2. to indulge, give oneself up to 3. to leap 4. to pamper, spoil 5. to shoot (an arrow) 6. even if 7. vertical, longitudinal 8. length from north to south
~容 **zòngróng** попусти́тельствовать; попусти́тельство	to connive
~队 **zòngduì** коло́нна; отря́д	column, file
~横 **zòng-héng** вдоль и поперёк	1. to traverse 2. in length and breadth; vertically and horizontally 3. with ease
众 **zhòng** мно́жество, ма́сса	crowd, multitude; numerous, many (of people)
~人 **zhòngrén** толпа́; ма́ссы; обще́ственность	everybody
认 **rèn 1.** различа́ть, распознава́ть **2.** признава́ть	1. to recognize, know 2. to admit, own up 3. to accept as unavoidable
~错 **rèncuò 1.** обозна́ться **2.** призна́ть оши́бки	to admit mistakes, apologize
~可 **rènkě** позволя́ть, разреша́ть	to approve; approval
~为 **rènwéi** счита́ть, полага́ть	to think/believe that
~真 **rènzhēn 1.** справедли́вый **2.** серьёзный, добросо́вестный	1. to take for real 2. serious, earnest
~识 **rènshi** знать, быть знако́мым; понима́ть	to know, recognize; knowledge, understanding
欠 **qiàn 1.** недостава́ть, не хвата́ть **2.** быть в долгу́	1. to owe 2. to lack, be short of 3. to raise slightly 4. to yawn
吹 **chuī 1.** дуть; игра́ть *(на*	1. to blow, puff 2. to play (a wind instr.) 3.

人队从纵众认欠吹

духовом инструменте)	(coll.) to boast, brag 4. to fall through (of
2. хвáстаться	plans)
砍 **kǎn** рубúть, разрубáть	1. to cut, chop, hack 2. to throw sth. at
欲 **yù** желáть, стремúться;	1. to wish, desire, want; wish, desire 2.
желáние, страсть	about to, on the point of
欣 **xīn** рáдость, удовóльст-	glad, happy, joyful
вие	-
～赏 **xīnshǎng** любовáться,	to appreciate, enjoy, admire
восхищáться	-
掀 **xiān** приподня́ть; откú-	1. to lift (a cover/etc.) 2. to surge,
нуть	cause to surge //to start (a mvt., etc.)
～起 **xiānqi** возникáть	1. to lift, raise 2. to (make) surge 3.//
软 **ruǎn 1.** мя́гкий; эластúч-	1. soft, weak, pliant 2. poor in quality
ный **2.** слáбый	-
歌 **gē** пéсня; гимн; мелóдия	to sing; song
～曲 **gēqǔ** пéсня; мелóдия	song
～舞团 **gēwǔtuán** ансáмбль	song and dance troupe
пéсни и пля́ски	-
～剧 **gējù** óпера	opera
歇 **xiē 1.** отдыхáть **2.** оста-	1. to have a rest 2. to stop (work,
новúть, прекратúть	etc.), knock off 3. to go to bed
炊 **chuī** готóвить пúщу	to cook a meal
欢 **huān 1.** рáдоваться, ве-	1. to enjoy 2. to love; love 3. happy,
селúться **2.** любúть; нрá-	cheerful, merry 4. vigorous, dynamic
виться	5. pleasure
～呼 **huānhū** привéтствен-	to hail, acclaim
ные вóзгласы	-
～乐 **huānlè** *см.* 欢 1	happy, joyous, gay
～迎 **huānyíng** встречáть	to welcome, greet
(торжественно); привéт-	-
ствовать; добрó пожáло-	-
вать!	-
～送 **huānsòng** провожáть	to see/send off
(торжественно); прóводы	-
欺 **qī 1.** обмáнывать **2.** ос-	1. to deceive, cheat 2. to bully, brow-
корбля́ть, унижáть	beat
～骗 **qīpiàn** обмáнывать	to cheat, dupe
～负 **qīfù** обижáть; третúро-	to browbeat, take advantage of, pick
вать	on
款 **kuǎn 1.** дéньги **2.** пункт,	1. a sum of money, fund 2. item, clause
парáграф	3. signature 4. sincere 5. leisurely
～项 **kuǎnxiàng 1.** дéнежная	a sum of money, fund
сýмма **2.** статья́, парáг-	-
раф	-

次 **cì 1.** слéдующий *(по счё-*	1. order, sequence 2. second, next 3.
ту) **2.** второстепéнный	inferior, second-rate 4. (M. for time,
3. порядок, очерёдность	occurrence)
4. *сч. сл. для событий*	-
～序 **cìxù** порядок, послéдо-	order, sequence
вательность	-
～等 **cìděng** вторóй сорт	inferior, second-rate, second-class
～要 **cìyào** второстепéнный	less important, secondary, subordi-\\
羡 **xiàn 1.** стрáстно желáть;	to admire, envy \\nate, minor
завидовать **2.** остáток, из-	-
быток	-
～慕 **xiànmù** *см.* 羡 1	to admire, envy //sults, etc.)
饮 **yǐn** пить; напиток	1. to drink; drinks 2. to swallow (in-//
尺 **chǐ** чи *(мера длины, рав-*	1. rule, ruler 2. (M. of length, =1/3
ная 0,33 м)	meter)
～寸 **chǐcun** размéр	measurement, dimension
～度 **chǐdù 1.** размéры; мас-	measure, scale
штáб **2.** мерило, критéрий	-
久 **jiǔ** продолжительное врé-	1. for a long time 2. of specified dura-
мя; давнó	tion
～仰 **jiǔyǎng** *вежл.* рад с	(court.) pleased to meet you
Вáми познакóмиться	-
爪 **zhǎo** нóгти; кóгти	claw, talon
～ **zhuǎ 1.** лáпа **2.** нóжка	1. claw, talon 2. paw of small animal
(мебели)	3. foot of utensil
抓 **zhuā 1.** хватáть, ловить	1. to grab, seize 2. to scratch 3. to ar-
2. царáпать; чесáть **3.** про-	rest, catch 4. to stress 5. to be re-
водить, осуществлять	sponsible for, take charge of
爬 **pá** ползти, карáбкаться	1. to crawl, creep 2. to climb, scramble
～山 **páshān** лезть, взби-	to climb a mountain
рáться *(на гору)*	-
～虫 **páchóng** пресмыкáю-	reptile
щиеся	-
瓜 **guā** тыква; бахчевые	melon; gourd
культýры	-
～子 **guāzǐ** сéмечки	melon seeds
孤 **gū 1.** сиротá; одинóкий	1. orphaned 2. solitary, isolated, alone
2. единичный; изолиро-	-
ванный	-
～立 **gūlì 1.** одинóкий **2.** изо-	isolated
лировать; изоляция; изо-	-
лированный	-
狐: 狐狸 **húli** лисá; лисий	1. fox 2. (derog.) bewitching woman
长 **cháng 1.** длинный; дли-	1. long 2. lasting 3. steadily, regularly

次羡饮尺久爪抓爬瓜孤狐长

нá **2.** длúтельный, продолжúтельный **3.** достóинство, плюс	4. length 5. strong point 6. to be good/ strong (in/at)
长 **zhǎng 1.** растú, развивáться **2.** увелúчиваться **3.** стáрший *(по возрасту)* **4.** главá; начáльник; дирéктор	1. to grow, grow up, increase 2. older, elder 3. eldest 4. senior 5. chief, head
～征 **chángzhēng 1.** дáльнее путешéствие **2.** похóд; экспедúция	1. expedition, long march 2. (Communist) Long March (1934—1935)
～短 **cháng-duǎn** достóинства и недостáтки; зá и прóтив	1. length 2. accident, mishap 3. right and wrong 4. strong and weak points
chángduan длинá	length
～篇小说 **chángpiān xiǎoshuō** ромáн	novel, long piece of fiction
～方形 **chángfāngxíng** прямоугóльник; прямоугóльный	rectangle
～度 **chángdù** длинá	length
～处 **chángchù** достóинство, преимýщество	strong/good points, forte
～途 **chángtú** длúнная дорóга; дáльний путь (рейс)	long distance
～途电话 **chángtú diànhuà** междугорóдный телефóн	long-distance (telephone) call
～城 **chángchéng** Велúкая китáйская стенá	1. Great Wall 2. impregnable bulwark
帐 **zhàng 1.** занавéска; пóлог; палáтка **2.** счёт **3.** óпись	1. curtain, canopy 2. military tent 3. accounts, account book 4. debt, credit
张 **zhāng 1.** раскрывáть, развёртывать **2.** смотрéть, глазéть **3.** *сч. сл. для плоских предметов*	1. to stretch, spread, expand 2. to set out, display 3. to magnify, exaggerate 4. to start a business 5. to look 6. (M. for flat objects)
～望 **zhāngwàng** смотрéть вокрýг, окúдывать взглядом	1. to look around 2. to peep (through a crack/etc.)
～开 **zhāngkāi** раскрыть; развернýть	to open, spread
～大 **zhāngdà 1.** расширять; расширéние **2.** преувелúчивать	to magnify, exaggerate

涨 **zhǎng** повыша́ться, подниматься	to rise, go up (of water/prices/etc.)
~ **zhàng** расширя́ться; разбуха́ть	1. to swell, bloat, distend 2. to exceed expectation(s)
大 **dà** **1.** большо́й; вели́кий; кру́пный **2.** си́льно, о́чень, весьма́	1. large, big, great, high, tall, vast 2. much, very 3. old 4. eldest 5. adult 6. father
~ **dài** *см.* 大夫	doctor, physician
~胆 **dàdǎn** сме́лый, хра́брый	audacious, bold, daring
~陆 **dàlù** контине́нт, матери́к	continent, mainland
~国沙文主义 **dàguó shāwénzhǔyì** великодержа́вный шовини́зм	great-power chauvinism
~半 **dàbàn** в основно́м; бо́льшей ча́стью	1. more than half, most 2. very likely
~街 **dàjiē** гла́вная у́лица; проспе́кт; магистра́ль	main street
~字报 **dàzìbào** дацзыба́о	big-character poster
~学 **dàxué** университе́т; институ́т; вуз	1. university, college 2. Confucian way/text of great (moral) learning
~约 **dàyuē** о́коло, приблизи́тельно	1. about, around 2. probably, likely
~众 **dàzhòng** наро́дные ма́ссы; ма́ссовый	1. the people/masses 2. popular
~夫 **dàifu** врач, до́ктор	physician, doctor
~米 **dàmǐ** рис	pearl/white rice
~家 **dàjiā** все, мы все, все вме́сте	1. all of us 2. everyone 3. rich and influential family 4. master
~衣 **dàyī** пальто́; ве́рхнее пла́тье	overcoat, topcoat
~厦 **dàshà** зда́ние	building, mansion
~使 **dàshǐ** посо́л	ambassador
~使馆 **dàshǐguǎn** посо́льство	embassy
~概 **dàgài** вероя́тно; приблизи́тельно; в о́бщем	1. general idea 2. appropriate 3. probably
~气层 **dàqìcéng** атмосфе́ра	atmosphere, atmospheric layer
~会 **dàhuì** собра́ние; съезд; конгре́сс; ассамбле́я	rally, plenary meeting, conference
庆 **qìng** пра́здник, торжество́; поздравля́ть, че́ствовать	1. to celebrate, congratulate 2. occasion for celebration
~祝(贺) **qìngzhù(hè)** **1.** по-	to celebrate

美摸膜模奠奥懊澳换

здравля́ть, че́ствовать **2.** пра́здновать	-
美 **měi** краси́вый; прекра́сный	1. beauty, perfection; beautiful, pretty 2. (coll.) self-satisfied
～ **měi** США (Соединённые Шта́ты Аме́рики); Аме́рика	U.S.A., United States; America
～学 **měixué** эсте́тика	aesthetics
～丽 **měilì** краси́вый; прекра́сный	beautiful
～术 **měishù** изобрази́тельные иску́сства	1. fine arts 2. painting
摸 **mō** **1.** щу́пать; осяза́ть **2.** иска́ть, иссле́довать	1. to feel, touch, grope for 2. to feel/ sound out
膜 **mò** плева́; оболо́чка; перепо́нка	1. membrane 2. film, thin coating
模 **mó** **1.** образе́ц; фо́рма **2.** подража́ть, имити́ровать	1. pattern, standard 2. to imitate
～ **mú** лите́йная фо́рма; моде́ль	mold, matrix, pattern
～型 **múxíng** моде́ль; маке́т	foundry mold, die, form
～样 **múyàng** вид, о́блик	1. appearance, look 2. approximately,\\ \\around, about
～仿 **mófǎng** подража́ть	to imitate, copy
～范 **mófàn** **1.** образе́ц, станда́рт **2.** уда́рник *(труда)*	1. exemplary person/thing, model 2. mold for casting bronze
奠 **diàn** учреди́ть, установи́ть	1. to establish, settle 2. to make offerings to the spirits of the dead
～基人 **diànjīrén** основополо́жник	founder
～立(定) **diànlì(dìng)** *см.* 奠	to establish, found, set up
奥 **ào** непоня́тный, таи́нственный	profound, abstruse, difficult to understand
～ **ào** А́встрия	(Abbr.) Austria
～林匹克 **àolínpǐkè** олимпи́йский	(loan w.) Olympic
～运会 **àoyùnhuì** *сокр.* олимпи́йские и́гры	(loan w.) Olympic Games
懊 **ào** сожале́ть, раска́иваться	1. regretful, remorseful 2. annoyed, vexed
澳 **ào** **1.** прича́л; при́стань **2.** Австра́лия **3.** Мака́о	sea inlet, bay
换 **huàn** **1.** меня́ть, обме́нивать; сменя́ть **2.** перемеща́ться; ～句话说 **huàn jù**	1. to exchange, trade 2. to change

huà shuō ины́ми слова́ми,	-
ина́че говоря́	-
换班 huànbān сменя́ть(ся);	1. to change shifts 2. changing of the
сме́на, ва́хта	guard
～车 huànchē пересá́живаться; переса́дка	to change trains/busses
	-
奖 jiǎng 1. хвали́ть, одоб-	1. to encourage, praise, reward 2. to
ря́ть 2. премирова́ть; наг-	give a prize/award; prize, award; re-
ражда́ть; пре́мия, награ́-	ward
да; приз	-
～金 jiǎngjīn пре́мия	money award, bonus, premium
～章 jiǎngzhāng меда́ль	medal, decoration
～励 jiǎnglì поощря́ть, одоб-	to encourage and reward; award
ря́ть	-
～赏 jiǎngshǎng премиро-	award, reward
ва́ть; награжда́ть	-
契 qì контра́кт	1. contract, deed 2. to agree, get along\\
～约 qìyuē контра́кт, согла-	contract, deed, charger \\well
ше́ние	-
类 lèi 1. род; вид; гру́ппа;	1. to resemble, be similar to 2. kind,
разря́д; катего́рия 2. по-	type, class, category 3. generally
хо́жий, подо́бный, анало-	-
ги́чный	-
～型 lèixíng тип; типово́й	type
～似 lèisì подо́бный, анало-	to be similar to; similar, analogous
ги́чный	-
尖 jiān 1. остриё, ко́нчик	(coll.) 1. point, tip, top 2. cream of the
2. отли́чный, превосхо́д-	crop 3. roadside meal
ный	-
～锐 jiānruì о́стрый, заост-	1. sharp-pointed 2. penetrating, incis-
рённый	ive 3. shrill, piercing 4. intense, acute
～锐化 jiānruìhuà обостре́-	to intensify, become more acute
ние	-
太 tài 1. сли́шком, чрезме́р-	1. too, excessively 2. extremely, very
но 2. почте́нный; уважа́е-	3. grand, supreme
мый	-
～阳 tàiyáng со́лнце	1. sun 2. sunshine, sunlight
～子 tàizǐ насле́дник прес-	crown prince
то́ла	-
～太 tàitài госпожа́, да́ма;	(trad.) 1. Mrs. , madame 2. wife
вежл. Ва́ша супру́га	-
头 tóu 1. голова́ 2. верху́ш-	1. head 2. hair (style) 3. top end 4.
ка 3. гла́вный; глава́	chief, head 5. leading, first, previous
4. пе́рвый, нача́льный	6. before, prior 7. (M. for livestock)

换奖契类尖太头

头一 **tóuyī** пéрвый	first
～脑 **tóunǎo** 1. головá 2. главá, руководи́тель	1. brains, mind 2. (coll.) head, leader 3. main threads, clue
～等 **tóuděng** пéрвый сорт	first class/rate
～子 **tóuz** главáрь	chieftain, boss
～发 **tóufa** вóлосы; причёска	hair (on a human head)
买 **mǎi** покупáть	1. to buy, purchase 2. to hire
～卖 **mǎi-mài** торговáть; торгóвля	buying and selling; business deal/ transaction //exert to the utmost
卖 **mài** продавáть	1. to sell 2. to betray, sell out 3. to//
～命 **màimìng** рисковáть жи́знью	1. to exhaust oneself for sb. 2. to die unworthily for
～力 **màilì** проявля́ть рвéние	to spare no effort
续 **xù** продолжáть; продолжéние	1. to be continuous/successive 2. to continue, extend, join 3. to add
赎 **shú** вы́купить; откупи́ться	1. to redeem, ransom 2. to atone for
～当 **shúdàng** вы́купить залóженное	to redeem sth. pawned
读 **dú** читáть; изучáть	1. to read (aloud) 2. to attend school
～者 **dúzhě** читáтель	reader
～书 **dúshū** 1. учи́ться 2. читáть	1. to read, study 2. to attend school
～本 **dúběn** хрестомáтия, кни́га для чтéния	1. reader, textbook 2. piece of writing
实 **shí** 1. и́стинный, пóдлинный 2. пóлный; цéльный 3. плод *(растения)*	1. solid, full, substantial 2. true, real, actual 3. practical 4. reality, fact 5. fruit, seed
～验 **shíyàn** óпыт, экспеpимéнт	to experiment, test; experiment, test
～在 **shízài** 1. действи́тельно, в сáмом дéле 2. реáльный	1. indeed, really, honestly 2. in fact, as a matter of fact
～行 **shíxíng** осуществля́ть	to put into practice/effect, implement
～事 **shíshì** факт, реáльность	true story, real things
～事求是 **shí shì qiú shì** реалисти́ческий подхóд	to seek truth from fact, be practical and realistic
～习 **shíxí** практиковáться	to practice, do fieldwork; practice
～践 **shíjiàn** прáктика, действи́тельность	to practice; practice
～施 **shíshī** осуществля́ть, проводи́ть в жизнь	to put into effect, implement
～现 **shíxiàn** осуществи́ть, вы́полнить	to achieve, realize, bring about

实际 **shíjì** реáльный, дейст-вúтельный; практúческий	reality, practice
状 **zhuàng** **1.** нарýжность, вид **2.** положéние, состоя́-ние **3.** документ	1. form, shape 2. state, condition 3. description 4. account, record 5. written complaint 6. certificate
～况 **zhuàngkuàng** положé-ние; обстоя́тельства	condition/state of affairs
～态 **zhuàngtài** состоя́ние, положéние вещéй	state (of affairs), condition
伏 **fú** **1.** лежáть ничкóм **2.** пря́таться; сидéть в за-сáде	1. to bend over, lie prostrate 2. to subside, go down 3. to hide, conceal 4. to subdue, tame 5. to admit
献 **xiàn** подносúть, препод-носúть	1. to offer, present, donate 2. to show, display
～媚 **xiànmèi** заискивать	to ingratiate oneself with
～词 **xiàncí** послáние, обра-щéние	congratulatory message
～身 **xiànshēn** посвятúть се-бя́ *чему*	1. to devote/dedicate oneself to 2. to give one's life for
～礼 **xiànlǐ** дар, подношéние	to present a gift
～花 **xiànhuā** дарúть (воз-лагáть) цветы́	to present flowers
获 **huò** **1.** добúться, достúчь **2.** убирáть *(урожай)*	1. to capture, catch 2. to obtain, win, reap 3. to be able to
～得 **huòdé** получúть, до-бúться	to gain, acquire, win, achieve
～得者 **huòdézhě** лауреáт; призёр	laureate, prize winner
默 **mò** молчáть	1. to keep silent 2. to write from memory
～书(写) **mòshū(xiě)** пи-сáть под диктóвку; дик-тáнт	
～契 **mòqì** молчалúвое сог-лáсие	tacit/secret agreement
狱 **yù** **1.** тюрьмá **2.** ад	1. prison, jail 2. lawsuit, criminal case
厌 **yàn** **1.** приéсться, надо-éсть **2.** удовлетворúться	1. to detest, loathe 2. to be disgusted/bored with 3. to be satiated
哭 **kū** плáкать	to cry, weep
臭 **chòu** **1.** вонь; вонючий **2.** негóдный; недостóйный	1. foul, stinking, malodorous 2. disgusting, disgraceful
～化 **chòuhuà** дискредитúро-вать	to discredit
突 **tū** **1.** прорвáть **2.** внезáп-но, неожúданно	1. to dash forward 2. to project, stick out 3. suddenly, abruptly 4. chimney

突跃妖奏凑笑天

突击 **tūjī** внезáпный удáр; удáрный	1. to assault 2. to do a crash job
~出 **tūchu** **1.** стáвить на пéрвое мéсто **2.** выступáть, торчáть	1. to give prominence to, stress 2. projecting 3. outstanding
~破 **tūpò** **1.** прорвáть *(оборону)* **2.** побúть *(рекорд)*	1. to make a breakthrough 2. to surmount
~然 **tūrán** вдруг, неожúданно, внезáпно	suddenly, abruptly
跃 **yuè** прыгать, подпры́гивать	to leap, jump
~进 **yuèjìn** скачóк	to leap forward
妖 **yāo** **1.** прúзрак, привидéние **2.** необы́чный, стрáнный	1. goblin, demon, evil spirit 2. supernatural, weird 3. seductive, bewitching
~怪 **yāoguài** прúзрак; чудóвище	monster, goblin, demon
~术 **yāoshù** мáгия, колдовствó	sorcery, witchcraft
奏 **zòu** игрáть *(на музыкальном инструменте)*	1. (mus.) to perform 2. to memorialize the emperor
凑 **còu** собирáть, накáпливать	1. to gather together, pool, collect 2. to happen by chance 3. to profit by
~巧 **còuqiǎo** удáчное совпадéние	luckily, fortunately, as luck would have it
~集 **còují** собирáть	to gather together
笑 **xiào** смея́ться; улыбáться	1. to smile, laugh 2. to ridicule, laugh at
~话 **xiàohua** шýтка; анекдóт	1. to laugh at, ridicule 2. joke, jest
天 **tiān** **1.** нéбо **2.** день; сýтки **3.** прирóдный, естéственный **4.** погóда	1. sky, heaven 2. overhead 3. day 4. season 5. weather 6. nature 7. God, Heaven
~空 **tiānkōng** нéбо, воздýшное прострáнство	sky, heaven
~桥 **tiānqiáo** пешехóдный мост	overpass, bridge (over)
~才 **tiāncái** талáнт; талáнтливый	genius; talent, gift
~文学 **tiānwénxué** астронóмия	astronomy
~线 **tiānxiàn** антéнна	antenna, aerial
~花 **tiānhuā** óспа	smallpox
~花板 **tiānhuābǎn** потолóк	ceiling

天气 **tiānqì** погóда; клúмат	weather
～然 **tiānrán** прирóда; естéственный	natural
误 **wù 1.** ошúбка; ошúбочный **2.** опáздывать, задéрживаться	1. to miss (due to delay) 2. to harm, injure 3. mistake, error 4. by mistake
关 **guān 1.** закрывáть; выключáть **2.** застáва; тамóжня **3.** касáться, относúться	1. to shut, close; turn off; lock up; close down 2. issue/receive (payment) 3. to concern, implicate 4. pass 5. barrier, crux, critical juncture, turning point
～节 **guānjié** сустáв; сустáвы	1. (anat.) joint 2. key links 3. bribe
～于 **guānyú** в отношéнии; что касáется	about, on, with regard to, concerning
～键 **guānjiàn** глáвный пункт; основнóе звенó	key, crux
～怀 **guānhuái** забóтиться; забóта	to show loving care/concern for
～系 **guānxi** отношéния, связь	1. to concern, affect; relation; bearing, impact 2. membership credentials
～心(念) **guānxīn(niàn)** забóтиться, беспокóиться	to be concerned about
联 **lián 1.** соединя́ть, свя́зывать; послéдовательно; непреры́вно **2.** союз, федерáция	1. to ally oneself with, unite 2. allied, joint, mutual 3. antithetical couplet; parallel, symmetrical
～盟 **liánméng** союз, лúга	alliance, coalition, league, union
～合 **liánhé 1.** соединéние; коалúция **2.** кóмплекс	1. to unite, ally 2. joint, combined 3. alliance, union, coalition
～合国 **liánhéguó** ООН (Организáция Объединённых Нáций)	United Nations
～合企业 **liánhé qíyè** комбинáт	(industrial) combine
～邦 **liánbāng** федерáция, союз	federation, union, commonwealth
～欢节 **liánhuānjié** фестивáль	festival
～系 **liánxì** свя́зи, контáкты	to integrate, relate, link; contact
疾 **jí** болéзнь, страдáние	1. disease, illness 2. suffering, difficulty
嫉: 嫉妒 **jídù** ревновáть; завúдовать	1. to envy, be jealous of 2. to hate
族 **zú** национáльность; род; плéмя	clan, race, tribe, group

候 喉 猴 挨 夫 扶 肤 失 跌 秩 铁

候 **hòu 1.** ждать **2.** вре́мя, сезо́н	1. to wait, await 2. to inquire after 3. to pay (bills) 4. time, season 5. con-\\
~补者 **hòubǔzhě** кандида́т	candidate \\dition, state, symptoms
~车室 **hòuchēshì** зал ожида́ния	waiting room (for busses/trains/etc.) -
~选人 **hòuxuǎnrén** кандида́т *(на выборах)*	candidate (for election) -
喉 **hóu** го́рло, горта́нь; гло́тка	throat, larynx -
~咙 **hóulong** *см.* 喉	throat //pish and naughty
猴 **hóu** обезья́на	1. monkey 2. clever/smart chap 3.im-//
挨 **ái** подверга́ться; перено-си́ть; страда́ть от	1. to suffer, endure 2. to drag out, delay, stall //in sequence
~ **āi** приближа́ться; ря́дом	to get close to, be next to, follow//
夫 **fū** мужчи́на; муж, супру́г	1. husband 2. man 3. person engaged in manual labor 4. (suf.) man
~妇 **fū-fù** супру́ги	husband and wife
~人 **fūrén** супру́га; госпожа́	Lady, Madame, Mrs. -
扶 **fú 1.** подде́рживать, подпира́ть **2.** помога́ть, выруча́ть	1. to support with the hand 2. to help sb. up, straighten sth. up 3. to help, relieve
肤 **fū** ко́жа, ко́жный покро́в	skin
失 **shī 1.** потеря́ть, утра́тить, лиши́ться **2.** оши́бка, упуще́ние	1. to lose 2. to miss, let slip 3. mistake, mishap, defect -
~望 **shīwàng** разочарова́ться; потеря́ть наде́жду	1. to become disappointed 2. to lose hope/faith
~业 **shīyè** потеря́ть рабо́ту; безрабо́тный	to lose one's job, be out of work -
~常 **shīcháng** ненорма́льный	abnormal, odd -
~败 **shībài** потерпе́ть пораже́ние	1. to be defeated, defeat, lose 2. to fail; failure
~眠 **shīmián** страда́ть бессо́нницей	to suffer from insomnia -
~踪 **shīzōng** пропа́сть бе́з вести; исче́знуть	to be missing -
~去 **shīqù** потеря́ть, лиши́ться	to lose -
跌 **dié** упа́сть	1. to fall, tumble 2. to drop, fall
秩: 秩序 **zhìxù** поря́док, после́довательность	order, sequence - //as iron 3. resolved 4. cruel, violent
铁 **tiě** желе́зо; желе́зный	1. iron 2. arms, weapon 3. firm, strong//

铁丝 **tiěsī** прóволока	iron wire
～匠 **tiějiang** кузнéц	blacksmith, ironsmith
～路 **tiělù** желéзная дорóга	railway, railroad
～矿 **tiěkuǎng** желéзная рудá	iron ore/mine
～道 **tiědào** желéзная дорóга	railway, railroad
～軌 **tiěguì** рéльсы	rail(s)
夹 **jiā** 1. сжимáть, зажимáть 2. нести́ под мы́шкой 3. щипцы́; тиски́ 4. футля́р; бумáжник	1. to press from both sides, place in between 2. to mix, mingle, intersperse 3. to carry secretly 4. pincers 5. folder
峡 **xiá** 1. проли́в 2. ущéлье	1. gorge, canyon 2. straight
狭 **xiá** ýзкий, тéсный	narrow
块 **kuài** 1. кусóк; глы́ба 2. *сч. сл. для основных денежных единиц*	1. piece; block 2. (M. for piece, lump, chunk)
缺 **quē** 1. недоставáть; недостáток 2. изъя́н, дефéкт	1. to be short of, lack 2. vacancy, opening
～席 **quēxí** отсýтствовать	to be absent (from a meeting/etc.)
～乏 **quēfá** недоставáть; недостáток, дефици́т	to lack, be short of
～点 **quēdiǎn** дефéкт, недостáток	shortcoming, defect, weakness
快 **kuài** 1. бы́стрый, скóрый 2. прия́тный; рáдостный, весёлый	1. fast, quick 2. soon 3. quickwitted, ingenious 4. sharp (of knives) 5. straightforward 6. pleased, elated
～活 **kuàihuó** весёлый, жизнерáдостный	1. happy, cheerful 2. thrilled
～车 **kuàichē** скóрый пóезд	1. express train/bus 2. vehicle travelling at high speed
～乐 **kuàilè** рáдостный, весёлый	happy, cheerful; happiness
筷: 筷子 **kuàiz** пáлочки для еды́	chopsticks
决 **jué** 1. реши́ть; решéние; реши́тельный 2. прорвáть; проби́ть	1. to decide, determine 2. definitely, certainly 3. to execute sb. 4. to bid farewell to 5. to be breached, burst
～口 **juékǒu** пробóина; брешь	to be breached, burst (of dikes, etc.)
～计 **juéjì** определённо	to decide, make up one's mind; definitely, certainly
～定 **juédìng** реши́ть; реши́тельный	1. to decide, resolve, make up one's mind 2. to determine 3. decision
～议 **juéyì** резолю́ция, решéние	resolution

决央映秧英胰木休林淋麻

决赛 juésài фина́льная встре́ча	(sports) finals
～心 juéxīn реши́мость; реше́ние	to make up one's mind to, be determined to; determination, resolution
央 yāng центр, середи́на	1. to entreat 2. to end, finish 3. center
映 yìng 1. отража́ть(ся) 2. демонстри́ровать *(фильм)*	1. to reflect, mirror, shine 2. to project (slides/etc.)
秧 yāng 1. расса́да, са́женцы 2. мальки́	1. seedling, sprout 2. rice seedling 3. vine 4. young (of food animals)
英 yīng 1. выдаю́щийся; му́дрый; 2. герои́ческий	1. hero, outstanding person 2. flower, petal
～ yīng А́нглия	England
～雄 yīngxióng геро́й	hero
～明 yīngmíng му́дрый	wise, brilliant
～勇 yīngyǒng до́блестный, герои́ческий	heroic, valiant
胰 yí *мед.* па́нкреас, поджелу́дочная железа́	pancreas
～子 yízi мы́ло	1. (coll.) pancreas (of animals) 2. soap
木 mù 1. де́рево; деревя́нный 2. одеревене́ть, онеме́ть	1. tree 2. timber, wood 3. wooden 4. numb, insensitive 5. stupid, silly
～匠 mùjiàng пло́тник; столя́р	carpenter
～器 mùqì ме́бель; деревя́нная у́тварь	wooden furniture/articles
休 xiū 1. отдыха́ть; о́тдых 2. прекрати́ть, переста́ть	1. to stop, cease; to rest 2. do not 3. good fortune
～业 xiūyè закры́ть предприя́тие	1. to suspend business 2. to end (a course/etc.)
～养所 xiūyǎngsuō дом о́тдыха	rest home, sanatorium
～假 xiūjià о́тпуск; кани́кулы	to have vacation/holiday/leave; vacation
～战 xiūzhàn переми́рие	to cease fire, have a truce
～息 xiūxi отдыха́ть; о́тдых; переры́в	to have/take a rest
林 lín лес; ро́ща	1. forest, woods, grove 2. forestry 3. circle, group 4. many, numerous
淋 lín полива́ть; ороша́ть	to pour, drench
～浴 línyù душ	shower, shower bath
麻 má 1. конопля́; лён; кунжу́т 2. онеме́ть	1. hemp 2. pitted, pockmarked 3. numbed, tingling
～雀 máquè воробе́й	1. sparrow 2. mahjong
～醉 mázuì быть под де́йст-	1. to anesthetize 2. to poison, drug 3. anesthesia

вием наркóза; анестезú-	-
ровать	-
麻痹 **mábì** парализовáть; па-	1. to benumb, blunt 2. to slacken vig-
ралúч	ilance 3. paralysis 4.palsy 5. numbness
～烦 **máfan** беспокóить, до-	to trouble/bother sb.; troublesome,
кучáть; беспокóйство	inconvenient //tudinous
森 **sēn** густóй лес	1. full of trees 2. dark, gloomy 3. multi-//
床 **chuáng** **1.** кровáть **2.** ста-	1. bed 2. (M. for bedding)
нóк	-
亲 **qīn** **1.** родúтели; роднá,	1. relatives 2. parents 3. marriage 4.
рóдственники **2.** быть	to kiss 5. close, intimate, dear 6. personal
блúзким; сближáться с	-
3. сам; лúчно	-
～密 **qīnmì** сердéчный, блúз-	close, intimate
кий	-
～嘴 **qīnzuǐ** целовáть(ся)	to kiss
～属 **qīnshǔ** рóдственники	1. kinsfolk, relatives 2. kinship 3. related
～切 **qīnqiè** блúзкий, сердéч-	cordial, genial, warm
ный	-
～爱 **qīn'ài** дорогóй, любú-	dear, beloved
мый	-
～戚 **qīnqì** рóдственники	relatives
集 **jí** **1.** собирáться; сбóри-	1. to gather, collect 2. country fair,
ще **2.** собирáть; собрáние,	market 3. collection of writings
коллéкция	-
～合 **jíhé** собирáться, сосре-	to gather, assemble, muster
дотóчиваться	-
～团 **jítuán** грýппа; группи-	group, clique, circle, bloc
рóвка; блок; клúка	-
～邮 **jíyóu** филателúя	to collect stamps; stamp-collecting
～中 **jízhōng** концентрúро-	1. to concentrate 2. to centralize 3. to
вать, сосредотóчивать	focus 4. to put together
～市 **jíshì** рынок; ярмарка	country fair/market
～体 **jítǐ** коллектúв; коллек-	collective
тúвный	-
～体农庄 **jítǐnóngzhuāng** кол-	collective farm
хóз	-
～会 **jíhuì** собирáться; собрá-	assembly, rally, gathering
ние; мúтинг	-
某 **mǒu** нéкто; нéкий; э́н-	1. some, a certain 2. reference to one-
ский	self
煤 **méi** кáменный ýголь	coal
～油 **méiyóu** керосúн	kerosene
～气 **méiqì** газ	coal gas

煤媒谋保操

煤气管 **méiqì guǎn** газопровóд	gas pipes
～炭 **méitàn** кáменный ýголь	coal
媒 **méi** сват; свáха; посрéдник	matchmaker, go-between, intermediary, vehicle, medium
谋 **móu** стрóить плáны, замышля́ть	1. to work for, seek, plot 2. to consult, discuss 3. plan, scheme, stratagem
～生 **móushēng** зарабáтывать на жизнь	to seek livelihood
～害 **móuhài** покушáться; покушéние	1. to plot murder 2. to plot against
保 **bǎo** **1.** защищáть; охраня́ть **2.** обеспéчить, гарантúровать **3.** содержáть, кормúть	1. to protect 2. to keep 3. to guarantee 4. to stand guarantor for sb. 5. guarantor
～卫 **bǎowèi** *см.* 保 1	to defend, safeguard
～险 **bǎoxiǎn** **1.** страховáть; страховáние **2.** безопáсный; предохранúтельный	1. to insure; insurance 2. to be sure 3. safe
～险箱 **bǎoxiǎnxiāng** сейф	(car) bumper
～证 **bǎozhèng** гарантúровать; ручáться; гарáнтия	1. cash deposit, down payment, earnest money 2. bail
～管 **bǎoguǎn** управля́ть; обслýживать	1. to take care of 2. certainly, surely
～留 **bǎoliú** сохраня́ть; резервúровать	1. to continue to have, retain 2. to hold back, reserve
～障 **bǎozhàng** **1.** *см.* 保 1 **2.** ручáться, гарантúровать	to ensure, guarantee, safeguard
～存 **bǎocún** **1.** хранúть, сохраня́ть **2.** спастúсь, остáться в живы́х	to preserve, conserve, keep
～持 **bǎochí** поддéрживать, соблюдáть	to keep, maintain, preserve
～守 **bǎoshǒu** **1.** защищáть **2.** консервативный; кóсный	1. to guard, keep 2. conservative
～护 **bǎohù** защищáть; охраня́ть; опекáть	to protect, safeguard
～健 **bǎojiàn** здравоохранéние	to care for one's health
操 **cāo** **1.** держáть в рукáх **2.** управля́ть **3.** тренировáться, упражня́ться	1. to grasp, hold 2. to act, do, operate 3. to speak 4. conduct, behavior 5. drill exercise

操纵 **cāozòng** распоряжа́ться; управля́ть; держа́ть в рука́х	1. to operate, control 2. to rig, manipulate
～心 **cāoxīn** беспоко́иться, забо́титься	1. to worry/trouble about, take pains to 2. to wrack one's brains
澡 **zǎo** мы́ться; купа́ться	bath //bath(house)
～堂 **zǎotáng** ба́ня	1. common bathing pool 2. public//
～盆 **zǎopén** ва́нна	bathtub
架 **jià 1.** подста́вка; по́лка; ра́ма **2.** устана́вливать, подве́шивать 3. *сч. сл. для машин, самолётов*	1. to put up, erect 2. to ward off, withstand 3. to support, prop, help 4. to kidnap 5. frame, rack, shelf, stand 6. fight, quarrel 7. (M. for planes, etc.)
～子 **jiàz** го́нор, высокоме́рие	1. frame, stand, rack, shelf 2. framework 3. airs 4. posture, stance
桌:桌子 **zhuōz** стол	table, desk
荣 **róng 1.** сла́ва, честь, почёт **2.** расцве́т, процвета́ние	1. honor; honorable, glorious 2. thriving
～誉 **róngyù** сла́ва, почёт	honor; honorary
～军 **róngjūn** ветера́н войны́	disabled veteran
柔 **róu** ги́бкий; мя́гкий, не́жный	to soften; soft, supple, gentle
～道 **róudào** дзюдо́	judo
蹂:蹂躏 **róulìn** посяга́ть	to trample over, ravage
梁 **liáng 1.** ба́лка, перекла́дина **2.** мост	1. roof beam 2. bridge 3. ridge 4. Liang dynasty (502—577)
茶 **chá** чай; ча́йный	tea
～壶 **cháhú** ча́йник	teapot
～叶 **cháyè** ча́йный лист	tea leaves
～碗 **cháwǎn** ча́шка; пиала́	teacup
～具 **chájù** ча́йный серви́з	tea things
桑 **sāng** ту́товое де́рево	mulberry
嗓 **sǎng** го́рло; горта́нь; го́лос	1. throat, larynx 2. voice
条 **tiáo 1.** ве́тка, ветвь **2.** статья́; пара́граф **3.** запи́ска **4.** *сч. сл. для продолговатых предметов и некоторых животных*	1. strip, slip, stripe, streak 2. sth. long and narrow 3. item, article, clause 4. short note 5. (M. for long narrow things)
～理 **tiáolǐ** поря́док, систе́ма	(proper) arrangement/presentation, orderliness, method
～件 **tiáojiàn** усло́вия; огово́рка	//ment, prerequisite, qualification 1. condition, term, factor 2. require-//

条例 **tiáolì** прáвила; устáв; наставлéние	regulations, rules, ordinances
～约 **tiáoyuē** пакт, договóр	treaty, pact
～令 **tiáolìng** устáв	regulations
探 **tàn** **1.** искáть **2.** шпиóнить; развéдывать	1. to look for, explore 2. to visit, call on 3. to stretch/pop forward 4. spy, \\
～矿 **tànkuǎng** развéдка недр	to prospect (for minerals) \\detective
～索 **tànsuǒ** дои́скиваться; развéдывать	to explore, probe; explorations
～照灯 **tànzhàodēng** прожéктор	searchlight
深 **shēn** **1.** глубóкий **2.** óчень, весьмá **3.** тёмный	1. deep 2. penetrating, profound
～刻 **shēnkè** глубóкий	deep, profound
～厚 **shēnhòu** глубóкий, крéпкий	1. deep, profound 2. solid, deep-seated
～度 **shēndù** глубинá	1. depth 2. profundity
杀 **shā** убивáть, умерщвля́ть	1. to kill, massacre 2. to fight 3. to\\
柴 **chái** дровá; хвóрост	firewood \\burn, smart (of medicine)
躲 **duǒ** скрывáться, прятáться; избегáть	1. to hide (oneself) 2. to dodge, avoid
～避 **duǒbì** *см.* 躲	1. to hide (oneself) 2. to elude, dodge
杂 **zá** **1.** смесь; смéшанный **2.** вся́кий, рáзный	1. to mix, mingle; mixed, composite 2. miscellaneous, sundry
～技团 **zájìtuán** цирковáя трýппа	acrobatic troupe
～货 **záhuò** галантерéя	groceries //cords, notes
～志 **zázhì** журнáл	1. magazine, journal, periodical 2. re-//
～耍 **záshuǎ** аттракциóн	variety show, vaudeville
染 **rǎn** **1.** крáсить, окрáшивать **2.** заражáться; инфекциóнный	1. to dye 2. to catch (a disease) 3. to soil, pollute 4. to make strokes (in painting, etc.)
采 **cǎi** **1.** собирáть; добывáть **2.** отбирáть, выбирáть	1. to gather, pick 2. to mine 3. to select 4. variegated color 5. facial color and\\
～纳 **cǎinà** **1.** принимáть *(предложение)* **2.** придéрживаться *(какого-л. мнения)*	to accept, adopt \\expression, spirit
～访 **cǎifǎng** репортáж	to cover, interview, gather news
～购 **cǎigòu** закупáть; заготáвливать	-
～取 **cǎiqǔ** принимáть *(меры)*; прибегáть к	to take, adopt

菜 **cài 1.** óвощи; зéлень **2.** блю́до, кýшанье *(всё, кроме риса и хлеба)*	1. vegetables, greens 2. (non-staple) food 3. dish, course
～园 **càiyuán** огорóд	vegetable garden/farm
～单 **càidān** меню́	menu
案 **àn 1.** дéло; доку́мéнт **2.** *юр.* дéло, [судéбный] процéсс	1. table, desk 2. case (of law, etc.) 3. record, file 4. proposal
～件 **ànjiàn** дéло; докумéнты	case (of law, etc.)
术 **shù** тéхника; умéние, мастерствó	1. art, skill, technique 2. method, tactics
～语 **shùyǔ** тéрмин; терминолóгия	technical term/terminology
乐 **lè** рáдость; весéлье; удовóльствие	1. to be glad to, enjoy 2. happy, joyful 3. to laugh, be amused
～ **yuè** мýзыка	music
～器 **yuèqì** музыкáльные инструмéнты	musical instrument
～谱 **yuèpǔ** нóты	music score, music
～队 **yuèduì** оркéстр	orchestra, band
～观主义 **lèguānzhǔyì** оптими́зм	optimism
～意 **lèyì** охóтно, с удовóльствием	to be willing/ready to; pleased, happy
东 **dōng 1.** востóк; востóчный **2.** хозя́ин	1. east 2. master, owner 3. host
～西 **dōngxi** вещь, предмéт	thing, creature
～家 **dōngjia** хозя́ин, владéлец	1. landlord 2. boss, master
陈 **chén** расставля́ть, раскла́дывать	1. to lay out, put on display 2. to state, explain 3. old, stale 4. Chen dynasty
～列 **chénliè** расставля́ть; выставля́ть, экспони́ровать	to display, exhibit
～列室 **chénlièshì** вы́ставочный зал; павильóн	showroom, exhibition room
～列品 **chénlièpǐn** экспонáт	articles on display, exhibits
～列馆 **chénlièguǎn** вы́ставка *(помещение)*	exhibition hall
冻 **dòng 1.** мёрзнуть, зя́бнуть **2.** покрывáться льдом **3.** заливнóй *(о кушанье)*	1. to freeze 2. to feel very cold, be frostbitten 3. jelly

练 **liàn** **1.** упражня́ться, практикова́ться **2.** обуча́ть	1. to boil and scour raw silk; white silk 2. to practice, train, drill 3. skilled,\\
～习 **liànxí** упражня́ться, тренирова́ться; упражне́ние	1. to practice, exercise \\experienced
拣 **jiǎn** **1.** выбира́ть, отбира́ть **2.** подбира́ть, поднима́ть *(с земли)*	1. to select, pick out 2. to pick up, collect, gather
本 **běn** **1.** ко́рень **2.** осно́ва, су́щность **3.** да́нный, настоя́щий	1. root/stem of plant 2. foundation 3. capital 4. book 5. edition 6. this 7. original 8. current 9. according to 10. (M. for\\
～性 **běnxìng** су́щность; хара́ктер, приро́да	1. natural instincts, nature \\books, etc.)
～位主义 **běnwèizhǔyì** ме́стничество	selfish departmentalism, chauvinism
～子 **běnz** тетра́дь	1. book 2. notebook 3. edition
～事 **běnshi** спосо́бности; уме́ние	skill, ability
～来 **běnlái** **1.** с са́мого нача́ла **2.** со́бственно говоря́; по существу́	1. originally, at first; original 2. of course //faculty
～能 **běnnéng** инсти́нкт	1. instinct; instinctive 2. native ability,//
～质 **běnzhì** су́щность, приро́да	essence, nature, intrinsic quality
～领 **běnlǐng** спосо́бности; тала́нт	skill, ability, capacity
体 **tǐ** **1.** те́ло; органи́зм **2.** субста́нция, вещество́ **3.** структу́ра, организа́ция	1. body 2. substance 3. style, form 4. system 5. to realize 6. aspect (of a verb)
～刑 **tǐxíng** теле́сное наказа́ние	type of (bodily) build/figure
～育 **tǐyù** физкульту́ра, спорт	physical education/training; sports
～操 **tǐcāo** гимна́стика	gymnastics, calisthenics
～现 **tǐxiàn** воплоща́ть(ся); воплоще́ние	to embody, reflect, give expression to
～系 **tǐxì** систе́ма	system, setup
～会 **tǐhuì** вника́ть; понима́ть; понима́ние	to know/learn from experience, realize
笨 **bèn** **1.** тупо́й, глу́пый **2.** неуклю́жий, нело́вкий	1. stupid, dull 2. clumsy, awkward 3. cumbersome
米 **mǐ** **1.** рис *(очищенный)* **2.** метр	1. ice 2. shelled/husked seed
～饭 **mǐfàn** варёный рис	cooked rice

未 **wèi** не; ещё не	1. have not yet 2. or not (at end of\\
~婚夫 **wèihūnfū** жених	fiancé \\sentence)
~婚妻 **wèihūnqī** невéста	fiancée
~来 **wèilái** бýдущее; бýдущий	future, time to come
~必 **wèibì** едвá ли, врядли; не обязáтельно	may not, not necessarily
味 **wèi** **1.** вкус; зáпах **2.** интерéс	1. taste, flavor 2. smell, odor 3. interest, delight 4. to distinguish the\\
妹 **mèi** млáдшая сестрá	younger sister \\flavor of
末 **mò** **1.** верхýшка, кóнчик **2.** конéц; послéдний	1. tip, end 2. nonessentials, minor details 3. powder, dust
抹 **mǒ** **1.** мáзать, намáзывать **2.** вытирáть, стирáть	1. to put on, apply, smear 2. to brush/wipe off, exclude 3. to play
~ **mò** штукатýрить	1. to daub, plaster 2. to skirt, bypass
~布 **mǒbù** тряпка; полотéнце	wiping rag/towel
袜 **wà** носкú; чулкú	socks, stockings, hose
珠 **zhū** **1.** жéмчуг **2.** шáрик; бýсинка	1. pearl 2. bead
来 **lái** **1.** приходúть; прибывáть **2.** бýдущий, наступáющий; слéдующий **3.** дéлать, поступáть **4.** *вспом. гл.*; *соответствует* для; для тогó, чтóбы; чтóбы; 母亲费了许多功夫来安慰我 мать потрáтила мнóго врéмени, чтóбы утéшить меня	1. to come, arrive 2. to take place 3. to bring 4. to do 5. future, next, coming 6. in order to, so as to, so that 7.(suf.) ability; worthwhile; beginning of an action; hypothetical action; direction toward the speaker; repetition; -ly; time (since)
~往 **láiwǎng** курсúровать; взад и вперёд	to come and go
láiwang общáться; общéние; свя́зи	social intercourse
~历 **láilì** **1.** биогрáфия **2.** происхождéние	origin, background, career
~宾 **láibīn** гость	guest, visitor
~源 **láiyuán** истóчник; происхождéние	to originate, stem from; source, origin
果 **guǒ** **1.** фрýкты; плодú **2.** плодú, результáты **3.** дéйствúтельно, в сáмом дéле **4.** отвáжно, смéло	1. fruit 2. effect, outcome, result, consequence 3. surely, truly, actually 4. if, if actually 5. to stuff, fill
~实 **guǒshí** *см.* 果 1	1. fruit 2. gains, fruit

果然 **guǒrán** действи́тельно, в са́мом де́ле	really, as expected, sure enough
裸 **luǒ** го́лый, обнажённый	bare, naked, exposed
课 **kè** 1. уро́к; заня́тия 2. отде́л; отделе́ние	1. subject, course, class, lesson 2. sub-office 3. to tax 4. to supervise
～堂(室) **kètáng(shì)** аудито́рия; класс	classroom
～本 **kèběn** уче́бник	textbook
策 **cè** за́мысел, план	1. plan, scheme, strategy 2. to whip; whip 3. to plan
～略 **cèlüè** пла́ны; та́ктика	
～划 **cèhuà** намеча́ть; замышля́ть	to plan, plot, engineer
～源地 **cèyuándì** 1. исхо́дный пункт 2. оча́г *(напр. заболеваний)*	1. place of origin 2. base (of a military/social movement)
束 **shù** 1. свя́зывать; свя́зка; буке́т 2. ограни́чивать	1. to bind, tie 2. to control, restrain 3. bundle, bunch, sheath
～缚 **shùfù** свя́зывать, ско́вывать; кабала́	to tie up, fetter
辣 **là** о́стрый; го́рький; те́рпкий	1. peppery, hot 2. sharp, spicy, biting (of smell/taste) 3. vicious, ruthless
～椒 **làjiāo** кра́сный пе́рец	hot pepper, chili
乘 **chéng** 1. е́хать *(на транспорте)* 2. воспо́льзоваться *(случаем)* 3. умножа́ть; умноже́ние	1. to ride 2. to take advantage of, avail oneself of 3. (math.) to multiply
兼 **jiān** соединя́ть; совмеща́ть; по совмести́тельству	1. to do concurrently; concurrently, both 2. double, twice
嫌 **xián** подозрева́ть; вызыва́ть подозре́ние	1. to dislike, mind 2. suspicion 3. ill will, grudge
谦 **qiān** скро́мный; такти́чный	modest
～虚 **qiānxū** скро́мный; скро́мность	to make modest remarks; modest, unassuming
火 **huǒ** ого́нь, пла́мя	1. fire 2. firearms, ammunition 3. anger, temper 4. fiery 5. urgent
～星 **huǒxīng** 1. Марс 2. и́скра	1. Mars 2. (coll.) spark
～炬 **huǒjù** фа́кел	torch
～山 **huǒshān** вулка́н	volcano
～器 **huǒqì** огнестре́льное ору́жие	firearms
～石 **huǒshí** креме́нь	flint
～车 **huǒchē** по́езд	train

火车站 **huǒchēzhàn** вокза́л;	railway station
ста́нция	-
～葬 **huǒzàng** крема́ция	to cremate; cremation
～箭 **huǒjiàn** раке́та; раке́т-	rocket
ный	-
～炉 **huǒlú** печно́е отопле́-	stove
ние; печь	-
～药 **huǒyào** по́рох	gunpowder
～柴 **huǒchái** спи́чки	match
～灾 **huǒzāi** пожа́р	fire disaster, conflagration
～腿 **huǒtuǐ** копчёный о́ко-	(smoked) ham
рок	-
～花 **huǒhuā** **1.** и́скра **2.** фей-	spark
ерве́рк	-
伙 **huǒ** компаньо́н, това́рищ	1. meals, board, mess 2. partner, mate
～计 **huǒji** **1.** прика́зчик **2.**	3. partnership, company, group, band 4.
разг. рабо́та, заня́тие	to combine, join 5. together, in common
～食 **huǒshi** пи́ща	food, meals, mess
秋 **qiū** о́сень	1. autumn, fall 2. time, period 3. year\\
～天(季) **qiūtiān(jì)** о́сень	autumn, fall \\4. harvest
～收 **qiūshōu** осе́нняя жа́тва	1. autumn harvest 2. limpid eyes (of a\\
灰 **huī** **1.** зола́, пе́пел **2.** и́з-	1. ash 2. dust 3. lime 4.\\ \\woman)
весть	- \\gray 5.disheartened
～尘 **huīchén** пыль	dust, dirt
～碟 **huīdie** пе́пельница	ashtray
～泥 **huīní** штукату́рка	plaster
～色 **huīsè** се́рый (пе́пель-	1. gray, ashy 2. pessimistic, gloomy 3.
ный) цвет	obscure, ambiguous
恢:恢恢 **huīhuī** широ́кий, об-	extensive, vast
ши́рный	-
～复 **huīfù** восстана́вливать;	1. to resume, renew 2. to recover, re-
реставри́ровать; воссоздa-	gain 3. to restore, reinstate, rehabilitate
ва́ть	-
炭 **tàn** древе́сный у́голь	1. charcoal 2. carbon
灭 **miè** **1.** уничтожа́ть, лик-	to extinguish, exterminate, put/go out
види́ровать **2.** туши́ть, га-	-
си́ть	-
～亡 **mièwáng** погуби́ть; по-	to be destroyed, die out
ги́бнуть	-
～火器 **mièhuǒqì** огнетуши́-	fire extinguisher
тель	-
灵 **líng** у́мный, спосо́бный;	1. quick, clever, sharp 2. effective 3.
сообрази́тельный	mysterious, divine 4. spirit, intelligence
～活 **línghuó** **1.** живо́й, по-	1. nimble, agile 2. flexible, elastic

灵灾熨烫炎淡谈水

дви́жный 2. сме́тливый,	-
сообрази́тельный	-
灵敏 **língmǐn** у́мный; прони-	sensitive, keen, agile, acute
ца́тельный	-
～魂 **línghún** 1. душа́ 2. пси́-	soul, spirit
хика, созна́ние	-
～感 **línggǎn** вдохнове́ние	inspiration
灾 **zāi** стихи́йное бе́дствие	1. disaster, calamity 2. misfortune
～难 **zāinàn** бе́ды, страда́-	calamity, misfortune
ния	-
～害 **zāihài** несча́стье; бе́д-	calamity, disaster
ствие	-
～民 **zāimín** пострада́вшие	disaster victims
(от стихийного бедствия)	-
～荒 **zāihuāng** стихи́йное	famine due to crop failures
бе́дствие; неурожа́й	-
熨 **yùn** гла́дить *(утюгом)*	to iron, press
～斗 **yùndǒu** утю́г	flatiron
烫 **tàng** 1. обже́чь(ся); об-	1. to scald, burn; scalding, boiling, hot
вари́ть(ся) 2. завива́ть	2. to warm in hot water 3. to iron,
(волосы) 3. гла́дить, утю́-	press 4. perm (hair)
жить	-
炎 **yán** 1. сжига́ть; пла́мя	1. inflammation, -itis 2. hot
2. горя́чий 3. воспале́ние	-
淡 **dàn** 1. пре́сный 2. сла́-	1. thin, light 2. tasteless, weak 3. pale
бый; жи́дкий 3. безраз-	4. indifferent 5. slack, dull
ли́чный, холо́дный	-
～水 **dànshuǐ** пре́сная вода́	fresh water
～气 **dànqì** азо́т	nitrogen
谈 **tán** бесе́довать; разгова́-	to talk, chat; chat
ривать	-
～判 **tánpàn** перегово́ры	negotiations, talks
～论 **tánlùn** обсужда́ть	to discuss
～心 **tánxīn** поговори́ть по	to have a heart-to-heart talk
душа́м	-
水 **shuǐ** 1. вода́; жи́дкость;	1. water 2. liquid 3. river
сок 2. во́дный, речно́й	-
～星 **shuǐxīng** Мерку́рий	Mercury
～痘 **shuǐdòu** ве́тряная о́спа	chicken pox
～稻 **shuǐdào** заливно́й рис	paddy (rice)
～管 **shuǐguǎn** водопрово́д-	water pipe
ная труба́; водопрово́д	-
～晶 **shuǐjīng** криста́лл; хру-	crystal; rock crystal
ста́ль	-

水猪 **shuizhū** дельфи́н dolphin
～田 **shuitián** заливно́е [ри́совое] по́ле paddy field
～平 **shuipíng** у́ровень 1. horizontal, level 2. standard/level (e.g., of living)
～平线 **shuipíngxiàn** горизо́нт horizontal line
～牛 **shuiniú** бу́йвол water buffalo
～车 **shuichē** водяно́е колесо́ 1. waterwheel 2. water cart/wagon
～库 **shuikù** водохрани́лище reservoir
～利 **shuilì** ирригáция 1. water conservancy 2. irrigation works
～手 **shuishǒu** моря́к; матро́с seaman, sailor
～产 **shuichǎn** во́дный про́мысел aquatic product
～彩画 **shuicǎihuà** акваре́ль *(рисунок)* watercolor (painting)
～果 **shuiguǒ** фру́кты fruit
～灾 **shuizāi** наводне́ние flood, inundation
～球 **shuiqiú** во́дное по́ло water polo
～银 **shuiyín** ртуть mercury, quicksilver
～泥 **shuiní** цеме́нт cement
～池 **shuichí** водоём, пруд pond, pool, cistern
～龙 **shuilóng** пожа́рный насо́с (fire) hose
冰 **bīng** лёд; ледяно́й; заморо́женный 1. ice 2. to put on ice 3. to feel cold
～鞋 **bīngxié** коньки́ 1. skating boots 2. skates
～山 **bīngshān** а́йсберг iceberg
～箱 **bīngxiāng** холоди́льник refrigerator, freezer
～川(河) **bīngchuān(hé)** ледни́к, глéтчер glacier
～球 **bīngqiú** хокке́й 1. ice hockey 2. puck
～雹 **bīngbáo** град hail(stone)
～淇淋 **bīngqilín** моро́женое ice cream
尿 **niào** моча́ to urinate; urine
泉 **quán** исто́чник, родни́к spring, fountain
腺 **xiàn** железа́; же́лезы gland
浆 **jiāng** 1. густа́я жи́дкость 2. крахма́лить; крахма́л 1. thick liquid 2. to starch; starch
～ **jiàng** отва́р; кле́йстер thick
～果 **jiāngguǒ** я́года berry
～洗 **jiāngxi** крахма́лить to wash and starch

永 **yǒng 1.** ве́чный; наве́чно,	perpetually, forever, always
навсегда́; *перед отриц.* ни-	-
когда́ **2.** дли́тельный; по-	-
стоя́нный	-
～恒 **yǒnghéng** ве́чный, по-	eternal, perpetual
стоя́нный	-
～垂不朽 **yǒng chuí bùxiǔ**	to be immortal, will last forever
ве́чный, неувяда́емый	-
～久 **yǒngjiǔ** долговре́мен-	permanent(ly), perpetual(ly), ever-
ный; постоя́нный	lasting(ly)
～远 **yǒngyuǎn** всегда́, ве́ч-	always, forever
но; навсегда́	-
脉 **mài** арте́рии; кровено́сные	1. arteries and veins 2. pulse 3. vein
сосу́ды	(of leaves, insect wings)
录 **lù** запи́сывать; перепи́-	1. to record, write down, copy 2. to
сывать	employ, hire 3. to tape-record 4. re-\\
～音 **lùyīn** звукоза́пись	to record sound \\cord, collection
～音机 **lùyīnjī** магнитофо́н	tape-recorder
绿 **lǜ 1.** зелёный **2.** хлор	green
膝:膝盖 **xīgài** коле́но, коле́н-	knee
ка	-
漆 **qī** ла́ковое де́рево; лак	to paint; paint, varnish, lacquer
～器 **qīqì** ла́ковые изде́лия	lacquerware
暴 **bào 1.** внеза́пный, неожи́-	1. sudden and violent 2. cruel, savage 3.
данный **2.** вспы́льчивый **3.**	short-tempered 4. to stick out, bulge
жесто́кий, свире́пый	-
～虐 **bàonüè** жесто́ко обхо-	brutal, tyrannical
ди́ться; му́чить; бесчело-	-
ве́чный	-
～露 **bàolù 1.** под откры́тым	to reveal, lay bare
не́бом; откры́тый **2.** обна-	-
ру́жить(ся); вскрыть, ра-	-
зоблачи́ть	-
～行 **bàoxíng** бесчи́нство-	savage act, outrage, atrocity
вать; бесчи́нства; зве́рства	-
～雨 **bàoyǔ** ли́вень; гроза́	torrential rain, cloudburst
～动 **bàodòng** восста́ть;	insurrection, rebellion
взбунтова́ться; восста́ние;	-
бунт	-
～发 **bàofā** разрази́ться, ра-	1. to break out, burst 2. to become
зыгра́ться	rich/important suddenly
～乱 **bàoluàn** беспоря́дки;	riot, rebellion, revolt
бунт	-
～风 **bàofēng** урага́н; шторм	1. storm wind, gale 2. storminess

爆 **bào** **1.** взрыва́ться; ло́паться, тре́скаться **2.** хлопу́шка, раке́та	1. to explode, burst 2. quick-fry, quick-boil
～炸 **bàozhà** взорва́ть(ся); взрыв	to explode, blow up
～竹 **bàozhú** хлопу́шка, раке́та	firecracker
～发 **bàofā** *см.* 爆炸	to explode, blow up
～破 **bàopò** взорва́ть, подорва́ть	to blow up, demolish, blast
泰 **tài** мир, споко́йствие	1. safe, peaceful 2. extreme, most
～ **tài** *сокр.* Таила́нд	(abbr.) Thailand
求 **qiú** **1.** проси́ть; тре́бовать; добива́ться; стреми́ться **2.** иска́ть, оты́скивать	1. to request, entreat 2. to strive for, seek, try
球 **qiú** шар; мяч; сфери́ческий	ball
隶 **lì** принадлежа́ть; подчиня́ться	1. to be subordinate to, be under 2. a person in servitude
～属 **lìshǔ** подчиня́ться; зави́сеть от; подчинённый; подве́домственный	to be subordinate to
康 **kāng** **1.** процвета́ние, благополу́чие **2.** здоро́вье	1. healthy 2. peaceful 3. abundant 4. easy
～乐 **kānglè** жизнера́достный	1. peaceful and happy 2. wholesome recreation
～健 **kāngjiàn** здоро́вый, кре́пкий	healthy, in good health
慷:慷慨 **kāngkǎi** **1.** возбуждённый, взволно́ванный **2.** с энтузиа́змом **3.** ще́дрый, широ́кий *(о нату́ре)*	1. to be generous/liberal/unselfish 2. vehement, fervent
聚 **jù** **1.** собира́ться, сходи́ться **2.** собира́ть, нака́пливать	to assemble, gather, get together
～集 **jùjí** *см.* 聚	to gather, assemble, collect
骤 **zhòu** бы́стро бежа́ть, мча́ться; стреми́тельный; внеза́пно, вдруг	1. abruptly, suddenly 2. to trot (of a horse)
承 **chéng** **1.** приня́ть, получи́ть **2.** взять на себя́ **3.** продолжа́ть *(чьё-л. де́ло)* **4.** признава́ть(ся); соглаша́ться	1. to bear, hold, carry 2. to undertake, contract 3. to be indebted (to sb. for a kindness), be granted a favor 4. to continue, carry on

承继 **chéngjì** наслéдовать, быть преéмником	1. (trad.) to be adopted as heir to one's uncle 2. to adopt a brother's son
～当 **chéngdāng** взять на себя́	to take, bear
～认 **chéngrèn** признавáть; признáние	1. to admit, acknowledge, recognize 2. to give diplomatic recognition (to)
蒙 **mēng** обмáнывать, дурáчить	1. to cheat, dupe 2. to make a wild guess 3. unconscious, senseless
～ **méng** тёмный, невéжественный	1. to cover 2. to receive, meet with 3. ignorant, illiterate
～住 **mēngzhu** вводи́ть в заблуждéние	to be momentarily stumped
豪 **háo 1.** выдаю́щаяся ли́чность; геро́й **2.** могу́чий, влия́тельный **3.** волосóк, щети́нка	1. a person of extraordinary powers or endowments 2. bold and unconstrained 3. despotic, bullying
～无(不) **háowú(bù)** нискóлько, абсолю́тно не	to completely lack
～杰 **háojié** выдаю́щаяся ли́чность; геро́й	demigod, hero
家 **jiā 1.** семья́, семéйство; дом **2.** дом, жили́ще **3.** мéбель **4.** инструмéнт	1. family, household, home 2. (suf.) -er/-ist/-ian 3. school of thought 4. belonging to family 5. my (of older family members)
～畜 **jiāchù** домáшние живóтные	domestic animal, livestock
～禽 **jiāqín** домáшняя пти́ца	domestic fowl, poultry
～属 **jiāshǔ** члéны семьи́	family members/dependents
～产 **jiāchǎn** домáшнее иму́щество	family property
～乡 **jiāxiāng** рóдина, мéсто рождéния	hometown, native place
～伙 **jiāhuo 1.** тип, субъéкт **2.** вещь, шту́ка	(coll.) 1. implement 2. whatchama-call-it 3. pistol, gat, dagger 4. penis 5. dishes 6. guy
～庭 **jiātíng** семья́	family, household
～具 **jiājù** мéбель, обстанóвка	furniture
稼 **jià** хлебá	1. to sow (grain) 2. cereals, crops
嫁 **jià 1.** вы́йти зáмуж **2.** свали́ть *(вину, ответственность)*	1. (of a woman) to marry 2. to marry off a daughter 3. to shift, transfer
缘 **yuán 1.** причи́на, пóвод **2.** край, каймá	1. reason, cause 2. fate, predestination 3. edge, fringe, hem 4. to go along; along
～故 **yuángù** причи́на	cause, reason
象 **xiàng 1.** слон **2.** изобра-	1. elephant 2. appearance, shape, im-

же́ние; вне́шний вид; о́браз	age 3. to imitate, be like, resemble, take after 4. to look as if, seem
象征 **xiàngzhēng** символизи́ровать; си́мвол	to symbolize, signify, stand for; symbol, emblem, token
～棋 **xiàngqí** ша́хматы	Chinese chess
像 **xiàng** **1.** вне́шний вид; о́браз **2.** быть похо́жим	1. to be like, resemble 2. to seem, look as if 3. such as, like 4. likeness, portrait\\ \\picture 5. image
橡 **xiàng** **1.** жёлудь **2.** каучу́ковое де́рево; каучу́к	1. oak 2. rubber tree
～胶 **xiàngjiāo** каучу́к	rubber
～皮 **xiàngpí** **1.** рези́на **2.** рези́нка, ла́стик	1. rubber 2. eraser
畏 **wèi** боя́ться; страх	1. to fear, dread 2. to respect
喂 **wèi** эй!; алло́!	1. to feed 2. hello, hey
馁 **wèi** корми́ть, содержа́ть *(скот)*	to feed, nurse (a baby); to keep, feed (livestock)
丧 **sāng** тра́ур; по́хороны	mourning
～ **sàng** **1.** умере́ть, поги́бнуть **2.** потеря́ть, лиши́ться	to lose
～命 **sàngmìng** поги́бнуть	to lose one's life
～事 **sāngshì** по́хороны	funeral arrangement(s)
～失 **sàngshī** утра́тить; утра́та	to lose
～气 **sāngqi** па́дать ду́хом; унывать	(coll.) to have bad luck
展 **zhǎn** **1.** раскры́ть(ся), разверну́ть(ся) **2.** расширя́ть(ся); увели́чивать(ся)	1. to open up, spread out, expand, develop 2. to postpone, extend 3. to exhibit ; exhibition 4. to visit 5. to blot
～望 **zhǎnwàng** **1.** наблю-да́ть; обозрева́ть **2.** перспекти́вы	1. to look into the distance/future 2. prospects
～开 **zhǎnkāi** *см.* 展	1. to spread out, unfold, open up 2. to// //launch, develop
～期 **zhǎnqī** отсро́чить, продли́ть срок; пролонги́ровать	1. to extend a time limit 2. exhibition period
～览 **zhǎnlǎn** выставля́ть, экспони́ровать	to exhibit, show, display; exhibit, show, display
～览会 **zhǎnlǎnhuì** вы́ставка	exhibition
振 **zhèn** **1.** трясти́, сотряса́ть **2.** возбужда́ть; воодушевля́ть	1. to shake, flap 2. to vibrate, activate 3. to relieve (famine/etc.) 4. to restore order 5. to terrify 6. to abandon
～动 **zhèndòng** потрясти́, всколыхну́ть	to vibrate

振兴 **zhènxīng** возрождáть; развивáть	to promote, develop vigorously
晨 **chén** ýтро; рассвéт	morning
震 **zhèn** сотрясáть, колебáть	1. to shake, quake 2. to shock 3. to be shocked/terrified
派 **pài** **1.** фрáкция, группирóвка **2.** посылáть, командировáть; направлять	1. group, school, faction, clique 2. style, manner, air 3. to send, assign, appoint 4. chic, hip 5. (M. for scenery, etc.)
～别 **pàibié** **1.** течéние, направлéние *(напр. в науке)* **2.** фрáкция, группирóвка	group, school, faction
～遣 **pàiqiǎn** посылáть, командировáть	to send, dispatch
旅 **lǚ** **1.** путешéствовать **2.** *воен.* бригáда	1. to travel, stay away from home 2. troops, force; brigade
～社 **lǚshè** гостúница	hotel
～客 **lǚkè** **1.** пассажúр **2.** путешéственник **3.** постоялец	hotel guest; traveler; passenger
～馆 **lǚguǎn** гостúница, отéль	hotel
～伴 **lǚbàn** спýтник, попýтчик	traveling companion, fellow passenger
～行 **lǚxíng** путешéствовать; путешéствие	to travel, journey, tour
衣 **yī** **1.** одéжда; плáтье; костюм **2.** чехóл; футляр	1. clothing, clothes, garment 2. coat, covering
～柜 **yīguì** гардерóб, шкаф	wardrobe, armoire
～裳(服) **yīshang(fu)** одéжда	(coll.) clothing, clothes
依 **yī** опирáться; оснóвываться на; в соотвéтствии с, соглáсно	1. to depend/count on 2. to comply with, agree, consent 3. according to, judging by
～靠 **yīkào** опирáться; полагáться на; зависеть от	to rely/depend on; support, backing
～附 **yīfù** завúсеть	to depend on, attach oneself to
～赖 **yīlài** завúсеть от; завúсимый	to depend/rely on
～照 **yīzhào** в соотвéтствии с, соглáсно	according to, in light of
～然 **yīrán** по-прéжнему; твёрдо, неизмéнно	still, as before
装 **zhuāng** **1.** одевáться; наряжáться; одéжда **2.** маскировáться, притворяться **3.** упакóвывать; наполнять; нагружáть **4.** оборý-	1. to play the part/role of, act 2. to dress up 3. to pretend, feign 4. to install, fit, assemble 5. to load, pack, hold 6. outfit, dress, clothing, costume 7. stage makeup/costume

довать; оснащáть; снаряжáть	-
装备 **zhuāngbèi** оборýдовать; оборýдование; снаряжéние	to equip, outfit; equipment, outfit
～饰 **zhuāngshì** украшáть; разукрáшенный	to decorate, adorn, ornament, deck; decoration, ornament
～饰品 **zhuāngshìpin** украшéния, безделýшки	ornament
～载 **zhuāngzài** грузи́ть, нагружáть; погрýзка	to load
裂 **liè 1.** разорвáть(ся); лóпнуть **2.** расщепи́ть	1. to split, crack 2. to divide up (profits) 3. to rend, rip open 4. to sever\\
～开 **lièkai** расколóть(ся); трéснуть	to split open, rend \\(a relationship)
～痕(缝) **lièhén(féng)** трéщина; разры́в	rift, crack, fissure
袋 **dài** мешóк; сýмка; кармáн	1. bag, sack, pocket, pouch 2. (M. for bags of sth.)
袭 **xí** нападáть; нападéние	1. to make a surprise attack on 2. to carry on as before 3. to plagiarize 4. (M. for clothes)
～击 **xíjī** удáр; налёт, нападéние	-
表 **biǎo 1.** нарýжный, внéшний; повéрхностный **2.** выражáть(ся), проявля́ть (-ся) **3.** табли́ца; шкалá; циферблáт **4.** анкéта **5.** счётчик; прибóр; часы́ **6.** двоюродный	1. surface, exterior 2. model, example 3. list, table, form 4. meter 5. watch 6. to indicate
～格 **biǎogé** графá	form, table
～面 **biǎomiàn** внéшняя (лицевáя) сторонá	surface, face, outside, appearance
～明 **biǎomíng** свидéтельствовать, покáзывать	to make known, indicate
～扬 **biǎoyáng** прославля́ть; поощря́ть; стáвить в примéр	to praise, commend
～决 **biǎojué** голосовáть; голосовáние	to vote, decide by vote
～现 **biǎoxiàn** обнарýживать(ся), выражáть(ся); выражéние, проявлéние	1. to show, display 2. to show off 3. manifestation, expression
～演 **biǎoyǎn** выступáть, давáть представлéние	1. to perform, act, play 2. to demonstrate; performance, exhibition

表衰衷滚农脓浓

表示 **biǎoshì** выража́ть; пока́зывать; свиде́тельствовать	to show, express, indicate
衰 **shuāi** дряхле́ть, слабе́ть; приходи́ть в упа́док	to decline, wane; feeble, declining
～落 **shuāiluò** упа́док; деграда́ция	to decline, go downhill
～弱 **shuāiruò** дря́хлый, не́мощный, сла́бый	weak, feeble
衷 **zhōng** и́скренний, чистосерде́чный	inner feelings, heart
～心 **zhōngxīn** чистосерде́чный; от всего́ се́рдца	heartfelt, cordial
滚 **gǔn** **1.** клокота́ть, бурли́ть; кипе́ть **2.** кати́ться; враща́ться; крути́ться	1. to roll, trundle; roll, turn 2. to get away, beat it 3. to boil 4. to bind, trim
～蛋 **gǔndàn** убира́йся вон!	(derog.) Beat it!, Scram!
农 **nóng** земледе́лие; се́льское хозя́йство; земледе́лец, крестья́нин	1. agriculture, farming 2. peasant, farmer
～庄 **nóngzhuāng** дере́вня; фе́рма, хозя́йство	farmstead
～业 **nóngyè** се́льское хозя́йство	agriculture, farming
～作物 **nóngzuòwù** сельскохозя́йственные культу́ры	crops
～学 **nóngxué** агроно́мия	agronomy, agriculture
～时 **nóngshí** вре́мя полевы́х рабо́т	farming season
～村 **nóngcūn** дере́вня	rural area, countryside, village
～户 **nónghù** крестья́нский двор	peasant household
～场 **nóngchǎng** *с.-х.* фе́рма	farm
～民 **nóngmín** крестья́нство; крестья́нин	peasant, peasantry
～艺 **nóngyì** агроно́мия	agronomy
～艺师 **nóngyìshī** агроно́м	agronomist
～具 **nóngjù** сельскохозя́йственные ору́дия, инвента́рь	farm implements
脓 **nóng** гной; гно́йный	pus
浓 **nóng** **1.** густо́й, пло́тный **2.** кре́пкий, концентри́рованный	dense, thick, concentrated

跟 **gēn 1.** пя́тка; каблу́к **2.** сле́довать (идти́) за; с; вме́сте с	1. to follow 2. to marry (of a woman) 3. with, to, from 4. and 5. heel
~前 **gēnqián** о́коло; пе́ред; при себе́	1. in front of, before 2. close to, nearby
~随 **gēnsuí** сле́довать за, сопровожда́ть	to follow
眼 **yǎn 1.** глаз **2.** глазо́к; про́резь; щель **3.** *муз.* такт; па́уза	1. eye 2. look, glance 3. small hole, aperture 4. salient/weighted point
~泪 **yǎnlèi** слёзы	tears
~看 **yǎnkàn 1.** в [оди́н] миг **2.** воо́чию уви́деть	1. to see sth. happen 2. to watch helplessly 3. soon, in a moment
~下 **yǎnxià** сейча́с, в да́нное вре́мя	at present, now
~睛 **yǎnjing** глаза́	eye
~皮 **yǎnpí** ве́ки	eyelid
~毛 **yǎnmáo** ресни́цы	eyelash
~镜 **yǎnjìng** очки́	glasses, spectacles
恨 **hèn** ненави́деть; не́нависть	1. to hate; hate 2. to regret 3. to be exasperated
~不得 **hènbude** не те́рпится *(что-л. сделать)*	to be very anxious to, itch to
很 **hěn** о́чень, весьма́	very, quite, awfully
限 **xiàn** ограни́чивать, сде́рживать; грани́ца, преде́л	to set a limit, restrict
~制 **xiànzhì** ограни́чивать, лимити́ровать; ограниче́ние	to restrict, confine
~期 **xiànqī** срок	to be within a definite/set time; time limit, deadline
~额 **xiàn'é** лими́т	limit, quota, norm
狠 **hěn** свире́пый, жесто́кий	1. ruthless, relentless 2. firm, resolute
根 **gēn 1.** ко́рень; основа́ние; фунда́мент **2.** нача́ло, исто́чник **3.** *сч. сл. для длинных предметов*	1. root 2. cause, origin, source 3. (M. for long and thin things)
~据 **gēnjù 1.** да́нные; основа́ния **2.** осно́вываться; согла́сно; по	1. basis, grounds, foundation 2. on the basis of, according to
~本 **gēnběn** основно́й, коренно́й; коренны́м о́бразом	1. essence, foundation 2. basic, essential, fundamental 3. at all, simply, utterly
~源 **gēnyuán** исто́ки; исто́чник	source, origin, root

根艰银痕良狼粮娘浪食

根除 **gēnchú** выкорчёвывать, искоренять	to eliminate, root out
艰:艰难 **jiānnán** трудный, тяжёлый	difficult, hard
银 **yín** 1. серебро; серебряный 2. деньги	silver
～行 **yínháng** банк	bank
～幕 **yínmù** экран	(motion-picture) screen
痕 **hén** 1. шрам, рубец 2. след, отпечаток	mark, trace
～迹 **hénjī** шрам	mark, trace, vestige
良 **liáng** добро; добрый; хороший, благородный	1. good, fine 2. instinctive, inborn, innate 3. very, very much 4. good people
～好 **liánghǎo** хороший, положительный; прекрасный	good, well
～心 **liángxīn** совесть	conscience
狼 **láng** 1. волк 2. хищный; хищник	1. wolf 2. cruel and greedy person
～心 **lángxīn** жестокий, бесчеловечный	cruel, brutal, savage, inhuman
粮 **liáng** зерно; провиант	1. grain, food, provisions 2. grain tax in kind
～食 **liángshi** зерно; продовольствие; продовольственный	grain, cereals, food
娘 **niáng** 1. девочка; девушка 2. мать	1. Ma, Mum, mother 2. elderly married woman, young woman
浪 **làng** 1. волна 2. беспутный, развратный 3. расточительный	1. wave, billow, breaker 2. dissolute, unrestrained
～潮 **làngcháo** прибой	tide, wave
～漫 **làngmàn** 1. распущенность 2. романтический	1. (loan w.) romantic 2. dissolute, debauched
～漫主义 **làngmànzhǔyì** романтизм	romanticism
～费 **làngfèi** транжирить деньги; расточительство	1. to waste, squander 2. extravagant
食 **shí** кушать; есть; еда, пища	1. to eat 2. to feed 3. meal, food; edible 4. eclipse
～堂 **shítáng** столовая	(institutional) dining room, canteen
～盐 **shíyán** поваренная соль	table salt
～器 **shíqì** столовый прибор	pots and pans, kitchen utensils
～品 **shípǐn** продукты питания	foodstuff(s), food

食言 **shíyán** не сдержа́ть сло́во	to go back on one's word
～指 **shízhǐ** указа́тельный па́лец	forefinger, index finger
～物 **shíwù** проду́кты пита́ния	food, edibles
～欲 **shíyù** аппети́т	appetite
～具 **shíjù** посу́да	tableware
走 **zǒu** **1.** идти́; е́хать **2.** ускользну́ть; сорва́ться **3.** пропуска́ть; проса́чиваться **4.** теря́ть, утра́чивать *(цвет, форму)*	1. to walk, go 2. to run, move 3. to leave, go away 4. to visit, call on 5. to go through 6. to leak, escape, let out 7. to lose (flavor/shape, etc.)
～话 **zǒuhuà** вы́болтать, разболта́ть	to let out a secret, leak out
～廊 **zǒuláng** галере́я; коридо́р	corridor, passage, passageway
～漏 **zǒulòu** *см.* ～话	1. to leak out, divulge 2. smuggling and\\ \\tax evasion
～狗 **zǒugǒu** приспе́шник	stooge, flunky, running-dog
～动 **zǒudòng** дви́гаться; ходи́ть	1. to walk about, stretch one's legs 2. to visit each other
～私 **zǒusī** занима́ться контраба́ндой	to smuggle
徒 **tú** **1.** идти́ пешко́м **2.** зря, напра́сно **3.** после́дователь, учени́к	1. disciple, pupil, apprentice 2. follower 3. (derog.) person, fellow 4. to go on foot 5. bare, empty 6. only 7. in vain
～弟 **túdi** учени́к; подмасте́рье	apprentice, disciple
～然 **túrán** зря, напра́сно	in vain, to no avail
趋 **qū** **1.** направля́ться **2.** стреми́ться к; име́ть тенде́нцию	1. to run/hasten forward 2. to incline/ tend towards
～向 **qūxiàng** **1.** устремле́ние; тенде́нция **2.** стреми́ться к	to tend/incline to; trend, tendency
～势 **qūshì** тенде́нция	1. trend, tendency 2. to follow a trend
超 **chāo** **1.** превыша́ть; превосходи́ть **2.** выходи́ть за преде́лы; пере=; над=; сверх=; ультра=	1. to surpass, overtake 2. to transcend 3. ultra-, super-, extra-
～音速 **chāo-yīnsù** сверхзвукова́я ско́рость	supersonic speed
～等 **chāoděng** вы́сшего со́рта	of superior grade, extra fine

超赴赶趁趣越起

超过 **chāoguò** превыша́ть; превосходи́ть	to strip, surpass, exceed
～额 **chāo'é** превыше́ние; пере=; сверх=	to exceed quota
赴 **fù** отправля́ться, направля́ться	to go, attend
赶 **gǎn** **1.** догоня́ть; торопи́ть(ся) **2.** погоня́ть **3.** гнать, выгоня́ть; изгоня́ть	1. to run after, pursue 2. to make a dash/rush for 3. to drive 4. to drive away, expel 5. to encounter 6. until, till
～上 **gǎnshàng** догна́ть; успе́ть	1. to overtake 2. to run into (a situation), be in time for
～快 **gǎnkuài** скоре́е; сро́чно; бы́стро	at once, quickly
～走 **gǎnzǒu** прогна́ть, вы́гнать; изгна́ть	to drive away, expel
～紧 **gǎnjǐn** сро́чно, неме́дленно	hurriedly, losing no time
趁 **chèn** по́льзоваться *(случаем)*	1. to take advantage of, avail oneself of 2. to be possessed of, be rich in 3. while
趣 **qù** интере́с; интере́сный	1. to hasten 2. interest, delight; inter-\\ \\esting
～味 **qùwèi** интере́с; вкус	fun, interest, taste, delight
越 **yuè** **1.** переходи́ть *(через)*; превыша́ть **2.** ещё бо́лее; 越…越… чем..., тем **3.** *сокр.* Вьетна́м	1. to get/jump over 2. to exceed, overlap 3. the more...the more... 4. (abbr.) Vietnam
～次 **yuècì** внеочередно́й	to skip a grade/rank
～轨 **yuèguǐ** **1.** сойти́ с ре́льсов **2.** экстрава га́нтный	to exceed bounds, transgress
起 **qǐ** **1.** встава́ть; поднима́ть(-ся) **2.** начина́ть(ся); возника́ть **3.** *суф. результативно-направленных гл., указывающих на: а) движение снизу вверх и б) на начало действия*	1. to rise, get up 2. to raise, build 3. to start 4. to unload, remove 5. to buy, obtain 6. (suf. with sense of "up") 7. (as a resultative ending)
～重机 **qǐzhòngjī** подъёмный кран; домкра́т	hoist, crane, derrick
～立 **qǐlì** встать, подня́ться с ме́ста	to stand up
～名 **qǐmíng** дать и́мя	to name sb./sth.
～草 **qǐcǎo** наброса́ть чернови́к; соста́вить план (прое́кт)	to draft, draw up
～初 **qǐchū** в са́мом нача́ле	at first, originally

起码 **qǐmǎ** как ми́нимум; по ме́ньшей ме́ре	rudimentary, minimum, elementary; at least
～义 **qǐyì** подня́ть восста́ние; восста́ние	to revolt; revolt
～点 **qǐdiǎn 1.** старт; исхо́дный пункт **2.** проло́г, нача́ло	starting point
足 **zú 1**. нога́; но́жка **2.** быть доста́точным; доста́точно, дово́льно	1. foot, base 2. sufficient(ly), enough, fully, as much as
～够 **zúgòu** доста́точно; доста́точный	sufficiently, enough, fully, amply
～球 **zúqiú** футбо́л	soccer (football)
促 **cù** побужда́ть; спосо́бствовать	1. to urge, promote 2. close to, near 3. short (of time), hurried, urgent
～进 **cùjìn** спосо́бствовать; стимули́ровать	to promote, accelerate
捉 **zhuō** схвати́ть, пойма́ть	1. to clutch, hold, grasp 2. to catch,//capture
～弄 **zhuōnòng** подшу́чивать, высме́ивать	to tease, make fun of
是 **shì 1**. есть; быть, явля́ться **2.** да, пра́вда	1. to be 2. matter, affair 3. this, all 4. right, true 5. certainly, for sure
～否 **shìfǒu** не... ли?	whether or not, is it so or not
～非 **shìfēi** и́стина и ложь	1. right and wrong 2. quarrel, dispute
～的 **shìde** да, так	that's it, yes, right
堤 **dī** да́мба; плоти́на	dike, embankment, levee
～防 **dīfang 1.** огражде́ние, барье́р **2.** принима́ть ме́ры предосторо́жности	to take precautions, be on guard against
提 **tí 1.** держа́ть **2.** поднима́ть; повыша́ть **3.** упомина́ть **4.** предлага́ть, выдвига́ть	1. to carry, take 2. to lift, raise, promote 3. to move up a date 4. to extract 5. to refer to, bring up 6. to bring (a prisoner) to court 7. to promote
～醒 **tíxǐng** напомина́ть	to remind, alert to, warn
～出 **tíchū** предлага́ть, выдвига́ть	to put forward, pose, raise
～倡 **tíchàng** предлага́ть, выдвига́ть; выступа́ть с инициати́вой	to advocate, encourage, recommend
～琴 **tíqín** скри́пка	violin family (viola, violin, cello, bass)
～前 **tíqián** досро́чно; зара́нее, заблаговре́менно	1. to advance a date 2. in advance, beforehand
～高 **tígāo** поднима́ть, повыша́ть	to raise, heighten, enhance, increase, improve

提题定旋疑

提案 **tí'àn** предложéние, проéкт	proposal, motion, draft resolution
～供 **tígōng** **1.** вручáть; выдавáть **2.** поставля́ть, снабжáть	to supply, furnish, offer
题 **tí** **1.** тéма; вопрóс **2.** надпи́сывать; подпи́сывать	1. topic, subject, title 2. problem 3. to inscribe
～目 **tímù** тéма; заглáвие, назвáние	1. title, subject, topic 2. exercise problems, exam questions
～材 **tícái** тéма; сюжéт	subject matter, theme
定 **dìng** **1.** твёрдый, стаби́льный, устóйчивый **2.** устанáвливать, определя́ть **3.** закáзывать, брони́ровать **4.** обязáтельно, непремéнно	1. calm, stable 2. fixed, settled 3. to decide 4. to subscribe to, order (merchandise/etc.) 5. surely, certainly
～理 **dìnglǐ** теорéма	theorem
～量 **dìngliàng** мéра, нóрма	1. fixed quantity 2. to quantify 3.//quantitative
～立 **dìnglì** вы́работать, установи́ть	1. to establish, set up 2. to elaborate, work out
～居 **dìngjū** жить осéдло; посели́ться, обосновáться	to settle down
～作 **dìngzuò** заказáть; сдéлать на закáз	to order, place an order for
～期 **dìngqī** регуля́рный; периоди́ческий	1. to fix a date 2. fixed (of time) 3. periodic, regular
～义 **dìngyì** определéние, формулирóвка	definition
～额 **dìng'é** нóрма	quota, norm
旋 **xuán** поворáчиваться; вращáться; возвращáться	1. to revolve, circle, spin 2. to return, come back 3. circle 4. soon, before long
～ **xuàn** **1.** кружи́ться, вихрь **2.** точи́ть, вытáчивать	1. to turn sth. on a lathe 2. whirl 3. turning, spinning 4. at the time
～工 **xuàngōng** тóкарь	(mach.) turner
～开 **xuánkāi** отви́нчивать	to unscrew
～床 **xuànchuáng** токáрный станóк	(mach.) turning lathe
～风 **xuànfēng** вихрь; смерч	whirlwind
疑 **yí** сомнéние, недовéрие; подозревáть	1. to doubt, suspect 2. to be doubtful/uncertain
～问 **yíwèn** вопрóс; сомнéние	question, doubt
～惑(忌) **yíhuò(jì)** сомневáться; сомнéние	to be perplexed/uncertain; uncertainty

凝 **níng** **1.** сгусти́ться; затверде́ть **2.** собира́ться, ска́пливаться	1. to congeal 2. to concentrate attention
~结(固) **níngjié(gù)** сгуща́ться; затвердева́ть	to coagulate, congeal, condense
捷 **jié** **1.** бы́стрый, прово́рный **2.** Че́хия; Чехослова́кия	1. prompt, nimble, quick 2. Czech

乂

驳 **bó** **1.** оспа́ривать; опроверга́ть **2.** перегружа́ть *(товары)*	1. to refute, contradict 2. to transport by lighter; barge, lighter 3. varicolored
~斥 **bóchì** **1.** опрове́ргнуть, отве́ргнуть **2.** раскритикова́ть	to refute, denounce
义 **yì** **1.** справедли́вость **2.** долг, обя́занность **3.** беспла́тный, безвозме́здный **4.** смысл, значе́ние **5.** назва́ный, приёмный	1. justice, righteousness 2. chivalry, sense of honor 3. meaning, significance 4. righteous, just 5. adopted, adoptive 6. artificial, false 7. volunteer
~务 **yìwù** **1.** долг, обя́занность; обяза́тельный **2.** доброво́льный **3.** безвозме́здный	1. duty, obligation 2. volunteer duty
仪 **yí** **1.** вне́шний вид; мане́ры **2.** обря́д, ритуа́л **3.** прибо́р, аппара́т	1. appearance, bearing 2. etiquette, ceremony, rite 3. present, gift 4. apparatus, instrument
~器 **yíqì** аппарату́ра; прибо́ры	instrument, apparatus
~仗队 **yízhàngduì** почётный карау́л	guard of honor
~式 **yíshì** церемониа́л, ритуа́л	ceremony, rite
议 **yì** **1.** обсужда́ть; сове́товаться; реша́ть **2.** предложе́ние; мне́ние	1. confer, discuss 2. to criticize 3. opinion, view 4. treatise, argumentation
~程 **yìchéng** пове́стка дня, поря́док веде́ния собра́ния	agenda
~案 **yì'àn** прое́кт; законопрое́кт	proposal, motion

议文坟蚊父交

议论 **yìlùn** обсуждáть, дискути́ровать	to discuss, debate; discussion
~员 **yìyuán** депутáт; член парлáмента	member of a legislative body
~会 **yìhuì** парлáмент; конгрéсс	parliament, legislative assembly
文 **wén** 1. пи́сьменность; язы́к; литератýра 2. культýра, цивилизáция 3. узóр, орнáмент	1. writing, script 2. language 3. literary/artistic/cultural pursuits 4. literary language 5. civil, civilian 6. cultural, cultured, literary 7. gentle, refined
~言 **wényán** вэнья́нь	classical language (Ch.)
~盲 **wénmáng** негрáмотный; негрáмотность	1. an illiterate 2. illiteracy
~章 **wénzhāng** статья́	1. essay, article 2. literary works, writings 3. hidden/implied meaning
~件 **wénjiàn** докумéнт	documents, file
~字 **wénzì** пи́сьменность	1. characters, script, writing style or phraseology
~学 **wénxué** литератýра	literature
~明 **wénmíng** цивилизáция; цивилизóванный	civilization, culture; civilized
~化 **wénhuà** культýра; культýрный	1. culture, civilization 2. education, literacy
~化革命 **wénhuà gémìng** культýрная революция	The Great Proletarian Cultural Revolution
~艺 **wényì** литератýра и искýсство	literature and art
坟 **fén** моги́ла; моги́льный холм	grave, tomb
~墓 **fénmù** моги́ла; склеп	grave, tomb
~地 **féndì** клáдбище	graveyard, cemetery
蚊 **wén** комáр; моски́т	mosquito
~子 **wénzi** *см.* 蚊	mosquito
~帐 **wénzhàng** моски́тная сéтка	mosquito net
父 **fù** отéц	1. father 2. male relative of father's generation
~母 **fù-mǔ** роди́тели	parents, father and mother
~亲 **fùqin** отéц	father
交 **jiāo** 1. вручáть, передавáть 2. имéть связь; соприкасáться 3. плати́ть, вноси́ть	1. to hand over, give up, deliver 2. to meet, join 3. to reach 4. to cross, intersect 5. to associate with 6. to mate 7. to fall 8. friendship 9. mutual, together, same time
~给 **jiāogěi** передавáть, отдавáть	to hand/give to
~界 **jiāojiè** грани́чить; грани́ца	to have a common boundary

交响乐 **jiāoxiǎngyuè** симфони́ческая му́зыка	symphony
～纳 **jiāonà** плати́ть, вноси́ть	to pay (to the state/etc.), hand in
～易 **jiāoyì** торго́вля; сде́лка; обме́н	deal, trade, transaction; to transact
～换 **jiāohuàn** обме́нивать (-ся); обме́н	to exchange, swap
～通 **jiāotōng** связь, сообще́ние; тра́нспорт; пути́ сообще́ния	1. traffic, communications, transportation 2. liaison
～通员 **jiāotōngyuán** связно́й	liaison person
～战 **jiāozhàn** быть в состоя́нии войны́	to fight, wage war
～流 **jiāoliú** **1.** обме́ниваться *(опытом)*; обме́н **2.** слива́ться, впада́ть	1. to exchange, interflow, interchange 2. (electr.) alternating
咬 **yǎo** куса́ть; укуси́ть; грызть	1. to bite, snap at 2. to bark 3. to incriminate 4. to pronounce clearly 5. to\\
较 **jiào** сра́внивать, сопоставля́ть; сравни́тельно, относи́тельно	1. rather, quite, more 2. to\\ \\nitpick \\compare 3. to dispute 4. clearly
胶 **jiāo** **1.** кле́ить; клей; кле́йкий **2.** рези́на	1. glue, gum 2. rubber 3. resin, sap 4. to glue 5. sticky 6. stubborn
～布 **jiāobù** клеёнка	1. rubberized fabric 2. adhesive plaster
～捲 **jiāojuǎn** фотоплёнка	(roll) film
狡:狡猾 **jiǎohuá** хитри́ть; хи́трый; кова́рный	sly, cunning
校 **jiào** сверя́ть, корректи́ровать	1. to check, proofread 2. to compare critically, collate 3. to contest
～ **xiào** шко́ла; учёбное заведе́ние	1. school 2. field officer
～正 **jiàozhèng** пра́вить, корректи́ровать	to proofread and correct, rectify
～对 **jiàoduì** сверя́ть, слича́ть; корректи́ровать	1. to proofread, proof; proofreader 2. to check against a standard, calibrate
～长 **xiàozhǎng** дире́ктор *(школы)*; ре́ктор	1. headmaster, principal 2. president, chancellor //...and...
又 **yòu** опя́ть, ещё, сно́ва	1. again, moreover 2. and 3. but 4. both//
叹 **tàn** вздыха́ть, печа́литься	1. to sigh 2. to exclaim (admiringly)
仅 **jǐn** то́лько, всего́ лишь	only, merely, barely
取 **qǔ** **1.** брать, получа́ть **2.** отбира́ть, выбира́ть **3.** добива́ться, достига́ть	1. to take, get, obtain 2. to select

取最撮权双轰

取得 **qǔdé** получи́ть; доби́ться, дости́чь	to gain, acquire, obtain
～消 **qǔxiāo** аннули́ровать, ликвиди́ровать; ликвида́ция	to cancel, abolish, nullify
～巧 **qǔqiǎo** быть иску́сным (ло́вким)	to wangle, finagle
～笑 **qǔxiào** насмеха́ться	to ridicule, make fun of
～决 **qǔjué** зави́сеть от	to be decided by, depend on
最 **zuì** са́мый; в вы́сшей сте́пени	most, superlatively
～后 **zuìhòu** оконча́тельный, после́дний	last, final
～高 **zuìgāo** **1.** наивы́сший; максима́льный **2.** верхо́вный	highest, supreme, tallest
～初 **zuìchū** первонача́льный, в са́мом нача́ле	initially, at first
～近 **zuìjìn** **1.** са́мый бли́зкий **2.** за после́днее вре́мя	1. recently, lately 2. soon, in the near future 3. nearest
撮 **cuō** горсть; щепо́тка, ничто́жное коли́чество	1. to gather, scoop up, take up with fingers 2. to extract 3. (1 ml.)
权 **quán** **1.** власть; пра́во **2.** авторите́т **3.** ги́бкость; подви́жность	1. right, power, authority 2. tentatively 3. to weigh, assess 4. to handle a task provisionally 5. steelyard weight
～利 **quánlì** права́	right, privilege
～力 **quánlì** власть, полномо́чия	power, authority
～变 **quánbiàn** лави́ровать; ги́бкость	to adjust to change; adaptability, flexibility, tact
～威 **quánwēi** авторите́т, прести́ж	authority
双 **shuāng** па́ра; па́рный; двойно́й; чётный	1. two, twin, both, dual 2. even (number) 3. double, twofold 4. pair
～生 **shuāngshēng** близнецы́	twin
～重 **shuāngchóng** двойно́й	double, dual, twofold
～方 **shuāngfāng** о́бе стороны́; двусторо́нний	both sides, two parties
轰 **hōng** **1.** гро́хот; гром **2.** взрыва́ть(ся); взрыв	1. to rumble, boom 2. (onom.) bang!, boom!
～炸 **hōngzhà** бомби́ть; бомбардиро́вка	bomb
～炸机 **hōngzhàjī** бомбарди́ро́вщик	bomb

轰动 **hōngdòng** всколыхну́ть, потрясти́	to cause a sensation, make a stir
～轰烈烈 **hōnghōnglièliè** **1.** оглуши́тельный **2.** грандио́зный	vigorous, dynamic
摄 **shè** **1.** брать, взять **2.** фотографи́ровать	1. to absorb, assimilate 2. to photograph, shoot 3. to act for 4. to conserve one's health
～制 **shèzhì** снять *(фильм)*	to produce (a film)
～影 **shèyǐng** фотографи́ровать, снима́ть; фотогра́фия	1. photograph 2. to film, shoot a film
叔 **shū** дя́дя	1. father's/husband's younger brother 2. third brother
～叔 **shūshu** дя́дя	father's younger brother, uncle
椒 **jiāo** пе́рец	pepper, spice plants
叙 **xù** излага́ть; изложе́ние	1. to talk, chat 2. to narrate, recount, relate 3. to assess, appraise 4. to arrange in order 5. preface
～述 **xùshù** излага́ть, переска́зывать; изложе́ние, переска́з	to narrate, relate
奴 **nú** раб; ра́бский	to enslave; bond servant, slave
～隶 **núlì** раб; ра́бский	slave
～役 **núyì** порабоща́ть; порабоще́ние	to enslave
汉 **hàn** **1.** Кита́й; кита́йский **2.** мужчи́на	1. Han people/language/dynasty 2. man
～语 **hànyǔ** кита́йский язы́к	Chinese/Sinitic language(s)
～字 **hànzì** кита́йские иеро́глифы	Chinese character(s)
～族 **hànzú** кита́йцы, ха́ньцы	Han ethnic group
叉 **chā** **1.** ви́лка **2.** ви́лы	1. fork, intersection 2. cross, X
～ **chǎ** раздви́нуть, расста́вить	to part so as to form a fork
报 **bào** **1.** сообща́ть; информи́ровать; докла́д; сообще́ние; извеще́ние **2.** газе́та **3.** отблагодари́ть	1. to report 2. to reply 3. to compensate 4. newspaper 5. periodical 6. bulletin 7. telegram
～答 **bàodá** отплати́ть, отблагодари́ть	to repay, requite
～告 **bàogào** докла́дывать; докла́д	1. to report, make known 2. report, speech 3. (student) term paper
～名 **bàomíng** записа́ться [в спи́сок], зарегистри́роваться	to sign up, enter one's name
～酬 **bàochou** отблагодари́ть, вознагради́ть; вознагражде́ние; гонора́р	reward, remuneration, pay

报服反

报刊 **bàokān** пре́сса, периоди́ческая печа́ть	periodical publications
～效 **bàoxiào** отда́ть, поже́ртвовать	to give service/money to repay sb.'s kindness
～复 **bàofù** отплати́ть, отомсти́ть; возме́здие	to retaliate
～纸 **bàozhǐ** газе́та	1. newspaper 2. newsprint
～仇 **bàochóu** отомсти́ть; месть	to revenge, avenge
服 **fú** **1.** оде́жда, пла́тье **2.** подчиня́ться, повинова́ться **3.** служи́ть **4.** принима́ть *(пищу, лекарство)*; глота́ть	1. to take (medicine) 2. to serve, obey, submit oneself to 3. to convince 4. to be used to 5. clothes, dress 6. mourning dress
～饰 **fúshì** галантере́я	dress and personal adornment
～务 **fúwù** **1.** служи́ть; нести́ слу́жбу **2.** обслу́живать; обслу́живание	to serve, be in the service of; service
～务处 **fúwùchù** бюро́ обслу́живания	service bureau
～务员 **fúwùyuán** официа́нт; обслу́живающий персона́л	attendant, clerk
～从 **fúcóng** слу́шаться, подчиня́ться; повинове́ние, послуша́ние	to obey, submit (oneself) to, be subordinated to
～气 **fúqì** смири́ться, подчини́ться	to feel that things are fair
反 **fǎn** **1.** переверну́ть; перевёрнутый **2.** напро́тив, наоборо́т **3.** выступа́ть про́тив; анти=, противо=; контр=	1. to turn over 2. to return, counter 3. to revolt, rebel 4. to oppose, combat 5. upside down, inside out, in the reverse direction 6. on the contrary, instead 7. counterrevolutionaries, reactionaries\\
～应 **fǎnyìng** **1.** реаги́ровать; отклика́ться; о́тклик **2.** *хим.* реа́кция	to react, respond; reaction; \\8. contra-response; repercussion
～正 **fǎnzheng** так и́ли и́на́че; всё равно́	1. in any case, anyway, anyhow 2. rebel turning to join government's side
～击 **fǎnjī** контруда́р, отпо́р	to beat back, counteract
～省 **fǎnxǐng** самоана́лиз	introspection, self-questioning
～面 **fǎnmiàn** оборо́тная сторона́, изна́нка	1. reverse/wrong side, back 2. opposite, negative side
～作用 **fǎnzuòyòng** противоде́йствие	opposite reaction
～革命 **fǎngémìng** контрре-	counterrevolutionary

волю́ция; контрреволюцио́нный	-
反对 **fǎnduì** быть про́тив; протестова́ть; проти́виться	to oppose, be against, combat, dispute
～对党 **fǎnduìdǎng** оппозицио́нная па́ртия	opposition party, the opposition
～动 **fǎndòng** реа́кция; реакцио́нный	reactionary; reaction
～动派 **fǎndòngpài** реакционе́ры, реа́кция	reactionaries
～映 **fǎnyìng** отража́ть; отраже́ние	1. to reflect, mirror 2. to report, make known
～驳 **fǎnbó** опрове́ргнуть; опроверже́ние	to refute, retort, negate
～复 **fǎnfù** 1. неоднокра́тно 2. повторя́ться; повторе́ние, рециди́в	1. repeatedly, again and again 2. reversal, relapse
～抗 **fǎnkàng** отпо́р, сопротивле́ние	to revolt, resist
～感 **fǎngǎn** отвраще́ние, антипа́тия	to dislike, be disgusted with; dislike
版 **bǎn** 1. доска́ для печа́тания; клише́ 2. изда́ние 3. полоса́, страни́ца	1. printing plate (block) 2. edition 3. page (of newspaper)
～画 **bǎnhuà** гравю́ра	etching, engraving, block print
叛 **pàn** взбунтова́ться, восста́ть; измени́ть	to betray, rebel, revolt
～徒 **pàntú** мятёжник; изме́нник, ренега́т	traitor, renegade, turncoat
～变 **pànbiàn** измени́ть, преда́ть	to turn traitor, defect
～乱 **pànluàn** мятёж; беспоря́дки	armed rebellion
板 **bǎn** доска́; пла́нка	1. board, plank, plate; paddle 2. shutter// //3. hard, stiff, unnatural
贩 **fàn** торгова́ть; торго́вец	to buy to resell; dealer, peddler
饭 **fàn** 1. варёный рис; ка́ша 2. еда́, пи́ща	cooked rice or other cereals
～店 **fàndiàn** 1. рестора́н 2. гости́ница	1. hotel 2. restaurant
～厅 **fàntīng** столо́вая	dining hall/room, mess hall
～铺 **fànpù** заку́сочная	(small) restaurant, eating house
友 **yǒu** друг; прия́тель; дру́жеский, дру́жественный	friend; associate
～谊 **yǒuyì** дру́жба	friendship

友好 **yǒuhǎo** дру́жба; дру́жеский	close friend; friendly, amicable
爱 **ài 1.** люби́ть; любо́вь; люби́мый **2.** пристрасти́ться к **3.** быть подве́рженным	1. to love, like, be fond of, be keen on, cherish; love 2. to be apt to
～国主义 **àiguózhǔyì** патрио́тизм	patriotism
～好 **àihào** люби́ть	1. to love, like, be fond of, be keen on// //2. interest, hobby
～情 **àiqíng** любо́вь	romantic love
～护 **àihù** бере́чь, оберега́ть	to cherish, treasure, take good care of
～人 **àirén** люби́мый; муж; жена́	1. husband, wife 2. sweetheart
～克司光线 **àikèsī guāngxiàn** рентге́новские лучи́	(loan w.) X-ray
拔 **bá 1.** вытаскивать; выдёргивать **2.** выдвига́ть; повыша́ть *(в должности)*	1. to uproot; to pull out, draw 2. to choose 3. to surpass 4. to lift 5. to capture 6. to cool in water 7. (mach.) drawing
～掉 **bádiào** вы́дернуть; вы́корчевать; уничто́жить	
发 **fā 1.** выпуска́ть; выбра́сывать **2.** отправля́ть, посыла́ть **3.** начина́ть; приходи́ть в де́йствие **4.** обнару́живать(ся), проявля́ть (-ся)	1. to send out, deliver, distribute 2. to utter, express 3. to shoot, emit 4. to develop, expand 5. to rise/expand (of food) 6. to come/bring into existence 7. to open up, discover, expose 8. to become 9. to show one's feeling; to\\ \\feel 10. to start, set out, begin
～ **fà** во́лосы; причёска	hair
～生 **fāshēng** возника́ть; происходи́ть	to happen, occur, take place
～出 **fāchū** издава́ть, испуска́ть	to issue, send/give out
～言 **fāyán** выступа́ть, произноси́ть речь	to speak, make a statement/speech
～誓 **fāshì** дава́ть кля́тву; принима́ть прися́гу	to vow, pledge
～给 **fāgěi** выдава́ть	to issue, distribute, grant
～音 **fāyīn** произноси́ть; произноше́ние	to pronounce; pronunciation, articulation
～挥 **fāhuī 1.** развива́ть; распространя́ть **2.** выявля́ть; проявля́ть	1. to bring into play, give free rein to 2. to develop (an idea/etc.), elaborate
～射 **fāshè 1.** вы́стрелить; вы́пустить; запусти́ть **2.** излуча́ть	1. to launch, project, discharge, shoot 2. (phys.) to emit, transmit
～财 **fācái** разбогате́ть	to get rich, make a pile

发芽 **fāyá** распуска́ться; всходи́ть	to germinate, sprout
～明 **fāmíng** изобрета́ть; открыва́ть; изобрете́ние; откры́тие	1. to invent; invention 2. to expound
～育 **fāyù** расти́, развива́ться; рост, разви́тие	to grow, develop; growth, development
～扬 **fāyáng** развива́ть; распространя́ть	1. to develop, carry out 2. to make the most of
～动 **fādòng** нача́ть, разверну́ть	1. to start, launch 2. to mobilize, arouse
～动机 **fādòngjī** дви́гатель, мото́р	engine, motor
～展 **fāzhǎn** развива́ть(ся), развёртывать(ся); разви́тие	1. to develop, expand, grow 2. to recruit, admit
～表 **fābiǎo** **1.** опубликова́ть **2.** вы́разить, вы́сказать	to publish, issue
～达 **fādá** развива́ть(ся); ра́звитый	developed, flourishing
～电站 **fādiànzhàn** электроста́нция	generator, dynamo
～烧 **fāshāo** температу́рить; жар	to have a fever/temperature
～光 **fāguāng** свети́ться; светя́щийся	1. to shine, give out light 2. luminescence
～现 **fāxiàn** обнару́живать (-ся), выявля́ть(ся)	to find, discover; discovery
～觉 **fājué** **1.** обнару́жить; раскры́ть **2.** почу́вствовать	to find, detect, discover
～疯 **fāfēng** сойти́ с ума́	to go mad/crazy
拨 **bō** **1.** переставля́ть, передвига́ть **2.** гру́ппа; па́ртия *(товара)* **3.** ассигнова́ть, выдава́ть	1. to move with hand/foot/stick/etc.; to turn, stir, poke 2. to allocate 3. (M. for groups)
废 **fèi** **1.** прекрати́ть; аннули́ровать; изъя́ть, исключи́ть **2.** него́дный, нену́жный; брако́ванный	1. to give up, abandon, abolish, abrogate 2. waste
～址(墟) **fèizhi(xū)** разва́лины, руи́ны	ruins; deserted/neglected place
～品 **fèipǐn** брако́ванная проду́кция, брак	1. waste product, reject 2. scrap, waste

废缓暖援假搜

废话 **fèihuà** болтовня́, вздор	superfluous words, nonsense, rubbish
～物 **fèiwù** отбро́сы, ути́ль	good-for-nothing
～人 **fèirén** инвали́д	1. disabled person 2. good-for-nothing
～除 **fèichú** отмени́ть, аннули́ровать	to abolish, abrogate, repeal
缓 **huǎn** **1.** ме́длить; отложи́ть, отсро́чить; ме́дленный **2.** смягчи́ть; примири́ть	1. to delay, postpone 2. to recuperate, revive 3. late, tardy, slow 4. relaxed
～和 **huǎnhé** смягчи́ть, осла́бить	to relax, ease up, mitigate, appease
～慢 **huǎnmàn** ме́длить; медли́тельный; ме́дленно	slow
暖 **nuǎn** гре́ть(ся); тёплый	to warm up; warm, genial
～和 **nuǎnhuo** тёплый, ла́сковый	(nice and) warm; to warm up
～气 **nuǎnqì** отопле́ние	central heating
援 **yuán** поддéрживать, помога́ть	1. to pull by hand 2. to rescue, help 3. to cite, quote
～助 **yuánzhù** помога́ть; по́мощь	to support, aid; support, aid
假 **jiǎ** **1.** ло́жный; подде́льный, фальши́вый **2.** предполага́ть; е́сли; при усло́вии **3.** заи́мствовать, перенима́ть	1. false, fake, artificial, phony 2. to borrow, avail of 3. if, supposing 4. (law) conditional, tentative
～ **jià** о́тпуск; кани́кулы	1. vacation, holiday 2. leave of absence, furlough
～如 **jiǎrú** е́сли; е́сли бы	if, supposing, in case
～借 **jiǎjiè** заи́мствовать; брать взаймы́	1. to make use of 2. phonetic loan characters, homophonous substitution
～冒 **jiǎmào** подде́лывать, фальсифици́ровать	1. to pose as 2. to palm off (a fake as genuine)
～面具 **jiǎmiànjù** ма́ска	mask, false front
～扮(装) **jiǎbàn(zhuāng)** притворя́ться, маскирова́ться	to masquerade as
～定(设) **jiǎdìng(shè)** предположи́ть; предположе́ние, гипо́теза	1. to suppose, assume, grant, presume 2. hypothesis 3. (math) postulate
～使 **jiǎshǐ** е́сли бы; пусть да́же	if, in case, in the event that
搜 **sōu** иска́ть, разы́скивать	1. to search 2. to collect, gather
～查 **sōuchá** **1.** обы́скивать **2.** рассле́довать	to search, ransack, rummage

搜寻 **sōuxún** *см.* 搜	to search/look for, seek
～索 **sōusuǒ** искáть; обы́скивать; пóиск; óбыск	to search/hunt for, scout around
瘦 **shòu** 1. худóй, тóщий 2. пóстный 3. ýзкий *(об одежде)*	1. thin, emaciated 2. lean (of meat) 3. tight (of clothing) 4. barren, unproductive (of land)
度 **dù** 1. мéра; стéпень; грáдус 2. закóн, закономéрность 3. проводи́ть *(время)*	1. to spend (holidays), pass (time) 2. occasion, time 3. intensity 4. linear measure 5. limit, tolerance, magnanimity
渡 **dù** 1. переправля́ться чéрез рéку́; переправа 2. проходи́ть чéрез 3. проводи́ть *(время)*	1. to cross (water) 2. to tide over 3. to ferry across
～口 **dùkǒu** перепрáва	ferry, pier/crossing
～船 **dùchuán** парóм	ferryboat
慢 **màn** мéдленный; медли́тельный	1. slow 2. supercilious, rude 3. to postpone, defer
～性 **mànxìng** 1. медли́тельный 2. хрони́ческий	1. chronic 2. slow (in taking effect)
漫 **màn** 1. разливáться; разли́в 2. пóлный, безграни́чный	1. to fill 2. to reach a limit, expire, be over 3. full, complete 4. satisfied 5. conceited 6. entirely, wholly 7. Manchus
～画 **mànhuà** карикатýра, шарж	caricature, cartoon
侵 **qīn** захвáтывать; вторгáться	1. to invade, intrude into 2. to approach, get near to
～略 **qīnlüè** вторгáться; агрéссия; агресси́вный	to invade; agression, encroachment
～夺 **qīnduó** захвáтывать, отнимáть си́лой	to seize by force
～入 **qīnrù** вторгнуться; вторжéние	to invade, intrude into
～犯 **qīnfàn** 1. вторгáться, нападáть; нарушáть *(границу)* 2. нашéствие	to violate , infringe on (sb.'s rights)
寢 **qǐn** спать; спáльня	1. to sleep 2. to stop, end 3. bedroom
受 **shòu** 1. принимáть; получáть 2. подвергáться; терпéть; испы́тывать 3. быть пригóдным (подходя́щим)	1. to receive, accept 2. to endure, suffer, be subjected to 3. to be pleasant
～苦 **shòukǔ** мýчиться, страдáть	to suffer hardship
～罪 **shòuzuì** подвéргнуться наказáнию	to endure hardship/torture/etc.

受伤 **shòushāng** получи́ть ране́ние, быть ра́ненным	to be injured/wounded
授 **shòu** дава́ть; передава́ть, вруча́ть	1. to confer, give 2. to instruct
～权 **shòuquán** уполномо́чить	to empower, authorize
～课 **shòukè** преподава́ть	to give lessons //overcharge, fleece
敲 **qiāo** стуча́ть(ся); бить	1. to strike, beat (drums/etc.) 2. to//
支 **zhī** **1.** подде́рживать **2.** выде́рживать, выноси́ть **3.** выпла́чивать; выдава́ть *(деньги)* **4.** получа́ть, брать *(деньги)* **5.** ветвь, ответвле́ние	1. to support, sustain, bear 2. to send away, put sb. off, dispatch 3. to pay/draw (money) 4. branch, offshoot 5. the 12 Earthly Branches 6. (M. for slender objects, military contingents, songs, wattage, etc.)
～部 **zhībù** ячéйка *(партийная)*	branch (of Party/etc.) //port, back, stand by
～持 **zhīchí** подде́рживать	1. to sustain, hold out, bear 2. to sup-//
～援 **zhīyuán** подде́рживать, помога́ть	to support, assist, help; support, help
～线 **zhīxiàn** *ж.-д.* ве́тка	branch/feeder line
～配 **zhīpèi** **1.** распределя́ть **2.** управля́ть, кома́ндовать	1. to arrange, allocate, budget 2. to control, dominate, govern 3. government
～流 **zhīliú** прито́к, рука́в *(реки́)*	1. tributary, affluent 2. minor aspects, nonessentials
～票 **zhīpiào** де́нежный чек	(bank) check
歧 **qí** **1.** ответвле́ние доро́ги **2.** расходи́ться; различа́ть (-ся)	1. branch of a road 2. to differ; differences (in views)
～视 **qíshì** дискримина́ция	discrimination, one-sided approach
鼓 **gǔ** **1.** бараба́н **2.** бить, ударя́ть **3.** возбужда́ть; воодушевля́ть	1. to beat/play; drum 2. to arouse, inspire
～舞 **gǔwǔ** воодушевля́ть (-ся)	1. to inspire, hearten 2. to rejoice, dance for joy
～掌 **gǔzhǎng** аплоди́ровать; аплодисме́нты	to applaud, clap one's hands
～励 **gǔlì** поощря́ть, воодушевля́ть	to encourage, urge
～动 **gǔdòng** **1.** агити́ровать **2.** стимули́ровать	1. to agitate, arouse 2. to instigate, incite
技 **jì** мастерство́, уме́ние; те́хника	skill, ability
～师 **jìshī** те́хник	technical expert

技巧 **jìqiǎo 1.** иску́сный, уме́лый **2.** ло́вкий; хи́трый	technique, skill, craftsmanship, dexterity
～术 **jìshù 1.** те́хника; техни́ческий **2.** мастерство́, уме́ние	1. technology 2. skill, technique
肢 **zhī** коне́чности	limb, extremity
枝 **zhī** ве́тка, ответвле́ние	1. branch 2. (M. for slender items)
翅 **chì** кры́лья; плавники́	1. wing 2. shark's fin
皮 **pí 1.** ко́жа; ко́жаный; коже́венный **2.** кора́; оболо́чка; кожура́ **3.** мех; мехово́й **4.** пласти́на **5.** упря́мый	1. skin 2. leather, hide 3. wrapper 4. surface 5. thin/flat pieces/sheets 6. rubber 7. soft and soggy 8. case-hardened; indifferent 9. naughty
～鞋 **píxié** ко́жаная о́бувь; боти́нки	leather shoes
～匠 **píjiang** скорня́к	1. cobbler 2. farmer
～箱 **píxiāng** чемода́н	leather suitcase
～革 **pígé** ко́жа	leather, hide
～带 **pídài** ко́жаный по́яс; реме́нь	1. leather belt 2. (mach.) driving belt
～袄 **pí'ǎo** шу́ба	fur-lined jacket
～肤 **pífū** ко́жный покро́в, ко́жа	skin
～球 **píqiú** мяч *(кожаный)*	rubber ball
～包 **píbāo** портфе́ль; су́мка	leather handbag/briefcase
～货 **píhuò** меха́	fur, pelt //3. large low-lying field
坡 **pō** склон, скат	1. to slant, slope incline; slope 2. plain//
玻:玻璃 **bōli** стекло́	1. glass 2. (coll.) nylon, plastic
皱 **zhòu** морщи́ны; мо́рщить; хму́рить	to wrinkle; wrinkle
～痕(纹) **zhòuhén(wén)** морщи́ны	wrinkles
破 **pò 1.** разби́ть; разру́шить; полома́ть; порва́ть **2.** нанести́ уще́рб **3.** растра́тить; обанкро́титься	1. to break, cleave, cut 2. get rid of, eradicate 3. to defeat, capture 4. to expose 5. broken, damaged, torn 6. inferior, poor, lousy 7. (suf.) through
～烂 **pòlàn** изорва́ть; изо́рванный	1. tattered, ragged, worn-out 2. (coll.) junk, scrap
～产 **pòchǎn** обанкро́титься, разори́ться; банкро́тство	to go bankrupt; to come to naught; bankruptcy
～冰船 **pòbīngchuán** ледоко́л	icebreaker
～裂 **pòliè** расколо́ть(ся); разорва́ть(ся)	1. to burst, split, rupture 2. plosion; plosive //clarify, show light
～晓 **pòxiǎo** рассве́т	1. dawn, daybreak 2. (coll.) to explain,//

技肢枝翅皮坡玻皱破

破彼被披波疲没

破坏 **pòhuài** разруша́ть; подрывно́й, диверсио́нный	1. to destroy, wreck, smash 2. to violate (an agreement/etc.)
彼 **bǐ** друго́й, ино́й; тот	1. that, those, the other, another 2. the
~此 **bǐcǐ** взаи́мно	other party 3. there
被 **bèi** 1. одея́ло 2. покрыва́ться; покро́в 3. *показатель пассива*; 他被打死了	1. quilt 2. cover 3. by 4. (signifier of passive)
он был уби́т	-
~告 **bèigào** обвиня́емый; отве́тчик	1. defendant, the accused 2. to be sued
~单 **bèidān** простыня́	(bed) sheet
~褥 **bèirù** посте́льные принадле́жности	bedding, bedclothes
~动 **bèidòng** пасси́вный	passive
披 **pī** 1. наки́нуть; накры́ть 2. раскры́ть, разверну́ть	1. to drape over one's shoulders 2. to open, unroll 3. to split open, crack
波 **bō** 1. волна́; во́лны 2. волнова́ть(ся); волне́ние	1. wave 2. unexpected turn of events
~ **bō** По́льша	Poland
~折 **bōzhé** тру́дности, невзго́ды	twists and turns
~动 **bōdòng** всколыхну́ть; взволнова́ть	1. to undulate, fluctuate; fluctuation, rise and fall 2. (phys.) wave motion
~长 **bōcháng** *радио* длина́ волны́	wavelength
~浪 **bōlàng** волна́; во́лны	wave
疲:疲劳(倦) **píláo(juàn)** уста́ть, утоми́ться	tired, weary; fatigue
没 **méi** 1. не име́ть; нет 2. *отриц. частица прош. вр.* не	1. not 2. there are no
~ **mò** 1. погружа́ться в во́ду; тону́ть 2. исчеза́ть 3. отбира́ть, конфискова́ть	1. to drown, submerge 2. to vanish 3. to overthrow 4. to confiscate 5. to die
~落 **mòluò** зака́т; упа́док	to decline, wane
~什么 **méi shénme** ничего́, пустяки́	it doesn't matter, never mind
~事 **méishì** 1. быть без де́ла 2. ничего́ не случи́лось	1. to have nothing to do, be free 2. it doesn't matter, it's nothing, never mind
~有 **méiyǒu** не име́ть; нет	not to have, there is not to be
méiyou *отриц. прош. вр.* не	without
~关系 **méi guānxi** ничего́, не име́ет значе́ния	1. to have no relation/relevance 2. it doesn't matter, never mind

没收 **mòshōu** изъя́ть, конфискова́ть; конфиска́ция	to confiscate, expropriate
毁 **huǐ** **1.** уничто́жить; разру́шить **2.** оклевета́ть, оговори́ть	1. to destroy, ruin, damage 2. to burn up 3. to defame, slander 4. to refashion
～谤 **huǐbàng** клевета́ть; клевета́	to slander, libel
～灭 **huǐmiè** уничто́жить	to destroy, exterminate
～坏 **huǐhuài** разру́шить; повреди́ть	to destroy, damage
～损 **huǐsǔn** по́ртить; вреди́ть	to damage, impair
役 **yì** **1.** сраже́ние; вое́нная опера́ция **2.** слу́жба	1. labor, service 2. military service 3. servant 4. to use as a servant
段 **duàn** **1.** отре́зок; уча́сток **2.** абза́ц	1. section, part 2. paragraph
锻 **duàn** **1.** зака́ливать **2.** кова́ть **3.** пла́вить	to forge
～炼 **duànliàn** зака́ливать(-ся), тренирова́ть(ся); зака́лка, трениро́вка	1. to engage in physical exercise 2. to temper, steel, toughen
投 **tóu** **1.** мета́ть, броса́ть **2.** бро́ситься, ки́нуться **3.** отпра́вить, напра́вить **4.** подходи́ть, соотве́тствовать	1. to throw, fling 2. to send, deliver 3. to go to, join 4. to lodge, stay 5. to fit in with
～降 **tóuxiáng** капитули́ровать; капитуля́ция	to surrender, capitulate
～奔 **tóubèn** убежа́ть к, иска́ть прибе́жища	to seek refuge
～考 **tóukǎo** сдава́ть экза́мен	to sign up for an examination
～入 **tóurù** попа́сть, оказа́ться в	1. to throw/put into 2. to participate in
～机 **tóujī** **1.** спекули́ровать; спекуля́ция **2.** приспоса́бливаться	1. to speculate 2. to be opportunistic 3. to get along well
～资 **tóuzī** вкла́дывать капита́л; капиталовложе́ние	to invest
～票 **tóupiào** голосова́ть; голосова́ние	to vote, cast a vote
股 **gǔ** **1.** бедро́; бёдра **2.** а́кция; пай	1. thigh 2. section 3. strand, ply 4. share (of) 5. (M. for, e.g., thread, groups, etc.)
般 **bān** гру́ппа; класс; род; вид	(suf.) sort, kind, way
搬 **bān** передвига́ть(ся), пе-	1. to take away, remove 2. to apply in-

搬设变攻致

ремещáть; перемещáться; переезжáть	discriminately 3. to move (house) -
搬移 **bānyí** переезжáть, переселя́ться	to move, transport -
～家 **bānjiā** переселя́ться	to move from one home to another
～运 **bānyùn** перевози́ть, транспорти́ровать	to move, transport -
设 **shè** учреди́ть, основáть; установи́ть	1. to set up, found 2. to work out 3. if 4. (math.) given, suppose
～立(置) **shèlì(zhì)** *см.* 设	to establish, found
～备 **shèbèi** обору́дование, оснащéние	equipment, facilities -
～计 **shèjì** **1.** плани́ровать; проекти́ровать **2.** замышля́ть	design, plan - -
～施 **shèshī** **1.** устрóйство; сооружéние **2.** мероприя́тие	installation, facilities - -
～法 **shèfǎ** изы́скивать спóсобы	to try; to think up a method -
变 **biàn** изменя́ть(ся); превращáть(ся); изменéние	1. to change; change, adaptation 2. to become 3. to transform 4. to perform
～节分子 **biànjié fēnz** ренегáт, отсту́пник	to recant politically, be a turncoat -
～革 **biàngé** преобразовáние	transformation, change
～形 **biànxíng** измéнчивый, меня́ющийся; деформáция	to be out of shape, become deformed -
～换 **biànhuàn** перемени́ть	to vary, alternate
～成 **biànchéng** превращáть (-ся) в	to change into -
～化 **biànhuà** изменя́ться; перемéна	to change, vary; change, transformation
～质 **biànzhì** перерождáться; перерождéние	to go bad, deteriorate -
～态 **biàntài** видоизменéние, деформáция	1. abnormal, anomalous 2. (physiol.) metamorphosis
攻 **gōng** нападáть, атаковáть, штурмовáть	1. to attack, assault 2. to censure, accuse 3. to study, specialize in sth.
～击 **gōngjī** **1.** атаковáть; атáка; наступлéние **2.** нападáть; напáдки	1. to attack, assault 2. to accuse, vilify - -
致 **zhì** **1.** направля́ть, посылáть; адресовáть **2.** доводи́ть до; приводи́ть к	1. to send, extend, deliver 2. to incur, cause 3. to invite, collect (scholars, etc.) 4. charm 5. fascination, interest

致辞 **zhìcí** обращáться с рéчью; привéтствие	to make a speech -
～敬 **zhìjìng** с привéтом, с уважéнием *(в письме)*	to pay tribute/respects to -
政 **zhèng 1.** управля́ть, прáвить; прави́тельственный; администрати́вный **2.** поли́тика; полити́ческий	1. government 2. politics; political - - -
～治 **zhèngzhì** *см.* 政 2	politics, political affairs
～府 **zhèngfǔ** прави́тельство; прави́тельственный	government -
～协 **zhèngxié** Нарóдный полити́ческий консультати́вный совéт *(КНР)*	Chinese People's Political Consultative Conference (CPPCC) -
～策 **zhèngcè** поли́тика; полити́ческий курс	policy -
～权 **zhèngquán** власть *(политическая)*	political/state power, regime -
～变 **zhèngbiàn** государ́ственный переворóт	coup d'état -
～党 **zhèngdǎng** полити́ческая пáртия	political party -
故 **gù 1.** собы́тие, происшéствие **2.** причи́на **3.** намéренно, нарóчно **4.** стáрый, прéжний	1. reason 2. friend, acquaintance 3. incident, event 4. deliberately, on purpose 5. hence, so, therefore, as a result 6. to die, pass away 7. original, former, old
～事 **gùshi 1.** скáзка; расскáз **2.** происшéствие, инцидéнт	story, tale, plot -
～乡 **gùxiāng** рóдина, родны́е местá	- -
～意 **gùyì** намéренно, нарóчно	intentionally, willfully -
敌 **dí** враг, проти́вник; сопéрник; врáжеский; враждéбный	1. enemy, foe 2. match, equal - -
～对 **díduì** враждéбный	hostile, antagonistic
～人 **dírén** враг, проти́вник	enemy
～视 **díshì** ненави́деть	to regard with hostility
牧 **mù** пасти́(сь); пасту́х	to herd, tend, pasture
～业 **mùyè** скотовóдство	animal husbandry
～畜 **mùxù** занимáться скотовóдством	animal husbandry -
～场 **mùchǎng** пáстбище, вы́гон	grazing land, pasture -

收敢教散

收 **shōu** 1. получáть, принимáть 2. прибирáть, приводи́ть в порядок 3. убирáть урожáй; жáтва; урожáй	1. to receive, accept 2. to take in/back 3. to collect 4. to harvest, gather in 5. to conclude, stop - //to repair 4. to punish, settle with
~拾 **shōushi** *см.* 收 2	1. to put in order, tidy up 2. to pack 3.//
~据 **shōujù** распи́ска, квитáнция	receipt -
~音机 **shōuyīnjī** радиоприёмник	radio (set) -
~押 **shōuyā** взять под арéст, арестовáть	to take into custody, detain -
~割 **shōugē** убирáть урожáй; жáтва	to reap, gather in -
~获 **shōuhuò** 1. собрáть урожáй 2. достижéния, результáты	1. to bring in crop/harvest 2. gains, results -
~入 **shōurù** дохóд, поступлéния	1. income 2. to include -
~成 **shōucheng** урожáй	harvest, crop
敢 **gǎn** сметь, осмéливаться, решáться	1. to dare, have courage to 2. to have confidence to, be sure
教 **jiào** 1. учи́ть, обучáть; обучéние, учёба 2. заставля́ть; давáть возмóжность 3. рели́гия	1. to teach 2. to cause/ask to 3. religion - -
~ **jiāo** обучáть; преподавáть	to teach
~堂 **jiàotáng** цéрковь, храм	church, cathedral
~室 **jiàoshì** аудитóрия, класс	classroom, schoolroom
~科书 **jiàokēshū** учéбник	textbook
~导 **jiàodǎo** учи́ть; наставля́ть	to instruct, give guidance; teaching, guidance
~育 **jiàoyù** просвещéние, образовáние	to teach, educate, inculcate; education -
~条 **jiàotiáo** дóгма	dogma, doctrine, creed, tenet
~条主义 **jiàotiáozhǔyì** догмати́зм	dogmatism, doctrinairism -
~授 **jiàoshòu** 1. преподавáть; преподавáние 2. профéссор	1. to instruct, teach 2. professor - -
~员 **jiàoyuán** учи́тель, преподавáтель	teacher, instructor -
散 **sǎn** 1. распускáть(ся); рассыпáть(ся); рассы́панный 2. разрóзненный	1. to come loose 2. scattered 3. (Ch. med.) medicine in powder form -

散 **sàn 1.** разойти́сь, рассе́яться **2.** разбра́сывать; распространя́ть **3.** разве́ивать, разгоня́ть	1. to break up 2. to distribute 3. to let out 4. to fire, discharge
～开 **sànkai** рассе́ивать(ся), рассредото́чивать(ся)	to dispense, scatter
～布 **sànbù** распространя́ть (-ся)	1. to disseminate, scatter, diffuse
～步 **sànbù** гуля́ть, прогу́ливаться	to take a walk
～漫 **sǎnmàn** распу́щенный; расхля́банный	1. careless and sloppy 2. unorganized, scattered
～心 **sànxīn** развле́чься, разве́яться	to seek distraction
～会 **sànhuì** закрыва́ть собра́ние	to adjourn a meeting
撒 **sā 1.** ста́вить, расставля́ть *(сети)* **2.** разбра́сывать; распространя́ть	1. to let go, release 2. to let oneself go
～ **sǎ** разбра́сывать семена́, се́ять	1. to scatter, sprinkle, spread 2. to spill, drop
～种 **sǎzhǒng** разбра́сывать семена́, се́ять	to sow seeds
～娇 **sājiāo** капри́зничать	1. to act like a spoiled child 2. to act// //coquettishly
～谎 **sāhuǎng** лгать; врать	(coll.) to tell a lie
撤 **chè 1.** отменя́ть; ликвиди́ровать **2.** отводи́ть наза́д; выводи́ть **3.** снима́ть, отстраня́ть	1. to remove, take away 2. to withdraw, evacuate
～军 **chèjūn** отво́д (вы́вод) войск	to withdraw troops
～销 **chèxiāo** отменя́ть, аннули́ровать, упраздня́ть	to cancel, rescind, revoke
～退 **chètuì** отступа́ть; отводи́ть войска́	to withdraw, pull out
撇 **piē** отбра́сывать; выбра́сывать	to cast aside, abandon
放 **fàng 1.** освобожда́ть, отпуска́ть **2.** запуска́ть; стреля́ть **3.** положи́ть; поста́вить	1. to put, place 2. to set free, release 3. to let off, give out 4. to put out to pasture 5. to let oneself go, let sb. have his own way 6. to expand 7. to\\ \\bloom 8. to lend\\ \\9. to add 10. to lay aside
～肆 **fàngsì** распу́щенный, развя́зный	unbridled, wanton
～弃 **fàngqì 1.** броса́ть, ос-	to abandon, give up, renounce

тавля́ть **2.** возде́рживать-ся, отка́зываться	-
放射 **fàngshè** излуча́ть; радиоакти́вный; радиа́ция	to radiate, emit
~映 **fàngyìng** демонстри́ровать *(фильм)*	to show, project (a film)
~火 **fànghuǒ** поджига́ть	1. to set on fire, commit arson 2. to create a disturbance
~假 **fàngjià** отпусти́ть на кани́кулы; предоста́вить о́тпуск	to have/be on a holiday/vacation, have a day off
~心 **fàngxīn** успоко́иться	to set one's mind at rest, rest/feel assured
缴 **jiǎo 1.** вноси́ть, упла́чивать **2.** забира́ть, отбира́ть	1. to pay, hand over/in 2. to capture
~纳 **jiǎonà** вноси́ть, плати́ть *(взносы, налоги)*	to pay (to state/etc.); to hand in
~获 **jiǎohuò** захвати́ть, взять *(трофеи)*	to capture, seize
激 **jī 1.** би́ться, ударя́ться *(о волнах)* **2.** возбужда́ть; раздража́ть **3.** бу́рный; я́ростный, ожесточённый	1. to surge, dash 2. to arouse, stimulate, excite 3. to fall ill from getting wet 4. chill 5. sharp(ly), fierce(ly), violent(ly) 6. extreme(ly)
~动 **jīdòng** возбужда́ть; стимули́ровать	stirred, agitated
~化 **jīhuà** интенсифика́ция	to sharpen, intensify, become acute
~烈 **jīliè** ожесточённый, я́ростный	intense, sharp, fierce, acute
敬 **jìng** почита́ть, уважа́ть	1. to respect; respectfully 2. to offer politely
~爱 **jìng'ài** уважа́емый, дорого́й	1. to respect and love 2. esteemed and beloved
~礼 **jìnglǐ** приве́тствовать; приве́т	1. to salute, give a salute 2. to extend one's greetings 3. respectfully yours
敏 **mǐn** у́мный, сообрази́тельный	quick, nimble, agile
枚 **méi** *сч. сл. для тонких и круглых предметов*	1. stick used as a mouth gag 2. (M. for coins, etc.)
嫩 **nèn 1.** молодо́й, неокре́пший **2.** мя́гкий, не́жный	1. tender, delicate 2. inexperienced, unskilled
救 **jiù** спаса́ть; выруча́ть; помога́ть	1. to rescue, save, salvage 2. to help, relieve
~星 **jiùxīng** спаси́тель, избави́тель	liberator, emancipator
~命 **jiùmìng** спаса́ть *(от гибели)*; спаса́тельный; спаси́те!	1. to save sb.'s life 2. Help!, Save me!

救济 **jiùjì** оказывать по́мощь; по́мощь	to relieve, succor
～护 **jiùhù** спаса́ть; ока́зывать по́мощь *(медицинскую)*; спаса́тельный; санита́рный	to give first aid; to rescue, relieve
～急 **jiùjí** 1. помога́ть в беде́ 2. ока́зывать пе́рвую по́мощь	to help meet an urgent need
效 **xiào** 1. стара́ться; отдава́ть все си́лы 2. результа́т, эффе́кт 3. подража́ть, копи́ровать	1. effect, result 2. efficiency 3. to imitate 4. to devote oneself to, render service
～率 **xiàolǜ** эффекти́вность; коэффицие́нт поле́зного де́йствия, кпд	efficiency, productiveness
～力 **xiàolì** эффе́кт, де́йствие	1. to serve 2. effect
～劳 **xiàoláo** 1. прилага́ть уси́лия, стара́ться 2. заслу́га	to work for
～果 **xiàoguǒ** результа́т, эффе́кт	1. effect, result 2. sound effects
改 **gǎi** изменя́ть, переде́лывать; исправля́ть; пере=; ре=	1. to change, transform 2. to amend, revise 3. to correct, put right
～正 **gǎizhèng** исправля́ть; исправле́ние	to correct, amend
～善 **gǎishàn** улучша́ть(ся), соверше́нствовать(ся)	to improve, perfect
～革 **gǎigé** преобразо́вывать, реформи́ровать; рефо́рма	to reform; reform
～良 **gǎiliáng** улучша́ть; улучше́ние	to reform, ameliorate; reform
～良主义 **gǎiliángzhǔyì** реформи́зм	reformism
～变 **gǎibiàn** измени́ть(ся), перемени́ть(ся); измене́ния, переме́ны	to change, reform
～造 **gǎizào** реконструи́ровать, перестра́ивать; реконстру́кция, перестро́йка	to transform, reform, remold, remake
～进 **gǎijìn** улучша́ть, соверше́нствовать	to improve; improvement

微败赦数麦复

微 **wēi** **1.** ма́ленький, кро́шечный; микро= **2.** слегка́, немно́го	1. minute, tiny, slight 2. profound, abstruse, subtle
～生物 **wēishēngwù** микроорганизмы	microorganism, microbe
～妙 **wēimiào** многозначи́тельный, глубокомы́сленный	delicate, subtle
～笑 **wēixiào** улыба́ться; улы́бка	to smile
败 **bài** разби́ть; нанести́ (потерпе́ть) пораже́ние; прийти́ в упа́док	1. to lose, be defeated 2. to beat 3. to spoil 4. to counteract 5. to decay
赦 **shè** амнисти́ровать; амни́стия	to pardon, remit (punishment)
数 **shù** **1.** число́, коли́чество; ци́фра **2.** не́сколько	1. number, figure 2. fate 3. plan, project 4. several 5. talent, skill
～ **shǔ** счита́ть, пересчи́тывать	1. to count 2. to be reckoned as 3. to enumerate, list 4. to scold, rebuke
～量 **shùliàng** число́, коли́чество	quantity, amount
～目 **shùmù** число́; су́мма	number, amount //amount
～字 **shùzì** ци́фра	1. numeral, figure, digit 2. quantity, //
～学 **shùxué** матема́тика	mathematics
麦 **mài** пшени́ца; рожь; хле́бные зла́ки	wheat
复 **fù** **1.** возвраща́ться **2.** восстана́вливать; реставри́ровать **3.** отвеча́ть; отве́т **4.** сно́ва, опя́ть **5.** закрыва́ть; покрыва́ть; заслоня́ть **6.** переве́ртывать(ся), опроки́дывать(ся) **7.** сло́жный; составно́й **8.** повто́рный, втори́чный	1. to turn round/over 2. to answer 3. to recover, restore 4. to revenge 5. compound, complex 6. duplicate 7. again
～盖 **fùgài** закрыва́ть *(крышкой)*	to cover; cover
～活 **fùhuó** ожи́ть, воскре́снуть	to bring back to life, revive; Resurrection
～辟 **fùbì** реставри́ровать; восстана́вливать; реставра́ция	to restore a dethroned monarch or old order
～习 **fùxí** повторя́ть; повторе́ние	to review, revise

复仇 **fùchóu** отомсти́ть; месть; возме́здие	to revenge, avenge
～仇主义 **fùchóuzhǔyì** реванши́зм	revanchism
～兴 **fùxīng** восстановле́ние, возрожде́ние	to revive, resurge, rejuvenate
履 **lǚ** 1. ступа́ть; наступа́ть *(ногами)* 2. о́бувь 3. выполня́ть, осуществля́ть	1. to step/tread on, follow 2. shoes
～行 **lǚxíng** выполня́ть, осуществля́ть	to perform, fulfill, carry out
～历 **lǚlì** биогра́фия	curriculum vitae, antecedents
腹 **fù** живо́т; брюшна́я по́лость	belly, abdomen, stomach
夏 **xià** ле́то; ле́тний	1. summer 2. ancient name for China 3.//Xia dynasty
～季(天) **xiàjì(tiān)** ле́то	summer
厦 **shà** зда́ние; дворе́ц; небоскрёб	tall building, mansion
陵 **líng** 1. холм, курга́н 2. мавзоле́й	1. hill, mound 2. imperial tomb, mausoleum
～墓 **língmù** мавзоле́й	mausoleum, tomb
傻 **shǎ** глу́пый; дура́к; идио́т	1. stupid, muddle-headed 2. stunned
唆 **suō** подстрека́ть	to instigate, abet
～使 **suōshǐ** *см.* 唆	to instigate, abet
酸 **suān** 1. прокиса́ть; ки́слый; кислота́ 2. ныть, ломи́ть	1. sour, tart 2. sick at heart, grieved, distressed 3. pedantic, impractical 4. aching, tingling 5. acid
～痛 **suāntòng** *см.* 酸 2	aching
～味儿 **suānwèir** ки́слый	tart flavor, acidity
处 **chǔ** 1. помеща́ться, располага́ться 2. жить, существова́ть 3. реша́ть, определя́ть	1. to get along (with sb.) 2. to be situated in, be in a certain condition 3. to manage, handle, deal with 4. to punish, sentence 5. to dwell, live
～ **chù** 1. ме́сто 2. управле́ние; отде́л	1. place 2. point, part 3. department, office 4. (M. for homesteads)
～理 **chǔlǐ** 1. руководи́ть, управля́ть 2. принима́ть ме́ры; ула́живать; разреша́ть *(вопросы)*	1. to handle, deal with, dispose of 2. to process 3. to sell at a reduced price
～罚 **chǔfá** налага́ть взыска́ние; подверга́ть наказа́нию	to punish, penalize
～女 **chǔnǚ** де́вственница; де́вственный	virgin, maiden

夜液及级吸极八入丈

夜 **yè** ночь; ночно́й	night, evening
～校 **yèxiào** вече́рняя шко́ла	night/evening school
液 **yè** жи́дкость; сок	liquid, fluid, juice
及 **jí 1.** доходи́ть до, достига́ть **2.** а та́кже, и	1. and 2. in/on, to 3. to reach, come up to 4. to be in time for
～格 **jígé** подходи́ть, соотве́тствовать; отвеча́ть *(требованиям)*	to pass (a test) - -
～时 **jíshí** успе́ть; своевре́менно, во́время	1. timely, in time 2. promptly -
级 **jí 1.** ступе́нь; сте́пень; разря́д **2.** год обуче́ния; курс; класс	1. level, rank, grade 2. school grade/ class/form 3. (M. for stages/steps) 4. degree
吸 **xī 1.** вдыха́ть; впи́тывать; вса́сывать **2.** привлека́ть, вовлека́ть	1. to inhale, breathe in 2. to absorb, suck up 3. to attract, draw to oneself -
～烟 **xīyān** кури́ть	to smoke (a pipe/etc.)
～引 **xīyin** *см.* 吸 **2**	to attract, draw, fascinate
～收 **xīshōu** втя́гивать; поглоща́ть; вовлека́ть	1. to absorb, suck up, assimilate 2. to recruit, enroll, admit
极 **jí 1.** верши́на **2.** по́люс **3.** в вы́сшей сте́пени, кра́йне	1. to reach the end of 2. the utmost point, pole 3. ridge, beam 4. throne 5. extreme(ly)
～力地 **jílìde** изо все́х сил	doing one's utmost, sparing no effort

㇏

八 **bā** во́семь	eight
～月 **bāyuè** а́вгуст	August
入 **rù 1.** входи́ть, вступа́ть **2.** поступле́ния, дохо́ды	1. to enter 2. to receive, take in 3. to conform with 4. to descend, set 5. in-\\
～口 **rùkǒu 1.** вход **2.** импорти́ровать; и́мпорт	1. to enter the mouth 2. entrance \\come -
～学 **rùxué** поступа́ть учи́ться; приступа́ть к заня́тиям	1. to start school 2. to enter school/college - -
～场券 **rùchǎngquàn** входно́й биле́т	admission ticket -
～迷 **rùmí 1.** гре́зить; забы́ться **2.** пристрасти́ться; быть одержи́мым	to be fascinated - -
～党 **rùdǎng** вступа́ть в па́ртию	to join a political party - //length, = 3.33 meters)
丈 **zhàng 1.** чжан *(мера дли-*	1. to measure land 2. (measure of//

ны, равная 3,3 м) **2.** поч-	-
тéнный человéк	-
丈夫 **zhàngfu** муж	husband
史 **shǐ** истóрия; лéтопись	history
使 **shǐ** **1.** испóльзовать, при-	1. to send (as envoy); envoy 2. to have
менять **2.** посылáть **3.** по-	sb. do sth. 3. to use, employ, apply 4.
сóл; послáнник; послáнец	to make, cause, enable 5. if
4. *служ. гл.* побуждáть,	-
заставля́ть	-
～馆 **shǐguǎn** посóльство;	legation, embassy
представи́тельство	-
～命 **shǐmìng** ми́ссия, назна-	mission
чéние	-
～用 **shǐyòng** испóльзовать,	to use, employ, apply
употребля́ть, применя́ть	-
～劲 **shǐjìn** изо всéх сил; под-	to exert all one's strength
натýжиться	- //experience, undergo
更 **gēng** меня́ть, сменя́ть	1. to change, replace, transform 2. to//
～ **gèng** **1.** ещё бóлее, тем бó-	1. more, still/even more 2. further,
лее **2.** снóва, повтóрно	furthermore
～生 **gēngshēng** возрож-	to regenerate, revive
дáться, обновля́ться	-
～加 **gèngjiā** ещё бóлее, тем	(even) more
бóлее	-
硬 **yìng** **1.** жёсткий, твёрдый	1. hard, stiff 2. firm, tough, obstinate
2. упóрный, настóйчивый	3. doggedly
～席 **yìngxí** жёсткое мéсто *(в*	-
вагоне)	-
～说 **yìngshuō** утверждáть	-
便 **biàn** **1.** удóбный; удóбст-	1. then, in that case 2. as early/little as
во **2.** обы́чный, простóй;	3. even if 4. then 5. convenient 6. infor-
неофициáльный	mal, plain 7. convenience 8. to relieve\\
～ **pián** дешёвый	cheap \\oneself 9. urine, excrement
～宜 **piányi** дешёвый	1. cheap 2. small advantages 3. to let\\
～所 **biànsuǒ** убóрная, туа-	toilet, lavatory, privy \\sb. off lightly
лéт	-
～利 **biànlì** удóбный; вы́год-	1. convenient, easy 2. to facilitate
ный	-
～衣 **biànyī** штáтская одéж-	1. civilian/plain clothes 2. plainclothes-
да	man
～是 **biànshì** **1.** и́менно **2.**	1. is (exactly) 2. even if
дáже éсли	-
之 **zhī** *служ. сл.; заменяет*	1. (modifier-modified part.) 2. (as
的 *или* 以	obj.) it, him, her, this 3. this 4. to go

之一 **zhī yī** оди́н из	one of
～间 **zhījiān** ме́жду, среди́	(suf.) among, between
乏 **fá** 1. утомля́ться, устава́ть 2. не хвата́ть, недостава́ть	1. to lack 2. tired, weary 3. exhausted, worn out
贬 **biǎn** 1. унижа́ть 2. снижа́ть, понижа́ть	1. to demote, relegate 2. to reduce, devalue 3. to censure, depreciate
～值 **biǎnzhí** *эк.* девальва́ция	1. to devalue, devaluate 2. to depreciate
逞 **chěng** 1. пока́зывать, проявля́ть 2. своево́льничать	1. to show off, flaunt 2. to carry out (a plot), succeed (in) 3. indulge
逗 **dòu** 1. остана́вливаться, заде́рживаться 2. вызыва́ть *(смех, интерес)* 3. дразни́ть	1. to tease, play with 2. to amuse 3. amusing 4. (slight pause in reading)
遥 **yáo** отдалённый, далёкий	distant, remote, far
造 **zào** 1. создава́ть, твори́ть; стро́ить 2. подде́лывать, фальсифици́ровать	1. to make, build, create, establish 2. to concoct, fabricate 3. to go to, arrive at 4. epoch, period 5. parties in a lawsuit 6. crop
～谣 **zàoyáo** измышля́ть, клевета́ть	to start a rumor
～反 **zàofǎn** бунтова́ть; бунта́рь; цзаофа́нь	to rebel, revolt
适 **shì** 1. быть подходя́щим, соотве́тствовать; подходя́щий 2. как раз, кста́ти	1. fit, suitable, proper 2. just, right 3. to go, follow, pursue 4. to marry
～应 **shìyìng** 1. годи́ться, соотве́тствовать 2. приспоса́бливаться	1. to suit, adapt, fit 2. to get used to
～当 **shìdàng** надлежа́щий, соотве́тствующий; подходя́щий	suitable, proper
～合 **shìhé** соотве́тствовать, подходи́ть	to suit, fit; suitable
遣 **qiǎn** посыла́ть, командирова́ть	1. to send, dispatch 2. to dispel, dissipate, divert 3. to banish, exile
谴:谴责 **qiǎnzé** осужда́ть; укоря́ть	to condemn, denounce, censure
追 **zhuī** 1. гна́ться, пресле́довать 2. торопи́ть, подгоня́ть	1. to chase, pursue 2. to trace, look into, find out 3. to seek, go after 4. to recall, reminisce 5. retroactively 6. posthumously
～击 **zhuījī** пресле́довать; пресле́дование	to pursue and attack

追悼 **zhuīdào** отдавáть последний долг, прощáться *(с покóйным)*	to mourn a death
～求 **zhuīqiú** стреми́ться к, добивáться	1. to seek, pursue 2. to woo, court
遭 **zāo** **1.** встрéтиться, столкнýться **2.** подвергáться; испы́тывать	1. to encounter 2. round 3. (M. for times/turns)
迫 **pò** **1.** вынуждáть, заставля́ть; настáивать **2.** угнетáть	1. to compel, force, coerce 2. to approach, come near 3. urgent, pressing
～害 **pòhài** приводи́ть к ги́бели, губи́ть	to persecute; persecution
～切 **pòqiè** настоя́тельный; актуáльный	urgent, pressing, imperative
～使 **pòshǐ** вынуждáть, заставля́ть	to force, compel
道 **dào** **1.** путь, дорóга **2.** э́тика, морáль **3.** и́стина; справедли́вость **4.** при́нципы; учéние **5.** даоси́зм; даóсский	1. road 2. channel 3. way 4. doctrine 5. Daoism 6. line 7. to say, speak 8. to think, suppose 9. (M. for rivers/topics, etc.)
～理 **dàoli** **1.** при́нцип; доктри́на **2.** и́стина; справедли́вость **3.** резóн, смысл	1. reason, rationality 2. the right way
～路 **dàolù** путь, дорóга	road, way, path
～义 **dàoyì** э́тика, морáль	morality and justice
～教 **dàojiào** даоси́зм	Daoism
～德 **dàodé** нрáвственность, морáль; добродéтель	morality, ethics, morals
逼 **bī** вынуждáть, заставля́ть; доводи́ть до	1. to force, compel, press 2. to press for, extort 3. to press on 4. to close in on
近 **jìn** **1.** бли́зкий; вблизи́ **2.** недáвний; за послéднее врéмя **3.** бли́зкий, роднóй	1. near, close 2. similar/close to 3. intimate, closely related 4. easy to understand 5. recent 6. to approach
～卫 **jìnwèi** ли́чная охрáна; гвáрдия	guards
～视 **jìnshi** близорýкий	myopia, nearsightedness
逝 **shì** скончáться; кончи́на	1. to pass 2. to die, pass away
～世 **shìshì** скончáться, умерéть	to pass away, die
迎 **yíng** **1.** встречáть, выходи́ть навстрéчу **2.** быть обращённым к	1. to welcome, receive, meet 2. to face

迎迁避连逢缝进

迎接 **yíngjiē** встречáть; встрéча	to meet, welcome
迁 **qiān 1.** переселя́ть(ся); переезжáть **2.** переводи́ть на другóе мéсто рабóты	to move, change
～居 **qiānjū** меня́ть мéсто жи́тельства	to change dwelling/address
～移 **qiānyí** перемещáться; переселя́ться	to move, remove, migrate
～就 **qiānjiù** приспосáбливаться	to accommodate, compromise
避 **bì** пря́таться, скрывáться; избегáть, уклоня́ться	1. to avoid, evade, shun 2. to prevent, keep away, repel
～难 **bìnán** спасáться от бéдствия	to take refuge, seek asylum
～暑 **bìshǔ** жить на дáче	1. to be away for summer holidays 2.//to prevent sunstroke//
～孕 **bìyùn** противозачáточный	contraception
～免 **bìmiǎn** избежáть, избáвиться от	to avoid, refrain from, avert
连 **lián 1.** соединя́ть(ся); соприкасáться; свя́зывать (-ся); связь, отношéние **2.** непреры́вный; подря́д **3.** дáже	1. to join, link, connect 2. (mil.) company 3. endless succession 4. in succession, one after another 5. even
～忙 **liánmáng** поспéшно, торопли́во	promptly, at once
～络 **liánluò** свя́зываться с; связь	to connect, tie, link
～带 **liándài** соединённый, совмещённый; совмéстный	to be related, to involve
～续 **liánxù** непреры́вный	continuous, successive, running
～系 **liánxì** связь, отношéния	connection, link, tie; relation(ship)
～接 **liánjiē** свя́зывать, соединя́ть; примыкáть	to join, connect, untie, link
逢 **féng** встрéтиться, натолкнýться; случи́ться	to meet, come upon
缝 **féng** шить; чини́ть; штóпать	to stitch, sew
～ **fèng 1.** щель; трéщина **2.** шов; рубéц	1. seam 2. crack, crevice, fissure
～纫 **féngrén** шить	to sew, tailor
进 **jìn 1.** идти́ вперёд, про-	1. to advance 2. to enter, come/go in-

двигáться **2.** входи́ть; вступáть	to 3. to receive 4. to eat, drink, take 5. to submit, introduce 6. courtyard\\
进一步 **jìnyībù** дальнéйший; ещё дáльше	to go a step further \\7. into, in
～口 **jìnkǒu 1.** вход **2.** импортúровать; и́мпорт	1. to enter port 2. to import 3. entrance
～行 **jìnxíng** осуществля́ть, выполня́ть	1. to be in progress, go on 2. to carry on/out 3. to be on the march; advance
～步 **jìnbù** прогресси́вный; прогрéсс	1. to progress, advance, improve; progress, improvement 2. progressive
～攻 **jìngōng** наступáть; наступлéние	to attack, assault
过 **guò 1.** проходи́ть (*через*) **2.** проходи́ть (*о времени*); проводи́ть (*время*) **3.** встречáть (*праздник*) **4.** чересчу́р, сли́шком **5.** *гл. суф. завершённо-многократного вида*	1. to pass, cross 2. to transfer (e.g., ownership) 3. to undergo a process, go through 4. to surpass, exceed 5. to celebrate, observe 6. fault, mistake 7. too, excessively 8. after
～程 **guòchéng** процéсс, ход	course, process
～节 **guòjié** отмечáть, встречáть (*праздник*)	to celebrate a festival
～年 **guònián 1.** встречáть Нóвый год **2.** на бу́дущий год	to celebrate/spend New Year's
～期 **guòqī** просрóчить; просрóчка	1. to exceed a time limit, be overdue 2. too old
～分 **guòfèn** чересчу́р, сли́шком	excessive, undue; over-, excessively
～渡 **guòdù** перехóдный; перехóд (*процесс*)	to go beyond the normal limit, overdo; excessive, undue
遵 **zūn** в соотвéтствии с; подчиня́ться; руковóдствоваться	to abide by, obey, observe
～循 **zūnxún** руковóдствоваться; слéдовать *чему*; в соотвéтствии с	to follow, abide by, adhere to
～守 **zūnshǒu** соблюдáть, придéрживаться	to observe, abide by
随 **suí 1.** слéдовать, сопровождáть **2.** имéть при себé **3.** по желáнию; произвóльно	1. to follow 2. to comply with, adapt to 3. to let (sb. do as he likes) 4. to go along with (some action) 5. to look like, resemble 6. as soon as
～后 **suíhòu** затéм	soon afterwards

随 通

随行 **suíxíng** сопровожда́ть, сле́довать за	1. to accompany/follow sb. on a trip 2. retinue, suite, entourage //necessary
～时 **suíshí** в любо́е вре́мя	1. at any time, at all times 2. whenever//
～身 **suíshēn** име́ть при себе́	(to take/have) with oneself
～便 **suíbiàn** **1.** свобо́дно, поудо́бнее **2.** небре́жно, ко́е-ка́к	1. casually, randomly 2. carelessly 3. wantonly, willfully 4. to do as one pleases
～地 **suídì** где попа́ло	anywhere, everywhere
～意 **suíyì** по жела́нию; произво́льно	as one pleases
通 **tōng** **1.** проходи́ть сквозь, проника́ть; пропуска́ть **2.** доводи́ть до, сообща́ть **3.** обща́ться **4.** находи́ться в обраще́нии **5.** весь, це́лый	1. to communicate/connect (with) 2. to join, share 3. to master, understand thoroughly 4. to be interchangeable with 5. open, through 6. general, all, entire 7. (suf.) authority, expert
～知 **tōngzhī** сообща́ть, информи́ровать, уведомля́ть; сообще́ние, извеще́ние	to notify, inform; notice, circular
～信 **tōngxìn** перепи́сываться; перепи́ска	to communicate by letter, correspond
～告 **tōnggào** сообще́ние, изве́стие; объявле́ние	to give public notice, announce; public notice, circular
～俗 **tōngsú** популя́рный; общедосту́пный	popular, common
～行 **tōngxíng** **1.** ходи́ть, курси́ровать **2.** пропуска́ть; проходи́ть	1. to pass/go through 2. to be current, be of general use
～行证 **tōngxíngzhèng** про́пуск	travel pass/permit
～常 **tōngcháng** **1.** обы́чный, норма́льный **2.** всегда́	general, usual, normal
～报 **tōngbào** **1.** уведомля́ть, информи́ровать **2.** бюллете́нь, ве́стник	1. to circulate a notice 2. circular 3. bulletin, journal
～过 **tōngguò** **1.** проходи́ть; пропуска́ть; прохо́д **2.** принима́ть *(резолюцию)* **3.** в хо́де *чего* **4.** посре́дством	1. to traverse, get past 2. to adopt, pass, carry (motion/legislation)
～讯 **tōngxùn** сообще́ние, информа́ция	1. communication 2. news report, newsletter
～风 **tōngfēng** прове́тривать, вентили́ровать	1. to ventilate, be well ventilated 2. to divulge information
～货膨胀 **tōnghuò péngzhàng** инфля́ция	inflation

遍 **biàn** **1.** повсю́ду, повсеме́стно **2.** раз, разо́к	1. all over, everywhere 2. (M. for times/occurrences)
遇 **yù** встре́титься, столкну́ться	1. to meet, encounter 2. to treat, receive 3. treatment
逆 **nì** идти́ наперекóр; вопреки́	1. to go against, disobey 2. (pref.) contrary, counter 3. traitor 4. inverse,\\ \\converse
逻:逻辑 **luóji** ло́гика	(loan w.) logic
迈 **mài** идти́ уве́ренным ша́гом; шагну́ть	1. to step, stride 2. old
违 **wéi** преступа́ть, наруша́ть; идти́ вразре́з	1. to disobey, violate 2. to be separated 3. to avoid 4. to miss, lose
～背 **wéibèi** отступа́ть от; изменя́ть; наруша́ть	to violate, go against
～反 **wéifǎn** наруша́ть; вопреки́	to violate, transgress, infringe
～犯 **wéifàn** наруша́ть, преступа́ть	to violate, infringe
透 **tòu** проходи́ть наскво́зь, проника́ть	1. to penetrate, seep through 2. to disclose secretly 3. thorough(ly)
～露 **tòulù** очеви́дный, я́вный	to divulge, leak, reveal
～明 **tòumíng** просве́чивать (-ся); прозра́чный	transparent
～漏 **tòulòu** **1.** протека́ть, проса́чиваться **2.** разглаша́ть	to divulge, leak
递 **dì** передава́ть, вруча́ть; адресова́ть	1. to forward, transmit 2. to alternate 3. successively
边 **biān** **1.**край; кайма́; опу́шка **2.** окра́ина; грани́ца; погранѝчный	1. side 2. margin, edge, rim 3. border, boundary 4. limit 5. by the side of
～疆 **biānjiāng** грани́ца; пограни́чный райо́н	border area
～区 **biānqū** пограни́чный райо́н	border area/region
～界 **biānjiè** грани́ца	border, boundary
～防军 **biānfángjūn** пограни́чные войска́	frontier force
～境 **biānjìng** *см.* 边界	border, frontier
迟 **chí** ме́длить; опа́здывать; промедле́ние, заде́ржка	1. slow, tardy 2. late
～到 **chídào** опозда́ть, задержа́ться	to be/come/arrive late
～疑 **chíyí** быть в нереши-	to hesitate

тельности, колебáться; нерешúтельный	-
达 **dá 1.** достúчь, дойтú до **2.** постúчь, познáть **3.** сообщúть, довестú до свéдения	1. intelligible 2. prominent 3. to reach 4. to inform 5. until
送 **sòng 1.** посылáть, пересылáть; перевозúть, доставлять **2.** провожáть **3.** дарúть, преподносúть	1. to deliver, carry 2. to give as a present 3. to see sb. off/out, accompany, escort
～给 **sòng gěi 1.** послáть **2.** подарúть	to send/present to
～行 **sòngxíng** провожáть *(в дорогу)*	to see sb. off, wish sb. bon voyage
述 **shù** расскáзывать, излагáть	to state, relate, narrate
迷 **mí 1.** прийтú в смятéние **2.** обворожúть, очаровáть **3.** стать одержúмым; мáния	1. confused, lost 2. enchanted/enamored with 3. to enchant 4. enthusiast, fan 5. to lose one's bearings
～信 **míxìn 1.** суевéрие, предрассýдки; культ **2.** слéпо вéрить; заблуждáться	1. superstition, blind faith/worship 2. to have blind faith in, make a fetish of
～路 **mílù** заблудúться	1. to lose one's way, get lost 2. inner ear
～糊 **míhu** смýтный, тумáнный	labyrinth, maze
～惑 **míhuò 1.** ввестú в заблуждéние **2.** прийтú в замешáтельство	to puzzle, confuse, baffle
谜 **mí** загáдка	riddle, conundrum; enigma, mystery
～语 **míyǔ** загáдка	riddle, conundrum
～底 **mídǐ** разгáдка	1. answer/solution to a riddle 2. truth
速 **sù** бы́стрый, скóрый; скóрость	1. fast, rapid, quick, speedy 2. speed, velocity 3. to invite
～度 **sùdù** скóрость; тéмпы	speed, rate, pace, velocity, tempo
～记 **sùjì** стенográфия; стенограмма	to take shorthand; shorthand, stenography
逮:逮捕 **dàibǔ** арестовáть; арéст	to make an arrest
逐 **zhú 1.** изгонять, выгонять **2.** постепéнно, послéдовательно	1. to pursue 2. to expel, banish 3. one by one, one after another
～渐 **zhújiàn** *см.* 逐 2.	gradually, by degrees
～字 **zhúzì** буквáльный	word for word, verbatum

隧:隧道 **suìdào** тоннéль	tunnel
退 **tuì** 1. отступáть; отхóд 2. уйти́ из; остáвить *(службу)* 3. возвращáть, сдавáть обрáтно	1. to retreat, retire 2. to decline, ebb 3. to return, give back, refund 4. to cede
～伍 **tuìwǔ** демобилизовáться; демобилизóванный	to be demobilized
～却 **tuìquè** отступáть, отходи́ть; отхóд	1. to retreat, withdraw 2. to shrink back, flinch
～换 **tuìhuàn** обменя́ть	to exchange/replace a purchase
～休 **tuìxiū** уйти́ на пéнсию; вы́йти в отстáвку	to retire, become pensioned
～还 **tuìhuán** возвращáть	to return
～化 **tuìhuà** 1. деградúровать; регрéсс, деградáция, упáдок 2. атрофúроваться	to degenerate, deteriorate; degeneration, deterioration
～色 **tuìsè** линя́ть, теря́ть цвет	to fade (of colors)
～职 **tuìzhí** уйти́ в отстáвку	to withdraw from office, quit a job
腿 **tuǐ** 1. ногá; бедрó 2. нóжка *(мебели)* 3. óкорок	1. leg 2. ham
这 **zhè** э́то; э́тот; такóй; так	1. this 2. now
～些 **zhèxiē** э́ти	these
～里 **zhèli** здесь, тут	here //(part. for hesitation)
～个 **zhège** э́то; э́тот	1. this one, this 2. (coll.) so, such 3.//
～样 **zhèyàng** такóй; так, таки́м óбразом	so, such, like this, this way
～么 **zhème** так, таки́м óбразом	so, such, this way, like this
返 **fǎn** возвращáть(ся); обрáтный; отвéтный	to return
邀 **yāo** приглашáть; приглашéние	1. to invite, request 2. to solicit, seek 3. to intercept
～请 **yāoqǐng** *см.* 邀	to invite; invitation
远 **yuǎn** 1. далёкий, отдалённый; далекó 2. дли́тельный, продолжи́тельный	far, distant (lit./fig.)
～视 **yuǎnshì** дальнозóркий	(med.) farsightedness
～景化 **yuǎnjǐnghuà** прогнози́рование	long-term/-range plan
选 **xuǎn** избирáть, выбирáть; отбирáть, подбирáть	to select, choose, elect; selection, anthology
～择 **xuǎnzé** отбирáть; отбóр; селéкция	to select, opt; selection, option

选逃迅还遗途遮运

选举 **xuǎnjǔ** выбира́ть; вы́боры	to elect (by vote)
～举权 **xuǎnjǔquán** избира́тельное пра́во	franchise, right to vote
～手 **xuǎnshǒu** чемпио́н	player selected as contestant; athlete
～集 **xuǎnjí** и́збранные произведе́ния	selected works, anthology
逃 **táo** скрыва́ться; пря́таться; бежа́ть; побе́г	1. to escape, flee 2. to evade, shirk, escape
～走(跑) **táozǒu(pǎo)** бежа́ть, спаса́ться бе́гством	to run away, flee
迅:迅速 **xùnsù** ско́рый, бы́стрый	rapid, speedy, prompt
还 **huán** возврати́ть(ся), верну́ть(ся)	1. to go/come back 2. to give back, return, repay 3. to give/do sth. in return
～ **hái 1.** ещё, всё ещё **2.** всё-таки, всё же	1. still, yet 2. even more 3. also, as well, besides, too 4. passably, fairly 5. even
～是 **háishi 1.** и́ли **2.** всё-таки, всё же	1. still, nevertheless 2. had better 3. or
遗 **yí 1.** оста́вить *(в наследство)*, завеща́ть; посме́ртный **2.** потеря́ть, утра́тить	1. to lose 2. to leave behind, keep back 3. to omit, leave out 4. to bequeath 5. sth. lost 6. incontinence
～留 **yíliú** оставля́ть в насле́дство	to leave behind, hand down
～产 **yíchǎn** насле́дство; насле́дие	legacy, inheritance
～书 **yíshū** завеща́ние	1. posthumous papers 2. deathbed note
～失 **yíshī** потеря́ть, утра́тить	to lose
～体 **yítǐ** оста́нки, труп	remains (of dead)
～憾 **yíhàn** сожале́ть; к сожале́нию	regret, pity
途 **tú** путь, доро́га	road, route, journey, way
遮 **zhē 1.** заслоня́ть, загора́живать **2.** препя́тствовать	1. to conceal, cover 2. to block, impede
运 **yùn 1.** дви́гаться; передвига́ть **2.** перевози́ть **3.** судьба́	1. to carry, transport 2. to use, wield, utilize 3. to revolve 4. fortune, luck, fate
～输 **yùnshū** перевози́ть; тра́нспортный; тра́нспорт	to transport; transport
～河 **yùnhé** кана́л	canal
～用 **yùnyòng** испо́льзовать, применя́ть; примене́ние	to utilize, wield, apply
～动 **yùndòng 1.** дви́гаться;	1. to move, turn around 2. movement, campaign, drive 3. sports, exercise

движéние **2.** движéние за; кампáния **3.** спорт; занимáться спóртом	- - -
运动场 **yùndòngchǎng** стадиóн	sports/athletic ground, playground -
~动会 **yùndònghuì** спартакиáда	sports meet, games -
~送 **yùnsòng** перевози́ть; перевóзка	to transport, convey -
~载火箭 **yùnzài huǒjiàn** ракéта-носи́тель	(mil.) carrier rocket -
~气 **yùnqi** **1.** судьбá **2.** удáча, счáстье	fortune, luck -
巡 **xún** **1.** патрули́ровать **2.** инспекти́ровать	1. to patrol, make one's rounds 2. round of drinks //one's rounds
~查 **xúnchá** патрули́ровать	to make a tour of inspection, make//
~回 **xúnhuí** **1.** выезднóй; передвижнóй **2.** турнé	to tour, make a circuit of -
挺 **tǐng** **1.** вы́тащить; вы́двинуть **2.** вы́прямиться	1. to stick/bulge out 2. to endure 3. erect, firm 4. very, rather, quite
庭 **tíng** **1.** двор; дом, семья́ **2.** суд	1. hall 2. front (court)yard 3. law court -
~长 **tíngzhǎng** председáтель судá	presiding judge, president of a law court
延 **yán** отклáдывать, отсрóчивать	1. to prolong, extend, protract 2. to postpone, delay 3. to engage, send\\
~期 **yánqī** продлевáть срок; отсрóчка	to postpone, defer \\for, invite -
诞:诞生(辰) **dànshēng(chén)** роди́ться; рождéние	to be born, come into being, emerge -
建 **jiàn** **1.** основáть, учреди́ть **2.** стрóить, сооружáть	1. to build, construct, erect 2. to establish, set up, found 3. to propose,\\
~立 **jiànlì** учреждáть, оснóвывать	to establish, set up, found \\advocate -
~议 **jiànyì** вноси́ть предложéние; предложéние	to propose, suggest, recommend -
~设 **jiànshè** стрóить, сооружáть; строи́тельство	to build, construct; construction -
~筑 **jiànzhù** стрóить; строи́тельный	1. to build, construct, erect 2. building, structure, edifice 3. architecture
健:健康 **jiànkāng** здорóвый, крéпкий; здорóвье	healthy, sound; health, physique -
鼠 **shǔ** кры́са; мышь	mouse; rat
纸 **zhǐ** бумáга; бумáжный	1. paper 2. (M. for piece/sheet)

纸低抵底民眠代

纸烟 **zhǐyān** сигаре́та; папиро́са	cigarette
低 **dī 1.** опуска́ть(ся); низ; ни́зкий; внизу́ **2.** наклоня́ть(ся)	1. low 2. to let droop, hang down, lower
抵 **dǐ 1.** сопротивля́ться; отража́ть нападе́ние **2.** закла́дывать	1. to support, prop 2. to resist, withstand 3. to compensate for 4. to mortgage 5. to balance 6. to be equal to 7. to arrive at
～押 **dǐyā** закла́дывать, отдава́ть в зало́г	mortgage
～抗 **dǐkàng** сопротивля́ться; дава́ть отпо́р; противостоя́ть	to resist, stand up to
底 **dǐ 1.** осно́ва; дно; низ **2.** набро́сок, черновик	1. bottom, base 2. ins & outs 3. rough draft 4. file copy 5. end 6. ground
民 **mín** наро́д; наро́дный	1. people, humanity, masses 2. civilian
～望 **mínwàng** ча́яния наро́да	1. the people's hope 2. the people's role model
～主主义 **mínzhǔzhǔyì** демокра́тия; демократи́ческий	democracy
～间 **mínjiān** наро́дный	1. among the people, popular, folk 2. nongovernmental, people-to-people
～用 **mínyòng** гражда́нский	civil
～众 **mínzhòng** наро́дные ма́ссы	the masses
～族 **mínzú** на́ция; национа́льность; национа́льный	1. ethnic minority/group 2. nation, nationality
～族主义 **mínzúzhǔyì** национали́зм; националисти́ческий	nationalism
～兵 **mínbīng** наро́дное ополче́ние; ополче́нец	1. people's militia 2. militiaman
眠 **mián** спать; спя́чка	1. sleep 2. dormancy
代 **dài 1.** заменя́ть, замеща́ть; заме́на **2.** представля́ть; от и́мени; представи́тель **3.** эпо́ха **4.** поколе́ние, сме́на	1. to take the place of 2. acting 3. period 4. generation
～理 **dàilǐ** замеща́ть; исполня́ть обя́занности; представля́ть *(чьи-л. интересы)*	1. to act as an agent/proxy 2. acting, (pref.) sub-
～替 **dàitì** заменя́ть; вме́сто	to take the place of, substitute for
～表 **dàibiǎo** представля́ть; от и́мени; представи́тель; депута́т; делега́т	to represent; representative, delegate

代表团 **dàibiǎotuán** делегáция; мúссия	delegation, mission, deputation
～表大会 **dàibiǎodàhuì** съезд; конгрéсс	congress, conference, convention
式 **shì 1.** прáвило; образéц; тип **2.** обря́д, церемóния	1. model, standard 2. form, pattern, formula, style 3. ceremony, ritual 4. (ling.) mode, mood
试 **shì 1.** прóбовать; испы́тывать; эксперименти́ровать; óпыт, экспери́мент **2.** экзаменовáть; экзáмен	to try, test; test
～验 **shìyàn** проводи́ть óпыт (испытáние); óпыт; эксперментáльный, прóбный	to attempt, experiment, test; attempt, experiment, test
～验室 **shìyànshì** лабораторúя	laboratory
～用 **shìyòng** проверя́ть на прáктике; прóбный	to try out
武 **wǔ 1.** воéнный; вооружённый **2.** вои́нственный	1. military, martial, valiant 2. footstep
～器 **wǔqì** орýжие	weapons, arms
～官 **wǔguān** воéнный атташé	military officer/attaché
～装 **wǔzhuāng** вооружáть(-ся); вооружéние; вооружённый	1. to arm 2. arms, military equipment/uniform 3. armed forces 4. armed
战 **zhàn 1.** сражáться; войнá; бой **2.** дрожáть от стрáха	1. to fight; war, warfare, battle 2. to shiver, tremble
～士 **zhànshì** боéц, вóин	soldier, combatant, warrior
～胜 **zhànshèng** победи́ть, одержáть побéду	to defeat, vanquish
～斗 **zhàndòu** сражáться; бой; боевóй	to fight; fight
～利品 **zhànlìpǐn** трофéи	spoils of war
～争 **zhànzhēng** войнá; воéнный	war, warfare
～友 **zhànyǒu** сорáтник	comrade-in-arms
～犯 **zhànfàn** воéнный престýпник	war criminal
找 **zhǎo 1.** искáть **2.** обращáться к *комý* **3.** давáть сдáчу; сдáча	1. to look for, seek 2. to call on, approach, ask for 3. to give change
我 **wǒ** я; мой; мы; наш	1. I 2. we, our 3. self
俄 **é 1.** вдруг, внезáпно **2.** *сокр.* Росси́я; рýсский	1. presently 2. short name for Russia

俄语(文) **éyǔ(wén)** ру́сский	Russian language
язы́к	-
饿 **é** голода́ть; го́лод	1. to starve 2. hungry
戏 **xì** **1.** игра́; шу́тка; развле-	1. to play, sport 2. to make fun of, joke 3.
че́ние **2.** теа́тр; спекта́кль	drama, play, show
～剧 **xìjù** пье́са; дра́ма	drama, play, theater
～院 **xìyuàn** теа́тр	theater //ther...or... 3. someone
或 **huò** и́ли, ли́бо	1. perhaps, maybe, probably 2. or, ei-//
～者 **huòzhě** **1.** и́ли, ли́бо **2.**	1. perhaps, maybe 2. or, either...or...
возмо́жно, вероя́тно	-
域 **yù** **1**. грани́ца, преде́л **2.**	domain, region, area
райо́н; террито́рия	-
贼 **zéi** **1.** разбо́йник; банди́т	1. thief 2. traitor, enemy 3. harm, mur-
2. преда́тель; мятéжник	der 4. wily, deceitful 5. extremely
戒 **jiè** **1.** предостерега́ть **2.**	1. to guard against 2. to exhort, warn,
возде́рживаться от; обе́т,	admonish 3. to give up, drop, stop
заро́к	4. (finger) ring 5. prohibition
～指 **jièzhi** кольцо́, пе́рстень	ring (for the finger)
～备 **jièbèi** принима́ть ме́ры	to guard, take precautions
предосторо́жности	-
截 **jié** отре́зать; пресе́чь; пе-	1. to cut, sever; length, section, chunk
рехвати́ть	2. to stop, check 3. by (a set time)
载 **zài** **1.** нагружа́ть **2.** пере-	1. to transport 2. to record, publish 3.
вози́ть; груз **3.** помеща́ть	to fill
(в газете) **4.** запи́сывать;	-
вноси́ть в	-
栽 **zāi** сажа́ть дере́вья; вы-	1. to plant, grow, raise 2. to tumble,
са́живать расса́ду	fall 3. to frame (sb.) 4. to lose face
～培 **zāipéi** выра́щивать,	1. to cultivate, grow 2. to foster, train,
культиви́ровать	educate 3. to give/receive patronage
裁 **cái** **1.** крои́ть, ре́зать **2.**	1. to cut 2. to reduce, dismiss 3. to
сокраща́ть, уреза́ть **3.** ре-	judge, decide
ша́ть, определя́ть	-
～军 **cáijūn** *сокр.* сокраще́-	to disarm; disarmament
ние вооруже́ний	-
～判 **cáipàn** суди́ть; пригo-	1. judgment 2. judge, referee, umpire
во́р	3. to act as referee
～制 **cáizhì** ограни́чивать;	to curtail, restrict
применя́ть са́нкции	-
～决 **cáijué** реша́ть; реше́ние	to adjudicate; ruling
～缝 **cáifeng** портно́й	tailor, dressmaker
戴 **dài** носи́ть *(головной*	1. to wear, put on (of accessories) 2.
убор, очки и др.)	respect, honor, support
咸 **xián** солёный	1. salty 2. all

咸菜 **xiáncài** солёные óвощи, солéнья	salted vegetable
喊 **hǎn** грóмко кричáть, звать	1. to cry out, yell 2. to call (sb.)
减 **jiǎn** **1.** уменьшáть(ся), сокращáть(ся) **2.** вычитáть; мúнус	1. to subtract 2. to reduce, decrease, cut 3. to lessen, diminish, deduct
～省 **jiǎnshěng** экономúть; экономия	to reduce waste, economize
～少 **jiǎnshǎo** уменьшáть, убавлять	to reduce, decrease
成 **chéng** **1.** закóнчить(ся), завершúть(ся) **2.** созрéть, поспéть; быть готóвым; готóвый **3.** стать, превратúться в **4.** весь, цéлый	1. to accomplish, succeed 2. to become, turn into 3. achievement, result 4. fully developed/grown, mature 5. established, ready-made 6. able 7. considerable 8. whole 9. all right 10. 1/10
～立 **chénglì** **1.** основáть, учредúть **2.** успéшно закóнчить	1. to found, establish 2. to be tenable, hold water
～语 **chéngyǔ** идиóм	set phrase, idiom
～年 **chéngnián** **1.** весь год **2.** совершеннолéтний	1. to grow up, come of age; adult, grown-up 2. year after year
～分 **chéngfèn** **1.** составнáя часть, элемéнт **2.** социáльное положéние	1. composition, component part, ingredient 2. class/economic status, profession
～功 **chénggōng** успéх	to succeed; success
～为 **chéngwéi** стать, превратúться в	to become, turn into
～长 **chéngzhǎng** повзрослéть, вы́расти; рост	to grow up, mature
～家 **chéngjiā** женúться	to get married
～衣 **chéngyī** **1.** шить плáтье **2.** готóвое плáтье	1. tailoring 2. ready-made clothes
～就(绩) **chéngjiù(jī)** успéхи, достижéния; результáт	to achieve, accomplish; achievement, accomplishment, success
～员 **chéngyuán** состáв, учáстники, члéны	member
～熟 **chéngshú** созревáть; созрéвший	ripe, mature
城 **chéng** гóрод; городскóй	1. wall 2. city wall 3. city, town
～市 **chéngshì** гóрод	town, city
诚 **chéng** **1.** чéстный, добросóвестный; úскренний **2.** úстинный, действúтельный	1. sincere, honest 2. really, actually, indeed

诚威藏线践残贱浅钱洩

诚实 **chéngshí** че́стный, пра́вдивый	honest
威 **wēi** **1.** вели́чие; авторите́т **2.** пуга́ть, внуша́ть страх	1. greatness, power, might, authority, prestige; imposing, impressive 2. to menace, imperil, threaten
～信 **wēixìn** авторитéт, прести́ж	prestige, popular trust
～力(势) **wēilì(shì)** си́ла; вели́чие	power, might
～胁 **wēixié** угрожа́ть; угро́за	to menace, imperil
藏 **cáng** **1.** пря́тать(ся), скрыва́ть(ся) **2.** храни́ть, сберега́ть	1. to hide, conceal 2. to store, lay by
～ **zàng** **1.** склад, храни́лище **2.** *сокр.* Тибе́т; тибе́тский	short name for Xizang (Tibet)
线 **xiàn** **1.** нить **2.** ли́ния, черта́ **3.** тра́сса	1. thread, string, wire 2. route, line 3. demarcation line, boundary 4. clue
践 **jiàn** ходи́ть по, ступа́ть	1. trample 2. to fulfill, perform
～踏 **jiàntà** попира́ть, топта́ть	to tread on, trample underfoot
残 **cán** **1.** по́ртить; кале́чить **2.** жесто́кий, бесчелове́чный **3.** неполноце́нный; дефе́ктный	1. incomplete, deficient 2. savage, ferocious 3. remaining, remnant 4. to injure, damage
～酷 **cánkù** *см.* 残 3	brutal, ruthless
～暴 **cánbào** зве́рства; бесчелове́чный, зве́рский	ruthless, brutal
～废 **cánfèi** кале́чить(ся); кале́ка, инвали́д	(derog.) 1. handicapped; handicapped person 2. too short a man
～余 **cányú** пережи́тки	remnants, remains, vestiges
贱 **jiàn** **1.** дешёвый **2.** ничто́жный, незначи́тельный	1. inexpensive, cheap, low-priced 2.lowly, humble 3. base, despicable 4. my
浅 **qiǎn** **1.** ме́лкий **2.** пове́рхностный **3.** све́тлый, бле́дный	1. shallow, superficial 2. easy, simple 3. light (of color)
钱 **qián** де́ньги	1. copper coin 2. cash, money, fund, sum
～币 **qiánbì** де́ньги; валю́та	coin, money, currency
洩 **xiè** **1.** проса́чиваться, проника́ть **2.** обнару́живаться, получа́ть огла́ску	1. to let out, discharge, release 2. to leak (news/secret, etc.) 3. to give vent to
～漏 **xièlòu** разгласи́ть, получи́ть огла́ску	to leak, divulge

L

乱 **luàn 1.** беспоря́док, хао́с; в беспоря́дке **2.** смеша́ть (-ся), спу́тать(ся)	1. in disorder/confusion 2. confused, in a turmoil 3. indiscriminate, random 4. to confuse, mix up, riot 5. disorder
礼 **lǐ 1.** но́рмы поведе́ния **2.** этике́т; обря́д, церемо́ния **3.** пода́рок	1. ceremony, rite, ritual 2. courtesy, etiquette, manners 3. gift, present -
～堂 **lǐtáng** а́ктовый зал	assembly hall, auditorium
～品 **lǐpǐn** пода́рок	gift, present
～拜 **lǐbài 1.** воскресе́нье **2.** неде́ля	1. religious service 2. week 3. day of week 4. Sunday
～拜堂 **lǐbàitáng** це́рковь, храм	church -
～物 **lǐwù** пода́рок	gift, present
～服 **lǐfú** (выходно́й) костю́м; пара́дная оде́жда	ceremonial robe/dress, formal attire -
～炮 **lǐpào** салю́т *(артиллерийский)*	gun salute -
～貌 **lǐmào** этике́т; ве́жливый	courtesy, politeness, manners -
轧 **yà 1.** нае́хать, перее́хать, раздави́ть **2.** прока́тывать *(металл);* прессова́ть	1. to crush, run/roll over 2. (onom.) humming sound -
孔 **kǒng 1.** щель; дыра́, отве́рстие **2.** Конфу́ций; конфуциа́нский	1. hole, aperture 2. badly 3. very 4. Confucius, Confucian 5. (M. for holes) -
乳 **rǔ 1.** гру́ди; вы́мя **2.** молоко́; моло́чный	1. breast 2. milk 3. newborn, suckling -
～品 **rǔpǐn** моло́чные проду́кты	dairy products -
扎 **zhā 1.** уколо́ть; вонзи́ть **2.** вти́снуться	1. to prick, pierce 2. to plunge into -
～ **zhá 1.** из после́дних сил; че́рез си́лу **2.** остана́вливаться; квартирова́ть	(to be) hardly able to - -
～ **zā** свя́зывать; перевя́зывать	to tie, bind -
～针 **zhāzhēn** де́лать уко́л	to give/have acupuncture treatment
比 **bǐ 1.** сра́внивать; сравни́тельный, относи́тельный **2.** *сокр.* Бе́льгия	1. to compare, contrast 2. to emulate 3. to draw an analogy 4. to copy 5. to gesture 6. ratio 7. compared with
～重 **bǐzhòng** уде́льный вес	1. proportion 2. specific gravity

比 批 鹿 棍 混 此 化

比如 **bǐrú** напримéр	for example/instance
～例 **bǐlì** 1. примéр; аналóгия 2. пропóрция; масштáб	1. proportion 2. scale
～方 **bǐfang** примéр; напримéр	analogy, instance
～较 **bǐjiào** срáвнивать; сравнéние; сравнúтельно, бóлее úли мéнее	1. to compare, contrast 2. over, than 3. relatively, fairly
～赛 **bǐsài** состязáться, соревновáться; состязáние, соревновáние; кóнкурс	match, competition
批 **pī** 1. решáть, выносúть решéние; резолю́ция 2. оптóвый; пáртия *(напр. товара)*	1. to slap (sb.'s face) 2. to comment, criticize, refute 3. to write comments on a document 4. batch, lot 5. (coll.) cloth fibers not yet twisted
～准 **pīzhǔn** утвердúть; ратифицúровать	to ratify, approve, sanction
～评 **pīpíng** критиковáть; крúтика	to criticize; criticism
～判 **pīpàn** давáть оцéнку, рецензúровать; критúческий	to criticize; critique
～驳 **pībó** отвергáть, опровергáть; откáзывать	1. to veto an opinion/request from a subordinate body 2. to refute, rebut
～示 **pīshì** резолю́ция, решéние; указáние	memo from superior to inferior
鹿 **lù** олéнь	deer
棍 **gùn** пáлка; трость	1. rod, stick 2. villain
混 **hùn** 1. смéшивать; смéшанный 2. беспоря́дочный, хаотúческий 3. мýтный, нечúстый	1. to mix, confuse 2. to pass for, pass off as 3. to muddle/drift along 4. to get along with sb. 5. thoughtlessly, recklessly
～血种(儿) **hùnxuèzhǒng('ér)** метúс	mixed race
～和(合) **hùnhé(hé)** смéшивать(ся); составнóй; комбинúрованный; сбóрный	to mix, blend, mingle
～凝土 **hùnníngtǔ** бетóн	concrete
～乱 **hùnluàn** пýтать; беспоря́док; беспоря́дочный	chaos, confusion, disorder; confused, chaotic
此 **cǐ** э́то; э́тот, дáнный	this
化 **huà** 1. изменя́ться; превращáться 2. хúмия; химú-	1. to change, transform, convert 2. to melt, dissolve, thaw 3. to digest, re-

ческий **3.** таять; плавиться **4.** *суф.* -изация	move 4. to burn up, incinerate 5. to disguise 6. to die 7. culture 8. chemistry 9. (suf.) -ize
化粧 **huàzhuāng** гримироваться; косметика	to make up (as)
～学 **huàxué** химия; химический	chemistry
～学化 **huàxuéhuà** химизация	(extensive) use of chemical fertilizers and other farm chemicals
～装 **huàzhuāng** переодеваться *кем;* маскироваться; гримироваться	1. (theatr.) to make up 2. to disguise oneself
靴 **xuē** сапоги	boots
～鞋 **xuēxié** обувь	footwear
讹 **é 1.** ошибка; ошибочный **2.** вымогать; шантажировать	1. to blackmail 2. erroneous
～诈 **ézhà** шантаж	1. to defraud 2. to extort
花 **huā 1.** цветок; цветной, пёстрый **2.** тратить, расходовать	1. flower, blossom 2. pattern, design 3. fireworks 4. essence, cream 5. wound 6. courtesan, prostitute 7. to spend 8. flowery 9. profligate
～生 **huāshēng** арахис	peanut
～圈 **huāquān** венок	wreath, garland
～柳病 **huāliǔbìng** венерические болезни	venereal disease
～样 **huāyàng 1.** красочный **2.** фигурный	1. pattern, variety 2. trick 3. variations in performance
～费 **huāfèi** тратить; расходы	to spend, expend; expenditure(s)
北 **běi** север; северный	1. north 2. to be defeated
～方 **běifāng** север	1. north 2. northern part of country
死 **sǐ 1.** умереть; смерть; смертельный **2.** прочно, крепко **3.** *словообр. элемент* насмерть, до смерти	1. to die 2. desperately, to the death 3. extremely 4. implacable, deadly 5. rigid, fixed, inflexible 6. closed, impassable
～亡 **sǐwáng** погибнуть, умереть; смерть	to be dead/doomed
～刑 **sǐxíng** смертная казнь	death penalty, capital punishment
屍 **shī** труп; покойник	corpse, dead body
毙 **bì** убить	1. to die, get killed 2. to shoot (to death)
呢 **ní** сукно; шерстяная ткань	woolen cloth
～ **ne** *частица, выражающая подчёркнутое утверждение или вопрос, напр.:* 天	(part.) 1. (marking questions about a subject already mentioned) 2. (indicating continued state/action) 3.

化
靴
讹
花
北
死
屍
毙
呢

气好呢! хоро́шая пого́да!; 你呢? а Вы?	(indicating deliberate pause) 4. (indicating strong affirmation)
泥 **ní** гли́на; грязь; ил	1. mud, clay 2. mashed vegetables/fruit
～ **nì** ма́зать; штукату́рить	1. to cover/daub with plaster 2. stubborn, bigoted
～土 **nítǔ** гли́на	1. earth, soil 2. clay
～炭 **nítàn** торф	peat
～水匠 **níshuǐjiàng** штукату́р	bricklayer, plasterer
老 **lǎo 1.** ста́рый; стари́к; ста́рость **2.** уважа́емый, почте́нный **3.** да́вний; застаре́лый; и́здавна	1. old, aged 2. of long standing 3. outdated 4. overgrown 5. dark (of colors) 6. old people 7. parents 8. very 9. always 10. (pref. to indicate friendship)
～百姓 **lǎobǎixìng** просто́й наро́д; крестья́не	common people, civilians
～爷 **lǎoye 1.** дед, де́душка **2.** ба́рин, господи́н	1. master, lord 2. maternal grandfather, grandpa
～早 **lǎozǎo** давно́ уже́; давны́м-давно́	(coll.) very early, long ago
～半天 **lǎobàntiān** до́лгое вре́мя, до́лго	a long time
～师 **lǎoshī** учи́тель, наста́вник	teacher
～病 **lǎobìng 1.** хрони́ческая боле́знь **2.** привы́чка	1. old and ailing 2. old ailment
～乡 **lǎoxiāng** земля́к	1. fellow villager 2. friendly address 3. (derog.) country bumpkin
～大哥 **lǎodàgē** ста́рший брат	elder brother
～实 **lǎoshi** скро́мный, просто́й; че́стный	1. honest, frank 2. well-behaved, good 3. simple-minded, naive
～是 **lǎoshi** всегда́, постоя́нно	always
～板 **lǎobǎn** хозя́ин, владе́лец	shopkeeper, proprietor, boss
～虎 **lǎohǔ** тигр	tiger
～兵 **lǎobīng** ветера́н	old soldier, veteran
～婆 **lǎopo** жена́	(coll.) wife
它 **tā** он, она́, оно́ *(о неодушевлённых предметах)*	1. it, they 2. this, that
舵 **duò** руль	rudder, helm
～手 **duòshǒu** рулево́й, ко́рмчий	pilot, helmsman
蛇 **shé** змея́	snake, serpent
伦:伦理 **lúnlǐ** э́тика	ethics, moral principles
轮 **lún 1.** колесо́; круг; диск;	1. wheel (-like), disc, ring 2. steam-

вращáться **2.** сменя́ться; по óчереди	boat, steamer 3. to take turns 4. round (e.g., of talks)
轮船 **lúnchuán** пароxóд	steamer, steamship
～到 **lúndào** óчередь за	to approach (in turns/order)
～流 **lúnliú** по óчереди, поочерёдно	by turns, in turn
论 **lùn 1**. теóрия, учéние **2.** обсуждáть, дискути́ровать **3.** о, об *(в названиях работ)*	1. to discuss, talk about 2. to decide on, determine 3. to mention, regard, consider 4. view, statement, opinion 5. theory 6. essay, dissertation 7. by
～理 **lùnlǐ** лóгика; логи́ческий	1. to reason things out, have it out 2. logic 3. normally, as things should be
～断 **lùnduàn** выскáзывать суждéние; определéние	inference, judgment, thesis
～争 **lùnzhēng** ди́спут; дискýссия	to argue, debate; argument, debate, controversy
～文 **lùnwén 1.** статья́ **2.** диссертáция; диплóмная (курсовáя) рабóта	thesis, dissertation, treatise, paper
～战 **lùnzhàn** спор, полéмика	to debate; debate, polemic
～坛 **lùntán 1.** трибýна **2.** прéсса; общéственное мнéние	forum, tribune
能 **néng 1.** мочь, быть в состоя́нии; умéть **2.** спосóбности; умéние; талáнт **3.** энéргия, си́ла	1. to be able to, be capable of; ability, capability, skill 2. energy
～干 **nénggàn** умéлый; спосóбный	1. able, capable, competent 2. clever, ingenious
～手 **néngshǒu** мáстер *(своего дела)*, умéлец	expert, master hand
～够 **nénggòu** мочь, быть в состоя́нии	to be able to, be capable of
～力 **nénglì 1.** умéние; спосóбность **2.** энéргия	ability, capacity
～人 **néngrén** *см.* 能手	able person
犯 **fàn 1.** нарушáть, преступáть *(закон)*; преступлéние; престýпник **2.** совершáть оши́бку	1. to violate, offend 2. to attack, assail, work against 3. to commit 4. to recur (of an old illness), revert (to a bad habit) 5. criminal
～罪 **fànzuì** соверши́ть преступлéние; преступлéние; престýпный	to commit a crime/offense

犯案 **fàn'àn** уголо́вное де́ло	to be discovered and brought to justice
～境 **fànjìng** наруша́ть грани́цу	to invade the frontiers of another country
～禁(忌) **fànjìn(jì)** наруша́ть запре́т	to violate a ban
碗 **wǎn** ча́шка; пиала́	bowl
范 **fàn** образе́ц, станда́рт; ра́мки	1. model, example; pattern, matrix 2. limits; restriction
～围 **fànwéi** сфе́ра, о́бласть; ра́мки	scope, range, extent, parameter
危 **wēi** быть в опа́сности; угрожа́ть; опа́сный	danger
～险 **wēixiǎn** опа́сность; опа́сный	danger, peril; dangerous, perilous
～害 **wēihài** губи́ть; вреди́ть	to harm, endanger
～机 **wēijī** кри́зис; опа́сный (крити́ческий) моме́нт	crisis
仓 **cāng** склад; кладова́я	warehouse, storehouse
～库 **cāngkù** *см.* 仓	warehouse, storehouse
抢 **qiǎng 1.** отнима́ть; гра́бить **2.** торопи́ться, спеши́ть **3.** стира́ть; ста́чивать	1. to pillage, loot 2. to vie for (work, etc.) 3. to rush (harvest, etc.) 4. to scrape (a pot, etc.) 5. to sharpen
～夺 **qiǎngduó** *см.* 抢 1	to pillage, plunder
～救 **qiǎngjiù** спаса́ть; выруча́ть	to rush to save
舱 **cāng** каби́на; каю́та	1. cabin 2. module
枪 **qiāng** ружьё, винто́вка	rifle, gun
～杆子 **qiānggǎnz** винто́вка	gun barrel, gun, arms
～决(毙) **qiāngjué(bì)** расстреля́ть	to execute by shooting
疮 **chuāng** нары́в; я́зва; ра́на	1. sore, skin ulcer 2. wound
苍 **cāng** тёмно-голубо́й; си́зый; зелёный	1. dark green 2. blue 3. gray, ashy
～蝇 **cāngying** му́ха	fly
卷 **juàn 1.** сви́ток *(книга, картина)* **2.** том; разде́л **3.** канцеля́рское де́ло	1. book 2. examination paper 3. file, documents, dossier 4. roll
～ **juǎn** свёртывать, скру́чивать	1. to roll up; roll 2. to sweep off, carry along 3. spool, reel, roll //Stems
己 **jǐ** сам; ли́чно	1. oneself 2. sixth of the 10 Heavenly//
纪 **jì 1.** запи́сывать; за́писи **2.** усто́и, осно́вы **3.** эпо́ха, пери́од	1. historical records, annals, chronicles, 2. to write down, record 3. century 4. geological period 5. discipline

纪年 **jìnián** хро́ника, ле́топись	to record chronologically; chronological record of events //regulations
～律 **jìlǜ** дисципли́на	1. discipline, morale 2. laws and//
～元 **jìyuán** нача́ло э́ры	1. beginning of a reign/era 2. epoch, era
～念 **jìniàn** отмеча́ть *(годовщину)*; па́мятный; юбиле́йный	1. to commemorate, mark 2. souvenir - -
～念品 **jìniànpǐn** сувени́р	souvenir
～念日 **jìniànrì** годовщи́на, юбиле́й	commemoration/memorial day -
～念碑 **jìniànbēi** монуме́нт, па́мятник; мемориа́льная доска́	monument, memorial - -
配 **pèi** **1.** соединя́ть(ся), сочета́ть(ся) **2.** подбира́ть; подгоня́ть **3.** быть приго́дным	1. to join in marriage 2. to mate (of animals) 3. to mix, compound 4. to distribute according to plan 5. to match 6. to deserve 7. to deserve, be suited
～合 **pèihé** сочета́ться; в сочета́нии с	to coordinate, cooperate; cooperative -
～套 **pèitào** компле́кт	to form a complete set
记 **jì** **1.** запомина́ть; па́мять **2.** запи́сывать, де́лать заме́тки; за́пись **3.** знак, ме́тка	1. to remember, bear in mind, commit to memory 2. write down, record 3. notes, records 4. mark, sign 5. birthmark 6. seal
～性 **jìxìng** па́мять	memory
～者 **jìzhe** корреспонде́нт; журнали́ст	reporter, correspondent -
～号 **jìhào** знак, си́мвол	mark, sign
～录 **jìlù** **1.** запи́сывать; прото́кол; документа́льный **2.** реко́рд	1. to take notes, keep minutes; minutes, notes, record 2. note-taker -
～录片 **jìlùpiàn** документа́льный фильм, хро́ника	documentary film -
～载 **jìzǎi** запи́сывать, де́лать за́писи; за́пись	to put down in writing, record; record, account
～忆 **jìyì** па́мять	to remember, recall; memory
岂 **qǐ** ра́зве?, неуже́ли?	how could...? //terward 4. too
已 **yǐ** уже́	1. already 2. to stop, cease, end 3. af-//
～经 **yǐjīng** уже́	already
巷 **xiàng** переу́лок	lane, all //(Hong Kong)
港 **gǎng** **1.** га́вань; порт; зали́в **2.** *сокр.* Гонко́нг	1. port, harbor 2. (abbr.) Xianggang// -
包 **bāo** **1.** обёртывать; упако́вывать; свёрток **2.** окру-	1. to wrap 2. to surround, encircle 3. to include, contain 4. to undertake all 5.

жáть, охвáтывать; заключáть *(в себе)*	to assure, guarantee 6. bundle, package 7. bag, sack 8. swelling
包括 **bāokuò** включáть, охвáтывать	to include, consist of, comprise, incorporate
～含 **bāohán** заключáть, содержáть	to contain, embody, include; inclusion -
～管 **bāoguǎn** гарантúровать, обеспéчивать	to assure, guarantee -
～厢 **bāoxiāng** лóжа *(в театре)*	box (in a theater) -
～围 **bāowéi** окружáть; окружéние, осáда	to surround, encircle; encirclement -
～装 **bāozhuāng** обёртывать; упакóвывать	1. to pack 2. to dress up 3. package, packing, packaging //package
～裹 **bāoguǒ** посы́лка	to wrap/bind up; bundle, parcel,//
～扎 **bāozā** перевя́зывать; перевя́зка	to wrap/bind up, pack; packing, (cloth) bandage //walk 4. to be away/off
跑 **pǎo** бéгать; бежáть	1. to run 2. to run away, escape 3. to//
抱 **bào 1.** обнимáть; держáть на рукáх **2.** затаúть в душé	1. to hold/carry in the arms 2. to have a first child 3. to adopt 4. to cherish 5. to hatch, brood 6. to handle together
～歉 **bàoqiàn** сожалéть; извиня́ться; óчень жаль	to be sorry/apologetic -
～怨 **bàoyuàn** таúть обúду	to complain, grumble
胞 **bāo 1.** утрóба; дéтское мéсто, послéд **2.** *биол.* клéтка	1. afterbirth 2. sibling - -
炮 **pào** пýшка; орýдие	roast in pan
～灰 **pàohuī** *обр.* пýшечное мя́со	cannon fodder -
泡 **pào 1.** пузырú *(на воде)* **2.** электролáмпа **3.** смáчивать; пропúтывать **4.** завáривать *(чай)*	1. spongy, not solid 2. sth. puffy and soft 3. (M. for urine/feces) - -
～沫 **pàomò** пéна; пузырú	foam, froth
饱 **bǎo 1.** насыщáться; наедáться **2.** пóлный, достáточный	1. full, plump 2. satiated, full 3. to satisfy 4. fully -
～满 **bǎomǎn** довóльный, удовлетворённый	full, plump -
雹 **báo** град	hail //near 4. (loan w.) bar
巴 **bā** *фон. знак*	1. to hope for 2. to cling to 3. to be//
吧 **bā** *частица, выражающая предположение или при-*	(part. expressing: 1. mild imperative 2. acknowledgment 3. uncertainty 4.

глашение к совместному действию, напр.: 在这里吧 здесь!; 走吧 пошли́!	pause)
把 **bǎ** **1.** схвати́ть; держа́ть **2.** *служ. сл. для инверсии дополн.*	1. to grasp 2. to hold 3. to dominate 4. to guard 5. to tie up 6. about 7. handle 8. bunch, bundle 9. (M. for handfuls)
～ **bà** ру́чка, рукоя́тка	1. grip, handle 2. stem (of plants)
～握 **bǎwò** гара́нтия; уве́ренность	1. to grasp firmly 2. assurance, certainty
～守 **bǎshǒu** охраня́ть	to guard
～戏 **bǎxì** **1.** у́личное представле́ние; цирк **2.** трюк, уло́вка	1. acrobatics, jugglery 2. cheap trick, game 3. impish person
肥 **féi** **1.** жи́рный; плодоро́дный; оби́льный **2.** удобря́ть; удобре́ние	1. to fertilize; fertilizer, manure 2. fat 3. fertile, rich 4. loose, loose-fitting, large
～料 **féiliào** удобре́ние	fertilizer, manure
～沃 **féiwò** плодоро́дный, ту́чный *(о почве)*	fertile, rich
～皂 **féizào** мы́ло	soap
爸 **bà**, 爸爸 **bàba** па́па, оте́ц	papa, dad, father
色 **sè** **1.** цвет, окра́ска **2.** сорт; ка́чество **3.** катего́рия; разря́д	1. color 2. look, expression 3. kind, sort 4. feminine charm 5. sexual appetite 6. theatrical role 7. metallic content
绝 **jué** **1.** оборва́ть(ся); прерва́ть(ся), прекрати́ть(ся) **2.** категори́чески; абсолю́тно	1. to cut off, sever 2. exhausted, used up 3. desperate, hopeless 4. unique, superb, matchless 5. uncompromising 6. extremely, most 7. absolutely
～望 **juéwàng** отча́яться	to give up all hope, to despair
～路 **juélù** тупи́к, безвы́ходное положе́ние	blind alley, impasse
～对 **juéduì** абсолю́тный; безусло́вный; категори́ческий	absolute(ly), perfect(ly), definite(ly)
～食 **juéshí** объяви́ть голодо́вку	to fast, go on a hunger strike
七 **qī** семь	seven
～月 **qīyuè** ию́ль	July
皂 **zào** мы́ло	1. soap 2. black
托 **tuō** **1.** подноси́ть, подава́ть; подно́с **2.** поруча́ть, доверя́ть **3.** уви́ливать	1. to hold in the palm, support from under 2. to serve as a foil, set off 3. to plead 4. to rely on 5. to entrust
～拉斯 **tuōlāsī** трест	(loan w.) trust
～管 **tuōguǎn** опека́ть; опе́ка	trusteeship

托 宅 诧 毛 耗 尾 毫 笔 毯 纯 吨 也

托儿所 **tuō'érsuǒ** дéтские я́сли	nursery, child-care center, crèche
宅 **zhái** жили́ще; кварти́ра	residence, house
诧:诧异 **chàyì** удивля́ться, изумля́ться	astonished
毛 **máo 1.** шерсть; вóлос; пух; шерстянóй; мохнáтый **2.** грýбый, необрабóтанный **3.** растеря́ться	1. hair, feather, down, wool 2. mildew, mold 3. semifinished (product) 4. gross (profit) 5. little, small 6. careless, crude 7. alarmed 8. depreciated\\
～重 **máozhòng** вес брýтто	gross weight \\9. 1/10 yuan, dime
～巾 **máojīn** махрóвое полотéнце	towel
～病 **máobìng** недостáток, порóк, изъя́н	1. trouble, mishap, breakdown 2. defect, shortcoming, fault, mistake 3.\\
～衣 **máoyī** шерстянóй трикотáж	woolen sweater \\illness
～皮 **máopí** мех, пушни́на	fur, pelt
～笔 **máobǐ** кисть, ки́сточка	writing brush
耗 **hào 1.** трáтить, расхóдовать **2.** тянýть, оття́гивать *(время)*	1. to consume, cost, expend 2. to waste time, dawdle 3. bad news
尾 **wěi 1.** хвост; хвостовóй **2.** конéц; конéчный	1. tail 2. end 3. remaining part, remnant 4. (M. for fish, etc.)
毫 **háo 1.** волосóк **2.** крóшечный, ничтóжный	1. writing brush 2. fine long hair 3. in the least, all 4. milli-
～无(不) **háowú(bù)** нискóлько не, совершéнно не	to completely lack
笔 **bǐ 1.** кисть; перó; карандáш **2.** писáть, запи́сывать	1. pen 2. technique of writing/calligraphy/drawing 3. stroke 4. to write
～名 **bǐmíng** псевдони́м	pen name, pseudonym
～记本 **bǐjìběn** записнáя кни́жка, блокнóт	notebook
毯 **tǎn 1.** ковёр **2.** одея́ло *(шерстяное)*	1. blanket 2. carpet, rug
纯 **chún** чи́стый, очи́щенный	1. pure, unmixed 2. simple 3. skillful,// //practiced, well-versed
～洁 **chúnjié** чи́стый; чистотá	pure, clean and honest
～粹 **chúncuì** чи́стый, без при́меси, настоя́щий	pure, unadulterated
吨 **dūn** тóнна	(loan w.) ton
也 **yě** тóже, тáкже	1. also, too, as well, either 2. even
～许 **yěxǔ** возмóжно, мóжет быть	perhaps, probably, maybe

地 **dì 1.** Земля́, земно́й шар **2.** земля́, по́ле **3.** райо́н, ме́сто **4.** основа́ние; фон	1. the earth 2. land, soil 3. fields 4. ground 5. place 6. position 7. background 8. distance
~ **de** *суф. наречий*	(adverbial-forming suf., -ly)
~主 **dìzhǔ** поме́щик, землевладе́лец	1. landlord 2. host
~理 **dìlǐ** геогра́фия	1. geography 2. geographical features//of a place
~址 **dìzhǐ** а́дрес; местонахожде́ние	address, location
~位 **dìwèi** положе́ние; ме́сто, пост	position, status
~区 **dìqū** райо́н	1. area, district, region 2. prefecture
~名 **dìmíng** географи́ческое назва́ние	place name
~图 **dìtú** ка́рта *(географическая)*	map
~面 **dìmiàn 1.** пове́рхность земли́ **2.** ме́стность	1. (earth's) surface, ground 2. (archi.) ground floor 3. (coll.) region
~下 **dìxia** под землёй; подзе́мный	on the ground
dìxià подпо́льный, нелега́льный	1. underground 2. secret activity
~平线 **dìpíngxiàn** горизо́нт	horizon
~带 **dìdài** зо́на, по́яс	zone, belt, district, region
~步 **dìbù** положе́ние, состоя́ние	1. condition, situation, state 2. extent
~形 **dìxíng** релье́ф ме́стности	topography, terrain
~方 **dìfāng** ме́сто, ме́стность; ме́стный	local, regional; place, space
~球 **dìqiú** земно́й шар	the earth/globe
~球仪 **dìqiúyí** гло́бус	(terrestrial) globe
~震 **dìzhèn** землетрясе́ние	earthquake, seism
~板 **dìbǎn** пол; насти́л	1. floorboard 2. floor
~段 **dìduàn** уча́сток земли́	areal sector/section
~道 **dìdào** подзе́мная доро́га	1. tunnel 2. causeway
dìdao по-настоя́щему, до́лжным о́бразом	1. genuine 2. pure, authentic, typical 3. well done, thorough
~毯 **dìtǎn** ковёр	carpet, rug
~质 **dìzhì** геоло́гия (строе́ние) земли́	geology
~质学 **dìzhìxué** геоло́гия	geology
~点 **dìdiǎn** пункт, ме́сто	place, site, locale

他 她 池 拖 施 绳 蝇 龟 电

他 **tā** **1.** он **2.** другóй, посторóнний	1. he 2. she 3. it 4. they (inanimate things in object position) 5. other,\\
她 **tā** онá	she \\another 6. elsewhere
池:池塘 **chítáng** пруд, водоём	pond, pool
拖 **tuō** **1.** тянýть, тащи́ть **2.** отклáдывать, оття́гивать	1. to pull, drag, haul 2. to delay, drag on, procrastinate
～鞋 **tuōxié** шлёпанцы	slippers, sandals, flip-flops
～拉机 **tuōlājī** трáктор	(loan w.) tractor
～延 **tuōyán** затя́гивать; отклáдывать	to delay, put off
施 **shī** **1.** осуществля́ть, проводи́ть в жизнь **2.** применя́ть; испóльзовать	1. to execute, carry out 2. to bestow, give 3. to use, apply
～政 **shīzhèng** управля́ть; администрати́вный	to govern, administer
～肥 **shīféi** вноси́ть удобрéния	to apply fertilizer //reprimand 4. to continue
绳 **shéng** верёвка	1. rope, string 2. guideline 3. to correct,//
蝇 **yíng** мýха	fly
龟 **guī** черепáха	tortoise, turtle
电 **diàn** **1.** электри́чество; электри́ческий **2.** телегрáмма; телегрáфный **3.** мóлния	1. electricity 2. telegram 3. to give/ get an electric shock 4. to send a telegram
～压 **diànyā** *эл.* напряжéние	voltage
～汇 **diànhuì** телегрáфный перевóд	to telegraph money; remittance by telegram
～器 **diànqì** электроаппаратýра	electrical equipment/appliance
～话 **diànhuà** телефóн	1. telephone 2. phone call
～台 **diàntái** радиостáнция; рáция	1. transmitter-receiver, transceiver 2. broadcasting station
～焊 **diànhàn** электросвáрка	electric welding
～车 **diànchē** трамвáй; электри́чка	1. streetcar, tram, tramcar 2. trolley-bus, trolley
～灯 **diàndēng** электри́ческая лáмпа	electric lamp/light
～子 **diànz** электрóн	electron; electronic
～子计算机 **diànzi jìsuànjī** электрóнная вычисли́тельная маши́на, ЭВМ	electronic computer
～扇 **diànshàn** вентиля́тор	electric fan
～影 **diànyǐng** кинó	film, movie

电影院 **diànyǐngyuàn** кинотеа́тр	cinema, movie (house)
~梯 **diàntī** лифт; эскала́тор	elevator
~报 **diànbào** телегра́мма; телегра́фный	telegram, cable
~线 **diànxiàn** 1. электропрово́дка 2. ли́ния электропереда́чи	(electric) wire
~池 **diànchí** *эл.* батаре́я; элеме́нт	(electric) cell, battery
~视 **diànshì** телеви́дение	television, TV
~流 **diànliú** электри́ческий ток	electric current
~气 **diànqì** электри́чество; электри́ческий	electricity
掩 **yǎn** 1. закрыва́ть; покрыва́ть 2. пря́тать, скрыва́ть	1. to cover, hide 2. to shut, close 3. to ambush 4. to get pinched/nipped
~盖 **yǎngài** прикрыва́ть, маскирова́ть	to cover, conceal
~护 **yǎnhù** охраня́ть, прикрыва́ть	to screen, shield, cover, be defensive about sth.
~蔽 **yǎnbì** *см.* 掩盖	to screen, shelter, cover
淹 **yān** погружа́ть(ся) в во́ду; тону́ть	1. to flood, submerge 2. to delay 3. to stay, be stranded 4. erudite, well-read
~没 **yānmò** утону́ть, затону́ть	to flood, inundate
甩 **shuǎi** 1. броса́ть, мета́ть 2. покида́ть	1. to move backward and forward 2. to throw 3. to leave sb. behind, throw off

儿

儿 **ér** 1. сын; ребёнок 2. *суф. сущ. и наречий*	1. child 2. youth 3. son 4. male 5. (suf. for non-syllabic diminutive)
~童 **értóng** де́ти; де́тский	children
~子 **érz** сын	son
~女 **érnǚ** сыновья́ и до́чери; де́ти	1. sons and daughters, children 2. young males and females
元 **yuán** 1. нача́ло; первонача́льный 2. глава́; гла́вный 3. дина́стия Юа́нь 4. юа́нь; до́ллар; ие́на; во́на	1. first, primary 2. basic, fundamental 3. old, eminent 4. vital state, vitality 5. origin 6. Yuan dynasty (1279—1368)
~旦 **yuándàn** пе́рвый день Но́вого го́да	New Year's Day
~帅 **yuánshuài** ма́ршал; кома́ндующий	1. marshall 2. supreme commander

元玩完院冠寇绕晓

元素 **yuánsù** *хим.* элемéнт	(chem.) element
玩 **wán** игрáть, забавля́ться, развлекáться	1. to play, have fun 2. to employ 3. to trifle with 4. to enjoy, appreciate
~弄 **wánnòng 1.** забавля́ться **2.** насмехáться	1. to play/juggle with 2. to resort to, employ
~笑 **wánxiào** смея́ться, шути́ть	joke, jest
~具 **wánjù** игрýшка; безделýшка	toy, plaything
~意儿 **wányìr 1.** игрýшка **2.** шýтка	1. toy, plaything 2. thing
完 **wán 1.** пóлный, цéлый; сполнá **2.** закóнчить; закóнченный; конéц, окончáние **3.** *гл. суф. завершённости действия*	1. to exhaust, use up 2. to finish, complete 3. to pay (taxes) 4. whole, complete
~全 **wánquán 1.** пóлный; целикóм, пóлностью **2.** закóнченный	1. complete, whole 2. completely, fully, wholly, absolutely
~整 **wánzhěng 1.** пóлный, в пóлном состáве **2.** цéльный; цéлостность	complete, integrated, intact
~善 **wánshàn** превосхóдный, совершéнный	perfect, consumate
~毕 **wánbì** закóнчить	to finish, complete
~好 **wánhǎo** совершéнный, безупрéчный	1. intact, whole 2. in good condition
~成 **wánchéng** заверши́ть, вы́полнить	to accomplish, complete, fulfill
院 **yuàn 1.** двор; сад **2.** инститýт; акадéмия; кинотеáтр; больни́ца	1. courtyard, compound 2. branch of government 3. public facility 4. institute, college
~长 **yuànzhǎng** председáтель; дирéктор; президéнт	1. director/president (of museum/institute, etc.) 2. gov't. branch head
冠 **guàn** выделя́ться; превосходи́ть	1. to put on a hat 2. to precede, crown with 3. first place, best
~军 **guànjūn** пéрвое мéсто; чемпиóн	champion
寇 **kòu** грáбить	1. bandit 2. invader, enemy 3. to in-//vade, harass
绕 **rào 1.** обвя́зывать, обмáтывать **2.** обходи́ть; в обхóд	1. to wind, coil, entwine 2. to revolve around sth. 3. to detour, go around 4. to become entangled
晓 **xiǎo 1.** рассвéт **2.** знать; понимáть	1. dawn, daybreak 2. to know 3. to tell

晓得 **xiǎode** знать, понимáть; я́сно, поня́тно	to know
挠 **náo** **1.** беспокóить, тревóжить **2.** чесáть; царáпать	1. to scratch 2. hinder 3. yield, flinch
烧 **shāo** **1.** сжигáть; горéть **2.** жáрить, поджáривать **3.** кипяти́ть; вари́ть **4.** нагревáть, подогревáть	1. to burn 2. to cook, heat, roast, stew 3. to run a fever; fever
饶 **ráo** **1.** богáтый, оби́льный **2.** прости́ть, поми́ловать	1. to spare (from harsh treatment), to give sth. extra 3. rich, plentiful
光 **guāng** **1.** свет; лучи́; излучéние **2.** слáва; слáвный **3.** блеск; блестя́щий **4.** дóчиста, без остáтка	1. light, ray, brightness 2. honor, glory, luster 3. scene 4. smooth, glossy 5. gracious 6. to be used up 7. to be bare/naked 8. solely, merely, only 9. to glorify
～辉 **guānghuī** сверкáть, блестéть	radiant, brilliant; radiance
～学 **guāngxué** óптика	optics
～明 **guāngmíng** свет; свéтлый	1. light 2. bright, promising 3. open-hearted, guileless
～滑 **guānghuá** глáдкий, зеркáльный	smooth, glossy, sleek
～荣 **guāngróng** слáва; почёт; слáвный	honor, glory, credit; glorious, honored, honorable
～线 **guāngxiàn** естéственное освещéние, луч свéта	light, ray
～景 **guāngjǐng** **1.** вид, пейзáж **2.** обстанóвка, положéние дел	1. scene 2. circumstances, conditions 3. surroundings 4. (coll.) about, around 5. very probably, quite likely
晃 **huǎng** я́ркий, ослепи́тельный	1. to dazzle 2. to flash past
～ **huàng** качáться; неустóйчивый	to shake, sway
先 **xiān** **1.** прéжний; прéжде, рáньше **2.** впереди́ **3.** сначáла; предвари́тельно, зарáнее **4.** прéдки; предшéственники	1. before, earlier, in advance 2. elder generation, ancestor 3. late, deceased
～生 **xiānshēng** учи́тель, настáвник	1. teacher 2. mister, Mr., gentleman, sir 3. husband 4. Ms. 5. doctor
～后 **xiānhòu** в рáзное врéмя	1. early or late, priority, order 2. successively
～锋 **xiānfēng** авангáрд	vanguard
～例 **xiānlì** прецедéнт	precedent
～决 **xiānjué** предвари́тельный	prerequisite

先 洗 宪 霓 兄 祝 况 竟 党

先进 **xiānjìn** передовóй, прогрессúвный	to advance; advance
～觉 **xiānjué** – предчýвствовать	social/political reform visionary
洗 **xǐ** **1.** мыть; стирáть **2.** купáть(ся); умывáть(ся) **3.** *фото* проявлять	1. to wash, bathe 2. to redress, right 3. to kill and loot, sack 4. to develop (film) 5. to shuffle (cards, etc.) 6. to baptize
～澡 **xǐzǎo** купáться; принимáть вáнну	to take a bath
～染店 **xǐrǎndiàn** ателье́ химчúстки	cleaner and dyer, laundering and dyeing shop
宪 **xiàn** закóн; конститýция	1. statute 2. constitution
～兵 **xiànbīng** жандáрм; жандармéрия	military police
～法 **xiànfǎ** конститýция	constitution, charter
霓 **ní** рáдуга	secondary rainbow
～虹 **níhóng** неóновый	(loan w.) neon //between men
兄 **xiōng** стáрший брат	1. elder brother 2. courteous address//
～弟 **xiōngdì** брáтья; брáтский	brothers; fraternal, brotherly //ble servant
xiōngdi млáдший брат	1. (coll.) younger brother 2. your hum-//
祝 **zhù** поздравля́ть, желáть *чего*	1. to bless, invoke a blessing 2. to express good wishes, wish
～寿 **zhùshòu** поздравля́ть с днём рождéния	to congratulate (an elderly person) on his/her birthday
～词 **zhùcí** поздравлéние, привéтствие	congratulatory speech, congratulations
～贺 **zhùhè** поздравля́ть	to congratulate
况 **kuàng** положéние, ситуáция	1. condition, situation 2. to compare 3. moreover, besides 4. much less, let \\
～且 **kuàngqiě** притóм; бóлее тогó	moreover, besides, in addition \\alone
竞 **jìng** состязáться; конкурúровать	1. to compete, contend, vie 2. strong, forceful
～争 **jìngzhēng** сопéрничать, конкурúровать; конкурéнция	to compete; competition
～选运动 **jìngxuǎn yùndòng** предвы́борная (избирáтельная) кампáния	election campaign
～赛 **jìngsài** соревновáние; состязáние; кóнкурс	to compete, contest; competition, contest //KMT 3. clique 4. to be partial
党 **dǎng** пáртия; партúйный	1. political party 2. The Party, CCP,//
～性 **dǎngxìng** партúйность	Party spirit

党证 **dǎngzhèng** парти́йный биле́т, партбиле́т	Party card
~组织 **dǎngzǔzhī** парторганиза́ция	CP organization
~章 **dǎngzhāng** уста́в па́ртии	Party constitution/regulations
~纲 **dǎnggāng** програ́мма па́ртии	Party program/platform
~代表大会 **dǎng dàibiǎo dàhùi** партсъе́зд	Party Congress
~派 **dǎng-pài** па́ртии и группиро́вки	factions, parties, cliques
~员 **dǎngyuán** член па́ртии	Party member
~龄 **dǎnglíng** партста́ж	Party standing/seniority
~委 **dǎngwěi** партко́м	Party committee
克 **kè** **1.** быть в состоя́нии, мочь; преодолева́ть **2.** грамм	1. to be able to, can 2. to restrain 3. to overcome, subdue, capture 4. to digest 5. to set a time limit 6. gram
~服 **kèfú** преодолева́ть	1. to surmount 2. to put up with
兑 **duì** меня́ть, обме́нивать	1. to exchange, convert 2. add
脱 **tuō** **1.** снима́ть *(одежду)*; сбра́сывать *(кожу)* **2.** уходи́ть от; покида́ть, оставля́ть	1. to cut meat off bones 2. to cast/come off, shed, take off 3. to omit (words) 4. to escape from 5. to neglect, slight 6. if, in case
~落 **tuōluò** упа́док, деграда́ция	to drop, fall/come off
~离 **tuōlí** **1.** покида́ть; расстава́ться **2.** отходи́ть, отрыва́ться	to separate oneself from
税 **shuì** нало́г; по́шлина, сбор	tax, duty
蜕 **tuì** **1.** линя́ть; сбра́сывать ко́жу **2.** меня́ться, перерожда́ться	to slough off, molt, exuviate; exuvia
~变(化) **tuìbiàn(huà)** перерожда́ться; перерожде́ние	1. to transform, transmute 2. (phys.) to decay
说 **shuō** **1.** говори́ть, разгова́ривать **2.** расска́з **3.** уче́ние, тео́рия	1. to speak, talk 2. to explain 3. to scold 4. theory, teachings, doctrine
~话 **shuōhuà** говори́ть, разгова́ривать	1. to speak, talk, say, chat 2. to gossip 3. (coll.) in a minute, right away
~明 **shuōmíng** объясня́ть; объясне́ние	to explain, illustrate, show

说服 **shuōfú** убеди́ть; уговори́ть	to persuade, convince
~不上 **shuōbushàng** не зна́ю, не могу́ сказа́ть	1. can't say/tell 2. not to be worth mentioning
锐 **ruì** о́стрый, отто́ченный	1. sharp, keen 2. rapid, fast
竟 **jìng** 1. коне́ц, преде́л 2. всё-таки; вопреки́ ожида́ниям	1. frontier, limit 2. eventually 3. actually 4. throughout, whole 5. to go to the length of 6. to finish, complete
境 **jìng** 1. грани́ца 2. ме́сто; сторона́ 3. обстано́вка, ситуа́ция	1. border, boundary 2. place, area, territory 3. condition, situation, circumstances
镜 **jìng** 1. зе́ркало 2. ли́нза; очки́	1. mirror 2. lens, glass
~头 **jìngtóu** объекти́в	1. camera lens 2. shot, scene
见 **jiàn** 1. ви́деть; увиде́ть 2. взгля́ды; мне́ние	1. to see, catch sight of 2. to meet with, be exposed to 3. to seem 4. to refer to 5. opinion, view
~怪 **jiànguài** 1. удивля́ться 2. обижа́ться	take offense, mind
~面 **jiànmiàn** ви́деться, встреча́ться	to meet, see
~解 **jiànjiě** взгля́ды, воззре́ния	view, opinion, understanding
现 **xiàn** 1. тепе́рь, сейча́с; совреме́нный 2. нали́чный 3. проявля́ться, обнару́живаться; очеви́дный	1. to show, appear, display 2. ready, on hand 3. present, current 4. just, at the time, extempore
~在 **xiànzài** тепе́рь, сейча́с, ны́не	now, at present, today
~款 **xiànkuǎn** нали́чные де́ньги	ready money, cash
~实 **xiànshí** 1. реа́льный; реалисти́ческий 2. актуа́льный; насу́щный	1. reality, actually 2. practical, pragmatic
~象 **xiànxiàng** проявле́ние; при́знак	phenomenon, appearance
~役 **xiànyì** действи́тельная вое́нная слу́жба	1. active service/duty 2. on active duty, active
~代 **xiàndài** совреме́нность; совреме́нный	modern times, contemporary age; contemporary, modern
~成 **xiànchéng** гото́вый, сде́ланный	ready-made
~钱 **xiànqián** нали́чные де́ньги	(coll.) ready money, cash
视 **shì** 1. смотре́ть; осма́три-	1. to regard, look at/upon 2. to inspect, watch

вать; инспекти́ровать 2.	-
рассма́тривать как	-
视觉 **shìjué** зре́ние	visual sense, vision
～察 **shìchá** осма́тривать; ин-	to inspect
спекти́ровать	-
舰 **jiàn** вое́нный кора́бль	warship, naval vessel
规 **guī** 1. норми́ровать; но́р-	1. dividers, compasses 2. regulation 3.
ма; пра́вило 2. ци́ркуль	to admonish, advise 4. to plan 5. gauge
～矩 **guīju** пра́вила поведе́-	1. rule, custom 2. compass and square
ния; поря́док	3. well-behaved 4. gentleman-like,\\
～格 **guīgé** станда́рт, обра-	standard, specification \\honest
зе́ц	-
～律 **guīlǜ** зако́н; закономе́р-	law, regular pattern
ность	-
～则 **guīzé** пра́вила; регла́-	1. rule, regulation 2. regular, fixed
мент	-
～模 **guīmó** масшта́б; разме́р	scale, scope
～定 **guīdìng** устана́вливать,	1. to stipulate, provide 2. to fix, set,
определя́ть	formulate
观 **guān** 1. наблюда́ть, смот-	1. to look at, watch, observe 2. sight,
ре́ть; обозре́ние, обзо́р 2.	view 3. outlook, concept 4. (suf.)
взгля́ды; мне́ние; иде́я	point of view
～看 **guānkàn** смотре́ть, на-	to watch, view
блюда́ть	-
～众 **guānzhòng** зри́тели; ау-	spectator, audience
дито́рия; пу́блика	-
～察 **guānchá** наблюда́ть;	to observe, survey, inspect
обозрева́ть; обозре́ние	-
～察员 **guāncháyuán** наблю-	observer
да́тель	-
～念 **guānniàn** взгляд, пред-	sense, idea, conception
ставле́ние; иде́я	-
～点 **guāndiǎn** то́чка зре́ния	point of view, standpoint
觉 **jué** 1. чу́вствовать, ощу-	1. to sense, feel 2. to wake (up) 3. to
ща́ть 2. сознава́ть, пони-	become aware/awakened, discover 4.
ма́ть	feeling, sensation
～ **jiào** спать; сон	sleep
～悟 **juéwù** сознава́ть; со-	to come to understand, realize; con-
зна́ние	sciousness, awareness, understanding
览 **lǎn** осма́тривать; осмо́тр	1. to look at, see, view 2. to read
宽 **kuān** 1. просто́рный, ши-	1. wide, broad 2. generous, lenient 3.
ро́кий 2. распусти́ть, осла́-	comfortably/well off 4. breadth,
бить 3. великоду́шный,	width 5. to relax, relieve 6. to extend
ще́дрый	-

鬼魂魔虎允充统跳

鬼 guì 1. привидéние; чёрт 2. злой; опáсный 3. подви́жный; лóвкий	1. ghost, spirit 2. sinister plot 3. secret(ly) 4. terrible, too bad 5. smart 6. evil 7. (suf.) term of abuse
～脸 guiliǎn гримáса	1. funny face, grimace 2. toy mask
～话 guihuà враньё; сплéтни	lie
魂 hún душá; дух	soul, spirit, mood
魔 mó 1. злой дух, чёрт, дья́вол 2. чáры; ми́стика	1. evil spirit, demon, monster 2. magic, mystic
～术 móshù мáгия, колдовствó	magic, conjuring, sleight of hand
虎 hǔ тигр	1. tiger; tiger-like, brave 2. to bluff, intimidate 3. to deceive, cheat
允: 允许 yǔnxǔ разрешáть, позволя́ть	to permit, allow
充 chōng 1. заполня́ть; пóлный, напóлненный 2. исполня́ть обя́занности	1. to fill, charge 2. to serve/act as 3. to pretend to be, pose as, pass sth. off as 4. sufficient, full
～当 chōngdāng исполня́ть обя́занности; служи́ть	to serve/act as
～满 chōngmǎn 1. наполня́ть; напóлненный 2. быть преиспóлненным, преиспóлниться	to be brimming/permeated with
～分 chōngfèn пóлностью; пóлный	full, ample, abundant
统 tǒng 1. объединя́ть, соединя́ть; целикóм 2. систéма; послéдовательность	1. order, system 2. to unite 3. all, together
～一 tǒngyī еди́нство; еди́ный	to unify, unite, integrate; unified, centralized
～括 tǒngkuò подводи́ть итóг; резюми́ровать	to generalize, sum up, summarize, recapitulate
～治 tǒngzhì управля́ть; госпóдствовать; госпóдствующий	to rule, dominate
～计 tǒngjì стати́стика; статисти́ческий	1. statistics 2. to add up, count
～制 tǒngzhì контрóль; диктáт	to control; control
跳 tiào 1. пры́гать, скакáть 2. танцевáть	1. to jump 2. to palpitate 3. to skip (over)
～伞 tiàosǎn пры́гать с парашю́том	to parachute, bail out; parachute jumping
～舞 tiàowǔ танцевáть; тáнцы	to dance

跳板 tiàobǎn 1. трампли́н 2. трап	gangplank, springboard
挑 tiāo 1. нести́ на коромы́сле 2. выбира́ть, подбира́ть	1. to select, pick 2. to carry 3. to prick/lance 4. carrying-pole load
～ tiǎo подстрека́ть, провоци́ровать; дразни́ть	1. to push/poke sth. up 2. to instigate, incite, provoke 3. rising stroke (in calligraphy)
～衅 tiǎoxìn провоци́ровать; провока́ция	to provoke
～拨 tiǎobō подстрека́ть, провоци́ровать	to incite, sow discord
～选 tiāoxuǎn выбира́ть	to choose, select
～战 tiǎozhàn 1. провоци́ровать войну́ 2. вызыва́ть на соревнова́ние; броса́ть вы́зов	to challenge to battle/contest; challenge
桃 táo пе́рсиковое де́рево; пе́рсик	peach
抛 pāo отбро́сить, бро́сить, вы́бросить	1. to throw, toss, fling 2. to leave behind, cast aside
～弃 pāoqì оста́вить; отказа́ться от	to abandon, forsake, cast aside
尤:尤其 yóuqí в осо́бенности; тем бо́лее	especially, particularly
优 yōu отли́чный, прекра́сный, превосхо́дный	1. excellent, superior 2. ample, abundant 3. free, leisurely
～胜 yōushèng превосходя́щий, подавля́ющий	winning, superior
～待 yōudài 1. хорошо́ обраща́ться 2. льго́ты	to give preferential/special treatment; preference
～等 yōuděng первокла́сный, отли́чный	high-class, first-rate
～秀 yōuxiù лу́чший; прекра́сный; отли́чно	outstanding, excellent
～越 yōuyuè превосходи́ть; преиму́щество, превосхо́дство	superior, outstanding
～先权 yōuxiānquán приорите́т	priority, preference
～点 yōudiǎn досто́инство; плюс	merit, strong/good point, advantage
扰 rǎo меша́ть, беспоко́ить; производи́ть беспоря́док	to disturb, bother
～乱 rǎoluàn дезорганизо́вывать; наруша́ть	to throw into disorder

跳挑桃抛尤优扰

犹: 犹太复国主义 **yóutài fùguózhǔyì** сиони́зм	Zionism
就 **jiù 1.** и́менно, как ра́з; сейча́с же, неме́дленно **2.** относи́тельно, что каса́ется **3.** приступи́ть *(к исполне́нию)*	1. to move towards 2. to undertake, engage in 3. to accomplish, make 4. to accommodate oneself to, suit 5. to go with 6. concerning 7. then 8. at once 9. exactly 10. only, just 11. even if
～任 **jiùrèn** приступи́ть к исполне́нию обя́занностей	to take up one's post
～业 **jiùyè** быть при де́ле; за́нятость; за́нятый	to get or take up a job
～是 **jiùshì 1.** и́менно; то́ есть **2.** то́лько	1. to be 2. quite right, exactly, precisely 3. even if, even
～寝 **jiùqǐn** лечь спать; усну́ть	to retire for the night, go to bed
～地 **jiùdì** на ме́сте	on the spot
龙 **lóng** драко́н	1. dragon 2. dinosaur 3. imperial
～头 **lóngtóu** кран *(водопрово́дный)*	1. tap, faucet 2. leader of sect, secret society, etc. 3. bicycle handlebar
无 **wú** не име́ться, отсу́тствовать; не-, без-	1. there is not, not to have 2. no, not, without 3. nothing, nil
～耻 **wúchǐ** бессты́дный, на́глый	shameless, brazen
～益 **wúyì** бесполе́зный	useless, unprofitable
～所谓 **wúsuǒwèi** всё равно́, безразли́чно	1. to be indifferent 2. not to matter 3. can't be considered as
～聊 **wúliáo** мра́чный, уны́лый; неинтере́сный	1. bored 2. senseless, silly, stupid 3. boring
～神论 **wúshénlùn** атеи́зм	atheism
～价 **wújià** бесце́нный	priceless
～谓 **wúwèi** беспо́мощный	pointless, senseless
～用 **wúyòng** бесполе́зный, нену́жный	useless
～产者 **wúchǎngzhe** пролета́рий; пролета́рский	proletarian
～产阶级 **wúchǎnjiējí** пролетариа́т; пролета́рский	Proletariat
～限 **wúxiàn** безграни́чный, беспреде́льный	infinite, limitless
～疑 **wúyí** несомне́нно	beyond doubt, undoubtedly
～故 **wúgù** беспричи́нный	without cause/reason
～敌 **wúdí** непобеди́мый	unmatched, invincible
～效 **wúxiào** недействи́тельный	1. of/to no avail 2. null and void

无线电 **wúxiàndiàn** ра́дио	radio
～比 **wúbǐ** несравни́мый, беспримéрный	unparalleled, matchless
～论 **wúlùn** незави́симо от; без разли́чия	no matter what/how, etc., regardless
～机 **wújī** неоргани́ческий	inorganic
～軌电车 **wúguǐ diànchē** тролле́йбус	trackless trolley, trolley bus
～私 **wúsī** бескоры́стный	disinterested, unselfish
～偿 **wúcháng** безвозме́здный	free, gratis, gratuitous
抚 **fǔ 1.** бере́чь, забо́титься; подде́рживать **2.** успока́ивать, утеша́ть **3.** гла́дить, погла́живать	1. to comfort, console 2. to nurture, foster 3. to stroke
～恤 **fǔxù** помога́ть, подде́рживать	to comfort the bereaved
～养 **fǔyǎng** опека́ть	to foster, raise, bring up
～摩 **fǔmó** гла́дить, погла́живать	to stroke, fondle
既 **jì** поско́льку	1. already, then, later on 2. complete, full
～然 **jìrán** поско́льку	since, as, now that
概 **gài** обобща́ть; обобще́ние; в о́бщем	1. without exception, categorically 2. general, approximate
～括 **gàikuò** обобща́ть; обобще́ние	to summarize, generalize; briefly, in broad outline
～念 **gàiniàn** поня́тие, представле́ние	concept, conception, notion, idea
耽:耽误 **dānwu 1.** заде́рживаться, опа́здывать **2.** вреди́ть де́лу *(промедлением)*	to delay, hold up
枕:枕头 **zhěntou** поду́шка	pillow
免 **miǎn** освобожда́ть(ся); быть свобо́дным от	1. to exempt, excuse 2. to dismiss, fire 3. to avoid, refrain from 4. not to be\\ \\allowed to
～得 **miǎnde** во избежа́ние; что́бы не	so as not to, so as to avoid
～职 **miǎnzhí** освободи́ть от до́лжности	to remove sb. from office
～费 **miǎnfèi** беспла́тный	to be free of charge; gratis
晚 **wǎn 1.** ве́чер **2.** по́здно; по́здний **3.** по́сле, пото́м	1. evening, night 2. late, far on in time 3. younger, junior
～上(间) **wǎnshang(jiān)** ве́чером	evening
～饭 **wǎnfàn** у́жин	supper, dinner

晚会 **wǎnhuì** вéчер, вечери́н-	evening entertainment/party
ка	-
挽 **wǎn 1.** тяну́ть, тащи́ть **2.**	1. to pull, draw 2. to roll/coil up 3. to
восстанáвливать *(поло-*	lament sb.'s death
жение)	-
～救 **wǎnjiù** спасти́ положé-	to save, remedy
ние	-
勉 **miǎn 1.** старáться, прила-	1. to strive to 2. to exhort to
гáть уси́лия **2.** воодушев-	-
ля́ть; побуждáть	-
～励 **miǎnlì** *см.* 勉 2	to encourage, urge
～强 **miǎnqiǎng 1.** чéрез си́-	1. to force sb. to do sth. 2. to do with
лу, с трудóм **2.** постарáть-	difficulty 3. unconvincing, strained 4.
ся	reluctantly, grudgingly
兔 **tù** зáяц; крóлик	hare, rabbit
蔬:蔬菜 **shūcài** óвощи	vegetables, greens
梳 **shū** причёсываться, рас-	to comb; comb
чёсывать; грéбень; расчёс-	-
ка	-
流 **liú** течь; течéние; потóк	1. to flow 2. to drift 3. to spread 4. to
～星 **liúxīng** метеóр	degenerate 5. to banish 6. flow 7. rate,\\
～血 **liúxuè** проливáть кровь;	to bleed, shed blood \\class, grade
кровопроли́тие; кровопро-	-
ли́тный	-
～亡 **liúwáng** эмигрáция	to go into exile
～利 **liúlì** глáдкий, плáвный;	fluent, smooth
свобóдный, бéглый *(о ре-*	-
чи)	-
～行 **liúxíng** имéть хождé-	to spread, rage (of a contagious dis-
ние; распространённый,	ease)
общепри́нятый	-
～行病 **liúxíngbìng** эпидé-	epidemic disease
мия	-
～动 **liúdòng 1.** течь, ли́ться	1. to flow 2. to go from place to place
2. передвижнóй	3. mobile
～派 **liúpài** направлéние,	school, sect
шкóла	-
～放 **liúfàng** ссылáть; ссы́л-	1. to banish, exile 2. to float logs down-
ка	stream
～通 **liútōng** находи́ться в	to circulate
обращéнии; циркули́ро-	-
вать	-
～氓 **liúmáng** бродя́га, бо-	1. hoodlum, hooligan, gangster 2. hooli-
ся́к; хулигáн	ganism, indecency

荒 **huāng** **1.** неурожа́й; го́лод **2.** пусты́рь; запу́щенный, забро́шенный	1. waste 2. desolate 3. famine, lean year 4. rusty, out of practice 5. short of, wanting 6. fantastic, absurd 7. waste-\\ \\ land 8. to neglect
～年 **huāngnián** неурожа́йный год	famine/lean year -
～谬 **huāngmiù** оши́бочный, абсу́рдный, вздо́рный	absurd, preposterous -
～地 **huāngdì** целина́	wasteland, undeveloped land
慌 **huāng** быть в смяте́нии	1. to lose self-possession, panic 2. fran-\\ \\tic 3. frightfully
～忙 **huāngmáng** поспе́шно, торопли́во; растеряно	in a great hurry -
谎 **huǎng** лгать; ложь, обма́н	lie, falsehood -
～言(话) **huǎngyán(huà)** ложь; сплётни	lie, falsehood -

⺄, ⺃, 乙

讯 **xùn** спра́шивать; запра́шивать; допра́шивать; опро́с; запро́с; допро́с	1. message, dispatch 2. to interrogate, question -
～问 **xùnwèn** допра́шивать; допро́с	1. to interrogate, question 2. to ask about, inquire
气 **qì** **1.** газ; во́здух; пар; возду́шный **2.** дыха́ние **3.** настрое́ние; хара́ктер, нрав **4.** кли́мат; пого́да	1. air, gas 2. smell 3. spirit, vigor, morale 4. tone, atmosphere, attitude 5. anger 6. to anger 7. to get angry -
～压 **qìyā** атмосфе́рное давле́ние	atmospheric pressure -
～温 **qìwēn** температу́ра во́здуха	air temperature -
～节 **qìjié** времена́ го́да	integrity, moral courage
～候 **qìhòu** кли́мат; климати́ческий	climate -
～体 **qìtǐ** газ; газообра́зный	gas
～味 **qìwèi** **1.** за́пах **2.** вкус, накло́нности	flavor, smell -
～象 **qìxiàng** пого́да; метеорологи́ческий	1. prevailing spirit/atmosphere 2. climatic phenomenon
～氛 **qìfēn** атмосфе́ра	atmosphere, ambiance
汽 **qì** пар; газ; парово́й; га́зовый	vapor, steam -
～船 **qìchuán** теплохо́д; парохо́д; ка́тер	steamship, steamer -

汽氢氧佩风讽疯几

汽油 **qìyóu** бензи́н	gasoline
～车 **qìchē** автомоби́ль	motor vehicle, auto
～水 **qìshuǐ** газиро́ванная вода́	soft drink, soda water
氢 **qīng** водоро́д	hydrogen
氧 **yǎng** кислоро́д	oxygen
佩 **pèi** носи́ть *(на поясе, на груди)*	1. to wear 2. to admire
～服 **pèifú** уважа́ть, почита́ть	to admire
风 **fēng 1.** ве́тер **2.** нра́вы, обы́чаи; мо́да; мане́ры; стиль	1. wind 2. common practice, custom, general mood, style 3. news, information 4. to winnow 5. to put out to dry/air
～土 **fēngtǔ** приро́дные усло́вия	local conditions
～俗 **fēngsú** нра́вы, обы́чаи	custom
～格 **fēnggé** хара́ктер; мане́ра; стиль	style
～扇 **fēngshàn** вентиля́тор	electric fan
～潮 **fēngcháo 1.** волне́ния, беспоря́дки **2.** тенде́нция, тече́ние	agitation, unrest
～头 **fēngtou 1.** положе́ние, ситуа́ция **2.** изве́стность	1. trend of events 2. limelight
～味 **fēngwèi** вкус; интере́с	special flavor, local color
～光(景) **fēngguāng(jǐng)** вид; пейза́ж, ландша́фт	scene, view, sight
讽:讽刺 **fěngcì** высме́ивать; сати́ра; сарка́зм	to satirize, mock
疯 **fēng** сойти́ с ума́; сумасше́ствие; сумасше́дший	1. to spindle (of plants) 2. insane, mad
～狂 **fēngkuáng** сумасше́дший; бе́шеный	1. insane 2. frenzied,unbridled
～人 **fēngrén** сумасше́дший, умалишённый	insane (person)
飞 **fēi** лета́ть; лету́чий; лета́ющий	1. to fly 2. to hover/flutter in the air 3. to volatilize 4. unexpected, accidental 5. unfounded 6. swiftly
～船 **fēichuán** дирижа́бль	airship, dirigible
～行 **fēixíng** лета́ть; полёт	to fly; flying, flight
～快 **fēikuài** быстро, стреми́тельно	1. very fast, at lightning speed 2. extremely sharp
～机 **fēijī** самолёт	aircraft, airplane
～机场 **fēijīchǎng** аэродро́м	airport
几 **jǐ** ско́лько?	1. how many 2. a few, several, some

几 **jī 1.** почти́, о́коло **2.** не́сколько	nearly, almost, practically -
～时 **jìshí** когда́?	what time?, when?
～乎 **jīhū** почти́, о́коло; едва́ не	almost, nearly -
肌 **jī** мы́шцы, му́скулы	muscle
～肉 **jīròu** мы́шцы, му́скулы; мя́со	muscle -
机 **jī 1.** маши́на; механи́зм **2.** слу́чай, возмо́жность **3.** подви́жный; ло́вкий	1. machine 2. chance 3. occasion 4. crucial point, key link 5. organic -
～密 **jīmì** соверше́нно секре́тно	top secret -
～器 **jīqi** маши́на; механи́зм; механи́ческий	machine, machinery, apparatus -
～警 **jījǐng** ло́вкий, нахо́дчивый	sharp-witted, vigilant -
～车 **jīchē** локомоти́в; мото́рный ваго́н	1. locomotive 2. engine -
～构 **jīgòu 1.** механи́зм; аппара́т **2.** структу́ра, организа́ция, устро́йство	1. mechanism 2. office, organ, body 3. internal structure of an organization -
～场 **jīchǎng** аэродро́м	airport, airfield
～关 **jīguān 1.** организа́ция, учрежде́ние **2.** аппара́т; механи́зм	1. mechanism 2. office, organ, body 3. stratagem, scheme, intrigue 4. machine-operated
～床 **jīchuáng** стано́к	machine tool //mechanical
～械 **jīxiè** *см.* 机器	machine, machinery, mechanism;//
～能 **jīnéng** назначе́ние, роль, фу́нкция	function -
～会 **jīhuì** удо́бный слу́чай	chance, opportunity
～会主义 **jīhuìzhǔyì** оппортуни́зм	opportunism -
饥 **jī** голода́ть; го́лод; неурожа́й	to starve; hungry -
抗 **kàng** сопротивля́ться, противоде́йствовать; возража́ть	1. to resist, fight 2. to defy 3. to contend with, be a match for -
～拒 **kàngjù** сопротивля́ться	to resist, defy
～议 **kàngyì** протестова́ть; проте́ст	to protest; protest -
肮:肮脏 **āngzāng** гря́зный	dirty, filthy
航 **háng** пла́вать *(на судне)*; лета́ть *(на самолёте)*; су-	to navigate; boat, ship -

дохóдство; воздухоплáва-	-
ние	-
航空 **hángkōng** авиáция;	aviation
авиа=; аэро=	-
～行 **hángxíng** навигáция	1. to sail; sailing 2. to fly; flight
～海 **hánghǎi** мореплáвание	1. to sail the seas 2. maritime navigation
炕 **kàng** кан *(лежанка)*	brick bed warmed by fire underneath
凭 **píng** **1.** опирáться; пола-	1. to lean on/against 2. to rely/depend
гáться; на основáнии **2.**	on 3. evidence, proof, testimony 4. ac-
свидéтельство; докумéнт	cording to 5. no matter what/how
～证 **píngzhèng** доказáтель-	proof, evidence
ство, свидéтельство	-
～据 **píngjù** **1.** доказáтельст-	evidence, proof
во, свидéтельство **2.** доку-	-
мéнт; спрáвка	-
沉 **chén** **1.** утонýть; исчéз-	1. to sink 2. to keep down, to lower 3.
нуть; пропáсть **2.** глубó-	deep, profound 4. heavy
кий, сúльный	-
～重 **chénzhòng** **1.** серьёзный,	1. heavy 2. serious
вáжный **2.** тяжёлый *(о бо-*	-
лезни, положении)	-
～默 **chénmò** молчáние, ти-	1. reticent, taciturn 2. silent
шинá	-
～没 **chénmò** утонýть	to sink
壳 **ké** оболóчка; скорлупá;	1. shell 2. housing, casing, case
пáнцирь	-
亮 **liàng** свет; свéтлый, бле-	1. bright, light 2. loud and clear 3. en-
стя́щий	lightened 4. to shine 5. to show
秃 **tū** **1.** лы́сый, плешúвый;	1. bald, bare 2. blunt 3. incomplete
облысéть **2.** дефéктный, с	-
изъя́ном	-
凡 **fán** **1.** все, всё; вся́кий,	1. this mortal world, the earth 2. out-
кáждый **2.** обы́чный, зау-	line 3. commonplace, ordinary 4. all,
ря́дный	every, any 5. altogether
巩 **gǒng** укрепля́ть; крéпкий,	to consolidate
прóчный	-
～固 **gǒnggù** *см.* 巩	to consolidate, strengthen, solidify
帆 **fān** пáрус	sail
～布 **fānbù** парусúна; бре-	canvas
зéнт	-
赢 **yíng** вы́играть, победúть	to gain, win; gain, win
九 **jiǔ** дéвять	1. nine 2. many, numerous
～月 **jiǔyuè** сентя́брь	1. September 2. 9th lunar month/moon
仇 **chóu** ненавúдеть; мстить	1. enemy, foe 2. hatred, enmity

仇恨 **chóuhèn** ненави́деть; вражда́, не́нависть	to hate; hatred, enmity
～视 **chóushì** ненави́деть, вражде́бно относи́ться	to regard as an enemy, look upon with hatred
轨 **guǐ** ре́льсы; колея́	1. rail, track 2. course, path
～道 **guǐdào** 1. ре́льсы, путь 2. орби́та	1. track 2. orbit, trajectory 3. course, path
究 **jiū** иссле́довать, рассле́довать	1. to study carefully, investigate, go into 2. actually, really, after all
～竟 **jiūjìng** в конце́ концо́в	1. actually 2. after all 3. outcome
执 **zhí** держа́ть(ся); бра́ть (-ся)	1. to hold in the hand 2. to persist in 3. to implement, carry out 4. to direct
～行 **zhíxíng** исполня́ть, приводи́ть в исполне́ние; исполни́тельный	to carry out, execute; executive
～政 **zhízhèng** стоя́ть у вла́сти; пра́вящий	to hold power, govern
瓦 **wǎ** 1. черепи́ца, гонча́рные изде́лия 2. *сокр.* ватт	1. tile 2. earthenware 3. (loan w.) watt
～斯 **wǎsī** газ	(loan w.) gas
～解 **wǎjiě** распада́ться, разлага́ться; распа́д	to disintegrate, collapse
瓶 **píng** буты́лка; флако́н; ва́за	1. bottle, vase, flask 2. (M. for bottles, etc.)
瓷 **cí** фарфо́р; фарфо́ровые изде́лия	porcelain, china
亿 **yì** сто миллио́нов	hundred million
乞 **qǐ** проси́ть, выпра́шивать	to beg (for alms, etc.), supplicate
～丐 **qǐgài** ни́щий	beggar
吃 **chī** 1. есть; пить 2. впи́тывать, поглоща́ть; втя́гивать 3. подверга́ться; переноси́ть, терпе́ть	1. to eat 2. to have one's meals 3. to live on 4. to annihilate, wipe out 5. to absorb, soak up 6. to suffer, incur 7. to exhaust, be a strain
～苦 **chīkǔ** му́читься, страда́ть	to bear hardship
～亏 **chīkuī** понести́ убы́ток	1. to suffer loss, come to grief 2. unfortunately
～力 **chīlì** трудоёмкий; с трудо́м, че́рез си́лу	to entail strenuous effort, be a strain
～饭 **chīfàn** ку́шать, есть	1. to eat, have a meal 2. to keep alive, make a living
～惊 **chījīng** пуга́ться	to be startled, shocked/amazed
艺 **yì** иску́сство; мастерство́; те́хника	1. skill, craftsmanship 2. art
～术 **yìshù** иску́сство; худо́жественный	1. art 2. skill

挖
不

挖 **wā** рыть, копа́ть; ковыря́ть	to dig, excavate
不 **bù** не; нет	1. not 2. no
～但 **bùdàn** не то́лько; 不但...而且... не то́лько..., но и...	not only
～堪 **bùkān** невыноси́мо	1. utterly 2. can't bear/stand
～如 **bùrú** 1. *перед сущ.* уступа́ть в, быть ху́же 2. *перед гл.* лу́чше [уж]	1. to be unequal/inferior to 2. it would be better to
～管 **bùguǎn** 1. не име́ть отноше́ния 2. несмотря́ на, вопреки́	1. no matter, regardless of 2. to pay no heed to
～惜 **bùxī** не остана́вливаться пе́ред; не бре́згать, не гнуша́ться	1. not to stint 2. not to hesitate (to do sth.)
～错 **bùcuò** 1. пра́вильно, ве́рно 2. неплохо́й; непло́хо	1. correct 2. yes 3. (coll.) not bad, pretty good
～相容 **bùxiāngróng** несовмести́мый	incompatible
～断 **bùduàn** непреры́вный; непреры́вно	unceasingly, continuously
～行 **bùxíng** нельзя́; не годи́тся	1. won't do/work 2. to be no good 3. not be permitted
～得不 **bùdé bù** быть вы́нужденным	cannot but, to have to
～同 **bùtóng** ра́зница, отли́чие; ра́зный	not alike, different; difference
～朽 **bùxiǔ** неувяда́емый, бессме́ртный	immortal (of fame, etc.)
～久 **bùjiǔ** недо́лго; вско́ре	1. soon, before long 2. soon after
～足 **bùzú** нехва́тка; недоста́точный	1. not to be enough 2. not to be worth (doing) 3. cannot, should not
～是 **bùshì** не, нет, не явля́ется	no, not be
bùshi оши́бка; вина́	fault, blame
～仅 **bùjǐn** не то́лько	not only
～过 **bùguò** 1. но, одна́ко 2. то́лько, всего́ лишь	1. but, however, only 2. merely, only
～通 **bùtōng** 1. не сообща́ться с; не пропуска́ть 2. быть непоня́тным	1. to be obstructed 2. not to make sense

不论 **bùlùn** безразли́чно, что бы ни́; незави́симо	no matter (how/who/what, etc.)
～顾 **bùgù** пренебрега́ть; вопреки́, несмотря́ на	1. to ignore 2. in spite of, regardless of
～必 **bùbì** не обяза́тельно, не ну́жно	need not, not have to
～然 **bùrán** в проти́вном слу́чае, и́на́че	1. not so 2. no 3. or else, otherwise, if not
坏 **huài** 1. плохо́й, него́дный 2. испо́ртиться, слома́ться	1. bad 2. evil, harmful 3. spoiled 4. awfully, very 5. to spoil 6. dirty trick,\\evil idea
～处 **huàichu** поро́ки; недоста́тки	harm, disadvantage, defect
环 **huán** 1. кольцо́; кольцево́й 2. окружа́ть	1. ring 2. link 3. to surround, encircle //around
～绕 **huánrào** окружа́ть	1. to surround, encircle 2. to revolve//
～境 **huánjìng** обстано́вка, ситуа́ция; среда́, окруже́ние	environment, surroundings, circumstances
怀 **huái** 1. па́зуха 2. содержа́ть в себе́, таи́ть 3. ду́мы, забо́ты	1. bosom 2. mind, heart, state of mind 3. to think of, miss 4. to cherish 5. to conceive (a child)
～孕 **huáiyùn** быть бере́менной	to be pregnant
～疑 **huáiyí** сомнева́ться; относи́ться с подозре́нием (недове́рием)	to doubt, suspect; doubt, suspicion
～抱 **huáibào** 1. держа́ть на рука́х; обнима́ть 2. жела́ть, стреми́ться к	1. to cherish 2. ambition 3. embrace
～念 **huáiniàn** ду́мать о, мечта́ть	to cherish the memory of, think of
杯 **bēi** рю́мка; стака́н	1. cup 2. (prize) cup, trophy
以 **yǐ** 1. *предлог; употр. при дополн.:* 给农民以土地 дать зе́млю крестья́нам 2. *союз* что́бы; для того́, что́бы; ввиду́ того́, что	1. using, taking 2. from a point on (e.g., in a text) 3. because of 4. in order to, so as to 5. take/regard (as) (i.e., indicator of direct/indirect object)
～上 **yǐshàng** 1. вы́ше; све́рху; над 2. бо́лее, свы́ше	1. more than, over, above 2. the above/foregoing/above-mentioned
～至 **yǐzhì** вплоть до	1. down/up to 2. to such an extent as to
～后 **yǐhòu** по́сле; по́сле того́, как	after, afterwards, later, hereafter
～外 **yǐwài** 1. кро́ме; кро́ме того́ 2. снару́жи, вне	beyond, outside, other than, except

以下 **yǐxià** **1.** ни́же; сни́зу **2.**	(suf.) 1. below, under 2. the following
ме́нее	-
～前 **yǐqián** ра́ньше, пре́жде;	before, formerly, previously
до	-
～内 **yǐnèi** внутри́; в преде́-	(suf.) within, less than
лах	-
～为 **yǐwéi** полага́ть, счита́ть	to think/believe/consider erroneously
～来 **yǐlái** с того́ вре́мени,	(suf.) since
как	-
～及 **yǐjí** а та́кже; и	as well as, along with, and
～便 **yǐbiàn** для того́, что́бы	so that, in order to, with the aim of
～免 **yǐmiǎn** во избежа́ние;	in order to avoid, so as not to
что́бы не	-
似 **sì** **1.** быть похо́жим, по-	1. to be similar/like 2. to seem, appear
ходи́ть на **2.** как бу́дто,	-
ка́жется	-
拟 **nǐ** **1.** плани́ровать, наме-	1. to draw up, draft 2. to intend, plan
ча́ть **2.** предполага́ть, на-	3. to imitate
мерева́ться **3.** подража́ть,	-
копи́ровать	-
～订(定) **nǐdìng(dìng)** наме́-	to draw up, formulate
тить, заплани́ровать	-
咳 **ké** ка́шлять	to cough
～嗽 **késòu** ка́шлять; ка́шель	to cough
孩 **hái** ребёнок, дитя́	child
～子 **háiz** *см.* 孩	child, children, son, daughter
核 **hé** **1.** ко́сточка **2.** *физ., би-*	1. nut, kernel 2. nucleus 3. to investi-
ол. ядро́ **3.** рассма́тривать	gate, verify
～算 **hésuàn** рассчи́тывать;	business accounting
вычисля́ть	-
～子 **héz** **1.** ко́сточка **2.** ядро́;	(phys.) nucleon
я́дерный	-
～桃 **hétao** гре́цкий оре́х	walnut
～心 **héxīn** сердцеви́на; яд-	nucleus, core, kernel
ро́	-
该 **gāi** **1.** сле́дует, необходи́-	1. ought to, should 2. to be sb.'s turn
мо, до́лжно **2.** заслу́жи-	to do sth. 3. to deserve 4. to owe 5.
вать, сто́ить **3.** да́нный;	this, that, the said/given
вышеука́занный	-
六 **liù** шесть	six
～月 **liùyuè** ию́нь	1. June 2. sixth lunar month
兴 **xīng** **1.** поднима́ть, разви-	1. to prosper, rise, prevail 2. to start,
ва́ть; возрожда́ть **2.** про-	begin 3. to encourage, promote 4. to
цвета́ть; подъём, расцве́т	get up, rise 5. to permit 6. perhaps

兴 **xìng 1.** ра́доваться **2.** интере́с	mood/desire to do sth., interest, excitement
～奋 **xīngfèn** воодушевля́ть(-ся), вдохновля́ть(ся); воодушевле́ние, подъём	1. excited 2. (physiol.) excitation, stimulation
～趣 **xìngqù** интере́с, заинтересо́ванность	interest(s), tastes
～建 **xīngjiàn** стро́ить, прокла́дывать *(дорогу)*	to build, construct
兵 **bīng** солда́т; во́йско	1. weapons, arms 2. (rank-and-file) soldier 3. army, troops 4. military
～士 **bīngshì** солда́т	
～役 **bīngyì** вое́нная слу́жба	military service
宾 **bīn** гость	guest
～馆 **bīnguǎn 1.** гости́ница **2.** резиде́нция	guesthouse
共 **gòng 1.** о́бщий, совме́стный **2.** всего́, итого́	1. together 2. altogether, in all 3. common, general 4. to share, possess in common
～和国 **gònghéguó** респу́блика	republic
～计 **gòngjì** всего́, итого́	to amount to, add up to, total
～存 **gòngcún** *см.* 共处	to coexist
～青团 **gòngqīngtuán** комсомо́л	(abbr.) Communist Youth League
～青团员 **gòngqīngtuányuán** комсомо́лец	(abbr.) Communist Youth League member
～同 **gòngtóng** совме́стный, о́бщий	1. common 2. joint
～产主义 **gòngchǎnzhǔyì** коммуни́зм	communism
～产党 **gòngchǎndǎng** коммунисти́ческая па́ртия	Communist Party
～产党员 **gòngchǎndǎngyuán** коммуни́ст, член коммунисти́ческой па́ртии	Communist Party member
～处 **gòngchǔ** сосуществова́ть; сосуществова́ние	to coexist
供 **gōng 1.** снабжа́ть, поставля́ть **2.** дава́ть показа́ния	1. to supply, feed 2. to be for (the use/convenience of)
～ **gòng** подноше́ние, приноше́ние	1. to offer sacrifices; sacrifices 2. to confess, own up to 3. deposition
～应 **gōngyìng** снабжа́ть; удовлетворя́ть *(спрос)*	to supply
～给 **gōngjǐ** снабжа́ть; снабже́ние; *воен.* дово́льствие	to supply, provide, furnish

供烘洪翼粪其棋旗舆具俱真填

供词 gōngcí *юр.* показáния	statement/confession made under\\
烘 hōng печь; жáрить; сушить	1. to dry/warm by fire \\interrogation 2. to bake 3. to contrast
洪 hóng разли́в; наводнéние	1. big, vast 2. flood
翼 yì крылó; кры́лья	1. wing 2. flank 3. to protect, assist
粪 fèn кал; помёт; навóз	1. excrement, dung 2. to apply manure
其 qí егó; их; тот; те	his, hers, its, their, he, she, it, that
~中 qízhōng среди́ них, в том числé	in/among (it/them/which, etc.) -
~实 qíshí факти́чески, в действи́тельности, на сáмом дéле; по существý	as a matter of fact, actually, in fact - -
~他 qítā прóчие, други́е	1. others, the rest 2. other, else
~余 qíyú остальны́е	others, the rest //in a board game
棋 qí шáхматы; шáшки	chess/chess-like game, piece used//
旗 qí флаг; знáмя	banner, emblem
~手 qíshǒu знаменóсец	standard-bearer, flagman
~帜 qízhì *см.* 旗	1. banner, flag 2. rallying point, stand
舆 yú 1. мáссы; мáссовый 2. кýзов *(машины)*; *ж.-д.* платфóрма	1. public, popular 2. carriage, chariot 3. area, territory -
~论 yúlùn общéственное мнéние	public opinion -
具 jù 1. орýдие; ýтварь; инвентáрь 2. имéть, обладáть	1. utensil, tool, implement 2. talent 3. to possess, have 4. to provide 5. fully
~备 jùbèi имéть(ся) в нали́чии	to possess, have, be provided with -
~有 jùyǒu *см.* 具 2	to possess, have, be provided with
~体 jùtǐ конкрéтный	concrete, specific, particular
俱 jù всё, целикóм	all, complete
~乐部 jùlèbù клуб	(loan w.) (social) club
真 zhēn 1. настоя́щий, пóдлинный, и́стинный 2. и́скренний, правди́вый	1. true, real, genuine 2. really, truly, indeed 3. clearly -
~理 zhēnlǐ прáвда, и́стина	truth
~正 zhēnzhèng настоя́щий, пóдлинный, и́стинный	genuine, true, real -
~实 zhēnshí действи́тельный, реáльный	true, real, authentic -
~诚 zhēnchéng и́скренний, чистосердéчный	sincere, genuine, true -
填 tián 1. наполня́ть; начиня́ть 2. заполня́ть *(бланк, анкету)*	to fill in, stuff - -

填写 **tiánxiě** *см.* 填 2	to fill in a form
镇 **zhèn** подавля́ть, усмиря́ть; репресси́ровать	to press down, keep down - //execute a counterrevolutionary
～压 **zhènyā** *см.* 镇	1. to suppress, repress, put down 2. to//
典 **diǎn 1.** образцо́вый; класси́ческий **2.** зако́н; пра́вила	1. to mortgage 2. to be in charge of 3. standard 4. allusion 5. ceremony 6. dictionary 7. canon
～型 **diǎnxíng** образе́ц, приме́р; класси́ческий	1. typical case, model, type 2. typical, representative
～礼 **diǎnlǐ** торжество́, церемо́ния	ceremony, celebration -
～范 **diǎnfàn** образе́ц, станда́рт	model, example -
只 **zhī 1.** оди́н из па́ры; едини́чный **2.** *сч. сл. для единичных предметов*	1. single 2. (M. for animals/vessels/one of a pair of things/some utensils) -
～ **zhǐ** то́лько, лишь	only, merely
～好 **zhǐhǎo** лу́чше всего́; остаётся лишь	to have to, be forced to, can only, may as well just, have no choice but (to)
织 **zhī 1.** ткать; тка́ный **2.** организо́вывать	1. to weave 2. to knit -
职 **zhí** обя́занности; слу́жба; до́лжность	1. duty, job 2. post, office -
～工 **zhígōng** рабо́чие и слу́жащие	workers and staff members -
～业 **zhíyè** заня́тие, профе́ссия	occupation, profession, vocation -
～位 **zhíwèi** до́лжность; пост	position, post
～员 **zhíyuán** слу́жащий	office worker, staff member, functionary
积 **jī** собира́ть, скла́дывать; нака́пливать	1. to amass, store up, accumulate 2. long-standing, age-old 3. product
～极 **jījí** акти́вный	1. positive 2. active, energetic, vigorous
～肥 **jīféi** загота́вливать удобре́ния	to collect farmyard manure -
～累 **jīlěi** нака́пливать; скопле́ние	to accumulate -
识 **shí** знать; познава́ть; зна́ния	to know, recognize; recognition -
～字 **shízì** быть гра́мотным	to learn to read, be/become literate
贝 **bèi 1.** двуство́рчатая ра́ковина **2.** сокро́вище, драгоце́нность	1. shellfish 2. cowrie - -
坝 **bà** да́мба; плоти́на	1. dam 2. dike, embankment 3. sandbar
贡 **gòng** подноси́ть, дари́ть	tribute

贡献 **gòngxiàn** сде́лать вклад *(в общее дело)*; вклад	to contribute, dedicate, devote; contribution
责 **zé 1.** быть отве́тственным за; отве́тственность; обя́занность **2.** порица́ть, осужда́ть	1. duty, responsibility 2. to demand 3. to interrogate 4. to blame, reprove 5. to punish
～任 **zérèn** *см.* 责 1	1. duty, responsibility 2. blame
～备 **zébèi** укоря́ть, упрека́ть, выгова́ривать	to blame, reprove; blame, reproof
～罚 **zéfá** нака́зывать; налага́ть взыска́ние	to punish
～成 **zéchéng** поручи́ть; обяза́ть	to enjoin, charge (sb.) with a task
债 **zhài** долг; заём	debt
贵 **guì 1.** дорого́й, це́нный **2.** уважа́емый; зна́тный; Ваш	1. expensive, costly 2. highly valued 3. noble, of high rank 4. (abbr.) Guizhou
～姓 **guìxìng** как Ва́ша фами́лия?	(May I ask) your (family) name?
～重 **guìzhòng** высоко́ цени́ть; уважа́ть	valuable, precious
～族 **guìzú** аристокра́тия	aristocrat, noble
溃 **kuì** прорва́ть(ся), ло́пнуть; разру́шиться; слома́ться	1. to burst (dam) 2. to break through (an encirclement) 3. to be routed 4. to fester, ulcerate
～败 **kuìbài** потерпе́ть пораже́ние	1. to be defeated/routed 2. to fester
员 **yuán 1.** слу́жащий; персона́л **2.** член *(организации)* **3.** *суф. сущ. со знач. профессии, напр.:* 车务员 проводни́к	(suf.) member, -er, -ist, etc.
损 **sǔn 1.** уменьша́ть(ся); сокраща́ть(ся) **2.** вреди́ть, по́ртить; наноси́ть уще́рб	1. to decrease, lose 2. to harm, damage 3. to be sarcastic/caustic 4. to be mean/shabby
～害 **sǔnhài** *см.* 损 2	to harm, damage, injure
～伤 **sǔnshāng** испо́ртить, полома́ть	1. to harm, damage, injure 2. loss
～失 **sǔnshī** поте́ря, убы́ток, уще́рб	to lose; loss
～坏 **sǔnhuài** *см.* 损伤	to damage, injure
贺 **hè** поздравля́ть	to congratulate
～年 **hènián** поздравля́ть с Но́вым го́дом	to extend New Year's greetings, pay a New Year's call

贺电 **hèdiàn** поздрави́тельная телегра́мма	congratulatory telegram -
贯 **guàn** прони́зывать, проходи́ть насквозь	1. to pass through, cross 2. to be versed in 3. to link up 4. to hit a target
~穿 **guànchuān** *см.* 贯	1. to run through, penetrate 2. to connect
~彻 **guànchè** доводи́ть до конца́	to carry out, implement - //habitual, customary
惯 **guàn** привы́чка; обы́чай	1. to be used to 2. to indulge, spoil 3.//
侦 **zhēn** следи́ть; разузнава́ть	to detect, scout, investigate -
~探 **zhēntàn** разве́дывать; разве́дка; разве́дчик	to do detective work; detective; spy -
~察 **zhēnchá** разве́дывать; разве́дка	to investigate (a crime) -
质 **zhì** 1. вещество́, мате́рия 2. ка́чество, сво́йство	1. nature, character 2. quality, matter 3. to question 4. to pledge 5. simple\\
~量 **zhìliàng** ка́чество	1. quality 2. (phys.) mass \\6. sincere
~问 **zhìwèn** сде́лать запро́с, запра́шивать; запро́с	to question, call to account -
喷 **pēn** бры́згать; изверга́ть; источа́ть	1. to spurt, spout, gush 2. to spray, sprinkle
~水 **pēnshuǐ** 1. фонта́н 2. душ	fountain -
~气式 **pēnqìshì** *тех.* реакти́вный	jet-propelled -
愤 **fèn** возмуща́ться, негодова́ть	indignation, anger, resentment -
~慨 **fènkǎi** возмуща́ться; возмущённо	to be indignant (at injustice) -
~怒 **fènnù** возмуще́ние, гнев, негодова́ние	indignant, angry - //3. to covet, seek, hanker after
贪 **tān** жа́дный, а́лчный	1. to be corrupt 2. to desire insatiably//
~污 **tānwū** брать взя́тки; корру́пция	corrupt, venal; corruption, graft -
~欲(心) **tānyù(xīn)** жа́дность, а́лчность	to take bribes, practice graft -
负 **fù** 1. нести́ на себе́ 2. быть отве́тственным; отве́тственность; отве́тственный 3. подверга́ться 4. наруша́ть *(слово)* 5. проигра́ть, потерпе́ть пораже́ние	1. to carry on the back/shoulder, bear 2. to bear (responsibility) 3. to rely on 4. to suffer 5. to enjoy 6. to owe (money) 7. to betray, abandon, go against 8. to lose, be defeated 9. minus, negative - //cumbrance
~担 **fùdān** 1. но́ша, бре́мя,	to bear, shoulder; burden, load, en-//

тя́готы **2.** нести́ отве́тствен-	-
ность	-
负约 **fùyuē** наруша́ть дого-	to break a promise
во́р	-
～伤 **fùshāng** получи́ть ра-	to be wounded/injured
не́ние	- //of 2. conscientious
～责 **fùzé** *см.* 负 2	1. to be responsible for, be in charge//
懒 **lǎn** лени́ться; лени́вый	1. lazy 2. sluggish, languid
～惰 **lǎnduò** лени́ться; лень;	lazy, indolent
лени́вый	-
贸:贸易 **màoyì** торгова́ть;	tirade
торго́вля	-
贫 **pín** **1.** нужда́, бе́дность;	1. poor, impoverished 2. inadequate,
бе́дный, неиму́щий **2.** не-	deficient 3. garrulous, loquacious
доста́точный	-
～苦 **pínkǔ** *см.* 贫 1	poverty-stricken
～农 **pínnóng** крестья́нин-	poor peasant
-бедня́к	-
～乏 **pínfá** недоста́точный,	poor, lacking
ску́дный	-
费 **fèi** тра́тить, расхо́довать;	1. to cost, spend, expend 2. fee, dues,
расхо́ды	expenses, charge 3. wasteful
～事 **fèishì** обремени́тельный,	to give/take a lot of trouble
хло́потный	-
～用 **fèiyòng** расхо́ды, из-	cost, expenses
де́ржки	-
～力 **fèilì** трудоёмкий	to need great effort, be strenuous
～心 **fèixīn** **1.** беспоко́иться	1. to give/take a lot of trouble 2. May I
2. *вежл.* весьма́ обя́зан!,	trouble you (to do sth.)
премно́го благода́рен	-
资 **zī** **1.** сре́дства; капита́л;	1. money, expenses 2. endowment, na-
ресу́рсы **2.** приро́дные да́н-	tural ability 3. qualifications, record
ные, спосо́бности	of service 4. to subsidize, support 5.\\
～金 **zījīn** фо́нды; капита́лы	fund \\to provide, supply
～格 **zīgé** **1.** приро́дные да́н-	1. qualifications 2. seniority
ные **2.** квалифика́ция	-
(*степень подготовленно-*	-
сти); ка́чества	-
～料 **zīliào** материа́лы; сре́д-	1. means 2. data, material
ства	-
～产 **zīchǎn** иму́щество, со́б-	1. property 2. capital 3. assets
ственность	-
～产阶级 **zīchǎnjiējí** буржу-	capitalist class, bourgeoisie,
ази́я; буржуа́зный	propertied class

资本 **zīběn** капитáл	1. capital 2. sth. capitalized on
～本主义 **zīběnzhǔyì** капитали́зм	capitalism
～本家 **zīběnjiā** капитали́ст	capitalist
～源 **zīyuán** ресýрсы	natural resources
贷 **dài** давáть (дать) взаймы́	1. to loan 2. to borrow, lend 3. shift, shirk 4. to pardon
～款 **dàikuǎn** кредитовáть; креди́т	to grant a loan; loan, credit
货 **huò** товáр; груз	1. goods, commodity 2. money 3. blockhead, idiot 4. to sell
～品 **huòpǐn** товáры; товáр	types of goods/products
～币 **huòbì** дéньги; валю́та; дéнежный	money, currency
～物 **huòwù** товáр; груз; грузовóй	goods, commodity, merchandise
赞 **zàn** хвали́ть, одобря́ть	1. to support, assist 2. to praise, commend 3. eulogy
～同 **zàntóng** одóбрить, согласи́ться	to approve of, endorse
～扬 **zànyáng** хвали́ть, давáть хорóший óтзыв	to praise, commend
～美 **zànměi** восхищáться; хвали́ть	to praise, eulogize
～成 **zànchéng** одобря́ть, соглашáться	1. to approve, endorse 2. to assist
锁 **suǒ** запирáть; замóк; запóр	1. to lock up 2. to chain up 3. locksmith 4. lock 5. fetters
页 **yè** лист, страни́ца	page, leaf
项 **xiàng** 1. пункт; статья́ 2. вид; род	1. nape (of neck) 2. sum (of money) 3. (math.) term 4. (M. for items/clauses)
～目 **xiàngmù** пункт; статья́; рýбрика; раздéл	1. item, article, clause 2. project
颈 **jǐng** шéя; гóрло	neck
顺 **shùn** 1. попýтный; благоприя́тный; удóбный 2. вдоль, по 3. послéдовательный; по поря́дку 4. приводи́ть в поря́док	1. to obey, follow, submit to 2. to arrange, put in order 3. to take the opportunity to 4. to steal
～利 **shùnlì** успéшный, благоприя́тный	smooth(ly), successful(ly), without a hitch
～从 **shùncóng** повиновáться, подчиня́ться; послýшный	to submit/yield to
～便 **shùnbiàn** попýтно, при слýчае, заоднó	conveniently, in passing

资贷货赞锁页项颈顺

顶 **dǐng** **1.** верши́на, маку́шка **2.** кры́ша **3.** о́чень, весьма́	1. the crown of the head 2. top 3. to carry on the head 4. to gore, butt 5. to go against 6. to equal 7. very, most
预 **yù** зара́нее, заблаговре́менно	in advance, beforehand
～言 **yùyán** предска́зывать; предсказа́ние	to prophesize, predict, foretell; prophecy, prediction
～告 **yùgào** предупрежда́ть, предостерега́ть; предупрежде́ние	to announce in advance, herald; advance notice
～备 **yùbèi** пригото́вить; подгото́вить(ся); запасно́й, резе́рвный	to prepare, get ready; preparation
～算 **yùsuàn** сме́та; бюдже́т	1. budget 2. to calculate in advance
～防 **yùfáng** предохраня́ть, предотвраща́ть; профилакти́ческий	to prevent, guard against
～定 **yùdìng** **1.** зара́нее намеча́ть **2.** зака́зывать, резерви́ровать	to predetermine, schedule
～报 **yùbào** предска́зывать; прогно́з	to forecast; forecast
～先 **yùxiān** зара́нее, заблаговре́менно	in advance, beforehand
须 **xū** **1.** до́лжно, сле́дует, необходи́мо **2.** усы́; у́сики	1. to have to, must 2. beard, mustache 3. palpus, tassel 4. to await, wait till
～要 **xūyào** ну́жно, необходи́мо	to have to, must
颜 **yán** **1.** лицо́; нару́жность, вне́шний вид **2.** цвет, окра́ска	1. face, countenance, facial expression 2. prestige, dignity 3. color
～色 **yánsè** цвет	1. color 2. countenance, facial expres-// //sion 3. (coll.) dyestuff, pigment
烦 **fán** **1.** надоеда́ть; надое́дливый **2.** затрудня́ть, обременя́ть	1. vexed, irritated, annoyed 2. tired of 3. superfluous and confusing 4. to trouble (sb. to/for)
～杂 **fánzá** сло́жный, запу́танный	miscellaneous, complex
～扰 **fánrǎo** беспоко́ить, трево́жить	1. to bother, disturb 2. to feel disturbed
倾 **qīng** **1.** наклоня́ться; накло́н **2.** име́ть скло́нность (тенде́нцию) **3.** перевора́чиваться, опроки́дываться	1. to incline 2. to exhaust, use up 3. to admire

倾听 **qīngtīng** прислу́шиваться	to listen attentively to
～销 **qīngxiāo** продава́ть по бро́совым це́нам; де́мпинг	to dump (goods/etc.); cutthroat sale, dumping
～向 **qīngxiàng** име́ть скло́нность; тенде́нция, стремле́ние, скло́нность; укло́н	to be inclined to, side with, prefer; tendency, trend, inclination, deviation
顾 **gù** **1.** забо́титься, уделя́ть внима́ние **2.** огля́дываться	1. to turn around and look at 2. to attend to 3. to call on 4. on the contrary, instead 5. however, but 6. really
～客 **gùkè** клие́нт; покупа́тель	customer, shopper, client
～问 **gùwèn** сове́тник	adviser, consultant
顽 **wán** **1.** упря́мый, ко́сный, твердоло́бый **2.** озорно́й; непослу́шный	1. stupid, dense, insensate 2. stubborn, obstinate 3. naughty, mischievous //set against change, die-hard
～固 **wángù** *см.* 顽 1	1. obstinate, stubborn, headstrong 2.//
～皮 **wánpí** непослу́шный; озорно́й	naughty, mischievous
～强 **wánqiáng** упо́рный, насто́йчивый	indomitable, tenacious
颠 **diān** **1.** упа́сть, опроки́нуться **2.** трясти́(сь)	1. to jolt, bump 2. to fall 3. top of the head 4. summit 5. to run/go away
～倒 **diāndǎo** **1.** переверну́ть, поста́вить вверх дном **2.** извраща́ть, искажа́ть	1. to put upside down, reverse 2. confused, disorderly, topsy-turvy
～覆 **diānfù** **1.** опроки́нуться **2.** подрывно́й *(о деятельности)*	to overturn, subvert
颂 **sòng** прославля́ть, воспева́ть; о́да, похвала́	to praise, extol, laud; song, ode, eulogy
～歌 **sònggē** канта́та; гимн	song, ode
领 **lǐng** **1.** ше́я; воротни́к **2.** вести́ за собо́й, руководи́ть **3.** подве́домственный **4.** получа́ть, принима́ть	1. neck; collar, neckband 2. outline, main point 3. to lead 4. to have jurisdiction over 5. to receive, draw, get 6. to understand, grasp, comprehend
～空 **lǐngkōng** возду́шное простра́нство *(страны)*	territorial airspace
～土 **lǐngtǔ** террито́рия	territory
～袖 **lǐngxiù** вождь, ли́дер	leader
～子 **lǐngz** воротни́к; воротничо́к	collar //ship; leader
～导 **lǐngdǎo** руководи́ть; ру-	to lead, exercise leadership; leader-//

ководство	-
领导权 **lǐngdǎoquán** гегемо́ния	leadership, authority, overall control
～事 **lǐngshì** ко́нсул	consul
～带 **lǐngdài** га́лстук	1. necktie, tie 2. to lead
～海 **lǐnghǎi** территориа́льные во́ды	territorial waters
～域 **lǐngyù** о́бласть, сфе́ра	1. territory, domain, realm 2. field, sphere
黄 **huáng** жёлтый	1. yellow 2. spoiled, withered 3. (coll.) to fizzle out, fall through
～金 **huángjīn** зо́лото	gold
～昏 **huánghūn** су́мерки	dusk
～油 **huángyóu** сли́вочное ма́сло	1. butter 2. grease
～瓜 **huángguā** огуре́ц	cucumber
横 **héng** попере́чный; горизонта́льный; поперёк	1. horizontal, transverse 2. sideways, across 3. to move crosswise 4. violently 5. unrestrainedly
～ **hèng** **1.** бесчи́нствовать; своево́льный **2.** противоесте́ственный	1. harsh and unreasonable, perverse 2. unexpected
～行霸道 **héngxíng-bàdào** бесчи́нствовать	to tyrannize, domineer
～暴 **hèngbào** лю́тый, жесто́кий	cruel, tyrannical
演 **yǎn** **1.** пока́зывать, демонстри́ровать; игра́ть на сце́не; выступа́ть **2.** трениро́ваться, практикова́ться	1. to develop, evolve 2. to drill, practice 3. to perform a play, act
～习 **yǎnxí** **1.** репети́ровать, отраба́тывать; репети́ция **2.** манёвры, уче́ния	to maneuver, drill, exercise, practice
～奏 **yǎnzòu** игра́ть, исполня́ть	to give an instrumental (musical) performance
～变 **yǎnbiàn** измене́ния, переме́ны	to develop, evolve; development, evolution
～说 **yǎnshuō** речь, выступле́ние	to deliver a speech, make an address; speech, address
～员 **yǎnyuán** арти́ст, актёр	performer
小 **xiǎo** **1.** ма́ленький; ме́лкий; ма́лый **2.** незначи́тельный, сла́бый	1. small, little, pretty, minor 2. young, 3. for a moment, for a little while 4. the young 5. concubine
～型 **xiǎoxíng** миниатю́р-	small-sized, small-scale, miniature

ный; портати́вный; мини=	-
小组 **xiǎozǔ** кружо́к; гру́п-	group
па; брига́да	-
～看 **xiǎokàn** презира́ть,	(coll.) to look down upon, belittle
пренебрега́ть	-
～学 **xiǎoxué** нача́льная шко́-	primary/elementary school
ла	-
～时 **xiǎoshí** час	hour
～册子 **xiǎocèz** брошю́ра	booklet, pamphlet
～卖部 **xiǎomàibù** буфе́т;	1. small shop attached to a theater, etc.
кафе́	2. buffet, snack counter
～米 **xiǎomi** пшено́; чуми́за	millet
～麦 **xiǎomài** пшени́ца	wheat
～说 **xiǎoshuō** расска́з; по́-	fiction
весть; рома́н	-
～孩 **xiǎohái** ребёнок; де́ти	(coll.) child
～心 **xiǎoxīn** быть осторо́ж-	to be careful, take care
ным; осторо́жно!, бере-	-
ги́сь!	- //of grandchild
孙 **sūn** внук	1. grandson 2. generations below that//
示 **shì** **1.** пока́зывать; де-	1. to show, indicate 2. letter, instructions
монстри́ровать **2.** ука́зы-	-
вать; уведомля́ть	-
～威 **shìwēi** демонстри́ро-	1. to put on a show of force 2. to dem-
вать; демонстра́ция; ма-	onstrate, march; demonstration
нифеста́ция	-
标 **biāo** выража́ть, обозна-	1. to mark, sign, label 2. prize, award
ча́ть; знак, отме́тка; ма́р-	3. outward sign 4. superficiality
ка; этике́тка	-
～准 **biāozhǔn** но́рма, стан-	standard, criterion; standard
да́рт; нормати́вный; стан-	-
да́ртный	-
～语 **biāoyǔ** ло́зунг, плака́т	slogan; poster
～本 **biāoběn** образе́ц, мо-	1. specimen, sample 2. (Ch. med.) root
де́ль	cause and symptoms of disease
～题 **biāotí** загла́вие	title, heading, headline, caption
～记 **biāojì** отме́тка, знак,	token, souvenir
си́мвол	-
～识(志) **biāoshì(zhì)** зна-	to identify
менова́ть, символизи́ро-	-
вать; си́мвол	-
蒜 **suàn** чесно́к	garlic
票 **piào** **1.** биле́т; квита́н-	1. ticket 2. ballot 3. note 4. check 5.

ция; тало́н **2.** бюллете́нь *(для голосования)*	certificate 6. hostage 7. business deal 8. fast, agile, vigorous 9. to write\\ \\a ticket
漂 **piāo** пла́вать на пове́рхности	to drift, float about
～ **piǎo** промыва́ть, прополаскивать; отбе́ливать	1. to bleach 2. to rinse
～ **piào** краси́вый	to come to nothing, fall through
～亮 **piàoliang** краси́вый	1. handsome, beautiful 2. remarkable
宗 **zōng** 1. пре́дки; род **2.** уче́ние, шко́ла; се́кта	1. forefathers, ancestors 2. clan 3. faction, sect, school 4. principal aim 5.\\ \\to venerate
～派 **zōngpài** се́кта	faction; sect
～派主义 **zōngpàizhǔyì** секта́нтство	sectarianism; factionalism
～教 **zōngjiào** рели́гия	religion
综 **zōng** свя́зывать, объединя́ть; обобща́ть	to put together, sum up
～合 **zōnghé** 1. обобща́ть; обобще́ние **2.** синтези́ровать; ко́мплекс; ко́мплексный; поли=	1. to synthesize 2. comprehensive, multiple, composite
崇 **chóng** 1. возвы́шенный, благоро́дный **2.** уважа́ть; почита́ть	1. high, holy, sublime 2. to esteem, worship
～拜 **chóngbài** почита́ть; поклоня́ться; культ	to worship, adore
禁 **jìn** 1. запреща́ть; запре́т; запре́тный **2.** взять под стра́жу	to endure, stand; endurable
～止 **jìnzhǐ** запреща́ть	to prohibit, ban
～区 **jìnqū** 1. запре́тная зо́на **2.** запове́дник	1. forbidden/restricted zone 2. (wildlife/plant) preserve, reserve, natural park
～闭 **jìnbì** 1. взять под стра́жу, арестова́ть **2.** закры́ть, запрети́ть	to confine sb. (as punishment)
～运 **jìnyùn** эмба́рго	embargo; embargoed
～地 **jìndì** *см.* 禁区	forbidden/restricted area
察 **chá** иссле́довать; рассле́довать	to inspect, scrutinize
擦 **cā** вытира́ть, стира́ть; натира́ть	1. to rub, scrape, scrub 2. to polish, wipe/spread on, apply 3. to brush by
京 **jīng** столи́ца; столи́чный	1. capital of a country 2. Beijing
惊 **jīng** испуга́ть(ся), перепуга́ть(ся)	1. to startle, alarm 2. to be startled/shy, stampede 3. violent, fierce
～异(奇) **jīngyì(qí)** изум-	surprised, astounded

ля́ться, поража́ться; изумле́ние, удивле́ние	-
惊动 **jīngdòng** **1.** потрясти́; перепуга́ть **2.** трево́жить (-ся)	to alarm, disturb
～人 **jīngrén** порази́тельный	astonishing, amazing, alarming
～慌 **jīnghuāng** растеря́ться; па́ника	alarmed, scared
～心 **jīngxīn** производи́ть впечатле́ние	to make an impression
掠 **lüè** отнима́ть; похища́ть; гра́бить	1. to pillage, sack 2. to sweep/brush past, graze, skim over
～夺 **lüèduó** захва́тывать; отнима́ть, отбира́ть	to plunder, rob, pillage
凉 **liáng** **1.** охлажда́ть; остыва́ть; прохла́дный **2.** ле́тний, лёгкий	to make/become cool
～鞋 **liángxié** санда́лии	scandals
～台 **liángtái** балко́н	balcony; veranda
～快 **liángkuai** прохла́дный	to cool off; pleasantly cool
～菜 **liángcài** холо́дные заку́ски	cold dish
景 **jǐng** **1.** вид, пейза́ж **2.** обстоя́тельства, обстано́вка	1. view, scene 2. situation, condition 3. (theatr.) scenery, scene 4. to admire, esteem 5. great, grand
原 **yuán** **1.** исто́чник, нача́ло; первонача́льный; перви́чный **2.** осно́ва; причи́на **3.** равни́на **4.** проща́ть, извиня́ть	1. primary, original 2. to pardon, forgive 3. plain, plateau 4. origin, source 5. graveyard
～理 **yuánlǐ** при́нцип, основно́е положе́ние	principle, tenet
～告 **yuángào** *юр.* исте́ц	plaintiff
～始 **yuánshǐ** **1.** нача́ло; первонача́льный; перви́чный **2.** первобы́тный; примити́вный	1. original, firsthand 2. primeval, primitive
～因 **yuányīn** причи́на	cause, reason
～料 **yuánliào** сырьё; сырьево́й	raw material
～则 **yuánzé** при́нцип, пра́вило	principle
～子 **yuánzǐ** а́том; а́томный	atom

原稿 **yuángǎo** ру́копись; черно́вик	original manuscript, master copy
～状 **yuánzhuàng** ста́тус-кво́	original/previous state, status quo ante
～本 **yuánběn** оригина́л, по́длинник; первонача́льный; основно́й	1. origin 2. original copy 3. original (for a translation) 4. original bill 5. causes of an incident 6. originally, formerly
～来 **yuánlái 1.** на са́мом де́ле; ока́зывается **2.** первонача́льный; первонача́льно	1. originally, formerly 2. as a matter of fact
～谅 **yuánliàng** извиня́ть, проща́ть	to excuse, pardon (oneself)
源 **yuán** исто́чник, ключ, родни́к	1. source (of a river), fountainhead 2. source, origin
你 **nǐ** ты; твой	you
称 **chēng 1.** звать, называ́ть; назва́ние **2.** хвали́ть, одобря́ть **3.** взве́шивать на веса́х	1. to call 2. to say, state 3. to commend, praise 4. to weigh 5. name
～ **chèn** подходи́ть, соотве́тствовать	to fit, match, suit
～许 **chēngxǔ** одобря́ть	1. to praise 2. commendation
～呼 **chēnghū** называ́ть; назва́ние	1. to call, address 2. form of address
～号 **chēnghào 1.** наименова́ние, назва́ние; кли́чка **2.** зва́ние	title, name, designation
～职 **chènzhí** соотве́тствовать своему́ назначе́нию	to be competent, fill a post with credit
～赞 **chēngzàn** *см.* 称 2	to praise, acclaim, commend
素 **sù 1.** просто́й, обы́чный, повседне́вный **2.** основно́й; элемента́рный **3.** расти́тельная пи́ща; вегетариа́нский	1. white 2. plain, simple, quiet 3. vegetarian 4. native 5. basic element 6. usually, habitually, always
～性 **sùxìng** приро́да, хара́ктер	(one's) disposition/temperament
～菜 **sùcài** вегетариа́нская пи́ща	vegetarian dish
累 **lèi** устава́ть, утомля́ться	1. tired, weary 2. to tire, strain, wear//out 3. to work hard, toil
～ **lěi 1.** нава́ливать, нагроможда́ть **2.** многокра́тно; подря́д	1. to pile up, accumulate 2. to involve 3. to build by piling up

骡 luó мул	mule
螺 luó 1. ули́тка 2. спира́ль; винт; винтово́й	1. spiral shell; snail 2. fingerprint whorl
～丝 luósī резьба́; винтово́й; нарезно́й	screw
索 suǒ 1. кана́т 2. иска́ть 3. добива́ться, тре́бовать	1. to search 2. to demand, exact 3. large rope
～引 suǒyǐn и́ндекс	index
紧 jǐn 1. ту́го связа́ть; туго́й; пло́тный 2. сро́чный, э́кстренный 3. ва́жный, значи́тельный	1. to tighten; tight, taught 2. close at hand 3. urgent, tense 4. strict, stringent 5. hard up
～密 jǐnmì 1. бли́зкий, те́сный 2. пло́тный	1. close together, inseparable 2. rapid and intense
～张 jǐnzhāng обостря́ться; напряже́ние; напряжённый, о́стрый	1. nervous, keyed up 2. strained, intense, tense 3. scarce, in short supply
～急 jǐnjí сро́чный; ва́жный; крити́ческий	urgent, critical
繁 fán 1. сло́жный 2. многочи́сленный; мно́го	1. in great numbers, numerous, manifold 2. complicated 3. to propagate
～殖 fánzhí размножа́ться; размноже́ние	to breed, reproduce, propagate
～华 fánhuá пы́шный, роско́шный	flourishing, bustling, busy
～荣 fánróng процвета́ть; процвета́ние; цвету́щий	1. to make sth. prosper 2. flourishing, prosperous, booming
紫 zǐ фиоле́товый; лило́вый; бордо́; кори́чневый	purple, violet
系 xì 1. связь; генеало́гия 2. факульте́т	1. system, series 2. (college) department , faculty 3. to tie, fasten 4. to relate to 5. to be anxious
～列 xìliè се́рия; ряд	series, set
～统 xìtǒng систе́ма, поря́док	system
余 yú 1. оста́ток, изли́шек 2. свобо́дный, неза́нятый	1. surplus, remainder 2. (suf.) -odd 3. (wr.) I, me
除 chú 1. исключа́ть, не счита́ть; кро́ме; ～了…以外 за исключе́нием 2. устраня́ть, удаля́ть	1. to get rid of, eliminate, remove 2. (math) to divide 3. except 4. besides 5. doorstep
～非 chúfēi за исключе́нием, кро́ме; е́сли то́лько не	1. only if/when 2. unless
～去 chúqù отбра́сывать, устраня́ть	1. to eliminate 2. except

涂赤恭添心德志

涂 **tú** кра́сить; ма́зать; зама́зывать; штукату́рить	1. to apply, spread on 2. to scrawl 3. to blot/cross out
～改 **túgǎi** исправля́ть *(написанное)*; пра́вить, корректи́ровать	to alter
赤 **chì** **1.** кра́сный; а́лый **2.** наго́й, го́лый	1. red 2. loyal, sincere, single-hearted 3. bare, naked
～字 **chìzì** дефици́т	deficit
～道 **chìdào** эква́тор; экватори́альный	equator
恭 **gōng** почита́ть; почти́тельно, с уваже́нием...	respectful, reverent
～喜 **gōngxǐ** поздравля́ю!	congratulations
～敬 **gōngjìng** уважа́ть; почита́ть	respectful; respect
～贺 **gōnghè** поздравля́ть	to congratulate
添 **tiān** увели́чивать, прибавля́ть	1. to add, increase 2. to have a baby
心 **xīn** **1.** се́рдце **2.** чу́вства; настрое́ния **3.** середи́на, центр	1. heart 2. mind, feeling 3. center, core
～脏 **xīnzàng** се́рдце	heart
～里 **xīnli** в душе́; в уме́	in the heart, at heart, in mind
～理 **xīnlǐ** пси́хика	psychology, mentality
～理学 **xīnlǐxué** психоло́гия	psychology
～绪 **xīnxù** настрое́ние	state of mind
～机 **xīnjī** **1.** смека́лка **2.** моти́вы, побужде́ния	thinking, scheming
～急 **xīnjí** **1.** волнова́ться, не́рвничать **2.** нетерпели́вый	impatient, short-tempered
～思 **xīnsī** мне́ние; наме́рение; мы́сли	1. thought, idea 2. thinking 3. state of mind, mood
～疼 **xīnténg** боле́ть душо́й; принима́ть бли́зко к се́рдцу	1. love dearly 2. to be distressed, feel sorry
德 **dé** доброде́тель, мора́ль, нра́вственность	1. morality, virtue 2. heart, mind 3. kindness
～ **dé** Герма́ния; неме́цкий	Germany; German
志 **zhì** **1.** стремле́ние; во́ля; реши́мость **2.** за́пись; заме́тки; обзо́р	1. will, aspiration, ideal, ambition 2. records 3. mark, sign 4. to remember 5. to be devoted to 6. measure, weight
～向 **zhìxiàng** стремле́ние; поры́в	aspiration, ideal, ambition

志愿 **zhìyuàn** желáние, стремлéние; доброво́льный	1. aspiration, wish, ideal 2. to pledge to do sth., volunteer
惩:惩罚 **chéngfá** накáзывать; налагáть взыскáние; накáзание; взыскáние	to punish, penalize
恶 **ě** тошни́ть; тошнотá	1. to feel sick/nauseated 2. to be nau-//seating/disgusting
～ **è** преступлéние; зло; дурнóй, сквéрный	1. evil 2. fierce 3. to dislike
～ **wù** надоéсть	to loathe, hate
～性 **èxìng** злокáчественный	1. viciousness 2. malignancy
～霸 **èbà** тирáн; и́зверг; самодýр	local despot
～劣 **èliè** сквéрный, отврати́тельный	vile, nasty
～毒 **èdú** свирéпый, жестóкий; злóбный	venomous
～化 **èhuà** ухудшéние	to worsen
～心 **èxīn** испы́тывать отвращéние	1. to feel nauseated, become sick 2. to be fed up 3. disgusting, nauseous
忘 **wàng** забывáть; забы́вчивый	to forget, overlook, neglect
～我 **wàngwǒ** самозабвéнно	selfless, oblivious of oneself
～记 **wàngjì** забывáть	to forget, overlook
急 **jí** **1.** срóчный, э́кстренный **2.** óстрый, крити́ческий **3.** волновáться, нéрвничать **4.** бы́стрый, поспéшный	1. impatient, anxious 2. rapid, fast; violent 3. irritated, annoyed 4. urgent 5. hard up 6. eager to help
～性 **jíxìng** **1.** горя́чность; торопли́вость **2.** óстрый *(о заболевании)*	1. acute (of diseases) 2. quick-tempered
～忙 **jímáng** поспéшно, торопли́во	in haste, hurriedly
～于 **jíyú** спеши́ть с	eager/anxious to (do sth.)
～需 **jíxū** нýжный, крáйне необходи́мый	1. to require (sth.) urgently 2. urgent need
～救 **jíjiù** неотлóжная пóмощь	first aid, emergency treatment
隐 **yǐn** скрывáть, пря́тать; скры́тый, тáйный	1. to conceal, hide 2. to live as a recluse 3. latent, dormant 4. hidden 5. painful
稳 **wěn** **1.** крéпкий, прóчный; стаби́льный **2.** вéрный, надёжный	1. firm, stable, steady 2. sedate, staid 3. certain, sure
～当 **wěndāng** надёжный; устóйчивый	reliable, secure, safe

稳惹总聪怠意

稳固 **wěngù** крéпкий, прóчный; стаби́льный	firm, stable
～定 **wěndìng** упрóчить; стабилизи́ровать	to stabilize; stable, steady
惹 **rě** вызывáть, навлекáть	1. to cause (sth. bad) to happen 2. to provoke
～事 **rěshì** навлéчь на себя́ неприя́тность	to cause trouble
总 **zǒng** 1. соединя́ть; обобщáть; в цéлом; всеóбщий 2. глáвный, основнóй, генерáльный 3. всегдá 4. в конéчном счёте	1. total, comprehensive, general, overall 2. chief, head, general 3. always, invariably 4. anyway, after all, inevitably, sooner or later 5. to assemble, put together, sum up
～理 **zǒnglǐ** премьéр-мини́стр	premier, prime minister
～结 **zǒngjié** обобщáть; вы́воды; итóговый, заключи́тельный	to sum up, summarize; summary, summing up
～结报告 **zǒngjié bàogào** отчётный доклáд	summary/final/concluding report
～路线 **zǒnglùxiàn** генерáльная ли́ния	(pol.) general line
～部 **zǒngbù** штаб-кварти́ра	1. headquarters 2. head office
～而言之 **zǒng'éryánzhī** одни́м слóвом, корóче говоря́	in short, in a word
～局 **zǒngjú** центрáльное (глáвное) бюрó (управлéние)	directorate, chief, central administrative board
～是 **zǒngshì** всегдá, вообщé, в любóм слу́чае	always
～统 **zǒngtǒng** президéнт	president (of a republic)
～会 **zǒnghuì** генерáльный совéт	1. central administrative body 2. headquarters 3. club 4. collection 5. to be inevitable
聪:聪明 **cōngming** у́мный; спосóбный	intelligent, bright, clever
怠 **dài** лени́ться; лень; лени́вый	1. idle, remiss, slack, negligent 2. to treat coldly
～工 **dàigōng** саботи́ровать; саботáж	to slow down (work)
意 **yì** 1. мысль, идéя; желáние 2. ду́мать, полагáть	1. meaning, idea 2. wish, desire, intention 3. suggestion, hint, trace 4. attention 5. to think, expect
～ **yì** Итáлия	Italy
～图 **yìtú** намéрения	intention; intent
～外 **yìwài** неожи́данный, непредви́денный	1. unexpected, unforeseen 2. accident, mishap

意料 **yìliào** предполага́ть; предположе́ние	to anticipate, expect
~味 **yìwéi** 1. стремле́ние; интере́с 2. означа́ть, зна́чить	1. meaning, significance, implication 2. interest, flavor, overtone
~义 **yìyì** смысл, значе́ние	meaning, sense, significance
~见 **yìjiàn** 1. мне́ние, взгля́ды 2. возраже́ния; недово́льство; прете́нзии	1. idea, view, opinion, suggestion 2. objection, complaint
~识 **yìshì** созна́ние; созна́тельность; идеоло́гия	consciousness, mentality
~志 **yìzhì** во́ля	will, determination
~思 **yìsi** 1. значе́ние, смысл; интере́с 2. мне́ние, то́чка зре́ния	1. meaning, idea 2. opinion, wish, desire 3. hint, trace 4. interest, fun 5. token of affection/appreciation
想 **xiǎng** 1. ду́мать, мы́слить 2. жела́ть, хоте́ть 3. скуча́ть по, тоскова́ть	1. to think 2. to suppose, reckon, consider 3. to want to, feel like (doing sth.), would like to
息 **xī** 1. дыша́ть; дыха́ние 2. прекраща́ть(ся), перестава́ть; отдыха́ть; о́тдых	1. to cease 2. to rest 3. to grow, multiply 4. breath 5. news 6. interest 7. one's children
熄 **xī** гаси́ть, туши́ть	to extinguish, put out
~灯 **xīdēng** 1. гаси́ть свет 2. отбо́й *(отход ко сну)*	to put out a light
思 **sī** ду́мать, мы́слить; мысль; иде́я	1. to think, consider, deliberate 2. to think of, long for 3. thought
~索 **sīsuǒ** обду́мывать; мы́слить	to think deeply, ponder
~想 **sīxiǎng** 1. мысль; иде́я 2. идеоло́гия; идеологи́ческий, иде́йный	1. thought, thinking, idea 2. ideology
恩 **ēn** доброта́; ми́лость, благодея́ние	kindness, favor
~惠 **ēnhuì** доброта́; ми́лость	favor, grace
怎 **zěn** как?, каки́м о́бразом?	why?, how?
~么 **zěnme** как?; почему́?	how?, what?
~么[一]回事 **zěnme [yī]huíshì** в чём де́ло?, что случи́лось?	What's the matter?, What's happened?
~[么]样 **zěn[me]yàng** 1. как?, каки́м о́бразом?; како́в? 2. как дела́?	1. how?, what? 2. How are things?
~么办 **zěnmebàn** как быть?	What's to be done?
忠 **zhōng** ве́рность, пре́данность; ве́рный, пре́данный	loyal, devoted, faithful, honest

忠患悲念愈慰愚滤忿忍

忠实(诚) **zhōngshí(chéng)**	true, faithful
пре́данность; пре́данный	-
患 **huàn** **1.** страда́ть; горе-	1. to worry, be anxious 2. to become ill
ва́ть **2.** несча́стье, бе́дствие	3. scourge, peril, disaster 4. trouble,\\
～病 **huànbìng** боле́ть	to fall ill \\worry
悲 **bēi** горева́ть; сожале́ть;	1. sad, melancholy 2. compassion
скорбь, печа́ль	-
～剧 **bēijù** траге́дия, дра́ма	tragedy (drama)
～惨 **bēicǎn** го́рестный, тра-	miserable, tragic
ги́ческий	-
～伤 **bēishāng** горева́ть, уби-	sad, sorrowful
ва́ться	-
～观主义 **bēiguānzhǔyì** пес-	pessimism
сими́зм; упа́дочничество	-
念 **niàn** **1.** ду́мать; вспоми-	1. to think of, miss 2. to read aloud 3.
на́ть **2.** чита́ть *(вслух)*;	to study, attend school 4. thought,
учи́ться	idea 5. care, remembrance
～书 **niànshū** **1.** учи́ться **2.**	to read, study
чита́ть вслух	-
愈 **yù** **1.** превосходи́ть **2.** ещё	1. the more... 2. to be better 3. to re-
бо́лее; тем бо́лее; 愈...	cover
愈... чем..., тем...	- //(that)
慰 **wèi** успока́ивать, утеша́ть	1. to console, comfort 2. to be relieved//
～问 **wèiwèn** **1.** справля́ться	to comfort, console, convey sympathy/
о здоро́вье **2.** выража́ть со-	greetings
боле́знование (сочу́вст-	-
вие)	-
～劳 **wèilao** ше́фствовать	to requite with gifts/thanks, etc.
愚 **yú** **1.** глу́пый, тупо́й **2.** ду-	1. foolish, stupid 2. (humb.) I, my 3. to
ра́чить, обма́нывать	make a fool of, dupe
滤 **lǜ** проце́живать, фильтро-	to strain, filter
ва́ть	-
忿 **fèn** возмуща́ться; гне́ваться-	indignation, anger, resentment
ся; возмуще́ние; гнев, не-	-
годова́ние	-
～恨 **fènhèn** ненави́деть; не́-	to detest, resent indignantly
нависть; возмуще́ние	-
～怒 **fènnù** *см.* 忿	indignant, angry
忍 **rěn** терпе́ть, сноси́ть;	1. to bear, endure 2. to hold back, for-
сде́рживать(ся)	bear 3. cruel, merciless
～让 **rěnràng** терпе́ние; тер-	to be conciliatory
пели́вый	-
～耐 **rěnnài** терпе́ть, выно-	patient, forbearing; patience
си́ть	-

忍受 **rěnshòu** стерпе́ть, снес-ти́, вы́держать	to endure, bear
忽 **hū 1.** пренебрега́ть, прези-ра́ть **2.** внеза́пно, неожи́-данно	1. to neglect, overlook 2. to disdain 3. suddenly 4. now...
～略 **hūlüè** упусти́ть из ви́ду; игнори́ровать	to neglect, overlook, lose sight of
～视 **hūshì** пренебрега́ть, иг-нори́ровать	to ignore, overlook, neglect
～然 **hūrán** вдруг, внеза́пно, неожи́данно	suddenly
葱 **cōng** лук *(растение)*	1. onion, scallion 2. green
恣:恣意 **zìyì** произво́льно	recklessly, willfully
态 **tài 1.** состоя́ние, положе́-ние **2.** вид, о́блик **3.** пове-де́ние	1. appearance, state, condition 2. attitude, demeanor 3. (ling.) voice 4. (comput.) mode
～度 **tàidu 1.** пози́ция; под-хо́д, отноше́ние **2.** поведе́-ние; мане́ры	1. manner, bearing 2. attitude, approach
愁 **chóu** грусти́ть; грусть, пе-ча́ль; гру́стный	to worry, be anxious/grieved
恳 **kěn** и́скренне, серде́чно	1. earnestly, sincerely 2. to request,\\
～请 **kěnqǐng** проси́ть, умо-ля́ть	to request earnestly \\entreat
～切 **kěnqiè** и́скренне, сер-де́чно	earnest, sincere
～求 **kěnqiú** *см.* 恳请	to implore, entreat
怒 **nù** серди́ться, гне́ваться; гнев, я́рость; гне́вный	anger, fury //3. melancholy 4. absurd
悠 **yōu** далёкий, до́лгий	1. (coll.) to swing 2. remote in time/space//
～久 **yōujiǔ** до́лгий, продол-жи́тельный	long in time
惑 **huò 1.** сомнева́ться; подо-зрева́ть **2.** вводи́ть в за-блужде́ние	1. to confuse, delude, mislead 2. to doubt, suspect
感 **gǎn 1.** чу́вствовать, ощу-ща́ть; чу́вство, ощуще́ние **2.** возбуди́ть; растро́гать	1. to feel, sense 2. to move, touch 3. sense, feeling 4. (Ch. med.) to be affected (by cold)
～冒 **gǎnmào** грипп; просту́-да	1. to catch cold 2. common cold
～谢 **gǎnxiè** благодари́ть; благода́рность	to thank, be grateful
～情 **gǎnqíng** чу́вство; чу́вст-ва; взаимоотноше́ния	emotion, feeling, sentiment

忍忽葱恣态愁恳怒悠惑感

感动 **gǎndòng** растрóгать (-ся)	to move, touch
～染 **gǎnrǎn** **1.** заразúться; инфéкция **2.** влиять; увлекáть	1. to infect 2. to influence, affect
～觉 **gǎnjué** ощущáть, чýвствовать	to feel, perceive, become aware of; sense, perception, feeling
～想 **gǎnxiǎng** впечатлéние, ощущéние	impressions, reflections, thoughts
怨 **yuàn** **1.** быть озлóбленным; озлоблéние **2.** быть недовóльным; упрекáть, укорять	1. to blame, reproach, reprove 2. resentment, grudge, enmity
忌 **jì** **1.** завúдовать; ревновáть **2.** боя́ться, опасáться **3.** дать зарóк; запрéт, табý	1. to be jealous of, envy 2. to fear, dread 3. to avoid, shun 4. to quit, give up 5. taboo 6. anniversary of sb. esteemed
恐 **kǒng** **1.** боя́ться; пугáться **2.** пожáлуй; боюсь, что	1. to fear, dread 2. to terrify, intimidate 3. perhaps, I'm afraid (that)
～怕 **kǒngpà** **1.** пожáлуй; вероя́тно; как бы не **2.** боя́ться, опасáться	1. to fear 2. perhaps, I'm afraid (that), I fear (that)
～吓 **kǒnghè** запýгивать, устрашáть	to threaten, intimidate
～怖 **kǒngbù** террóр	1. fearful, horrible 2. terror
～惧 **kǒngjù** страх	-
您 **nín** Вы; Ваш	(court.) you
恋:恋爱 **liàn'ài** любóвь; влюблённость	love, romantic attachment
悬 **xuán** **1.** висéть; подвеснóй; вися́чий **2.** далёкий; далекó	1. to hang, suspend 2. to feel anxious, be solicitous 3. outstanding, unresolved 4. far apart 5. dangerous
～空 **xuánkōng** пустóй; необоснóванный; нереáльный	1. to hang in the air, suspend in midair 2. to be divorced from reality
～念 **xuánniàn** дýмать; беспокóиться	1. to be concerned (about sb. who is elsewhere) 2. suspense in a film/play
必 **bì** непремéнно, обязáтельно	1. certainly, surely 2. to have to, must
～需 **bìxū** необходúмый; необходúмо	1. to need, require 2. essential, indispensable
～定 **bìdìng** обязáтельно, непремéнно; определённо	certainly, surely
～须 **bìxū** необходúмо, дóлжно	to have to, must, it is necessary

必然 **bìrán** непреме́нно; неизбе́жно	1. inevitable, certain 2. certainly 3. necessity
～要 **bìyào** необходи́мый, ну́жный; сле́дует	1. necessary, indispensable 2. need
秘 **mì** та́йный, секре́тный; нелега́льный; та́йна, секре́т	1. secret 2. secretary
～密 **mìmì** *см.* 秘	secret, confidential; secret
～书 **mìshū** секрета́рь *(технический)*	secretary
～书长 **mìshūzhǎng** генера́льный секрета́рь	secretary general
泌 **bì** выделя́ться; секре́ция	to secrete
蒸 **zhēng** **1.** пар; испаре́ние **2.** вари́ть на пару́	1. to evaporate 2. steam
糕 **gāo** пиро́жное; торт; кекс	cake, pudding
黑 **hēi** **1.** чёрный; тёмный; мра́чный **2.** скры́тый, та́йный **3.** зло́стный; злоде́йский	1. black 2. dark 3. secret, shady, covert 4. wicked, sinister, vicious 5. to blacken 6. to hide 7. to exhort 8 . (slang) to be greedy
～暗 **hēi'àn** **1.** мрак, темнота́ **2.** реа́кция; реакцио́нный	1. dark 2. dark aspect, seamy side
～板 **hēibǎn** кла́ссная доска́	blackboard
～麦 **hēimài** рожь	rye
～心 **hēixīn** бесче́стный, бессо́вестный; зло́бный	black heart, evil mind
熏 **xūn** копти́ть; прокопти́ть (-ся)	1. to smoke, fumigate 2. to cure meat, etc. with smoke 3. to assail the nostrils 4. smoked 5. warm
～ **xùn** угоре́ть	to poison by gas
焦 **jiāo** **1.** пригоре́ть; сжечь; проже́чь **2.** волнова́ться, беспоко́иться	1. burnt, scorched 2. worried, anxious 3. coke
～急 **jiāojí** волнова́ться, беспоко́иться	anxious, worried
礁 **jiāo** риф; подво́дный ка́мень	reef
瞧 **qiáo** гляде́ть, смотре́ть	to see, look at
～不起 **qiáobuqǐ** презира́ть, смотре́ть свысока́	(coll.) to look down upon, despise
蔗 **zhè** са́харный тростни́к	sugar cane
点 **diǎn** **1.** то́чка; пятно́; ка́пля; немно́жко **2.** пункт; ме́сто **3.** час; вре́мя **4.** зажига́ть	1. drop 2. spot 3. dot, point 4. place 5. aspect, feature 6. a little/bit 7. o'clock; hour; time 8. to light, burn 9. to touch on, hint 10. to select 11. to drip

点照煮煎烈然

点名 **diǎnmíng** де́лать перекли́чку; перекли́чка	1. to call a roll 2. to mention sb. by name
～菜 **diǎncài** выбира́ть меню́	to order dishes, choose dishes from//a menu
～心 **diǎnxīn** сла́дости; десе́рт	1. light refreshments 2. pastry 3. dim sum
照 **zhào 1.** освеща́ть, свети́ть **2.** отража́ть(ся); смотре́ть (-ся) *(в зеркало)* **3.** извеще́ние; уведомле́ние; но́та **4.** удостовере́ние; па́спорт **5.** согла́сно, в соотве́тствии с **6**. забо́титься	1. to shine, illuminate 2. to reflect, mirror 3. to take a photograph 4. to take care of, look after 5. to notify 6. illumination, glow 7. photograph, picture 8. license, permit 9. towards 10. according to, in accordance with -
～耀 **zhàoyào** озаря́ть, освеща́ть	to shine, illuminate -
～相 **zhàoxiàng** фотографи́ровать; фотогра́фия	to photograph -
～相机 **zhàoxiàngjī** фотоаппара́т	camera -
～样 **zhàoyàng** по устано́вленному образцу́	1. after a pattern/model 2. in the same old way, as before
～料 **zhàoliào** хлопота́ть; забо́титься	to take care of, comfort -
～片 **zhàopiān** фотока́рточка, фотогра́фия	photograph, picture -
～例 **zhàoli** по обыкнове́нию, как пра́вило	according to precedent/practice -
～明 **zhàomíng** освеща́ть; освеще́ние; иллюмина́ция	to illuminate; illumination -
～顾 **zhàogù** забо́титься	to look after, care for, attend to
～会 **zhàohuì** *дип.* но́та	to recall (e.g., a diplomat)
煮 **zhǔ** вари́ть; варёный	to boil, cook
煎 **jiān** поджа́ривать; подсу́шивать	1. to fry in shallow oil 2. to simmer in water 3. to decoct 4. to be very vexed
烈 **liè 1.** жа́ркий, зно́йный **2.** я́ростный, неи́стовый **3.** стра́стный, пы́лкий **4.** до́блестный, герои́ческий	1. strong, violent, intense 2. staunch, upright, stern, just 3. sacrificing oneself for a just cause 4. merits, achievements
～士 **lièshì** поги́бший геро́й	1. martyr 2. person of high endeavor
然 **rán 1.** так; тако́в **2.** *суф. наречий*	1. right, correct 2. so 3. however, but 4. (adj./adv. suf.)
～后 **ránhòu** зате́м, по́сле э́того	and then, after that -
～而 **rán'ér** но, одна́ко; всё-таки	even so, but -

燃 **rán** жечь; зажигáть(ся);	to burn, ignite
воспламенять(ся)	-
～料 **ránliào** тóпливо, горю́-	fuel
чее	-
～烧 **ránshāo** жечь; поджи-	to burn
гáть; горéние; сгорáние	-
杰 **jié** выдающийся, талáнт-	outstanding person, hero; outstand-
ливый	ing, prominent
～作 **jiézuò** шедéвр	masterpiece
熬 **áo 1.** терпéть, переноси́ть	1. to boil, stew 2. to decoct 3. to hold
2. вывáривать; туши́ть	out, endure 4. to stay up late/all night
燕 **yàn** лáсточка	swallow
熊 **xióng** медвéдь	1. to bear 2. to scold, oppress, tyran-\\
热 **rè 1.** греть, нагревáть; жа-	hot \\nize 3. mean, malicious 4. oafish
рá; жар **2.** рвéние, энтузи-	-
áзм	-
～闹 **rènao** оживлённый,	to have a lively time; lively, buzzing with
шу́мный, лю́дный	excitement; excitement, lively scene
～情 **rèqíng** энтузиáзм; пá-	enthusiastic
фос; страсть	-
～带 **rèdài** трóпики; тропи́че-	the tropics
ский	-
～水瓶 **rèshuipíng** тéрмос	thermos bottle
～核武器 **rèhé wǔqì** термо-	thermonuclear weapons
я́дерное ору́жие	-
～心 **rèxīn** энтузиáзм; пыл,	enthusiastic, ardent
рвéние	-
～烈 **rèliè** горя́чий, пы́лкий,	ardent
стрáстный	-
熟 **shú 1.** созрéть, поспéть;	1. ripe 2. cooked, done 3. processed 4.
спéлый, зрéлый; готóвый	familiar 5. skilled, experienced 6. deep
(о пище) **2.** хорошó знать;	(sleep/thoughts, etc.)
знакóмый, привы́чный	-
～练 **shúliàn** квалифици́ро-	skilled, practiced, proficient
ванный, óпытный	-
～悉 **shúxī** знать досконáль-	to know sth./sb. well
но; быть осведомлённым	-
私 **sī 1.** чáстный, ли́чный; не-	1. personal, private 2. illegal 3. selfish
официáльный **2.** тáйный;	-
контрабáндный	-
～信 **sīxìn** ли́чная корреспон-	personal letter
дéнция	-
～营 **sīyíng** чáстный *(о пред-*	privately owned/operated
прия́тии)	-

私宏云层尝会

私利 **sīlì** эгоисти́ческие интере́сы; ли́чная вы́года	private/selfish interest, personal gain
～有制 **sīyǒuzhì** систе́ма ча́стной со́бственности	private ownership (of means of production)
～人 **sīrén** ча́стное лицо́; ча́стный, ли́чный	1. personal friend/relative 2. confidant 3. one's own man
～货 **sīhuò** контраба́нда *(това́ры)*	smuggled/contraband goods
～心 **sīxīn** **1.** эгоисти́ческие побужде́ния, эгои́зм **2.** заве́тный, задуше́вный	selfish motive/idea, selfishness
宏 **hóng** обши́рный, огро́мный	great, grand
～伟 **hóngwěi** вели́чественный, грандио́зный	magnificent, grand
～大 **hóngdà** огро́мный, обши́рный	grand, great
云 **yún** о́блако; ту́ча	1. cloud 2. (abbr.) Yunnan 3. to say
～彩 **yúncai** облака́	(coll.) clouds
层 **céng** **1.** слой, пласт; эта́ж **2.** повторя́ться; насла́иваться	layer, story, floor
～次 **céngcì** поря́док, после́довательность	1. rank order 2. administrative levels 3. arrangement of ideas 4. (ling.) stratification
尝 **cháng** **1.** про́бовать [на вкус]; испы́тывать **2.** не́когда, когда́-то	1. to taste 2. to experience, come to know 3. ever, once
会 **huì** **1.** собира́ть(ся); встреча́ться **2.** мочь, уме́ть **3.** собра́ние, заседа́ние **4.** о́бщество, сою́з **5.** миг, моме́нт	1. to assemble 2. to meet 3. to understand, grasp 4. can 5. to be skillful in 6. be likely/sure to 7. to pay/foot a bill 8. meeting, party 9. association, society 10. capital, chief city 11. opportunity
～ **kuài** вычисля́ть; учи́тывать; учёт	to count, compute, calculate
～合 **huìhé** собира́ться, сходи́ться	to join, meet, converge, assemble; confluence, fusion
～话 **huìhuà** диало́г; у́стная речь	to converse (as in a language course); conversation
～客室 **huìkèshì** приёмная; гости́ная	reception room
～面 **huìmiàn** встре́ча, свида́ние	to meet
～计 **kuàiji** счетово́дство; бухгалте́рия	1. accounting 2. bookkeeper, accountant

会商 huìshāng совеща́ться; вести́ перегово́ры	to hold a conference/consultation, consult
～谈 huìtán бесе́да; перегово́ры	to hold talks; talks
～议 huìyì собра́ние, совеща́ние; конфере́нция; пле́нум	meeting, conference
～费 huìfèi чле́нские взно́сы	membership fees/dues
～演 huìyǎn фестива́ль	(theatr.) joint performance
绘 huì рисова́ть; карти́на; жи́вопись	to paint, draw
～画 huìhuà рисова́ть; карти́на	to draw, paint; drawing, painting
～图 huìtú черти́ть; рисова́ть	1. to draw pictures 2. to prepare engineering drawings
县 xiàn уе́зд; уе́здный	country
套 tào 1. покрыва́ть; надева́ть; обёртывать; футля́р; чехо́л; обёртка 2. компле́кт; набо́р; серви́з	1. sheath, case 2. bend, curve 3. padding 4. traces, harness 5. knot, noose, trap 6. cliché, formula 7. to encase 8. to overlap, interlink 9. to copy, model
～鞋 tàoxié гало́ши	overshoes, rubbers, galoshes
去 qù 1. уходи́ть, отправля́ться 2. про́шлый, проше́дший 3. удаля́ть; отбра́сывать	1. to go (to), leave 2. to remove, get rid of 3. to send 4. to be apart 5. past, last 6. extremely, very, really 7. (part.) so as to 8. (suf.) away
～世 qùshì скончáться; кончи́на	to die, pass away
～年 qùnián про́шлый год	last year, the year past
法 fǎ 1. зако́н; пра́вило 2. спо́соб, ме́тод, приём	1. law 2. method, way, mode 3. standard, model 4. to follow, model 5. magical arts
～ fǎ Фра́нция	France
～宝 fǎbǎo 1. талисма́н, амуле́т 2. маги́ческое сре́дство; панаце́я	talisman
～官 fǎguān судья́	judge, justice
～西斯 fǎxīsī фаши́ст; фаши́стский	(loan w.) fascist
～律 fǎlǜ зако́н; пра́во	law, statute
～律学 fǎlǜxué юриспруде́нция	jurisprudence, law
～制 fǎzhì законода́тельство	legal systems/institution, legality
～则 fǎzé пра́вила; зако́ны	1. standard method 2. binding agreement 3. (math) formula
～子 fǎz спо́соб, ме́тод, сре́дство	way, method
～案 fǎ'àn законопрое́кт	proposed law/bill

法庭(院) **fǎtíng(yuàn)** суд; трибунáл	court, tribunal
~令 **fǎlìng** укáз; закóн; декрéт	laws, decrees
罢 **bà 1.** прекращáть, переставáть **2.** увольня́ть	1. to cease 2. to quit 3. to dismiss 4. to finish 5. to refuse to attend
~工 **bàgōng** бастовáть; забастóвка	to go on strike; strike
~了 **bàle** и всё; лáдно, хвáтит	forget it
摆 **bǎi 1.** расставля́ть, располагáть, стáвить **2.** качáть (-ся), шатáть(ся)	1. to place, put, arrange 2. to state clearly 3. to assume, put on 4. to sway, swing, wave 5. pendulum
~设 **bǎishè** *см.* 摆 1	to furnish and decorate (a room)
~脱 **bǎituō** сбрóсить; освободи́ться, отдéлаться от *когó-чегó*	to cast/shake off
丢 **diū 1.** потеря́ть, утрáтить **2.** отбрóсить; опусти́ть	1. to lose, misplace 2. to discard 3. to put aside
~脸 **diūliǎn** осрами́ться, оскандáлиться	to lose face
~掉 **diūdiào** потеря́ть; брóсить, вы́кинуть	1. to lose 2. to throw away
公 **gōng 1.** справедли́вый, беспристрáстный **2.** óбщий; общéственный; коммунáльный **3.** официáльный, госудáрственный **4.** самéц	1. public affairs, official duties 2. to make public 3. public, state-owned, collective 4. common, accepted 5. just, fair, impartial 6. metric 7. male (of animals)
~社 **gōngshè** коммýна	1. primitive commune 2. commune 3. people's commune
~墓 **gōngmù** брáтская моги́ла	cemetery
~里 **gōngli** киломéтр	kilometer
~理 **gōngli 1.** и́стина; аксиóма **2.** справедли́вость	1. generally acknowledged or self-evident truth 2. (math) axiom
~正 **gōngzhèng** справедли́вый, прáвильный	just, fair, impartial
~证 **gōngzhèng** нотариáльно засвидéтельствованный	1. notarization 2. acknowledgment
~告 **gōnggào** объявлéние; коммюникé	announcement, proclamation
~路 **gōnglù** шоссé; магистрáль	highway, road
~园 **gōngyuán** парк	1. park 2. garden
~斤 **gōngjīn** килогрáмм	kilogram

公平 **gōngping** чéстный; справедли́вый	fair, just, impartial
~开 **gōngkāi** публи́чный, откры́тый; легáльный	to make public, make known to the public; open, overt, public
~升 **gōngshēng** литр	liter
~司 **gōngsī** фи́рма, компáния	company, corporation
~有(用) **gōngyǒu(yòng)** общéственный; коммунáльный	1. to possess jointly 2. total 3. common, public
~布 **gōngbù** опубликовáть; публикáция	to promulgate, announce, publish
~分 **gōngfēn 1.** сантимéтр **2.** грамм	1. centimeter 2. gram
~约 **gōngyuē** пакт	1. convention, pact 2. joint pledge
~务 **gōngwù** государственная слу́жба	public affairs, official business
~众 **gōngzhòng** пу́блика; публи́чный	(the) public
~尺 **gōngchǐ** метр	meter
~报 **gōngbào 1.** прави́тельственный вéстник **2.** официáльное сообщéние, коммюникé	bulletin
~使 **gōngshi** послáнник	envoy, minister
~道 **gōngdào** справедли́вый, чéстный	justice
~民 **gōngmín** граждани́н	citizen
~式 **gōngshì** фóрмула	formula, form
~论 **gōnglùn** общéственное мнéние	public opinion
~元 **gōngyuán** нóвая э́ра	Christian era (A.D.)
~共 **gōnggòng** óбщий; общéственный	public, common, communal
~共汽车 **gōnggòng qìchē** автóбус	(local) bus
~债 **gōngzhài** государственный заём	government bond
~顷 **gōngqing** гектáр	hectare
~私合营企业 **gōng-sī héyíng qìyè** госудáрственно-чáстные предприя́тия	joint state-private ownership of enterprises/business
~然 **gōngrán** откры́то, я́вно	openly, brazenly

公安 **gōng'ān** общéственный порядок, общéственная безопáсность	public security
松 **sōng 1.** соснá; соснóвый **2.** распустúть, ослáбить **3.** свобóдный, вольгóтный **4.** небрéжный	1. pine 2. dried minced meat 3. to loosen, slacken; loose, slack 4. to let go, untie 5. light and flaky, soft 6. not hard up
~树 **sōngshù** соснá	pine tree, pine
~手 **sōngshǒu** вы́пустить из рук	to loosen one's grip, let go
~劲 **sōngjìn** охладевáть; ослаблять усúлия	to relax one's effort, slacken (off)
磁 **cí 1.** магнúт **2.** фарфóр; фаянс	1. (phys.) magnetism 2. porcelain, china
虫 **chóng** насекóмое; червяк; пресмыкáющееся	insect, worm
触 **chù 1.** задевáть; касáться, дотрáгиваться **2.** осязáть	1. to touch, contact 2. to strike, hit 3. to move sb., stir up sb.'s feelings
~觉 **chùjué** осязáние	sense of touch
融 **róng 1.** тáять; плáвить (-ся) **2.** быть в обращéнии	1. to melt, thaw 2. to blend, merge
~解(化) **róngjiě(huà)** тáять; плáвить(ся)	to thaw
独 **dú 1.** одинóкий; едúнственный; одно=; моно= **2.** самостоятельный, независúмый	1. alone, in solitude 2. only, singly 3. old people without offspring
~立 **dúlì** независúмость; независúмый, самостоятельный	to stand alone; independent; independence
~占 **dúzhàn** монополизúровать; монопóльный; монополистúческий	to monopolize
~唱 **dúchàng** сóльное пéние, сóло	(vocal) solo
~创 **dúchuàng** оригинáльный; индивидуáльный	original creation
~特 **dútè** осóбый; оригинáльный, своеобрáзный	unique, distinctive
~幕剧 **dúmùjù** одноáктная пьéса	one-act play
~奏 **dúzòu** исполнять сóло	instrumental solo
独裁 **dúcái** деспотúческий;	dictatorship, despotism

диктáторский	-
烛 **zhú** свечá; светúльник	1. candle 2. watt 3. to illuminate, light up
蚀 **shí** **1.** откýсывать; отлáмывать **2.** *астр.* затмéние	1. to lose 2. to erode, corrode
虽 **suī** хотя́; несмотря́ на то, что	though, although, even if
～然 **suīrán** хотя́, хоть; несмотря́ на то, что	though, although
强 **qiáng** **1.** мóщный, сúльный; здорóвый **2.** быть лýчшим, превосходúть **3.** бóлее, сверх	1. strong, powerful, vigorous 2. better 3. slightly more than, plus
～ **qiǎng** заставля́ть, принуждáть	to strive, make an effort, force
～ **jiàng** настáивать на своём, упря́миться	stubborn, unyielding
～壮 **qiángzhuàng** крéпкий, здорóвый	strong and sturdy
～盗 **qiángdào** грабúтель, бандúт; грабúтельский	robber, bandit
～加 **qiángjiā** навя́зывать; вынуждáть	to impose, force (upon)
～国 **qiángguó** сúльное госудáрство, держáва	powerful country
～制 **qiángzhì** принуждáть; принудúтельный	1. to force, compel, coerce 2. (ling.) obligatory
～调 **qiángdiào** подчёркивать, акцентúровать	1. to stress 2. to underline
～大 **qiángdà** могýщественный, мóщный	big and powerful, formidable
～暴 **qiángbào** безжáлостный, жестóкий	1. violent, brutal 2. to rape
～迫 **qiǎngpò** принуждáть, вынуждáть; навя́зывать	to force (sb. to do sth.)
～烈 **qiángliè** сúльный; я́ростный	strong, intense, violent
蚕 **cán** шелковúчный червь	silkworm
蛋 **dàn** яйцó	1. egg 2. an egg-shaped object
骚 **sāo** **1**. беспокóить, тревóжить **2.** бунтовáть; бунт	1. lascivious (of women) 2. to disturb, upset
～动 **sāodòng** беспоря́дки, волнéния	1. to become restless 2. to disturb, upset 3. disturbance
蛮 **mán** дúкий, вáрварский	1. barbaric, fierce 2. quite, very

蜜 **mì** мёд; медо́вый	1. honey 2. sweet 3. crystallized
～蜂 **mìfēng** пчела́	honeybee, bee
令 **lìng** **1.** прика́зывать; прика́з; ука́з; декре́т **2.** заставля́ть	1. command, decree 2. season 3. drinking game 4. short lyric 5. to make, cause 6. good 7. (court.) your
龄 **líng** во́зраст, го́ды	1. age, years 2. length of time, duration
岭 **lǐng** го́рный хребе́т	1. mountain range 2. mountain, ridge
怜 **lián** жале́ть, сочу́вствовать	1. to sympathize with, pity 2. to love
冷 **lěng** **1.** хо́лод; холо́дный; хо́лодно **2.** равноду́шный **3.** неожи́данно, внеза́пно, вдруг	1. cold 2. frosty (in manner) 3. cool 4. unfrequented, deserted, out-of-the-way 5. strange, rare 6. shot from hiding
～淡 **lěngdàn** равноду́шный, апати́чный; вя́лый; ску́чный	1. cheerless, desolate 2. cold, indifferent 3. to treat coldly, cold-shoulder, slight
～战 **lěngzhàn** холо́дная война́	cold war
铃 **líng** звоно́к; колоко́льчик	1. bell 2. sth. bell-shaped 3. bud
零 **líng** **1.** ме́лочь; ме́лкий **2.** нуль; нулево́й	1. zero, naught, nil 2. odd, a little extra 3. fractional part 4. to wither and fall
～星 **língxīng** ме́лкий; разро́зненный	1. fragmentary, odd, piecemeal 2. scattered, sporadic
～售 **língshòu** ро́зничная прода́жа	to (sell) retail
～件 **língjiàn** дета́ли; запасны́е ча́сти	spare parts, spares, components
～钱 **língqián** ме́лкие де́ньги, ме́лочь	1. small change 2. pocket money
专 **zhuān** **1.** специа́льный, осо́бый **2.** абсолю́тный; еди́нственный	1. special, focused, concentrated 2. arbitrary, tyrannical 3. to monopolize
～业 **zhuānyè** специа́льность; специализи́рованный; отраслево́й	1. special field of research, specialty, discipline 2. major (in a university)
～门 **zhuānmén** специа́льный	special, specialized
～修 **zhuānxiū** специализи́роваться	to specialize in (an area of study)
～修生 **zhuānxiūshēng** стажёр	on-the-job trainee, trial employee, apprentice
～约 **zhuānyuē** конве́нция	compact, convention
～家 **zhuānjiā** специали́ст	expert, specialist
～政 **zhuānzhèng** диктату́ра	dictatorship

专心 **zhuānxīn** сосредото́читься; увле́чься	to be absorbed in, concentrate effort
砖: 砖头 **zhuāntóu** кирпи́ч	1. brick fragment 2. brick
传 **chuán** **1.** передава́ть; сообща́ть **2.** распространя́ть; заража́ть **3.** звать, вызыва́ть	1. to pass (on), hand down 2. to teach, impart 3. to spread 4. to transmit, conduct, convey, express 5. to summon 6. to infect, be contagious
~ **zhuàn** **1.** биогра́фия **2.** ле́топись, хро́ника **3.** по́весть	1. biography 2. historical novel 3. commentaries on the classics
~播 **chuánbō** **1.** распространя́ть(ся) **2.** трансли́ровать	1. to disseminate, propagate, spread 2. (phys.) propagation
~单 **chuándān** **1.** листо́вка **2.** пове́стка	leaflet, handbill
~染 **chuánrǎn** заража́ть(ся); инфе́кция	to infect, be contagious
~染病 **chuánrǎnbìng** **1.** эпиде́мия **2.** инфекцио́нная боле́знь	infectious/contagious disease
~达 **chuándá** **1.** доста́вить по назначе́нию **2.** довести́ до све́дения	1. to pass on, transmit, communicate 2. reception and registration at a public establishment 3. janitor
~送 **chuánsòng** передава́ть; транспорти́ровать	to transmit, deliver
~统 **chuántǒng** тради́ция; традицио́нный	tradition; traditional
~真电报 **chuánzhēn diànbào** фототелегра́мма	phototelegram
~票 **chuánpiào** **1.** пове́стка в суд **2.** о́рдер	1. subpoena, summons 2. voucher
转 **zhuǎn** **1.** враща́ть(ся), верте́ть(ся); повора́чивать(ся) **2.** передава́ть; пересыла́ть	1. to turn, revolve, rotate 2. (M. for turns/revolutions)
~告 **zhuǎngào** пересказа́ть	to transmit (a message), communicate, pass on (word)
~移 **zhuǎnyí** перемеща́ть, передвига́ть	1. to shift, transfer, divert 2. to change, transform 3. metastasis
~弯 **zhuǎnwān** поверну́ть, сверну́ть	to turn a corner, make a turn
~动 **zhuǎndòng** **1.** враща́ть(-ся); враще́ние **2.** перемести́ть(ся), передви́нуть(ся)	to turn (around), move
~变 **zhuǎnbiàn** измене́ние, превраще́ние; перело́м; сдвиг	to change, transform; change, transformation

转女接

转达 **zhuǎndá** передава́ть, доводи́ть до све́дения	to pass on, convey, communicate
～运 **zhuǎnyùn** перевози́ть; перево́зки	1. to forward, transship 2. to have luck turn in one's favor
～载 **zhuǎnzài** 1. перепеча́тывать; перепеча́тка 2. перегружа́ть; перегру́зка	to reprint elsewhere

丶，乛

女 **nǚ** 1. же́нщина; же́нский 2. дочь 3. де́вочка; де́вушка	1. woman, female 2. daughter, girl
～工 **nǚgōng** 1. рабо́тница 2. же́нская рабо́та	woman worker
～士 **nǚshì** да́ма, госпожа́	1. educated girl/woman 2. Ms., Miss
接 **jiē** 1. соединя́ть(ся); сходи́ться, сближа́ться; соедине́ние 2. непреры́вно, после́довательно 3. получа́ть; принима́ть	1. to come in contact with, come close to 2. to connect, join, put together 3. to catch, take hold of 4. to receive 5. to meet, welcome 6. to take over
～应 **jiēyìng** по́мощь, подде́ржка	1. to come to sb.'s aid, coordinate with, reinforce 2. to supply
～任 **jiērèn** приня́ть дела́	to take over a job
～班 **jiēbān** приня́ть сме́ну	to take one's turn of duty, succeed, carry on
～班人 **jiēbānrén** сме́на (*поколение*)	successor
～洽 **jiēqià** согласова́ть, договори́ться; нала́дить конта́кты	to take up a matter with, arrange (business/etc.) with
～管 **jiēguǎn** брать на себя́ управле́ние (контро́ль)	to take over management
～着 **jiēzhe** вслед за, зате́м, да́лее	1. to catch 2. to follow, carry on 3. next, immediately after
～待 **jiēdài** принима́ть (*госте́й*)	to receive, admit
～吻 **jiēwěn** целова́ть(ся); поцелу́й	to kiss
～受(收) **jiēshòu(shōu)** 1. приня́ть, получи́ть; поступле́ние 2. восприним́ать	to accept, receive (honors, etc.)
～近 **jiējìn** сближа́ться; приближа́ться	1. to be close to; to approach, near 2. to be on intimate terms with
～见 **jiējiàn** приня́ть, дать	to receive sb., grant an interview to

аудие́нцию; приём	-
妄触 **jiēchū** вступа́ть в конта́кт	1. to come into contact with, get in touch with 2. to engage 3. to contact
～ **wàng** безрассу́дный; бестолко́вый	1. absurd, unreasonable 2. presumptuous, rash
～图 **wàngtú** безуспе́шно пыта́ться	to attempt vainly
～想 **wàngxiǎng** несбы́точные мечты́	1. to hope vainly 2. wishful thinking, vain hope
妻 **qī** жена́	wife
凄 **qī** **1.** хо́лод; холо́дный **2.** печа́литься; скорбь, печа́ль	1. chilly, cold 2. bleak and desolate 3. sad, miserable, wretched
～惨 **qīcǎn** скорбе́ть, печа́литься; печа́ль	wretched, miserable, tragic
宴 **yàn** угоща́ть; пирова́ть; пир; банке́т	1. banquet, dinner party 2. pleasure, joy 3. leisure 4. to give a dinner
～请 **yànqǐng** устро́ить банке́т *(в честь кого-л.)*	to fete, entertain (at a dinner)
～会 **yànhuì** банке́т; приём	banquet, dinner party
要 **yào** **1.** хоте́ть, жела́ть; намерева́ться **2.** необходи́мый, ну́жный; ва́жный **3.** е́сли	1. to want/wish (to), ask (for) 2. to have to 3. to need 4. be about to, shall, will 5. important, essential, vital 6. if, suppose, in case 7. to summarize
～ **yāo** тре́бовать	1. to demand 2. to coerce 3. to invite
～塞 **yàosài** кре́пость, форт	fort, fortification, strategic spot
～命 **yàomìng** ужа́сно, невыноси́мо	1. to drive sb. to death, kill 2. extremely, awfully, terribly 3. aggravating,\\
～求 **yāoqiú** тре́бовать; тре́бование; прете́нзия	to demand, request; demand \\annoying
～是 **yàoshì** е́сли; е́сли бы	if, in case //ous 3. anxious to
～紧 **yàojǐn** ва́жный; ва́жно	1. important, essential 2. critical, seri-//
～点 **yàodiǎn** ва́жный пункт; гла́вное	1. main points, essentials, gist 2. key strongpoint //strait, isthmus 5. pass
腰 **yāo** та́лия; поясни́ца	1. waist 2. pocket 3. middle part 4. //
～子 **yāoz** *анат.* по́чка	(coll.) kidney
～带 **yāodài** по́яс; реме́нь	waistband, belt, girdle
安 **ān** **1.** успоко́ить; ми́рный, споко́йный **2.** устро́ить, помести́ть; установи́ть	1. to set (sb.'s mind) at ease 2. to rest content 3. to place suitably 4. to fix, install 5. peaceful 6. safe 7. where, how
～全 **ānquán** безопа́сность; безопа́сный	safe, secure; security, safety
～置 **ānzhì** устана́вливать; монти́ровать; монта́ж	to find a place for, help settle down, arrange for

安排 **ānpái** **1.** расста́вить, расположи́ть **2.** нала́дить; устро́ить	1. to arrange, plan, fix up; arrangement 2. to provide (meals, etc.) -
~乐 **ānlè** **1.** ра́дость **2.** комфо́рт **3.** споко́йный, ми́рный	peace and happiness; happy - -
~装 **ānzhuāng** *см.* 安置	to install, erect, fix, mount
~定 **āndìng** усто́йчивый, стаби́льный	1. stable, quiet, settled 2. to stabilize 3. (coll.) tranquilizer
~心 **ānxīn** успоко́иться; споко́йный	1. to feel at ease, be relieved 2. to keep one's mind on sth.
~慰 **ānwèi** утеша́ть, успока́ивать	to comfort, console; comforting -
按 **àn** **1.** нажима́ть; тро́гать руко́й **2.** в соотве́тствии с; согла́сно; по **3.** примеча́ние, спра́вка, сно́ска	1. to press, push down 2. to leave aside, shelve 3. to restrain 4. to keep one's hand on 5. to check, refer to 6. note, notation 7. according to, in ac-\\
~时 **ànshí** своевре́менно; по часа́м	on time/schedule \\cordance with -
~摩 **ànmó** растира́ть, масси́ровать; масса́ж	to massage; massage -
~照 **ànzhào** в соотве́тствии с; согла́сно; по	according to, in the light of, on the basis of
耍 **shuǎ** **1.** забавля́ться, развлека́ться **2.** дава́ть представле́ние	1. to play (a role/tricks, etc.) 2. to gamble -
~弄 **shuǎnòng** обма́нывать, дура́чить	to make a fool of, deceive -
~笑 **shuǎxiào** подшу́чивать; шути́ть; забавля́ться	1. to joke, have fun 2. to play a joke on - //riage, posture
姿 **zī** вид, о́блик; мане́ра	1. looks, appearance 2. gesture, car-//
~势(态) **zīshì(tài)** по́за; мане́ра держа́ться	1. posture, carriage 2. attitude, pose -
楼 **lóu** **1.** многоэта́жный дом **2.** эта́ж **3.** балко́н, я́рус *(в театре)*	1. storied building 2. story, floor 3. superstructure -
~房 **lóufáng** многоэта́жный дом	multi-storied building -
~梯 **lóutī** ле́стница *(между этажами)*	stairs, staircase -
委 **wěi** **1.** поручи́ть; назна́чить, уполномо́чить **2.** сложи́ть с себя́, перепоручи́ть **3.** криво́й **4.** *сокр.* комите́т,	1. to entrust, designate 2. to abandon, discard 3. to accumulate 4. end 5. committee 6. committee member 7. indirect, winding 8. listless, dejected 9.

комиссия	actually, certainly
委屈 **wěiqu** оби́да, недово́льство	1. to feel wronged 2. to be obstructed (in a career) 3. to inconvenience (sb.)
～曲 **wěiqū** искажа́ть, извраща́ть	1. winding, tortuous (roads, etc.) 2. ins and outs, the full story
～托 **wěituō** поруча́ть, уполномо́чивать	to entrust, trust
～员 **wěiyuán** член сове́та (комите́та, коми́ссии)	committee member
～员会 **wěiyuánhuì** сове́т; комите́т; коми́ссия	committee
矮 **ǎi** коро́ткий; низкоро́слый	1. short (of stature) 2. low
娶 **qǔ** жени́ться	to take a wife
樱:樱桃 **yīngtao** ви́шня; чере́шня	cherry
妥 **tuǒ** 1. надлежа́щий, соотве́тствующий 2. уве́ренный	1. appropriate, proper 2. (suf.) ready, settled, finished
～当 **tuǒdàng** как сле́дует, надлежа́щим о́бразом	appropriate, proper
～协 **tuǒxié** соглаша́ться; компроми́сс	to come to terms, compromise
尽 **jǐn** 1. кра́йний; после́дний 2. по́лностью, целико́м 3. пусть, пуска́й	1. to the greatest extent 2. utmost 3. to give priority to 4. within the limits of 5. to keep on doing sth.
～ **jìn** 1. зако́нчить; вы́полнить 2. всё; целико́м 3. кра́йний, са́мый	1. to the utmost/limit 2. to end 3. to use up, exhaust 4. to try one's best, put to best use 5. all
～量 **jǐnliàng** максима́льно; всеме́рно, вся́чески; все́ми си́лами	1. to the best of one's ability 2. (to drink/eat) to the full
～管 **jǐnguǎn** 1. то́лько и знать, что 2. несмотря́ на; пусть да́же, хотя́	1. to feel free to, not hesitate to 2. even though, despite
尽力 **jìnlì** изо всех сил; отда́ть все си́лы	to try one's best
～职 **jìnzhí** вы́полнить долг до конца́	to fulfill one's duty
枣 **zǎo** фи́ник	jujube, Ch. date (fruit)
搀 **chān** 1. подде́рживать, помога́ть 2. сме́шивать; разбавля́ть	1. to help by the arm, support sb. with one's hand 2. to mix
寒 **hán** 1. зима́; хо́лод; холо́дный 2. бе́дный, убо́гий	1. cold, glacial 2. poor, needy 3. (humb.) my 4. to shiver 5. to ignore, flout
～假 **hánjià** зи́мние кани́кулы	winter vacation

寒冬终疼

寒冷 **hánlěng** хóлод; морóз	cold, frigid
冬 **dōng** зимá; зи́мний	1. winter 2. (onom.) rat-a-tat
～季(天) **dōngjì(tiān)** зимá	winter
终 **zhōng** **1.** закóнчить(ся); конéц, финáл **2.** до концá; весь, цéлый	1. end, finish 2. to end, die 3. whole, en-\\ \\tire 4. eventually, after all, in the end
～生 **zhōngshēng** всю жизнь	all one's life
～止 **zhōngzhǐ** останови́ть, пресéчь	1. to stop, end 2. termination, annulment, abrogation 3. (mus.) cadence
～结 **zhōngjié** закóнчить, заверши́ть; конéц, финáл	end, final stage
～于 **zhōngyú** в концé концóв; заверши́ться, закóнчиться	at (long) last, in the end, finally
～身 **zhōngshēn** всю жизнь	1. all one's life, lifelong 2. marriage
～究 **zhōngjiū** в конéчном счёте	eventually, in the end, after all
～点 **zhōngdiǎn** конéчный пункт, фи́ниш	1. terminal point, destination 2. (sports) finish line
疼 **téng** **1.** боли́т; боль **2.** люби́ть	1. to hurt, ache, pain 2. to love dearly
～爱 **téng'ài** горячó люби́ть	to love dearly

APPENDIX A

GEOGRAPHICAL NAMES

(1975)

兰州 **lánzhōu** *г.* Ланьчжо́у	Lanzhou
坦桑尼亚 **dānsǎnníyā** Танза́ния	Tanzania
上海 **shànghǎi** *г.* Шанха́й	Shanghai
江西 **jiāngxī** *пров.* Цзянси́	Jiangsi (prov.)
江苏 **jiāngsū** *пров.* Цзянсу́	Jiangsu (prov.)
土耳其 **tǔěrqí** Ту́рция	Turkey
基多 **jīduō** *г.* Ки́то	Quito
塞浦路斯 **sàipǔlùsī** *гос-во и о-в* Кипр	Cyprus
圣地亚哥 **shèngdìyàgē** *г.* Сантья́го	Santiago
墨西哥 **mòxīgē** Ме́ксика	Mexico
墨西哥城 **mòxīgēchéng** *г.* Ме́хико	Mexico City
渥太华 **wòtàihuā** *г.* Отта́ва	Ottawa
金沙萨 **jīnshāsà** *г.* Кинша́са	Kinshasa
金边 **jīnbiān** *г.* Пномпе́нь	Phnom Penh
里斯本 **lǐsīběn** *г.* Лиссабо́н	Lisbon
亚洲 **yàzhōu** А́зия	Asia
亚丁 **yàdīng** *г.* А́ден	Aden
亚松森 **yàsōngsēn** *г.* Асунсьо́н	Asunçion
纽约 **niǔyuē** *г.* Нью-Йо́рк	New York
拉萨 **lāsà** *г.* Лха́са	Lhasa
拉巴斯 **lābāsī** *г.* Ла-Пас	La Paz
孟加拉国 **mèngjiālāguó** Бангладе́ш	Bangladesh
堪培拉 **kānpéilā** *г.* Ка́нбе́рра	Canberra
维也纳 **wéiyěnà** *г.* Ве́на	Vienna
雅加达 **yǎjiādá** *г.* Джака́рта	Jakarta
雅典 **yǎdiǎn** *г.* Афи́ны	Athens

山西 **shānxī** *пров.* Шаньси́	Shansi (prov.)
山东 **shāndōng** *пров.* Шань-	Shandong (prov.)
ду́н	-
甘肃 **gānsù** *провинция* Гань-	Gansu (prov.)
су́	-
加拉加斯 **jiālājiāsī** *г.* Кара́-	Caracas
кас	-
加拿大 **jiānádà** Кана́да	Canada
加纳 **jiānà** Га́на	Ghana
加德满都 **jiādémǎndū** *г.* Кат-	Katmandu
манду́	-
合肥 **héféi** *г.* Хэфэ́й	Hefei (city)
哈巴罗夫斯克 **hābāluófūsīkè**	Khabarovsk
г. Хаба́ровск	-
哈瓦那 **hāwǎnà** *г.* Гава́на	Havana
哈尔滨 **hāěrbīn** *г.* Харби́н	Haerbin (city)
塔那那利佛 **tǎnànàlìfó** *г.* Ан-	Antananarivo
тананари́ву (Тананари́ве)	-
吉隆坡 **jílóngpō** *г.* Куа́ла-	Kuala Lumpur
-Лу́мпур	-
吉林 **jílín** *пров. и г.* Цзили́нь	Jilin (prov. & city)
(Гири́н)	-
喜马拉雅山脉 **xīmǎlāyǎ shān-**	The Himalayas
mò Гимала́и	-
古巴 **gǔbā** Ку́ба	Cuba
喀布尔 **kābùěr** *г.* Кабу́л	Kabul
洛伦索马贵斯 **luòlúnsuǒ - mǎ-**	Lourenço Marques (Maputo)
guìsī *г.* Ло[у]ре́нсу-Ма́р-	-
киш	-
台拉维夫 **táilāwéifū** *г.* Тель-	Tel Aviv
-Ави́в	-
台湾 **táiwān** 1) *о-в* Тайва́нь	Taiwan
(Формо́за) 2) *пров.* Тай-	-
ва́нь	-

台北 **táibĕi** *г.* Тайбэ́й	Taipei
日内瓦 **rìnèiwǎ** *г.* Жене́ва	Geneva
日本 **rìbĕn** Япо́ния	Japan
日本海 **rìbĕnhǎi** Япо́нское мо́ре	Sea of Japan
旧金山 **jiùjīnshān** *г.* Сан-Франци́ско	San Francisco
智利 **zhìlì** Чи́ли	Chile
香港 **xiānggǎng** Сянга́н (Гонко́нг)	Hong Kong
柏林 **bólín** *г.* Берли́н	Berlin
福州 **fúzhōu** *г.* Фучжо́у	Fuzhou (city)
福建 **fújiàn** *пров.* Фуцзя́нь	Fujian (prov.)
四川 **sìchuān** *пров.* Сычуа́нь	Sichuan (prov.)
缅甸 **miǎndiàn** Би́рма	Burma
西班牙 **xībānyá** Испа́ния	Spain
西伯利亚 **xībólìyà** Сиби́рь	Siberia
西宁 **xīníng** *г.* Сини́н	Xining (city)
西藏自治区 **xīzàng zìzhìqū** Тибе́тский автоно́мный райо́н	Tibetan Autonomous Region
西藏高原 **xīzàng gāoyuán** Тибе́тское наго́рье	Tibetan Plateau
西贡 **xīgòng** *г.* Сайго́н	Saigon
西安 **xīān** *г.* Сиа́нь	Xian (city)
浙江 **zhèjiāng** *пров.* Чжэ́цзя́н	Zhejiang (prov.)
新加坡 **xīnjiāpō** *гос-во, о-в и г.* Сингапу́р	Singapore
新疆维吾尔族自治区 **xīnjiáng-wéiwúĕrzú zìzhìqū** Синьцзя́н-Уйгу́рский автоно́мный райо́н	Xinjiang Autonomous Region
新西兰 **xīnxīlán** *гос-во и о-ва* Но́вая Зела́ндия	New Zealand
斯里兰卡 **sīlì lánkā** *гос-во и о-в* Шри Ла́нка	Sri Lanka
斯德哥尔摩 **sīdégē'ĕrmó** *г.* Стокго́льм	Stockholm
印度 **yìndù** И́ндия	India
印度半岛 **yìndù bàndǎo** *п-ов* Индоста́н	Hindustan
印度洋 **yìndùyáng** Инди́йский океа́н	Indian Ocean

印度尼西亚 **yìndùníxīyà** Ин-	Indonesia
донéзия	-
仰光 **yǎngguāng** *г.* Рангýн	Rangoon
挪威 **nuówēi** Норвéгия	Norway
郑州 **zhèngzhōu** *г.* Чжэн-	Zhengzhou (city)
чжóу	-
华盛顿 **huáshèngdùn** *г.* Ва-	Washington
шингтóн	-
华沙 **huáshā** *г.* Варшáва	Warsaw
千岛群岛 **qiāndǎoqúndǎo** Ку-	Kuril(e) Islands
рúльские островá	-
平壤 **píngrǎng** *г.* Пхеньян	Pingrang (city) (Korea)
中国 **zhōngguó** Китáй; 中华	China
人民共和国 **zhōnghuá rén-**	People's Republic of China (PRC)
mín gònghéguó Китáйская	-
Нарóдная Респýблика	-
(КНР)	-
中印半岛 **zhōngyìn bàndǎo**	Indochina
п-ов Индокитáй	-
科伦坡 **kēlúnpō** *г.* Колóмбо	Colombo
济南 **jìnán** *г.* Цзинáнь	Jinan
非洲 **fēizhōu** Áфрика	Africa
菲律宾 **fēilǜbīn** *гос-во и о-ва*	Philippines
Филиппúны	-
开罗 **kāiluó** *г.* Каúр	Cairo
刚果 **gāngguǒ** Кóнго	Congo
列宁格勒 **lièninggélē** *г.* Ле-	Leningrad
нингрáд	-
利雅得 **lìyǎdé** *г.* Эр-Рияд	Riyadh
利马 **lìmǎ** *г.* Лúма	Lima
利比亚 **lìbǐyà** Лúвия	Libya
宁夏回族自治区 **níngxiàhuízú**	Ningxiahuizu Autonomous Region
zìzhìqū Нинся-Хуэйский	-
автонóмный райóн	-
荷兰 **hélán** Нидерлáнды	Netherlands
(Голлáндия)	-
阿拉伯埃及共和国 **àlābó āijí**	Arab Republic of Egypt
gònghéguó Арáбская Рес-	-
пýблика Егúпет (АРЕ)	-
阿富汗 **àfùhàn** Афганистáн	Afghanistan
阿穆尔河 **àmùěrhé** *р.* Амýр	Amur (river)
(Хэйлунцзян)	-
阿根廷 **āgēntíng** Аргентú-	Argentina
на	-

阿尔及利亚 **àěrjílìyà** *гос-во*	Algeria
Алжи́р	-
阿尔及尔 **àěrjíěr** *г.* Алжи́р	Algiers
阿尔巴尼亚 **àěrbāníyà** Алба́-	Albania
ния; 阿尔巴尼亚人民共和国	People's Republic of Albania
àěrbāníyà rénmín gònghé-	-
guó Наро́дная Респу́бли-	-
ка Алба́ния	-
河南 **hénán** *пров.* Хэна́нь	Henan (prov.)
河内 **hénèi** *г.* Хано́й	Hanoi
河北 **héběi** *пров.* Хэбэ́й	Hebei (prov.)
哥本哈根 **gēběnhāgēn** *г.* Ко-	Copenhagen
пенга́ген	-
哥伦比亚 **gēlúnbǐyà** Колу́м-	Colombia
бия	-
符拉迪沃斯托克 **fúlādíwòsī-**	Vladivostok
tuōkè *г.* Владивосто́к	-
呼和浩特 **hūhéhàotè** *г.* Хух-	Huhehaote (Huhehot)
-Хо́то	-
湖南 **húnán** *провинция* Ху-	Hunan (prov.)
на́нь	-
湖北 **húběi** *провинция* Хубэ́й	Hubei (prov.)
朝鲜 **cháoxiān** Коре́я	Korea
朝鲜民主主义人民共和国 **chāo-**	Korean People's Democratic
xiān mínzhǔzhǔyì rénmín	Republic
gònghéguó Коре́йская На-	-
ро́дно - Демократи́ческая	-
Респу́блика (КНДР)	-
青海 **qīnghǎi** *провинция* Цин-	Qinghai (prov.)
ха́й	-
瑞士 **ruìshì** Швейца́рия	Switzerland
瑞典 **ruìdiǎn** Шве́ция	Sweden
南昌 **nánchāng** *г.* Наньча́н	Nanchang (city)
南斯拉夫 **nánsīlāfū** Югосла́-	Yugoslavia
вия; 南斯拉夫社会主义联邦	Socialist Federal Republic of
共和国 **nánsīlāfū shèhuì-**	Yugoslavia
zhǔyì liánbāng gònghéguó	-
Социалисти́ческая Феде-	-
рати́вная Респу́блика Юго-	-
сла́вия (СФРЮ)	-
南非共和国 **nánfēi gònghé-**	Republic of South Africa
guó Южно-Африка́нская	-
Респу́блика (ЮАР)	-
南宁 **nánníng** *г.* Наньни́н	Nanning (city)

南朝鲜 **náncháoxiān** Ю́жная	South Korea
Коре́я	-
南海 **nánhǎi** Ю́жно-Кита́й-	South China Sea
ское мо́ре	-
南越南共和国 **nányuènàn**	Republic of South Vietnam
gònghéguó Респу́блика	-
Ю́жный Вьетна́м (РЮВ)	-
南京 **nánjīng** *г.* Нанки́н	Nanjing (city)
布隆迪 **bùlóngdí** Буру́нди	Burundi
布拉格 **bùlāgé** *г.* Пра́га	Prague
布拉柴维尔 **bùlācháiwéiěr** *г.*	Brazzaville
Браззави́ль	-
布宜诺斯艾利斯 **bùyínuòsī**	Buenos Aires
àilìsī *г.* Буэ́нос-А́йрес	-
布加勒斯特 **bùjiālēisītè** *г.* Бу-	Bucharest
харе́ст	-
布鲁塞尔 **bùlǔsàiěr** *г.* Брюс-	Brussels
се́ль	-
布达佩斯 **bùdápèisī** *г.* Буда-	Budapest
пе́шт	-
希腊 **xīlà** Гре́ция	Greece
内蒙古自治区 **nèiměnggǔ zì-**	Inner Mongolian Autonomous Region
zhìqū Автоно́мный райо́н	-
Вну́тренняя Монго́лия	-
丹麦 **dānmài** Да́ния	Denmark
沙特阿拉伯 **shātèālābó** Сау́-	Saudi Arabia
довская Ара́вия	-
广西壮族自治区 **guǎngxī-**	Guangxi-Zhuangzu Autonomous Region
-zhuàngzú zìzhìqū Гуанси́-	-
-Чжуа́нский автоно́мный	-
райо́н	-
广州 **guángzhōu** *г.* Гуанчжо́у	Guangzhou (Canton) (city)
(Канто́н)	-
广东 **guǎngdōng** *пров.* Гуан-	Guangdong (prov.)
ду́н	-
萨哈林岛 **sàhālíndǎo** *о-в* Са-	Sakhalin
хали́н	-
萨那 **sànà** *г.* Сана́	San'a
卢森堡 **lúsēnbǎo** *гос-во и г.*	Luxembourg
Люксембу́рг	-
伊拉克 **yīlākè** Ира́к	Iraq
伊斯兰堡 **yīsīlánbǎo** г. Ислам-	Islamabad
аба́д	-
伊朗 **yīlǎng** Ира́н	Iran

罗马 **luómǎ** *г.* Рим	Rome
罗马尼亚 **luómǎníyà** Румы́ния; 罗马尼亚社会主义共和国 **luómǎníyà shèhuìzhǔyì gònghéguó** Социалисти́ческая Респу́блика Румы́ния (СРР)	Romania Socialist Republic of Romania - - - -
芬兰 **fēnlán** Финля́ндия	Finland
万象 **wànxiàng** *г.* Вьентья́н (Вьентя́н)	Vientiane -
约旦 **yuēdàn** Иорда́ния	Jordan
匈牙利 **xiōngyálì** Ве́нгрия; 匈牙利人民共和国 **xiōngyálì rénmín gònghéguó** Венге́рская Наро́дная Респу́блика (ВНР)	Hungary Hungarian People's Republic - - -
葡萄牙 **pútáoyá** Португа́лия	Portugal
锡兰 **xílán** *гос-во и о-в* Цейло́н; *см.* 斯里兰卡	Ceylon (Sri Lanka) -
马里 **mǎlǐ** Мали́	Mali
马来西亚 **mǎláixīyà** Мала́йзия	Malaysia -
马尼拉 **mǎnílā** *г.* Мани́ла	Manila
马德里 **mǎdélǐ** *г.* Мадри́д	Madrid
马尔加什共和国 **mǎěrjiāshí gònghéguó** Малагаси́йская Респу́блика	Malagasy Republic (Madagascar) - -
乌兰巴托 **wūlán-bātuō** *г.* Ула́н-Ба́тор	Ulan Bator (Ulaanbaatar) -
乌拉圭 **wūlāguī** Уругва́й	Uruguay
乌鲁木齐 **wūlǔmùqí** *г.* Урумчи́	Urumchi (city) -
乌苏里 **wūsūlǐ** *р.* Уссу́ри	Ussuri (river)
苏維埃社会主义共和国联盟 **sūwēiāi shèhuìzhǔyì gònghéguó liánméng** Сою́з Сове́тских Социалисти́ческих Респу́блик (СССР)	Union of Soviet Socialist Republics (USSR) - -
苏丹 **sūdān** Суда́н	Sudan
苏联 **sūlián** Сове́тский Сою́з	Soviet Union
海牙 **hǎiyá** *г.* Гаа́га	The Hague
海南岛 **hǎinándǎo** *о-в* Хайна́нь	Hainan (island) -
海地 **hǎidì** Гаи́ти	Haiti

欧洲 **ōuzhōu** Евро́па	Europe
长江 **chángjiāng** *р.* Чанцзя́н	Changjian (Yangtze) (river)
(Янцзы[цзя́н], Голуба́я ре-	-
ка́)	-
长春 **chángchūn** *г.* Чанчу́нь	Changchun (city)
长沙 **chángshā** *г.* Чанша́	Changsha (city)
大西洋 **dàxīyáng** Атланти́-	Atlantic Ocean
ческий океа́н	-
大洋洲 **dàyángzhōu** Океа́ния	Oceana
大不列颠 **dàbùlièdiān** Вели-	Great Britain
кобрита́ния	-
美国 **měiguó** Соединённые	United States of America (USA)
Шта́ты Аме́рики (США)	-
美洲 **měizhōu** Аме́рика	America
莫三鼻给 **mòsānbíji** Мозам-	Mozambique
би́к	-
莫斯科 **mòsīkē** *г.* Москва́	Moscow
奥斯陆 **àosīlù** *г.* О́сло	Oslo
奥地利 **àodìlì** А́встрия	Austria
澳洲 **àozhōu** Австра́лия	Australia
澳门 **àomén** Аомы́нь (Мака́о)	Aomin (Macao)
澳大利亚 **àodàlìyà** Австра́-	Australia
лия	-
澳大利亚联邦 **àodàlìyà lián-**	Australian Union
bāng Австрали́йский Сою́з	-
太平洋 **tàipíngyáng** Ти́хий	Pacific Ocean
океа́н	-
太子港 **tàizǐgǎng** *г.* Порт-о-	Port-au-Prince
-Пренс	-
太原 **tàiyuán** *г.* Тайюа́нь	Taiyuan (city)
天山 **tiānshān** Тянь-Ша́нь	Tianshan (mountains)
天津 **tiānjīn** *г.* Тяньцзи́нь	Tianjin (city)
埃塞俄比亚 **āisāiébǐyà** Эфи-	Ethiopia
о́пия	-
陕西 **shǎnxī** *пров.* Шэньси́	Shanxi (prov.)
英国 **yīngguó** А́нглия	England
保加利亚 **bǎojiālìyà** Болга́-	Bulgaria
рия; 保加利亚人民共和国	People's Republic of Bulgaria
bǎojiālìyà rénmín gònghé-	-
guó Наро́дная Респу́бли-	-
ка Болга́рия (НРБ)	-
东海 **dōnghǎi** Восто́чно-Ки-	East China Sea
та́йское мо́ре	-
东京 **dōngjīng** *г.* То́кио	Tokyo

柬埔寨 **jiǎnpǔzhài** Камбóджа	Cambodia
黎巴嫩 **líbānùn** Ливáн	Lebanon
泰国 **tàiguó** Таилáнд	Thailand
蒙古 **měnggǔ** Монгóлия; 蒙	Mongolia
古人民共和国 **měnggǔ rén-**	Mongolian People's Republic
mín gònghéguó Монгóль-	-
ская Нарóдная Респýбли-	-
ка (МНР)	-
蒙得维的亚 **měngdéwéidìyà** *г.*	Montevideo
Монтевидéо	-
蒙罗维亚 **měngluówéiyà**	Monrovia
г. Монрóвия	-
旅大 **lǚdà** *г.* Люйдá	Lüda (Darien) (city)
银川 **yínchuān** *г.* Иньчуáнь	Yinchuan (city)
越南 **yuènán** Вьетнáм	Vietnam
越南民主共和国 **yuènán mín-**	Democratic Republic of Vietnam
zhǔ gònghéguó Демокра-	-
ти́ческая Респýблика Вьет-	-
нáм (ДРВ)	-
捷克斯洛伐克 **jiékèsīluòfákè**	Czechoslovakia
Чехословáкия; 捷克斯洛伐	Czechoslovak Socialist Republic
克社会主义共和国 **jiékèsīluò-**	-
fákè shèhuìzhǔyì gònghé-	-
guó Чехословáцкая Социа-	-
листи́ческая Респýблика	-
(ЧССР)	-
叙利亚 **xùlìyà** Си́рия	Syria
汉城 **hànchéng** *г.* Сеýл	Seoul
曼谷 **màngǔ** *г.* Бангкóк	Bangkok
玻利维亚 **bōlìwéiyà** Боли́вия	Bolivia
波兰 **bōlán** Пóльша; 波兰人	Poland
民共和国 **bōlán rénmín**	Polish People's Republic
gònghéguó Пóльская На-	-
рóдная Респýблика (ПНР)	-
波哥大 **bōgēdà** *г.* Боготá	Bogota
波罗的海 **bōluòdìhǎi** Балти́й-	Baltic Sea
ское мóре	-
波恩 **bō'ēn** *г.* Бонн	Bonn
辽宁 **liáoníng** *пров.* Ляони́н	Liaoning (prov.)
达卡 **dákǎ** *г.* Дáкка	Dacca
达马士革 **dámǎshìgē** *г.* Да-	Damascus
мáск	-
达累斯萨拉姆 **dálèisī-sàlāmǔ**	Dar es Salaam
г. Дар-эс-Салáм	-

远东 **yuǎndōng** Да́льний Восто́к	Far East
武汉 **wǔhàn** *г.* Уха́нь	Wuhan (city)
戈壁 **gēbì** *пустыня* Го́би	Gobi (desert)
成都 **chéngdū** *г.* Чэнду́	Chengdu
扎伊尔 **zāyīěr** Заи́р	Zaire
比利时 **bǐlìshí** Бе́льгия	Belgium
昆明 **kūnmíng** *г.* Куньми́н	Kunming (city)
北冰洋 **běibīngyáng** Се́верный Ледови́тый океа́н	Arctic Ocean
北京 **běijīng** *г.* Пеки́н	Beijing (city)
尼日利亚 **nírìlìyà** Ниге́рия	Nigeria
尼泊尔 **nípòr** Непа́л	Nepal
尼科西亚 **níkēxīyà** *г.* Никоси́я (Никози́я)	Nicosia
老挝 **lǎowō** Лао́с	Laos
伦敦 **lúndùn** *г.* Ло́ндон	London
厄瓜多尔 **èguāduōěr** Эквадо́р (Экуадо́р)	Ecuador
巴基斯坦 **bājīsītǎn** Пакиста́н	Pakistan
巴拉圭 **bālāguī** Парагва́й	Paraguay
巴格达 **bāgédá** *г.* Багда́д	Baghdad
巴西 **bāxī** Брази́лия	Brasilia
巴西利亚 **bāxīlìyà** *г.* Брази́лия	Brasilia
巴拿马 **bānámǎ** *гос-во и г.* Пана́ма	Panama
巴黎 **bālí** *г.* Пари́ж	Paris
也门 **yěmén** Йе́мен	Yemen
也门阿拉伯共和国 **yěmén ālābó gònghéguó** Йе́менская Ара́бская Респу́блика	Yemen Arab Republic
也门民主人民共和国 **yěmén mínzhǔ rénmín gònghéguó** Наро́дная Демократи́ческая Респу́блика Йе́мен	People's Republic of Yemen
地拉那 **dìlànà** *г.* Тира́на	Tirana
地中海 **dìzhōnghǎi** Средизе́мное мо́ре	Mediterranean Sea
沈阳 **shěnyáng** *г.* Шэнья́н	Shenyang (city)
几内亚(比绍) **jīnèiyà (bìshào)** Гвине́я-Биса́у	Guinea-Bissau
杭州 **hángzhōu** *г.* Ханчжо́у	Hangzhou (city)
以色列 **yǐsèliè** Изра́иль	Iran

贝鲁特 **bèilǔtè** *г.* Бейру́т	Beirut
贝尔格莱德 **bèiěrgéláidé** *г.* Белгра́д	Belgrade
贵阳 **guìyáng** *г.* Гуйя́н	Guiyang (city)
贵州 **guìzhōu** *пров.* Гуйчжо́у	Guizhou (prov.)
黄河 **huánghé** *р.* Хуанхэ́ (Жёлтая река́)	Huanghe (Yellow) (river)
黄海 **huánghǎi** Жёлтое мо́ре	Huanghai (Yellow) (sea)
索非亚 **suǒfēiyà** *г.* Софи́я	Sofia
赫尔辛基 **hè'ěrxīnjī** *г.* Хе́льсинки	Helsinki
德里 **délǐ** *г.* Де́ли	Delhi
德意志联邦共和国 **déyìzhì liánbāng gònghéguó** Федерати́вная Респу́блика Герма́нии (ФРГ)	Federal Republic of Germany
德意志民主共和国 **déyìzhì mínzhǔ gònghéguó** Герма́нская Демократи́ческая Респу́блика (ГДР)	German Democratic Republic
德黑兰 **déhēilán** *г.* Тегера́н	Teheran
意大利 **yìdàlì** Ита́лия	Italy
惠灵顿 **huìlíngdùn** *г.* Ве́ллингтон (Уэ́ллингтон)	Wellington
秘鲁 **bìlǔ** Перу́	Peru
黑海 **hēihǎi** Чёрное мо́ре	Black Sea
黑龙江 **hēilóngjiāng** 1. *пров.* Хэйлунцзя́н 2. *р.* Хэйлунцзя́н (Аму́р)	1. Heilongjiang (prov.) 2. Heilongjiang (Amur) (river)
云南 **yúnnán** *пров.* Юньна́нь	Yunnan (prov.)
法国 **fǎguó** Фра́нция	France
安卡拉 **ānkǎlā** *г.* Анкара́	Ankara
安哥拉 **āngēlā** Анго́ла	Angola
安曼 **ānmàn** *г.* Амма́н	Amman
安徽 **ānhuī** *пров.* Аньхо́й	Anhui (prov.)
委内瑞拉 **wěinèiruìlā** Венесуэ́ла	Venezuela

APPENDIX B

PINYIN (ALPHABETICAL) INDEX

This index provides a second means of entry into the main body of the dictionary, the first being the direct entry via the Rosenberg (Russian) Graphical System itself (see Guide to the Use of the Rosenberg Graphical System).

The index includes all of the 2,278 entries in the body of the dictionary, which, with very few exceptions, appear in their simplified form.

The sequence of the pinyin entries in the *first column* is alphabetical and then by tone 1–4 (ˉ, ˊ, ˇ, ˋ), the fifth or neutral tone (no tone sign is indicated) appearing after the fourth tone. The corresponding character(s) appear in the *second column*. In those instances in which a single pinyin entry corresponds to two or more characters, the sequence of the latter is the same as that in the body of the dictionary, i.e., that of the Graphical System itself. The *third column* indicates the page number.

INDEX FOR FINDING CHARACTERS IN THE DICTIONARY[1]

	SECTION[2]	GROUP AND PAGE NUMBER	
I →	1. 一	1	1一兰坦鱼 5卫上应 8俭 9工经 14士土在 20至王 26金生垂 30里
		2	32止业互五 36丑立豆 39且 40直盖监孟 43益血
		3	44继亡区 47世痱归彗当 50维屆画凶齿 54山击搖 55出甘臼
	2. 口	4	58口石 64言合晤 69培占 72古告唐 75名 76召 77谷各 80沿台 81营官
		5	82日普 83借 89者 90白百 91目 95自临 97田由 101曲国 106面西
II ↓	3. 丨	6	107引丨个下 111斤昨卸节 116部十千 121干平 124午辛奉举 126半牛车
		7	129羊舞丰拜 131律革单 132中甲申斗纠耳
	4. 刂	8	137介侨齐非 138开并异升 142井川州肃
	5. ㇕	9	144今片
	6. 亅	10	144到剂 146刑 150丁街 153可予 155了子 158寸 165才于呼 牙 167手 争事
	7. 𠃌	11	169门习司羽 173月丽角 180用辅而编 183高 184同摘周 186商南
		12	187纲网向 188巾布市雨 191内两离册 193再身
III ↙	8. 丿	13	194步少形 197厂广严产 199戶声伊岁多
	9. ㇇	14	200梦乡
	10. ㇆	15	200幻刀分万方 204约竭匈陶 205句物 207易场书巧号 208污考与
		16	209马乌鸟岛仍 210粥鸾弱弟佛力 214办 215为母

1. The beginning page number for the subsequent characters/graphemes is shown in boldface type in each instance.
2. i.e. basic graphic element.

INDEX FOR FINDING CHARACTERS IN THE DICTIONARY[1]

1. The beginning page number for the subsequent characters/graphemes is shown in boldface type in each instance.
2. i.e. basic graphic element.